APPLIED STATISTICS
FOR PUBLIC AND NONPROFIT ADMINISTRATION

NINTH EDITION

APPLIED STATISTICS

FOR PUBLIC AND NONPROFIT ADMINISTRATION

KENNETH J. MEIER

TEXAS A&M UNIVERSITY

JEFFREY L. BRUDNEY

UNIVERSITY OF NORTH CAROLINA WILMINGTON

JOHN BOHTE

UNIVERSITY OF WISCONSIN–MILWAUKEE

❖❖ Cengage

Australia • Brazil • Canada • Mexico • Singapore • United Kingdom • United States

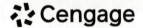

Applied Statistics for Public and Nonprofit Administration, **Ninth Edition**
Kenneth J. Meier, Jeffrey L. Brudney and John Bohte

Product Director: Suzanne Jeans

Product Manager: Carolyn Merrill

Content Developer: Lauren Athmer, LEAP Publishing, Inc.

Content Coordinator: Eireann Aspell

Product Assistant: Abigail Hess

Senior Media Developer: Laura Hildebrand

Rights Acquisitions Specialist: Jennifer Meyer Dare

Manufacturing Planner: Fola Orekoya

Art and Design Direction, Production Management, and Composition: PreMediaGlobal

Cover Image: © Rob MacDougall/ Getty Images

Library of Congress Control Number: 2013952525

Student Edition:
ISBN-13: 978-1-285-73723-2
ISBN-10: 1-285-73723-7

Cengage
200 Pier 4 Boulevard
Boston, MA 02210
USA

Cengage is a leading provider of customized learning solutions with employees residing in nearly 40 different countries and sales in more than 125 countries around the world. Find your local representative at: **www.cengage.com.**

To learn more about Cengage platforms and services, register or access your online learning solution, or purchase materials for your course, visit **www.cengage.com.**

Instructors: Please visit **login.cengage.com** and log in to access instructor-specific resources.

Printed at CLDPC, USA, 04-23

To Diane and Nancy

About the Authors

Kenneth J. Meier is the Charles H. Gregory Chair in Liberal Arts and Distinguished Professor of Political Science at Texas A&M University. He is also a professor of Public Management in the Cardiff School of Business, Cardiff University, Wales, United Kingdom, and the research fellow at the Danish National Centre for Social Research. He is the editor in chief of the *Journal of Public Administration Research and Theory*, a former editor of the *American Journal of Political Science* (1994–1997), and a former associate editor of the *Journal of Politics* (1991–1994) and the *Journal of Public Administration Research and Theory* (2000–2009). He served as president of the Southwest Political Science Association; the American Political Science Association sections on State Politics and Policy, Public Policy, and Public Administration; the Public Management Research Association; and the Midwest Political Science Association. He has received the John Gaus Award for career contributions to public administration scholarship (2006), the Dwight Waldo Award from the American Society for Public Administration for career contributions to the literature (2010), and the H. George Frederickson Award from the Public Management Research Association for lifetime achievement in public management research. He currently lives with the love of his life, Diane Jones Meier, in Bryan, Texas, and spends his free time comparing the merits of California zinfandels with Australian shirazes.

Jeffrey L. Brudney, Ph.D., is the inaugural holder of the Betty and Dan Cameron Family Distinguished Professorship of Innovation in the Nonprofit Sector at the University of North Carolina Wilmington. Previously, he held the Albert A. Levin Chair of Urban Studies and Public Service at Cleveland State University. According to a study in the *Journal of Public Administration Education*, he ranks tenth in research productivity based on articles published over the past decade in journals affiliated with the American Society for Public Administration. He is the author of *Fostering Volunteer Programs in the Public Sector: Planning, Initiating, and Managing Voluntary Activities*, for which he received the John Grenzebach Award for Outstanding Research in Philanthropy for Education. In 2010, he served on the United Nations Volunteers Programme Technical Advisory Board on the first study ever of the *State of the World's Volunteerism Report*, and in 2008 he was invited to the White House by President Bush to hear his "Remarks on Volunteering." He has received the Herbert Kaufman Award from the Public Administration Section of the American Political Science Association, the Academy of Management Public and Nonprofit Division Best Article Award, and the William E. Mosher and Frederick C. Mosher Award for the best article written by an academician in *Public Administration Review*. Dr. Brudney is the editor in chief of *Nonprofit and Voluntary Sector Quarterly*, the premier journal in nonprofit-sector studies.

John Bohte is associate professor of Political Science at the University of Wisconsin–Milwaukee. Dr. Bohte enjoys teaching courses on public budgeting, statistics, and state politics.

Brief Contents

Contents

List of Symbols

μ	population mean
σ	population standard deviation
Σ	summation of all listed numbers
!	factorial
C_r^n	combination of n things taken r at a time
p^r	probability p raised to the r-th power
EV	expected value
$\overline{X}$	sample mean
s	sample standard deviation
n	size of the sample
N	size of the population
λ	lambda for the Poisson distribution
α	population regression intercept
β	population regression slope
a	sample regression intercept
b	sample regression slope
$\hat{Y}$	predicted value of Y
e	error
s.e.	standard error of the mean
$S_{y|x}$	standard error of the estimate
r^2	coefficient of determination (bivariate)
R^2	multiple coefficient of determination (multivariate)
Adj. R^2	adjusted R^2 (coefficient of determination adjusted for variables with little or no explanatory power)
s.e.$_b$	standard error of the slope
z	standard normal score
t	t-distribution score

List of Symbols

population mean

population standard deviation

summation of all listed numbers

factorial

combination of n things taken r at a time

probability p raised to the r-th power

expected value

sample mean

sample standard deviation

size of the sample

size of the population

lambda for the Poisson distribution

population regression intercept

population regression slope

sample regression intercept

sample regression slope

predicted value of Y

error

standard error of the mean

standard error of the estimate

coefficient of determination (bivariate)

multiple coefficient of determination (multivariate)

adjusted R^2 (coefficient of determination adjusted for variables with little or no explanatory power)

standard error of the slope

standard normal score

t-distribution score

Preface

The first edition of this book was not the product of years of planning. It was written out of necessity. Assigned to teach a master's degree course entitled "Measurement and Analysis for Public Administrators," the original two authors could find no suitable text, so we wrote one. Since the initial publication of this book in 1981, other textbooks have appeared intended for the "methods" course(s) in master of public administration (MPA) degree programs. With this ninth edition, we believe that *Applied Statistics for Public and Nonprofit Administration* continues to possess unique advantages for study and practice in this field.

The first advantage—long a hallmark of the book—is accessibility. Because MPA students as well as those with an interest in the nonprofit sector come from disparate backgrounds, their prior exposure to statistics and quantitative methods is generally weak and varies widely. For many, if not most, students with an interest in public and/or nonprofit sectors, the last time they took a mathematics course was in high school. Given this audience, a rigorous presentation of statistical methods would have proved too threatening, difficult, and off-putting. Instead, we wanted a volume that would assume little familiarity with the subject but one that would teach quantitative novices a great deal in very little time. We also wanted to adopt a tone that would invite readers rather than intimidate them.

A second advantage of the book is that it addresses substantive problems illustrative of those faced by practicing administrators in the public and nonprofit sectors. Methods and statistics textbooks in political science and sociology and other disciplines rely predominantly on academic, rather than practitioner-oriented, examples. Although a number of excellent methods textbooks for business administration are available, they typically focus, understandably, on a different set of issues and problems (e.g., manufacturing production, market analysis, etc.) than those that normally concern and activate public and nonprofit administrators. We wanted a methods statistics book with examples that would be relevant for this audience.

A third advantage of the book is that it can help colleges, schools, and departments meet the accreditation standards for master's degree programs established by the National Association of Schools of Public Affairs and Administration, or NASPAA.* In addition, with respect to nonprofit studies, the book can help

---

*http://www.naspaa.org/accreditation/standard2009/docs/NS2009FinalVote10.16.2009.pdf

schools in meeting the *Curricular Guidelines for Graduate Study in Nonprofit Leadership, the Nonprofit Sector and Philanthropy.* ** Published by the Nonprofit Academic Centers Council, or NACC (which at this writing does not have authority or responsibility to accredit academic programs in nonprofit studies), the guidelines are instructive nevertheless in suggesting a solid curriculum in this domain. Of particular relevance here, Section 16.0 provides guidelines relating to "Assessment, Evaluation and Decision-Making Methods" in the nonprofit sector. Chapter 1 discusses in greater detail how *Applied Statistics for Public and Nonprofit Administration* addresses the standards for curricula in public administration and nonprofit studies.

In preparing this ninth edition, we have again followed these guidelines that motivated the original edition and all subsequent editions of this book. In fact, the ninth edition is more faithful to them than the original edition, for in the past 30 years or so we have had the opportunity to use this book—and receive valuable feedback from a great many students and practitioners—at several major research universities, as well as at numerous off-campus locations. The new edition benefits from this experience and "field testing."

Over the years since initial publication, a constituency of valued students and colleagues has arisen around *Applied Statistics for Public and Nonprofit Administration.* We are grateful for their guidance and help. They have kindly provided us with comments and suggestions, both positive and negative, but always with an eye toward improving the book for students of public affairs and nonprofit administration. We welcome you to join this group by contacting us either directly or through the publisher, Cengage Learning/Wadsworth (www.cengage.com).

New to This Edition

At the suggestion of the reviewers for this edition, we have incorporated many changes into this edition. We thank these individuals for their suggestions. Several improvements to the text are especially noteworthy.

First, the ninth edition offers a leaner (but not meaner!) version of *Applied Statistics for Public and Nonprofit Administration.* We have eliminated multiple chapters that instructors informed us that they rarely have time to cover in class and devoted greater attention to the more important chapters remaining. In addition, we rewrote Chapter 1 to welcome new users, both faculty and students, and to reintroduce the book to old friends.

The ninth edition continues to make substantial progress on a process that schools and departments of public administration and affairs are also undertaking: incorporating greater recognition and discussion of problems and examples relevant and important to the nonprofit sector and organizations. More than

---

**http://www.urban.csuohio.edu/nacc/documents/GradCG07.pdf

any other academic unit (such as social work or business administration), public administration schools and departments offer their students concentrations in nonprofit management, leadership, or organizations and consequently attract students with these interests. A few universities also have freestanding master's degree programs in this burgeoning domain of research and practice. We feel that this book should reflect these emerging trends in public administration and affairs. Accordingly, we have tried to make the discussion, examples, and problems in this ninth edition more responsive and interesting to students with a background in nonprofit organizations or aspirations to work in the nonprofit sector. Our growing appreciation of the elements and processes important to the nonprofit sector makes the book more relevant for these students, as well as for MPA students who will increasingly encounter nonprofit organizations in their studies and profession.

This ninth edition of *Applied Statistics for Public and Nonprofit Administration* continues to illustrate the increasing role of the nonprofit sector in interacting and working with the public sector.

As recommended by the reviewers of this edition and by faculty members and students, in this edition we continue to focus on updating problems at the end of the chapters, including problems pertaining to nonprofit organizations. As in previous editions, answers to odd-numbered computational problems appear at the end of the book. In addition, instructors can access answers to all problems, and much other useful material for teaching courses in applied statistics for public and nonprofit administration, in our ***Instructor's Manual***.

Among the problems at the end of the chapters, you will find more computer-based problems (clearly marked with an icon), based on practice and experience in the public and nonprofit sectors. We have also made the relevant datasets available for instructor and student use. We have not tied the book to any particular software because across schools, levels and types of government, and nonprofit organizations, great variety exists with respect to both computer support and statistical software. We provide datasets for practice and problem solving on *your* technology so that the text and problems are not bound to a particular choice.

The ninth edition incorporates more examples to guide use and interpretation of statistics for public and nonprofit managers. We have added more examples to the text and present them more completely. This edition also includes more figures and other graphical displays. The summaries presented at the end of several chapters have been improved.

Our guiding philosophy continues to be to make the book accessible, practical, and useful, even at the expense of statistical rigor. In their program of study, MPA students and those with an interest in the nonprofit sector will have plenty of time to pick up that *second* course in statistics if they are interested. But first they must get through their *initial* exposure. We wrote this book to assist them. Our goal is to help students make good sense and good use of data with appropriate statistics, recognize the strengths as well as the limitations of the results obtained, and communicate these findings and insights clearly and persuasively to others.

Toward these ends, the ninth edition maintains the tone, level of presentation, and approach featured in the eight previous editions. We have also updated, corrected, amended, clarified, and elaborated the material as necessary to make it more readable, current, and interesting.

We are grateful to students, colleagues, and reviewers for suggesting many of these changes. We look forward to hearing your ideas.

Teaching Enhancements

Instructor's Manual Online for *Applied Statistics for Public and Nonprofit Administration, 9th Edition*

ISBN-13: 9781285737294

The Instructor's Manual contains for each chapter: an outline and summary; critical thinking questions; in-class activities; lecture launching suggestions; a list of key terms with definitions; and suggested readings and Web resources.

Free Companion Website for *Applied Statistics for Public and Nonprofit Administration, 9th Edition*

ISBN-13: 9781285737263

The free student companion website for *Applied Statistics and Public and Nonprofit Administration* is accessible through cengagebrain.com, which allows access to chapter-specific interactive learning tools including flashcards, quizzes, glossaries, and more. Instructors may access these resources by logging into their account at www.cengage.com/login.

Acknowledgments

A task of this magnitude could not have been accomplished without the assistance of others. We are grateful to the many students and colleagues who have kindly given us feedback that informs this ninth edition.

Over the editions of this book, a great many students at Texas A&M University, the University of Georgia, Cleveland State University, the University of North Carolina Wilmington, the University of Oklahoma, Oakland University, and the University of Wisconsin–Milwaukee have provided us with a diverse teaching laboratory. They, too, have offered comments and suggestions that proved helpful in improving this book. We appreciate their tolerance not only for errors that appeared in earlier editions but also for a sense of humor that occasionally goes awry on the printed page. (Otherwise reasonable people may disagree over the frequency of the latter occurrence.)

Thanks are due to the reviewers of this ninth edition for their very helpful comments and suggestions: Steven Bourassa, University of Louisville; Jayce

Farmer, Florida State University; Kenneth Kickham, University of Central Oklahoma; Gina Reinhardt, Texas A&M University; and Eva Witesman, Brigham Young University.

We are also grateful to a lengthy list of colleagues who have reviewed and improved previous editions of the book: William C. Adams, George Washington University; Kristian Alexander, University of Utah; Akpan Akpan, Texas Southern University; Robert Aldinger, Valdosta State University; Nolan J. Argyle, Valdosta State University; George Antunes, University of Houston; Dave Armstrong, University of Wisconsin–Milwaukee; Charles Barrilleaux, Florida State University; Brady Baybeck, University of Missouri–St. Louis; Cindy Bennett-Boland, University of Arkansas; R. M. Bittick, California State University–Dominguez Hills; Nancy Brooks, Cornell University; Gerald R. Bushee, George Mason University; Gary Copeland, University of Oklahoma; Paul J. Culhane, Northern Illinois University; Mark Daniels, University of Memphis; Matthew Dull, Virginia Tech; Warren Eller, West Virginia University; Jeff Fine, Clemson University; Jody Fitzpatrick, University of Colorado–Colorado Springs; Barry D. Friedman, North Georgia College and State University; John Forrester, University of Missouri–Columbia; James F. Guyot, Baruch College–City University of New York; Uk Heo, University of Wisconsin–Milwaukee; Tom Holbrook, University of Wisconsin–Milwaukee; Deniz Leuenberger, Bridgewater State College; Steve Percy, University of Wisconsin–Milwaukee; John Piskulich, Oakland University; Steven Rhiel, Old Dominion University; Bruce D. Rogers, Tennessee State University; Arthur Sementelli, Stephen F. Austin State University; Soo Geun Song, West Virginia University; Brian Stipak, Portland State University; Jon R. Taylor, University of St. Thomas (Houston, Texas); Chris Toppe, Georgetown University; Meredith Weinstein, North Carolina State University; Robert Wrinkle, University of Texas–Pan American; and Lin Ye, Roosevelt University.

We thank our editor, Lauren Athmer, for her work on and dedication to this book. We are also grateful to the staff of Cengage Learning. The authors thank Rebecca A. Peter for her excellent assistance in the revision process. Although we appreciate the help rendered by all of these people, they share none of the blame for any errors of commission or omission. That responsibility rests solely with us.

Kenneth J. Meier
Texas A&M University

Jeffrey L. Brudney
University of North Carolina Wilmington

John Bohte
University of Wisconsin–Milwaukee

Foundations of Quantitative Analysis

Statistics and Public and Nonprofit Administration

The Advantages of a Statistical Approach

Can the study of statistics be interesting and rewarding? We think it can be. Can learning to use statistics make you a more accomplished and professional public or nonprofit administrator? Without a doubt. Our commitment to these principles led us to write this book.

As we have revised and improved each edition of this textbook, we have been able to demonstrate more convincingly the advantages of statistics for the study and practice of public and nonprofit administration. Most important, by offering insight into issues and problems in a field that would otherwise go unnoticed and unheeded, statistics will help you to become a better decision maker.

First, statistics have great power to describe systematically a body of information or data to provide the background you need for decision making. No other approach matches the precision and quantification that statistics bring to this task. Statistics can show very precisely the average, as well as the variability, in a subset or *sample* of data or in the population as a whole. Consider a local food pantry, for example. The nonprofit manager would like to know how many hours volunteers donate to the organization in a typical week. How much do the hours donated vary week by week? Or, consider the regional office of the department of motor vehicles. The director needs to know how many clients on average visit in a typical day. How much does this number vary day to day? This information is essential for decision makers, for example, for planning and staffing. Answering such questions is the descriptive function of statistics.

Second, statistics are very useful for testing ideas *empirically*—that is, against actual data or observations. Statistics subject our intuitive ideas about how a process or phenomenon operates to empirical testing. Confronting our informed conjectures and speculations with data and observation is called *hypothesis testing*. A *hypothesis* is an informed guess or conjecture about an issue or problem of interest. For example, we might hypothesize or conjecture that as nonprofit organizations become more involved in the delivery of publicly financed services, more jobs will become available in these sectors, or that developing skills in statistics in a master of public administration (MPA) program or in a concentration in nonprofit management will enhance students' prospects in the job market upon graduation. Statistics are helpful for evaluating the extent to which the data available support or refute our hypotheses. This use constitutes the hypothesis-testing function of statistics.

Third, statistics are the foremost method for drawing an accurate inference from a subset or sample of data to its parent, the full population. Rarely does a public or nonprofit administrator have the luxury of working with the complete population; instead, the data available are almost always a sample of observations. Nevertheless, administrators would like to use the sample of data to generalize or infer to the entire population. Public and nonprofit administrators need to know what the sample suggests about the population. For example, based on a random sample of residents, a nonprofit administrator may want to estimate the likely number of financial donors in the county. Based on a sample of agency records, a public administrator may need to estimate the number of housing units that are vacant in the city. Statistics provide an excellent methodology for drawing this linkage. Because we do not have the data from the entire population, we can still make an error in inferring from the sample to the population. Yet statistics are valuable, for they enable the analyst to estimate the probability or extent of this error. This function is the essence of statistical inference.

To these classic uses of statistics we can add two others. First, in public and nonprofit administration, managers face situations and challenges of daunting complexity, such as homelessness, poverty, illiteracy, crime, drug and alcohol dependency, and child and spousal abuse. We entrust to public and nonprofit managers the most difficult problems in society. A major advantage of statistics is that they can help the manager keep track of an almost innumerable collection of measured characteristics or attributes, called *variables*, at the same time. Statistics allow the manager to manipulate the variables and evaluate the strength of their influence on desired outcomes, such as raising agency performance and citizen satisfaction in the public sector or increasing success in obtaining grant funding and retaining volunteers in the nonprofit sector. The ability to examine a large number of variables simultaneously—and to sort out and make sense of the complicated interrelationships among them—is a great advantage of statistical methods for dealing with the highly complex problems that confront the public and nonprofit sectors.

An appreciation of statistics can also help the public and the nonprofit manager become a much more discerning consumer of quantitative information. Like it or not, managers in all sectors are bombarded with "facts" or assertions based on statistical analysis. There is no escape from them. They appear regularly in myriad sources, including reports, evaluations, memoranda, briefings, hearings, press releases, newspaper accounts, electronic communications, books, academic journals, and many other outlets. Public and nonprofit managers need the skills to evaluate the conflicting claims and representations often made, and to avoid being misled. Statistics offer major benefits in this area. Perhaps this reason is the best one of all for the study and application of statistics in public and nonprofit administration.

As reflected in the MPA curriculum, statistics are certainly not all there is to know about public or nonprofit organizations and management. One must acquire or hone additional skills as well as develop a general understanding of broader political, legal, economic, and social forces. But statistics, too, have a rightful place in the program of study for the MPA, as well as in academic concentrations and degree programs in nonprofit organizations and management.

Statistics and Options for Managers

For these reasons, statistics and quantitative analysis have become a major element of public and nonprofit management. The organizations and agencies in which you will likely work routinely use data and statistics to help understand complex situations and make decisions. Human resources managers receive personnel projections to schedule recruitment efforts. Transportation planners rely on complex computer simulations to design urban transportation systems. Budget officers and accountants scour economic projections and analyses. Program evaluators are charged with making quantitative assessments of a program's effectiveness. Nonprofit managers weigh the benefits against the costs of hiring a fund-raising firm. They compare volunteer recruitment and turnover rates by age and education level. They distribute surveys to donors and potential donors to learn about them and encourage further giving. Quantitative analyses have become so prevalent that no midlevel manager in the public or nonprofit sector can—or should—hope to avoid them.

The increasing sophistication of quantitative techniques affords public and nonprofit managers few options with regard to statistics. At one extreme, a manager untutored in statistical methods can act as if they did not exist and ignore reports containing statistics. Unfortunately, this option is exercised all too often and at considerable cost: The public or nonprofit manager loses valuable information presented in quantitative form. This option is not acceptable.

At the other extreme, public and nonprofit managers may choose to accept, uncritically, the findings of the data analyst or statistical report. This option leads to an error as serious as the first. Although quantitative analysts will almost certainly possess a stronger background in statistics than does the manager (that's their job), the analysts lack the experience and skills—and the responsibility—to make managerial decisions. Those decisions rest with public and nonprofit managers, based on the best statistical (and other) advice available. We wrote this book for students who consider public or nonprofit management their present or future occupation.

The third option open to the manager—the one endorsed by the authors—is to receive training in quantitative techniques. The training advocated and offered in this book, however, is *not* a standard course in statistics, which often remains a required (and dreaded) element of most MPA programs and nonprofit education degrees. Instead, we seek to develop appreciation for, and intuitive understanding of, basic elements of statistics and quantitative analysis for managers in the public and nonprofit sectors.

Reading this book and working the problems presented (which we recommend you do!) will not transform you from quantitative novice to master statistician. Such a transformation is not desired, nor necessary. By and large, public and nonprofit managers do not select and calculate the appropriate statistics. Far more often, they receive statistical information and are expected to make reasoned and responsible decisions based on it (and other factors). For this task, a rigorous course in mathematical statistics is not required. It is essential, however, that managers become intelligent and critical consumers of quantitative information. Toward that end, this book stresses the application, interpretation, and evaluation of basic statistics.

This book is intended primarily for students who have no, or only a very limited, background in mathematics, statistics, or other quantitative methods. We present the material in an applied, nonrigorous, easily readable format that focuses on practical problems faced by public and nonprofit managers. The book is designed to engage readers in the discussion of these problems and to help you see how statistics can be useful in managerial decision making. Often we present a step-by-step approach to learning the different statistical techniques to build your confidence and mastery. Statistical theory is discussed only rarely, and the computational formulas that pepper most statistics books are reserved for those instances in which they enlighten rather than mystify.

We hope that the advantages of our approach will become evident as you read and use the book. As noted before, it is not intended to be a comprehensive text in formal statistics. Instead, we have written the book as an introduction to statistics for managers in the public and nonprofit sectors. Too often, students in our field are alienated by more formal methods courses that emphasize precision over application, or theory over data, with the result that a first course in statistics becomes an eminently disliked and forgettable last one. We have worked to develop a text that will engage and hold the interest of students in public and nonprofit administration and, hopefully, whet their appetite for further training in this area. For those who seek a more mathematical and theoretical approach to managerial statistics, several good books are available (see the Annotated Bibliography at the end of the text).

The Role of Calculation

Whenever possible in this book, we have provided step-by-step instructions for performing statistical procedures and evaluating the results. We strongly recommend that you do these calculations and follow along. Statistics is not a spectator sport: You learn by doing.

But with laptop and desktop computer programs featuring an entire repertoire of statistics seemingly available at the click of a computer mouse, why worry about calculating statistics? Why go to the trouble?

Precisely because statistics have become so immediately accessible, it is all the more important to see how they are derived and computed. We know of no better way to understand the various statistics, their advantages and limitations, and their assumptions and anomalies than to experiment with a few data points, make the appropriate calculations, and observe what values of the statistic are generated in return. Whatever the strengths or peculiarities of the statistic, they will soon become apparent to you. You will see how the statistic can assist you in decision making.

Given the profusion of user-friendly statistical package programs available on laptop and desktop computers, however, many students and managers in the public and nonprofit sectors are becoming exposed to them through a different mechanism: Instead of learning about the statistics beforehand and then applying them, they may plunge into using them simply because they are so accessible. Unfortunately, though, they may not understand them. We do not want to discourage healthy curiosity or interest in statistics; nurturing it is difficult enough. But, in effect, these students and managers practice a tempting statistical version of the popular television quiz show *Jeopardy*; for those who are not aware, in this quiz show contestants are given the answer but must state the question (instead of the reverse—fun, huh?). For instance, you can easily obtain "the regression" (answer) on the computer, but what regression is, how you should interpret it, and why are questions that require prior study for correct application and use. In this book we pose the important questions before explaining the answers.

With statistical package programs increasingly loaded onto computers, students untrained in quantitative techniques can easily generate the statistical "answers" on their computer—but then can only guess at the question, use, or purpose behind those answers. In our judgment, these students have not learned statistics but have acquired a computer skill. There is a big difference. In this book, we emphasize building foundational knowledge of statistics for public and nonprofit managers.

Academic Standards for Master's Degree Programs in Public Affairs and Curricular Guidelines for Nonprofit Academic Programs

We can offer you one more reason for learning and using applied statistics in public administration and nonprofit administration: the accreditation standards in the field. The National Association of Schools of Public Affairs and Administration (NASPAA) has formulated standards for accreditation of master's degree programs in public affairs, policy, and administration. Many public administration programs also offer concentrations or certificates in nonprofit administration and include pertinent courses in the curriculum.

NASPAA adopted the revised *Standards for Accreditation for Master's Degree Programs* in 2009.[1] NASPAA Standard 5, "Matching Operations with the Mission: Student Learning," section 5.1, "Universal Required Competencies," states that an MPA program, "As the basis for its curriculum … will adopt a set of required competencies related to its mission and public service values" in five domains. The domains encompass the ability to

- lead and manage in public governance;
- participate in and contribute to the policy process;
- analyze, synthesize, think critically, solve problems, and make decisions;
- articulate and apply a public service perspective; and
- communicate and interact productively with a diverse and changing workforce and citizenry.

The chapters and material presented in this book are intended especially to raise the ability of students in public administration to "analyze, synthesize, think critically, solve problems, and make decisions." Increasing and honing this ability, in turn, will contribute to the other four required NAPAA competencies of leading and managing in governance, participating and contributing in the policy process, articulating and applying a public service perspective, and communicating and interacting with the workforce and citizenry. This book will help to create and refine the ability of students in public and nonprofit administration to synthesize information, understand and perform crucial data analysis and interpret the results, and support problem solving and decision making that underlie sound and effective practice in the other domains specified by NASPAA in its accreditation standards.

Although it does not yet have authority or responsibility to accredit academic programs in nonprofit studies, the Nonprofit Academic Centers Council (NACC) published revised *Curricular Guidelines for Graduate Study in Nonprofit Leadership, the Nonprofit Sector and Philanthropy* in 2007.[2] Section 16.0 treats "Assessment, Evaluation and Decision-Making Methods" and includes three guidelines for nonprofit academic programs to meet in this area:

1. methods and modes to evaluate performance and effectiveness at both organizational and programmatic levels;
2. decision-making models and methods and how to apply them in nonprofit organizational settings; and
3. the use and application of both quantitative and qualitative data for purposes of strengthening nonprofit organizations, the nonprofit sector, and society at large.

This book can assist MPA programs and students in meeting the NASPAA Standards for Accreditation with regard to the ability to "analyze, synthesize,

---

[1] http://www.naspaa.org/accreditation/standard2009/docs/NS2009FinalVote10.16.2009.pdf
[2] http://www.naccouncil.org/pdf/GradCG07.pdf

think critically, solve problems, and make decisions." Likewise, this book offers coverage of the NACC Curricular Guidelines for "Assessment, Evaluation and Decision-Making Methods."

This book can provide the basis for courses that satisfy the NASPAA Accreditation Standards and the NACC Curricular Guidelines relating to quantitative techniques of analysis and requisite skills in program evaluation, information synthesis, decision making, and problem solving. The book elaborates statistical methods as a tool for assisting public and nonprofit managers in making decisions. By focusing on the assumptions underlying the various techniques, the careful interpretation of results, and the limitations as well as the strengths of the information conveyed, the text stresses the ethical and effective utilization of statistics and quantitative analysis.

With respect to the competencies identified by NASPAA and NACC, Part 1 of the book addresses "Foundations of Quantitative Analysis." The chapters in this section set out the rationale for a statistical approach in public and nonprofit administration and provide essential background in measurement and research design. The chapters elaborate on research methodology and treat a wide range of related issues, including problem diagnosis, the logic of inquiry, causal inference, and threats to the validity of a quantitative study.

Part 2, "Descriptive Statistics," introduces basic statistical analysis. The chapters here are also useful for acquainting students with the presentation and interpretation of statistical charts, graphs, and tables to inform themselves as well as other decision makers.

Part 3, "Probability," explores the many uses of this tool in public and nonprofit management. The chapters in this section assist students in defining and diagnosing decision situations and selecting and evaluating a course of action.

The chapters in Part 4, "Inferential Statistics," not only develop sophisticated analytic skills but also help in the definition of problems, formulation of alternatives, choice of decision, and evaluation of results. They help the manager to understand the promise—and the limitations—of a sample of data for reaching conclusions about the entire population.

Part 5, "Analysis of Nominal and Ordinal Data," introduces another set of quantitative skills useful for the public and nonprofit administrator. This type of analysis is employed frequently in written memoranda and technical reports and in the evaluation of survey data. These data distinguish public administration and nonprofit administration (and other social science fields) from the natural, physical, and biological sciences, in which measurement is typically much more precise.

Part 6 presents "Regression Analysis." Regression is one of the most flexible and frequently utilized statistical techniques in the social sciences. The chapters in this section greatly enhance the decision-making, analytic, and evaluative capabilities of public and nonprofit managers. The chapters in this section discuss the methods of regression analysis and the varied applications of regression-based techniques in public and nonprofit management. The last chapter in this section, Chapter 21, explains how to read and interpret regression output generated by computer programs, which is often complicated and difficult to understand. The chapter provides a needed skill that is too often overlooked. In sum, this book provides essential coverage pertaining to the NASPAA Standards for Accreditation in Public Affairs and Administration and the NACC Curricular Guidelines for Nonprofit Administration.

A Road Map for This Book

This book is designed so that each of its parts is self-contained, yet builds on the other parts.

Part 1 lays the foundations for the use of statistics and quantitative analysis in public and nonprofit administration. Chapter 1 explains why statistics have become important to this enterprise, and Chapter 2 elaborates how to measure critical *concepts* such as organizational effectiveness, job satisfaction, volunteer competence for a task, and public trust in an agency. Chapter 2 also provides the twin evaluative criteria for assessing measurement: reliability and validity.

Chapter 3 shows how to depict or model a problem or issue of importance in public or nonprofit administration—for example, the reorganization of an agency to increase productivity—and how to follow up with a systematic study based on data. The chapter elaborates different research plans, called *research designs*, that direct how and when the data are to be collected, analyzed, and interpreted to answer questions about topics of interest, such as how to improve service delivery, recruit volunteers more effectively, integrate the work of paid and nonpaid (volunteer) human resources, or redesign public or nonprofit organizations. The chapter provides the context for understanding the uses, advantages, and limitations of the statistics presented in the other chapters of the book.

Part 2 covers basic descriptive statistics. This part of the book is devoted to the analysis of *univariate statistics* or one variable at a time. Chapter 4, "Frequency Distributions," begins this discussion with a treatment of how to categorize and display a large volume of data, or a (frequency) distribution, in a graphical format, such as a table, chart, or figure, and how to work with percentages. The chapter following, "Measures of Central Tendency," is concerned with finding and interpreting the average in a distribution of data: You may be familiar with the main measures of central tendency: the mean, median, and mode. The chapter shows how to calculate these statistics both for data that have been arranged in a table or chart and for data that have not, which we affectionately term "raw data." Once you have calculated or read the average for a group or distribution of data, the next question to ask is how closely the data cluster or spread about this average—that is, whether the observed values or observations are relatively concentrated or dispersed about the measure of central tendency. Chapter 6, "Measures of Dispersion," introduces the two major statistics for measuring dispersion in a sample of data: the variance and its close relative, the standard deviation. It also discusses the range and other statistics.

The next part of the book addresses probability. Chapter 7 presents the most common probability distribution, the normal curve. The familiar bell-shaped curve has numerous uses and applications in public and nonprofit administration. When data follow a normal distribution, it is practical and easy (OK, maybe not easy, but surely within your reach) to determine, for example, the percentage of job applicants who fall above or below a criterion score on a test of job-related skills. Or you can find the score that distinguishes the top 5% of applicants who warrant further consideration, such as a follow-up interview.

Have you ever wanted to know the probability that an agency could hire three minorities for 10 positions when 50% of the job applicants were minorities? For problems similar to this one, Chapter 8 introduces the binomial probability distribution. The chapter also shows how the normal distribution can be applied to simplify complex binomial problems, provided certain conditions are met. Chapter 9 discusses other useful probability distributions for public and nonprofit managers. The hypergeometric probability distribution is used when the manager wants to make a generalization from a sample to a finite population. The Poisson and the exponential probability distributions are used whenever the manager needs to include time or distance in a probability judgment—for example, the probability of having two computer failures per day at the agency, or encountering 15 potholes per 100 meters in a sample of city streets.

Part 4 explores statistical inference and focuses on the issue of how the manager can generalize (infer) results from a small sample of data to the much larger population from which the sample was drawn. This technique is useful in its own right and also to support advanced statistical procedures presented later in the book, such as regression analysis. Because the public or nonprofit manager almost always works with a sample of data rather than the full population—but seeks reliable information about the entire population—knowledge of statistical inference is essential. To learn how to estimate the value of the mean or average for a population from a sample of data, consult Chapter 10. This chapter also discusses procedures for constructing confidence bands or intervals around the mean estimate.

Chapter 11 applies the techniques of statistical inference to testing hypotheses. Although it is not possible to avoid the risk of error in inferring from a sample of data to the population (we cannot be sure of our estimates if we do not have population information), public or nonprofit managers may be willing to take an acceptable risk in drawing an inference. The chapter shows how, by using the techniques of classical hypothesis testing on a sample of data, the manager can make a decision regarding the full population—for example, that the average number of times the population of agency clients seeks assistance is four times or more per year, or that the average is less—with a risk of error of, say, 5%. You will thus learn a technique that in the long run will allow you to make the correct decision 95% of the time but be in error the remaining 5% (remember, because we do not know the "answers" in the population, we cannot be right all the time). Chapter 12 shows how to estimate population proportions, rather than mean or average values, from a sample—for example, the proportion (or percentage) of motorists in a county who drive faster than 65 miles per hour on a stretch of highway. For those situations in which the manager needs to compare the performance or characteristics of two groups (e.g., experimental and control groups, a group before [pre-] and after [post-] the implementation of a program), Chapter 13 explains how to test for differences between groups using the statistical technique called *analysis of variance*.

Beginning with Part 5, the remainder of the book deals with relationships between two or more variables. The study of relationships between two variables is called *bivariate analysis*. Bivariate statistical techniques can help to answer myriad research and practical questions for the public and nonprofit manager: Is agency budget related to performance? Do police patrols reduce crime? Does greater inclusiveness in government hiring lead to a more responsive bureaucracy? Does government contracting with nonprofit organizations produce more efficient delivery of services? Do employees in nonprofit organizations display greater job motivation than those in other sectors of the economy? Do smaller nonprofit organizations adapt more quickly to their environments than larger ones? Is there a relationship between delegating decision-making authority to lower levels of the organization and innovativeness of employees?

Part 5 explains how to construct tables and analyze data measured at the nominal or ordinal levels—that is, information measured in terms of categories (nominal variables include gender and race) or rating scales (ordinal variables encompass attitudes, such as attitude toward balancing the federal budget or clients' evaluations of the training provided by a volunteer center). Chapter 14 shows how to use percentages to analyze and interpret tables called *contingency tables* or *cross-tabulations* that pair data from two nominal or ordinal variables. Chapter 15 builds on this foundation to provide more sophisticated techniques for analyzing tables, including statistical inference (chi-square) and measures of association (gamma, lambda, and so forth). Chapter 16 discusses statistical control table analysis, a procedure for examining the relationship between two variables while taking into account, or "controlling for" or "holding constant," a third variable. The analysis of three or more variables simultaneously presented in this chapter introduces *multivariate analysis*, a topic covered more extensively in later chapters of the text.

Part 6 is concerned with relationships between variables assessed on equal interval scales, or "interval" data, such as variables measured in years, dollars, or miles. Chapter 17 begins the discussion with an "Introduction to Regression Analysis," a highly flexible and often used statistical technique that is helpful in a variety of managerial situations in the public and nonprofit sectors. The chapter shows how a line or linear relationship depicted in a graph can summarize the relationship between two interval variables—for instance, the relationship between the number of intake workers at a government facility and the number of clients who receive service in a given day. Chapter 18 explains the assumptions and limitations of regression analysis. Estimating and predicting trends in the future based on past data is the subject of Chapter 19 on time series analysis. This chapter is concerned with forecasting over time trends important to public and nonprofit managers, such as future population, the number of people likely to volunteer to government agencies, service clients, sewage output, and the number of organizations that will participate in the community walk-a-thon to raise cancer awareness.

Chapter 20, "Multiple Regression," extends this technique to the multivariate context: It shows how to use regression to analyze and understand relationships among three or more variables. For example, how well can the average age of housing and the percentage of renter-occupied buildings in a neighborhood explain or predict the incidence of fires across a city? To what extent do the number of volunteers working in nonprofit agencies and the number of community events sponsored by these organizations affect the amount of money collected in their annual fund-raising campaigns?

Chapter 21 focuses on the interpretation of regression output—that is, output generated by statistical software package programs. The earlier chapters in this section present a variety of regression examples in equation form to illustrate how relationships between variables can be summarized using linear equations. Regression analysis is almost always performed with computers. Statistical software packages generally do not present regression results in equation form, however—which can make the leap from textbook to computer printout confusing. This chapter explains how to write up regression results based on a summary table of statistics, which constitute most statistical software package programs' presentations.

Following the chapters in the book, you will find other materials useful for the study of applied statistics for public and nonprofit administration. For those motivated to learn more about statistics (do not laugh—by the time you have read a chapter or two, this student could be you!), we have included an annotated bibliography with a brief description of each entry. The bibliography contains a wide assortment of texts valuable for assistance and reference. For ease of use of the book, you will also find, at the back, a glossary of key terms that have been boldfaced at their first appearance in the text (except in the first chapter, where they are highlighted in italics to draw attention to later use). To make the book self-contained, you will find all of the statistical tables (normal, *t*-test, etc.) essential for applied statistics for public and nonprofit administration—both in your coursework and in your careers. Finally, you will quickly make friends with the section containing answers to the odd-numbered computational questions from the problem sets at the end of each chapter. We encourage you to work these problems and check your results.

Whenever possible, we have attempted to include problems faced by public and nonprofit administrators in the real world. Many of our midcareer as well as more senior students have suggested problems and examples for the book. Although all the data and problems are hypothetical, they represent the types of situations that often confront practicing public and nonprofit administrators. We hope that you find them useful and interesting.

Now you have a road map for the book. Good luck on the journey!

Measurement

U sing a statistical approach in public and nonprofit administration begins with measurement. **Measurement** is the assignment of numbers to some phenomenon that we are interested in analyzing. For example, the effectiveness of army officers is measured by having senior officers rate junior officers on various traits. Educational attainment may be measured by how well a student scores on standardized achievement tests. Good performance by a city bus driver might be measured by the driver's accident record and by his or her record of running on time. The success of a nonprofit agency's fund-raising drive might be measured by the amount of money raised. How well a nonprofit agency's board of directors represents client interests might be measured by the percentage of former or current clients on the board.

Frequently, the phenomenon of interest cannot be measured so precisely but only in terms of categories. For example, public and nonprofit administrators are often interested in characteristics and attitudes of the general populace and of various constituency groups. We can measure such things as the racial and gender composition of the individuals in these groups; their state of residence or their religious preferences; their attitudes toward a particular agency or government in general; their views on space exploration, public spending, or the tax treatment of nonprofit organizations; and so on. Although such variables do not have quantitative measurement scales, it is still possible to measure them in terms of categories—for instance, white versus nonwhite; female versus male; favor tax decrease, favor no change, favor tax increase; and so on. Although these phenomena cannot be measured directly with numerical scales, they are important variables nonetheless. Public and nonprofit administrators need to know how to measure, describe, and analyze such variables statistically.

In many managerial situations, the manager does not consciously think about measurement. Rather, the manager obtains some data and subjects them to analysis. Of course, problems arise with this approach. For example, in Chapter 11 we discuss a program where the Prudeville police department cracks down on prostitution in the city, and arrests by the vice squad increase from 3.4 to 4.0 on average per day. Based on these numbers, the police chief claims a successful program. This example illustrates a common measurement problem. The city council of Prudeville was concerned about the high level of prostitution activity, not the low level of prostitution arrests. Conceivably the number of prostitution arrests could be positively related to the level of prostitution activity (i.e., more prostitution arrests indicate greater prostitution activity). In this situation the police chief's data may reveal increased prostitution, not decreased prostitution. In fact, the only thing an analyst can say, given the police chief's data, is that the number of prostitution arrests increased.

In this chapter, we discuss some of the important aspects of measurement, both in theory and in application. The chapter presents the theory of measurement and discusses operational definitions and indicators. Following this discussion, the chapter explores the concept of measurement validity and then turns to increasing reliability and the types of measures, such as subjective indicators, objective indicators, and unobtrusive indicators. Next, the chapter presents levels of measurement: nominal, ordinal, and interval. It follows with a discussion of the implications of selecting a particular level of measurement and concludes by considering performance measurement techniques and benchmarking.

Theory of Measurement

Measurement theory assumes that a concept that interests an analyst cannot be measured directly. Army officer effectiveness, educational achievement, bus driver performance, level of prostitution activity, social capital, program success, and civic engagement are all concepts that cannot be measured directly. Such concepts are measured indirectly through indicators specified by operational definitions. An **operational definition** is a statement that describes how a concept will be measured. An **indicator** is a variable, or set of observations, that results from applying the operational definition. Examples of operational definitions include the following:

- Educational attainment for Head Start participants is defined by the achievement scores on the Iowa Tests of Basic Skills.
- Officer effectiveness is defined by subjective evaluations by senior officers using form AJK147/285-Z.
- Program success for the Maxwell rehabilitation program is defined as a recidivism rate of less than 50%.
- A convict is considered a recidivist if, within 1 year of release from jail, the convict is arrested and found guilty.
- Clients' satisfaction with the service of the Department of Human Resources is measured according to the response categories that clients check on a questionnaire item (high satisfaction, medium satisfaction, and low satisfaction).
- An active volunteer in the Environmental Justice Association is defined as a person who donates his or her time to the association at least 5 hours per week, on average.

- One measure of board director activity of the Nature Society is the number of hours devoted by board members to this organization each month.
- The efficiency of a fund-raising firm is defined as the money raised divided by the costs paid to the firm.

Operational definitions are often not stated explicitly but are implied from the research report, the memo, or the briefing. A manager should always encourage research analysts to state explicitly their operational definitions. Then the manager can focus on these definitions and answer a variety of measurement questions, such as the ones we will discuss later. It is important for public and nonprofit managers to know how the complicated concepts they deal with are measured. Without this knowledge, they will be hard-pressed to understand quantitative analyses or explain them to others.

Reading the preceding operational definitions, you may have been troubled by the lack of complete congruence between the concept and the indicator. For example, assume the city transit system evaluates the job performance of its bus drivers by examining each one's accident record and on-time rate. A driver may well have a good accident record and be on time in her bus runs and yet be a poor bus driver. Perhaps the on-time record was achieved by not stopping to pick up passengers when the driver was running late. Or perhaps the driver's bus was continually in the shop because the driver did not see to maintaining the bus properly.

This example suggests that observed indicators may not offer a complete measure of the underlying concepts. Most students of measurement accept the following statement:

$$\text{Indicator} = \text{concept} + \text{error}$$

A good indicator of a concept contains very little error; a poor indicator is only remotely related to the underlying concept.

In many cases several indicators are used to measure a single concept. One reason for using **multiple indicators** is that a concept may have more than one dimension. For example, the effectiveness of a receptionist may be related to the receptionist's efficiency and the receptionist's courtesy to people. To measure effectiveness adequately in this instance, we would need at least one indicator of efficiency and one of courtesy. To measure nonprofit financial standing would require several indicators of, for example, funds in reserve, diversity in funding sources, and operating efficiency. The term *triangulation* is sometimes used to describe how multiple indicators enclose or "hone in" on a concept.

Multiple indicators are also needed when the indicators are only poor or incomplete representations of the underlying concept. For example, a measure of a nonprofit agency's receptivity to volunteers might include the presence of a volunteer coordinator, procedures in place to welcome new volunteers, and an explicit orientation for new volunteers. The success of a neighborhood revitalization program would require several indicators. The increase in housing values might be one indicator. The decrease in crime, reduction in vandalism, willingness to walk outside at night, and general physical appearance might be other indicators. The start of a neighborhood association or of a day care cooperative could be additional indicators. Each indicator reflects part of the concept of neighborhood revitalization but also reflects numerous other factors, such as economic growth in the entire city, demand for housing, street lighting, and so on. The theory behind multiple indicators in this situation is that the errors in one indicator will cancel out the errors in another indicator. What remains will measure the concept far better than any single indicator could alone. For these reasons, a multiple-indicator strategy to measure important concepts comes highly recommended in public and nonprofit management.

Measurement Validity

A **valid indicator** accurately measures the concept it is intended to measure. In other words, if the indicator contains very little error, then the indicator is a valid measure of the concept. The measurement validity of an indicator often becomes a managerial problem. For example, many governments administer civil service examinations that are supposed to be valid indicators of on-the-job performance. If minorities or women do not do as well as white males on these examinations, the agency is open to discrimination lawsuits. The agency's only defense in such a situation is to prove that the civil service examination is a valid indicator of on-the-job performance (not an easy task).

Validity can be either convergent or discriminant. The preceding paragraph discusses **convergent validity**: Do the indicator and the concept converge? Does the indicator measure the concept in question? **Discriminant validity** asks whether the indicator allows the concept to be distinguished from other similar, but different, concepts. For example, using achievement scores on standardized tests may lack discriminant validity if the tests have some cultural bias. A good indicator of educational achievement will distinguish that concept from the concept of white, middle-class acculturation. A culture-biased test will indicate only educational achievement that corresponds with the dominant culture. As a result, such an indicator may not be valid.

Social scientists have long grappled with the idea of **measurement validity**. They have suggested several ways that validity can be established. An indicator has **face validity** if the manager using the indicator accepts it as a valid indicator of the concept in question. For example, years spent by students in school is accepted as a valid indicator of formal education. An indicator has **consensual validity** if numerous persons in different situations accept the indicator as a valid indicator of the concept. The recidivism rate, for example, has consensual validity as a good measure of a prison's ability to reform a criminal. Often, consensual validity is established through finding a published research study in which the indicator has been used, thus suggesting its acceptance by scholars. An indicator has **correlational validity** if it correlates strongly with other indicators that are accepted as valid.

For example, community satisfaction with a nonprofit organization as assessed in a survey might be strongly related to the amount of monetary donations received by the agency or the number of donors. (In Chapter 17 we discuss correlation and how it is measured.) Finally, an indicator has **predictive validity** if it correctly predicts a specified outcome. For example, if scores on a civil service examination accurately predict on-the-job performance, the exam has predictive validity.

These four types of validity offer ways in which a public or nonprofit manager can accept, or argue, that an indicator is valid. They do not, however, guarantee that the indicator is a particularly effective measure of the concept in question. An indicator may have face validity, consensual validity, correlational validity, and predictive validity and still not be as effective as other measures. Consider the Law School Admission Test (LSAT). The LSAT has face validity (it seems to make sense) and consensual validity (numerous law schools use it to screen applicants). It also has correlational validity (it correlates with undergraduate grades) and predictive validity (it correlates with law school grades). And yet the LSAT is not as strong a predictor of law school performance as is the socioeconomic status of the student's family.

With all of the tests for validity and all of the different ways that an indicator can be validated, developing valid indicators of concepts remains an art. It requires all of the skills that a public or nonprofit manager has at his or her disposal. To be sure, in some cases, such as finding indicators of lawn-mower efficiency, valid indicators can be easy to derive. By contrast, developing valid indicators of community police effectiveness or of the "health" of the nonprofit community in a city is a very difficult task. Scholars and practitioners continually debate the meaning and measurement of crucial concepts, such as social capital, civic engagement, military preparedness, and board of directors' leadership.

One approach to finding or developing valid indicators is to review the published literature in a field. Or you may check studies or reports from other jurisdictions or consult with experts in the field. In general, if an indicator is used in the published literature, it has at a minimum both face and consensual validity, and it may meet other validity criteria as well. Before (or while) you create your own indicators of an important concept, it is a good idea to consult the relevant literature. A review of the literature carries additional benefits, such as making you aware of how other researchers have approached related problems or issues and what they have found. Such information can make your analytical task easier. You may also find that the "answer" to your research question, for which you had planned to develop indicators, already exists, thus saving you the time and effort of conducting your own study.

Measurement Reliability

A **reliable indicator** consistently assigns the same number to some phenomenon that has not, in fact, changed. For example, if a person measures the effectiveness of the police force in a neighborhood twice over a short period of time (short enough so that change is very unlikely) and arrives at the same value, then the indicator is termed *reliable*. Or, if the rate of volunteering to a volunteer center remains constant from one day to the next, it is probably a reliable indicator. If two different people use an indicator and arrive at the same value, then, again, we say that the indicator is reliable. Another way of defining a reliable indicator is to state that an indicator is a reliable measure if the values obtained by using the indicator are not affected by who is doing the measuring, by where the measuring is taking place, or by any other factors than variation in the concept being measured.

Increasing Reliability

The two major threats to **measurement reliability** are subjectivity and lack of precision. A **subjective measure** relies on the judgment of the measurer or of a respondent, for example, in a survey. A general measure that requires the analyst to assess the quality of a neighborhood or the performance of a nonprofit board of directors is a subjective measure. Subjective measures have some inherent unreliability because the final measures must incorporate judgment. Reliability can be improved by rigorous training of the individuals who will do the measuring. The goal of this training is to develop consistency. Another method of increasing reliability is to have several persons assign a value, and then select the consensus value as the measure of the phenomenon in question. Some studies report a measured *inter-rater reliability* based on the consistency of measurement performed by several raters. Often, judgments about the effectiveness of nonprofit boards of directors are based on the ratings provided by multiple knowledgeable actors—for example, the board chairperson, the chief executive officer of the nonprofit, and nonprofit stakeholders such as funders, donors, and other similar nonprofits in the community.

Reliability can also be improved by eliminating the subjectivity of the analyst. Rather than providing a general assessment of the quality of the neighborhood, the analyst might be asked to answer a series of specific questions. Was there trash in the streets? Did houses have peeling paint? Were dogs running loose? Did the street have potholes? How many potholes? Or consider the performance of the local volunteer center. How many volunteers does it attract? What work do the volunteers perform? What are the results of their efforts for the community? Does the volunteer center recruit any new volunteers or only those already active in the community?

Reliability problems often arise in survey research. For example, suppose that you were asked to respond to survey questions concerning the performance of one of your instructors—or a local political figure, or "bureaucrats," or the volunteers assisting in your agency—on a day that had been especially frustrating for you. You might well evaluate these subjects more harshly than on a day when all had seemed right with the world. Although nothing about these subjects had changed, extraneous factors could introduce volatility into the ratings, an indication of unreliability. If your views of these subjects had actually changed though, and the survey instrument picked up the (true) changes, the measurement would be considered reliable. (For that reason, reliability is often assessed over a short time interval.) By contrast, a reliable measure, such as agency salaries or number of employees and volunteers, is not affected by such extraneous factors.

Unfortunately, although removing the subjective element from a measure will increase reliability, it may decrease validity. Certain concepts important to public and nonprofit managers—employee effectiveness, citizen satisfaction with services, the impact of a recreation program—are not amenable to a series of objective indicators alone. In such situations a combination of objective and subjective indicators may well be the preferred approach to measurement.

Lack of precision is the second major threat to reliability. To illustrate this problem, we use the example of Mrs. Barbara Kennedy, city manager of Barren, Montana (fictional cities are used throughout the book), who wants to identify the areas of Barren with high unemployment so that she can use the city's federal job funds in those areas. Kennedy takes an employment survey and measures the unemployment rate in the city. Because her sample is fairly small, neighborhood unemployment rates have a potential error of $\pm 5\%$. This lack of precision makes the unemployment measure fairly unreliable. For example, neighborhood A might have a real unemployment rate of 5%, but the survey measure indicates 10%. Neighborhood B's unemployment rate is 13.5%, but the survey measure indicates 10%. Thus, the manager has a problem with measurement imprecision.

One way to improve the precision of these measures is to take larger samples. But in many cases, having a larger sample is insufficient. For example, suppose the city of Barren has a measure of housing quality that terms neighborhood housing stock as "good," "above average," "average," or "dilapidated." Assume that 50% of the city's housing falls into the dilapidated category. If the housing evaluation were undertaken to designate target areas for rehabilitation, the measure lacks precision. No city can afford to rehabilitate 50% of its housing stock. Barren needs a more precise measure that can distinguish among houses in the dilapidated category. This need can be met by creating measures that are more sensitive to variations in dilapidated houses (the premise is that some dilapidated houses are more dilapidated than others; for example, "dilapidated" and "uninhabitable"). Improving precision in this instance is more difficult than simply increasing the sample size.

Measuring Reliability

Unlike validity, the reliability of a measure can be determined objectively. A common method for assessing measurement reliability is to measure the same phenomenon or set of indicators or variables twice over a reasonably short time interval and to correlate the two sets of measures. The *correlation coefficient* is a measure of the statistical relationship or association between two characteristics or variables (see Chapter 17). In this instance, the higher the correlation between the two measures over time, the higher the reliability. This procedure is known as **test-retest reliability**.

Another approach to determining reliability is to prepare alternative forms that are designed to be equivalent to measure a given concept, and then to administer both of them at the same time. For example, near the beginning of a survey, a researcher may include a set of five questions to measure attitudes toward government spending or trust in nonprofit fund-raisers, and toward the end of the survey, he or she may present five more questions on the same topic, all parallel in content. The correlation between the responses obtained on the two sets of items is a measure of **parallel forms reliability**. Closely related is **split-half reliability**, in which the researcher divides a set of items intended to measure a given concept into two parts or halves; a common practice is to divide them into the even-numbered questions and the odd-numbered questions. The correlation between the responses obtained on the two halves is a measure of split-half reliability. *Cronbach's alpha*, a common measure of reliability, is based on this method.

In all three types of reliability measurement—test-retest, parallel forms, and split-half—the higher the intercorrelations or statistical relationships among the items, the higher the reliability of the indicators.

If several individuals are responsible for collecting and coding data, it is also good practice to assess **inter-rater reliability**. Inter-rater reliability is based on the premise that the application of a measurement scheme should not vary depending on who is doing the measuring (see above). For example, in screening potential applicants for a food and clothing assistance program, a nonprofit community center might use a 10-item checklist for assessing the level of need for each client. To determine whether agency staff are interpreting and applying the checklist consistently, we could ask five employees to screen the same group of 20 clients using the checklist. High inter-rater reliability would exist if all five employees came up with very similarly scored (or even identical) checklists for each client. Alternatively, if the scored checklists for each client turned out to be dramatically different, we would have low inter-rater reliability. Low inter-rater reliability can indicate that confusion exists over how a measurement instrument should be applied and interpreted.

Types of Measures

We have already presented examples of two types of indicators—subjective and objective. The **subjective indicator** requires some judgment to assign a value, whereas the **objective indicator** seeks to minimize discretion. Assume that the city manager wants to know the amount of city services delivered to each neighborhood in the city. Objective measures of city services would be acres of city parks, number of tons of trash collected, number of police patrols, and so on. Subjective measures of city services could be obtained by asking citizens whether the levels of various city services were adequate. A subjective measure of nonprofit organizational effectiveness—a difficult concept to assess—might be the reputation of these organizations as assessed by local funding agencies.

A third type of measure, an **unobtrusive indicator**, is intended to circumvent the so-called *Hawthorne effect*, in which the act of measuring a phenomenon can alter the behavior being assessed. In the Hawthorne studies, employees who were observed by a research team seemed to change their workplace behavior as a result of being observed. For example, when you call the county services hotline and hear the message that "your call may be monitored and recorded," you are likely to receive different (better) treatment than if no message were issued. As another example, asking city residents about the quality of police services may sensitize them to police actions. If an individual is asked his or her opinion again, the answer may be biased by earlier sensitizing. A city employment counselor, for example, will likely know that her evaluation is based on the number of individuals who are placed in jobs. She may then focus her efforts on the easiest persons to place, rather than devote time to all clients, to build up a favorable record. Any reactive measure (a measure that affects behavior when it is taken) has some inherent reliability and validity problems.

One way to circumvent this problem is through the use of unobtrusive measures (see Webb et al., 1999). A library, for example, could determine its most useful reference books (which do not circulate) by asking patrons which reference books they use most frequently. Among the problems in this situation is that many people who do not use reference books might answer the question nevertheless. An unobtrusive measure of reference book popularity would be the amount of wear on each book. To gauge public interest in its operations, a nonprofit organization could count the number of Web "hits" on its home page.

Suppose the head of the Alcoholic Beverage Control Board in a state wants to know how much liquor is consumed "by the drink." Because it is illegal to serve liquor by the drink in many counties in certain states, sending a survey questionnaire to private clubs would yield little (valid) response. An unobtrusive measure would be to count the number of empty liquor bottles found in the trash of private clubs. An unobtrusive measure of the interest of service volunteers in the governance of a nonprofit board would be a simple count of how many volunteers attend open board sessions over a calendar year.

Unobtrusive measures can be used in a variety of situations and can take on as many different forms as the creative manager can devise. They do, however, have some limitations. Unless care is taken in selection, the measures may lack validity. For example, a manager may decide that she can determine the amount of time an office spends in nonproductive socializing by measuring the office's consumption of coffee and fountain water (this fountain uses bottled water). She assumes that more coffee and more water fountain meetings imply less productivity. In fact, one office might consume more coffee than another because it has older workers (who are more likely to drink coffee) or because the office puts in more overtime and needs more coffee to make it through the night.

Levels of Measurement

In many cases public and nonprofit managers can use actual numbers to measure phenomena: tons of garbage collected in a given town, number of arrests made by the police per week, response times in minutes of a local fire department, number of children attending a daily church after-school program, miles driven in a week by Meals on Wheels volunteers, and so forth. Because this information consists of real numbers, it is possible to perform all types of arithmetic calculations with the data— addition, subtraction, multiplication, and division. As we will learn in Chapter 5 on measures of central tendency, when we have numerical data, we can readily compute average scores, such as the mean or average number of tons of garbage collected per week, the average response time of the fire department, and so forth.

Unfortunately for public and nonprofit administrators, available data are often not measured in nearly as precise a fashion as are these variables. There are several reasons for the lack of precision. In some cases it is a reflection of the state of the art of measurement. For instance, although it may be possible to say that a client is "very satisfied," "satisfied," "neutral," "dissatisfied," or "very dissatisfied" with a new job training program contracted out to a nonprofit agency, it usually is *not* possible to state that his or her level of satisfaction is exactly 2.3—or 5 or 9.856 or 1.003. Most measures of attitudes and opinions do not allow this level of exactitude. In other instances, loss of precision results from errors in measurement or, perhaps, from lack of foresight. For example, you may be interested in the number of traffic fatalities in the town of Berrysville over the past few years. As a consequence of incomplete records or spotty reporting in the past, you may not be able to arrive at the exact number of fatalities in each of these years, but you may be quite confident in determining that there have been *fewer* fatalities this year than *last year*.

Finally, some variables inherently lack numerical precision: One could classify the citizens of a community according to race (white, African American, Hispanic, or other), gender (male or female), religion (Protestant, Catholic, Jewish, Buddhist, or other), and many other attributes. It would be futile to attempt to calculate the arithmetic average of race or religion, however, and it would be meaningless to say that a citizen is more female than male: A person is classified as either one or the other.

In discussing these different types of variables, social scientists usually refer to the concept of **levels of measurement**. Social scientists conventionally speak of three levels of measurement. The first or highest (most precise) level is known as the **interval level** of measurement. The name derives from the fact that the measurement is based on a unit or interval that is accepted as a common standard and that yields identical results in repeated applications. Weight is measured in pounds or grams, height in feet and inches, distance in miles or kilometers, time in seconds or minutes, and so on. The variables discussed at the beginning of this section are all measured at the interval level: *tons* of garbage, *number* of arrests, response times in *minutes*. As a consequence of these standard units, it is possible to state not only that there were more arrests last week than this week but also that there were exactly *18* more arrests. (Some texts discuss a fourth level of measurement—*ratio*—but for our purposes it is effectively the same as interval measurement.)

The second level of measurement is called **ordinal**. At this level of measurement it is possible to say that one unit or observation (or event or phenomenon) has *more* or *less* of a given characteristic than another, but it is not possible to say *how much* more or less. Generally, we lack an agreed-on standard or metric ("interval") at this level of measurement. Almost all assessments of attitudes and opinions are at the ordinal level.

Consider the previous example, which focused on client satisfaction with a new job training program contracted out to a nonprofit agency specializing in this function. At this writing no one is quite sure how to measure satisfaction or how a unit of satisfaction may be defined. Nevertheless, an interviewer could be dispatched to the field to ask clients: "How satisfied are you with the new job training program recently instituted in this community? Very satisfied, satisfied, neutral, dissatisfied, or very dissatisfied?" To create an ordinal-level variable, we might attach numbers to the response categories for this survey question as a rank ordering. The numbered categories might look like those displayed in Table 2.1.

A participant who is "very satisfied" is assigned a score of "1," a participant who is "satisfied" is assigned a score of "2," and so on. Table 2.2 shows what the satisfaction variable would look like if we entered data for a small sample of participants into a spreadsheet or statistical software package.

Table 2.1	An Ordinal Measure of the Concept "Satisfaction"
	1 = very satisfied
	2 = satisfied
	3 = neutral
	4 = dissatisfied
	5 = very dissatisfied

© Cengage Learning

| Table 2.2 | An Example of an Ordinal Variable |

Name	Satisfaction
Jones	2
R. Smith	3
Franklin	1
Barnes	2
A. Smith	3

© Cengage Learning

Of course, it would not be possible to ascertain from a client his or her exact numerical level of satisfaction (e.g., 4.37; 16.23). For example, if a "1" is assigned to the response of one participant and a "3" to another, the precise magnitude of difference between the participants cannot be determined (for more on why precise distances across cases cannot be determined using nominal- and ordinal-level measures, see the section titled "Some Cautions" in Chapter 5). If one citizen answers that he or she is "very satisfied" with the program, however, it is safe to conclude that he is *more* satisfied than if he had stated that he was "satisfied" (or "neutral," "dissatisfied," or "very dissatisfied"); similarly, a response of "very dissatisfied" indicates *less* satisfaction than one of "dissatisfied" (or "neutral," "satisfied," or "very satisfied"). How *much* more or less remains a mystery. As another example, a polling firm might ask a representative sample of citizens how good a job they believe the mayor is doing in running the city (very good, good, average, poor, or very poor) and to what extent they are interested in community affairs (very interested, interested, neutral, uninterested, or very uninterested). These variables are also ordinal-level and are subject to the same limitations as is the measure of satisfaction with the job training program.

The name *ordinal measurement* derives from the ordinal numbers: first, second, third, and so on. These numbers allow the *ranking* of a set of units or observations (or events or phenomena) with respect to some characteristic or attribute, but they do not indicate the exact distances or differences between the objects. For example, in an election the order of finish of the candidates does not say anything about the number of votes each one received. The order of finish indicates only that the winner received more votes than did the runner-up, who in turn received more votes than the third-place finisher. By contrast, the exact vote totals of the candidates are interval information that reflects how many more or fewer votes each candidate received than the other candidates.

At the third level of measurement one loses not only the ability to state exactly how much of a trait or characteristic an object or event possesses (interval measurement) but also the ability to state that it has more or less of the characteristic than has another object or event (ordinal measurement). In short, the **nominal level** of measurement lacks any sense of relative size or magnitude: It allows one to say only that things are the same or different. Measurement notwithstanding, some of the most important variables in the social sciences are nominal. These were mentioned before: race, gender, and religion. It is easy to expand this list to public and nonprofit management: occupation, type of housing, job classification, sector of the economy, employment status. A nominal coding scheme for employee gender appears in Table 2.3.

If we entered data for a number of employees of a nonprofit agency into a spreadsheet or statistical software package program, the values for employee gender would look like those displayed in Table 2.4. In this example, employee Jones is female, whereas R. Smith is male.

Now that you have some idea of the three levels of measurement, write several examples of interval, ordinal, and nominal variables in the margins. After

Table 2.3	A Nominal Measure of Employee Gender
	1 = female
	0 = male

© Cengage Learning

Table 2.4	An Example of a Nominal Variable	
Name		**Employee Gender**
Jones		1
R. Smith		0
Franklin		1
Barnes		1
A. Smith		0

© Cengage Learning

you have finished, fill in the level of measurement for each of the variables listed in Table 2.5.

Whether you were aware of it or not, if you are like most people, before you read this chapter, you probably assumed that measurement was easy and accurate: All you needed to do was to count whatever it is that interests you or rely on technology to do the same thing. From the number of dollars a person makes (income) to the number of people in your city (population) to the amount of degrees registered on a thermometer (temperature) to the number of miles recorded by your automobile odometer as you drive to and from work (commute mileage), measurement was straightforward and precise. In (management) practice, measurement is more challenging—and more interesting.

The Implications of Selecting a Particular Level of Measurement

When deciding what level of measurement to collect and use as a public or nonprofit manager, keep in mind that variables originally coded at a higher level of measurement can be transformed into variables at lower levels of measurement because more precise measurements can be grouped into broader categories. The opposite is generally not true, however. Variables originally coded at lower levels of measurement cannot be transformed into variables at higher levels of measurement because higher levels of measurement call for more information and more precise information than is built into lower levels.

For example, let's say that the director of a nonprofit organization decides to collect data on the dollar amount of supplies and services spent on each client to get a sense of how efficiently services are provided. He can measure the cost per client at either the interval or the ordinal level. The director takes data for

Table 2.5	Some Variables: What Is the Level of Measurement?
Variable	**Level of Measurement**

1. Number of children
2. Opinion of the way the president is handling the economy (strongly approve, approve, neutral, disapprove, strongly disapprove)
3. Age
4. State of residence
5. Mode of transportation to work
6. Perceived income (very low, below average, average, above average, very high)
7. Income in dollars
8. Interest in statistics (low, medium, high)
9. Sector of economy in which you would like to work (public, nonprofit, private)
10. Hours of overtime per week
11. Your comprehension of this book (great, adequate, forget it)
12. Number of memberships in clubs or associations
13. Dollars donated to nonprofit organizations
14. Perceived success of animal rights association in advocacy (very high, high, moderate, low, very low)
15. Years of experience as a supervisor
16. Your evaluation of the level of "social capital" of your community (very low, low, moderate, high, very high)

© Cengage Learning

10 recent clients and constructs both ordinal and interval variables just to see what the different data would look like. The results are displayed in Table 2.6.

If you were the director, how would you measure the cost variable? Think about the advantages of measuring cost at the interval level. With the interval-level variable, we know exactly how much money was spent on each client. With the ordinal-level variable, we only know that a client falls into a particular cost range. If we construct the measure at the interval level, we can also determine the exact distance or numerical difference between individual cases. For example, it cost $19 more to serve the first client than it did to serve the second client. In contrast, the ordinal-level measure would tell us only that the first client was in the "moderate" cost range, whereas the second client was in the "low" cost range.

Table 2.6	Different Levels of Measurement for the Same Concept	
Cost per Client in $ (interval)	**Cost per Client (ordinal)**	
57	2	where 1 = low (less than $50)
38	1	2 = moderate ($50 to $100)
79	2	3 = high ($100 or more)
105	3	
84	2	
159	3	
90	2	
128	3	
103	3	

In terms of flexibility, note that we can always recode or convert the interval-level version of the variable into the ordinal-level variable if we want or need to present the data differently at a later time. But what if we originally constructed the variable at the ordinal level and later found it necessary to report data on the actual dollar amount spent per client—for example, for a program evaluation or grant proposal? We would be unable to obtain this information because ordinal-level data cannot be transformed into interval-level data. Although we would know that the cost per client was between $50 and $100 in four cases, we would be unable to determine the exact cost per client if our data were originally measured at the ordinal level.

As a public or nonprofit manager, sometimes you will not be able to choose the level of measurement for the variables to be examined. This limitation often arises when working with data originally collected by another party, such as a government agency or private firm. In those cases where you are able to choose, keep in mind the many advantages of collecting and constructing variables at higher rather than lower levels of measurement.

In Parts 5 and 6 of this book, you will see that levels of measurement have important implications for data analysis. If you plan on using a particular statistical method to analyze data, you need to make sure to use an appropriate level of measurement when constructing the variables. Otherwise you may spend a lot of time collecting data only to find that you are unable to analyze the data with the intended statistical technique. Contingency tables (the topic of Chapters 14–16) are used to analyze nominal- and ordinal-level data. Regression analysis (covered in Chapters 17–21), one of the most commonly used techniques in statistical analysis, generally requires the use of interval-level data.

In public or nonprofit administration, measurement can be a challenge. In the first place, as elaborated in the theory of measurement discussed earlier in the chapter, measurement often contains error. We do not have perfect measures of bureaucratic or organizational performance or employee morale or citizen satisfaction—or many of the other concepts that you may want to measure and use. Evaluating the quality and accuracy of measurement through validity and reliability assessment is desirable and frequently demanding. In the second place, the richness of public and nonprofit administration calls for several different types of measures. Thus, you will need to use subjective, objective, and unobtrusive indicators. In addition, you will confront different levels of measurement. The interval level corresponds most closely to our typical understanding of measurement as counting things—for example, the number of hours of class attended in a week or the number of pages of reading required for an assignment are interval measures. The other two levels of measurement, ordinal and nominal, do not allow such ready accounting. Nevertheless, you may have to assess work attitudes in your organization (ordinal) for an organizational development effort or identify five areas of social need in your community (nominal) for a grant proposal. Bringing the full menu of measurement concepts to bear on a problem or issue is a useful technique in public and nonprofit administration.

Performance Measurement Techniques

No treatment of measure in public or nonprofit organizations can ignore performance measurement. Performance measurement has become increasingly important in both government and nonprofit settings. Performance measurement yields information necessary for explaining program results to external audiences and stakeholders. Donors to nonprofit organizations want to see evidence that their contributions are being spent on worthwhile activities. Citizens want to know that government agencies are putting their tax dollars to good use. The efficient use of funding is only one dimension of performance. External constituencies also want to know whether government and nonprofit organizations are making progress toward their stated goals. Is a government agency adequately addressing the problem it was created to address? Is a nonprofit organization generating results consistent with its mission statement, or is it having problems meeting key objectives?

In addition to presenting program operations to external constituencies, performance measurement provides organizations with information that can be used to adjust internal operations. Performance measurement can reveal how efficiently resources such as time and money are being used. Performance data can also help managers spot problems such as inconsistencies in how policies are being applied or implemented.

Defining Inputs, Outputs, and Outcomes

To apply statistical tools to performance measurement the public or nonprofit manager first needs to know what to measure and why.

In performance measurement the critical variables are *inputs*, *outputs*, *outcomes*, and *efficiency*.

Inputs

Inputs are resources that an organization uses to achieve its goals. Common examples of inputs include the following:

- annual agency appropriations or funding for the organization
- dollar amount of donations received annually by the organization
- number of employees at the organization
- number of volunteers at the organization

Organizations acquire resources so that they can pursue their goals. Collecting data on resource variables such as these is crucial if we want to see how resources affect performance. Information about core resources like money and the work of employees provide the beginning for understanding organizational performance.

Outputs versus Outcomes

How do we measure or operationalize the concept of performance? To understand performance, we must first explain the difference between outputs and outcomes. **Outputs** are tangible indicators that show how an organization uses its resources. Common examples of outputs in public and nonprofit organizations include the following:

- number of cases processed per employee
- number of forms processed per day
- number of clients each employee has served
- number of overtime hours worked per week
- number of times an agency stays within its spending targets
- average cost of serving a client
- average amount of time (minutes, hours, days) spent per client

Outputs are sometimes called *workload measures* because they show what organizations have produced with the inputs they have. Are outputs indicators of performance? They can be, but measuring performance solely in terms of outputs has some serious drawbacks. Although outputs provide tangible evidence of what inputs such as money or employees can produce, they generally provide little information about quality. For example, an agency that processes 25% more forms than it did last month might appear to be making large gains in efficiency, but if the error rate in processing forms has tripled as a result, the higher output would not be very impressive. No organization wants to live by the motto "We may make a lot of errors, but at least we're fast."

When employees are sensitized to the fact that performance is being measured in terms of outputs, they may also feel pressured to produce desirable levels of output while ignoring the larger question of whether organizational goals are actually being achieved. For example, if counselors at a domestic abuse shelter are evaluated primarily by how quickly they serve each client, they may feel pressure to move from one client to the next without adequately assessing the circumstances of each client. If teachers feel pressure to produce high student scores on standardized achievement tests, they may "teach to the test" instead of focusing on broader learning objectives. When too much attention is placed on outputs, we sometimes lose sight of whether key organizational goals are being met.

Outcomes are more precise indicators of performance than outputs because they focus more on quality than on quantity and more on results outside the organization than inside. Impressive output or workload statistics are not necessarily evidence that organizational goals are being achieved. For example, an output for a parole officer is the number of parolees supervised per year, a measure of organizational workload. By contrast, an outcome is the recidivism rate for the parolees being supervised. If a parole officer is supervising a large number of parolees (output) but more than 90% return to jail within a year (outcome), it is questionable whether progress toward core organizational goals is being made.

How do we determine outcomes? A nonprofit organization can identify important outcomes by looking at its mission statement. Foundations and major grantmakers sometimes define outcomes that must be measured to ensure continued funding. In the case of government agencies, legislative bodies such as city councils and state legislatures often select the outcomes to be achieved. Legislatures appropriate funds to public agencies with the expectation that certain goals will be achieved. Examples of outcomes include the following:

- percentage of job training participants (out of all program participants) who receive full-time jobs
- percentage of alcohol treatment patients who remain sober for 2 years after completing the program
- percentage of low-income students who graduate from college
- percentage of new immigrants who pass an English-language proficiency test after 1 year
- percentage of sixth-grade students who maintain healthy eating habits for 3 months

Measuring outcomes is particularly important for human services organizations that deal with complex social problems. Domestic abuse shelters, alcoholism treatment centers, homeless shelters, unemployment offices, agencies for the blind or disabled, and other social welfare agencies are all examples of human services organizations. The number of clients processed usually is not as important as whether the cases have been handled correctly to achieve the desired results when understanding and addressing complex social problems.

Defining performance in terms of outputs is usually more acceptable for "bottom-line" organizations, where tasks are very clear and little controversy exists over the meaning of performance. For example, the tasks of a municipal recycling facility are well-defined (collecting and processing recyclable material). A public transit department may have slightly more complicated performance goals, but the outputs—riders transported and fares collected—are still fairly easy to measure.

Outputs and outcomes are valid indicators of organizational performance, but outputs are generally much easier to measure than outcomes. Outcomes are more challenging because they typically unfold over time, take more effort to compile and verify, and pertain to results achieved external to the organization (e.g., overcoming drug dependency). Measuring performance in organizations addressing complex social problems typically goes beyond simple output or workload measures to outcome, the extent to which organizational goals have been achieved.

Inputs, Outputs, and Efficiency

Organizations often measure **efficiency** using data on inputs and outputs. One of the most common methods for evaluating efficiency involves dividing inputs by outputs to determine the average level of inputs per output (sometimes referred to as *unit cost*). For example, if a drug abuse treatment facility spends $750,000 in staff time and supplies (inputs) to serve 580 patients (outputs), the average cost per patient is $1,293 (i.e., 750,000/580). A public works department that spends $340,000 in salaries and supplies to complete 297 minor patching and repair jobs on city streets (outputs) spends an average of $1,144 per job (i.e., 340,000/297).

Efficiency measures provide information about costs on a per-client or per-event basis. They can be especially useful for comparison and assessment over time. For example, if a drug abuse treatment center spent $1,293 per client last year and $1,480 per client this year, officials would probably want to examine the factors responsible for the increase.

Relying heavily on efficiency measures to evaluate performance has serious drawbacks. First, efficiency measures generally cannot measure quality. If the cost of treating a client improves (decreases) from $1,293 to $920 but the percentage of cases successfully resolved goes down (worsens), the improvement in efficiency comes at a high price. Average cost data can also be misleading if the level of resources used varies dramatically per client or event. Costs for minor street repairs might vary from $200 to $4,900. Small changes in the number of high- or low-cost repairs from year to year could result in substantial fluctuations in the average cost per job.

Measuring efficiency can help a manager determine whether resources are being wasted. Efficiency, however, is rarely *the* central focus of most nonprofit and government organizations. If the average cost of putting out a fire goes up from one year to the next, it would be silly to tell the fire department to find a cheaper way to fight fires. If the average cost of treating a mental health patient increases by 10% from one year to the next, cutting corners to improve efficiency may result in reduced quality of care. Measuring organizational performance is more concerned with whether the job is done right rather than with how inexpensively work is completed.

Outcome Measures from External Sources

One limitation of outcome measures generated by organizations is that employees may overstate the number of successes and understate the number of failures to portray themselves and their agencies in a better light. An advantage of externally generated outcome measures is that individuals who do not have a vested interest in the success of an organization may provide more honest assessments of organizational performance.

Many agencies use client surveys for this reason. Survey data can provide a wealth of information about performance because clients may view an agency differently from how the agency's employees view the agency. Clients can raise awareness of problems that managers might not know exist. For example, client survey questions might focus on how promptly services were provided, whether the client would be willing to use agency services in the future, and whether counselors did a good job explaining agency policies and answering client questions. Similarly, the head of a public works department could validate job completion data reported by snowplowing crews by asking citizens when and how often their streets were plowed and whether the crews did a good job clearing the roads.

In addition to survey data, other examples of outcome measures based on external data might include the number of complaints an agency receives each month, the number of newspaper articles about an organization that take a negative tone, certification by an accreditation agency, any awards or citations received by the agency, and the number of deficiencies in performance identified by an outside auditor.

The Importance of Using Multiple Output and Outcome Measures

A single output or outcome measure is rarely adequate for assessing the performance of an entire organization. Organizations typically address a variety of problems and thus have a variety of goals.

Having multiple output and outcome measures makes it possible to measure performance more comprehensively and to spot inconsistencies more easily. If we know that two output measures should be highly correlated but the data reveal that they are not, performance problems may exist. If a social services agency asks both agency staff and clients to answer the question "Was the problem adequately solved?" large differences in the response patterns across the two groups would be undesirable. Public schools often measure performance in terms of the percentage of students who pass state-mandated standardized tests. A comparison performance measure in this case would be dropout rates. Increasing pass rates accompanied by increasing dropout rates might mean that performance gains are taking place not because the quality of education is improving but because weak test takers are dropping out of school.

Finally, performance is usually a multidimensional concept. Organizations sometimes have short-, medium-, and long-term performance goals. If a nonprofit agency is receiving grant money from several different foundations, each foundation may require information on different outputs and outcomes. Defining performance using multiple measures helps avoid an all-or-nothing mentality, where success is determined by looking at only a single criterion.

Benchmarking

The rationale for **benchmarking** is that a public or nonprofit organization can gain a better understanding of its own performance by comparing itself to similar organizations. The following examples illustrate the logic of benchmarking:

- A police department for a city of 500,000 residents compares its crime clearance rate to those of police departments in 10 similarly sized cities.
- A sanitation department compares its average cost for collecting a ton of trash to cost data for five other municipal sanitation departments within the county.
- A drug treatment center compares its success rate in treating patients to those of three other drug treatment facilities across the state.
- A YMCA branch compares its customer satisfaction rates to those of 10 other branch locations across the state.
- A nonprofit job training center compares its job placement rate with the placement rates of 12 other job training centers in similar communities in the region.

Comparative performance data allow an organization to determine how well it is doing relative to its peers. Once top performers have been identified, organizations with performance problems can study the strategies used by their more successful peers and adopt similar strategies themselves. The term *best practice* is often used in conjunction with benchmarking because the process can provide organizations with strategies that can lead to better performance. The steps in the benchmarking process are as follows:

Step 1. Select the variable or performance measure to be used as a benchmark. Benchmarking is not feasible if data for a performance measure are unavailable for the organizations in the peer group. Before selecting the measures to be used as benchmarks, the public or nonprofit manager must make sure that the desired data are available.

Because the results obtained from benchmarking are often presented to external audiences, benchmarks should be defined in units or increments that are easily understood and interpreted. For example, a highly aggregated measure such as total expenditures in millions of dollars is more difficult to interpret than average expenditures per person (or citizen or client, etc.).

Descriptive statistics are useful in benchmarking because we want to know how close or far values for a particular variable or performance indicator are to a desired value or target. Averages or measures of central tendency such as means (see Chapter 5) and measures of dispersion such as standard deviations (Chapter 6) convey summary information about performance in ways that most people understand. The mean can often serve as a useful performance target.

Step 2. Select a peer group of organizations. You should always be prepared to explain why particular organizations have been chosen. Because benchmarking is about making comparisons, the peer group should consist of similar organizations. For example, a police department in a rural Illinois town of 5,000 people would not want to benchmark its performance against that of the police department in the city of Chicago because the scale and nature of policing in a large metropolitan area are much different than in a small rural town. Similarly, a homeless shelter that handles 25,000 clients a year might have unique scale advantages in purchasing food and supplies over a shelter that serves only 2,500 people a year. If the circumstances of different organizations vary dramatically, it is usually difficult to make valid comparisons.

Some examples of criteria that can be used to select peer organizations are the number of employees (such as organizations with 1,000 employees or more), size in dollars (cities with annual budgets between $10 and $15 million), function (human services), location (urban, suburban, or rural), and program status (established programs versus new demonstration or pilot programs).

Step 3. Collect the benchmark data for each member (often organization) in the peer group. You may need to consult a variety of sources to obtain the desired information on performance. Budgets and comprehensive annual financial reports (CAFRs) provide detailed information about the activities of city and county governments. References such as the *Statistical Abstract of the United States*, the *Book of the States*, and the *Municipal Year Book* provide a wide array of data useful for benchmarking purposes. Detailed information on the financial performance of nonprofit organizations can be obtained from annual reports and Internal Revenue Service (IRS) Form 990 tax returns. Other systematic information on nonprofit organizations can be found in *The New Nonprofit Almanac and Desk Reference: The Essential Facts and Figures for Managers, Researchers, and Volunteers* (Jossey-Bass).

Step 4. Assess where your organization ranks in the peer group. The data for each member of the peer group should be summarized and displayed in a table. Comparing your organization's score to the average score for the peer group can be very helpful in assessing its performance.

Step 5. Determine what steps should be taken to correct performance deficiencies if they occur. Look to better-performing peers for strategies that might help improve performance.

Benchmarking is best illustrated with an example. A group called Citizens Against Taxing and Spending (CATS) has gone before the media to complain about the "bloated bureaucracy" in the city of Dorchester, Michigan. The group feels that the city employs too many people compared to similar cities in the area. Mayor

Sandra Jackson believes that CATS's claims are exaggerated and that staffing levels in Dorchester are quite reasonable. She decides to benchmark Dorchester against nearby cities, using the number of government employees for every 1,000 citizens as the performance measure.

The mayor uses two criteria in choosing the other cities for comparison: population and size in square miles. Mayor Jackson decides that the population of each city should be within 10% above or below 52,000, the population of Dorchester. The size of the city also must be within 10% of Dorchester's 42.5 square miles because geographic size has a major impact on the number of police and fire employees a city needs.

The mayor's assistant reviews the annual budgets and CAFRs for 12 nearby cities and finds four that meet the above criteria. Data on the number of employees were also obtained from each city's annual budget.

The assistant divides the number of employees by the total residents for Dorchester and obtains a result of 0.0056. He sees nothing wrong with presenting the results in terms of the number of employees per resident, but the mayor explains that 0.0056 employees per resident is not a number the typical citizen is likely to find very meaningful. He agrees and multiplies the results for all cities by 1,000 to facilitate interpretation so that the measure used becomes government employees per 1,000 residents. The final results are displayed in Table 2.7.

The mayor is pleased with the results because they support the view that Dorchester is not that much different from nearby peer cities when it comes to the ratio of city employees to residents. In fact, Dorchester is slightly below the average of 5.78 employees per 1,000 residents for cities in the peer group (see Figure 2.1). The mayor's assistant comments that "it looks like CATS has been declawed," but the mayor expects CATS to raise other questions. She begins thinking about additional benchmarks that would help illustrate how fiscally responsible her administration has been, such as the ratio of supervisory personnel to line personnel and tax revenues per 1,000 residents. Can you think of any other benchmarks to use?

Table 2.7	Comparison of Government Employees per 1,000 Residents for Five Cities		
City	Number of Residents	Number of City Employees	Employees per 1,000
Auburn Park	49,000	298	6.08
Nova City	51,000	280	5.49
Dorchester	**52,000**	**290**	**5.58**
Royal Pine	53,900	299	5.55
Southville	55,000	340	6.18
Average employees per 1,000 residents for cities in peer group = 5.78.			

© Cengage Learning

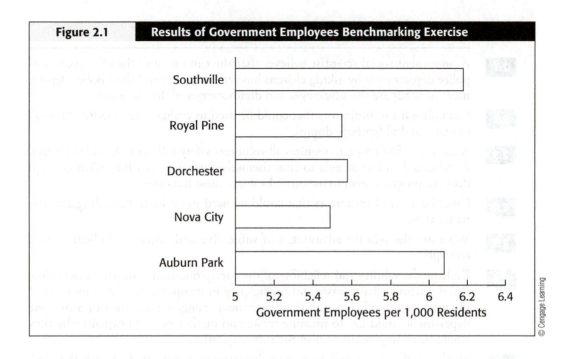

Figure 2.1 | **Results of Government Employees Benchmarking Exercise**

© Cengage Learning

Chapter Summary

Measurement is the assignment of numbers or category labels to some phenomenon. Some variables cannot be measured so precisely with numbers but require category labels. An operational definition tells the analyst how a concept will be measured. An indicator is a variable linked to a concept through an operational definition. The two key issues in measurement are reliability, or consistency of measurement, and validity, or meaningfulness of measurement (are we measuring what we think we are measuring?). The chapter discusses types of validity, types of reliability, and kinds of measures (subjective, objective, and unobtrusive).

In public and nonprofit management we use three levels of measurement: interval, ordinal, and nominal. Interval measurements are based on a standard unit or interval and are the most precise (e.g., population, income, tax assessments). Ordinal measurements lack such an agreed-on standard or unit but allow rank ordering. Nominal measurements lack any sense of relative size or magnitude; they allow us to say only that observations fall into the same or different categories. Despite the differences in the precision of measurement, many important variables in public and nonprofit management are measured at the ordinal level (e.g., attitudes and opinions) or at the nominal level (race, gender, religion, etc.). The chapter concluded with a discussion of performance measurement and benchmarking in public and nonprofit organizations. The chapter explained inputs, outputs, outcomes, and efficiency and other aspects of measuring organizational performance.

Problems

2.1 A prominent social scientist believes that she can measure the effectiveness of police departments by asking citizens how effective they feel their police department is. What are the advantages and disadvantages of this measure?

2.2 Compile a list of indicators that could be used to evaluate the quality of a city's sanitary landfill (garbage dump).

2.3 A campus safety program requires all volunteer safety officers to be at least 5 feet, 8 inches tall and to be able to chin themselves on an 8-foot bar. What concept does the program seem to measure? Evaluate these indicators.

2.4 Compile a list of indicators that could be used to evaluate a building maintenance crew.

2.5 What are the relative advantages of subjective and objective indicators of a concept?

2.6 Evaluate the validity and reliability of the survey question, "To what extent does this department have waste and inefficiency in its operations?" as a measure of the waste and inefficiency in the department. Suggest other measures that the department could use to measure waste and inefficiency and explain why they would be an improvement over the survey question.

2.7 The head of a municipal recreation department is not satisfied with the city's standardized performance evaluation form for employees. The form consists largely of a rating system that includes five categories: far above expectations, above expectations, meets expectations, below expectations, and far below expectations. The department head wants to develop improved measures of employee performance. Help him by suggesting improved measures and by evaluating their validity and reliability. Consider objective as well as subjective measures and obtrusive as well as unobtrusive measures of employee performance.

2.8 Identify a crucial concept in public administration, such as bureaucracy, professionalism, or responsiveness, and explain how this concept has been measured in the literature.

(a) What are some of the ways that researchers have measured the concept?

(b) To what degree have researchers established valid and reliable measures of the concept?

(c) Suggest new indicators that might improve on the measurement of the concept.

2.9 The director of the Art Institute would like to present some data on the size of donations in this year's annual report. He selects the following four categories to summarize donations:

Friend of the Institute	($25 to $99)
Silver Member	($100 to $249)
Gold Member	($250 to $499)
Platinum Member	($500 and above)

To get a sense of what the data will look like, the director gives you a sample of donations measured at the interval level and asks you to apply the coding scheme. Create an ordinal-level variable for donations using the data below. (*Hint:* To get started, you first need to assign a numerical code to each category.)

Interval Version (in $)	Ordinal Version
25	
150	
75	
450	
100	
750	
90	
175	
250	
50	

2.10 The director of the West Arbor Senior Center decides to put together a database on the center's activities. The center currently takes written records of services provided to clients, but the director feels that program information will be easier to access and analyze if the records are computerized. The program director generates the following sample data for 10 current clients:

	Service Provided	
Gender	Home Delivery of Meals	Assistance with Transportation
Male	Yes	Never
Female	Yes	Frequently
Female	No	Never
Male	No	Rarely
Female	Yes	Never
Male	Yes	Rarely
Male	Yes	Frequently
Female	No	Never
Male	Yes	Never
Female	No	Frequently

The director asks you to develop a measurement scheme and turn the data into numbers that can be put into a computerized database. Show the director how much you know about measurement, and develop a numerical coding scheme for each of the variables. Is a nominal-level coding scheme sufficient for all three variables, or does one variable need to be constructed using a higher level of measurement?

2.11 The Wildlife Conservation Center has put together a database to keep track of the attributes of its employees. Specifically, numerical codes are assigned to variables as follows:

Gender	1 = female	2 = male
Job Status	1 = full time	2 = part time
Job Description	1 = professional	2 = administrative 3 = general labor

Employee	Gender	Job Status	Job Description
1	1	1	1
2	2	1	3
3	1	2	2
4	2	1	2
5	1	2	1
6	1	2	1
7	2	2	3
8	1	1	3

Use the variable codes above to describe in words the attributes of each employee.

2.12 The city manager of Snook, Texas, wants to generate some statistics on a voluntary free flu shot clinic for city employees. Specifically, she has the following data on whether employees received shots and whether they took sick leave during the winter months:

Received Shot	Took Sick Leave
Yes	No
No	Yes
No	Yes
Yes	No
Yes	Yes
Yes	No
No	No
Yes	No
Yes	No
No	Yes

The city manager asks you to come up with a numerical coding scheme so that these data can be placed in a statistical program for analysis. Develop a coding scheme for each variable.

2.13 Tex Anderson has just been appointed director of the Roads Department in Gak, Texas. He knows that the last director was "urged to explore other career opportunities" due to performance problems in the department. The former director never collected data on performance, frequently exceeded spending ceilings, and rarely followed up on citizen complaints. Tex asks his staff to come up with performance measures for the following key program areas:

> Minor street repairs and pothole patching
> Street signage and traffic light repair
> Animal carcass removal

Tex tells his staff that the mayor will "chew him up and spit him out like a bad piece of brisket" if performance does not improve. Help Tex develop two output indicators and two outcome indicators for each of these programs.

2.14 The board of directors of Earth Rocks!, a nonprofit organization focused on environmental protection, hypothesizes that individuals are more likely to donate if they see evidence that their donations are used primarily for program activities rather than administrative and fund-raising costs. To get a sense of how its own cost structure compares to other groups, the board decides to benchmark the financial performance of Earth Rocks! against several other environmental organizations. The data for Earth Rocks! and the other environmental organizations appear below.

	Program Expenditures ($)	Fund-raising Costs ($)	Administrative Costs ($)	Total Costs ($)
Earth Rocks!	374,900	98,000	121,400	594,300
Weed Lovers	421,000	104,300	98,350	623,650
Flora and Fauna	353,400	97,600	71,840	522,840
Leaf It Be	501,900	89,000	109,750	700,650
Nature's Gift	455,470	71,000	82,450	608,920

Use these data to benchmark Earth Rocks! against the other environmental organizations. How does Earth Rocks! compare to the other environmental groups?

3

Research Design

W inston Lewis, mayor of the city of Kettering, Kansas, is upset. The showcase of his community pride program, "Stand Up for Kettering," is a failure. The program was intended to upgrade the quality of life of senior citizens in Kettering by relocating those living below the poverty line to new federally subsidized public housing, operated by a consortium of nonprofit housing agencies. Because termination of the program means a loss not only of federal funds but also of local jobs, Mayor Lewis is especially perturbed.

To add to the mayor's problems, in a blistering front-page editorial, the local newspaper, the *Kettering News*, blamed the failure of the community pride program on the incompetence of Lewis and his staff. The editorial claimed that the mayor did not take a personal interest in running the program and instead delegated its administration largely to cronies, none of whom had education or training in the needs and problems of senior citizens. As a result, the editorial contended, the senior citizens were treated shabbily—"as a product"—by the program, and insufficient attention was paid to their rights, convenience, and welfare. The editorial also suggested that the housing program might be more effective were the nonprofit providers given greater funding.

Lewis's initial reaction was to counterattack in the public media. He and his staff assembled information intended to refute the charges made in the editorial, and a press conference was tentatively scheduled.

Before the press conference took place, however, the mayor's chief strategist, Dick Murray, informed Lewis of his misgivings about this type of response to the editorial. In the first place, argued Murray, it would be certain to occasion a rejoinder from the newspaper, further publicity, and perhaps an official investigation of the program. Understandably, the mayor would prefer to avoid all of these. Second, even if the mayor were able to refute the newspaper charges, the nagging question would remain: What *did* cause the program to fail? Murray maintained that if he could demonstrate that factors *other* than those pertaining to the mayor and his staff were responsible for the failure of the program, then he could limit the adverse publicity and take the heat off Lewis—a nice solution to the mayor's problems. Suitably impressed, Lewis canceled the press conference and told Murray to proceed.

Murray first undertook his research. A telephone call to Washington, D.C., yielded the information that the federal government had funded the same program for senior citizens in Virtuous, Montana, a city similar to Kettering in area, population, and other crucial characteristics (economic base, form of government, and so forth). In contrast to the experience in Kettering, however, the federal government was quite pleased with the program in Virtuous; the Washington bureaucrat quipped that the program has enjoyed a success "as big as the sky." Murray reasoned that if Lewis and his staff have comparable levels of interest and competence in running the program as their counterparts in Virtuous, then these factors *cannot* be the cause of the failure of the program in Kettering, for the program has succeeded in Virtuous with the *same* level of official involvement. Murray checked with the Virtuous authorities and found that in both cities, the levels of interest and of competence of the mayor and staff were very similar. Thus, Murray concluded that some other factor must be responsible for the failure of the program in Kettering.

What might this factor be? Murray thought that the newspaper editorial might be on to something with regard to the need for greater funding. With more funding for the nonprofit housing providers, the results might look far different. Murray checked again with the Virtuous authorities and learned that Kettering was awarded far less in federal funds to run the senior citizen program than was Virtuous. This information provided support for Murray's hunch. He concluded that the program in Kettering failed not because of lack of official involvement—recall that the program in Virtuous succeeded with the same level of involvement—but because of a lack of sufficient federal funding. He reasoned that had the program in Kettering received the same level of funding as that in Virtuous, it would have been a success. After all, look at the experience in Virtuous, where more money was made available.

Murray delivered his findings to Mayor Lewis, who naturally was pleased. At a newly scheduled press conference, the mayor presented Murray's evidence to refute the allegations of the *Kettering News* editorial and to establish a new possible cause of the failure of the program in Kettering: inadequate federal funding. The press conference had the desired impact. Murray was also given a raise.

The process in which Murray was engaged—attempting to determine the cause of a relationship or event—is at the core of all social research. Social scientists seek to discover the causes of phenomena and rule out possible rival causes. The nature of this enterprise provides the focus for this chapter.

The first section of this chapter introduces the process and terminology commonly used by social scientists in constructing causal explanations. The second portion of the chapter discusses the formal criteria necessary to establish a relationship as causal. In other words, what evidence must the researcher present in order to demonstrate that A causes B? The final chapter segment is devoted to research design. A research design is a systematic program intended to evaluate proposed causal explanations on the basis of data. The two major types of design—experimental and quasi-experimental—are distinguished and elaborated. As you will see, a solid research design is essential to public and nonprofit managers in introducing and assessing administrative changes for maximum impact.

Constructing Causal Explanations

In contrast to Mayor Lewis's strategist Dick Murray—who sought the causes of a single event (the failure of the senior citizens program in Kettering)—social scientists are typically interested in accounting for *entire classes* of events or relationships. For example, what are the causes of success or failure of social programs? Does congressional oversight lead to a more responsive bureaucracy? Does regulation of utilities result in lower prices? Does government contracting with nonprofit agencies for service delivery lead to greater efficiency? Does contracting, however, weaken public sector accountability? Does government spending on social services tend to lessen nonprofit activity—or increase it? Does mandated community service (e.g., as a requirement for high school graduation) increase—or decrease—volunteering later in life? Do more open and fluid structures in public and nonprofit organizations lead to more effective agencies? These broad questions go far beyond isolated outcomes and lead us to think more generally about causation.

The basic building block in answering these questions and, more generally, in constructing causal explanations is the **concept**. From the mass of detail, and often confusion, surrounding the particular events in a class, the concept pinpoints an idea or element thought to be essential in accounting for the entire class. Concepts abstract or summarize the critical aspects in a class of events. For example, in his research, Murray isolated official involvement and level of funding as important elements in the senior citizens program in Kettering. These are concepts on the basis of which he might have attempted to explain the success or failure of *all* social programs. The concept points out a common trait or characteristic shared by the members of a class: In this case, social programs have varying levels of official involvement and funding.

To provide a more complete explanation of program success, Murray could have highlighted more abstract concepts. These might include power, social class (of clientele groups), and organizational goals. Because broader concepts potentially allow the researcher to account for a greater number of events, the more abstract the concept, and the more applicable to a wide range of phenomena, the more useful it is. Thus, a relatively small array of concepts tends to appear repeatedly in social science research, such as power, role, motivation, environment, system, exchange, sector, network, and organization.

Concepts act as a perceptual screen that sensitizes researchers to certain aspects of objects or events and leaves them oblivious to others. For this reason, the process of abstraction to arrive at concepts is perhaps the most critical element in the research process. In one sense, abstraction is a process similar to one used in everyday life: Inevitably, we tune in to some characteristics and tune out others. For example, after you meet a person for the first time, you are almost certain to remember his or her sex; you are less likely to recall elements of personal appearance, and less likely still to recall specific attitudes, opinions, and preferences. In another sense, however, abstraction in everyday life is quite different, because in scientific research, conceptualization is a much more self-conscious, painstaking endeavor.

To construct explanations of events or relationships, concepts must be defined. Two types of definitions are necessary for empirical or data-based research. The first is called a **nominal** or **conceptual definition**. It is the standard dictionary definition that defines the concept in terms of other concepts. For example, *patriotism* may be defined as love for one's country; *intelligence* may be defined as mental capacity; *occupation* may be defined as the type of work that an individual primarily performs; *volunteer* may be defined as donating one's time without pay.

In social research, nominal definitions must satisfy a set of conditions. Concepts should be defined as clearly and precisely as possible. A concept must not be defined in terms of itself. For example, to define *happiness* as the state of being happy is meaningless. Also, the definition should say what the concept is rather than what it is not. For example, to define *duress* as the absence of freedom does not distinguish it from several other concepts (coercion, imprisonment, compulsion, and so on). Inevitably, many other concepts will fit the description of what the concept is not. Furthermore, unless there is good reason, the definition should not constitute a marked departure from what has generally been accepted in the past. A good reason might be that you feel that previous definitions have misled research in the area. Whereas nominal definitions are arbitrary—they are neither right nor wrong—in order to advance knowledge, researchers attempt to make definitions as realistic and sensible as possible. Although it could not be proved incorrect to define a cat as a dog, it would be counterproductive.

The second type of definition is called an **operational definition** (sometimes called a *working definition*). The operational definition translates the nominal definition into a form in which the concept can be measured empirically—that is, with data. As discussed in Chapter 2, the process of operationalizing a concept results in indicators, or variables designed to measure the concept.

By converting abstract ideas (concepts) into a form in which the presence or absence, or the degree of presence or absence, of a concept can be measured for every individual or case in a sample of data, operational definitions play a vital role in research. They allow researchers to assess the extent of empirical support for their theoretical ideas. For example, *civic involvement* might be defined as the number of clubs, groups, or associations to which a person belongs.

In the prior example, Dick Murray felt that the degree of success attained by federal programs is determined by the level of funding rather than by local involvement. He operationalized these concepts as the size of the federal allotment to each city in the program and the level of interest and training of the local mayor and staff in the program, respectively. Program success is a difficult concept to operationalize, but Murray might have used a variety of indicators: the perceived satisfaction with the program (assessed in a survey) felt by public housing residents and by the larger community, the number of new housing units constructed, the cost per square foot, the degree to which the housing met federal standards, and so forth. He would be using a multiple indicator strategy, as explained—and recommended—in Chapter 2. By comparing the cities of Kettering and Virtuous, he was then able to demonstrate that although local involvement seemed to make no difference in the success of the senior citizens program (because the cities rated about the same on this dimension), the level of funding (on this factor the cities diverged) did make a difference.

Once a concept has been operationalized and measured in a sample of data, it is called a **variable**. A variable assigns numerical scores or category labels (such as female, male; married, single) to each case in the sample on a given characteristic (see Chapter 2 for a discussion of measurement). For example, in a study examining the job-related behavior of bureaucrats, a researcher may obtain data for five bureaucrats on the variables "race," "sex," "time wasted on the job per day" (minutes), and "attitude toward the job" (like, neutral, dislike). These data are displayed in Table 3.1, with each column representing a variable.

Often in research, variables are classified into two major types. It is the goal of most research to explain or account for changes or variation in the **dependent variable**. For example, Dick Murray sought to explain the failure of the senior citizens program in Kettering (and, implicitly, to understand how the program might be made a success). What factors could account for the different outcomes of the programs in Kettering and Virtuous? A variable thought to lead to or produce changes in the dependent variable is called independent. An **independent variable** is thought to affect, or have an impact on, the dependent variable. Murray examined the effects on program success of two independent variables: "interest and training of mayor and staff" and "federal funding." For terminological convenience, independent variables are sometimes referred to as *explanatory*, *predictor*, or *causal* variables, and the dependent variable as the *criterion*.

To account for changes in the dependent variable, researchers link the criterion explicitly to independent variables in a statement called a **hypothesis**. A

Table 3.1	Data for Five Bureaucrats			
	Variable			
Case	Race	Sex	Time Wasted on Job (minutes)	Attitude toward Job
Bureaucrat 1	White	Female	62	Dislike
Bureaucrat 2	White	Male	43	Neutral
Bureaucrat 3	African American	Male	91	Like
Bureaucrat 4	Hispanic	Male	107	Like
Bureaucrat 5	White	Female	20	Dislike

© Cengage Learning

hypothesis formally proposes an expected relationship between an independent variable and a dependent variable.

The primary value of hypotheses is that they allow theoretical ideas and explanations to be tested against actual data. To facilitate this goal, hypotheses must meet two requirements. First, the concepts and the variables that they relate must be measurable. Although propositions connecting unmeasurable concepts (or those for which data are currently unavailable) are important in research, they cannot be evaluated empirically and must be treated as assumptions. Second, hypotheses must state in precise language the relationship expected between the independent and dependent variables. For example, two hypotheses guided the research of Dick Murray:

1. The greater the local involvement in a program, the greater is the chance of program success.

2. The greater the level of federal funding for a program, the greater is the chance of program success.

In both hypotheses, the expected relationship is called *positive* because increases (decreases) in the independent variable are thought to lead to increases (decreases) in the dependent variable. Note that in a positive relationship, the variables move in the same direction: More (less) of one is thought to lead to more (less) of the other. In contrast, a *negative* or *inverse* relationship proposes that increases in the independent variable will result in decreases in the dependent variable, or vice versa. In a negative relationship, the variables move in opposite directions: More (less) of one leads to less (more) of the other. The following hypothesis is an example of a negative relationship:

3. The higher the degree of federal restrictions on administering a program, the less is the chance of program success.

Once the concepts specified by these hypotheses have been operationalized (measured), data can be brought to bear on them to evaluate the degree of empirical support for the anticipated relationships.

Hypotheses intended to provide an explanation for a phenomenon of interest (e.g., success or failure of federal programs) most often propose a positive or a negative relationship between an independent and a dependent variable. One merit of this procedure is that because the direction of the relationship (positive or negative) is made explicit, it is relatively easy to determine the degree of confirmation for (or refutation of) the hypothesis. Researchers are not always this circumspect in stating hypotheses, however, and it is not unusual to find in the literature examples in which the independent variable is said to "affect," "influence," or "impact" the dependent variable without regard for direction. This practice not only condones imprecision in thinking and hypothesis formulation but also creates difficulties in assessing empirical support for a hypothesis. For these reasons, this practice should be avoided.

An integrated set of propositions intended to explain or account for a given phenomenon is called a **theory**. The propositions link the important concepts together in anticipated relationships so that the causal mechanisms underlying the phenomenon are elucidated. In some of these propositions, it will be possible to operationalize the concepts and collect the data necessary to evaluate the hypothesized relationships empirically. As a consequence of difficulties in measuring some concepts or lack of available data, however, it may not be possible to test all propositions. Untested propositions constitute **assumptions**. Although assumptions lie outside the boundaries of empirical testing, they should not be accepted uncritically. Evidence from past research, as well as logical reasoning, can be used to assess their validity. For example, budget projections based on an assumption that all Americans will give contributions to charitable organizations in the next year are unreasonable. Also untenable is an assumption that the amount of volunteer hours will quadruple next year, even if a nonprofit needs them.

A full-blown theory to explain an important phenomenon, such as representativeness in public bureaucracy, relationships between political appointees and career civil servants, or the effect of volunteering on building social capital, can be highly abstract and comprehensive. It may contain numerous assumptions not only about how concepts are related but also about how they are measured. Because of difficulties in specifying and operationalizing all relevant elements and collecting all necessary data, theories are rarely, if ever, tested directly against actual data or observations. Instead, a simplified version of the theory called a **model** is developed and put to an empirical test. Usually the relationships proposed by the theory are depicted as a set of equations or, equivalently, as an arrow diagram; each arrow represents a hypothesis (see Figure 3.1). Regardless of the form, the model is a compact version of the theory intended for an empirical test. It identifies the essential concepts proposed by the theory and the interrelationships among them, and it presumes the existence of adequate measurement and relevant data. Ultimately, it is the model that is tested statistically, but the results will be brought to bear indirectly on the validity and utility of the theory.

As an example of a model, consider again the question of the determinants of success of social programs. Perhaps the activity of clientele groups leads to high levels of federal funding, which, in turn, increase the likelihood of program success. In addition, the activity of clientele groups may help to achieve program success directly through support at the local level. Federal funding, however, may be a mixed blessing. Although high levels of funding may enhance the prospects of success, they may also bring increased federal restrictions on administration of the program. These restrictions may reduce the chance of program success. This heuristic theory is by no means complete. To yield a more satisfactory explanation, we might want to add several components, such as the interest of elected officials in the program (recall the example of Kettering, Kansas, and Dick Murray with which this chapter began), the organizational structure of the program, and how well the means of achieving program success are understood (e.g., issuing checks for unemployment compensation versus improving mental health). The relationships with program success that have been proposed formally here can be displayed schematically in an arrow diagram, in which each arrow represents an expected causal linkage between a pair of concepts. A negative sign above an arrow indicates an inverse relationship, and an unmarked arrow corresponds to a positive relationship. Figure 3.1 presents the resulting heuristic model of the success of social programs.

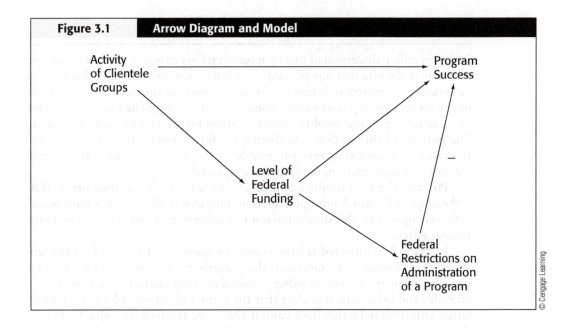

Figure 3.1 **Arrow Diagram and Model**

Activity of Clientele Groups

Program Success

Level of Federal Funding

Federal Restrictions on Administration of a Program

© Cengage Learning

To the extent that data confirm the relationships proposed by a theory and tested in the model, support is obtained for the theory, and its validity is enhanced. Analogously, the failure to find empirical support for a theory detracts from its validity and suggests the need for revisions. Researchers, however, are usually more willing to subscribe to the first of these principles than to the second. Whereas they rarely question data that offer support for their theoretical ideas, in the face of apparent empirical disconfirmation, revision of the theory is seldom their immediate response. Instead, operational definitions are critically evaluated; possible problems in the selection, collection, and recording of the sample of data are considered; numerical calculations are checked; and so on. As a result of the state of the art of social science research, these are reasonable steps to take prior to revising the theory. If these measures fail to lead to alternative explanations for the lack of empirical support obtained (such as a biased sample of data) or possible procedures to amend this situation (for instance, by devising new operational definitions for some concepts), however, the researcher has no choice but to reconsider and revise the theory.

The revision usually leads to new concepts, definitions, operationalizations, and empirical testing, so that the process begins all over again. Generally, it is through a series of repeated, careful studies, each building on the results of earlier ones, that researchers come to understand important subject areas.

In public and nonprofit management, you are unlikely to develop a theory. Often, however, you will propose a model, obtain the necessary data, and test it using the statistical methods you will learn in this book.

Causal Relationships

In the preceding discussion of theory, repeated reference was made to the concept of causality, the idea that one phenomenon is the cause of another. A theory may be considered a system of interrelated causal statements intended to account for or to explain a given phenomenon. These are tentative (hypothesized) statements of a relationship whose validity cannot be taken for granted but must be tested. The purpose of this section is to discuss the four formal criteria identified by most social scientists as necessary to establish a relationship as causal. The criteria are time order, covariation, nonspuriousness, and theory.

Probably the most intuitive of these criteria is the notion of **time order**. If A is the cause of B, then A must precede B in time; that is, changes in A must occur before changes in B. This stipulation is just another way of saying that cause must precede effect.

In many hypothesized relationships, the question of time order between variables is obvious. For example, if the researcher is interested in the effect of sex, race, country of birth, or other so-called ascribed characteristics on certain attitudes and behaviors, it is clear that the former set of variables precedes the latter. Unfortunately, this issue cannot always be resolved so easily. Consider the relationship between tenure on the job and job satisfaction: Does tenure lead to satisfaction, or does satisfaction lead to tenure? Both viewpoints seem reasonable. Or consider the relationship between attitude toward bureaucrats and attitude toward a particular government agency. Which variable comes first? Again, the question of temporal priority is problematic. In most relationships between attitudes and behaviors, it is difficult to establish time order with certainty. For this reason, causal statements linking these types of variables should be considered carefully.

The second criterion that must be satisfied for the relationship between two variables to be considered causal is **covariation**, or statistical *association* between the variables. *Covariation* means that the two variables move, or vary, together. That is, if A changes and B also changes, this covariation provides some evidence that A is the cause of B. Analogously, if changes in A are never accompanied by changes in B (no covariation), then A cannot be the cause of B. One way to understand this idea is to consider that if as A changes, B always remains constant, then A can have no impact on B. In that case, changes in A do not matter with respect to B.

For example, suppose a researcher hypothesized that higher salaries lead to more productive workers. If in a sample of data she found that salary and productivity covaried—that is, those paid higher salaries were more productive than those paid less—then she would have evidence for a causal relationship. If she found that as salaries increased, productivity showed no concomitant change, however, then the hypothesized causal relationship would be in jeopardy.

Of the four criteria of causality, perhaps the most difficult to comprehend is **nonspuriousness**. A nonspurious relationship is a covariation or association between two variables or phenomena that cannot be explained by a third factor. A nonspurious relationship implies that there is an *inherent* link between the two variables in the sense that changes in one produce changes in the other, and that their observed covariation is not the result of an accidental connection with some associated (third) variable.

For example, just about everyone knows people who claim to predict the weather—usually rain—based on "a feeling in their bones." Interestingly enough, these predictions may turn out to be correct more often than not. Thus, one would observe a covariation between the prediction and the weather. A moment's reflection though will show that there is no inherent link between these two phenomena. Instead, changes in pressure and moisture in the atmosphere cause both changes in the state of the human body (such as a feeling in the bones) and changes in the weather (such as rain). The original covariation between "feeling in the bones" and "rain" is observed not because the variables are causally related but because both of them are associated with a third factor, changes in the atmosphere. Hence, the original relationship is **spurious**: It can be explained by the effects of a third variable.

Although it may be relatively easy to think of examples of likely nonspurious relationships (fertilizer use and crop yield, exposure to sunlight and tan skin), it is far more difficult to *demonstrate* that an observed covariation is nonspurious. Establishing a relationship as nonspurious is an inductive process that requires that the researcher take into account *all* possible sources of an observed covariation between two variables. If, after the effects of all third factors are eliminated, the original covariation remains, then the relationship is nonspurious.

Because the condition requiring the elimination of all possible third variables is based on logical grounds (one would be incorrect in claiming a causal relationship between two variables if it could be explained by the effects of *any* other factor), nonspuriousness cannot be proved by data analysis alone. To the extent that a researcher explicitly takes into account possible sources of an observed covariation between two variables and is able to eliminate them as alternative explanations for the covariation, however, the validity of the causal inference is enhanced. In other words, the greater the number of relevant third variables considered and eliminated, the greater is the confidence that the original relationship is causal. For example, the researcher who finds that a covariation between interest in public affairs and performance in an MPA program persists after the effects of prior undergraduate education, occupation, amount of time available for study, and so on have been taken into account would have more confidence in the causal inference than if only one of these third factors had been considered.

The final criterion for establishing a relationship as causal is **theory**. As discussed earlier in the chapter, theories are meant to explain important phenomena. To establish a causal relationship, not only must the conditions of time order, covariation, and nonspuriousness be satisfied but also a theoretical or substantive justification or explanation for the relationship must be provided. Theory interprets the observed covariation; it addresses the issue of how and why the relationship occurs. In one sense, theory serves as an additional check on nonspuriousness. It lends further support to the argument that the link between two phenomena is inherent rather than the artifact of an associated third factor.

Many of the techniques used to assess causal relationships can be performed on computers using statistical software packages. Although computers can quickly generate sophisticated statistical analyses, they do not have the capability to judge whether results are plausible or meaningful in real-world settings. Statistical software packages see numbers for what they are—numbers. They cannot tell you whether a relationship between two variables is actually plausible. This is why theory is such an important component of causality.

Parts 4 through 6 of this book deal with statistical techniques used to test hypotheses. As you learn about these techniques, you should remember that even if a relationship is *statistically* significant, that does not necessarily mean it is significant in the sense of being meaningful or important. The job of a data analyst is to explain the substantive meaning of statistical relationships; computers alone are not capable of making such judgments.

As this discussion has illustrated, the criteria necessary for proof of a causal relationship are demanding. It is essential to balance this view with the idea that the determination of causation is not a yes–no question but a matter of degree. Satisfaction of each criterion lends further support to the causal inference. Additionally, for each criterion, there are varying levels of substantiation. Confidence in the time order of phenomena is variable, observed covariations can assume a range of magnitude from small to large, demonstrating nonspuriousness is nearly always problematic, and the validity of a given theory is usually the subject of debate. Evidence for a causal relationship is based on the extent to which all of these criteria are satisfied.

In this context, two final points merit consideration. First, social scientists accept the concept of **multiple causation**. It is widely acknowledged that an event or phenomenon may have several causes, all of them contributing to the result. For example, explanations of why a person continues to volunteer for an agency are complicated, based on a variety of organizational, social, and personal factors. Consequently, social researchers rarely speak of *the* cause; instead, they seek the *causes*, or determinants, of a phenomenon. Thus, it can and does happen that an observed covariation between an independent variable and a dependent variable turns out to be neither totally nonspurious nor totally spurious but partially spurious. Data analysis frequently suggests that both the independent variable and a third variable (as well as other explanatory variables) are potential causes of the dependent variable. The chapters on multivariate statistical techniques (Chapters 16 through 21) explain how to assess such effects.

Second, in developing and evaluating causal explanations, it can be extremely useful to construct an arrow diagram like the one in Figure 3.1. Depicting graphically a system of proposed causal relationships helps to uncover possible interrelationships among expected causes, sources of spuriousness, and omitted variables whose effects should not be ignored. It is also a quick and easy procedure. For all these reasons, the arrow diagram is a highly recommended technique, no matter how simple or complicated the model may be.

In normal conversation and managerial practice, people speak easily, sometimes too easily, about causation. These statements are interesting as conjectures or hypotheses about what leads to ("causes") what. If you intend to use or apply these statements in public and nonprofit management, be sure to evaluate them against the four criteria discussed above. Much of this book teaches you how to do so.

Research Design

A **research design** is a systematic program for empirically evaluating proposed causal relationships. The design specifies a model of proof for testing the validity of these relationships. The research design guides the collection, analysis, and interpretation of the relevant data. There are many types of research design, and they differ in their ability to generate reliable inferences concerning causality.

The concept of causality has long been a source of controversy among social scientists. Partly for this reason, several different conceptions of the validity or viability of a causal relationship have been proposed and utilized. The two most important of these are internal validity and external validity. **Internal validity** addresses the question of whether, *in a given study or research project*, the independent variable did indeed cause or lead to changes in the dependent variable. The criteria for assessing internal validity are those considered in the previous section: time order, covariation, nonspuriousness, and theory.

External validity captures a different idea: it is concerned with the issue of whether and to what extent results obtained in a given study can be *inferred* or generalized to hold true in settings, time periods, and populations different from the ones used in the study. For instance, are the findings of a study of college sophomores generalizable to the population of all U.S. citizens? Are the results of a study conducted 20 years ago still applicable today? To what extent might findings from a program evaluation in one state be generalizable to the same type of program in a different state? To what degree are supervisory techniques that seem to work well in a study of paid employees equally effective for volunteers? With what confidence can findings of a report on nonprofit agencies in the arts be extended to other domains, such as literacy, adult recreation, and nutrition? The names of the two key types of validity can be remembered easily because they refer to contexts that are internal and external to a study, respectively.

A major distinction can be made between *experimental* research designs and *quasi-experimental* designs. Nearly everyone has some familiarity with the setup of an experiment. A researcher assembles two groups of subjects; to ensure a valid comparison, the groups should be as similar as possible. The *experimental* group receives some treatment or stimulus, whereas the second or *control* group does not; instead, it serves as a baseline or reference point for evaluating the behavior of the first group. Before and after administration of the experimental stimulus, both groups are measured on relevant variables, particularly the dependent variable or criterion. These two measurements are referred to as the *pretest* and *posttest*, respectively. By comparing the scores of the experimental group with those of the control group, over time (pretest versus posttest), the researcher is able to determine whether the treatment led to a difference in areas of interest (attitude, behavior, performance). This procedure is called the classical **experimental design**.

Suppose, for example, that a researcher wanted to examine whether inspection of automobiles reduced the rate of traffic accidents. One way to do so would be to select two random samples of drivers in a given state. The first group would be required to have their automobiles inspected within 6 months (experimental group); the second group would be left alone (control group). Data would be collected regarding the past driving records of the drivers in both groups, and after 2 years, data would be collected again to encompass the period of the study. If in this period the rate of accidents decreased in the experimental (inspection) group relative to the rate in the control group, then the researcher would have some evidence for inferring that automobile inspections reduce traffic accidents. Conversely, if the data failed to show this pattern, the proposed causal relationship would be rejected.

Quasi-experimental designs of research have been given this appellation because they fail to incorporate one or more of the features of experimental designs. In particular, in many research designs it is difficult to control exposure to the experimental stimulus or independent variable. Consider a television information program funded by the federal government and intended to promote energy conservation. To examine the effectiveness of this program, the researcher would ideally want to study the behavior of two random samples of people: one that viewed the program and another that did not. In this situation, it would be relatively easy to determine whether the program led to energy conservation. In actuality, however, people interested in conservation will tend to watch the program, and those not interested in conservation will tend to seek other diversion—and there is little reason to assume that these two groups are random or matched in any sense. (For one thing, the groups differ dramatically in interest in energy conservation.) Thus, although the researcher may find that those who viewed the program were subsequently more likely to conserve energy than those who did not, it is not clear whether the program or the viewers' initial attitude was responsible for the impact.

A second aspect of the classical experimental research design that is often lacking in quasi-experimental designs is repeated measurement. To evaluate whether the independent variable produces changes in the dependent variable, it is very helpful to know respondents' scores on the variables prior to a change in the independent variable—that is, their scores on the pretest. Then one can determine whether this change is accompanied by a change in the dependent variable. In the experiment, this function is served by measurement before and after the experimental treatment, which is intended to affect or change the level of the independent variable in the experimental group (for instance, auto inspections are intended to increase the safety of automobiles).

Unfortunately, repeated measurements are not always available or feasible. For example, a researcher may be interested in the determinants of the effectiveness of an agency, but data on effectiveness may not have been collected until very recently, or relevant data from the past may not be comparable to current information. Or a researcher may be interested in the determinants of public opinion toward a nonprofit agency, but funding may limit the study to a single survey of respondents, so that repeated measurement is not possible. In both situations, the researcher is likely to obtain only one set of data for one point in time. Although it may be possible with such data to observe covariations between variables (such as between the funding of agency divisions and their performance), establishing time order between variables is necessarily problematic.

In the following sections, we discuss experimental and quasi-experimental designs of research in greater detail. Our primary objective is to assess the internal and external validity of these two major families of design. Within the category of the quasi-experiment, some texts further distinguish research designs, such as "descriptive" and "preexperimental" designs. Unfortunately, different authors and texts define these terms differently, and the terms are not standard. To avoid confusion, we do not use them here but simply refer to them as members of the family of quasi-experimental designs.

Experimental Designs of Research

Internal Validity

Experimental research designs offer the strongest model of proof of causality. The basic components of the classical experimental design can be summarized briefly.

Step 1: Assign subjects to two or more groups, with at least one "experimental" and one "control," so that the groups are as comparable as possible. The best way to assemble comparable groups is through random assignment of subjects to groups. *Random* means that there is no bias in the assignment so that, within the limits of statistical probability, the groups should not differ.

Step 2: Measure all subjects on relevant variables. Although a preexperiment measurement, or pretest, is usually administered, some experimental designs do not require a pretest. We present some of these designs below.

Step 3: Expose the experimental group(s) to the treatment or stimulus, the independent variable. Ensure that the control group(s) is(are) not exposed. Exposure to the treatment should constitute the only difference between the groups.

Step 4: Measure the groups again on the requisite variables in a postexperiment measurement, or posttest.

Step 5: Compare the measurements of the groups. If the independent variable does lead to changes in the dependent variable, this result should be evident in pretest–posttest comparisons between the experimental and control groups. Or, if the groups are large and known to be equivalent through random assignment, the analyst can simply compare posttest scores between the two groups. If the causal inference is valid, these comparisons should bear out predicted differences between the experimental and control groups.

Table 3.2	Classical Experimental Design				
Group	Random Assignment	Observation 1	Treatment	Observation 2	Comparison
Experimental	R_e	O_{e1}	X	O_{e2}	$O_{e2} - O_{e1}$
Control	R_c	O_{c1}		O_{c2}	$O_{c2} - O_{c1}$

© Cengage Learning

The classical experimental design is outlined in Table 3.2. In the table, O stands for observation or measurement, X for administration of the experimental treatment, R for random assignment, c for control group, e for experimental group, time subscript 1 for pretest, and time subscript 2 for posttest.

Intuitively, we know that the strength of experimental research designs with respect to internal validity arises from the fact that when these experiments are conducted properly, the experimental and control groups are identical except for a single factor—exposure to the experimental treatment. Thus, if, at the conclusion of the experiment, the former group is significantly different from the latter with respect to the dependent variable, the cause *must* be the treatment, or the independent variable. After all, this factor was the only one that distinguished the two groups.

The strength of the experimental design in internal validity can be shown more formally in connection with the elements of causality discussed before. First, consider the criterion of time order. Because the researcher controls administration of the experimental stimulus, and measurements are obtained prior to and after its introduction, the time order of variables is clear. Through exposure to the stimulus, the level of the independent variable is first altered (for subjects in the experimental group), and then, through pretest versus posttest comparison, any resulting changes in the dependent variable are readily observed.

Second, consider the criterion of covariation. If the independent variable is the cause of the dependent variable, then subjects exposed to higher levels of the former should manifest greater change in the latter. Operationally, this means that the experimental group should show greater change in the dependent variable than does the control group—or, equivalently, that exposure to the experimental treatment *covaries* with change in the dependent variable. The analyst can establish covariation by comparing pretest and posttest scores (if both are available) or by comparing the posttest scores alone, provided that members of the experimental group and control group were assigned to the groups at random.

Third, consider the criterion of nonspuriousness. As noted earlier, if the experimental and control groups are identical, with the exception of exposure to the treatment, then observed differences between the groups with respect to changes in the dependent variable can reliably be attributed to the independent variable rather than to other potential causes. After all, if the experimental design is implemented correctly, the independent variable is the only difference between the groups.

You may ask why the control group should manifest *any* changes in the dependent variable because these subjects are denied exposure to the experimental treatment. It is in this area especially that the advantages of the control group become apparent. With the passage of time, subjects in both the experimental and control groups may show changes in the dependent variable for reasons quite unrelated to the independent variable. For example, subjects may develop biologically and emotionally; they may react to the fact that they are being observed or measured; they may learn of dramatic events that transpire outside the experimental setting that may affect their scores on the dependent variable. The general name for developments such as these that could jeopardize the causal inference is *threats to internal validity*. The three threats just delineated are the threats of "maturation," "reactivity," and "history," respectively. (This listing is illustrative; refer to research design texts for a more complete inventory.)

The impact of these threats may be felt in any experiment, but assuming that the experimental and control groups are equated to begin with (through a procedure such as random assignment of subjects to groups), there is no reason to suspect that the threats should affect the groups differently. Hence, when the measurements of the two groups are compared, these effects should *cancel* one another. If the independent variable is a cause of the dependent variable though, the effect of the treatment should be manifested in an *additional* increment of change in the dependent variable—but only in the experimental group. Thus, although both groups may exhibit change, the experimental group should demonstrate greater change. In this manner, the control group serves as an essential baseline for interpreting and evaluating change in the experimental group.

Care must be taken in assembling experimental and control groups that are as comparable as possible. In particular, assigning subjects to the experimental or control groups arbitrarily, or segregating them according to scores on a criterion (low achievers versus high achievers, regular voters versus occasional voters), or allowing them to volunteer for either group creates obvious *selection biases* that result in a priori differences between the groups. Consequently, if the experiment reveals a difference in the dependent variable between the experimental group and the control group in the end, the researcher cannot rule out the possibility that it was the initial differences between the groups—rather than the experimental stimulus (independent variable)—that led to this result. Because the causal inference is thereby weakened, these (biased) selection procedures must be avoided.

The technique of choice in constructing equivalent experimental and control groups is **random assignment** of subjects to those groups. Random assignment removes *any* systematic difference between the groups. Randomization is an extremely powerful technique because it controls for factors both known *and* unknown to the researcher. For good reason, then, random assignment is the foremost method for equating experimental and control groups. Equating is fundamental to establishing the validity of the causal inference.

The manager needs to understand that random assignment does not mean haphazard or arbitrary assignment. It has a precise statistical meaning: Each subject or case has an equal chance of being assigned to the experimental group or to the control group. As a result, the groups will have very similar (if not equivalent) composition and characteristics, within the limits of statistical probability. It is this quality that leads to the comparability of the experimental and control groups. If you ever need to draw a random sample for research or other purposes, consult a table of random numbers (contained in the appendices of most statistics texts) or an expert in the field of sampling.

The final criterion of causality is theory. Unfortunately, no research design—and no statistical technique—can establish a causal relationship as substantively meaningful, credible, or important. This evaluation must be made on other grounds, such as logic, experience, and previous research. The criterion of theory reinforces the adage that statistics are no substitute for substantive knowledge of a field.

External Validity

The preceding discussion supports the conclusion that experimental designs of research are relatively strong with respect to internal validity—the causal inference based on the experimental setting and the selected sample of subjects. They are not as strong, however, with respect to external validity—the ability to generalize the results of a study to other settings, other times, and other populations. Primarily two factors limit the external validity of experimental designs.

The first is the **context** of these designs. To isolate subjects from extraneous variables, experimenters frequently place them in a laboratory setting. Although the laboratory works admirably in sealing off subjects from possibly confounding factors, it also removes them from a real-life setting, to which the researcher usually seeks to generalize results. Thus, one can question how closely the situation simulated in the laboratory resembles the processes of everyday life. For example, as part of the experimental treatment, the researcher may systematically expose subjects to new ideas, problems, information, or people. In the normal course of events, however, people exercise a great deal more personal choice and control regarding their exposure to and handling of these influences. Consequently, the results obtained in the experiment may hold under the experimental conditions, but their application to less artificial (more realistic) situations may be problematic.

Closely related to this type of difficulty is the argument that because premeasurement (pretesting) may sensitize subjects to the experimental treatment, results may apply only to pretested populations. This problem, however, is more tractable than the first. If the experimental and control groups have been randomly assigned, then the researcher can eliminate the pretest procedure because random assignment should remove any initial differences between the groups; a posttest is then sufficient to assess the effect of the experimental treatment. This research design is called the *posttest only—control group design*. Or, if time and resources allow, an additional set of experimental and control groups that are *not* pretested can be incorporated into the classical experimental design. With this addition, it is possible to determine not only whether the experimental stimulus has an effect on nonpretested samples but also the magnitude of any reactive

Table 3.3	Posttest Only-Control Group Design		
Group	Randomization	Treatment	Observation 1
Experimental	R_e	X	O_{e1}
Control	R_c		O_{c1}

© Cengage Learning

Table 3.4	Solomon Four-Group Design			
Group	Randomization	Observation 1	Treatment	Observation 2
Experimental	R_{ep}	O_{ep1}	X	O_{ep2}
Control	R_{cp}	O_{cp1}		O_{cp2}
Experimental	R_e		X	O_{e2}
Control	R_c			O_{c2}

© Cengage Learning

effects of premeasurement. This design is known as the *Solomon four-group design.* Letting O stand for observation or measurement, X for administration of the experimental treatment, R for random assignment of subjects to groups, c for control group, e for experimental group, and p for pretest, these two experimental designs can be outlined as shown in Tables 3.3 and 3.4.

The second factor that threatens the external validity of experimental designs of research is the sample of subjects on which findings are based. Because of ethical and financial considerations, experiments conducted on a random sample of individuals drawn from a well-defined population (such as U.S. citizens) have been rare. Institutional review boards (IRBs) are in place at most universities and research centers to evaluate ethical issues in research. They weigh the advantages and disadvantages of research carefully and probe the use of deception, which may be employed to make an experimental setting seem more realistic to participants. Sometimes the potential knowledge to be gained by the experiment is judged so vital that these objections are put aside (as with medical research on life-threatening diseases). In addition, the cost and practical problems of conducting an experiment on a random sample of subjects can be prohibitive. As a result, experiments traditionally have been conducted on "captive" populations—prison inmates, hospital patients, and especially students. The correspondence between these groups and more heterogeneous, "natural" populations is necessarily problematic, thus threatening the external validity of many experiments.

It is important to note, however, that this situation is beginning to change. As social science researchers have grown more familiar with the use and advantages of experimental designs, they have become attuned to naturally occurring experiments—such as changing traffic laws and their enforcement, implementing new government programs, turning over a part of nonprofit agency operations to volunteers, contracting with a fund-raising firm to increase donations to an agency, and so on. With adequate foreknowledge of such developments, the severity of threats to the external validity of experimental designs posed by problems of sampling and context can be attenuated significantly. In the future, social science researchers will probably become increasingly adept at warding off threats to the external validity of experiments.

Quasi-Experimental Designs of Research

Internal Validity

The most fundamental difference between quasi-experimental research designs and experimental designs centers on the ability of the researcher to control exposure to the experimental treatment, or independent variable. This control is much greater in experimental designs than in quasi-experimental designs. This section discusses the internal validity of several of the most common quasi-experimental designs.

Perhaps the most widely used quasi-experimental design is the **cross-sectional study** (sometimes called a *correlational study*). This type of study is based on data obtained at one point in time, often from a large sample of subjects. Most surveys of public opinion or attitudes toward government or nonprofit agencies are cross-sectional studies. For example, suppose a researcher collected information in a large-sample survey concerning the annual income of citizens, the amount of their charitable giving in the past year, the amount of their volunteering (hours) in the past year, their feelings of trust toward the nonprofit sector (low trust, medium trust, high trust), their feelings of trust toward the federal government (low trust, medium trust, high trust), and various other attitudes and behaviors of the respondents. The researcher would then analyze the relationships among these attitudes and behaviors using the statistical techniques you will learn later in this book. Such a study is called a cross-sectional study because it captures and analyzes data from one cross-section or point in time. With X representing the independent variable and O representing observation or measurement, the research design might be diagrammed as follows:

$$X \quad O$$

Another research design is the **case study**. As opposed to the cross-sectional design, the case study provides a much more in-depth examination of an event or locale, usually undertaken after something dramatic has transpired (such as Hurricane Katrina, "Super Storm" Sandy, or the tragic shooting in Newton, Connecticut). Although a case study may rest (at least partially) on data obtained from a random sample of respondents, more often the researcher relies on information from carefully selected individuals (informants) and archival records. We might diagram a case study similarly to the cross-sectional design, but the O or measurement or observation is very different in the two types of design, with the case study providing much more depth and detail than the cross-section:

$$X \quad O$$

A **panel study** is a series of cross-sectional studies based on the same sample of individuals over time; that is, a group of individuals is surveyed repeatedly over time. An examination of the effects of college that followed incoming students until their graduation would be a panel study. Or, a study that periodically interviewed a sample (or "panel") of executive directors of nonprofit agencies over time is a panel study. If the researcher collected data at six time points denoted by the subscripts, her research design could be diagrammed as follows:

$$O_1 \quad O_2 \quad O_3 \quad X \quad O_4 \quad O_5 \quad O_6$$

Finally, **trend studies** monitor and attempt to account for shifts over time in various indicators, such as gross national product, unemployment, attitude toward the president, number of nonprofit organizations registered with the Internal Revenue Service (IRS), and so on. Examples are plentiful; regularly published reports chart the course of myriad economic measures (consumer price index, inflation rate), as well as indicators of public opinion (Harris poll, Gallup poll). The diagram for the trend study would appear similar to the panel study, but again the O or measurement or observation would differ (the panel study collects information from the same individual respondents over time). If the trend study had eight time points, as denoted by the subscripts, it could be diagrammed as follows:

$$O_1 \quad O_2 \quad O_3 \quad O_4 \quad X \quad O_5 \quad O_6 \quad O_7 \quad O_8$$

Some studies combine elements from several research designs in a **mixed research design**. For example, a researcher may conduct a large sample survey and include in the study an analysis of a particularly interesting or noteworthy case(s). Similarly, a researcher may supplement a trend study with a survey or an in-depth case study at one or more program sites. It is also possible to combine in the same study highly qualitative information (such as in-depth interviews with officials at a nonprofit organization) with quantitative analysis (e.g., organizational performance measurement at the same agency) to evaluate the implementation and effectiveness of efforts to measure performance.

Quasi-experimental research designs can be evaluated with respect to three of the four criteria for establishing a relationship as causal (internal validity): covariation, time order, and nonspuriousness. The remaining criterion is theory. As discussed before, the substantive plausibility of a causal relationship stands apart from considerations of research design or statistical techniques.

Quasi-experimental designs are relatively strong in demonstrating covariation between independent and dependent variables. Many statistics have been developed for assessing the magnitude of covariation or association between two variables (see Chapters 14 through 20). As long as the independent and dependent variables are measured across a sample of subjects, the researcher can use statistics to assess the degree of covariation.

An exception to this general conclusion should be noted. Because most case studies are based on a single unit of analysis (the case), establishing covariation may be problematic. For example, in a given case study, both the independent and the dependent variables may assume high values, thus tempting the researcher to conclude that one is the cause of the other. Because other cases in which the independent variable takes on different values are *not* examined, however, it is not possible to observe how the dependent variable changes with changes in the independent variable—the essence of the concept of covariation. This situation resembles an experiment in which a control group is mistakenly omitted: Without the control group, it is very difficult to evaluate the effect of the experimental treatment on the dependent variable.

In quasi-experimental designs that employ repeated measurements over time—called *longitudinal studies*—the time order of the independent and dependent variables is relatively clear. Thus, in panel studies, the criterion of time order for demonstrating causality is usually substantiated because changes can be tracked over time. In-depth studies that seek to reconstruct the chronology of important events may also be able to establish time order.

This conclusion does *not* hold for static or single-point-in-time studies, however. In cross-sectional studies especially, because of the lack of data collected over time, except in the most obvious cases (relationships between ascribed characteristics such as sex, race, or age and various attitudes and behaviors), the time order of a relationship may be a matter of faith or assumption (such as relationships between attitudes or between attitudes and behaviors). On the one hand, we can be confident that such variables as race and age may lead to particular attitudes and behaviors, and not the reverse. On the other hand, the direction of relationship between years in a job and attitude toward the work is open to debate. As a consequence, in many static (i.e., cross-sectional) studies the causal inference is weakened. For example, if all variables are measured just once, it is unclear whether employee work motivation leads to self-confidence or vice versa, or whether either variable is the cause or the result of employee productivity.

The major threat to the internal validity of quasi-experimental designs is spuriousness. The nonspuriousness criterion requires that the relationship between the independent variable and the dependent variable hold in the presence of all third variables. In experimental designs, control over exposure to the experimental treatment, random assignment of subjects to experimental and control groups, and isolation of subjects from extraneous influences enhance significantly the ability of the researcher to satisfy this condition. In quasi-experimental designs, circumstances are not as fortuitous. Exposure to the independent variable is beyond the control of the investigator; there is no reason to assume that those exposed are otherwise identical to those not exposed; and in the real world, confounding factors abound.

A researcher interested in the determinants of efficiency in public organizations, for example, may conduct a survey of state agencies. The results of the survey may show that efficiency covaries with agency size, measured according to personnel and budget. Might this relationship be causal? The answer is complicated. Many other variables covary with efficiency and may be responsible for the observed relationship. The type of technology used in an agency will affect both its efficiency and its size. Similarly, the training of agency employees will affect how efficiently the agency operates and the amount of personnel and budget needed. The structure of the agency may influence the degree of efficiency attained, as well as the level of personnel and budget. In order to determine whether the relationship between agency size and efficiency is nonspurious, the researcher would have to show that even after the effects of third variables such as agency technology, employee training, and organization structure have been taken into account, this relationship persists in the survey data. Chapter 16 presents an extensive discussion of nonspuriousness and appropriate statistical procedures to examine this criterion of causality for nominal and ordinal data.

To test for nonspuriousness in a quasi-experimental design, researchers attempt to compensate statistically for their lack of control over the actual situation. They employ *statistical control techniques* that assess the magnitude of relationship between the independent and dependent variables, taking into account (controlling for) the effects of plausible third variables (see Chapters 16 and 20). Unfortunately, these techniques are complex. Also, it is not possible *logically* to eliminate all third variables as the putative cause of an observed relationship. Moreover, to control statistically for their effects, the researcher must hypothesize in advance the likely third variables and collect data on them. This task is difficult, time-consuming, and expensive—but essential nonetheless. Because statistical control techniques require data from several cases or subjects, case studies are especially vulnerable with respect to the nonspuriousness criterion of causality. Although case studies are not typically strong with respect to validity, they can be very useful in uncovering important factors and suggesting hypotheses for further study.

External Validity

Although quasi-experimental designs of research must overcome serious challenges to internal validity, they tend to be relatively strong with respect to external validity. Two major reasons account for this fact. First, it is easier to obtain representative samples of the population for quasi-experimental designs. Consequently, in these designs more confidence can be placed in inferring findings from sample to population.

Second, in general, quasi-experimental designs are conducted in more natural (less artificial) settings than are experimental designs. Experiments often place subjects in a contrived environment controlled and monitored by the researcher. In contrast, in quasi-experimental designs, subjects may not realize that they are the focus of study (as in the use of highly aggregated statistics pertaining to the economy, traffic fatalities, and so on), or relevant information may be ascertained from them in comfortable and familiar surroundings (as in surveys of public attitudes and behaviors administered in the home or office). Whereas few would contend that these settings are totally free of possible bias, there is consensus that they are less reactive than most experimental designs—subjects are less likely to react to the context of the study itself. Hence, the results obtained are more likely to hold outside the study in other settings, thereby increasing external validity.

Again, exceptions must be appended to these conclusions. Because in panel studies the same respondents are interviewed repeatedly over time, they may grow sensitized to the fact that they are under study and thus become less typical of the population they were originally chosen to represent. This problem may be alleviated by limiting participation in the panel to a short period of time. Case studies are less tractable with respect to external validity. The case is usually selected precisely because there is something distinctive, atypical, or particularly interesting about it (e.g., a failure of a nuclear power plant, or a "whistleblower" whose courageous persistence saves a state government millions of dollars). As a consequence, it is difficult to judge the extent to which the results of a case study have relevance for other cases. Case study researchers should devote serious attention to considering the population of cases to which they may legitimately generalize their results. Unfortunately, researchers and readers alike often are so captivated by the details of an arresting case that they fail to ask the important question: What can be learned from this case to apply to other cases?

Research Designs and Validity

In the discussion of research design, two general points stand out. First, there is a trade-off between internal validity and external validity. In a given design, it is very difficult to increase one type of validity without decreasing the other. In experimental designs, although the control exercised by the researcher enhances internal validity, it jeopardizes external validity. In quasi-experimental designs, more natural settings and representative samples contribute to external validity, but these same factors make it more difficult to establish internal validity. In a given study, the researcher should work to achieve an acceptable balance between the two types of validity.

Some research procedures can enhance both internal validity and external validity simultaneously. For example, larger samples increase both internal validity and external validity. Replication increases internal and external validity. Mixed designs combining elements of experimental and quasi-experimental designs can also assist. So the researcher can take steps, but they are expensive and require additional care and effort.

Second, drawing reliable causal inferences is a serious, painstaking, and difficult enterprise. For example, after decades of research and thousands of studies on job attitudes and performance, experts continue to disagree over the causes and effects. This instance is not an isolated one; in many other fields in the social sciences, the causes of important phenomena remain elusive. By contrast, in everyday life one hears a great deal of loose talk regarding the cause or causes of an event or a phenomenon. Most of it is just that—talk. Nevertheless, critical decisions are often made on this basis. Remember that the same criteria used to establish a relationship as causal in research apply *outside* this environment as well. Unless these criteria are reasonably satisfied, one can—and should—question the causal inference.

Chapter Summary

Research designs involve setting up a research project so that the research questions can be answered as unambiguously as possible. The objective of a good research design is to establish causal relationships and to assess their generalizability.

The basic building block in constructing causal explanations is the concept, which pinpoints an idea or element thought to be essential in accounting for the class of events under study. Concepts are defined in two ways: with a nominal definition, which is the standard dictionary definition, and with an operational definition, which translates the nominal definition into a form in which the concept can be measured empirically. Once concepts have been operationalized and measured in a sample of data, they are called variables. The two major types of variables are independent (anticipated causes) and dependent (the variables thought to be affected by them). A hypothesis formally proposes an expected relationship between an independent and a dependent variable.

Social scientists have identified four criteria as necessary for establishing a relationship as causal: time order, covariation, nonspuriousness, and theory. A research design is a program for evaluating empirically proposed causal relationships. The evaluation is based on two criteria: internal validity (did the independent variable lead to changes in the dependent variable?) and external validity (can the results obtained in the study be generalized to other populations, times, and settings?). Two major families of research design were outlined: experimental designs and quasi-experimental designs. Both types were evaluated with regard to the four criteria for causal relationships that define internal validity and with regard to external validity. Briefly, the experimental design has its primary strengths in internal validity, and the quasi-experimental design has its strengths in external validity.

Problems

3.1 A researcher asserts that the relationship between attitude toward the field of public administration and taking courses in a public administration degree program is causal.

(a) What evidence must the researcher provide about this relationship to prove that it is causal?

(b) Given your answer, what aspects of the researcher's argument are likely to be strongest, and what aspects of her argument are likely to be weakest? Your discussion should include clear definitions of each element of a causal relationship.

3.2 Develop a model that includes at least four concepts. Elaborate any theoretical or literature support underlying it. Present the model in an arrow diagram that shows schematically the relationships the model proposes. Provide operational definitions for all concepts, and state hypotheses derived from the model.

(a) Which types of research designs would be best suited to testing the model?

(b) Which types of research designs would be least suited to testing the model?

3.3 Professor George A. Bulldogski has taught social graces to athletic teams at a major southeastern university for the past 15 years. Based on this experience, he insists that table manners are causally related to leadership. Professor Bulldogski has data showing that athletes who have better table manners also demonstrate greater leadership in athletic competition. The university gymnastics coach, who wants to build leadership on her team, is considering asking Professor Bulldogski to meet regularly with her team. She hopes that after he teaches table manners to team members, they will become better leaders. Should she invite Professor Bulldogski to meet with the gymnastics team? If she does so, can she expect his involvement to develop greater leadership on the team? Explain your answers.

3.4 For the entire month of January 2014, the local domestic violence shelter ran a series of ads on the government access cable television channel. The director of the shelter hypothesized that the ads would bring more attention to the problem of domestic violence and make victims of domestic violence more aware of the shelter's programs. The director has monthly data on the number of new clients. At the end of April 2014, the director asks you to come up with a research design to help assess whether the ads had an effect on the number of clients served.

(a) What type of research design would you use to test the hypothesis?

(b) The director has monthly figures for the number of clients served in 2013. Are these data relevant for testing the above hypothesis? If so, why?

3.5 The head of the Teen Intervention Center believes that troubled youth are not getting the message if they complete the center's 5-week education program but still have subsequent encounters with law enforcement. When they first come to the center, teens are broken up into groups of 15 to meet with a counselor and answer questions about what society defines as acceptable versus unacceptable behaviors.

(a) If you were the head of counseling at the center, what knowledge might you gain by asking each group of teens similar questions at the end of the 5-week program?

(b) Is there any reason to expect different responses to the initial questions and those asked at the end of the program? Explain.

(c) What type of research design would you be using if you administered a questionnaire to the same group of individuals at the outset of treatment, at the end of treatment, and 6 months after treatment?

Descriptive Statistics

PART

2

Descriptive Statistics

Frequency Distributions

Descriptive statistics is nothing more than a fancy name for numbers (statistics) used to summarize a group of data. These data can be the number of arrests each police officer makes, the amount of garbage collected by city work crews, the number of fund-raising events held by a nonprofit organization in a year, the number of volunteers assisting a government agency, the number of high school students participating in community service projects, or the size of various government agencies (measured by personnel or budget). In their unorganized or nontabulated form, data (affectionately known as "raw data") are difficult to comprehend. This chapter explains how to convert raw data into frequency and percentage distributions and related data displays.

We begin with an example that shows how to construct a frequency distribution, then discuss percentage distributions, followed by cumulative frequency distributions. The chapter presents graphical presentations and gives examples of how to construct frequency polygons and histograms. It concludes with tips for effective graphical presentations.

Constructing a Frequency Distribution

We begin by presenting some (really) raw data. The listing below gives the number of tons of trash collected by the Normal, Oklahoma, sanitary engineer teams for the week of June 8, 2014. Each entry is the number of tons of trash collected by a team during the week.

57	70	62	66	68	62	76	71	79	87
82	63	71	51	65	78	61	78	55	64
83	75	50	70	61	69	80	51	52	94
89	63	82	75	58	68	84	83	71	79
77	89	59	88	97	86	75	95	64	65
53	74	75	61	86	65	95	77	73	86
81	66	73	51	75	64	67	54	54	78
57	81	65	72	59	72	84	85	79	67
62	76	52	92	66	74	72	83	56	93
96	64	95	94	86	75	73	72	85	94

Clearly, presenting these data in their raw form would tell the administrator little or nothing about trash collection in Normal. For example, how many tons of trash do most teams collect? Do the teams seem to collect about the same amount of trash, or does their performance vary?

The most basic restructuring of raw data to facilitate understanding of what they mean is the **frequency distribution**. A frequency distribution is a table that pairs data values—or ranges of data values—with their frequency of occurrence. For example, Table 4.1 is a frequency distribution of the number of arrests each Morgan City police officer made in March 2014. Note that the entire table is labeled, as is each column. Here, the data values are the number of arrests, and the frequencies are the number of police officers. This procedure makes it easy to see that most Morgan City police officers made between 16 and 20 arrests in March 2014.

Public and nonprofit managers use a standard vocabulary to describe data. A **variable** is a trait or characteristic that we wish to measure; in the preceding example, the variable is the number of arrests per police officer. A **class** is one of the grouped categories of the variable. The first class, for example, is from 1 to 5 arrests. Classes have **class boundaries** (the lowest and highest values that fall within the class) and **class midpoints** (the point halfway between the upper and lower class boundaries). The class midpoint of the third class, for example, is 13; it can easily be found by adding the lower class boundary (11) and the upper class boundary (15) and dividing by half (2) to identify the midpoint. The **class interval** is the difference or distance between the upper limit of one class and the upper limit of the next higher class. In our example the class interval is 5. The **class frequency** is the number of observations or occurrences of the variable within a given class; for example, the class frequency of the fourth class (16–20) is 132. The **total frequency** is the total number of observations or cases in the table—in this case, 244. In the remainder of this chapter, we will discuss some important characteristics of frequency distributions and the procedures for constructing them.

Table 4.1	Arrests per Police Officer: Morgan City, March 2014
Number of Arrests	**Number of Police Officers**
1–5	6
6–10	17
11–15	47
16–20	132
21–25	35
25+	7
	244

© Cengage Learning 2015

Constructing a frequency distribution is a relatively straightforward task. To illustrate this process we will use the Normal, Oklahoma, garbage collection data listed previously. You may prefer to use *Excel*™ or another computer program to create the frequency distribution. Our goal is that you understand the technique and its use and can answer the proverbial question, "Where/how did you get those numbers?"

Step 1: Scan the data to find the lowest and highest values of the variable. The lowest value in these data is 50 (column 3, the third value), and the highest value is 97 (column 5, the fifth value).

Step 2: List all the values from the lowest to the highest and then mark the number of times each value appears. This process is illustrated below.

50 /	60	70 //	80 /	90
51 ///	61 ///	71 ///	81 //	91
52 //	62 ///	72 /////	82 //	92 /
53 /	63 //	73 ///	83 ///	93 /
54 //	64 /////	74 //	84 //	94 ///
55 /	65 ////	75 //////	85 //	95 ///
56 //	66 ///	76 //	86 ////	96 /
57 //	67 //	77 //	87 /	97 /
58 /	68 //	78 ///	88 /	98
59 //	69 /	79 ///	89 //	

Step 3: The tabulations in Step 2 could be called a frequency distribution because each data value (tons of trash) is now paired with its frequency of occurrence. For a better visual presentation, however, the data should be grouped into classes. The rule of thumb is to collapse data into no fewer than 4 and no more than 20 classes. Fewer than 4 classes obscures the variation in the data; more than 20 presents too complex a picture to grasp quickly. The analyst chooses the number of classes in a table so that the table reflects the data as closely as possible. Other tips for constructing frequency distribution classes are as follows:

1. Avoid classes so narrow that some intervals have zero observations.

2. Make all the class intervals equal unless the top or bottom class is open-ended. An open-ended class has only one boundary. In the Morgan City arrest table, for example, the last category (251) is an open-ended category.

3. Use open-ended intervals only when closed-ended intervals would result in class frequencies of zero. This result usually occurs when some values are extremely high or extremely low.

4. Try to construct the intervals so that the midpoints are whole numbers.

For the present example, let us collapse the data into five categories. Constructing the remainder of the table results in the frequency distribution shown in Table 4.2.

Table 4.2	Tons of Garbage Collected by Sanitary Engineer Teams in Normal, Oklahoma, Week of June 8, 2014	
	Tons of Garbage	Number of Teams
	50–60	16
	60–70	24
	70–80	30
	80–90	20
	90–100	10
		100

© Cengage Learning 2015

Note in the table that the upper limit of every class is also the lower limit of the next class; that is, the upper limit of the first class is 60, the same value as the lower limit of the second class. This format is typically used when the data are continuous. A **continuous variable** can take on values that are not whole numbers (the whole numbers are 1, 2, 3, . . .); some examples are temperature (for instance, 98.6 degrees), miles per gallon (for instance, 18.1 mpg), and time spent at work (for instance, 9.25 hours per day). In the situation given in Table 4.2, statisticians interpret the first interval as running from 50 tons up to but not including 60 tons (that is, 59.999 tons). In this way no data value can fall into more than one class. When you see tables like this one in which interval limits appear to overlap, remember that the upper limit means up to but not including the value and that the lower limit begins with this value. Tables 4.3 and 4.4 are constructed in the same manner.

The Percentage Distribution

Suppose the Normal city manager wants to know whether Normal sanitary engineer crews are picking up more garbage than the city crews in Moore. The city manager may want to know because Moore crews collect only garbage that residents place curbside in front of their houses, whereas Normal crews collect trash cans located in residents' yards. The city manager's goal is to collect more garbage while holding down garbage collection costs.

Table 4.3 shows the frequency distributions of garbage collection in both cities. But from the frequency distributions, the city manager cannot tell which method of trash collection is more efficient. Because Moore has a larger workforce, it has a larger number of crews in all five of the classes. The data must be converted so that the two cities can be compared.

The easiest way to make the data comparable is to convert both columns of data into percentage distributions. A **percentage distribution** shows the percentage of the total observations that fall into each class. To convert the data of Table 4.3 to

Table 4.3	Tons of Garbage Collected by Sanitary Engineer Teams, Week of June 8, 2014		
		Number of Teams	
Tons of Garbage		Normal	Moore
50–60		16	22
60–70		24	37
70–80		30	49
80–90		20	36
90–100		10	21
		100	165

© Cengage Learning 2015

percentage distributions, the frequency in each class should be divided by the total frequency for that city. In this instance, all Normal class frequencies should be divided by 100, and all Moore class frequencies should be divided by 165. (Chapter 14 presents a more detailed discussion of percentage distributions.) Table 4.4 shows the resulting percentage distributions. Is the Moore method of trash collection more efficient than the method used in Normal?

Table 4.4 pairs each class with the percentage that class constitutes of all observations. Note that some new items are included in the percentage distribution table that were not included in the frequency distribution table. At the bottom of each column, a number is found, $N = 100$ or $N = 165$. N stands for the total number of observations; it represents the total frequency (or number of observations) on which the percentages are based. Given this number, you can calculate the original class frequencies (multiply the percentage times N). Try it. You should get the frequency distributions shown in Table 4.3.

Table 4.4	Tons of Garbage Collected by Sanitary Engineer Teams, Week of June 8, 2014		
		Percentage of Work Teams	
Tons of Garbage		Normal	Moore
50–60		16	13
60–70		24	22
70–80		30	30
80–90		20	22
90–100		10	13
		100	100
		$N = 100$	$N = 165$

© Cengage Learning 2015

Cumulative Frequency Distributions

Frequency distributions and percentage distributions show the number and percentage, respectively, of observations that fall in each class of a variable. Sometimes the administrator needs to know how many observations (or what percentage of observations) fall below or above a certain standard. For example, the fire chief of Metro, Texas, is quite concerned about how long it takes fire crews to arrive at the scene of a fire. The *Metro Morning News* has run several stories about fires in which it claimed the Metro fire department was slow in responding. Because the Metro fire department automatically records the time of fire calls on its computer and also records the dispatched fire truck's report that it has arrived at the fire, the response times to all fires are available. An analyst has made a frequency distribution of these response times (Table 4.5). The Metro fire chief considers 5 minutes to be an excellent response time, 10 minutes to be an acceptable response time, 15 minutes to be an unsatisfactory response time, and 20 minutes to be unacceptable. As a result, the fire chief wants to know the percentage of fire calls answered in under 5 minutes, under 10 minutes, under 15 minutes, and under 20 minutes. To provide the fire chief with the information she wants, the analyst must construct a cumulative percentage distribution.

Table 4.5	Response Times of the Metro Fire Department, 2014		
Response Time (Minutes)	Number of Calls	Running Total	Cumulative Percentage
0–1	7		
1–2	14		
2–3	32		
3–4	37		
4–5	48		
5–6	53		
6–7	66		
7–8	73		
8–9	42		
9–10	40		
10–11	36		
11–12	23		
12–13	14		
13–14	7		
14–15	2		
15–20	6		
	500		

Table 4.6	Response Times of the Metro Fire Department, 2014	
Response Time		Percentage (Cumulative) of Response Times
Under 5 minutes		27.6
Under 10 minutes		82.4
Under 15 minutes		98.8
Under 20 minutes		100.00
	N = 500	

© Cengage Learning 2015

The first step in developing a **cumulative percentage distribution** is to prepare a running total of responses to fire calls. To the right of the "Number of Calls" column in Table 4.5, you will find a blank column labeled "Running Total." In this column, we will calculate the total number of responses made that were less than each interval's upper limit. For example, how many fires were responded to in less than 1 minute? From the table we can see seven fires had response times of under a minute. Enter the number 7 for the first class in the "Running Total" column. How many fire responses were under 2 minutes? There were 21, with 7 under 1 minute, plus 14 between 1 and 2 minutes. Enter 21 as the value for the second class. Using this logic fill in the rest of the values in Table 4.5.

The second step is to construct a cumulative percentage column. This step is performed by dividing each frequency in the "Running Total" column by the total frequency (in this case, 500). In the fourth column of Table 4.5, "Cumulative Percentage," enter the following numbers. The first entry should be 1.4 (7 ÷ 500); the second entry should be 4.2 (21 ÷ 500); the third entry should be 10.6 (53 ÷ 500); fill in the remaining values for this column.

You now have a **cumulative frequency distribution** and a cumulative percentage distribution for the fire chief. The distribution is a bit awkward, however, because it has so many categories. The next step would be to collapse the cumulative percentage distribution into fewer categories. Because the fire chief is concerned with response times of 5, 10, 15, and 20 minutes, these times would be the best categories. Table 4.6 should result from your calculations. From this table, what can you tell the chief about fire department response times in Metro? How good are the department's response times?

Graphical Presentations

Often a public or nonprofit administrator wants to present information visually so that leaders, citizens, clients, staff, and others can get a general feel for a problem without reading a table. Two methods of visual presentation will be described here: the frequency polygon and the histogram.

Let us say that the Normal city manager, as part of her budget justification, wants to show the city council the number of complaints that the city animal control office receives about barking dogs. An assistant has prepared the frequency distribution shown in Table 4.7.

To construct a **frequency polygon**, follow these steps:

Step 1: On a sheet of graph paper, write the name of the variable across the bottom and the frequency along the side. Here, the variable is the number of complaints about dogs, and the frequency is the number of weeks. See Figure 4.1.

Table 4.7	Complaints per Week about Barking Dogs, 2014	
	Number of Complaints	Number of Weeks
	5–9	7
	10–14	6
	15–19	15
	20–24	17
	25–29	5
	30–34	2
		52

© Cengage Learning 2015

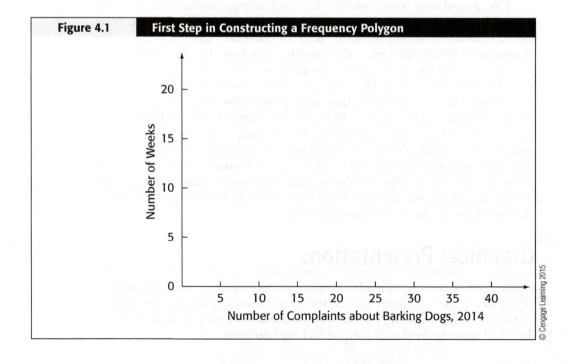

Figure 4.1 **First Step in Constructing a Frequency Polygon**

Number of Weeks (vertical axis: 0, 5, 10, 15, 20)

Number of Complaints about Barking Dogs, 2014 (horizontal axis: 5, 10, 15, 20, 25, 30, 35, 40)

© Cengage Learning 2015

Step 2: Calculate the midpoint for each class interval. Add the two boundaries for each class and divide by 2. For the first class, the midpoint is $(5 + 9) \div 2$, or 7. The midpoints for the other classes are 12, 17, 22, 27, and 32.

Step 3: On the horizontal dimension or axis of the graph, find the first class midpoint (7). Directly above this point, mark the frequency for this class (also 7) with a dot. Repeat this procedure for the five other classes. Your graph should look like the one in Figure 4.2.

Step 4: Calculate the midpoint for the class below the lowest class observed (this class would be 0–4 complaints) and for the class above the highest class served (35–39). Plot these midpoints with a frequency of 0 on your graph (i.e., on the horizontal axis).

Step 5: Draw a line connecting the points in sequence. Your first frequency polygon should look like the one in Figure 4.3. (Note that whereas the frequency polygon presents a useful visual representation of the data, the line segments do not correspond to actual data points.)

One nice aspect of frequency polygons is that the analyst can draw more than one on the same graph. For example, suppose that the Normal city manager wants to show how complaints about barking dogs have changed over time. The city manager gives you the data shown in Table 4.8. In Figure 4.4, graph frequency polygons for both years on the same graph. What does the graph tell you about barking dog complaints in 2014 as opposed to those in 2013?

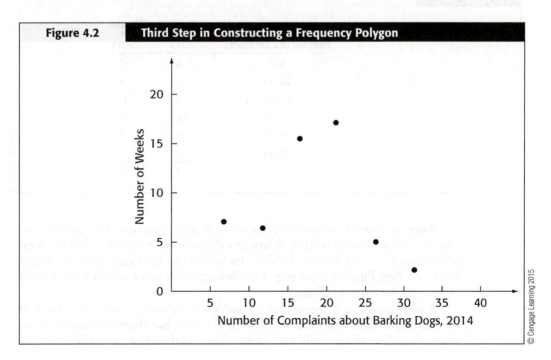

Figure 4.2 **Third Step in Constructing a Frequency Polygon**

Number of Weeks

Number of Complaints about Barking Dogs, 2014

© Cengage Learning 2015

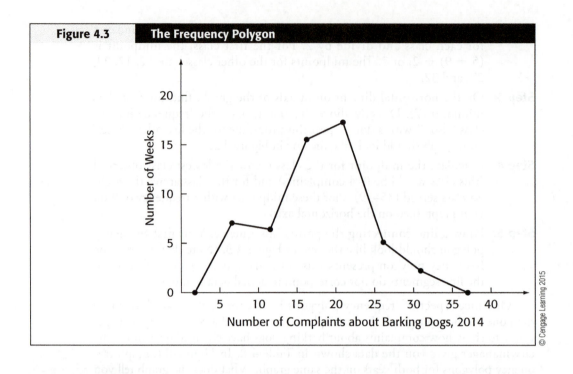

Figure 4.3 **The Frequency Polygon**

Number of Weeks (y-axis)
Number of Complaints about Barking Dogs, 2014 (x-axis)

© Cengage Learning 2015

Table 4.8 Complaints per Week about Barking Dogs, 2013 and 2014

| | Number of Weeks | |
Number of Complaints	2013	2014
5–9	8	7
10–14	12	6
15–19	14	15
20–24	10	17
25–29	6	5
30–34	2	2
	52	52

© Cengage Learning 2015

Note: Whenever two or more frequency polygons are drawn on the same set of axes, each polygon should be drawn in a different color or with a different type of line (such as solid, broken, bold) so the reader can tell them apart. Be sure to label each line. Figure 6.1 on page 110 illustrates this point using different types of lines on the same set of axes.

A **histogram** is a bar graph for a variable that takes on many values (such as income or gross national product [GNP]). The term **bar chart** is sometimes used when a variable can take only a very limited set of values (e.g., a variable assessing

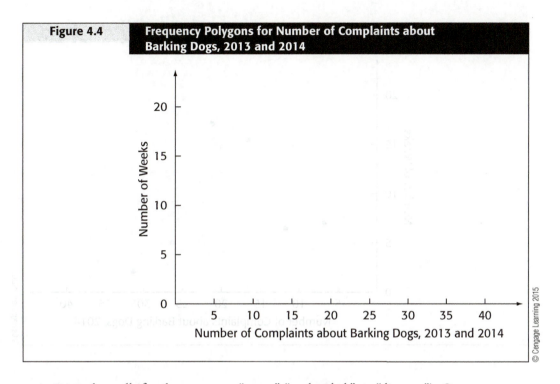

Figure 4.4 **Frequency Polygons for Number of Complaints about Barking Dogs, 2013 and 2014**

© Cengage Learning 2015

an opinion that calls for the responses "agree," "undecided," or "disagree"). Our intention is not to multiply terms (or confusion), but some statistical package programs do make this distinction. You will use these packages in public and nonprofit administration.

To construct a histogram of barking dog complaints in Normal for 2014, complete the following steps.

Steps 1–3: Follow the same procedures given for constructing frequency polygons in Steps 1, 2, and 3 above. Following this procedure should yield the graph shown in Figure 4.5.

Step 4: Using the points on the graph, first draw a horizontal line from the lower to the upper class boundary for each class. Then draw in the vertical lines along the class boundaries from these horizontal lines to the horizontal axis of the graph. Each class is now represented by a bar.

Step 5: Shade in the bars you have drawn in Step 4. Your graph should appear as shown in Figure 4.6.

You should use histograms rather than frequency polygons whenever you want to emphasize the distinctiveness of each class. As you can see by looking at the graphs, the frequency polygon tends to smooth out class differences. Frequency polygons should be used whenever you want to emphasize a smooth trend or when two or more graphs are placed on a single chart, table, or pair of coordinate axes.

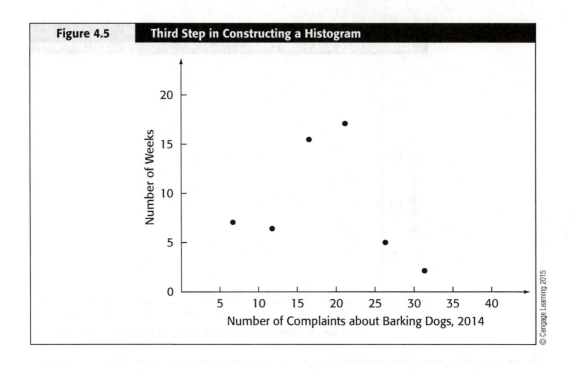

Figure 4.5   **Third Step in Constructing a Histogram**

Number of Weeks (y-axis)

Number of Complaints about Barking Dogs, 2014 (x-axis)

© Cengage Learning 2015

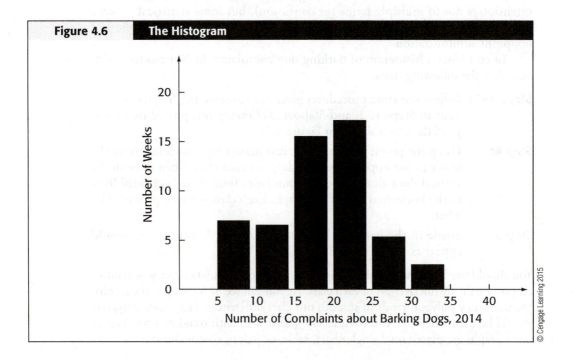

Figure 4.6   **The Histogram**

Number of Weeks (y-axis)

Number of Complaints about Barking Dogs, 2014 (x-axis)

© Cengage Learning 2015

Figure 4.7	Cumulative Frequency Polygons

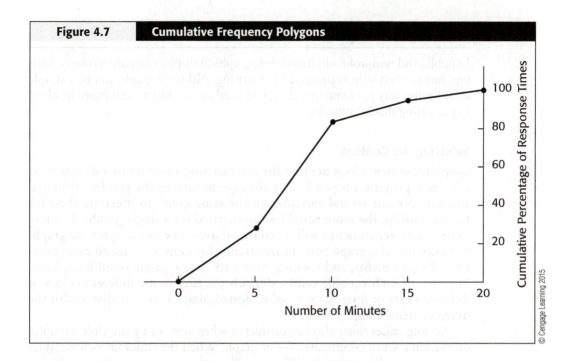

© Cengage Learning 2015

Cumulative frequency distributions can also be graphed. For example, the cumulative distribution for the Metro fire department response times shown in Table 4.6 can be made into a frequency polygon. For each response time in the table (under 5 minutes, under 10 minutes, and so on), simply plot the corresponding percentage and connect the consecutive points. Your graph should look like the one in Figure 4.7. For comparative purposes, make a second frequency polygon in Figure 4.7 for the city of Atlantis fire department; the response times are presented in Table 4.9. Be sure to label the two lines for clarity.

A frequency polygon for a cumulative distribution is called an **ogive**. Compare the ogives in Figure 4.7. Which fire department appears to respond more quickly to fires? Why do you think so?

Table 4.9	Response Times of Atlantis Fire Department, 2014	
Response Time		Percentage (Cumulative) of Response Times
Under 5 minutes		21.2
Under 10 minutes		63.9
Under 15 minutes		86.4
Under 20 minutes		100.0

© Cengage Learning 2015

Tips for Graphical Presentations

In public and nonprofit administration, graphical displays can often convey findings just as effectively as paragraphs of writing. Although graphs can be a simple and effective way to summarize data, you need to consider several issues involved in presenting this information.

Selecting the Content

Graphical presentations are best for summarizing variables that do not need a lot of explanation beyond what already appears on the graphs. Although you may present several variables on the same graph to illustrate their interrelationship, the more variables summarized on a single graph, the more likely the target audience will be confused over how to interpret the graph. For example, if a graph summarizes trends for employee health care, overtime, fringe benefits, and training costs with four separate trend lines, keeping track of each variable can be difficult (be sure to use different colors or different types of lines, such as solid, dotted, dashed, etc., to distinguish the different trend lines).

Scaling issues must also be considered when presenting multiple variables on the same set of coordinate axes or graph. When the scales for two variables are not comparable, it may be difficult to illustrate changes for each variable. For example, if the values for one variable are measured in hundreds of thousands (annual budget) and the values for another are well below 100 (number of organizational departments), the dramatic differences in scale are likely to obscure trends for the variable with the much smaller scale.

Another approach is to express data for two closely related variables in ratio terms. For example, a common measure of financial performance for nonprofit organizations is the **current ratio**. The current ratio is calculated by dividing current assets by current liabilities. Similarly, an organization could summarize information about the number of employees and the number of clients served by tracking changes by means of an employee–client ratio.

Selecting the Format

Spreadsheets and statistical software packages offer a wide variety of formats for presenting data graphically. Ideally, the format you choose should be suited to the dimension of performance you wish to highlight. For example, pie charts work well for breaking down aggregate categories into component parts. If an organization's budget is broken down into several functional areas, a pie chart can show the percentage of the total budget allocated to each area. Line graphs are useful if the goal is to present changes in performance measures over time. Histograms or bar charts or graphs are useful for ranking data or making comparisons across different observations.

We will illustrate the use of line graphs and histograms with an example. Joseph Copp is the police chief of Groton, Georgia. In early 2013, Chief Copp asked the mayor and city council for more funding so that the police department could initiate a "Click It or Ticket" campaign to combat the problem of drivers who do not wear seat belts. The chief's funding request was approved for the 2014 fiscal year (which begins in October 2013). To show the mayor and city council the effect of increased funding, the chief asks his assistant to construct a histogram for the number of citations issued for drivers not wearing seat belts from June 2013 through May 2014. Figure 4.8 displays the graph.

The graphical evidence reveals a general downward trend in the number of citations issued for seat-belt violations. Chief Copp believes that this graph will help him make a convincing case to the mayor and city council that the increase in funding has helped the police department address the problem more effectively. The manager should be sure to consider the "research design" step to rule out alternative explanations (see Chapter 3).

Selecting the Scale

If the default settings of the graphics software do not fit the range of your data, you should change the scale to better fit the data. Inappropriate scales can obscure

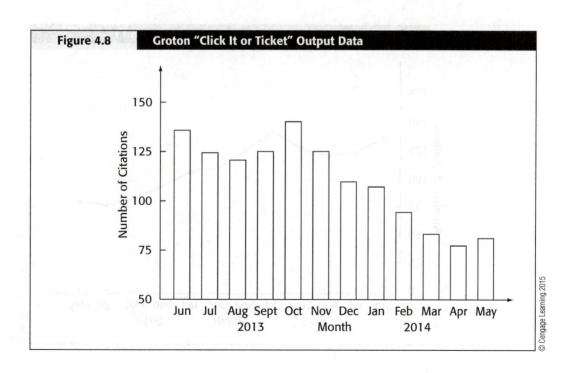

Figure 4.8 **Groton "Click It or Ticket" Output Data**

© Cengage Learning 2015

findings, which negate the benefits of using graphs to summarize data. This issue is especially problematic when the values for a measure fall in a relatively narrow range. For instance, if the values for a variable range from 10 to 25, and your graph ranges instead from 0 to 100, trends and changes in the data will be difficult to spot.

To illustrate the effects of differences in scale, we will present the Groton "Click It or Ticket" program data using two different line graphs. In Version A (Figure 4.9), the scale for the P-axis ranges from 0 to 175. In Version B (Figure 4.10), the scale ranges from 50 to 150.

Notice how differences in scale affect the presentation of results. Although the data are the same in both cases, the effect of the program looks more pronounced in Version B than it does in Version A. An important point about spreadsheets and other computer graphics tools is that these programs often apply default settings that do not necessarily fit the data in question. In the present case, the data values range from 77 to 140, but the graphics program automatically selected a scale of 0 to 175. Is a range of 0 to 175 necessary? Because the data range from 77 to 140, a graph with a minimum value of 0 and a maximum value of 175 for the P-axis obscures findings. Assessing trends and changes in variables is easier when the minimum and maximum points on a scale more closely match the actual range of the data.

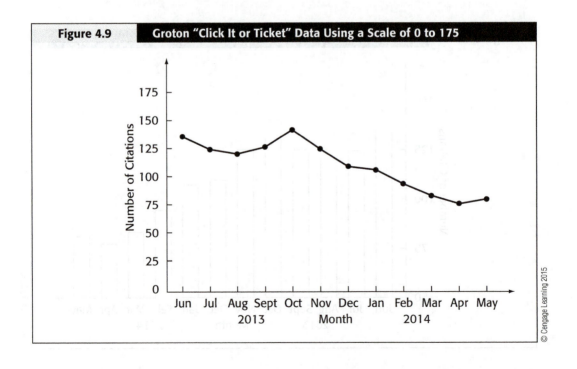

Figure 4.9 — **Groton "Click It or Ticket" Data Using a Scale of 0 to 175**

© Cengage Learning 2015

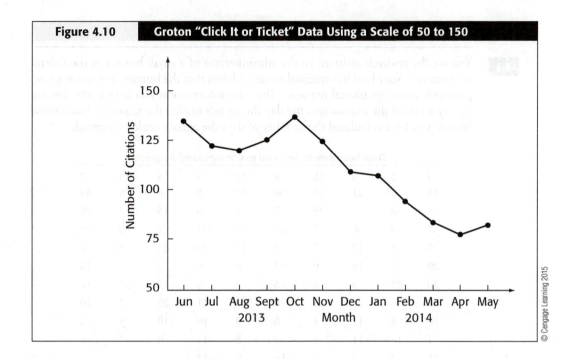

Figure 4.10 — **Groton "Click It or Ticket" Data Using a Scale of 50 to 150**

© Cengage Learning 2015

Chapter Summary

Descriptive statistics summarize a body of raw data (i.e., data that have not been organized or tabulated) so that the data can be more easily understood. Frequency distributions, percentage distributions, and cumulative frequency distributions are three ways to condense raw data into a table that is easier to read and comprehend. A frequency distribution displays the number of times each value, or a range of values, of a variable occurs. The frequency distribution shows the number of data points or observations that fall into each class of a variable. A percentage distribution displays the percentage of observations that fall into each class. A cumulative frequency (or percentage) distribution shows the number (or percentage) of observations that fall above or below a certain class.

To add visual appeal and increase interpretability, graphical presentations of data are used. Graphical techniques discussed in this chapter include the frequency polygon, the histogram and bar chart, and the ogive. The frequency polygon is a plot of the frequency distribution information (class versus frequency) with the plotted points connected in sequence by line segments. The histogram is a bar graph of a frequency distribution; each class is represented by a horizontal bar, and its frequency corresponds to the height of the bar from the horizontal axis. The term *bar chart* is sometimes used in place of *histogram* when the variable can take on only a very limited set of values. An ogive is a frequency polygon for a cumulative frequency distribution.

Problems

4.1 You are the research assistant to the administrator of a small bureau in the federal government. Your boss has received some criticism that the bureau does not respond promptly to congressional requests. The only information you have is the day the agency received the request and the day the agency mailed the response. From those figures, you have calculated the number of days the agency took to respond.

Days Necessary to Respond to Congressional Requests

9	1	6	10	8	12	9	14	15	7
19	8	21	10	50	37	9	4	28	44
9	18	8	39	7	1	4	15	7	28
47	9	6	7	24	10	41	7	9	29
6	4	12	7	9	15	39	24	9	2
20	31	18	9	33	8	6	3	7	16
20	26	9	9	16	5	3	12	36	11
8	6	28	35	8	10	11	20	3	10
16	8	12	4	6	9	10	10	9	16
4	14	11	8	5	8	11	9	7	6
11	9	7	8	10	9	11			

Do the following:

(a) Prepare the frequency distribution.

(b) Present the distribution graphically.

(c) Prepare a cumulative frequency distribution.

(d) Present the cumulative distribution graphically.

(e) Write a paragraph explaining what you have found.

4.2 Rebecca Peter, the mayor of Sunny, Alaska, feels that the productivity of meter butlers has declined in the past year. Mayor Peter's research assistant provides her with the accompanying data. Convert the frequency distributions to comparable distributions. What can you tell Mayor Peter about the productivity of her meter butlers?

Parking Tickets Issued per Meter Butler	Number of Butlers May 2013	Number of Butlers May 2014
21–30	5	6
31–40	7	9
41–50	9	12
51–60	5	7
61–70	3	1
	29	35

4.3 James Hartwell, the civil service director for Nova, South Carolina, compiles the accompanying frequency distribution of scores on the Nova civil service exam. Construct a cumulative frequency distribution and a cumulative frequency polygon for Mr. Hartwell.

Exam Score	Number of Applicants
61–65	20
66–70	13
71–75	47
76–80	56
81–85	33
86–90	27
91–95	41
96–100	34

4.4 The incumbent governor of a large state is campaigning on the platform that he eliminated a great many large, "do-nothing" bureaucracies. As the research assistant for the challenger, you are asked to present the accompanying data (numbers are the size of bureaus eliminated under the incumbent and under his predecessor) graphically in the manner most favorable for the challenger.

Incumbent		Predecessor
6	16	15
14	5	28
7	3	48
3	7	104
24	19	37
6	21	56
3	12	15
1	4	6
2	3	3
21	6	27
41	1	39

4.5 Refer to Problem 4.4. Construct a frequency distribution, and present it to reflect favorably on the incumbent.

4.6 The city clerk has received numerous complaints over the past year that couples applying for a marriage license have to wait too long to receive one. Although the clerk is skeptical (couples applying for a license are usually young and impatient), she pulls a representative sample of marriage licenses issued in the past year. Because a machine stamps each license application with the time the application is received and the time it is issued, she can tell how long the young (and old) lovers had to wait for the marriage license. The clerk considers service received in less than 10 minutes good and service received in less than 15 minutes acceptable. Her tabulation of the license data shows the following:

Minutes Waited for Marriage License	Number of Couples
Less than 5	28
5–9	36
10–14	60
15–19	82
20–24	44
25–29	39

Prepare the percentage distribution for the marriage license data and the appropriate graphical displays. Write a short memorandum explaining the results and addressing the issue of whether couples have to wait too long for marriage licenses.

4.7 The city clerk from Problem 4.6 is intrigued by the findings of her survey of marriage licenses issued in the past year (data analysis often has this effect). Accordingly, she decides to pull another representative sample of marriage licenses, this time from 2 years ago. She is interested in determining whether service to the public from her unit has improved or declined over the past 2 years. As before, the clerk considers service received in less than 10 minutes good and service received in less than 15 minutes acceptable. Her tabulation of the sample of marriage licenses issued 2 years ago shows the following:

Minutes Waited for Marriage License	Number of Couples
Less than 5	112
5–9	87
10–14	31
15–19	27
20–24	29
25–29	3

Prepare the percentage distribution for the marriage license data and the appropriate graphical displays. Write a short memorandum explaining the results and addressing the question of whether service to the public from her unit has improved or declined over the past 2 years.

4.8 Because of cutbacks in agency funding, the United Way of Megopolis has had to forgo routine maintenance of its computer terminals for the past 5 years. (The equipment is made by the Indestructible Computer Company.) The head of the agency is concerned that the agency will face a major equipment crisis this year because the recommended maintenance schedule for the terminals is once every 3 years. Over the past 5 years, the agency has been able to purchase new terminals.

In an effort to obtain more funding from the state legislature, the agency chief compiles the following data. The data show the time since the last routine maintenance of the terminal or, if the terminal was purchased in the last 2 years, the time since the terminal was purchased.

Years since Last Maintenance	Number of Terminals
1 or less	103
2	187
3	97
4	56
5	37
6	12
7 or more	5

Prepare the percentage distribution for the terminal maintenance data and the appropriate graphical displays. Write a short memorandum both explaining the results and trying to convince the state legislature to provide funding for routine maintenance of computer terminals.

4.9 Assume that you are a staff analyst working for the head of the United Way of Megopolis in Problem 4.8. Write a short memorandum both explaining the results of the data tabulation in Problem 4.8 and trying to convince the agency head that the equipment "crisis" at the agency is overblown.

4.10 The local humane society is concerned about available space for impounded animals. The agency keeps careful count of the number of animals it shelters each day. To determine the load on the agency, its head, Anna Trueheart, selects a representative sample of days from the last 2 years and records the number of animals impounded on each day. Her data appear as follows:

65	49	84	72	43	91
57	46	77	69	90	64
85	67	52	44	95	79
48	63	55	96	75	48
88	81	93	67	58	72
51	49	96	79	73	80
65	54	86	98	42	63
92	71	79	84	59	45

Prepare the frequency and percentage distributions for the animal impoundment data and the appropriate graphical displays for Ms. Trueheart. Write a short memorandum explaining both the results and the demands on the humane society to shelter animals.

4.11 The director of the state Department of Public Works wants to upgrade the department's automobile fleet; she claims that the fleet is too old. The governor appoints a staff analyst to investigate the issue. The analyst compiles data on both the age and the odometer readings (mileage) of the department's automobile fleet. Her data appear as follows:

Age (in years)	Number of Automobiles
Less than 2	16
2–4	24
4–6	41
6–8	57
8–10	64
10 or more	39

Mileage	Number of Automobiles
Less than 10,000	76
10,000–20,000	63
20,000–30,000	51
30,000–40,000	32
40,000–50,000	12
50,000 or more	17

Prepare percentage distributions for the age and mileage data and the appropriate graphical displays. Write a short memorandum to the governor both explaining the results and making a recommendation regarding whether the department's automobile fleet should be upgraded.

4.12 The mayor of Prominent, South Dakota, has received complaints about the city's "outrageously high" levels of general obligation debt (debt backed by the full faith and credit of the city). She asks her assistant to obtain data on the dollar amount of outstanding general obligation debt for four nearby cities so she can benchmark Prominent's debt burden. The assistant produces the following table:

City	Debt ($)	Population
Auburn Park	38,665,200	49,000
Nova City	36,464,000	51,000
Prominent	41,801,025	52,000
Royal Pine	44,856,200	53,900
Southville	45,485,175	55,000

Upon reviewing the table, the mayor comments, "If the numbers speak for themselves, this must be a foreign language." She tells her assistant that few people will understand the meaning of the table if they are forced to interpret all of these large numbers. She asks her assistant to calculate one summary benchmark measure using the data on both debt and population.

(a) Create a summary measure that is based on both the total debt and population data. What is the commonsense interpretation of the measure? How does Dorchester compare to the other cities on this measure?

(b) The mayor asks her assistant to create a graph or chart summarizing the results based on the new measure. What would be a good graphical format for presenting the findings on the new measure?

Measures of Central Tendency

The most commonly used descriptive statistics are measures of central tendency. As you can guess from this title, measures of central tendency attempt to locate the midmost or center point in a group of data. For example, what was the average starting salary of the students who graduated from the MPA program last year? On average over the past 5 years, how many MPA students accepted job offers from nonprofit organizations? On last week's midterm examination, what was the midmost score (i.e., the score that divided the observations in half)? On average, how many employees of the Mechanicsburg city government report job-related accidents every month? What was the midmost amount of monetary donations received by the Agency for Civic Renewal such that half the donations received were larger and half were smaller? The measures of central tendency give a shorthand indication of the main trends in the data.

A **measure of central tendency** is a number or score or data value that represents the average in a group of data. Three different types of averages are calculated and used most often in public and nonprofit management. The first is the *mean*, which is the arithmetic average of the observations; the second is the *median*, which is the observation that falls in the middle of the group so that half the responses are above it and half below it; and the third is the *mode*, or the data value that occurs with greatest frequency. This chapter shows how to calculate the three measures of central tendency for lists of data and for data that have been assembled into a frequency distribution, and it discusses the use and interpretation of these measures. It concludes with a discussion of the relationship between the measures of central tendency and the different levels of measurement—interval, ordinal, and nominal—you learned about in Chapter 2.

The Mean

The first measure of central tendency is the mean. The **mean** is the arithmetic average of a set of data points or observations. To calculate the mean, add all of the data points or observations and divide this new number (the sum) by the total number of observations in the set, which we labeled **N** in Chapter 4.

To illustrate, suppose that the head of the Bureau of Records wants to know the mean length of government service of the employees in the bureau's Office of

Table 5.1	Years of Government Service			
	Employee	Years	Employee	Years
	Bush	8	Obama	9
	Clinton	15	Gore	11
	Reagan	23	Cheney	18
	Kerry	14	Carter	20

© Cengage Learning

Computer Support. Table 5.1 displays the number of years that each member of the office has been employed in government.

To calculate the mean length of government service of the employees in the bureau's Office of Computer Support, add the years of service of each of the employees (i.e., the data points or observations). You should get a total of 118 years. Divide this sum by **N**, the (total) number of employees in the office (**N** = 8). This procedure yields the mean number of years of government service of the employees in the office (14.75).

The procedure for calculating the mean can be presented as a formula:

$$\mu = \frac{\sum_{i=1}^{N} X_i}{N}$$

This formula is not as formidable as it may seem. The Greek letter μ (mu) on the left side of the equal sign is the statistician's symbol for the population mean; it is pronounced "mew." The mean μ is equal to the formula on the right side of the equal sign. Another statistician's symbol is Σ; it means add (or sum) all the values of X (in our example, these were years of government service). The subscripts below and above the Σ indicate to sum all the Xs from the first, X_1, all the way through X_N, the last observation (here, the years of government service of the eighth employee). Finally, the formula says to divide the sum of all the Xs by **N**, the number of items being summed.

The formula for calculating the mean of a sample or subset of data, rather than the entire population, is identical except that different symbols are used to distinguish sample and population. The sample mean is denoted $\overline{X}$ ("x-bar"), and the number of observations in the sample **n**. Chapter 10 reviews these distinctions and elaborates their importance. That chapter introduces the topic of how the analyst can use a sample of data to make an inference to the larger population from which it is drawn (i.e., statistical inference).

The mean has several important properties:

1. Every item in a group of data is used to calculate the mean.
2. Every group of data has one and only one mean; as mathematicians would say, the mean is rigidly determined.

3. The mean can take on a value that is not realistic. For example, the average U.S. family had exactly 1.7 children, 2.2 pets, 1.1 automobiles, and made financial contributions to 3.4 charitable organizations in the past year.

4. An extreme value, sometimes called an **outlier**, has a disproportionate influence on the mean and thus may affect how well the mean represents the data. For example, suppose that the head of the Bureau of Records decides to shake up the Office of Computer Support by creating a new position in the office with responsibility to expedite operations. To fill the position, the head appoints a newly graduated MPA with a fine background in computers but only 1 year of prior service in government. In the space provided, calculate the mean years of government service of the employees in the expanded Office of Computer Support.

If you performed the calculations correctly, you should get a mean length of government service of 13.22 years. (The sum of the observations is 119; dividing by $N = 9$, the number of observations, yields a mean of 13.22.) This number tends to understate the years of government service of the employees in the office of Computer Support. Why?

The Median

The second measure of central tendency is the median. The **median** is the middle observation in a set of numbers when the observations are ranked in order of magnitude. For example, the Stermerville City Council requires that all city agencies include an average salary in their budget requests. The Stermerville City Planning Office has seven employees. The director is paid $62,500; the assistant director makes $59,500. Three planning clerks are paid $42,600, $42,500, and $42,400. The secretary (who does all the work) is paid $37,500, and a receptionist is paid $36,300.

The planning director calculates the mean salary and finds that it is $46,186. Check this result (you should get a total payroll of $323,300 for the seven employees for a mean of $46,186). This result disturbs the director because it makes the agency look fat and bloated. The secretary points out that the large salaries paid to the director and the assistant director are distorting the mean. The secretary then calculates the median, following these steps:

Step 1: List the salaries in order of magnitude. You may start with the largest or the smallest; you will get the same answer. The secretary prepares the following list:

Director	$62,500
Assistant	59,500
Clerk 1	42,600
Clerk 2	42,500
Clerk 3	42,400
Secretary	37,500
Receptionist	36,300

Step 2: Locate the middle item. With seven persons, the middle observation is easy to find; it is the fourth item, or the salary paid to clerk 2 ($42,500). For larger data sets, the rule is to take the number of observations (7, in this case) and add 1 to it (7 + 1 = 8). Divide this number by 2, and that number (8 ÷ 2 = 4) tells you that the median is the fourth observation (once data values have been put in order). Note that it makes no difference whether you select the fourth item from the top or the fourth from the bottom. The median is $42,500.

The planning director reports the median salary to the Stermerville City Council. It is lower than the mean—why? Nevertheless, the Stermerville mayor tells the planning director that because of the local tax revolt, the planning office must fire one person. The planning office responds, as all bureaucracies do, by firing the receptionist. After this action, what is the median salary of the planning office? Calculate it in the space provided.

After arranging the salaries in order, you may have discovered that with six observations, no middle item exists. The formula (N + 1) ÷ 2 seems to offer no help because (6 + 1) ÷ 2 = $3\frac{1}{2}$. But the median is actually that, the $3\frac{1}{2}$th item from the top (or bottom). Because observations cannot be split in half, we define the middle as halfway between the third and fourth items, in this case halfway between the salaries of clerk 2 and clerk 1. Because clerk 2 makes $42,500 and clerk 1 makes $42,600, the median is $42,550 [(42,600 + 42,500) ÷ 2]. Whenever the number of items (**N**) is an even number, the median will lie halfway between the two middle observations. This result is easy to remember if you think of the median as the measure of central tendency that divides a set of numbers so that half are smaller than the median and half are larger than the median.

The median has several important properties:

1. The median is not affected by extreme values.

2. Although every observation is used to determine the median, the actual value of every item is not used in the calculations. At most, only the two middle items are used to calculate the median.

3. If items do not cluster near the median, the median will not be a good measure of the group's central tendency.

4. The median usually does not take on an unrealistic value. The median number of children per family in the United States, for example, is 2.

5. The median is the 50th percentile in a distribution of data because half the observations fall above it and half fall below it. Percentiles are measures of relative ranking. You may have seen them reported on a standardized test, such as the Graduate Record Examination, or GRE. As with the median, they express what percentage of the scores fall below a given score. For example, 79% of the scores lie below the 80th percentile. In percentage distributions, you can use this fact to locate the median quickly by observing the data value at which the distribution of scores or observations crosses the 50th percentile. That value is the median.

Although the median conveys less precise information than the mean (knowing where the middle of a set of observations falls is less exact than is the precise numerical average), as you will see later in the chapter, the median is sometimes used in preference to the mean. In certain distributions of data, the median is more descriptive of the central tendency. For instance, an outlier typically has a much greater distorting effect on the mean than on the median. In addition, when a phenomenon cannot be measured on an (equal) interval scale but on an ordinal scale (e.g., job attitudes, client satisfaction, quality of life, volunteer interest in career development, and so forth), the median is especially useful as a measure of central tendency.

The Mode

The final measure of central tendency is the mode. The **mode** is the data value that occurs most often (with greatest frequency) in any distribution. In the frequency distribution in Table 5.2, what is the mode number of tickets issued? The value that occurs most often is 3 tickets issued, so 3 is the mode.

The distribution in Table 5.2 has only one mode; thus, it is called unimodal. The distribution in Table 5.3 is bimodal; it has two modes. Because Kapaun had 9 arrests for 14 weeks and 11 arrests for 14 weeks, the modes are 9 and 11. Distributions also can be trimodal, tetramodal, and so on.

Table 5.2	Tickets Issued by Woodward Police, Week of January 28, 2014
Number of Tickets	Number of Police Officers
0	2
1	7
2	9
3	14
4	3
5	2
6	1
	38

© Cengage Learning 2015

Table 5.3	Arrests per Week, Kapaun Air Station, 2014
Number of Arrests	Number of Weeks
7	2
8	4
9	14
10	8
11	14
12	10
	52

© Cengage Learning 2015

Statisticians generally relax the definition of the mode(s) to include the distinct peaks or clusters in the data that occur with high frequency. You should, too. Table 5.4 presents an example—the number of research methods and statistics courses required for graduation by a sample of MPA-granting schools with concentrations in nonprofit administration. The distribution is bimodal, with modes at one and three courses. Even though the latter mode occurs slightly less often (19 versus 23), it would be misleading to ignore it, so it, too, is considered a mode.

The mode has several important properties:

1. Because the most common value in a distribution of data can occur at any point, the mode need not be "central" or near the middle.

2. Unlike the mean and the median, the mode can take on more than one value. No other measure of central tendency has this characteristic. As a result, in some complex data distributions, such as a bimodal or

Table 5.4	Number of Required Courses in Research Methods and Statistics	
	Number of Courses	Number of Schools
	0	3
	1	23
	2	5
	3	19
		50

© Cengage Learning

trimodal distribution, the mode is the statistic of choice for summarizing the *central tendencies*. When a distribution has more than one distinct mode, it usually indicates something important in the data that cannot be captured so well by the mean or median.

3. More often than not, when a variable is measured on a numerical or interval scale (number of arrests, feet of snow plowed, and so forth), the mode may be of little interest. However, with variables measured at less precise levels—nominal (classifications, such as race or religion) and ordinal (rank orderings, such as responses on opinion questions)— the mode is much more useful and in certain instances is the preferred measure of central tendency. We return to this issue later in the chapter.

The Mean versus the Median

In most situations, numerical data can be summarized well with the mean. Because situations can arise in which the mean gives a misleading indication of central tendency, however, the median is preferred. When extreme values or outliers occur on a variable, the mean is distorted or pulled toward them. The statistical term is *skewed*. By contrast, because the median is the value of the middle case—once the data points have been arranged in order—it will remain in the middle of the distribution even if the variable has an extreme value. In this situation, the median is the preferred measure of central tendency. (Chapter 6 returns to this issue.)

For example, suppose that a nonprofit administrator needed to estimate the average price of houses in a city in order to apply for a federal grant. She takes a random sample of 10 homes sold recently and discovers 9 of them sold for between $180,000 and $220,000, and 1 home sold for well over $1 million. The mean housing price will be grossly inflated by the one outlying case and will yield a value unrepresentative of the price of houses in the city. The median will not be affected by the deviant case, however, and will have a value near the middle of housing prices, between $180,000 and $220,000. Thus, the median will be more typical of housing prices and should be used in preference to the mean. Remember that the purpose of measures of central tendency is to identify accurately the central point(s) in the distribution. Select and use the measures of central tendency that most clearly describe or represent the distribution of data.

Levels of Measurement and Measures of Central Tendency

Chapter 2, "Measurement," introduced the concept of levels of measurement. Students of public and nonprofit administration are most accustomed to interval measurement: variables that can be measured on a numerical scale, such as the budget of an agency or department in dollars, the number of clients assisted, or the amount of overtime hours logged by the cafeteria staff last week. Public and nonprofit managers (and those employed in for-profit businesses) also use variables measured at other, less precise levels. In discussing the median and the mode, we referred to these levels earlier in the chapter: Ordinal variables allow rank ordering of information—for example, how satisfied a client is with a nonprofit organization's response to her inquiry (very satisfied, satisfied, neutral, dissatisfied, or very dissatisfied) or a citizen's overall assessment of the services provided by the public library (very good, good, neutral, poor, or very poor). Nominal variables are classifications that have no metric information—for example, the gender of employees, their religion, their marital status, and so forth.

Why devote so much attention to the levels of measurement of the variables encountered in public and nonprofit administration? The answer is both simple and important: The statistics that can be appropriately calculated to summarize the distribution of single variables (the subject of this chapter) and to describe the relationship between variables (the subject of later chapters) differ from level to level. It is easy to see the source of the differences. Each of the levels expresses a different amount of information about a variable, and this idea is reflected directly in the kind of statistics that may be calculated and used.

For example, if a variable is measured at the interval level, we usually know everything about it that we may wish to know. It is possible to locate precisely all the observations along a scale: $32,749 yearly income; 4.57 prostitution arrests per week; 38 years of age; 247 cubic feet of sewage; 10,106 hours volunteered to United Way agencies last month. Because for these variables an equal distance separates each whole number on the measurement scale (dollars, arrests, years, cubic feet, and hours), all mathematical operations can be performed. Thus, as we saw earlier in the chapter, the scores of a group of cases or observations can be added and the sum divided by the number of observations to obtain the mean income, number of arrests, age, cubic feet of sewage, and hours volunteered. It is also possible to find the *median* or the middle score of the group for each of these variables. And, of course, the *mode*—the value occurring most frequently in a distribution—presents no problem.

Table 5.5	Pilots at Selected Air Bases	
	Air Base	Number of Pilots
	Minot	0
	Torrejon	2,974
	Kapaun	896
	Osan	0
	Andrews	6,531
	Yokota	57
	Guam	1,428

© Cengage Learning

Table 5.5 displays the number of pilots at selected air bases. At what level of measurement are these data? Be sure that you can calculate the mean (a total of 11,886 pilots ÷ 7 air bases = 1,698), median (896), and mode (0) for this distribution. If you have any problems, review the earlier portions of the chapter where these statistics are discussed. With interval-level data, the manager can calculate and use all three measures of central tendency.

Now consider *ordinal* data. At this level of measurement we are able to rank objects or observations, but it is not possible to locate them precisely along a scale. A citizen may "strongly disapprove" of the Springhill mass transit system's performance, but no number is available that expresses her exact level of disapproval or how much less she approves than if she had said "disapprove." Because there are no numerical scores or numbers attached to the responses—which, in the case of interval variables, are added and divided to compute the mean—it is not possible to calculate the mean for a variable measured at the ordinal level.

How about the median? Can it be calculated for ordinal data? Suppose an interviewer obtains from 11 citizens their responses to the question, "Do you approve or disapprove of the Springhill mass transit system's performance? Strongly approve, approve, neutral, disapprove, strongly disapprove?"

Ordinal data are commonly displayed in a frequency distribution. Table 5.6 presents the frequency distribution for the Springhill mass transit system. Consider the "cumulative total" column in the table. Note that the midmost case is the sixth citizen, who has the response "disapprove," which is, therefore, the median. As presented earlier in the chapter, the rule to find the midmost case is to add 1 to the total number of cases, or **N**, and divide this result by 2. In this example, 11 + 1 = 12 and 12 ÷ 2 = 6, so that the sixth case is in the middle of the distribution and has the median value, "disapprove."

It is important to note that the median is *not* "neutral." Although "neutral" is the middle response category, it does not tell us anything about the middle response given by the 11 citizens. "Neutral" falls in the middle of the scale but not in the middle of the 11 citizens. Note also that the median is the middle score of the 11 citizens, or the response "disapprove."

Table 5.6	Frequency Distribution of Citizens' Responses Concerning Springhill's Mass Transit System	
Response	Number of Citizens	Cumulative Total
Strongly approve	1	1
Approve	2	3
Neutral	2	5
Disapprove	2	7
Strongly disapprove	4	11

© Cengage Learning

We have now shown that the median can be calculated for ordinal variables. So can the mode. In Table 5.6, the most frequently mentioned response is "strongly disapprove," given by four citizens. Therefore, it is the mode or modal response.

Finally, at the *nominal* level of measurement, it is not possible to assign numerical scores to cases (interval level). A score of 1.7 on religion or 458 on nationality would be arbitrary and would make no sense. Thus, it is not possible to calculate the mean for nominal data.

Furthermore, the values of a group of cases on a nominal variable cannot be ranked in any kind of meaningful ordering of least to most, or vice versa (ordinal level). There is no meaningful or correct way to order the categories of race, religion, sex, or any other nominal variable. (Usually, we place them in alphabetical order for convenience, but that ordering is not a numerical or measurement scale.) Because the median is predicated on the ability to rank cases or observations of a variable so that the middle or median value may be found, it is not possible to calculate the median for nominal data.

The mode can, however, be found for nominal data. For the data in Table 5.7, which is the modal occupation of the employees of the Civil Service Commission?

Table 5.7	Civil Service Commission Employees by Occupation	
Occupation	Number of People	Percentage
Lawyer	192	61
Butcher	53	17
Doctor	41	13
Baker	20	6
Candlestick maker	7	2
Indian chief	3	1
	N = 316	100

© Cengage Learning

The mode is "lawyer" because it is the occupation of the largest number of people (192) in the distribution. Usually, the percentage of observations in the modal category is given, here 61%. Make sure that you can calculate the percentage distribution. If you have any difficulty, see Chapter 4.

Hierarchy of Measurement

We can summarize this discussion of levels of measurement and measures of central tendency in a convenient table. In Table 5.8, place an X in the column of a row if the designated measure of central tendency (mean, median, and mode) can be calculated for a given level of measurement (nominal, ordinal, and interval).

If you have completed the table correctly, the Xs will form a triangle pattern that slopes upward from the bottom left entry (Nominal–Mode) to the top right entry (Interval–Mean). If you did not find this pattern, you should review earlier parts of the chapter.

The lesson of Table 5.8 is that any statistic that can be calculated for a variable at a lower (less precise) level of measurement can also be calculated at all higher (more precise) levels of measurement. If the statistic can be calculated at a level that places fewer numerical restrictions on the data, it can be calculated at higher levels that meet these numerical requirements—and more. Thus, the mode is available at all three levels, the median at the ordinal and the interval levels, and the mean only at the interval level. This rule is usually stated as the "hierarchy of measurement" to indicate the ascending power of the higher levels of measurement. To the degree possible, then, it is always to your advantage to construct, collect, and use variables measured at higher levels.

With this knowledge, you are now in a position to describe the phenomena of interest in quantitative terms. For example, consider your work organization. The mean age of employees may be 37.1 years, the median 35, and the mode 39. The median opinion of employees with respect to contracting out for information technology services may be "disapprove"; perhaps the modal opinion is "strongly disapprove." Most of the employees may be white and male; and so on.

Table 5.8	Hierarchy of Measurement		
		Level of Measurement	
Measure of Central Tendency	Nominal	Ordinal	Interval
Mean			
Median			
Mode			

© Cengage Learning

Some Cautions

Two cautions regarding this discussion of levels of measurement should be kept in mind. First, most of the time you will not calculate statistics yourself; instead, a computer program will compute them for you. In order to store information compactly in a computer, the substantive category labels or names for ordinal variables—such as strongly agree, agree, neutral, disagree, and strongly disagree—as well as for nominal variables—such as white, African American, and Hispanic—are entered and stored in the computer as numbers. These numbers are usually called *codes*. The computer may also store the labels or names for the codes, but it performs all calculations based on the codes, not the value labels assigned to them. For example, the coding schemes in Table 5.9 may apply.

Because the computer calculates all statistics based on the numerical codes entered for the variables (not the value labels), strange things can happen to the unwary analyst. For example, if instructed to do so, the computer can and will calculate a mean or a median for nominal variables or a mean for ordinal variables based on the codes—even though these statistics have no meaning at these levels of measurement. It is up to you as the analyst to recognize such statistics as a mean attitude of 2.7 or a median race of 1 for what they are: garbage. Note that for interval variables the codes are the actual data values (7.123, 5.6, 10075.9,14, and so forth), so this problem does not arise.

The second caution is in part a consequence of the first. Because ordinal variables frequently are coded for computer utilization in the manner shown earlier (1 = strongly agree, 2 = agree, 3 = neutral, and so on) some students (and practicing managers) have jumped to the incorrect conclusion that these codes are actually meaningful numbers on a scale that expresses the precise level of an individual's agreement or disagreement with an interviewer's question. In other words, they have assumed that the coding categories are actual numbers and can be treated as such for statistical calculations—just as if they were interval data. This practice, which is rather common in all the social sciences, including political science and public and nonprofit administration, has led to the

Table 5.9	Examples of Two Coding Schemes			
Coding Scheme 1			**Coding Scheme 2**	
Code	Response		Code	Response
1	Strongly agree		1	White
2	Agree		2	African American
3	Neutral		3	Hispanic
4	Disagree			
5	Strongly disagree			

ordinal-interval debate. (Do not feel bad if you have missed it; it is not exactly a household term.) As the title suggests, the debate has focused on the justification for—or the lack of it—and the advantages of treating ordinal data as interval. Both sides have produced some persuasive evidence, and the debate has yet to be resolved definitively.

Our recommendation for students just starting out in quantitative work in public or nonprofit management is that you adopt the stance of the statistical purist—that you calculate and use for ordinal data only those statistics that are clearly appropriate for that level of measurement. For now, when you need to summarize or describe the distribution of an ordinal variable, rely on the median and mode. In the future, if you decide to continue your work in statistics, you can read some of the literature in the ordinal-interval debate and come to your own conclusions.

You may be wondering why we are placing such emphasis on the ordinal-interval debate. When you see the steps involved in examining and interpreting *relationships* among ordinal variables—as compared with those involved in the analysis of interval data (see Part 6 on regression)—the significance of this debate will become clear. But that is the purpose of Chapters 14 through 16.

Chapter Summary

Measures of central tendency are values used to summarize a body of data by indicating middle (or central) points in the distribution. Each measure of central tendency has a distinct meaning and method of calculation. The mean is the arithmetic average of all data points. The median is the data value that is greater than 50% of all the data points and less than 50% of all the data points. The mode is the data value that occurs most frequently in the distribution. This chapter illustrates the main features of all three measures of central tendency.

The chapter shows how the level of measurement of a variable (interval, ordinal, and nominal) determines the measures of central tendency that can appropriately be calculated for it. The hierarchy of measurement illustrates this concept. More specifically, the hierarchy of measurement indicates that the more precise the measurement, the more statistics that can be calculated and used. Thus, the mean, the median, and the mode can be calculated for internal-level data. The median and the mode can be calculated for ordinal-level data. Only the mode can be calculated for nominal-level data.

In the examples in this chapter and in the problems that follow, we use small numbers of cases to ease the burden of calculation of measures of central tendency while still illustrating the crucial concepts and points. In actual situations in public and nonprofit administration, you will typically deal with much larger numbers of cases, and a computer will perform the necessary calculations. The concepts and pointers for proper use and interpretation, however, remain the same.

Problems

5.1 During a recent crackdown on speeding, the Fort Pierce, Missouri, police department issued the following numbers of citations on seven consecutive days: 59, 61, 68, 57, 63, 50, and 55. Calculate the mean and median numbers of speeding citations.

5.2 The dean of Swiftwater State University is concerned that many faculty members at SSU are too old to be effective teachers. She asks each department to send her information on the average age of its faculty. The head of the sociology department does not wish to "lie" with statistics, but, knowing the preference of the dean, he would like to make the department appear youthful. The names and ages of the sociology department's members are listed in the accompanying table. Calculate both the mean age and the median age. Should the department send the dean the mean age or the median age?

Member	Age
Durkheim	64
Campbell	31
Weber	65
Likert	27
Stanley	35
Katz	40
Lazarsfeld	33

5.3 The average number of sick leave days used per employee per year in Bygones, Nebraska, is 6.7. The Normal city manager feels the Public Works Department is abusing its sick leave privileges. The frequency distribution for the department follows. Calculate the percentage distribution. In what categories do the mean and median of sick leave days fall? Is the Public Works Department abusing its sick leave?

Number of Days of Sick Leave Taken	Number of Employees
0–2	4
3–5	7
6–8	7
9–11	14
12–14	6

5.4 The U.S. Army is allowed only five test firings of the Lance missile. The following figures represent the number of feet by which the missiles missed the target: 26, 147, 35, 63, and 51. Calculate the mean and the median. Which should the army report?

5.5 The Department of Welfare wants to know the average outside income for all welfare recipients in the state. Use the data in the accompanying table to present the percentage distribution. In what category does the median fall? In what category does the mode fall?

Income	Number of Families
0–300	25
300–600	163
600–900	354
900–1,200	278
1,200–1,500	421
1,500–1,800	603
1,800–2,100	211
2,100–2,400	84
2,400–2,700	32
2,700–3,000	5

5.6 When should the median be used in preference to the mean?

5.7 The legislature has limited the Bureau of the Audit to a monthly average of 34 employees. For the first 9 months of the year, the employment figures were 31, 36, 34, 35, 37, 32, 36, 37, and 34. Does it appear that the bureau will make the target? How many employees can the bureau have over the next 3 months and still meet the target?

5.8 The collective bargaining agreement between Family Services Agency and the Federation of Social Workers specifies that the average case load for caseworkers cannot exceed 45. Using the accompanying data, the agency claims compliance, yet the union argues that the agency has violated the agreement. Who is correct?

Caseworker	Case Load
A	43
B	57
C	35
D	87
E	36
F	93
G	45
H	48
I	41
J	40

5.9 Refer to Problem 5.1. The Fort Pierce police chief is concerned that after the crackdown on speeding, the police department has not continued to enforce speed limits in town. She obtains data on speeding citations issued in the past 7 days. The numbers of citations issued over the past 7 days are 41, 48, 51, 47, 44, 45, and 49. Calculate the mean and median for these data. Based on your analysis, does the police chief appear to be correct?

5.10 The director of the doctor of public administration (DPA) program at Freedom University is developing a report to the faculty on the entering class of Ph.D. students. The director wants to present a statistical profile of the new students, including their grade point average (GPA) earned in master's degree programs. The GPAs for the eight entering students are 3.2, 3.6, 3.9, 3.3, 3.4, 2.8, 2.9, and 4.0. Calculate the mean GPA and median GPA earned by these students in their master's degree studies.

5.11 Some faculty members at Freedom University have complained to the director of the DPA program that Ph.D. students typically have strong verbal skills but lack mathematical preparation. (Fortunately, a statistics book is available in public administration to meet the needs of these students.) In response to the complaint, the Ph.D. director assembles the scores on the verbal and quantitative sections of the Graduate Record Examination (GRE) for the class of eight entering Ph.D. students. Each section is scored on a scale of 200 to 800. The GRE scores of each student are listed below.

GRE Verbal	GRE Quantitative
590	620
680	510
630	550
700	600
610	540
650	570
620	590
670	580

Based on your analysis of these data, evaluate the complaint lodged by the faculty members at Freedom University.

5.12 The head of the Data Processing Department in White Plains wants to estimate the amount of waste and inefficiency in her department. She conducts a survey of employees in the department. One question asks, "To what extent does this department have waste and inefficiency in its operations?" The responses to the item are given in the accompanying table.

Response	Number of Employees
To a very great extent	42
To a great extent	31
To a moderate extent	19
To some extent	12
Not at all	7

(a) At what level of measurement are these data?

(b) Calculate the percentage distribution and the appropriate measures of central tendency.

(c) According to these data, does the department appear to have a problem with waste and inefficiency? Explain your answer.

5.13 The civic center of Kulture City is badly in need of refurbishment. However, before the city council allocates funds for this purpose, its members want to get a better idea of how frequently the residents of Kulture City actually use the center. To find out, they hire a public opinion polling firm to survey citizens. The pollsters ask a random sample of residents the following question: "In the last year, how many times have you attended performances or activities at Kulture City civic center?" The responses of the sample are listed in the accompanying table.

Number of Performances or Activities Attended	Number of Citizens
0	587
1	494
2	260
3	135
4	97

(a) At what level of measurement are these data?

(b) Calculate the appropriate measures of central tendency and the percentage distribution.

(c) Should the city council allocate money to refurbish the civic center?

(d) Write a short memorandum in which you use these results to make a recommendation to the city council.

5.14 The head of a city's Recreation Department feels that the employees of the department are the best in the city. Each year, all city employees receive a standardized performance evaluation that rates them on a scale of performance: "far above expectations," "above expectations," "meets expectations," "below expectations," and "far below expectations." (Each rating has an operational definition.) The department head feels that his assessment of employees will be justified if at least 90% of them fall into the top two categories. The ratings received by department employees are shown in the accompanying table.

Rating	Number of Employees
Far above expectations	15
Above expectations	22
Meets expectations	77
Below expectations	9
Far below expectations	8

(a) At what level of measurement are these data?

(b) Calculate the percentage distribution and the appropriate measures of central tendency.

(c) What can you tell the head of the Recreation Department?

5.15 The director of a city's Personnel Office is concerned about racial diversity in the city's workforce. One variable she uses to measure diversity is race. According to records kept by the Personnel Office, the city employs 62 African Americans, 85 whites, 49 Hispanics, 33 Asians, and 21 from other ethnic groups.

(a) At what level of measurement are these data?

(b) Prepare the percentage distribution for these data, and calculate appropriate measures of central tendency.

(c) What can you tell the director of the Personnel Office?

6

Measures of Dispersion

A very useful descriptive statistic complementary to the measures of central tendency is a measure of dispersion. **Measures of dispersion** indicate how closely the data cluster about the mean. For example, the data listed in Table 6.1 show the number of daily arrests in Wheezer, South Dakota, for 2012, 2013, and 2014. The mean number of daily arrests for all 3 years is the same (2.75). How much the daily arrests cluster about the mean, however, varies. In 2013, the numbers cluster less about the mean than they do in 2012. In 2014, the arrests cluster closer to the mean than do either the 2013 or the 2012 arrests. This clustering is illustrated by the frequency polygons in Figure 6.1; the mean is depicted vertically to facilitate interpretation. (If you need to review frequency polygons, please see Chapter 4.) As the figure shows, measures of dispersion are valuable descriptive statistics for analyzing a set of data.

Many statistics texts discuss a variety of dispersion measures, such as the range, the average deviation, the interquartile deviation, and the standard deviation. Of all these measures, only the standard deviation has broad use and great value statistically, and hence this statistic is the only one we will discuss in this chapter. Nevertheless, it is a good idea to know what the other measures of dispersion are because you may encounter them in public and nonprofit management.

Table 6.1	Number of Daily Police Arrests in Wheezer, South Dakota		
		Number of Days	
Number of Arrests	**2012**	**2013**	**2014**
0	24	36	10
1	36	54	36
2	95	65	109
3	104	74	118
4	66	84	66
5	40	52	26
	365	365	365

© Cengage Learning 2015

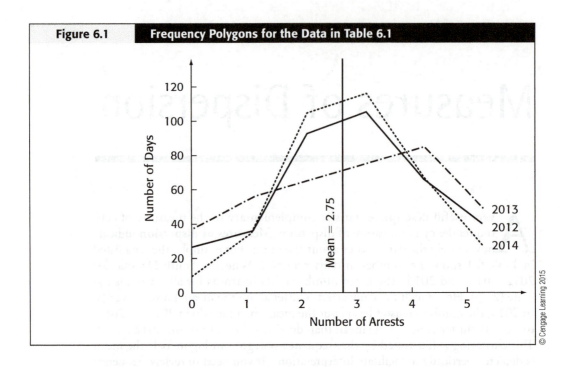

Figure 6.1 | **Frequency Polygons for the Data in Table 6.1**

The **range** is the difference between the largest value and the smallest value in a distribution of data. The **interquartile deviation** is the difference between two values in the distribution selected so that the middle 50% of all observations fall between them. The **average deviation** is the average difference between the mean and all other values. If these measures of dispersion seem appropriate for any particular use or project, consult a general statistics book to find out how to calculate and apply them [e.g., see the text by Johnson and Kuby (2006); a list of other suitable texts is given in the annotated bibliography at the end of the book].

The Standard Deviation

The standard deviation is the most commonly used measure of dispersion. The **standard deviation** is the average deviation or distance of each observation from the mean. Although the concept seems straightforward and useful, the computation is a bit cumbersome: It is the square root of the average squared deviation of the data from the mean. The standard deviation is based on the squared differences between every item in a data set and the mean.

An example can explain the formula far better than words. Normal, Oklahoma, has five street-cleaning crews. Because we have data for all five crews, we are working with the population rather than a sample and will calculate the population standard deviation. Later, we will explain the adjustment you would need to make if the five crews were a sample of the Normal, Oklahoma, street-cleaning crews (sample standard deviation). Listed in Table 6.2 are the numbers of blocks

Table 6.2	Blocks of Streets Cleaned by Work Crews

Work Crew	Number of Blocks
A	126
B	140
C	153
D	110
E	136
	665

© Cengage Learning

of city streets cleaned by the five crews. To determine the (population) standard deviation for these data, follow these steps:

Step 1: Calculate the mean from the data. Recall from Chapter 5 that to calculate the mean, you need to add the data values across the cases (here, the sum of the data values is 665 blocks) and divide that sum by the number of cases or **N** (here, the number of work crews, 5). The mean is 133.

Step 2: Subtract the mean from every item in the data set. In this situation, subtract 133 from the number of streets cleaned by each crew. Often a table like Table 6.3 is helpful in performing these calculations. Note that the sum of these differences equals *zero*. In fact, in any distribution of data, the sum of the differences of the data values from the mean will *always* equal zero. The reason is that the positive deviations above the mean will just balance the negative deviations below the mean such that the sum of the deviations is zero. Because the sum of the deviations is zero, we must adjust our calculations to derive a more useful measurement of dispersion in Step 3.

Step 3: Square the difference between each data value and the mean (the third column in Table 6.3). As noted in Step 2, the (nonsquared) differences

Table 6.3	Calculating the Differences

Number of Blocks	Subtract the Mean	Difference
126	133	−7
140	133	7
153	133	20
110	133	−23
136	133	3
		0

© Cengage Learning

Table 6.4	Calculating the Difference Squared		
Blocks	Mean	Difference	Difference Squared
126	133	−7	49
140	133	7	49
153	133	20	400
110	133	−23	529
136	133	3	9

© Cengage Learning

sum to zero, regardless of how condensed or dispersed the data values are about the mean. The reason is that the positive and negative differences will always balance each other out. Squaring the differences always yields a positive value and thus avoids this problem. Squaring is instrumental in measuring the actual amount of dispersion in the data (see Table 6.4).

Step 4: Sum the squared differences. You should get a sum of 1,036.

Step 5: Divide the sum by the number of items (**N** = 5). This number (207.2) is called the variance. The **variance** is the arithmetic average of the squared differences of the data values from the mean. The variance has little descriptive value because it is based on squared (not actual) units of measurement.

Step 6: Take the square root of the variance to find the standard deviation (here, the standard deviation is 14.4). Because we squared the differences between the mean and the data values in Step 3 (so that the differences would not sum to zero), it now makes sense to take the square root. In this manner, the standard deviation converts the variance from squared units to the original units of measurement. The standard deviation is the preferred measure of dispersion for descriptive purposes.

After calculating this relatively simple statistic, you should not be surprised to learn that statisticians have a complex formula for the standard deviation. The formula for σ (the Greek letter sigma, which statisticians use as the symbol for the standard deviation of a population) is

$$\sigma = \sqrt{\frac{\sum_{i=1}^{N}(X_i - \mu)^2}{N}}$$

This formula is not as formidable as it seems: $(X_i - \mu)$ is Step 2, subtracting the mean of the population from each data value. $(X_i - \mu)^2$ is Step 3, squaring the differences. $\sum_{i=1}^{N}(X_i - \mu)^2$ is Step 4, summing all the squared differences from the first case $i = 1$ to the last case $i = \mathbf{N}$. In Step 5 we divide the sum of the squared differences by the number of items (**N**). Finally, Step 6 is to take the square root of this quantity.

How would the calculations change if the five street-cleaning crews were a sample of the crews from Normal, Oklahoma, rather than the entire population? You would then need to calculate the sample standard deviation, denoted by the symbol *s*. To do so, you would follow the steps in the formula for the standard deviation, replacing the population mean μ with the sample mean, *X,* and **N** with $n - 1$, the number of cases in the sample (*n*) less 1. There are sound statistical reasons for making this adjustment, which we will discuss in Chapter 10 on statistical inference.

There are also good practical reasons. Dividing by $n - 1$ rather than *n* will yield a slightly larger standard deviation, which is the appropriate measure of care to take when you are using a sample of data to represent the population. In this example, the sample standard deviation would be 16.1 (1,036 ÷ 4 = 259; the square root of 259 = 16.1). When you are working with the population rather than a sample, there is no need to add this extra measure of caution. Thus, if the five Normal, Oklahoma, street-cleaning crews constitute the population, the (population) standard deviation is smaller, 14.4. You need to be aware that statistical package programs, spreadsheets, and hand calculators may assume that you are using the sample standard deviation rather than the population standard deviation (or vice versa). Depending on whether your data are a sample or a population, you may need to make an adjustment.

The smaller the standard deviation, the more closely the data cluster about the mean. For example, the standard deviations for the Wheezer, South Dakota, police arrests are 1.34 for 2012, 1.55 for 2013, and 1.16 for 2014 (see Figure 6.1). This calculation reinforces our perception that the 2013 data were the most dispersed and the 2014 data were the least dispersed. In general, when the data are closely bunched around the mean (smaller standard deviation), the public or nonprofit manager will feel more comfortable making a decision based on the mean.

Shape of a Frequency Distribution and Measures of Central Tendency

In addition to measuring the central tendency (see Chapter 5) and dispersion of a variable, public and nonprofit managers also need to know something about the "shape" of the frequency distribution of data values. The shape arises from plotting the values of the variable horizontally against their corresponding frequency of occurrence, which is plotted vertically. Several distinctive shapes of data distributions appear regularly in public and nonprofit administration and are important in analysis and interpretation. The shape of the distribution has implications for the usefulness of the different measures of central tendency.

Figure 6.2 shows a **symmetric distribution**. The data are evenly balanced on either side of the center or middle of the distribution. As you can see, each side is a reflection of the other. When a distribution is basically symmetric, the mean,

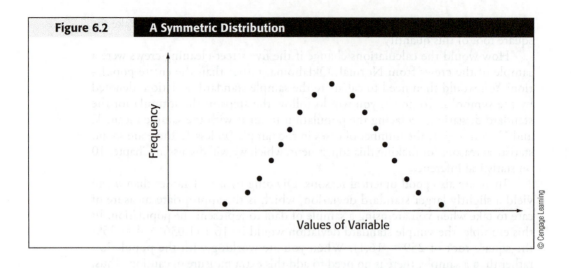

Figure 6.2 **A Symmetric Distribution**

Frequency

Values of Variable

© Cengage Learning

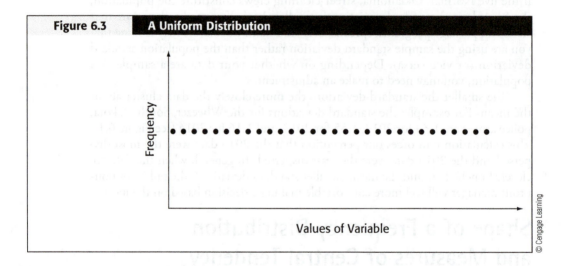

Figure 6.3 **A Uniform Distribution**

Frequency

Values of Variable

© Cengage Learning

median, and mode have very similar values at or near the center of the distribution. In this situation, the mean is the preferred measure of central tendency.

Figure 6.3 shows a **uniform distribution**. In a uniform distribution, each data value occurs with the same (or nearly the same) frequency. Because the data do not cluster around the middle or center of the distribution but are evenly spread across the variable, the dispersion, as measured by the standard deviation, will be large. The mean and median will be near the center of this distribution. Because many data values occur with the same or nearly the same frequency, however, the mode (or modes) is (are) generally not very useful in a uniform distribution.

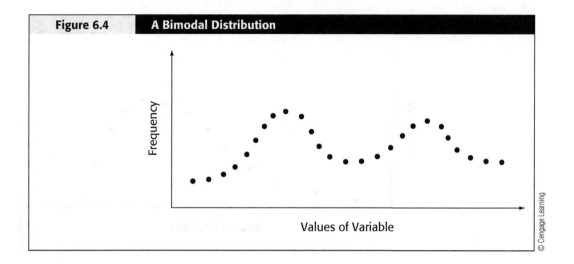

Figure 6.4 **A Bimodal Distribution**

Frequency

Values of Variable

© Cengage Learning

Chapter 5 introduced the idea of a **bimodal distribution**. The shape of such a distribution has two distinct peaks corresponding to data values that occur with high frequency, separated by other values that occur much less often. Figure 6.4 presents an example of a bimodal distribution. Note that in a bimodal distribution, the mean and the median fall near the center of the distribution, but relatively few cases fall there (note the low frequency). As a result, in a bimodal distribution the mean and the median are generally poor measures of central tendency. By contrast, consider the mode(s). The two modes (bimodal) capture the essence of the distribution and are preferred as measures of central tendency in this situation.

In an **asymmetric distribution**, the data fall more on one side of the center or middle of the distribution than on the other side. In that case, skewness exists in the data.

Negatively skewed data have a few extremely low numbers that distort the mean. Negatively skewed data form a frequency distribution like the one pictured in Figure 6.5.

Positively skewed data have a few very large numbers that distort the mean. The frequency distribution of positively skewed data resembles the one shown in Figure 6.6.

If data are strongly skewed, the mean is not a good measure of central tendency (see Chapter 5). The reason is that the mean is "pulled," or skewed, in the direction of the skewness away from the center of the distribution. A few very high or low values in a very asymmetric distribution will skew the mean. In that case, the median is the preferred measure of central tendency because it is largely unaffected by skewness. Recall that in calculating the median, the relative positions of the values are what matters rather than the actual magnitudes. The median is the midmost observation in the data when all the values have been placed in order of magnitude.

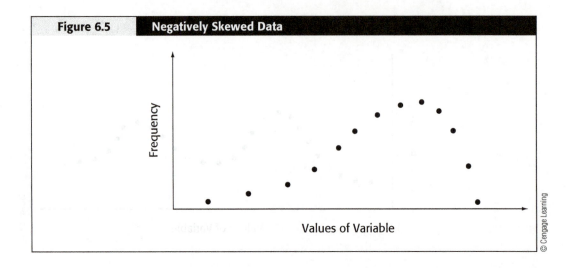

Figure 6.5 **Negatively Skewed Data**

Frequency

Values of Variable

© Cengage Learning

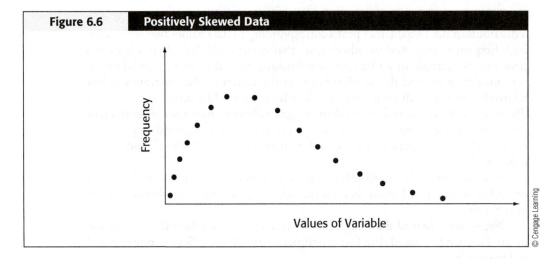

Figure 6.6 **Positively Skewed Data**

Frequency

Values of Variable

© Cengage Learning

Recall our discussion in Chapter 5 regarding the use of the median as a measure of central tendency. If the standard deviation for a set of data approaches or exceeds the value of the mean, the mean may not be a very representative measure of central tendency. When the standard deviation exceeds the mean, extreme values in the data are often responsible. Consider using the median in cases like this because it is not as sensitive to extreme values in the data.

A measure of skewness does exist and should be calculated by computer. Positive values of skewness indicate that the data are positively skewed and, therefore, the mean is artificially high. Skewness figures around zero indicate an unskewed (or symmetric) distribution. Negative numbers indicate negative skewness and, therefore, a mean that is artificially low.

Using Measures of Dispersion and Central Tendency Together

The standard deviation is an important complement to the mean. It is so important, in fact, that the public or nonprofit manager should be cautious in drawing conclusions about the data if she is given only the mean and not the standard deviation as well. In the absence of the standard deviation, the mean has limited value because it is difficult to see how much volatility or variability exists in the data.

For example, let's say that a supervisor is informed that the mean score for a group of employees on a job skills test is 90%. The supervisor is very pleased with the test scores. Without a standard deviation, though, how much does the supervisor really know about the mean score? To illustrate the value of the standard deviation when interpreting the mean, let's look at a couple of different scenarios:

$$\mu = 90 \qquad \sigma = 2$$
$$\mu = 90 \qquad \sigma = 9$$

In the first scenario, where the standard deviation is 2, most individual test scores are tightly clustered around the mean. In the second scenario, where the standard deviation is 9, the individual test scores are far more dispersed around the mean.

Depending on which of these standard deviations was associated with the mean, the supervisor might reach far different conclusions about her employees' performance. A standard deviation of 2 would suggest that most employees have scores close to the mean, whereas a standard deviation of 9 would suggest that the performance of individual employees is much more variable. The two situations are highly different—yet indistinguishable without having the standard deviation to accompany the mean.

Without the value of the standard deviation, it is difficult to evaluate how useful or descriptive a measure of central tendency the mean is. Therefore, the analyst should always provide both the mean and the standard deviation when describing data or reporting results.

Chapter Summary

Measures of dispersion indicate how closely a set of data clusters around the midpoint or center of the data distribution. Measures of dispersion include the range, the interquartile deviation, the average deviation, the variance, and the standard deviation. The first three of these measures are not as useful statistically as the last two.

For descriptive purposes, the standard deviation is used most often. The standard deviation is the square root of the average squared difference of the data values from the mean; it is the square root of the variance. This chapter illustrated the calculation and interpretation of the standard deviation. A small standard deviation (and variance) indicates that the data cluster closely around the mean. Conversely, a large standard deviation indicates much greater dispersion in the data, so that the public or nonprofit manager needs to be more careful in this instance in making decisions based on the mean.

The chapter discussed the characteristic shape of several data distributions common in public and nonprofit administration. These included symmetric, uniform, bimodal, and asymmetric distributions.

In an asymmetric distribution, skewness can present a problem. Negatively skewed data have a few very low values that distort the mean; conversely, positively skewed data have a few very large values that likewise distort the mean. Because it is basically unaffected by skewness, the median is the preferred measure of central tendency in this situation.

Problems

6.1 Dillon Russell, the local fire chief, wants to evaluate the efficiency of two different water pumps. Brand A pumps an average of 5,000 gallons per minute with a standard deviation of 1,000 gallons. Brand B pumps 5,200 gallons per minute with a standard deviation of 1,500 gallons. What can you say about the two types of pumps that would be valuable to Chief Russell?

6.2 Nicole Peter, a research analyst for the United Way of Chickasaw, is asked to provide information on the number of daily visits to food banks in Chickasaw for the past 2 weeks. For the accompanying data, calculate the mean, median, and standard deviation for Nicole.

6	9	0
11	12	5
4	7	10
3	3	12
9	8	

median = _____

mean = _____

standard deviation = _____

6.3 Helen Curbside, the chief custodial engineer for Placerville, has entered into the department computer the number of tons of garbage collected per day by all work crews in the city during a 1-week period. One statistic on the computer puzzles her: "Skewness 5 22.46." Interpret this result for Helen. What does it suggest about the performance of the city work crews?

6.4 Refer to Problem 5.4 (Chapter 5) on the Lance missile system. Five shots missed the target by 26, 147, 35, 63, and 51 feet, respectively. What is the standard deviation of the data?

6.5 The head of research and development for the U.S. Army must select for procurement one of the antitank weapons from the accompanying listing. The listed results indicate the distance away from the intended target that 100 test rounds fell. Which system should the army select, and why?

Weapon	Mean	Standard Deviation
A	22.4	15.9
B	18.7	36.5
C	24.6	19.7

6.6 The Whitehawk Indian Tribe believes the Bureau of Indian Affairs responds faster to grant applications from the Kinsa Tribe than it does to applications from the Whitehawk Tribe. From the accompanying data, what can you tell the Whitehawks?

Days to Respond to Grant Applications

Whitehawk	Kinsa
64	50
58	72
66	74
54	46
70	75
66	81
51	43
56	46

6.7 An audit of the Community Rehabilitation Agency reveals that the average "26 closure" (rehabilitation jargon for a successful effort) takes 193 days with a standard deviation of 49 days and a skewness of 3.15. What does this mean in English?

6.8 The U.S. Postal Service is concerned with the time it takes to deliver mail. It would like not only to deliver mail as quickly as possible but also to have as little variation as possible. Twenty letters are mailed from California state collection boxes to Onguard, Maine. From the following number of days for delivery, what can you tell the Postal Service? Calculate all measures of central tendency and dispersion.

5	4	5	4	6	3	4	8	5	4
3	6	4	5	4	3	7	2	4	4

6.9 An employee at the Purchasing Department claims that he and a few other employees do almost all the work. In support of his claim, he collects the accompanying data on the number of purchase orders cleared and processed by each of the 16 members of the department in a typical week. Calculate all measures of central tendency and dispersion for these data and evaluate this employee's claim. Do a few employees do almost all the work?

12	22	8	14	15	32	17	24
20	37	15	23	16	40	19	21

6.10 The director of the Kensington YMCA has become concerned about the health of the organization's employees. He issues a directive to all YMCA sites advising all managers to encourage employees to get at least 60 minutes of exercise per day. Following are the data on the number of minutes exercised per day (on average) by the 10 employees of the Kensington YMCA site. Calculate all measures of central tendency and dispersion for these data. How well do these employees meet the standard for exercise recommended by the director of the YMCA?

| 75 | 20 | 15 | 95 | 30 | 100 | 40 | 10 | 90 | 120 |

6.11 Complaints have reached the city manager of Foster that it is taking too long to pay bills submitted to the city. You are assigned to check how long it takes by looking at a few bills. Following are the lengths of time in days that it has taken the city to pay seven bills. Calculate the mean, median, and standard deviation. Would you report the mean or the median? Why?

| 34 | 27 | 64 | 31 | 30 | 26 | 35 |

6.12 The Mississippi State Penitentiary is concerned about the number of violent incidents in its prisons. After examining the eight prisons in the Mississippi system, a data analyst finds the following data for the numbers of violent incidents last month:

| 21 | 28 | 29 | 27 | 44 | 23 | 24 | 22 |

Calculate the mean, median, and standard deviation. Should the penitentiary use the mean or the median in its analysis? Why?

6.13 The city manager of Grosse Out Pointe wants to make sure that pay raises are distributed fairly to all employees. He asks his assistant to gather data on raises for a random sample of police and fire employees because he has received complaints that raises are not being distributed fairly in one of the departments.

The assistant calculates the mean for each group of employees. He tells the city manager that because the average pay raise is just about the same in each department, there is really no fairness issue to worry about. If you were the city manager, would you accept these results, or would you ask the assistant to provide you with more information? Explain.

Police	Fire
610	570
590	580
650	700
650	600
640	480
580	690
550	740
550	450
$\bar{X} = 603$	$\bar{X} = 601$

6.14 Jane Smart, director of the New Directions Youth Center, is planning a marketing campaign designed to attract more corporate donors. Because she has received several inquiries in the past regarding how much it costs to treat each client, Ms. Smart decides to collect these data so she can include this information in future promotional materials. She has data on 100 clients served over the past 6 months. Calculate the mean, median, and standard deviation for these data. Prepare a brief statement summarizing the cost data. *(Note: The data set for this problem is available on the book's companion website.)*

6.15 Data on spending per pupil across the entire population of Wisconsin public school districts are provided. Calculate the mean, median, and standard deviation for these data.

Next, use a statistical package program such as Statistical Package for the Social Sciences (SPSS), a statistical software program derived from "statistics" and "data" (STATA), or the like to create a frequency distribution for these data. Use your discretion when determining the number of categories in the distribution. To get started, make sure first to calculate the range for these data. *(Note: The data set for this problem is available on the book's companion website.)*

6.16 The Fowlerville, California, Department of Emergency Services is concerned about whether response times to 911 calls are within what the chief regards as an acceptable range. The head of emergency services has her intern collect data on response times for the most recent one hundred 911 calls and asks the intern to calculate the mean, median, mode, and standard deviation for these data. The head feels that average response times should be no greater than 5 minutes because Fowlerville is a relatively small community (in both population and geographic size). What can the intern tell the head about response times? *(Note: The data set for this problem is available on the book's companion website.)*

6.17 The city manager of Grand Rapids, Michigan, has instructed her assistant to compile data on employee travel reimbursement payments for the past year. There were a total of 250 reimbursement claims. As part of her cost management initiatives, the manager would like to get a better sense of what these reimbursement data look like—that is, to understand the important characteristics of the distribution, including range, average, and dispersion. Assist the manager by calculating the mean, median, mode, and standard deviation for these data (reimbursements per trip in dollars).

Next, use a statistical package program such as SPSS, STATA, or the like to create a frequency distribution for the reimbursement data. Use your discretion when determining the number of categories in the distribution. To get started, make sure first to calculate the range for these data. *(Note: The data set for this problem is available on the book's companion website.)*

6.18 The director of the Madison County jail is planning to testify before the Wisconsin state legislature with the goal of obtaining more state funds for the county jail system. In preparing his remarks, the director plans to present data on the average number of days that prisoners remain in jail. The director believes that his case will be more compelling if he can show that the average stay for prisoners is greater than 21 days. The director asks you, as chief operations officer for the jail, to calculate descriptive statistics for a random sample of 250 prisoners processed in the last 9 months. Calculate the mean and standard deviation for these data. What can you tell the director about his 21-day target? *(Note: The data set for this problem is available on the book's companion website.)*

 6.19 Data on the United Way of West Springfield's annual distributions to agencies and programs are provided on the companion website of this book. Calculate the mean, median, and standard deviation for these data. Which measure of central tendency (mean or median) does a better job of representing the data? *(Note: The data set for this problem is available on the book's companion website.)*

Probability

The Normal Probability Distribution

The most common probability distribution is the normal distribution. The normal distribution describes a great many phenomena: people's heights and weights, scores on numerous tests of physical dexterity and mental capability, psychological attributes, and so forth. Given this great range of phenomena, the normal probability distribution is very useful to managers in public and nonprofit organizations. This chapter elaborates the characteristics of the normal distribution and the calculation and use of standard normal scores or "z scores." It explains how to use the normal distribution table at the end of this book (see Statistical Table 1) to determine and interpret probabilities and discusses the application of the normal distribution to problems of public and nonprofit administration.

Characteristics of the Normal Distribution

The normal probability distribution pertains to continuous variables. A **discrete variable** takes on a countable number of distinct values, such as 0, 1, 2, 3, ... The number of job classifications in an agency, the number of employees in a department, and the number of training sessions conducted are all examples of discrete variables. The binomial distribution, the subject of the next chapter, is a discrete distribution. It is used to calculate the probability that a certain number of events will occur in a given number of trials—for example, the number of defective binoculars purchased by the Pentagon in a sample of 10.

By contrast, a *continuous variable* can assume a countless number (or at least a very large range) of numerical values in a given interval; good examples are temperature, pressure, height, weight, time, and distance. Note that all of these variables can take on fractional (or decimal) values. Other characteristics, such as those measured in dollars (budgets, fringe benefit costs, income, and so forth), are not, strictly speaking, continuous. In a given interval, however, they have so many values, and the values are so close to one another (consider incomes of $50,101, $50,102, $50,103, . . .) that it makes sense to treat them as continuous variables.

The normal curve characterizes such continuous variables—provided that their distribution of scores takes on a certain shape. The general "bell shape" curve is well known and probably familiar to you. It is shown in Figure 7.1.

| **Figure 7.1** | **The Normal Distribution** |

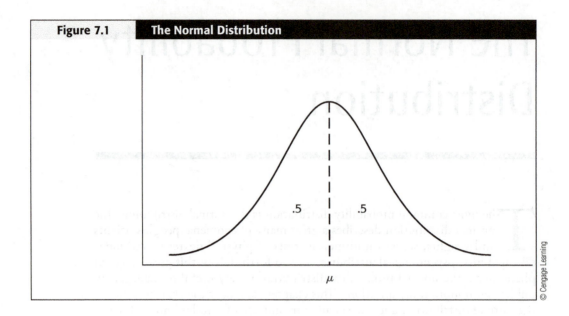

© Cengage Learning

As Figure 7.1 illustrates, the **normal curve** is a mounded distribution centered around a single peak at the mean. The curve is perfectly symmetric: Scores above and below the mean are equally likely to occur so that half of the probability under the curve (.5) lies above the mean and half (.5) below. Most values in a normal distribution fall close to the mean μ, and the curve tapers off gradually toward both of its ends or "tails." As values fall at a greater distance from the mean in either direction, the probability of their occurrence grows smaller and smaller. With respect to heights, weights, or other characteristics that have a normal distribution, most individuals cluster about the mean, and fewer and fewer individuals are found the farther one moves away from the central value in either direction. As shown in Figure 7.1, the normal curve does not touch the horizontal axis, which would indicate that a score at that point and beyond has zero probability of occurring. It is always possible, if not very likely, that a highly extreme value of a variable could occur. Nevertheless, as scores become more and more extreme, the probability of their occurrence becomes vanishingly small.

The normal curve is completely determined by its mean μ and standard deviation σ (Chapters 5 and 6 discuss these statistics in detail). As shown in Figure 7.1, the height of the curve is greatest at the mean (where the probability of occurrence is highest). Figure 7.2 shows that the standard deviation governs the clustering of the data about this central value. In a normal distribution, approximately 68.26% of all values fall within one standard deviation of the mean in either direction, approximately 95.44% of all values fall within two standard deviations of the mean, and approximately 99.72% of all values fall within three standard deviations of the mean in either direction. The shaded areas in Figures 7.2(a), 7.2(b), and 7.2(c) illustrate this phenomenon. Conversely, as shown by the unshaded areas in the figure, in a normal distribution about one-third of the data values lie beyond one standard deviation of the mean in either direction (1.0 − .6826 = .3174). Only about 5% of the data values lie beyond two standard deviations of the mean in either direction (1.0 − .9544 = .0456), and only about one-quarter of 1% of all values lie beyond three standard deviations (1.0 − .9972 = .0028).

| **Figure 7.2** | **The Normal Distribution and the Standard Deviation** |

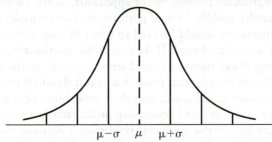

(a) 68.26% of all values lie within one standard deviation of the mean

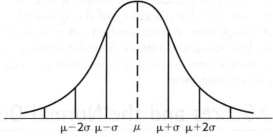

(b) 95.44% of all values lie within two standard deviations of the mean

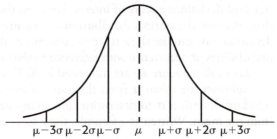

(c) 99.72% of all values lie within three standard deviations of the mean

The normal distribution is measured in terms of its standard deviation. Given a normal distribution, we can use the curve to find the probability of a data value falling within any number of standard deviations from the mean (although the probability of a data value exceeding three standard deviations is very small). If all the public or nonprofit manager had to be concerned about was the probability of scores falling within one, two, or three standard deviations from the mean, or beyond each of these limits, this would be a very short chapter (and many statistical consultants would need to find other employment). Figure 7.2 displays these probabilities only; that is, for data values falling exactly one, two, or three standard deviations from the mean.

The manager has a much broader range of needs and interests for the normal curve, however. She or he is often interested in identifying the data values that demarcate the top 5% of applicants, or the bottom quarter of the work group, or the middle 75% of performers. For example, what score on the innovation inventory should be used to select the top 10% of nominees for the Municipal Innovation Award? If the nonprofit coordinating council wants to recognize the top 2% of nonprofit social service agencies in the state with respect to number of clients served, what numerical cutoff should it use? Or, the manager may need to convert actual scores into their probability of occurrence. For instance, if scores on a test of word processing proficiency have a normal distribution, what percentage of the applicant pool scored between the mean and a particular score of interest (say, the score of an applicant who performed well in other aspects of the job interview), or surpassed this score, or fell below it? In what *percentile* did this applicant fall? If one nonprofit social service agency seemed to serve very few clients, what percentage of the agencies in the state did better—or worse? Although none of these questions refers to data values that fall exactly one, two, or three standard deviations from the mean, the normal distribution can be used to answer them—as well as many other questions important for public and nonprofit management.

z Scores and the Normal Distribution Table

The way that the manager goes about addressing these questions is to calculate, and interpret, a *z* score or standard normal score. A **z score** is the number of standard deviations a score of interest lies from the mean of the normal distribution. Because the normal distribution is measured with respect to the standard deviation, one can use the *z* score to convert raw data values into their associated probabilities of occurrence with reference to the mean.

Let's call the score we are interested in *X*. To calculate the associated *z* score, first subtract the mean μ from the score of interest *X,* and then divide by the standard deviation σ to determine how many standard deviations this score is from the mean. Written as a formula, the *z* score can be represented as

$$z = \frac{X - \mu}{\sigma}$$

As the formula illustrates, the *z* score is the number of standard deviations (σ) a score of interest (X) is from the mean (μ) in a normal distribution. According to the formula (and the definition of the *z* score), a data value X exactly one standard deviation above the mean will have a *z* score of 1.0, a value two standard deviations above the mean will have a *z* score of 2.0, and a value three standard deviations above the mean will have a *z* score of 3.0. Referring to Figure 7.2, we see that the probability associated with a *z* score of 1.0 is .3413—that is, in a normal distribution, just over one-third of the data values lie between the mean and a value one standard deviation *above* it. The respective *z* score for a data value one standard deviation *below* the mean will be the same in magnitude but negative in sign, or −1.0. (Note that for scores of interest below or less than the mean in value, $X - \mu$ will be a negative number.)

Because the normal curve is symmetric about the mean (half the probability lies above and half the probability below the mean; see Figure 7.1), the negative sign poses no difficulty: The probability associated with a *z* score of −1.0 is also .3413 (again, just over one-third of the data values fall between the mean and one standard deviation below it). In a normal distribution, then, .6826 of the data values lie within one standard deviation of the mean in either direction (.3413 + .3413), as shown in Figure 7.2(a). The associated probability for a *z* score of 2.0 (or −2.0) is .4772, and for a *z* score of 3.0 (or −3.0) the probability is .4986. Doubling these probabilities to take into account the scores below the mean and above the mean yields the aggregate probabilities shown in Figures 7.2(b) and 7.2(c) of .9544 and .9972 for data values within two or three standard deviations from the mean, respectively.

How does the manager deal with the myriad of other *z* scores that she or he will encounter in everyday work life in public or nonprofit administration? It would be impractical to have a graph or picture for each *z* score, as in Figure 7.2. Instead, for convenience, *z* scores are tabulated with their associated probabilities in a normal distribution table; the table appears as Table 1 in the Statistical Tables at the end of this book. As illustrated in Figure 7.3, the normal distribution table displays the percentage of data values falling between the mean μ and each *z* score, the area shaded in the figure. In the normal table (Statistical Table 1), the first two digits of the *z* score appear in the far left column; the third digit is read along the top row of the table. The associated probability is read at the intersection of these two points in the body of the table.

Refer to Statistical Table 1. In a normal distribution, what percentage of the data values lie between the mean μ and a *z* score of 1.33? That question is the same as asking what percentage of the cases lie between the mean and a point 1.33 standard deviations away (that is, one and one-third standard deviations). In the far left column of the table, locate the first two digits of the *z* score, 1.3, and read along this row until you reach the third digit, in the 0.03 column. The probability (for a *z* score of 1.33) is .4082. In a normal distribution, 40.82% of the data values lie between the mean and a *z* score of 1.33.

Given this result, we can use our knowledge of the normal distribution to answer several questions of interest. For instance, what percentage of the data

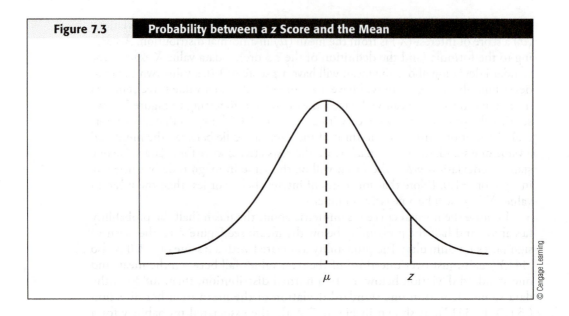

Figure 7.3 | **Probability between a z Score and the Mean**

values lie between the mean and a z score 1.33 standard deviations *below* it? A negative z score, in this case −1.33, indicates a score of interest less than the mean. Because the normal curve is symmetric, this z score bounds the same amount of area (probability) under the normal curve as a z score of 1.33. The probability is identical: .4082.

What percentage of the data values lies *above* a z score of 1.33? This area of the normal curve is shaded in Figure 7.4. How can we find this probability? Recall that in a normal distribution, half (.5) of the probability lies above the mean and half below. We know that .4082 of all the values lie between the mean and a z score of 1.33. The shaded area beyond this z score can be found by subtracting this probability from .5, giving an answer of .0918. So 9.18% of the data values lie above this score.

In a normal distribution, what percentage of the data values lies below a z score of 1.33? This portion of the curve is shaded in Figure 7.5. We can proceed in either of two ways. The easier is to subtract from 1.0 (the total probability under the curve) the percentage of data values surpassing this z score (.0918); the answer is .9082. Or, because we know that the area under the curve between the mean and this z score is .4082 and that the area below the mean is equal to .5, we can add these probabilities to find the same total probability of .9082.

In the normal distribution table at the end of the book (Statistical Table 1), practice finding the probabilities associated with the following z scores. Then, using the methods discussed earlier, calculate the percentage of data values in a normal distribution that falls above this z score and the percentage that falls below it.

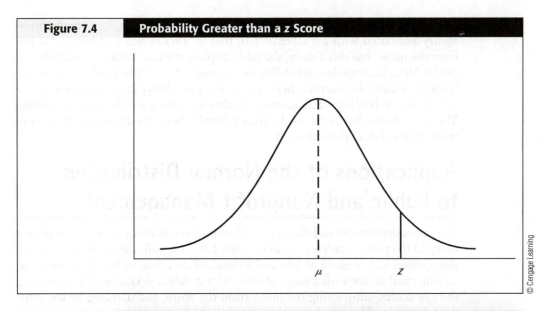

Figure 7.4   Probability Greater than a z Score

© Cengage Learning

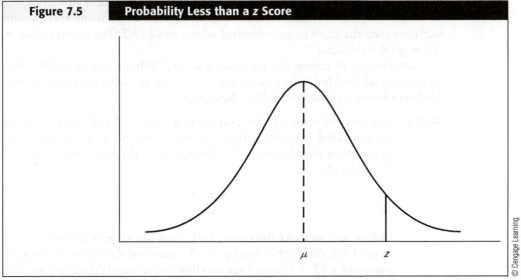

Figure 7.5   Probability Less than a z Score

© Cengage Learning

z	Table Probability	Percentage above z	Percentage below z
1.62			
0.73			
2.40			
−1.50			
−0.48			
−3.16			

For further practice in using the normal distribution table, look up the probability associated with a *z* score of 1.0; that is, a score one standard deviation from the mean. For this *z* score, the table displays the now familiar probability of .3413. Now, look up the probability for a *z* score of 2.0 (two standard deviations from the mean). No surprise here either: The probability is the equally familiar .4772. The probability for a *z* score of 3.0 also confirms our earlier understanding. The table shows that .4986 of the data values lie between the mean and a score three standard deviations above it.

Applications of the Normal Distribution to Public and Nonprofit Management

The police department in Jefferson, California, gives an exam to all who apply for entry to the police academy. Scores on the Jefferson police exam have a normal distribution with a mean of 100 and a standard deviation of 10. (Any exam can be converted to one with a mean of 100 and a standard deviation of 10 by taking the raw scores, subtracting the mean from the score, and dividing by the standard deviation. This number is then multiplied by 10, and that number is added to 100. This process is called *standardization*.) Assume that the recruitment examiner gives the exam to an individual who scores 119.2. The next question is, "How good is this score?"

Another way of stating this question is to ask, "What is the probability that a randomly selected individual would score 119.2 on the Jefferson police exam?" To determine this probability, follow these steps.

Step 1: Convert the score on the exam into a *z* score. Recall that a *z* score is calculated by subtracting the mean test score from the score in question and dividing the difference by the standard deviation. Symbolically,

$$z = \frac{X - \mu}{\sigma}$$

In this case, subtract the mean, 100, from the score of interest, 119.2, to get 19.2; divide this number by the standard deviation, 10, to get a *z* score of 1.92. A *z* score indicates how many standard deviations (and in what direction) a score is from the mean. Because this score is above the mean, the *z* score is positive. As explained earlier, values below the mean have negative *z* scores.

Step 2: Look up the value of a *z* score of 1.92 in a normal distribution table. Table 1 in the Statistical Tables at the end of the book is a normal distribution table designed to convert *z* scores into probabilities. The numbers in the first column and across the top of the table represent the values of the *z* scores. The values inside the table represent the area of the normal curve that falls between the *z* score in question and the mean (the total area under the curve is 1.0). In this example, proceed down the first column until you find a z score of 1.9. According to the numbers across the top of the table, the first number next to the 1.9 represents a z score of 1.90; the second number is for a z score of 1.91; the third number represents a z score of 1.92 and is the one that interests us. The value found here is .4726. This means that 47.26% of the police exam scores fall between the mean (100) and a z score of 1.92 (119.2). Because 50% (or half) of the scores fall below the mean, a total of 97.26% of the scores fall below a score of 119.2. In probability terms, the probability that a randomly selected individual will score 119.2 or better on the Jefferson police exam is .0274 (1.0 − .9726). Another way of stating this result is that the individual in question scored at the 97th percentile. In sum, the applicant did very well on the exam.

An important aspect of the normal distribution is its flexibility. The following examples illustrate some of the numerous applications of the normal distribution.

Suppose the Jefferson, California, police chief wants to know the percentage of job applicants who scored between 100 and 106 on the Jefferson police exam. Because the mean is 100 (and the standard deviation is 10), this question is equivalent to asking what percentage of the applicants score between 106 and the mean. To answer, follow the two-step procedure discussed earlier and repeated here.

Step 1: Convert the score of interest into a z score. Use the formula for the z score:

$$z = \frac{X - \mu}{\sigma}$$

$$= \frac{106 - 100}{10}$$

$$= .60$$

The z score corresponding to a raw score of 106 is .60. In other words, this score is six-tenths of a standard deviation above the mean.

Step 2: Look up a z score of .60 in the normal distribution table (Statistical Table 1) at the end of the book. The police chief wants to know the percentage of job applicants who fall between this z score (raw score =106) and the mean. We read this probability directly from the table; the table reveals a probability of .2257. Thus, about 22.6% of all applicants score between 100 and 106 on the exam. This area is shaded in Figure 7.6.

What percentage of applicants score above 106? This area, unshaded in Figure 7.6, is equal to .5 − .2257 = .2743, so about 27.4% of job applicants surpass this criterion.

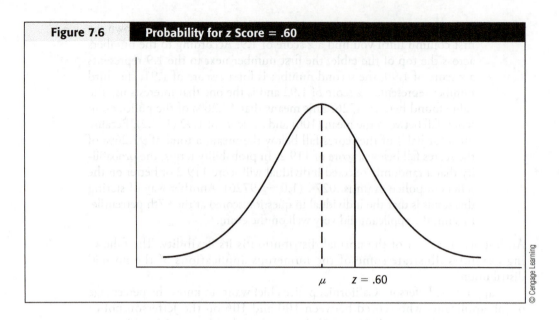

Figure 7.6   **Probability for z Score = .60**

μ z = .60

© Cengage Learning

What percentage of applicants score between 88 and 112 on the exam? Calculating this probability is easy if you split it into two questions with reference to the mean. First, what percentage of applicants fall between the mean of 100 and a score of 112? Calculate the z score in the space provided. Then, look up the corresponding probability in the normal distribution table.

Step 1: Convert the score of interest into a z score:

$$z = \frac{112 - 100}{10}$$

$$= \frac{12}{10}$$

$$= 1.20$$

Step 2: Look up a z score of 1.20 in the normal distribution table. The percentage of job applicants who fall between this z score and the mean is .3849. Thus, 38.49% of all applicants score between 100 (mean) and 112 on the police examination.

Now, consider the second part of the question: What percentage of applicants score between 88 and the mean of 100? Note that 88 is the same distance from the mean as 112, but in the opposite (negative) direction. Therefore, it will yield the same absolute z value with a negative sign, -1.20. The associated probability is the same, .3849. To find the percentage of applicants who score between 88 and 112, add these probabilities, for an answer of about 77 (.3849 + .3849 = .7698). This area of the normal curve is shaded in Figure 7.7.

What is the probability that a randomly selected applicant will score between 117 and 122 on the Jefferson police examination? Note that the probability of scoring between these two values is equal to the probability of scoring between the mean and 122 *minus* the probability of scoring between the mean and 117; this difference is highlighted in Figure 7.8. To find this area of the normal curve, follow the two-step procedure presented earlier. First, calculate the z scores for the two scores of interest, 117 and 122:

$$z = \frac{117 - 100}{10} \qquad\qquad z = \frac{122 - 100}{10}$$

$$= \frac{17}{10} \qquad\qquad\qquad = \frac{22}{10}$$

$$= 1.70 \qquad\qquad\qquad = 2.20$$

Next, look up the probabilities associated with z scores of 1.70 and 2.20 in the normal distribution table; .4554 of the area under the curve lies between 1.70 and the mean, and .4861 lies between 2.20 and the mean. As shown in Figure 7.8, the probability of scoring between 117 and 122, therefore, is equal to the difference between these two probabilities, or .0307 (.4861 − .4554).

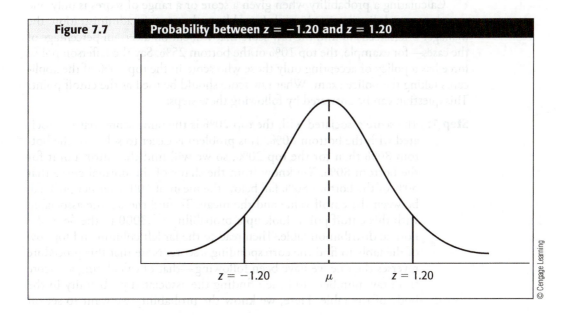

Figure 7.7	Probability between $z = -1.20$ and $z = 1.20$

$z = -1.20$ $\qquad$ μ $\qquad$ $z = 1.20$

© Cengage Learning

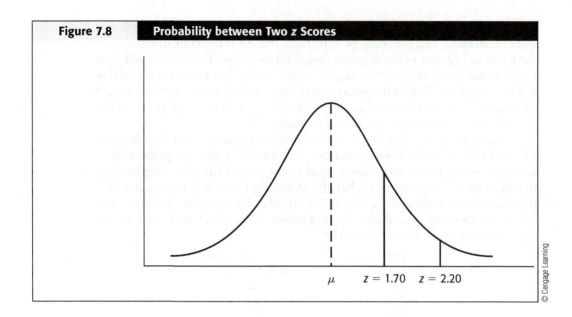

Figure 7.8 | **Probability between Two z Scores**

μ $z = 1.70$ $z = 2.20$

© Cengage Learning

What is the probability that an applicant will score 125 or more on the Jefferson police exam? Because we can calculate the probability that someone will score between the mean and 125, we can solve this problem. The probability of scoring between 100 and 125 (z score = ?) is .4938. Because 50% of all persons score below the mean, the probability of scoring 125 or below is .9938 (.50 + .4938). This result indicates the probability of scoring 125 or above is .0062 (1.0 − .9938).

Calculating a probability when given a score or a range of scores is only one way the normal distribution is used. In public and nonprofit administration, the manager often needs to find the raw score that will cut off a certain percentage of the cases—for example, the top 10% or the bottom 25%. Say the Jefferson police force has a policy of accepting only those who score in the top 20% of the applicants taking the police exam. What raw score should be used as the cutoff point? This question can be answered by following these steps:

Step 1: The score associated with the top 20% is the same score that is associated with the bottom 80%. This problem is easier to solve for the bottom 80% than for the top 20%, so we will find the cutoff point for the bottom 80%. We know from the shape of the normal curve that 50% of the bottom 80% fall below the mean of 100. Another 30% fall between the cutoff value and the mean. To find the z score associated with this cutoff point, look up a probability of .3000 in the *body* of a normal distribution table. Then read to the far left column and top row of the table to find the corresponding z score. Note that this procedure reverses the one we have been following—that of calculating a z score from raw numbers and then finding the associated probability in the body of the table. Here, we know the probability we want to set off

(.3000), and we need to find the associated z score. Therefore, we start in the body of the table.

Scanning the body of the normal distribution table, we find that the closest probability to .3000, without going under it, is .3023. The z score associated with this probability is .85 and is the one we seek. (If we had chosen a z score with an associated probability less than .3000, we would cut off slightly more than the top 20% of scores on the police examination.)

Step 2: Convert this z score to a raw score. Recall that a z score is the number of standard deviations a score of interest is from the mean. We want the raw score associated with a z score of .85. We multiply this z score times the standard deviation (10) to get 8.5; our score of interest is, thus, 8.5 above the mean. To complete the conversion, add this number to the mean to get $100 + 8.5 = 108.5$. If the police academy class is limited to the top 20% of all applicants, only those who score 108.5 or above on the examination should be admitted.

An example from nonprofit management will help to illustrate the normal distribution further. The Gold Star Mentoring Program selects peer mediators from among Cub Scouts in the area. To be eligible, a Cub Scout must score in the top 75% of applicants on a test of social knowledge and interest in helping other people. Because the Gold Star Mentoring Program would like to involve as many Cub Scouts as possible, it accepts the top 75% of all those taking the exam. Last year, the mean score on this exam was 80, with a standard deviation of 6. Exam scores were normally distributed. At what value should the minimum acceptable score be set to admit only the top 75% of Cub Scouts who apply?

Because we know 50% of the applicants will score above 80 (mean score), we need to know the score below the mean that will contain 25% of the scores between it and the mean (for a total of $50\% + 25\% = 75\%$). Looking up a probability of .25 in the normal table, we find a value of .2486 associated with a z score of .67. Because we are interested in scores below the mean, this z score is $-.67$. Converting a z score of $-.67$ to a raw score, we get a minimum acceptance score of 76 $[(-.67 \times 6) + 80 = 76]$. Thus, to admit the top 75%, the Gold Star Mentoring Program should accept Cub Scouts who score 76 or above on the test of social knowledge and interest in helping other people.

A Measurement Technique Based on Standard Normal Scores

To this point in the chapter, we have used standard normal scores or z scores to determine and interpret probabilities. We can also use z scores as an aid to measurement. In earlier examples, we showed how to use z scores to calculate the percentile in which a particular observation lies: Given a variable with a normal distribution and the resulting z scores, you can determine what percentage of observations lie above or below any score (i.e., the percentile). If you had such information, for example, on the responsiveness of public relations departments to citizen inquiries in cities of greater than 100,000 population, for example, you could use the normal distribution table to place the cities in percentiles on this variable.

You can also use normal scores to combine variables into scales or indices. A **scale** or **index** is a composite measure combining several variables into a single, unified measure of a concept. Because variables are usually measured on different scales, you should not simply add scores together to create a new scale. For example, if you needed to create and report an overall measure of the physical fitness of military troops, their height (inches), weight (pounds), age (years), speed (time to run a mile), and personal habits (frequency of smoking, drinking, and so on) might all be important—but simply summing scores across the different variables would be meaningless. The measurement scales for the variables are not comparable.

You can use standard normal z scores to overcome the problem of different scales of measurement. A z score converts any variable to the same unit of measurement; hence the name *standard* normal score. Regardless of the initial scale of measurement of a variable, all z scores are measured on the same normal curve or distribution and have the same probability interpretation. Thus, if variables are converted first to z scores to place them on the same measurement scale and then summed, the resulting scales or indices will not be distorted by any initial differences in measurement: Each variable will contribute appropriately, with the correct influence or weighting, to the composite scale or index.

Let's look at an example. John Pelissero, a data analyst for the city of Evansville, feels that excellent performance by city garbage collection crews can be summarized by two variables: tons of trash collected and the number of complaints received from citizens. Mr. Pelissero would like to combine these data into a single measure of performance, but he realizes that the variables are based on very different units of measurement (tons of trash and number of complaints). Because the tons of trash are so much larger in magnitude, they will dwarf the number of complaints, which are relatively small numbers. He knows that to create a meaningful index of performance, something must be done to place the two variables on the same measurement scale. Obviously, Mr. Pelissero has read this book and will go a long way in public or nonprofit management. In Table 7.1, he has assembled the data from each of the five city work crews on the number of tons of trash collected and the number of complaints lodged against them by citizens.

Table 7.1	Performance of City Garbage Collection Crews in Evansville	
Crew	Tons Collected	Complaints Against
A	127	6
B	132	8
C	118	4
D	170	9
E	123	3

Mr. Pelissero wants to combine these two variables into a single measure of performance, so he follows these steps.

Step 1: Calculate the mean (μ) and standard deviation (σ) for each variable. They are shown in Table 7.2.

Step 2: Convert each of the raw scores of trash collected and complaints received into z scores by taking the raw score, subtracting the mean, and dividing that difference by the standard deviation. The calculations are shown in Tables 7.3 and 7.4. Because complaints indicate poor performance (two complaints are worse, not better, than one complaint), the z scores for complaints were multiplied by -1 to reverse the scale.

Step 3: For each crew, add the z scores for trash collected and for complaints received, as shown in Table 7.5, to obtain performance scores. The performance scores can then be used to compare the trash collection crews with each other on a single measure. The z score procedure converts each variable to a common base (standard deviations from the mean) so that the variables can be added appropriately. Note that, as Table 7.3 shows, the highest-performing trash crew was fourth in total tons of trash collected but received the fewest complaints from citizens.

This procedure weights tons of trash collected and complaints received equally. If Mr. Pelissero felt that tons of trash collected was twice as important as complaints received, he would multiply the z scores for tons of trash by 2 before adding them to the z scores for complaints, as shown in Table 7.6. Note that some of the trash crews change ranking when tons of trash collected is given a higher weighting (twice as important).

Table 7.2	Mean and Standard Deviation for Each Variable		
	Crew	Tons	Complaints Against
	μ	134.0	6.0
	σ	18.6	2.3

© Cengage Learning

Table 7.3	z Scores for Tons of Trash Collected		
	Tons $-\ \mu$	$(X - \mu) \div \sigma$	z
	$127 - 134$	$-7 \div 18.6$	$-.38$
	$132 - 134$	$-2 \div 18.6$	$-.11$
	$118 - 134$	$-16 \div 18.6$	$-.86$
	$170 - 134$	$36 \div 18.6$	1.94
	$123 - 134$	$-11 \div 18.6$	$-.59$

© Cengage Learning

Table 7.4	z Scores for Complaints Received			
	Complaints − μ	$(X - \mu) \div \sigma$	z	− z
	6 − 6	0 ÷ 2.3	0	0
	8 − 6	2 ÷ 2.3	.87	−.87
	4 − 6	−2 ÷ 2.3	−.87	.87
	9 − 6	3 ÷ 2.3	1.30	−1.30
	3 − 6	−3 ÷ 2.3	−1.30	1.30

© Cengage Learning

Table 7.5	Performance Scores for Garbage Collection Crews		
Crew	Tons	Complaints	Performance
A	−.38	0	−.38
B	−.11	−.87	−.98
C	−.86	.87	.01
D	1.94	−.30	.64
E	−.59	1.30	.71

© Cengage Learning

A useful equal-weighting scheme is to weight the z scores for tons and the z scores for complaints by one-half, or .5. This procedure is equivalent to calculating the mean performance score for each garbage collection crew. The resulting performance scores retain the value of a z score in indicating how many units (standard deviations) a score is above or below the mean. Positive scores indicate performance above the mean, and negative scores indicate performance below the mean. As displayed in Table 7.7, performance scores calculated in this manner show that crews A and B are below the mean in performance, crew C is at the mean, and crews D and E are above the mean.

A public or nonprofit manager can assign any weights to the variables so long as the variables have been converted to z scores first and the weights can be explained and justified. The higher the weight assigned to a variable, the greater its influence in the composite scale or index. For example, the board of directors of a nonprofit food bank feels that dispensing meals is by far its most important activity. In comparing its performance with that of other food banks, it might weight meals served by a factor of 3.0, monetary donations by 2.0, and volunteer hours by 1.5. The number of variables that can be combined using the z score method has no limit. A manager can use 2, 4, 6, or 50 or more indicators and combine them by adding z scores. Of course, the variables or indicators should have relevance for the concept the manager wants to measure, and any weighting scheme must be explained and justified.

Table 7.6	Performance Scores When Tons Are Weighted Twice as Heavily as Complaints		
Crew	Tons × 2	Complaints	Performance
A	−.38 × 2 = −.76	0	−.76
B	−.11 × 2 = −.22	−.87	−1.09
C	−.86 × 2 = −1.72	.87	−.85
D	1.94 × 2 = 3.88	−1.30	2.58
E	−.60 × 2 = −1.20	1.30	.10

© Cengage Learning

Table 7.7	Performance Scores When Tons and Complaints Are Weighted by One-Half (.5)		
Crew	Tons × .5	Complaints × .5	Performance
A	−.38 × .5 = −.19	0 × .5 = 0	−.19
B	−.11 × .5 = −.055	−.87 × .5 = −.435	−.49
C	.86 × .5 = −.43	.87 × .5 = .435	.005
D	−1.94 × .5 = .97	−1.30 × .5 = .65	.32
E	−.59 × .5 = −.295	1.30 × .5 = .65	.355

© Cengage Learning

A note of caution is in order. The z score technique should be used only when the manager believes that the concept being measured has only one dimension. If the concept has two or more dimensions (as, for example, the effectiveness of a receptionist is a function of efficiency and courtesy), a more sophisticated statistical technique called *factor analysis* should be used to combine several indicators or variables into a new measure (see annotated bibliography for sources). When you want to combine multiple indicators of a multidimensional concept into new measures, consult a statistician.

Chapter Summary

The normal distribution is a very common and useful probability distribution in public and nonprofit administration. The general bell shape of the normal curve describes the distribution of many phenomena of interest to the public or nonprofit manager.

The normal distribution is measured in terms of its standard deviation. In a normal distribution, 68.26% of all values lie within one standard deviation of the mean in either direction, 95.44% of all values fall within two standard deviations of the mean, and 99.72% of all values fall within three standard deviations.

To use the normal distribution, the manager must calculate and interpret a z score. A z score is defined as the number of standard deviations a score of interest lies from the mean of the distribution. It is used to convert raw data values into their associated probabilities of occurrence with reference to the mean. Denoting the score of interest X, the mean μ, and the standard deviation σ, the formula for the z score is

$$z = \frac{X - \mu}{\sigma}$$

The normal distribution presented in Table 1 in the Statistical Tables at the end of this book displays the percentage of cases falling between any z score and the mean of the distribution (or the probability that falls under this region of the curve). Using this information, the public or nonprofit manager can answer a variety of important questions, such as the probability of observing a score less than or greater than, the score of interest, or the probability of a score falling between two scores of interest. She or he can also identify scores that will cut off portions of the normal curve of special interest, such as the top 5% of qualifiers.

One can also use standard normal (z) scores to combine variables into a composite scale or index. This technique is very useful to public and nonprofit managers, who often have several indicators of a concept (e.g., performance) and need to combine them into a single measure.

Problems

7.1 Vince Yosarian works for the Bureau of Forms. His manager has reprimanded Vince because she feels that he has not performed up to standard for processing forms at the bureau, the crucial part of the job. At the bureau, the number of forms processed by employees is normally distributed, with a mean of 67 forms per employee per day and a standard deviation of 7. His manager has calculated that Vince's average rate is 50 forms processed per day. What percentage of employees at the bureau process fewer forms than Vince? What percentage of employees at the bureau process more forms than Vince? Does the manager's complaint seem justified or not?

7.2 The average (mean) amount of time that a manager at the Cimaron Valley Department of Human Services spends in the annual performance review with an employee is 31.3 minutes, with a standard deviation of 5.7 minutes (normal distribution). What percentage of the annual performance reviews in the department take between 24.9 and 36.1 minutes? Between 26.4 and 30.6 minutes? Between 32.0 and 37.5 minutes? What percentage of the annual performance reviews take more than 40 minutes? What percentage take less than 20 minutes?

7.3 According to records kept by Mariposa County, the average (mean) amount of time that it takes for employees to be reimbursed for professional expenses incurred in service to the county is 36 days, with a standard deviation of 5 days. The distribution is normal. About 2 months ago, Latisha MacNeil attended a training conference for her job in the County Recreation Department. She filed for reimbursement of expenses that she incurred at the conference 42 days ago, but she has not received payment. What is the probability of receiving reimbursement within 42 days of filing? After 42 days? At this point, should Ms. MacNeil be apprehensive about receiving reimbursement?

7.4 Refer to Problem 7.3. The head of the Mariposa County Accounting Department wants to establish a standard regarding the length of time that employees can expect to wait to receive reimbursement for professional expenses. She wants to publish a standard that states the number of days it takes the department to process 98% of the claims filed. Help the department head find that standard.

7.5 Parnelli Jones, a vehicle manager for the northeast region of the forestry service, is charged with purchasing automobiles for service use. Because forestry service employees often have to drive long distances in isolated regions, Parnelli is very concerned about gasoline mileage for the vehicle fleet. One automobile manufacturer has told him that the particular model of vehicle that interests him has averaged 27.3 miles per gallon in road tests with a standard deviation of 3.1 (normal distribution). Parnelli would like to be able to tell his superiors at the forestry service that the cars will get at least 25 miles to the gallon. According to the road test data, what percentage of the cars can be expected to meet this criterion? Parnelli also thinks that his superiors might settle for cars that got 24 miles to the gallon or better. What percentage of the cars can be expected to meet this criterion?

7.6 Refer to Problem 7.5. During the negotiations with the automobile manufacturer, Parnelli gets a sinking feeling that some of the cars he is thinking of purchasing for the forestry service might average less than 20 miles to the gallon of gasoline. According to the road test data, what percentage of the cars can be expected to fall below this mileage level? Should Parnelli be very worried?

7.7 Butterworth, Missouri, is trying to increase its tourism, a great source of revenue. Among other things, Butterworth prides itself on its temperate climate. The tourism department would like to include in its glossy new brochure the middle range of temperatures that occur on 90% of the days there. A check with the National Weather Service finds that the average temperature in Butterworth is 76 degrees with a standard deviation of 5.7 (the temperatures were normally distributed). Help the tourism department by finding the two temperatures that cut off the middle 90% of temperatures in Butterworth.

7.8 The average (mean) paid by the Bureau of Indian Affairs (BIA) for a 5-day training workshop contracted with the private sector is $1,500 (standard deviation = $280; normal distribution). Perk Morgan, a BIA employee, would like to attend a sensitivity training workshop in Bermuda (he feels that he must go to an exotic location to get in touch with his true feelings); the government rate for the training workshop is $2,400. What percentage of 5-day training workshops funded by the BIA exceed this amount? Perk has also inquired about a sensitivity training workshop to be held in Sausalito, California (less exotic location, but Perk will still be able to get in touch with feelings); the cost for this workshop is $2,100.

What percentage of BIA-sponsored training workshops exceed this cost? What would you advise Perk to do?

7.9 Ima Fastrack is a data analyst at the Oakmont Civil Service Commission. When she was first hired 3 months ago, she was satisfied with her salary of $24,832. In the time since she was hired, Ima has talked with several others in similar positions with the Oakmont city government; all earn more than she does. Ima has obtained data on the salaries of data analysts with the city. The distribution of salaries is normal, with an average salary of $25,301 and a standard deviation of $986. Ima has come to believe that she is seriously underpaid relative to others in her position. Do you agree or disagree with her? Use the normal curve to support your answer.

7.10 The director of development at the Richman Children's Science Museum has recently collected data on donations for the past several years. She finds that the data are normally distributed with a mean of $51 and a standard deviation of $14. The director's ideal point for a minimum donation is $60. What percentage of individual donations are $60 or more? What percentage of individual donations are less than $60? The director's long-term goal for an average individual donation is at least $80. Based on the current data, does achieving this goal seem reasonable in the immediate future?

7.11 The Warrenville Empowerment Center has begun to track how many days of employment counseling its clients receive. The center's intern, Amanda Strom, finds that the average client receives 17 days of counseling with a standard deviation of 3.1 days (the data are normally distributed). The center's director has become more concerned about managing costs; so she asks Amanda to generate some information from these data. Because the director wonders if a target of 15 or fewer days of counseling is realistic, she asks Amanda to determine what percentage of clients receive 15 or fewer days of counseling. The director is especially concerned about clients needing 25 or more days of counseling and wonders what percentage of the current client base fits this profile. What should Amanda tell the director after analyzing the data?

7.12 Administrators at the national headquarters of the Center for the Display of Visual Arts are authorized to make small work-related purchases using purchasing cards. The average amount administrators charge to their cards per month is $278 with a standard deviation of 33 dollars. The data are normally distributed. The auditing staff at the center is concerned with the spending patterns of an administrator who has averaged $349 per month in charges. What percentage of balances are between $278 and $349 per month? What percentage of balances exceed $349 per month? Should the auditing staff be concerned about the spending habits of this particular administrator?

The Binomial Probability Distribution

The **binomial probability distribution** provides a method for estimating probability when events that concern the public or nonprofit manager take on certain characteristics. The binomial allows the manager to determine the probability that an event will occur a specified number of times in a certain number of trials. For example, if certain conditions are met, you can use the binomial distribution to estimate the probability that the mail will be delivered before a specified time every day for a week or the probability that a certain piece of equipment will remain operational throughout a 10-day inspection period. As these examples suggest, the binomial is a discrete distribution that deals with the probability of observing a certain number of events of interest in a set number of repeated trials. In this chapter we discuss the characteristics and use of the binomial probability distribution.

Binomial Probabilities

The binomial probability distribution can be used when the process under consideration is what is called a Bernoulli process. The first characteristic of a **Bernoulli process** specifies that the outcome of any trial (a trial being one attempt, whether or not successful) can be classified into one of two mutually exclusive and jointly exhaustive categories. One of these two categories (the one you want to examine) is referred to as a success; the other category is referred to as a failure.

Some examples will illustrate. Flipping an unbiased coin follows a Bernoulli process. Results of the flips can be classified as either a "head" or "not a head" (a tail). The solving of crimes by a police department can be described in a similar manner; a crime is either solved or not solved. Rolling a 6 on a die may be characterized as a 6 or not a 6 (any other number on the die).

The second characteristic of a Bernoulli process is that the probability of success must remain constant from trial to trial and be totally unaffected by the outcomes of any preceding trial. Each trial is **independent**, or not affected by the previous trials. Examples of independent events include the probability of obtaining a head on any flip of a coin. The probability on any given flip is not affected by the number of heads obtained on previous flips. The probability of a fire occurring in a community on a given night is not affected by whether a fire occurred in the community the previous night (assuming that there are no pyromaniacs living or visiting in the city).

Any process that exhibits these two characteristics is a Bernoulli process. When a Bernoulli process exists, the probability that any number of events will occur can be determined by using the binomial probability distribution. To determine a probability by using the binomial probability distribution, you must know three things: (1) the number of trials—that is, the number of times a certain event is tried or repeated; (2) the number of successes—that is, the number of times you achieve or want to achieve a given event; and (3) the probability that the event in question will occur in any trial. This probability might be known a priori (such as the probability of rolling a 6 on a die), or you might have to calculate it (for example, from the rates of equipment failures).

With the knowledge of these three factors, the following formula can be used to calculate the probability of any one event for the binomial probability distribution:

$$C_r^n p^r q^{n-r}$$

where

n = the number of trials

r = the number of successes

p = the probability that the event will be a success

$q = 1 - p$

Although this formula looks complex, in actuality it is not. The symbol C_r^n refers to what statisticians call a **combination** (read as "a combination of n things taken r at a time"). To illustrate a combination and its value, let us assume that we have four balls marked with the letters a, b, c, and d, respectively. We want to know how many different sets of three balls we could select from the four. In statistical language, we want to know the number of combinations of four balls taken three at a time. As the following illustration shows, a combination of four things taken three at a time equals 4; that is, there are four different combinations of four things taken three at a time.

Combination	Balls Selected
1	a, b, c
2	a, b, d
3	a, c, d
4	b, c, d

These four combinations of three balls represent all the possible ways that four items can be grouped into sets of three. In the space provided on page 147, use the same procedure to determine the value of a combination of four things taken two at a time.

If you found six combinations (*ab, ac, ad, bc, bd, cd*), congratulations.

Listing all possible combinations as a way to figure out this value often gets burdensome. For example, the following combination would take a long time to calculate by the combination-listing method:

$$C_6^{15}$$

The number of combinations of 15 things taken six at a time will be very large. To simplify, a shortcut method of determining the number of combinations has been found using the formula

$$C_r^n = \frac{n!}{r!\,(n - r)!}$$

where *n*! (called *n* factorial) is equal to $n \times (n - 1) \times (n - 2) \times (n - 3) \times \ldots \times 3 \times 2 \times 1$; *r*! and $(n - r)$! have the same interpretation. For example, $6! = 6 \times 5 \times 4 \times 3 \times 2 \times 1 = 720$.

In the preceding example, we find

$$C_6^{15} = \frac{15!}{6!9!}$$

$$= \frac{\overbrace{15 \times 14 \times 13 \times 12 \times 11 \times 10 \times 9 \times 8 \times 7 \times 6 \times 5 \times 4 \times 3 \times 2 \times 1}^{15!}}{\underbrace{(6 \times 5 \times 4 \times 3 \times 2 \times 1)}_{6!} \times \underbrace{(9 \times 8 \times 7 \times 6 \times 5 \times 4 \times 3 \times 2 \times 1)}_{9!}}$$

$$= 5{,}005$$

The use of the binomial distribution can best be illustrated by working a problem. Assume that we are going to flip an unbiased coin three times, and we want to know the probability of getting exactly three heads. In this example, the number of trials (*n*) is equal to 3, the number of coin flips. The number of successes (*r*) is equal to 3, the number of heads. The probability of obtaining a head on one flip of a coin (*p*) is equal to .5; *q*, then, is equal to $1 - p$, or .5. Recall that in a Bernoulli process, only two outcomes are possible. If the probability of success is *p*, then the probability of failure (i.e., nonsuccess) must be $1 - p = q$. Substituting these numbers into the binomial probability distribution formula, we get

$$C_r^n p^r q^{n-r} = \left(\frac{3!}{3!0!}\right) \times .5^3 \times .5^0 = .125$$

Calculating the combination term first, we find that the numerator (top) of the fraction is equal to 3!(3 × 2 × 1), or 6. This number is divided by the denominator (bottom) of the fraction, 3!, or 6, times 0!. To keep the universe orderly, *statisticians define 0! as equal to 1.* The combination term, therefore, is equal to 6 divided by 6, or 1; that is, there is only one way in which you could flip a coin three times and get three heads (the sequence head-head-head). The probability terms are easily calculated: $.5^3$ is equal to $.5 \times .5 \times .5$, or $.125$, and $.5^0$ is equal to 1. Note again that *statisticians define any number raised to the 0 power as equal to 1* to maintain an orderly universe. The probability of obtaining three heads in three flips of an unbiased coin, then, is $1 \times .125 \times 1$, or $.125$.

To test yourself, calculate the probability that in four flips of an unbiased coin, exactly two heads will occur. Calculate in the space provided.

You should have found a probability of .375 that two heads would occur on four flips of an unbiased coin. The problem may be defined as one where $n = 4$, $r = 2$, and $p = .5$ (the number of trials, the number of successes, and the probability of success, respectively). Again, q (probability of tails) $= 1 - p = .5$. The probability can be calculated as follows:

$$C_r^n p^r q^{n-r} = \left(\frac{4!}{2!2!} \right) \times .5^2 \times .5^2$$

$$= \left(\frac{4 \times 3 \times 2 \times 1}{2 \times 1 \times 2 \times 1} \right) \times .25 \times .25$$

$$= 6 \times .25 \times .25$$

$$= .375$$

Suppose you want to know the probability of obtaining *two or more* heads on four flips of an unbiased coin. In this situation, you would calculate the probability of obtaining four heads (.0625), the probability of obtaining three heads (.25), and the probability of obtaining two heads (.375). Because these three events are mutually exclusive, the probability of two, three, or four heads occurring is equal to the probability of two heads plus the probability of three heads plus the probability of four heads, or .6875 (i.e., $.375 + .25 + .0625 = .6875$). The calculations for two heads appear earlier; the calculations for three and four heads follow.

$$\text{Three heads: } C_4^4 \times .5^3 \times .5^1 = \left(\frac{4!}{3!1!} \right) \times .125 \times .5$$

$$= \left(\frac{4 \times 3 \times 2 \times 1}{3 \times 2 \times 1 \times 1} \right) \times .0625$$

$$= 4 \times .0625$$

$$= .25$$

Four heads: $C_4^4 \times .5^4 \times .5^0 = \left(\dfrac{4!}{4!0!}\right) \times .0625 \times 1$

$$= \left(\dfrac{4 \times 3 \times 2 \times 1}{4 \times 3 \times 2 \times 1 \times 1}\right) \times .0625$$

$$= 1 \times .0625$$

$$= .0625$$

The binomial probability distribution can assist the public or nonprofit manager. Suppose, for example, that the Stermerville Public Works Department has been charged with racial discrimination in hiring practices. Last year, 40% of the persons who passed the department's civil service examination and were eligible to be hired were minorities. From this group, the Public Works Department hired 10 individuals; 2 were minorities. What is the probability that if the Stermerville Public Works Department did *not* discriminate, it would have hired two or fewer minorities? (Note that we assume, as a personnel analyst would have to in this situation, that anyone who passed the examination was capable of successful job performance. In other words, we assume that every individual had the same chance to be hired.)

The easiest way for the public administrator to answer this question is to identify n, r, p, and q first and then perform the necessary calculations. In this case, p, the probability that a minority is hired, is equal to the proportion of minorities in the job pool, or .4. And q, of course, is equal to $1 - p = 1 - .4 = .6$. The number of trials (n) in this case is equal to the number of persons hired, or 10. The number of successes (r) is equal to the number of minorities selected in this group, or 2. We are interested in the probability of two or fewer minorities being selected, so we must calculate the binomial probability distribution for two minorities, one minority, and zero minorities.

The probability calculations for two minorities are as follows:

$$C_r^n p^r q^{n-r} = \left(\dfrac{10!}{2!8!}\right) \times .4^2 \times .6^8$$

$$= 45 \times .4^2 \times .6^8$$

$$= 45 \times .16 \times .6^8$$

$$= 7.2 \times .6^8$$

$$= 7.2 \times 0.168$$

$$= .120$$

The probability calculations for one minority are as follows:

$$C_1^{10} \times .4^1 \times .6^9 = \left(\frac{10!}{1!9!}\right) \times .4 \times .6^9$$

$$= 10 \times .4 \times .6^9$$

$$= 4 \times .6^9$$

$$= 4 \times .010$$

$$= .040$$

The probability calculations for zero minorities are as follows:

$$C_0^{10} \times .4^0 \times .6^{10} = \left(\frac{10!}{0!10!}\right) \times .4^0 \times .6^{10}$$

$$= 1 \times .4^0 \times .6^{10}$$

$$= 1 \times 1 \times .6^{10}$$

$$= .006$$

Statistically, the public administrator can conclude that the probability that the Stermerville Public Works Department could select two or fewer minorities out of 10 individuals hired from a pool that consists of 40% minorities is .166 (.120 + .040 + .006 = .166) if the department shows no preference in regard to hiring minorities. In other words, a pattern such as this one could occur about 1 time in 6.

This is a statistical statement. As a manager, you have to arrive at managerial conclusions. You need to know whether the department is engaged in discrimination. The statistical finding is only one piece of evidence that a manager uses in arriving at a conclusion.

After receiving statistical information, the manager should always ask whether anything else could have produced a result similar to this one other than discrimination (or whatever other question is involved). For example, perhaps more minorities were offered jobs, but they turned them down for some reason. Sometimes it is helpful to examine past behavior. If last year the department hired 42% minorities, you might not be too concerned. If it hired only 20% minorities last year, you might become more concerned. The manager's task at this point is to examine all potential reasons why the statistical pattern occurred and eliminate them. Can you think of other causes for these statistical results?

If no other reason can be found to account for the statistical result ($p = .166$) other than discrimination, then the manager must decide how sure he or she wants to be. Because this pattern could have occurred by chance 16.6% of the time, if the manager concludes that discrimination has occurred, there is a 1 in 6 chance that he or she is wrong. There is no "magic number" for how sure a manager should be. Social scientists often use a probability of less than

5% for making decisions. Setting an arbitrary standard and using it in every case regardless of circumstances, however, is generally not a good idea for a manager. In some cases, a 5% risk is far too high. For example, would you authorize the launch of the space shuttle if there were a 5% chance of an explosion? Such a decision would mean that the manager would find it acceptable if 1 of every 20 launches resulted in an explosion (i.e., 50%). Other decisions might not require levels as low as .05. A probability of .25, or even .35, might be acceptable in deciding between two alternative methods of collecting trash. In short, the manager must take the responsibility for establishing a level of risk based on how important the decision is. The manager should never let his or her statistical analyst set the probability level. This decision requires managerial judgment based on an individual's experience and willingness to take risks. Managers would do well to remember that statistical analysts are rarely fired when the manager they report to makes a bad decision. In Chapter 11 we revisit the issue of how sure the manager should be.

Although the binomial probability distribution provides a good method for estimating the probability that a given number of events will occur, often the task of calculating the binomial probability distribution becomes complex mathematically. For example, suppose that instead of hiring 2 minorities out of 10 persons, the Stermerville Public Works Department hired 43 minorities out of 150 persons. These figures would require the following probability to be estimated:

$$C_{43}^{150} \times .4^{43} \times .6^{107}$$

The estimation of this term for the probability of hiring exactly 43 minorities is complex. In addition, because the binomial is a discrete probability distribution, we would need to estimate the probability of hiring 42, 41, 40 … 0 minorities out of 150 and add all these probabilities together! The difficulty (and tedium) in estimating this probability exceeds the patience of most individuals. In situations like this, however, the binomial probability distribution can be estimated fairly well by using the continuous normal probability distribution, which we presented in Chapter 7.

The Normal Curve and the Binomial Distribution

The utility of the binomial distribution is somewhat limited when the number of trials or the number of successes becomes large. For example, Bill Povalla, the head of the Chicago Equal Employment Commission, believes that the Chicago Transit Authority (CTA) discriminates against Republicans. The civil service records show that 37.5% of the individuals listed as passing the CTA exam were Republicans; the remainder were Democrats (let's assume no one registers as an independent in Illinois). The CTA hired 30 people last year: 25 Democrats and 5 Republicans. What is the probability that this situation could exist if CTA did not discriminate?

The binomial distribution could be used to determine this probability, with the following information:

p = .375, the probability of randomly hiring a Republican

q = 1 − p = .625

n = 30, the number of persons hired

r = 5, 4, 3, 2, 1, or 0, the number of Republicans hired (you need to know the probability of hiring five or fewer Republicans)

Calculating this probability would take the normal human being several hours. Using the normal curve is much faster.

Recall from Chapter 7 that to use the normal curve to determine a probability, you need to know the mean (μ) and the standard deviation (σ) of the population, as well as the raw score in question (x).

The mean of a probability distribution is equal to its expected value. The **expected value** is a long-term average or expectation across many trials or events. In this situation, consider if numerous clusters of 30 CTA eligibles were selected randomly, what would be the average number of Republicans hired? The average is equal to the number of persons, that is, the number of trials (30 hirings), hired times the probability of selecting a Republican in any one trial (.375), or 11.25. Thus, the mean or expected value is equal to 11.25. If CTA hires 30 people, and the probability of hiring a Republican in any one trial (hiring decision) is .375, we would expect to hire a mean of just over 11 Republicans (mean = 11.25).

The standard deviation of a probability distribution is defined by statisticians as

$$\sigma = \sqrt{np(1 - p)}$$

In this case, we have

$$\sigma = \sqrt{30 \times .375(1 - .375)}$$

$$= \sqrt{11.25 \times .625}$$

$$= \sqrt{7.03}$$

$$= 2.65$$

To determine the probability that five or fewer Republicans would be selected if the CTA hiring were nonpartisan, convert the number actually hired into a z score. Recalling from Chapter 7 the formula for calculating a z score or standard normal score, we find that

$$z = \frac{X - \mu}{\sigma}$$

Here, X is the score of interest or 5 (Republicans hired), μ is the mean or 11.25, and σ is the standard deviation or 2.65. Thus, the z score is equal to

$$\frac{5 - 11.25}{2.65} = -2.36 \text{ or } 2.36$$

Looking up a z score of 2.36 in the normal table (Statistical Table 1 in the back of the book), we find a value of .4909, indicating that more than 49% of the values fall between a z score of 2.36 and the mean. Converting this score to a probability (.5000 − .4909), we find the probability that 5 or fewer Republicans would be hired by the CTA if it were nonpartisan in its hiring is .0091. That is, if the CTA does not discriminate, there is less than a 1% chance that it would hire 30 people and that 5 or fewer of them would be Republicans. In other words, the CTA probably gives preference to Democrats for its vacancies. If you were Mr. Povalla, what would you do with this information?

When to Use the Normal Curve

The normal curve is a good approximation to the binomial distribution when $n \times p$ is greater than 10 and $n \times (1 - p)$ is greater than 10. If either of these conditions is not met, the binomial distribution should be used instead of the normal curve. In addition, the normal curve is continuous: It tells you the probability that r or fewer events occurred, or that r or more events occurred. It does not tell you the probability of exactly r events occurring. If you need to know the probability of a certain number of events occurring (rather than the probability of r events), you must use the (discrete) binomial distribution.

Chapter Summary

The binomial probability distribution can be used whenever the outcome of any trial can be classified into one of two mutually exclusive and jointly exhaustive outcomes; one outcome is termed a success and the other a failure; and each trial is independent of the other trials. To determine a probability by using the binomial probability distribution, you must know the number of trials (n), the number of successes (r), the probability of a success in any one trial (p), and the probability of failure ($q = 1 - p$).

The probability of an event for the binomial probability distribution can be calculated by using the formula

$$C_r^n p^r q^{(n-r)}$$

where C_r^n is the number of combinations of n things taken r at a time. The formula for a combination is

$$C_r^n = \frac{n!}{r!(n - r)!}$$

In circumstances in which $n \times p$ is greater than 10 and $n \times (1 - p)$ is greater than 10, the normal probability distribution can be used to approximate the binomial probability distribution. As explained in Chapter 7, the z score is used to find probabilities in the normal distribution. The formula for the z score is

$$z = \frac{X - \mu}{\sigma}$$

where X is a score of interest (here, the number of successes), μ is the mean or expected value, and σ is the standard deviation. To use the normal distribution to approximate the binomial probability distribution, the mean (μ) is equal to $n \times p$, the standard deviation (σ) is equal to the square root of $n \times p \times (1 - p)$, and X is equal to the number of successes (r).

Problems

8.1 The state legislative council has been charged with sex discrimination in hiring. Last year it hired only 3 women out of 12 new employees. The civil service lists show that women comprise 40% of the qualified applicants for these jobs. What is the probability of hiring three or fewer women if the legislative council does not discriminate? Show all calculations.

8.2 The World Hunger Network administers a test to all applicants to measure their knowledge of the problem of world hunger. The name of the test is "The Hungry-I." The Hungry-I has been standardized so that it has a mean of 100 and a standard deviation of 10 (if you do not recall the process of standardizing a test, please refer to Chapter 7). What percent of applicants to the World Hunger Network score above 130? What percent score between 90 and 110? What percent score less than 80? What percent score between 120 and 130? Explain how you could use Figure 7.2 to answer these questions.

8.3 The foreign service exam gives a passing grade to only the top 10% of those taking the exam. The mean score is 84, with a standard deviation of 8. What should be the minimum passing grade?

8.4 In a grand jury case, a bookstore was indicted in Oklahoma County on several counts of selling an obscene book. The grand jury was composed of 22 Baptists and 8 other people. The defendant feels that Baptists are biased against free speech. What is the probability that 22 or more Baptists are selected on a jury if Oklahoma County is 40% Baptist?

8.5 Mary Doyle ran against Bernie Hobson for state senate. In one precinct, one of the two voting machines did not work, and 182 votes were cast on the broken machine. Mary needed to receive 177 of the 182 votes to win the election. On the other machine in the precinct, Mary received 51% of the votes. Assignment of voters to ballot boxes is independent. What is the probability that Mary won the election?

8.6 Over the past 50 years, one-half of all cities that apply have received mass transportation grants from the federal government. In the last round of grants, eight southern cities applied but none received a grant. Assume that all cities were equally qualified to receive the grants. What is the probability that no southern city receives a grant? The Southern Governors' Association is considering bringing a lawsuit against the federal government for discrimination in the awarding of the transportation grants. Do you think that the Southern Governors' Association would have a strong case or a weak case? How would you advise the association to proceed?

8.7 Seaman David Brady is one of 16 seamen in Petty Officer Rickels's unit. Every day four seamen are assigned to chip paint, and the others are assigned to screen movies to see if they are suitable for viewing. Seaman Brady believes that Rickels does not like him because he has been assigned to the paint detail 16 times in the past 20 days. What can you tell Seaman Brady?

8.8 The Procurement Bureau runs tests on 30 brand X teletype machines. It finds that an average of three machines fail in any 1 day period. Against the bureau's advice, the Public Affairs Department purchased 140 of these machines for all state offices. On the first day, 26 machines fail. What is the probability that this would happen if the true failure rate were 10%?

8.9 This year, 620 persons are nominated to participate in the president's Management Internship Program. After screening, 212 are selected for the program. Maxwell George University nominates five persons, and all five receive awards. What is the probability that this event would occur if the events were independent and all nominees are equally qualified?

8.10 Refer to Problem 8.9. Of the 620 nominees, 211 are women; and of these, 91 are selected. Is there any preference with regard to sex?

8.11 Past experience has shown that 60% of all captains are promoted to major. The 819th Infantry Division has 48 captains who are eligible for promotion. Nine of these captains are West Point graduates. Eight of the nine West Pointers are promoted. Is there any reason to suspect that West Point graduates are given preferential treatment? Why? Show your work.

8.12 If one-third of the University of Wisconsin teaching assistants (TAs) sign a petition calling for a collective bargaining election, an election will be held. A survey of 50 TAs indicates that 40% will sign the petition. What is the probability that a sample such as this could have occurred if one-third or fewer of the TAs in the population will sign such a petition?

8.13 The area supervisor of the Occupational Safety and Health Administration (OSHA) has heard a story that a certain inspector is not enforcing safety regulations. Past statistics reveal that inspectors find safety violations in 91% of all inspections. The supervisor pulls the files for the eight most recent inspections for the inspector whose behavior is questioned. These files reveal that safety violations were cited in two of the eight cases. Analyze these data and present a statistical conclusion.

8.14 The BFOQ Job Training Corporation believes that it has a new program that will increase job placements. Essentially, the corporation thinks that if it runs its trainees through a simulated interview before sending them out on a job interview, their likelihood of getting the job increases. BFOQ randomly selects 36 individuals of relatively equal skills on a matched-pair basis. Eighteen of these individuals are run through the simulation. BFOQ then sends one pair, one person who went through the training and one person who did not, to interview for one of 18 different jobs. (These individuals are the only ones to interview for the jobs.) Thirteen of the 18 persons who went through the simulation get the jobs. What is the probability that 13 of the 18 would get jobs if there were no difference between the two sets of 18 persons? Show your work.

8.15 The Bureau of Paperwork wants to know whether agency personnel prefer to use health maintenance organizations (HMOs) for their health care benefits. If more than 25% favor using HMOs, then the bureau will begin to set up procedures for this type of health care. A sample of 100 of the bureau's personnel reveals that 29 favor the use of HMOs. What is the probability that less than 25% of the bureau's employees favor the use of HMOs? [*Hint*: If 25% (mean) or less of all bureau employees favor use of HMOs, what is the probability of obtaining a sample in which 29 out of 100 personnel are in favor?]

8.16 The Bluefield Regional Employment Service needs to place five individuals in jobs this week to meet its yearly quota. During the past several years, the service's track record is that every person sent to interview for a job has a .6 probability of getting the job. The placements appear to be independent of each other. The service decides to send seven individuals for interviews this week. Based on what you know, what is the probability that the service will make its yearly quota this week?

8.17 The Department of the Treasury is concerned because one member of Congress has charged that by normal accounting standards, one-third of all savings and loans (S&Ls) in the country are bankrupt. To refute this claim, chief economist Tom Holbrook takes a sample of six S&Ls and finds that only one is insolvent (his staff had intended to gather a larger sample, but they were too busy processing S&L failures). If the true proportion of insolvencies is one-third, what is the probability that the Treasury Department would get the results that it did?

Some Special Probability Distributions

Although the normal curve and the binomial distribution cover a great many of the situations faced by nonprofit and public managers, in certain circumstances special probability distributions should be used. For example, assume that a finite number of persons apply for agency jobs and you want to know whether the agency discriminates. Or suppose that you need to determine the probability that an event will occur but have no idea about the number of trials. Or perhaps a fire department wants to know how long it can expect to wait between major fires. For situations similar to these, special probability distributions should be used. We will discuss three such distributions in this chapter: the hypergeometric probability distribution, the Poisson distribution, and the exponential probability distribution.

The Hypergeometric Probability Distribution

The Andersonville City Fire Department contends that its civil service examination for firefighters is valid; that is, it feels that anyone who passes the examination is qualified to be a firefighter. Last year, 100 persons passed the firefighter examination, 66 men and 34 women. From this list of 100 persons, a fire academy class of 30 was chosen: 24 men and 6 women. One woman who was not selected filed a complaint with the federal Equal Employment Opportunity Commission (EEOC), alleging discrimination. Three years later, the EEOC decided it will hear the case. The question is: How probable is it that Andersonville does not discriminate against women and would by chance admit six or fewer women to the fire academy class in question?

This question could be answered by using the normal curve to approximate the binomial probability distribution. The normal distribution, however, assumes that the population from which the trials are drawn is infinite. In the present situation, though, the population consists of those persons who passed the firefighter exam, and 100 is a long way from infinity. If the normal curve and the binomial probability distribution were used, in this case the probability estimates would be conservative—that is, the test would be less likely to show discrimination.

With a finite population, the **hypergeometric probability distribution** should be used. To use the hypergeometric distribution, you need to know the same things that were needed for the normal curve, plus the size of the population. The mean of the hypergeometric probability distribution is the distribution's expected value:

$$\mu = n \times p$$

In this case, μ equals 30 times .34 (the probability that a woman would be chosen at random), or 10.2. This mean is the same as the mean for the binomial distribution (see Chapter 8).

The standard deviation for the hypergeometric distribution is as follows:

$$\sigma = \sqrt{\left(\frac{N_p - n}{N_p - 1}\right)(np)(1 - p)}$$

where N_p is the size of the population, n is the number of trials, and p is the probability of success. The only difference between this standard deviation and the one for the binomial distribution is the ratio. $[(N_p - n)/(N_p - 1)]$.

Substituting the respective values into the formula for the standard deviation, we have

$$\sigma = \sqrt{\left(\frac{100 - 30}{100 - 1}\right) \times 30 \times .34 \times .66}$$

$$= \sqrt{\frac{70}{99} \times 30 \times .34 \times .66}$$

$$= \sqrt{.71 \times 30 \times .34 \times .66}$$

$$= \sqrt{4.78} = 2.19$$

Given a mean of 10.2 and a standard deviation of 2.19, is it probable that Andersonville could have randomly selected only six females for its firefighter class? Converting 6 into a z score, we find

$$z = \frac{x - \mu}{\sigma} = \frac{6 - 10.2}{2.19} = -1.92$$

Using the z score of -1.92 and the normal distribution table, we find the probability is .0274 that Andersonville could select six or fewer women given that it had no preference in regard to sex.

Had we used the binomial distribution in this example, the probability would have been higher. Calculate this probability in the space provided. Be sure to use the normal approximation to the binomial distribution with $n = 30$, $r = 6$ or less, and $p = .34$ (see Chapter 8).

If you found a probability of .0526, congratulations! If you did not, please refer to Chapter 8. Because most social scientists require a probability of .05 or less to reach a conclusion, why is it important to use the hypergeometric distribution in this situation?

The Poisson Distribution

The **Poisson distribution** is a probability distribution that describes a pattern of behavior when some event occurs at varying, random intervals over a continuum of time, length, or space. Such a pattern of behavior is called a **Poisson process**. For example, if we graphed the number of muggings in Chickasaw, Oklahoma, on a time dimension, we might find the following (where the Xs represent muggings):

```
+———— X —— X ——————————— XXX ———————— X ———— X —+
12:00 P.M.                                            12:00 A.M.
```

The number of potholes per foot on South Flood Street in Normal, Oklahoma, also follows a Poisson process, as shown in the following diagram:

```
+——— XX ——— XX — X ——— XXXX — X — X — X —+
0 feet                                      500 feet
```

In theory, each of these continuums can be divided into equal segments such that no more than one event (pothole, mugging) occurs in each segment. Every equal segment of Flood Street would either have a pothole or not have a pothole. In addition, for the process to be a Poisson process, the occurrence or nonoccurrence of any event must not affect the probability that other events will occur. That is, the fact that a pothole occurs at 621 South Flood Street does not affect whether or not a pothole occurs at 527 South Flood.

Up to this point, the process fits the description of a Bernoulli process: An event either occurs (success) or it does not (failure), and events are independent of each other. To determine the probability of any event when using the Bernoulli process, we need to know the probability of the event (p), the number of successes (r), and the number of trials (n). In the present situation, we could empirically determine the probability of a mugging occurring in Chickasaw during any time period (p). In this case, Chickasaw might experience .3 mugging per hour. Note that probabilities are based on time, length, or space. The number of successes (r) could also be determined. We can count the number of muggings in any period. We do not, however, know the number of trials. How many potential muggings were there in Chickasaw? This information cannot be determined. The major difference between a Poisson process and a Bernoulli process, then, is that the number of trials is not known in a Poisson process.

We illustrate the use of the Poisson distribution with an example. The Elazar Rape Crisis Center wants to staff its crisis hot line so that a center member will always be present if a rape victim calls. The Crisis Center operates between the hours of 6:00 P.M. and 6:00 A.M. By examining the past records of the center, the director has determined that the mean number of rapes per hour is .05. This information can be determined from police records.

The first question is: What is the probability that no rapes will occur on any given night? The steps in using the Poisson probability distribution are as follows:

Step 1: Adjust the mean to reflect the number of hours (length or space) you want to consider. In the present example, the mean number of rapes in an hour is .05. You want to know the mean number of rapes in 12 hours. Because these events are independent, the mean (or expected value) for a 12-hour period is .6 (.05 × 12). This new mean adjusted to the period of interest is called λ the Greek letter lambda (some texts refer to it as λ_t or "lambda t").

Step 2: To determine the probability of zero rapes, you need to refer to the Poisson distribution tables (Table 2 in the Statistical Tables at the end of the book). For those of you who feel that using a table is cheating, exact probabilities can be calculated with the following formula:

$$y = \frac{\lambda^x e^{-\lambda}}{x!}$$

where λ is the probability of the event, x is the number of occurrences, e is a constant (2.71828), and y is the probability of x occurrences. If you value your time, turn to Table 2. Scanning across the top of the table, locate λ equal to .6. You should find the following information:

x	$\frac{\lambda}{.6}$
0	.5488
1	.3293
2	.0988
3	.0198
4	.0030
5	.0004
6	.0000

This table gives a Poisson probability distribution for $\lambda = .6$. It tells you that if $\lambda = .6$, the probability of no (0) rapes in a single night is .5488. The probability of exactly one rape is .3293. The probability of exactly two rapes is .0988, and so on.

How might this information be used in a public or nonprofit management setting? Suppose that the director believes (based on past experience) that assisting a rape victim takes about 4 hours. One crisis center staff member remains with the victim for this period to assist with the medical treatment and police procedures. If the center had one staff member and two rapes occurred in a 4-hour period, then no one would be at the center to assist the second victim. The director wants to avoid this situation. How many staff members should be at the center?

Step 1: Adjust the mean to the time period. The mean is .05 for 1 hour, and you want to know about 4-hour periods (the amount of time a staff member will be away from the center). Therefore, λ is .2 (.05 $\times$ 4).

Step 2: Find the probabilities in the Poisson distribution table for 0, 1, 2, 3, 4, and 5 rapes when λ is .2.

Number of Rapes	Probability
0	.8187
1	.1637
2	.0164
3	.0011
4	.0001
5	.0000

To make the staffing decision, the director uses the preceding table. If 0 or 1 rape occurs in a 4-hour period, one staff member is sufficient. This situation will occur in 98% of the 4-hour periods (.8187 + .1637 = .9824). Because the director wants to minimize the time during which the crisis center cannot respond, the probability is interpreted as follows: If the crisis center staffs only one employee, this staffing arrangement will be inadequate 1.8% of the time periods (1 − .9324 = 0.176 or about 1.8%). Because the 12-hour day is equivalent to three 4-hour periods, a rape with no one present will occur on 5.4% (1.8% $\times$ 3) of the days (or about once every 3 weeks). The director considers this risk unacceptable.

If two staff members are stationed at the crisis center, the probability of sufficient staff is .9988. Translating this into days when a rape will occur with no one at the crisis center (.0012 $\times$ 3 = .0036, or .36%) reveals that the staff will be inadequate .36% of the days, or once every 278 days (36 times in 10,000 days). The staff director feels that this risk is tolerable and decides to staff two persons.

(**Note:** Staffing three persons would increase the probability of sufficient staff to .9999. This means inadequate staff problems would occur once every 10,000 days.)

You may have noticed that the Poisson probability tables give values only for λ less than or equal to 20. Poisson tables for larger λ values are not presented because the normal distribution table provides fairly accurate probabilities when λ is greater than 20. The normal distribution of this magnitude has a mean of λ and a standard deviation equal to the square root of λ. For a λ value of 30, therefore, you would use the normal table with a mean of 30 and a standard deviation of $5.5(\sqrt{30} = 5.5)$.

The Exponential Probability Distribution

The **exponential probability distribution** is used when the manager wants to know the most probable length of time between independent events. In the Elazar Rape Crisis Center example, the director might want to know the most probable length of time between rapes in order to plan procedures at the center. The exponential probability distribution is also used for scheduling. For example, it can be used to determine the time between arrivals at a municipal hospital, the time between fires in a city, the time between people's calls to the museum to find out how to volunteer, or the time between clients visiting the legal aid center. This information can be quite useful to a manager in scheduling her or his workforce.

The calculation procedures for the exponential probability distribution are complex. As a result, we will not discuss them in this book. But you should be aware that the exponential probability distribution exists and that it can be used to schedule activities when events occur randomly. If the need for this distribution arises, we suggest that a statistician be hired to deal with the problem. For large problems, such as scheduling police calls in a large city, computer programs are available.

Chapter Summary

This chapter introduced three special probability distributions used in public and nonprofit management. The hypergeometric probability distribution is used with finite populations when one knows the number of trials (each trial is independent), the number of successes, and the probability of a success. The Poisson probability distribution is used whenever events are independent and occur at varying random intervals of time, length, or space. The exponential probability distribution is used to estimate the length of time between independently occurring events. The chapter presented the formulas and examples for the hypergeometric probability distribution and the Poisson probability distribution to illustrate their application to public and nonprofit management. Because the calculations involved in the exponential probability distribution are more complex, we explained the distribution and recommended that you seek expert assistance should you need to apply it to managerial situations.

Problems

9.1 One hundred cities (60 are northern cities) apply for Comprehensive Employment and Training Act (CETA) grants to train the unemployed. Fifty grants are awarded, 40 to northern cities. Is there any anti–Sun Belt bias?

9.2 The mean number of crime reports filed per hour by the Millennium City Police Department is 0.833. What is the probability that in a 24-hour period 10 or fewer crime reports will be filed by the Millennium City Police Department? What is the probability that the Department will file 20 or more crime reports in a 24-hour period?

9.3 Police chief Lenny Lawnorder has heard through a normally reliable source that 30% of his officers are not using regulation handguns. To see whether this is true, Lenny randomly inspects 35 of his 200 officers. Seventeen have nonregulation handguns. If the true proportion is .3, what is the probability that this event will occur?

9.4 In Berksdale, Nebraska, the mean number of major fires is .071 on any given day. What is the probability that no major fires will occur in Berksdale in any given week (7 days)? What is the probability that more than four major fires will occur?

9.5 In the First Army, 150 first lieutenants were up for promotion to captain (35 of these were West Point graduates). Of these, 120 were promoted, including 24 West Pointers. Does the Army discriminate in promotions?

9.6 The mean number of teletype machines in the Bureau of Communications that break down is .625 in any given hour. If repairs take 8 hours, how many repair people should the Bureau of Communications staff?

9.7 Congressman Lester Asperin has charged that 50% of all IRS agents would fail a simple test on tax law. IRS Commissioner John Tight believes no more than 15% would fail. Of the 1,000 agents, 200 are randomly selected and given the test, and 60 fail. What is the probability that Asperin is correct? What is the probability that Tight is correct?

9.8 The mean number of murders reported in Metro City during the 8-hour graveyard shift is .5 for any hour. It takes two people 2 hours to investigate a homicide call. How many officers should be assigned to the homicide squad during these hours?

9.9 Refer to Problem 8.10 on page 155, where 91 of the 211 women nominated for the president's Management Internship Program are selected and 212 of the 620 total nominees are accepted. Use what you have learned in this chapter to determine the probability of this happening if all persons are equally qualified. What can you say if you do not assume equal qualifications?

9.10 The mean number of contracts that consulting firms receive with the Department of Human Services is .4 for any given year. Ecosystems Inc., a heavy contributor to political candidates, receives three contracts in 1 year. What is the probability that this event would occur by chance? What is the probability that Ecosystems will receive six contracts in 2 years?

9.11 The Madison Fire Department's files reveal that an average of six firefighters a year suffer heart attacks while on duty. The personnel office is concerned about this because it must budget funds for disabilities. There are some concerns that the physical condition of firefighters is getting worse. This year, nine firefighters suffered heart attacks. What is the probability that an event of this severity will occur? Given past history, what is the probability that no heart attacks will occur? Exactly one? Exactly two? Three or fewer?

9.12 The mean number of water main breaks is .4 per hour. In a 10-hour night shift, four mains break. What is the probability of exactly four mains breaking? Of four or more breaking? Which probability tells you the most about the chance of this situation happening?

9.13 The Nuclear Regulatory Commission estimates that the probability that a Westinghouse X-27 nuclear plant's warning system will fail in a year's time is .1. New York Power and Light operates six of the X-27 plants; last year one failed. What is the probability that one or more plants' warning systems will fail?

9.14 The mean number of fires per hour in Smallsville, Utah, is .1042. What is the probability that Smallsville will experience no fires on any given day? Five or more fires on any given day?

9.15 The Bureau of Paperwork has 1,000 employees, and the personnel division wants to know whether agency personnel prefer to use HMOs for their health care benefits. If more than 25% favor using HMOs, then the bureau will begin to set up procedures for this type of health care. A sample of 100 of the bureau's personnel reveals that 29 favor the use of HMOs. What is the probability that less than 25% of the bureau's employees favor the use of HMOs? [*Hint*: If 25% (mean) or less of bureau personnel favor use of HMOs, what is the probability of obtaining a sample in which 29 out of 100 are in favor?]

9.16 The University of Wisconsin employs 200 teaching assistants (TAs). If one-third of the TAs sign a petition calling for a collective bargaining election, an election will be held. A survey of 50 TAs indicates that 40% will sign the petition. What is the probability that a sample such as this could have occurred if one-third or fewer of the TAs in the population will sign such a petition?

9.17 Irena Blazes, the fire chief of Flares, Oregon, wants to introduce volunteers into the department but fears that employees will resist volunteers. Chief Blazes would like to use volunteers and wants to avoid potential labor problems. She has decided to introduce volunteers if 60% of the employees agree to work with them. She administers a survey to all 150 paid firefighters, and 90 respond. Among these 90 firefighters, 62 say that they agree to work with volunteers and accept them in the workplace. Given the results of this survey, should Chief Blazes proceed with her plans to introduce volunteer firefighters? What is the probability that she could obtain the survey results if 60% or fewer of the (paid) firefighters were willing to accept volunteers?

Inferential Statistics

Introduction to Inference

W hen statistics are used to summarize the distribution of a given sample or population, we call this summarizing **descriptive statistics**. In descriptive statistics, we use statistical techniques to describe and summarize data. **Inferential statistics** is the use of quantitative techniques to generalize from a sample to a population. In short, with inferential statistics, we hope to use a small subset or sample of data to infer what all the data or the population look like.

For example, the city officials in Pittsburgh, Pennsylvania, would like to know how pleased Pittsburgh citizens are with their new bus service. The best way to do this would be to ask every citizen of Pittsburgh how he or she feels about the transit system. Because the population of Pittsburgh is about 350,000 people, this interviewing could take forever (not to mention that it would cost more to do that than to run the transit system). An alternative is to randomly select a subset of persons (say, 100) and ask them about the mass transit system. From this sample, we will infer what the people of Pittsburgh think.

In this chapter, we begin the presentation of inferential statistics by reviewing some basic definitions and describing some simple inferential techniques.

Some Definitions

A **population** is the total set of items that we are concerned about. In the preceding example, the population is all the people who live in Pittsburgh, Pennsylvania.

A measure that is used to summarize a population is called a **parameter**. For example, the mean education level in Pittsburgh is 12.9 years. This measure is a parameter. Thus far in this book, we have discussed a variety of parameters, including the mean, the median, and the standard deviation of the population.

A **sample** is a subset of a population. In this text, we will assume that all samples are selected randomly. A random sample is a sample in which every member of the population has an equal chance of being included. If a sample is not a random sample, then the rules of statistical inference introduced here do not necessarily hold.

A **statistic** is a measure that is used to summarize a sample. The mean, the standard deviation, and the median of a sample are all statistics.

Table 10.1	Symbols for Parameters and Statistics	
Measure	Population Parameter	Sample Statistic
Mean	μ	$\overline{X}$
Standard deviation	σ	s
Number of cases	N	n

© Cengage Learning 2015

To create a bit more complexity in the interest of clarity, statisticians use different symbols for the mean and the standard deviation, depending on whether they are parameters or statistics. Table 10.1 illustrates the symbols.

The mean is always calculated the same way whether the data are taken from a sample or a population. The standard deviation, however, is calculated differently. Recall that the formula for calculating the standard deviation is

$$\sigma = \sqrt{\dfrac{\displaystyle\sum_{i=1}^{N}(X_i - \mu)^2}{N}}$$

The formula for the standard deviation of a sample is similar, with one slight twist:

$$s = \sqrt{\dfrac{\displaystyle\sum_{i=1}^{N}(X_i - \overline{X})^2}{n - 1}}$$

The difference here is that the sum of the squared deviations from the mean is divided by $n - 1$ rather than by N. Later in this chapter, we will explain why this correction is made.

Estimating a Population Mean

The best estimate of the population mean μ is the mean of the sample $\overline{X}$. To illustrate why this is true, we will use the data in Table 10.2, which lists the number of arrests by all 10 Yukon, Oklahoma, police officers in 2014.

The mean number of arrests by Yukon police officers is 15.0. But in circumstances where the population parameter cannot be calculated, either because the population is too large or because the data are not available, the mean of a sample can be used to estimate the population mean.

Assume that we took a random sample of five Yukon police officers and calculated the mean for those five as follows (the sample was selected by using a random number table):

Officers in Sample	Arrests	Mean
1, 3, 2, 8, 4	14, 10, 16, 20, 18	15.6

Table 10.2	Number of Arrests by Police Officers in Yukon, Oklahoma, 2014
Police Officer	Number of Arrests, 2014
1	14
2	16
3	10
4	18
5	8
6	15
7	17
8	20
9	19
10	13

© Cengage Learning 2015

The sample mean is one estimate of the population mean. Note that although our estimate is close (15.6 compared to 15.0), it is not exact. This discrepancy occurs because of sampling error—that is, our sample is not perfectly representative of the population. We would expect, however, that if we took numerous samples of five, the average sample mean (i.e., the average of the sample means) would approach the population mean. Let's try it. The data and calculations are shown in Table 10.3.*

Notice how the average sample mean quickly approaches the population mean and fluctuates around it. Statisticians have worked out this general problem and have logically demonstrated that the average sample mean over the long run will equal the population mean. The best estimate of the population mean, therefore, is the sample mean.

Estimating a Population Standard Deviation

The best estimate of the population standard deviation σ is the sample standard deviation s. Remember that s has $n - 1$ as a denominator rather than **N**. Again, let's use the Yukon police arrests example to illustrate the estimating accuracy of the sample standard deviation. The population standard deviation is 3.7. (If you do not believe us, calculate it from the data in Table 10.2.)

Drawing a sample of five officers, we get the estimate of the standard deviation shown in Table 10.4 (note that we use the same sample in this illustration that we used before).

---

*An entire field of statistics has developed around the idea of taking repeated samples with replacement. See Mooney and Duval (1993).

Table 10.3	Calculating the Average Sample Mean from Samples of Five			
	Officers in Sample	Number of Arrests	Sample Mean	Average of Means
	1, 3, 2, 8, 4	14, 10, 16, 20, 18	15.6	15.6
	1, 6, 8, 3, 4	14, 15, 20, 10, 18	15.4	15.5
	7, 4, 1, 5, 9	17, 18, 14, 8, 19	15.2	15.4
	2, 10, 7, 4, 6	16, 13, 17, 18, 15	15.8	15.5
	7, 10, 3, 6, 5	17, 13, 10, 15, 8	12.6	14.9
	10, 7, 2, 1, 4	13, 17, 16, 14, 18	15.6	15.0
	10, 3, 7, 4, 2	13, 10, 17, 18, 16	14.8	15.0
	10, 3, 8, 9, 4	13, 10, 20, 19, 18	16.0	15.1
	6, 4, 8, 9, 10	15, 18, 20, 19, 13	17.0	15.3
	2, 8, 4, 1, 5	16, 20, 18, 14, 8	15.2	15.3
	8, 3, 9, 10, 5	20, 10, 19, 13, 8	14.0	15.2
	2, 3, 7, 5, 1	16, 10, 17, 8, 14	13.0	15.0
	10, 8, 5, 6, 4	13, 20, 8, 15, 18	14.8	15.0
	9, 3, 6, 2, 7	19, 10, 15, 16, 17	15.4	15.0

© Cengage Learning

Table 10.4	Calculating s for a Sample of Five		
Officer	Arrests	Arrests − Mean	Squared
1	14	−1.6	2.56
3	10	−5.6	31.36
2	16	.4	.16
8	20	4.4	19.36
4	18	2.4	5.76
		$s = \sqrt{59.2 \div 4} = 3.85$	59.20 sum of squares

© Cengage Learning

Our estimate of the population standard deviation is 3.85, which is close to the population value of 3.7. Note that had we divided by n rather than by $n - 1$, the standard deviation estimate would have been 3.4. Dividing by n gives us a consistently low estimate of the population standard deviation. For this reason, the estimate *always* is made with a denominator of $n - 1$.

Most statistical programs calculate the sample standard deviation, not the population standard deviation. When you use a statistical package, you need to be aware of this fact.

The Standard Error

If you reported that the mean arrests per police officer in Yukon was 15.6, your supervisor might ask you if the mean was exactly 15.6. Your answer would be that you do not know but that your best estimate of the mean is 15.6. Your superior might then ask how good an estimate 15.6 is. Your superior really wants to know the range of values that the mean must fall within—that is, how much error can the mean estimate contain?

One way to answer this question is to take numerous samples, calculate a mean for each sample, and show the supervisor the range of mean estimates. If you wanted to be more sophisticated, you might calculate a standard deviation for all the mean estimates. The standard deviation for mean estimates has a special name; it is called the **standard error of the mean**.

Fortunately for the sanity of most management analysts, one does not need to take numerous samples, calculate a mean for each sample, and then calculate a standard deviation for the mean estimates to find the standard error of the mean. Statisticians have demonstrated that a good estimate of the standard error of the mean can be made with the following formula:

$$\text{s.e.} = \frac{\sigma}{\sqrt{n}}$$

where s.e. is the standard error of the mean, σ is the standard deviation of the population, and n is the sample size. Because we rarely know the population standard deviation, the estimated standard deviation can be used in computations:

$$\text{s.e.} = \frac{s}{\sqrt{n}}$$

Sometimes the symbol $S_{\bar{Y}}$ is used for the standard error of the mean to indicate that it is the standard deviation of mean estimates.

In the present example, we have a mean estimate of 15.6, a standard deviation estimate of 3.85, and a sample size of 5. Substituting these values into the equation for the standard error, we get

$$\text{s.e.} = \frac{3.85}{\sqrt{5}} = \frac{3.85}{2.236} = 1.7$$

How Sample Size Affects the Standard Error

The Yukon arrest data represent an ideal scenario as far as sampling is concerned. Because there were only 10 officers in the entire population, the chances of obtaining an accurate estimate of the population mean from a sample of 5 officers were very good. In the real world, we rarely have the time or resources to gather samples that are literally half the size of the population in question. For example, polling organizations typically use random samples in the range of 1,200 to 1,500 registered voters to make inferences about how tens of millions of voters are likely to vote in presidential elections. Because the goal of inference is to make a statement about the population based on one sample, what impact can sample size have on our results?

Statisticians have determined that larger samples generally provide better estimates of the population mean than smaller samples (provided the sampling method is not arbitrary or biased). This is true because the size of the standard error for larger samples is typically less than it is for smaller samples.

An example with real data will help illustrate this point. One of the authors has data on grades for a population of 283 public administration students. The data are normally distributed, with a mean of 79.3 and a standard deviation of 11.4. Using these data, we generated six random samples: three samples where $n = 5$ (for each sample) and three samples where $n = 35$ (for each sample). Table 10.5 presents the means, standard deviations, and standard errors.

Note that the means and standard deviations for the three larger samples are much closer to the true population values than the means and standard deviations for the smaller samples. The standard errors for the smaller samples are consistently larger than those for the larger samples. The results illustrate that larger samples typically do a better job at capturing the characteristics present in the population than do smaller samples.

Although there is no guarantee that we will always obtain a smaller standard error when using larger samples, well-known statistical principles called the **central limit theorem** and the **law of large numbers** form the basis for the idea that larger samples are generally more reflective of population characteristics than smaller samples.

If using larger samples is more desirable, how does an analyst determine the appropriate sample size? Statisticians have found that beyond a certain point,

Table 10.5	The Impact of Sample Size on the Standard Error	
	Three Samples ($n = 5$)	**Three Samples ($n = 35$) each)**
	Sample 1: $\overline{X} = 72.4$	Sample 1: $\overline{X} = 77.9$
	$s = 5.89$	$s = 10.88$
	s.e. $= 2.64$	s.e. $= 1.84$
	Sample 2: $\overline{X} = 87.6$	Sample 2: $\overline{X} = 78.43$
	$s = 9.20$	$s = 11.55$
	s.e. $= 4.11$	s.e. $= 1.95$
	Sample 3: $\overline{X} = 78.8$	Sample 3: $\overline{X} = 75.37$
	$s = 9.34$	$s = 11.22$
	s.e. $= 4.18$	s.e. $= 1.89$

© Cengage Learning

adding additional cases to a sufficiently large sample will have a limited effect on the quality and accuracy of the inferences we make about a population. How do we know when we have a sufficiently large sample? We will elaborate the formulas and steps used to determine appropriate sample size in Chapters 11 and 12.

The *t* Distribution

Sample estimates of a population mean fit a probability distribution called **Student's *t* distribution** or simply the **_t_ distribution**. The *t* distribution is a sampling distribution. In other words, if we repeatedly took samples, calculated means for each sample, and plotted them on a graph, the sample means would eventually take on a shape similar to that of the normal distribution.

The *t* distribution allows us to determine the probability of drawing a random sample with a particular mean and standard deviation, given a known or hypothesized population mean. In simpler terms, when we draw a random sample and calculate the mean, the *t* distribution enables us to evaluate which of the following statements is more likely to be correct:

The sample mean is statistically indistinguishable from the known (or hypothesized) population mean. As a result, there is a high probability that we could draw a sample with this mean from the given population.

The sample mean is statistically different from the known (or hypothesized) population mean. As a result, there is a low probability that we could draw a sample with this mean from the given population.

The interpretation of *t* scores is similar to that of *z* scores, or "standard normal scores" (see Chapter 7). Recall that as *z* scores become larger, the data points associated with the scores fall increasingly away from the mean. As *t* scores become larger, the values for the sample means in question fall increasingly away from the population mean to which they are being compared. In other words, as the distance between the sample mean and the population mean grows, it becomes less likely that the sample mean could have come from a population with that population mean. When we interpret *t* scores, we use this information to make judgments about whether a sample mean is similar to or different from a population mean.

When a sample has 30 cases or more, the normal distribution can be used in place of the *t* distribution. The *t* distribution resembles the normal distribution but has a flatter shape. Unlike the normal distribution, the *t* distribution differs for each sample size. To use the *t* distribution, the public or nonprofit manager needs to know the *degrees of freedom* (df), which corresponds to sample size and identifies the appropriate *t* values. For a sample mean, the degrees of freedom are $n - 1$. In our earlier example, we have four degrees of freedom. The *t* distribution is found in Table 3 in the Appendix of Statistical Tables. Note that rather than printing a large table for every sample size, only key values of the *t* distribution are printed.

To illustrate, if we wish to know between what two numbers 95% of the mean estimates will fall, we calculate the following estimates:

$$X \pm \text{s.e.} \times t$$

This formula is simply the mean estimate plus or minus the standard error times the appropriate t score. If we want the t score for a 95% **confidence limit**, we know that there must be 2.5% in each tail of the curve (to total 5%), so we look up the t score for .025 with four degrees of freedom. This figure is 2.78. The upper 95% confidence limit is $15.6 + (1.7 \times 2.78)$, or 20.3. The lower limit is $15.6 - (1.7 \times 2.78)$, or 10.9. We can be 95% sure (95% "confident") that the average number of arrests by Yukon police officers is between 10.9 and 20.3.

An Example

Several years ago, the Wiese school system was criticized because the average Wiese High School (WHS) graduate could read at only the ninth-grade level. After this report was made public, a special reading program was established to upgrade skills. The WHS principal wants to know whether the reading program has improved reading scores. If it has, she will request that an accreditation team visit the school. If the program has not improved the reading level to at least 10.0 (sophomore level), the administrator would like to avoid the embarrassment of a poor review.

To determine the average reading level of the senior class, we select 10 seniors at random. We assume that reading scores are normally distributed. The reading scores for these 10 seniors are shown in Table 10.6. We proceed as follows:

Step 1: Estimate the population mean. Calculate the sample mean reading score in the space provided next to Table 10.6. The answer should be 10.6.

Table 10.6	Reading Scores
Senior	Reading Score
1	13.4
2	12.1
3	11.4
4	10.6
5	10.3
6	10.2
7	9.8
8	9.7
9	9.4
10	8.6

Step 2: Estimate the population standard deviation. In this case, the estimated standard deviation is 1.4. Calculate in the space next to the table.

Step 3: Calculate the standard error of the mean:

$$\text{s.e.} = \frac{s}{\sqrt{n}} = \frac{1.4}{\sqrt{10}} = \frac{1.4}{3.16} = .44$$

Step 4: Provide an **interval estimate** of the mean. An interval estimate is an interval such that the probability that the mean falls within the interval is acceptably high. The most common interval is the 95% confidence interval (we are 95% sure that the mean falls within the interval). The t score (with nine degrees of freedom) for 95% confidence limits is 2.262 (.025 in each tail; see Table 3 in the Appendix). Using this t score, we find that the 95% confidence interval is equal to

$$10.6 \pm 2.262 \times .44$$
$$10.6 \pm 1.0$$
$$9.6 \text{ to } 11.6$$

We are 95% sure ("confident") that the mean reading level falls within the range of 9.6 to 11.6 years of school.

This answer bothers the principal because she wants to be certain that the mean is above 10.0. The principal wants us to calculate the probability that the population mean is 10.0 or less. The statistically correct way to ask this question is: If μ is 10.0 or less, what is the probability of drawing a sample with a mean of 10.6? This probability can be determined easily because we have both a mean and a standard error. We convert 10.6 into a t score:

$$t = \frac{\bar{X} - \mu}{\text{s.e.}} = \frac{10.6 - 10.00}{.44} = \frac{.6}{.44} = 1.36$$

Looking up a t score of 1.36 in Table 3, we find a probability greater than .10. In other words, the probability is greater than .1 that with a mean of less than 10.0 we could get a sample mean estimate of 10.6. To say this another way, the chance of a sample mean of 10.6 if the true (population) mean is only 10.0 is greater than 10%. Computer programs can calculate and report the exact probability for a t score. A t score of 1.36 with nine degrees of freedom has a probability of .103. To use the t table, one needs to know the degrees of freedom (in this case, 9) and compare the t scores with the listed values. A t score of 1.9, for example, is larger than 1.833 (the value for .05) and smaller than 2.262 (the value for .025), so the probability of a t score of 1.9 with nine degrees of freedom is less than .05 (but more than .025).

The principal decides that she would like to be more certain. Greater certainty can be achieved if the standard error of the mean can be reduced. The formula for the standard error of the mean

$$\text{s.e.} = \frac{s}{\sqrt{n}}$$

shows that the standard error can be reduced if the standard deviation can be reduced (which is not likely because this is a function of the population) or if the sample size can be increased. Let's increase the sample size to 100. By a quirk of fate, our sample of 100 has a mean of 10.6 and a standard deviation of 1.4. In the space provided, calculate the new standard error.

If you found the standard error to be .14, congratulations!

In the space provided, calculate the new 95% confidence limits for the Wiese High School senior class reading scores. (*Hint*: With 99 degrees of freedom, you may use the normal curve to approximate the *t* distribution.)

From this new information, what can you tell the principal?

Chapter Summary

Whenever the public or nonprofit manager wants to say something about a population of items or people based on a subset or sample of those items or people, the manager must engage in statistical inference. Inferential statistics use quantitative techniques to generalize from a sample (with summary measures called *statistics*) to a population (with summary measures called *parameters*). We normally use samples for our data and estimations because it is too difficult or too expensive to access or use the entire population. This chapter illustrated how to make and use estimates of the mean and standard deviation of a population based on sample data. The standard error of the mean tells us how much error is contained in the estimate of the mean—that is, how good the estimate is. Because larger samples tend to have smaller standard error values than smaller samples, larger samples generally allow more accurate inferences.

Problems

10.1   George Fastrack, head of the Bureau of Obfuscation's United Way drive, wants to know the average United Way pledge among Obfuscation Bureau employees (pledges are normally distributed). George takes a sample of 10 and gets the results shown in the accompanying table. What is George's best estimate of the mean donation? What is George's best estimate of the standard deviation of the donations? Between what two values can George be 95% sure the mean value lies?

Person	Pledge
1	$ 25
2	0
3	35
4	100
5	0
6	0
7	15
8	50
9	25
10	50

10.2 Captain E. Garth Beaver has been warned by Colonel Sy Verleaf that if the mean efficiency rating for the 150 platoons under Verleaf's command falls below 80, Captain Beaver will be transferred to Minot Air Force Base (a fate worse than Diego Garcias). Beaver wants to know in advance what his fate will be, so he will know whether to send change-of-address cards to his magazine subscriptions. Beaver takes a sample of 20 platoons and finds the following:

$$\overline{X} = 85 \quad s = 13.5$$

Would you advise Beaver to send change-of-address cards? (Assume that efficiency ratings are normally distributed.)

10.3 Last year, sanitation engineer crews in Buffalo, New York, collected 124 tons of trash per day. This year, larger, more efficient trucks were purchased. A sample of 100 truck-days shows that a mean of 130 tons of trash were collected, with a standard deviation of 30 tons. What is the probability that a sample with this mean could be drawn if the new trucks are no improvement (i.e., the population mean = 124)?

10.4 Current Tinderbox Park water pumps can pump 2,000 gallons of water per minute. The park tests 10 new Fastwater brand pumps and finds a mean of 2,200 and a standard deviation of 500. What is the probability that the Fastwater pumps were selected from a population with a mean no better than that of the present pumps?

10.5 If the absenteeism rates for a school district rise above 10%, the state reduces its aid to the school district. Stermerville Independent School District takes a sample of five schools within the district and finds the following absenteeism rates: 5.4%, 8.6%, 4.1%, 8.9%, and 7.8%. What is your best estimate of the absenteeism rate in Stermerville? Is it likely that the absenteeism rate is greater than 10%?

10.6 The Department of Animal Husbandry at State University believes that adding corn oil to cattle feed will increase the cattle's weight gain. The average weekly gain for State U cattle last year was 12.7 pounds. A sample of 30 cattle are fed corn oil-fortified feed with the following results:

$$\bar{X} = 14.1 \text{ pounds} \qquad s = 5.0$$

What can you tell the department?

10.7 Last year, there were 512 burglaries in Groton, Georgia. The police chief wants to know the average economic loss associated with burglaries in Groton and wants to know it this afternoon. There isn't time to analyze all 512 burglaries, so the department's research analyst selects 10 burglaries at random, which show the following losses:

$1,550	$1,874
$1,675	$2,595
$1,324	$1,835
$1,487	$1,910
$2,246	$1,612

What is the best estimate of the average loss on a burglary? Place 80% confidence limits around this estimate.

10.8 Last year, the Department of Vocational Rehabilitation was able to place people in jobs with an average salary of $40,600. This year, placement is handled by a private agency that charges $200 per placement. Using the following placement figures for this year (sample of 100), what can you tell the department?

$$\bar{X} = \$40,900 \qquad s = 2,000$$

10.9 The Government Accountability Office is auditing International Airways, a company that flies numerous charters for the government. The contract specifies that the average flight can be no more than 15 minutes late. A sample of 20 flights reveals the results in the accompanying table. Write a brief memo interpreting this information.

Flight Number	Status
217	On time
167	20 minutes late
133	17 minutes late
207	34 minutes late
219	On time
457	96 minutes late
371	30 minutes late
612	On time
319	6 minutes late
423	12 minutes late
684	11 minutes late

Flight Number	Status
661	61 minutes late
511	On time
536	On time
493	17 minutes late
382	12 minutes late
115	6 minutes late
107	3 minutes late
19	26 minutes late
123	19 minutes late

10.10 The Secretary of Welfare hypothesizes that the average district office has 5% or fewer fraudulent or ineligible recipients. A sample of 10 offices reveals a mean of 4.7% with a standard deviation of 1.2%. What can be said about the secretary's hypothesis?

10.11 The Department of Health and Human Services wants to know the average income of general assistance recipients. A sample of 60 recipients shows a sample mean of $17,400 with a standard deviation of $3,150. (a) Place a 90% confidence limit around your best estimate of the average income of general assistance recipients. (b) What is the probability that the average income could be $18,500 or more? (c) What is the probability that the average income might be as low as $17,000?

10.12 As an analyst for the Overseas Private Investment Corporation, you are required to report to Congress about guaranteed loans to companies doing business in Central American countries. You do not have time to find all the loans, so you take a sample of six loans. The loans have the following values, in millions of dollars:

$$223 \quad 247 \quad 187 \quad 17 \quad 215 \quad 275$$

Use this information to calculate a mean, and put 90% confidence limits around your estimate.

10.13 Complaints about how long it takes the city of Shorewood to pay its bills have reached the city manager. City policy requires that bills be paid within 30 days. A sample of 100 bills shows a mean of 34 days with a standard deviation of 15. Is it possible that a sample mean of 34 days could be generated from a population with a true mean of 30?

10.14 Last year, the Texas State Penitentiary averaged 14.1 violent incidents per day in its prisons. At the end of last year, the federal courts held that inmates could not supervise other inmates. Warden John Law thinks that this ruling will generate more violent incidents because, in the past, inmates used the supervision hierarchy to maintain a pecking order inside the prison. A sample of 40 days of records reveals a mean of 17.5 and a standard deviation of 2.0. What can you tell Warden Law?

10.15 The Metro City Bus system is concerned about the number of people who complain about the service. Metro City Bus managers suspect that many people do not know how to complain. Last year, complaints averaged 47.3 per day. This year, bus systems manager Ralph Kramden has posted a sign in all buses listing a number to call with complaints. Ralph would like to know whether this effort has generated any additional complaints. He takes a sample of 50 days and finds a mean of 54.7 and a standard deviation of 25.4. What can you tell Ralph?

10.16 The director of the Birkfield, California, Women's Shelter is planning the budget for next year and wants to know whether it's reasonable to assume an average stay of 21 days per client. The director asks her assistant to take a random sample of 35 clients who recently stayed at either of the shelter's two locations. The sample shows an average stay of 23 days with a standard deviation of 9.3 days. What should the assistant tell the director?

10.17 Last year, the average weight of babies born to clients of the Houston Women's Health Clinic was 7.5 pounds. The clinic's new director recently implemented an aggressive new educational program on the importance of proper nutrition during pregnancy. A random sample of 50 clients who took part in this program reveals an average birth weight of 8.1 pounds with a standard deviation of 1.1 pounds. What can the director conclude from these data?

10.18 Officials at the Special Inspector General for Afghanistan Reconstruction (SIGAR) are concerned about inventory management for parts used to repair U.S. military vehicles in the country. A comprehensive audit across all of the maintenance facilities last year revealed an average of 83 inventory errors (parts listed as available, but actually missing) per facility, per month. Officials at SIGAR want an update, but they do not have the time to do comprehensive inventory checks; accordingly, they select seven facilities for one-month reviews. Results show an average of 79 inventory errors per facility, with a standard deviation of 8.4. Can officials conclude that there has been a statistically significant improvement in the inventory error rate?

10.19 Janice Johnson, director of the Montana Bureau of Prisons, is concerned about the number of violent incidents among prisoners. Last year, the system averaged 1.5 violent incidents per day. In an attempt to lower this number, Director Johnson implemented an aggressive new training protocol to help prison staff better understand the conditions leading to the occurrence of such incidents. The director's assistant takes a random sample of 100 daily incident reports from the state's prisons to get a quick read of the situation. She finds an average incident rate of 1.41 per day with a standard deviation of .12. What should the assistant tell the director? *(Note: The data set for this problem is available on the book's companion website.)*

10.20 The Indiana Superintendent of Public Education is concerned about whether the state's schools will meet this year's achievement targets for performance on standardized tests. Specifically, this year's goal is an average pass rate of 81% at the state's 1,500 high schools. Because the state has not yet received all of the data from each school, the superintendent takes a random sample of 150 schools from the available reports to see whether this goal is within reach. The sample mean is 80.6 with a standard deviation of 7.6. What should the superintendent conclude from these data? *(Note: The data set for this problem is available on the book's companion website.)*

10.21 The National Council on Nonprofit Monitoring (NCNM) has issued guidelines stating that nonprofit organizations should spend at least 70% of all revenues collected from donations on direct program expenses. As part of an ongoing monitoring program, the Minnesota Lakes and Rivers Appreciation Foundation samples monthly expenditure reports from its offices throughout the state to see whether the local chapters are below the NCNM minimum. After taking a sample of 100 monthly expenditure reports from local chapters, the foundation's chief data analyst finds a mean of 77.4 with a standard deviation of 7.8. What can the foundation conclude about its conformance with the NCNM standard? *(Note: The data set for this problem is available on the book's companion website.)*

10.22 The mayor of Chud, Wisconsin, has faced criticism over the number of water quality advisories issued last year for the city's water supply. Specifically, Chud's average water contaminant score last year was .29 (a rating of "marginally acceptable" according to the Wisconsin Department of Natural Resources). The mayor and city council took a number of aggressive steps to improve the quality of the city's water supply this year. Ideally the mayor's target for this year is an average water contaminant score of no greater than .25 (an "acceptable" rating). The mayor hires an independent consultant to analyze 80 days' worth of water samples for contaminants. What can the consultant tell the mayor after analyzing these scores? *(Note: The data set for this problem is available on the book's companion website.)*

10.23 The director of the North Carolina Local Government Insurance Pool (NCLGIP) has implemented mandatory annual risk assessments for all members of the pool in hopes of reducing both the number of claims made by members and the average size of these claims. The average payout per claim last year was $34,000. To see whether the mandatory risk assessments are working, the director takes a random sample of 100 claims filed through the first 4 months of this year. What can the director conclude about the impact of this program? *(Note: The data set for this problem is available on the book's companion website.)*

10.24 Two years ago, the Harris County Nonprofit Council (HCNC) did a comprehensive study on the financial position of nonprofits in the Harris County area. The study revealed that budgetary operating reserves in the population of Harris County nonprofit organizations averaged 5.8 months. Officials at HCTNC have updated these data by surveying a random sample of 400 nonprofits in Harris County (150 organizations actually responded to the survey). Based on these data, can the staff at HCTNC conclude that the mean for budgetary operating reserves in the population is still at least 5.8 months? *(Note: The data set for this problem is available on the book's companion website.)*

10.25 In 2013, the average household income for micro-enterprise operators in Vermont was $36,752. Officials at the Vermont Foundation for Social Enterprise believe that household incomes among micro-entrepreneurs have gone up over time, but they do not have the time to contact all of the individuals in their micro-enterprise database to get an updated estimate. Accordingly, officials contact a randomly selected sample of 125 micro-entrepreneurs from their listings. Based on the data collected, can officials confidently conclude that the household incomes of the state's micro-entrepreneurs have gone up? *(Note: The data set for this problem is available on the book's companion website.)*

10.26 The Metro City Rescue Mission (MCRM) depends heavily on food donations from individuals. Last year, food donations at the MCRM's curbside collection program averaged 9.1 pounds per donation. The director of MCRM would like to know whether making assumptions based on a 9.1 pound average donation is still realistic. To find out, she asks two interns to randomly select and weigh 50 unprocessed donations from the curbside collection program currently in the MCRM's warehouse. Upon analyzing the data, what should the interns tell the director? *(Note: The data set for this problem is available on the book's companion website.)*

Hypothesis Testing

Public and nonprofit managers are often faced with decisions about program effectiveness, personnel productivity, and procedural changes. Decisions on such matters are based on the information relevant to them. Is the Chicago-area Head Start program upgrading the educational skills of its participants? Is Robert Allen an effective first-line supervisor? Will redesigning form SKL473/26 result in faster processing of equal employment complaints? A question that solicits information about managerial problems is called a **hypothesis**. When phrased as a statement rather than as a question, a hypothesis is nothing more than a statement about the world that may be tested to determine whether it is true or false. The following are examples of hypotheses:

- Following the Connecticut Highway Patrol's crackdown on speeders, the number of highway accident fatalities dropped.
- The average number of tons of trash collected by Jackson Hole, Wyoming, sanitation engineer crews is 247 tons per week.
- After implementation of the project team's management strategy, the productivity of the England County Welfare Department increased.

Hypotheses are traditionally presented in the negative. For example,

- Following the Connecticut Highway Patrol's crackdown on speeders, the number of highway accident fatalities *has not dropped*.

In the space provided, present the Jackson Hole and England County hypotheses in the negative.

A hypothesis expressed in the negative is referred to as a **null hypothesis** (the hypothesis that nothing changed or happened). As this chapter will illustrate, null hypotheses are easier to use in inferential statistics than are other types of hypotheses.

You will notice that prior to stating these null hypotheses, you had to interpret the original Jackson Hole and England County hypotheses. In order to test a null hypothesis, you must first state a **research hypothesis**. The research hypothesis is the opposite of the null. Put another way, if the null hypothesis is expressed in the negative, the research hypothesis is expressed in the positive. In policy evaluation, we often wonder whether policies have produced certain outcomes. Research hypotheses are generally constructed to reflect our expectations concerning policy outcomes.

For example, if a nonprofit organization institutes cost-cutting measures, the expectation is that costs will in fact go down. If a school district spends more money on teacher training, the expectation is that teacher performance will improve. If a state imposes tough new penalties on individuals convicted of driving under the influence, the expectation is that arrests for drunk driving will go down.

Just because we have expectations about the effects of policies or managerial decisions does not mean that those effects will always be realized. The goal of testing hypotheses statistically is to determine whether the data support or fail to support the research hypothesis in question. A research hypothesis is always paired with a null hypothesis so that we know what to conclude in those cases where the evidence fails to support the research hypothesis. Here are a few ways to conceptualize the difference between null and research hypotheses.

- If the research hypothesis states that an outcome *has been realized*, the null hypothesis states that an outcome *has not been realized*.

- If the research hypothesis states that a policy *had an effect*, the null states that the policy *did not have an effect*.

- If the research hypothesis states that *a change has occurred*, the null states that *a change has not occurred*.

- If the research hypothesis states that *a value will be greater than 50*, the null states that *a value will not be greater than 50*.

- If the research hypothesis states that the score for the experimental group *is lower than the score for the control group*, the null states that *the score for the experimental group is not lower than the score for the control group*.

The practical implications of testing a null hypothesis are important: If we are able to reject the null hypothesis, we accept the research hypothesis. If we are unable to reject the null hypothesis, we cannot accept the research hypothesis as true.

The research hypothesis is normally what the analyst believes is true and expects to find supported in the data analysis. The null hypothesis is the "foil," or comparison, that facilitates this statistical test. When writing null and research hypotheses, it is helpful to label the research hypothesis as H_1 and the null hypothesis as H_0 to avoid confusion over which hypothesis is which. Stating a null hypothesis is easier if you state the research hypothesis first. It is usually less difficult to understand what the opposite of the research hypothesis is if we already know the meaning of the research hypothesis.

This chapter discusses the logic of hypothesis testing. It also illustrates the process of testing hypotheses with both population parameters and sample statistics.

Steps in Hypothesis Testing

The logic of hypothesis testing is fairly simple.

Step 1: Formulate the hypothesis. Suppose that you have a research assistant, Thurman Truck, who is preparing a lengthy research report. Based on Truck's assurances, you develop the following hypotheses:

H_1 = Truck will complete the report by August.

H_0 = Truck will not complete the report by August.

Step 2: Collect data relevant to the hypothesis. You know that to complete the research report by August, Truck must complete a prospectus by January 15. On January 15, Truck tells you the prospectus will be done by January 22. On January 21, Truck promises you the prospectus on January 28. On January 27, Truck swears that the prospectus will be on your desk by February 5. On February 4, Truck ceases to come to work.

Step 3: Evaluate the hypotheses in light of the data. Are the data consistent with the null hypothesis or the research hypothesis? Does Truck's behavior indicate that the research report will not be completed by August (the null hypothesis)?

Step 4: Accept or reject the null hypothesis. Remember that the research hypothesis typically states that a hypothesized change *has* taken place. The null hypothesis typically states that a hypothesized change *has not* taken place. We must accept the null hypothesis that Truck will not finish his research report by August. If we accept the null hypothesis, this tells us that the data do not support the research hypothesis.

Step 5: Revise your decision in light of this new information. In this case, you decide to transfer Truck to your regional office in Lubbock, Texas, as a punishment for nonperformance.

The Importance of Stating the Null and Alternative Hypotheses Correctly

The ability to state null and research hypotheses correctly is essential to public and nonprofit managers. The statistical techniques that we cover later in the chapter will have little meaning if you do not understand the difference between null and research hypotheses. Stating the null hypotheses for the Jackson Hole and England County examples was relatively easy because we provided the research hypotheses. Practice stating both the null and research hypotheses for the management questions that follow. Do not worry about numbers or statistical calculations at this point. Concentrate on identifying the research question in each example and correctly stating the hypotheses. Sample null and research hypotheses for each research question are presented at the end of the chapter. Exact wording is not important, so you should not be concerned if the hypotheses you write are stated a bit differently than the ones found at the end of the chapter.

- Six months after the local newspaper ran a week-long series of articles on the Northlake, Virginia, Community Pride Center, the director wants to see whether this positive media coverage improved turnout at the center's after-school recreation programs compared to the turnout before the media coverage took place.

  H_1

  H_0

- The head of the Alton, New York, Public Works Department has installed security cameras in the public yard in hopes of lowering the large number of illegal after-hours dumping incidents. After 90 days, officials want to assess the impact this measure has had on the number of illegal dumping incidents.

  H_1

  H_0

- The director of philanthropy at the Art Institute of Cubs City, Illinois, is interested in assessing the impact recent changes in federal tax laws have had on donations. Because the changes gave potential donors favorable new tax benefits, the director would like to know whether the average donation amount is larger than it was prior to the change in the laws.

  H_1

  H_0

- The principal of the Oaklawn Charter School claims that the "Oaklawn method" of mathematics instruction produces higher scores on standardized math skills tests compared to those of students in the district who are taught the "old math."

  H_1

  H_0

Now that you have gained some experience in stating hypotheses, we demonstrate the statistical techniques used to test them.

Testing Hypotheses with Population Parameters

If the manager has access to population parameters, then hypothesis testing is as easy as deciding whom to start with if LeBron James plays for your basketball team. As an illustration, suppose that Jerry Green, governor of a large eastern state, wants to know whether a former governor's executive reorganization had any impact on the state's expenditures. After some meditation, he postulates the following research and null hypotheses:

H_1: State expenditures decreased after the executive reorganization compared with the state budget's long-run growth rate.

H_0: State expenditures did not decrease after the executive reorganization compared with the state budget's long-run growth rate.

Governor Green stated the null hypothesis in this way so that the test would be fair. He reasoned that one could not expect an absolute decrease in expenditures because the state's population was growing (and thus generating greater demands for state services). The average growth rate of state expenditures appears to provide a reasonable test.

A management review shows that the state's expenditures grew at the rate of 10.7% per year before the reorganization and 10.4% after the reorganization. What do these figures say about the null hypothesis? Because 10.4% is less than 10.7%, we reject the null hypothesis and conclude that the growth rate in state expenditures declined after the reorganization.

You may have objected to the preceding conclusion, thinking that a 0.3% decrease in the growth rate of expenditures was not significant. If you meant "statistically significant," you were incorrect. Because these are exact population parameters, statistical significance has no meaning (the probability that the state reduced its growth rate in expenditures is 1.0, or nearly so). If by "significance" you meant that the decrease was trivial, you are correct. Remember, however, that the hypothesis did not state that the change would be large, only that there would be a change.

Notice that we did not conclude that the reorganization *resulted in* a decline in the state budget's growth rate. That would be a causal statement. Statistics cannot come to this conclusion. Statistics can only determine whether the expenditure rate after the reorganization was less than the rate before the reorganization. To conclude that the reorganization resulted in the reduced rate, the manager must determine that no other variable could have caused the decline. This assessment is an evaluation of the research design (see Chapter 3) and cannot be made based on a single statistical test or finding. Finally, the manager must make a managerial assessment of this question based on the risks that the manager wishes to sustain.

To avoid overstepping the limits of statistics, we suggest that you approach all statistical problems in three steps.

Step 1: The statistics step: Did the growth rate in the budget decline after the reorganization?

Step 2: The research design step: Could factors other than the reorganization have caused the decline?

Step 3: The managerial step: What can I confidently conclude about the reorganization and the budget growth rate?

Hypothesis Testing with Samples

In most managerial situations population parameters are not available. This absence is the result of cost, inaccessibility, and a variety of other factors that prevent gathering data on the entire population. Although population parameters are the ideal data to use in hypothesis testing, circumstances almost always dictate the use of sample statistics. The Food and Nutrition Service of the Department of Agriculture, for example, may want to know the impact of food stamps on family nutrition. (The null hypothesis is that they have no impact.) Although the service might prefer data on all food-stamp recipients, costs of gathering the data restrict the Food and Nutrition Service to testing with samples.

Hypothesis testing with a sample can best be illustrated with an example. The police chief of Prudeville, Oklahoma, has received several complaints from the city council about prostitution in Prudeville. The council members all suggest a crackdown. The police chief issues orders to make more prostitution arrests and asks the department's research analyst to gather relevant data. After a month, the council is still upset and calls the police chief in to appear before the council. The chief asks his research assistant to assess the effectiveness of the crackdown so that the chief can present these data to the council.

Before the crackdown on prostitution, the Prudeville vice squad was making 3.4 prostitution arrests per day (arrests are normally distributed). The research assistant forms the following research and null hypotheses:

H_1: Following the Prudeville prostitution crackdown, prostitution arrests were greater than 3.4 per day.

H_0: Following the Prudeville prostitution crackdown, prostitution arrests were not greater than 3.4 per day.

How did we arrive at these hypotheses? If the research hypothesis states that the policy change had an effect, then the null hypothesis states that it did not have an effect. What is an effect in this case? The goal of the prostitution crackdown is to make more prostitution arrests. Accordingly, evidence of an effect would mean that prostitution arrests are rising above the pre-crackdown average of 3.4. If the policy did not have an effect, then we would expect to maintain the status quo of 3.4 arrests per day.

Because there is not enough time before the city council meeting to analyze all the data, the research analyst randomly selects 10 days of prostitution arrests for analysis. Table 11.1 presents the data.

Table 11.1	Sample Data for Prostitution Arrests
Day	Prostitution Arrests
1	3
2	5
3	7
4	2
5	3
6	6
7	4
8	3
9	6
10	1

© Cengage Learning

The analyst proceeds by the following steps:

Step 1: Estimate the population mean after the crackdown. Because the best estimate of the population mean is the sample mean, the analyst calculates the mean. His figure for the mean is 4.0.

Step 2: Estimate the population standard deviation. In this example, the estimated standard deviation is 1.94. (*Hint*: Divide by $n - 1$.)

Step 3: Calculate the standard error of the mean. Because we have only a sample, the mean estimate may be in error. As a result, we need to know how good an estimate of the mean we have. We use the formula

$$\text{s.e.} = \frac{s}{\sqrt{n}} = \frac{1.94}{\sqrt{10}} = .61$$

The standard error is .61.

Step 4: Test the hypothesis. Answer the following question: What is the probability of drawing a sample of 10 with a mean of 4.0 if the population mean is 3.4? This question can be answered by converting 4.0 into a *t* score and using the *t* table (arrests are normally distributed).

$$t = \frac{\bar{X} - \mu}{\text{s.e.}} = \frac{4.0 - 3.4}{.61} = .98$$

Looking up a *t* score of .98 in the *t* table (df = 9), we find that the probability of a sample of 10 with a mean of 4.0 coming from a population with a mean of 3.4 is greater than .1. The research assistant has access to a computer program that provides an exact probability. This probability is .176.

Step 5: The research assistant decides to accept the null hypothesis because he feels .17 is too large a probability to reject the null hypothesis. The police chief overrules the research assistant because he wants to show positive results (i.e., that prostitution arrests are increasing after the crackdown). He argues before the city council that this improvement in arrest rates has only a one-in-six chance of happening by chance. The research assistant is fired later that day.

Does the criterion used (arrest rates per day) accurately measure what the city council is concerned about (prostitution)? What does the city council want stopped? How could you measure this? How valid are the findings above given what you said about these measurements? Refer to Chapter 2. Apply the research design step to the alternative approach that you propose to assessing the level of prostitution in Prudeville.

How Sure Should a Person Be?

In the preceding example, a research analyst felt that a probability of .17 was not sufficiently small to reject a null hypothesis (because it allowed too great a risk of error), whereas the police chief felt that the risk of error was tolerable. Political considerations aside, how sure should a person be before rejecting the null hypothesis? In the words of Harvey Sherman, "It all depends." It all depends on how sure one needs to be to make a decision confidently.

When you make a decision about the probability for rejecting the null hypothesis, the general rule is that the t score obtained in testing the hypothesis must be larger than the t score associated with **alpha**, which is the probability you select for rejecting the null hypothesis. You should commit to memory the following decision rules for testing the null hypothesis:

- If the t score generated exceeds the t score associated with alpha, we can reject the null hypothesis. This means we are able to accept the research hypothesis.

- If the t score generated does not exceed the t score associated with alpha, we cannot reject the null hypothesis. This means we are unable to accept the research hypothesis.

Recall that the t score generated for the Prudeville arrests example is .98. If we decide to use an alpha of .05 for rejecting the null hypothesis (df = 9), the t score associated with alpha is 1.833. Because a t score of .98 is nowhere close to a score of 1.833, we clearly cannot reject the null hypothesis. In fact, the probability of .17 tells us that there is about a 17% chance that the null hypothesis is true in this case.

Social scientists routinely use a probability of .05 for rejecting the null hypothesis. But in many managerial situations, a .05 probability may be too great a risk. A rape crisis center may decide that the probability that one staff member cannot handle all the possible rape calls in any given day is .05. This means, however, that 1 day in 20, or once every 3 weeks, the rape crisis center will fail to meet a crisis. In this situation, a .05 level is too great a risk. A .001 level, one failure in 3 years, may be more acceptable.

A police department, by contrast, may be able to accept a .05 probability that one of its cars will be out of service. But the fire department may require a probability of only .0001 that a fire hose will fail to operate (that is, 1 chance in 10,000).

When we assign a probability of .05 for rejecting the null hypothesis, we are saying that if our t score exceeds the t score associated with alpha and we reject the null, there is still a 5% chance that the null hypothesis is actually true. Why are we willing to tolerate error? Because sample data do not give us a perfect sense of what is true in the population, we must be willing to accept a certain amount of error when making inferences about the population. We do not have perfect, or sometimes even very good, information about most populations.

Keep in mind that when you test a hypothesis using a small sample, the t scores associated with alpha values will be higher than those for larger samples. This is because estimates of the population obtained from small samples contain more error than those obtained from larger samples. If you look closely at the t table (Table 3, at end of book), you should see how alpha and degrees of freedom are related to sample size. Notice that as the number of degrees of freedom goes up, the t values for rejecting a null hypothesis go down. For example, if our sample contains 5 cases (df $= 4$), the t score for rejecting the null hypothesis with an alpha of .05 is 2.132. If our sample contains 25 cases (df $= 24$), the t score for rejecting the null hypothesis with an alpha of .05 is 1.711.

You may be wondering how to interpret the ∞ symbol at the foot of the degrees of freedom column on Table 3. The symbol ∞ means infinity, a very large limitless number. When a sample is smaller than 30, we generally cannot assume that the distribution of sample means is normally distributed. When a sample is 30 or greater, we can have greater confidence that the distribution of sample means is normally distributed. As a result, all we need to know for samples larger than 30 is one particular t score for the alpha in question. For example, when assigning a .05 probability for rejecting the null hypothesis, we use a t score of 1.645 (one-tailed) whenever our sample contains more than 30 cases.

Recall that in Chapter 10, we stated that when a sample has more than 30 observations, the normal distribution can be used in place of the t distribution. To see how the t distribution and the normal (z) distribution begin to converge when the number of cases exceeds 30, you can compare the t table (Statistical Table 3) and the normal table (Statistical Table 1) at the end of the book (Chapter 7 covers the normal probability distribution). When a sample has more than 30 cases, the t score (one-tailed; see below) for rejecting the null hypothesis at an alpha level of .05 is 1.645. Turning to the normal distribution table, which includes z scores only to two decimal places, we find that a z score of 1.64 has a probability of .4495 and a z score of 1.65 has a probability of .4505. Taking the mean of these two probabilities, we obtain a value of .4500 associated with a z score of 1.645. Subtracting .4500 from .50 (one-half of the normal distribution curve) yields an alpha value less than or equal to .05. Thus, we can say that 5% of the cases lie in one tail of the curve (that is, alpha $= .05$). The z and t values give us the same information about the percentage of observations found within the areas (assuming a one-tailed test) covered by the scores. In both cases, 5% of the data lie outside the range covered by the scores. The same logic applies for all of the other t-score values at ∞.

The lesson here is that larger samples are more likely to converge on the true characteristics of the population than are smaller samples. The smaller t scores for alpha associated with larger samples reflect this fact.

Finally, remember that when you generate a t score to test a hypothesis, you must always use the score to evaluate whether the null hypothesis, not the research hypothesis, should be rejected. Understanding the difference between null and research hypotheses is key to making correct substantive conclusions in interpreting t scores.

How certain one must be to reject a null hypothesis depends on the importance of the question involved. A public or nonprofit manager should never let his or her analyst make this decision. The analyst should provide the probability; it is the function of the manager to decide whether the probability is sufficient to reject the null hypothesis given the circumstances that are involved in the decision.

One- and Two-Tailed Tests

Determining the probability of an event is another way of assessing the statistical significance of an event. Another way of saying that the probability of event A is .01 is to say that A is statistically significant at the .01 level (that is, the probability that event A would occur by chance is .01). A significance test, therefore, is nothing more than a determination of the probability of an event.

Most statistics texts devote an extended discussion to one-tailed versus two-tailed tests of significance. This book will describe both briefly, but we will focus on the one-tailed test because it has much greater utility than the two-tailed test. A **one-tailed test** is applied whenever the hypothesis under consideration specifies a direction. In the previous Prudeville prostitution problem, the null hypothesis was that the arrest rate did not increase. We call this a one-tailed test because we are concerned with only one tail of the normal curve, the tail larger than 3.4 (see Figure 11.1).

A one-tailed test affects the probability assigned to the null hypothesis. Because we are interested only in values greater than 3.4, an $\overline{X}$ of 4.0 has a probability of .17. (*Reasoning:* If $\mu = 3.4$, 33% of all sample means fall between 3.4 and 4.0; 50% of all sample means fall below 3.4; this means 17% of all sample means fall at 4.0 or above; thus, the probability is .17.)

In rare circumstances, a public or nonprofit manager is interested in situations that differ greatly from the mean in either direction. For example, the Federal Railroad Administration (FRA) is purchasing railroad ties to recondition a railroad line from Bessmer, Michigan, to Rolla, Missouri. Because the railroad bed is unstable, only ties between 10 feet and 10 feet, 6 inches long can be used. The FRA administrator must inspect railroad tie shipments to decide whether they meet these standards. Because the FRA administrator cannot measure every tie, she decides to have a random sample of 10 pulled from every shipment. Any shipment

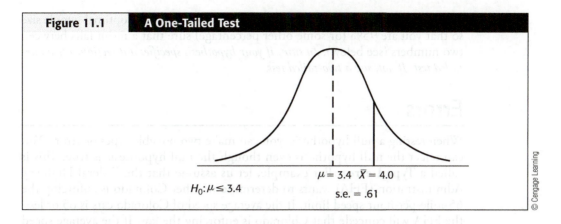

Figure 11.1 | **A One-Tailed Test**

$\mu = 3.4$ $\bar{X} = 4.0$

$H_0: \mu \le 3.4$

s.e. $= .61$

of ties in which more than 20% of the ties are either too large or too small will be rejected. From past experience, the administrator knows that the standard deviation of machine-cut ties is 1 inch. Based on the mean of each sample of 10, how can the administrator decide whether or not to accept a shipment?

Because this problem does not specify a direction for the hypothesis, it requires a **two-tailed test**. The first step is to determine the maximum mean value so that less than 10% of all ties are more than 10 feet, 6 inches long. (We use 10% because if 10% are too large and 10% are too small, 20% cannot be used.) To do this, look up a value of .1 in the t-score table (Table 3) (df = 9). The t score is 1.383. If the mean sample is within 1.383 standard deviations of 10 feet, 6 inches, then the shipment should be rejected. Converting this figure to a length in feet, we have

$$X = 10 \text{ feet, 6 inches} - (1.383 \times 1 \text{ inch}) = 10 \text{ feet, 4.62 inches}$$

In any sample whose mean is greater than 10 feet, 4.62 inches, probably 10% of the ties are longer than 10 feet, 6 inches.

Similarly, if the mean of the sample is 1.383 standard deviations from the lower limit of 10 feet, less than 10% of the ties will be too short. The lower limit for sample means, then, should be 10 feet, 1.383 inches. We now have a decision rule:

> If the mean length of 10 ties is between 10 feet, 1.38 inches and 10 feet, 4.62 inches, accept the shipment; if not, reject the shipment.

If shipments have a mean length of 10.3 inches and are normally distributed, using this decision rule will result in less than 20% of ties that are too long or too short. No more than 10% of the ties will be too long, and no more than 10% will be too short.

Although this problem uses both tails of the normal curve, it could easily be transformed into two separate problems, each with a one-tailed test (i.e., sample means for the railroad ties shorter than 10 feet, and sample means for the railroad ties longer than 10 feet, 6 inches). Because most management problems in the public and nonprofit sectors can be transformed into one-tailed problems, we suggest that you concentrate on learning how one-tailed tests are made.

The only exception to this rule is when you want to know the optimal sample size so that you are 95% (or some other percentage) sure that a mean falls between two numbers (see below). *In sum, if your hypothesis specifies a direction, use a one-tailed test. If not, use a two-tailed test.*

Errors

When testing a null hypothesis, you can make two possible types of errors. You can reject the null hypothesis even though the null hypothesis is true. This is called a **Type I error**. For example, let us assume that the Federal Highway Administration (FHA) wants to determine whether Colorado is enforcing the 65-mile-per-hour speed limit. If the average speed of Colorado cars is 65 or less, the FHA will concede that Colorado is enforcing the law. If the average speed is more than 65 miles per hour, then the FHA will begin proceedings to cut off some of Colorado's federal transportation funds. This is a serious step to take, so FHA officials want to be 99% certain before they act to cut off funds. Cost restrictions limit the sample of cars to be clocked to 100 cars.

Given this problem, the FHA analyst takes a preliminary survey and finds the standard deviation of Colorado car speeds to be 17.4 miles per hour. With a sample of 100, the standard error of any mean estimate would be

$$\text{s.e.} = \frac{s}{\sqrt{n}} = \frac{17.4}{\sqrt{100}} = \frac{17.4}{10} = 1.74$$

For a 99% confidence limit, the analyst scans the body of the normal table (to approximate a t table) for a probability value of .4900. This probability corresponds to a z score of 2.33. The analyst knows that if the sample mean of Colorado cars is 2.33 standard errors greater than 65, then she is 99% sure that the average speed of Colorado cars exceeds 65 miles per hour.

Translating this into a decision rule, she finds

$$X = 65 + (2.33 \times 1.74) = 65 + 4.05 = 69.05$$

If the average speed of the sample of cars is 69.05 miles per hour or above, the FHA will conclude that the average speed of Colorado cars is greater than 65 miles per hour and will begin withholding funds.

To illustrate the possibility of a Type I error, consider the following hypothetical situation. The average speed in Colorado is 65 miles per hour, but due to sampling error, the sample mean is 69.1. This situation will happen once in every 100 samples. The hypothesis of 65 miles per hour was rejected when it was actually true.

The second type of error, called, appropriately, a **Type II error**, occurs when you accept the null hypothesis as true when in fact it is false. Suppose that in the preceding example the population mean is 67 miles per hour and a sample revealed a mean of 67 miles per hour. (Clearly this can happen.) In this situation, you would conclude that the average speed of Colorado cars does not exceed 65 miles per hour when, in fact, it does.

Table 11.2	Calculations for Two Different Sample Sizes	
Statistic	Sample 1	Sample 2
n	100	500
$\overline{X}$	67.0	67.0
s	17.4	17.4
s.e.	1.74	.78
probability $X < 65$	.119	.0051

© Cengage Learning

The possibility of committing either a Type I error or a Type II error always exists. The probability of committing a Type I error can be reduced by increasing the probability required to reject the null hypothesis (e.g., by using alpha levels of .001 or .0001). Unfortunately, raising the alpha level increases the probability of a Type II error. This trade-off is resolved by deciding whether it would be worse to make a Type I or a Type II error. Is it worse to cut off Colorado's federal aid when it is complying with the law or to continue to aid Colorado if it is violating the law? Clearly the former is more dangerous in a political sense, so one would try to minimize the probability of a Type I error.

A method of minimizing Type II errors is to increase sample size. All other things being equal, the larger the sample size, the smaller is the standard error of the mean, and, therefore, the smaller is the likelihood of rejecting a true hypothesis. The data in Table 11.2 illustrate this point. The certainty of the analyst is increased by the larger sample. The probability of rejecting a true hypothesis with a sample mean of 67 is much less with a sample of 500 than with a sample of 100.

Determining Sample Size

Another research problem facing management analysts in the public and nonprofit sectors is deciding on how large a sample is necessary to adequately test the hypothesis. For example, Wisconsin State Welfare Department officials may want to know the average income of all Wisconsin Temporary Assistance for Needy Families (TANF) recipients. They would like to be 95% certain that their estimate of the average income is within $100 of the actual average (this information is needed for federal forms). Using a sample, we can get an estimate of the mean by using the sample mean. A 95% confidence interval can be placed around this estimate by adding and subtracting a number equal to 1.96 standard errors from the mean estimate (1.96 is the 95% confidence limit t score as n becomes large) and approaches infinity (see above):

$$\overline{X} \pm 1.96 \times \text{s.e.}$$

The amount of error in the estimate is represented by that part of the computation to the right of the plus or minus sign (1.96 × s.e.). Our problem is this: How large a sample is needed to reduce this error to $100? Mathematically, we can determine this sample size by setting $1.96 \times$ s.e. equal to $100:

$$100 = 1.96 \times \text{s.e.}$$

But

$$\text{s.e.} = \frac{s}{\sqrt{n}}$$

So

$$100 = \frac{1.96s}{\sqrt{n}}$$

$$\sqrt{n} = \frac{1.96s}{100}$$

$$n = \left(\frac{1.96s}{100}\right)^2$$

These calculations show that with an estimate of the standard deviation, we can calculate the desired sample size.

To estimate the standard deviation, the analyst takes a small sample of Wisconsin TANF recipients. The data in Table 11.3 result. In the space to the right of the data, calculate the standard deviation.

If you performed the calculations correctly, your answer should be 442. Substituting this value into the equation, we have

$$n = \left(\frac{1.96 \times 442}{100}\right)^2 = \left(\frac{866.3}{100}\right)^2 = (8.7)^2 = 75.7$$

Table 11.3	Data from a Sample of Wisconsin Welfare Recipients
Recipient	Income
1	$21,500
2	21,700
3	22,600
4	21,800
5	21,200
6	22,400
7	21,300
8	21,700
9	22,000
10	21,800

The optimum sample size in this situation is 76 people. This size should provide an estimate of the average income of Wisconsin welfare recipients to within $100.

To generalize this problem, the ideal sample size for any problem is a function of (1) the amount of error that can be tolerated, (2) the confidence one wants to have in the error estimate, and (3) the standard deviation of the population. Symbolically, this can be expressed as follows:

$$n = \left(\frac{t \times s}{E} \right)^2$$

where n is the sample size, t is the t score associated with the desired confidence limit, s is the estimated standard deviation, and E is the amount of error that can be tolerated.

For example, if you wanted to be 95% certain that the analyst's estimate in the previous example was within $50, you would perform the following calculations:

$$n = \left(\frac{1.96 \times 442}{50} \right)^2 = \left(\frac{866.3}{50} \right)^2 = (17.3)^2 = 300$$

The optimum sample size is 300 persons. (Always round up for sample sizes.)

Chapter Summary

Hypothesis testing is a statistical technique for evaluating whether a statement is more likely true or false. There are five steps involved: (1) formulate the hypothesis, (2) collect the relevant data, (3) evaluate the hypothesis in light of the data, (4) accept or reject the hypothesis, and (5) make your decision in light of the new information.

Hypotheses can be tested by using population parameters or sample statistics. Due to cost and feasibility factors, we most often have data drawn from a sample and use statistics calculated from the sample to test hypotheses. When statistics are used, the techniques of statistical inference are needed to test hypotheses. With statistical inference, we always face a risk of error because we use sample data to make a guess about (unknown) population conditions. We can make a Type I error—rejecting the null hypothesis when it is true—or a Type II error—failing to reject the null hypothesis when it is false. Unfortunately, decreasing one type of error tends to increase the other type. Tests of hypotheses can be either one-tailed or two-tailed: A one-tailed test specifies a direction (e.g., the average level of donations to nonprofit organizations is smaller this year than last), whereas a two-tailed test only states a difference (the average level of donations is no different this year than last).

The research hypothesis and the null hypothesis are essential to statistical inference. The research hypothesis proposes what we believe to be true or what we expect to find in the data analysis; the null hypothesis is a comparison or foil to the research hypothesis that includes all other results. When testing hypotheses, the statistical techniques described in the chapter are always used to assess whether the null hypothesis can or cannot be rejected. The *t* test, and the probabilities we interpret from this test, are always used to evaluate the null, not the research, hypothesis. If the null and research hypotheses are reversed or stated incorrectly, then the inferences made using *t* tests will be misleading.

This chapter also discusses the size of samples needed to ensure that there is only a given amount of error—that is, the sample size necessary to adequately test the hypothesis.

Problems

11.1 Last year, Normal, Illinois, had all car maintenance on the city's automobiles done by the city maintenance pool. The cost was $364 per car. This year, the city officials (and mothers) fired all the workers in the maintenance pool and are using Jack's Crash Shop to perform the maintenance. They would like to know, without a complete audit, whether Jack is saving them money. A random sample of 36 cars showed a mean repair cost of $330, with a standard deviation of $120. What can you tell the city officials?

11.2 The average grass maintenance engineer mows 1.4 acres of grass per day in Barron, Montana. Because labor costs are increasing, the city decides to try a new brand of mower. Ten randomly selected engineers are given these new mowers. After a test period, these 10 engineers cut an average of 2.1 acres per day, with a standard deviation of .6 acre. If the costs are similar, should the city purchase more new mowers?

11.3 It is contract negotiation time, and the Louisiana teachers union wants to argue that its salaries are the lowest in the region. Because the union has 20,000 members, it must rely on a survey. If the union wants to estimate its members' mean salary and be 95% sure that the estimate is within $200 of the real mean, how large a sample should the union use? Assume that a preliminary survey estimates the mean as $35,000, with a $1,000 standard deviation.

11.4 The departments at Bufford State University publish an average of 5.1 professional articles a year. The sociology department regularly averages about 3.5. The chairman of the sociology department, Steig Willick, feels her department does less well because it is harder to publish in sociology. Willick takes a survey of 12 other sociology departments and finds the following:

$$\overline{X} = 4.2 \qquad s = 1.6$$

What can Willick tell the dean?

11.5 The police chief of Kramer, Texas, reads a report that says the police clear 46.2% of all burglaries that occur in Kramer. The chief would like to know how good this figure is. She randomly selects 10 other Texas cities and asks them what percentage they clear. She gets the following numbers:

44.2%	36.4%	51.7%	32.9%	46.4%
40.3%	49.4%	32.1%	29.0%	41.0%

Is Kramer's clearance rate significantly different from those of other Texas cities?

11.6 The National TANF Recipients Organization has charged that state caseworkers are inexperienced. The Kansas State Social Welfare Department surveys its employees and finds that they have an average of 3.4 years of experience ($s = 3.9$, $n = 200$). What can the Kansas State Social Welfare Department claim?

11.7 Springdale University and the Springdale United Way jointly administer a student volunteerism program. Last year, students in the program volunteered an average of 7.3 hours of community service per month. Officials are concerned that students might not be putting in as many volunteer hours this year. A random sample of 75 student volunteers from the first 2 months of the year reveals an average of 6.8 hours of community service ($s = 1.5$ hours). Based on these data, what can program administrators conclude about their initial hypothesis (i.e., that student volunteering is decreasing)?

11.8 The Whitehawk Indian Tribe wants to know the average number of absences for each student at the elementary school run by the Bureau of Indian Affairs (BIA). The tribe members believe that the number of absences is at least 12 per student. A sample of 150 students reveals

$$\overline{X} = 11.8 \qquad s = 4.3$$

What can you tell from this information about the Whitehawk hypothesis?

11.9 The Bureau of Administration is concerned with high levels of employee absenteeism. Last year, the average employee missed 12.8 workdays. This year, there is an experimental program in which the agency pays employees for each sick day or personal day that they do not use. A preliminary survey of 20 persons reveals a mean of 8.7 days missed and a standard deviation of 4.6. Present a hypothesis and a null hypothesis, and evaluate them. State a conclusion in plain English.

11.10 The state of Michigan has just changed one of its toll roads from human collection of tolls to machine collection. The idea behind the change was to allow traffic to flow more smoothly through the toll plaza. With human attendants, the mean number of cars passing through the toll plaza was 1,253 per hour. A random sample of 100 hours under the new machine system of toll collection shows a mean of 1,261, with a standard deviation of 59. Present a hypothesis and a null hypothesis, and evaluate them. State a conclusion in plain English.

11.11 The Iowa State University Agriculture Research Team is concerned about the impact of the recent drought on the productivity of the state's corn crop. During the last 10 years, Iowa's corn crop has averaged 32.4 bushels per acre per year.

Final figures on this year's yields will not be in for another 6 months, but the team needs to estimate yields now in case the governor decides to apply for federal disaster aid. A sample of 100 acres reveals a mean of 22.4 bushels, with a standard deviation of 15.7. Based on this sample, present a hypothesis and a null hypothesis, and evaluate them. In plain English, state what you have found. Then place an 80% confidence limit around your best estimate of the mean yield.

11.12 The Heavenly Grace Christian Elementary School has decided to examine whether using biblical materials to teach reading has an impact on reading levels. Last year, a test revealed that the average sixth-grade student read at a 5.7 grade level. This year, after all secular humanist material was deleted from the curriculum, a 20-person sample of the sixth-grade student body was tested, with the following results:

$$\text{mean} = 6.4 \quad \text{standard deviation} = 1.9$$

Present a hypothesis and a null hypothesis, and evaluate them. State your conclusion in plain English.

11.13 The Wisconsin State Court system wants to assess the impact that punitive damages have on large tort awards. Using the court system's computer, 16 cases were selected at random from all those cases in which damages of $1 million or more were awarded. The sample revealed the following about the punitive damages in these cases:

$$\text{mean} = \$74,000 \quad \text{standard deviation} = \$55,000$$

Place a 99% confidence limit around your best estimate of the punitive damages for this type of case. One concern is that punitive damages for these cases might be in excess of $100,000. Present a hypothesis and a null hypothesis, and evaluate your hypotheses. Finish with a conclusion that a judge could understand.

11.14 The director of philanthropy at the Fleckman Institute of the Arts is interested in assessing the impact that recent changes in federal tax laws have had on donations. The average donor gave $580 last year. A random sample of 50 donations reveals that in the 5 months since the laws were changed, the average donor gave $625, with a standard deviation of $97. Present a hypothesis and a null hypothesis, and evaluate them. What can the director conclude about the effect the new tax laws are having on donations?

11.15 Six months after the local newspaper ran a week-long series of articles on the Northlake, Virginia, Community Pride Center, the director wants to see whether this positive media coverage improved turnout at the center's after-school recreation programs compared to the turnout before the media coverage took place. Prior to the media coverage, the center averaged 22.3 participants per day. The director has taken a random sample of daily attendance since the media coverage ended. Help the director evaluate the effects of the media coverage on program attendance. Present a hypothesis and a null hypothesis, and evaluate them. *(Note: The data set for this problem is available on the book's companion website.)*

11.16 John Witty, research analyst for the Wisconsin Department of Education, has begun work on a study examining the performance of charter schools in the state. Dr. Witty is particularly concerned about the relatively high dropout rates at these schools. Last year, the dropout rate for the state's charter schools averaged 15.1%. Dr. Witty believes that the rate has improved this year, but he does not have the data for the entire population of schools at this time. Accordingly, he collects data on dropout rates (expressed as the percentage of students who dropped out during the school year) for a random sample of 75 charter schools. Based on the data provided, what should Dr. Witty conclude? *(Note: The data set for this problem is available on the book's companion website.)*

11.17 The Chesterville, Montana, city council has criticized the city's Information Technology (IT) Division for creating a very user-unfriendly city website. As proof, the council points out that the city's website averaged only 200 unique "hits" (visits by nonrepeat users) per day over the last year. The city council asked the IT division to implement a number of changes in hopes of boosting traffic to the site. Three months after these changes were implemented, the city council asks the head intern to conduct a statistical evaluation of 90 randomly selected days' worth of data on visits (defined as unique hits) to the city's website. Help the city council evaluate the impact of these changes by conducting a statistical evaluation of these data. What should the intern report to the city council? *(Note: The data set for this problem is available on the book's companion website.)*

11.18 The Dean of the Graduate School at Eastern Seaboard State University (ESSU) believes that graduate programs at ESSU are at a competitive disadvantage to those at peer institutions as a consequence of the relatively low teaching assistantship stipends the university offers its graduate students. The dean plans to make a case to the chancellor that additional funding for teaching assistant salaries is needed to make ESSU more competitive with its peers. The current graduate student stipend at ESSU is $11,000. To bolster her case, the dean has her assistant select data on teaching assistantship stipends from 50 peer institutions. Based on these data, can the dean defend her position that stipends at ESSU are significantly different from those at peer institutions? *(Note: The data set for this problem is available on the book's companion website.)*

11.19 The mayor of Belmont, Texas (population, 800,000), is concerned about levels of prostitution in the city. Over the past year, the police department arrested an average of 8.9 individuals per day for solicitation. The mayor believes that these numbers are unacceptably high and would like to do something to address the problem. With the cooperation of the city council, the mayor authorizes a program to publicly identify individuals found guilty of solicitation on a weekly community affairs program airing on Belmont public access television. Several episodes of the program have aired, and the mayor would like to determine whether this initiative has had any impact on discouraging prostitution activity. The police department has been able to provide the mayor's office with 75 days' worth of arrest data since the first stated airing of the programs. Assist the mayor by analyzing the data on arrest rates. State both a null hypothesis and an alternative hypothesis for this problem, and provide a statistical evaluation of the data using a *t* test. What can the mayor's office conclude about the effectiveness of this program? *(Note: The data set for this problem is available on the book's companion website.)*

11.20 Several years ago, the Wisconsin Institute of Charitable Giving (WICG) conducted a comprehensive study on the grant-making activities of the nearly 1,300 charitable foundations in the state. The data collected showed an average grant size of $825,000. Officials at WICG are concerned that their data might be a bit dated, but they do not have the time or resources to update the data for the entire population of charitable foundations in the state. Accordingly, they collect data on the average size of grants in dollars for a randomly selected sample of 200 foundations. What can they conclude from their data? Present null and alternative hypotheses and evaluate them. *(Note: The data set for this problem is available on the book's companion website.)*

11.21 Sandy Parks, executive director of Be Kind Through In-Kind (BKTIK), is interested in using volunteers to perform some services normally handled by paid staff. Specifically, paid staff members are currently responsible for processing in-kind donations (such as clothing and appliances) received from donors. Donations need to be warehoused in the correct bins for further processing by paid employees. Teams of paid staff at BKTIK's five locations in Metro City process an average of 150 items per 3-hour shift. The director decides to let teams of volunteers periodically process in-kind donations over the next month (for a total of 50 three-hour shifts across the five locations). If the volunteers process the same number (or more) items on average as paid staff, Ms. Parks will reallocate paid staff to more complex work duties. What can Ms. Parks conclude from these data? Develop both null and alternative hypotheses and evaluate them. *(Note: The data set for this problem is available on the book's companion website.)*

11.22 The Northeast Foundation Association (NFA) is in the process of writing an informational bulletin on the advantages of Program Related Investments, or PRIs (typically defined as loans foundations make to support programmatic goals). Officials at NFA speculate that the default rate on PRIs is at least 5%, but they want a more precise estimate for their informational bulletin. Accordingly, the chief data analyst at NFA contacts a random sample of 250 foundations in the region (that are known PRI users) and asks them to supply data on their PRI default rates. Based on the data supplied, what can NFA officials conclude? Present both null and alternative hypotheses and evaluate them. *(Note: The data set for this problem is available on the book's companion website.)*

11.23 The Tennessee Board of Standards (TBS) is concerned about the issue of overcharges at grocery stores. An analysis of thousands of transactions from a study completed several years ago showed an average overcharge of $1.74 per $100 transaction. The TBS would like to get a read on whether the overcharge problem has improved or become worse since their last study. Accordingly, TBS inspectors complete 375 random shopping trips at grocery stores across the state (each inspector is asked to purchase approximately $100 worth of goods per transaction). A data analyst at the TBS parses out only those cases where overcharges occurred ($n = 130$ overcharges; there were undercharges too, but the TBS is only interested in studying the overcharge problem for now). What can the inspectors conclude from the data they've collected? *(Note: The data set for this problem is available on the book's companion website.)*

Answers to Sample Null and Research Hypotheses

Problem 1	H_1: Media coverage increased turnout at the Community Pride Center.
	H_0: Media coverage did not increase turnout at the Community Pride Center.
Problem 2	H_1: The installation of security cameras has led to a decrease in the number of illegal dumping incidents.
	H_0: The installation of security cameras has not led to a decrease in the number of illegal dumping incidents.
Problem 3	H_1: The size of the average donation has increased since the new tax laws were passed.
	H_0: The size of the average donation has not increased since the new tax laws were passed.
Problem 4	H_1: Math scores at Oaklawn are higher than those at other schools in the district.
	H_0: Math scores at Oaklawn are not higher than those at other schools in the district.

12

Estimating Population Proportions

O ften a manager does not want to know the mean score of some population but rather the percentage of some population that does something. A Department of Transportation official, for example, might want to know the proportion of motor vehicles that pass a state's vehicle inspection. A criminal justice planner might want to know what percentage of persons released from prison will be arrested for another criminal act within 1 year. A nonprofit manager might want to know the percentage of volunteers who show up when they are scheduled. All these situations require the analyst to estimate a population proportion rather than a population mean.

This chapter illustrates the procedure for estimating population proportions and demonstrates how to test hypotheses using proportions.

Estimating a Population Proportion

The procedure for estimating a population proportion and placing confidence limits around that estimate is relatively similar to that for estimating a population mean. We illustrate this process with an example.

The warden of Ramsey Prison wants to know the prison's recidivism rate. The warden wants to know this information because he believes that the Ramsey rehabilitation program is a rousing success that others might want to copy. If the recidivism rate is fairly low (say, under 70%), the warden will write an article on the Ramsey rehabilitation program for the *Journal of Law 'n' Order.* (The Ramsey rehabilitation program involves teaching each inmate a skill, such as making license plates, and then finding the inmate a job making license plates in the outside world.)

Because Ramsey is a large institution, calculating the recidivism rate for all past inmates would be difficult. The warden takes a sample of 100 former inmates who went through the rehabilitation program. These inmates are traced through the FBI's data system to find out whether they were arrested again within a year of release (recidivists). The warden considers anyone imprisoned again within a year a failure. The FBI search reveals that 68 of the 100 inmates became inmates again.

Question 1: What is the best estimate of the proportion of recidivists in this situation? The sample of 100 can be interpreted as 100 samples of 1.

The mean of these 100 samples is .68, which is the best estimate of the population proportion. In other words, the best estimate of a population proportion is the sample proportion.

Question 2: What is the standard deviation of the proportion? Recall that the standard deviation for a binomial probability distribution is

$$\sigma = \sqrt{n \times p \times (1 - p)}$$

where p is the probability and n is the number of trials.

If we treat this situation as a probability distribution, with $p = .68$ and one trial, the standard deviation is

$$\sigma = \sqrt{1 \times .68 \times .35} = \sqrt{.2176} = .47$$

The standard deviation is .47. In fact, this is how the standard deviation of a proportion is defined:

$$\sigma = \sqrt{p \times (1 - p)}$$

where σ is the standard deviation of the proportion and p is the proportion.

Because this is a sample, the formula is

$$s = \sqrt{p \times (1 - p)}$$

Actually, the standard deviation of a proportion makes no sense at all. All elements in the set have a value of 1 (recidivist) or 0 (not a recidivist). This means that the usual interpretation of a standard deviation as telling us the degree of clustering about the mean has little value. We calculate the standard deviation, however, because it permits us to calculate the standard error of the proportion.

Question 3: What is the standard error of the proportion? The standard error of a proportion has the same formula as the standard error of the mean:

$$\text{s.e.} = \frac{s}{\sqrt{n}}$$

where n is equal to the sample size. In our example, we have

$$\text{s.e.} = \frac{.47}{\sqrt{100}} = \frac{.47}{10} = .047$$

Question 4: What are the 95% confidence limits of the proportion? (Although proportions cannot be normally distributed—because individuals either are recidivists or are not—in this case, the sample size is larger than 30, so the normal curve can be used to approximate the t distribution for 99 degrees of freedom.) With a mean (read "proportion") and a standard error of the estimate, we can easily construct a 95% confidence limit. In this situation, the 95% confidence limits are

$$p \pm t \times \text{s.e.}$$
$$.68 \pm 1.96 \times .047$$
$$.68 \pm .092$$
$$.59 \text{ to } .77$$

Question 5: Using the 95% confidence limits, should the warden submit an article to the *Journal of Law 'n' Order*?

Proportions

Proportions problems have the same logic as means problems, and both are solved in a similar manner. For example, city council member Liver Smith argues that a majority of the people in Worcester oppose the continued funding of the Worcester Transit Bus System. Liver bases this argument on a random sample of 30 Worcester residents. Twenty-one residents opposed continued funding of the bus system. For Liver's data, what is the probability that this sample could be drawn if a majority of residents favor continuing the bus system?

This problem can be interpreted as an example of hypothesis testing. Liver's hypothesis is that the proportion of Worcester residents opposing the bus system is greater than .5:

$$H_1: p > .5$$

The null hypothesis may be expressed as

$$H_0: p \leq .5$$

or "The proportion of Worcester residents who oppose the bus system is less than or equal to .5." Clearly this hypothesis can be tested.

Step 1: Estimate the population proportion. In this case, it is .7, or $(21 \div 30)$.

Step 2: Estimate the population standard deviation. Because we are given a hypothetical population proportion $(p = .5)$, that proportion (not the sample proportion) should be used to estimate the standard deviation:

$$\sigma = \sqrt{p \times (1 - p)} = \sqrt{.5 \times .5} = .50$$

Step 3: Estimate the standard error of the proportion.

$$\text{s.e.} = \frac{\sigma}{\sqrt{n}} = \frac{.50}{\sqrt{30}} = \frac{.50}{5.5} = .091$$

Step 4: Test the hypothesis. What is the probability that a sample of 30 would result in a proportion estimate of .7 or greater if the true proportion were .5? Use a t table, and convert .7 to a t score:

$$t = \frac{X - \mu}{\text{s.e.}} = \frac{.7 - .5}{.091} = \frac{.2}{.091} = 2.20$$

Looking up a t score of 2.20 in Table 3 (Statistical Tables), we find a value of .025, which means that the probability of obtaining a sample that has a proportion of .7 or greater is less than .025.

Step 5: Reject the null hypothesis. Accept the alternative hypothesis that the proportion of Worcester residents opposing the bus system is greater than .5.

A Digression

Before examining some other uses of proportions, a digression is in order. (Digressions are in order only after a t score of 2.0 or more.) The perceptive reader might have seen another way to solve the previous problem. Another way to phrase the problem is this: If the probability of finding a person opposed to the Worcester bus system is .5, what is the probability that 21 or more of 30 randomly selected persons will oppose the bus system?

This problem is a binomial distribution problem, where $n = 30$, $r = 21$ or more, and $p = .5$. (If you need to refresh your memory regarding the binomial distribution, please see Chapter 8.) The mean in this case (or the expected value) is

$$\mu = n \times p = 30 \times .5 = 15$$

The standard deviation is

$$\sigma = \sqrt{n \times p \times (1 - p)} = \sqrt{30 \times .5 \times .5} = \sqrt{15 \times .5} = \sqrt{7.5} = 2.7$$

Converting r to a z score, we have

$$z = \frac{r - \mu}{\sigma} = \frac{21 - 15}{2.7} = \frac{6}{2.7} = 2.22$$

This z score corresponds to a probability of .0132 that 21 or more of 30 people oppose the bus system if $p = .5$. Although this probability is not the same as the probability found earlier (less than .025), the two probabilities are fairly close. The differences are the result of rounding error and the approximation of the t table.

Determining Sample Size

The director of the Office of Human Development wants to know the proportion of welfare recipients who own cars. She wants to know the proportion within 2% and wants to be 95% certain. Help her to determine the sample size necessary to find out this information.

This problem is identical to any other sample-size problem. Sample size is determined by the following formula:

$$n = \left(\frac{z \times \sigma}{E}\right)^2$$

where E is the amount of error tolerated. Because the director specified a 95% confidence limit and a 2% error, this formula becomes

$$n = \left(\frac{1.96 \times \sigma}{.02}\right)^2$$

The only thing we need to know in order to calculate sample size is the standard deviation. Although we could take a preliminary sample and estimate the standard deviation, there is an easier way. Statisticians have discovered that the standard deviation of a proportion is greatest when the proportion is equal to .5. You may verify this in a barefoot or intuitive way by calculating the standard deviations for the listed proportions in Table 12.1. Those of you with a calculus background, feel free to present a proof.

If you calculated the correct standard deviations, the largest standard deviation is .50 for a proportion of .5. This fact means that if we do not know a population proportion and we need to estimate a sample size, .5 is the best proportion estimate to use. Because all other proportions have smaller standard deviations, they will require smaller samples to have the same accuracy. So, in this case, we assume a proportion of .5 and thus a standard deviation of .5. Substituting the standard deviation of .5 into the formula, we get

$$n = \left(\frac{1.96 \times .5}{.02}\right)^2 = \left(\frac{.98}{.02}\right)^2 = 49^2 = 2{,}401$$

To be 95% confident that the proportion of welfare recipients who own cars is within 2% of the estimate, a sample of 2,401 is required.

Table 12.1	For What Proportion Is the Standard Deviation Greatest?		
Proportion	Standard Deviation	Proportion	Standard Deviation
p	$\sqrt{p(1-p)}$	.5	
.1		.6	
.2		.7	
.3		.8	
.4		.9	

To illustrate the need for a smaller sample if the proportion is smaller (or larger), assume that an earlier survey revealed that 10% of all welfare recipients owned cars. In this case, our estimate of the standard deviation is .3. Substituting this value into the sample-size formula, we get

$$n = \left(\frac{1.96 \times .3}{.02}\right)^2 = (29.4)^2 = 864$$

If interview costs run approximately $20 per interview, why is it sometimes helpful to estimate the population proportion in advance?

Decision Making

John Johnson, the warden at the Maxwell Federal Penitentiary, is considering a novel rehabilitation program. He believes that if certain types of nonviolent offenders are released early, they will have a very low recidivism rate. John considers a recidivism rate of 50% as an acceptably low rate. John would like to try the program for a few years and then, based on data from samples of inmates, decide whether or not to continue it. Because of the sensitive nature of experiments that release prisoners early, John wants to be 99% certain of his decision, and he can afford only a sample of 100. Given this information, construct a decision rule.

The procedure for a decision rule in this case is much like a decision rule based on means.

If $\mu > .5$, eliminate the program.

If $\mu < .5$, keep the program.

Translating this to a sample of 100 with 99% confidence, we have

If $X + t \times$ s.e. $< .5$, keep the program.

(Note that we need to consider only the "keep the program" option because the greatest danger is in keeping a program that lets hardened criminals loose on the streets. This means that we are interested in only one tail of the curve, so we look up a probability of .01 in the t table. Because $n = 100$, we use the normal curve approximation to look up .49.)

Because a 99% confidence limit has a t score of 2.33, and because the largest standard deviation possible is for $p = .5$ ($\sigma = .5$), we can substitute in these values:

$$\overline{X} + 2.33 \times \left(\frac{.5}{\sqrt{100}}\right) < .5$$

$$\overline{X} + 2.33 \times .05 < .5$$

$$\overline{X} + .1165 < .5$$

$$\overline{X} < .3835$$

From these calculations, we can formulate a new decision rule in which we have 99% confidence. Stated in terms of percentages:

If $\overline{X} < 38.35$, keep the program.

If $\overline{X} \leq 38.35$, terminate the program.

Therefore, whenever a sample of 100 inmates reveals a recidivism rate of 38.35% or greater, the release program should be terminated.

Chapter Summary

Often in public and nonprofit management, the analyst will have proportions, rather than mean scores, based on data from a sample and would want to estimate parameters for the entire population, such as the population proportion. Sample proportions can be used to estimate population parameters and to test hypotheses using procedures very similar to those used for means (see Chapter 11). The problems and pitfalls remain basically the same. In addition, the sample size needed for a particular management situation involving proportions can be determined in a manner similar to that shown in Chapter 11 for means.

Problems

12.1 The personnel department of a large government agency needs to know the percentage of employees who will retire this year. This information is essential to agency recruitment personnel. The agency determines this information with a random sample. If the agency wants to be 90% sure that its estimate of the retirement percentage is within 2%, how large a sample should it take?

12.2 If 33% of the members of the Sweetheart Union sign petitions to decertify the union, the National Labor Relations Board (NLRB) will call an election to determine whether Sweetheart will remain the exclusive bargaining agent. The union leadership takes a random sample survey of 40 and finds that 8 persons will sign the petition. What can you tell the union?

12.3 After a massive inventory, Central Library finds 12% of its volumes missing. As a result, Central institutes new procedures to prevent theft. After instituting these procedures for 1 year, Central Library wants to know whether they are working, but it cannot afford the cost of a complete inventory. The library takes a sample of 200 books and cannot locate 14 of them. These 14 are assumed to be lost to theft. What can you say about the new procedures?

12.4 Last year, 30% of all students at Wheezer School missed class during March because of illness. This year, the school board requires all teachers to dispense vitamin C tablets during the morning milk break. A sample of 60 children reveals that only 12 missed school during March. What can be said about the differences in absentee rates?

12.5 According to the Department of Transportation, 74% of all cars on Interstate 35 were exceeding the 55-mile-per-hour speed limit. The department runs a series of public service ads and then takes a sample of 2,000 cars. It finds that 72% of the cars are exceeding the speed limit. Write a memo discussing the possible impact of the department's ad program.

12.6 Bernie Belfry, the coordinator for Habitat for Humanity, wants to know the percentage of the population living in substandard housing. Belfry wants to be 99% certain that he is within 10 percentage points of the population percentage. How large a sample does Belfry need?

12.7 Refer to Problem 12.6. If an earlier survey revealed that 30% of the population was living in substandard housing, how large a sample should Belfry use?

12.8 The Department of Fish and Wildlife is under pressure to use poisons to kill coyotes. The department feels that poison will kill only those coyotes that would be killed by predators and harsh weather anyway. According to its records, an estimated 28% of all coyotes live through the winter. A pilot project is tried with poisons in the Lupus Wildlife Refuge. Of the 214 coyotes released there in the fall, 51 are found alive in the spring. What can you tell the department about the experiment?

12.9 Refer to Problem 10.9 (Chapter 10). What is your best estimate of the proportion of International Airways flights that arrive on time?

12.10 VISTA manager William Phogbound suspects that 50% of his volunteers are over 65 years old. A survey of 16 volunteers reveals that 7 are over age 65. What can be said about Phogbound's assertion?

12.11 If the error rate for TANF (Temporary Assistance for Needy Families) payments is greater than 5%, the federal government will cut off funding to the state of Utah. To see whether this is a problem, the agency director takes a sample of 250 TANF recipients and finds that errors have been made in 18 cases. What is your best estimate of the error rate in Utah? Place a 90% confidence limit around this estimate. Present a hypothesis and a null hypothesis, and evaluate them. State a conclusion in plain English.

12.12 The Milwaukee Independent School District (MISD) is concerned with white flight—the withdrawal of white students from MISD. Last year, 63% of all MISD students were white. To get a quick reading of the situation this year, a sample of 100 students is selected: 52 of those students are white. What is your best estimate of the proportion of white students in MISD? Present a hypothesis and a null hypothesis, and evaluate them. Present a conclusion in plain English.

12.13 The village of Whitefish Bay uses a private insurance carrier to cover its automobile fleet. The carrier contends that it pays 90% of all claims within 30 days after the claims are filed. The department wants to check this out without going through a complete audit. Analyst Susan Medford takes a sample of 100 claims from last year and finds that 82 were paid within 30 days. Present a statistical evaluation of these results.

12.14 When the State of Wisconsin directly administered its vehicle emissions testing system, the average monthly failure rate for vehicles tested in Milwaukee County was 10.8 percent. In 2013, the state contracted out with private automotive repair shops to perform vehicle emissions testing. Some state legislators have expressed concerns that this new system might create an incentive for providers to purposely inflate failure rates. The State Legislative Research Bureau (SLRB) is asked to gather a random sample of 150 inspection reports from Milwaukee County for the past month. The data reveal 19 vehicles with failed emissions tests. Based on these data, what can the SLRB tell these legislators?

12.15 A foundation that provides funding to the Metro City Teen Pregnancy Prevention Coalition (TPPC) has asked the organization to start collecting program outcomes data. Specifically, the foundation would like to know if the pregnancy rate for teen girls who participate in the educational programming at TPPC is significantly lower than the citywide average (currently 21%). The director of TPPC collects data for a random sample of girls who completed the Coalition's programming and finds that 8 out of the 65 clients contacted went on to become pregnant. Should the director be concerned about presenting her findings to the foundation?

Testing the Difference between Two Groups

Often a public or nonprofit administrator will have two samples and will want to know whether the values measured for one sample are different from those of the other sample on average. For example, a school administrator might want to know whether the reading levels of high school seniors improved after a special reading seminar was given: She wants a before-and-after comparison. A mental health counselor may want to know whether one type of treatment works better than another. A nonprofit executive may want to know whether agencies that contract with fund-raising firms net more donations than those that raise funds in-house. A librarian might want to know whether advertising affects circulation and thus might set up an experiment in which some branches advertise and others do not. In situations such as these, in which one would want to know whether two sample means are different or whether two sample proportions are different, the appropriate technique to use is a difference of means test.

Stating the Research and Null Hypotheses for Difference of Means Tests

In Chapters 10 and 11, we learned that when testing a hypothesis about a population using a single sample, the goal was to see whether a single sample with a particular mean could be drawn from a population with a known or hypothesized mean. The goal of testing hypotheses for two sample means is slightly different. When testing the difference between two sample means, the goal is to determine whether both sample means could have been drawn from the same population, or whether the two sample means are so different that they could not have been drawn from the same population.

For many management or policy evaluation issues, we expect the values for one sample to be different from those of the other sample. Research and null hypotheses are written to reflect this expectation. The general logic for the research hypothesis in a difference of means test is that one of the sample means is different (either smaller or larger) than the other sample mean. This statement is only a generic way of describing the underlying logic of a research hypothesis for a difference of means test. The actual hypotheses you write should be tailored to the specific research question at hand.

A thorough understanding of the research question helps clarify two important points necessary for carrying out a difference of means test: (1) the reason for hypothesizing a difference between the two groups (what makes one group different from the other?) and (2) the expected direction of the difference. For example, if we compare the academic performance of elementary school students who have participated in after-school learning programs to that of those who have not, it is simply too vague to hypothesize that the performance of the two groups will be different. Instead, we write the research hypothesis to reflect the expectation that the performance of program participants will be higher than that of nonparticipants.

Because we use samples to make inferences about larger populations, confirming the research hypothesis in a difference of means test indicates that the two population means are also different. In other words, there is a low probability that both samples could have been drawn from the same population. The general logic of the null hypothesis in a difference of means test is that the two sample means are *not* different. Failure to reject the null hypothesis indicates that the population means in question are not different.

To simplify, before examining the statistical issues involved in carrying out difference of means tests, we will illustrate how the process works using an example without data. Officials at the Bureau of Forms want to examine the effect that continuing education seminars have on employee performance. Half of the employees at the bureau have participated in continuing education seminars, whereas the other half have not. To see whether continuing education seminars are having an effect on performance, agency officials randomly select 50 employees who have participated in seminars and 50 who have not. After administering job skills tests to each of the samples, agency officials want to evaluate whether the test scores for the two groups of employees are different. The research and null hypotheses are as follows:

H_1: Employees who have taken continuing education seminars will have higher job skills scores.

H_0: There is no difference in job skills scores between employees who have taken continuing education seminars and those who have not.

In this case, if we were unable to reject the null hypothesis, the substantive conclusion would be that the mean test scores for the two populations of workers (those attending seminars and those not attending seminars) are not different. In other words, the population mean for both groups is the same, indicating that seminars are not leading to higher job skills scores.

If we were able to reject the null hypothesis, the substantive conclusion would be that the mean test scores for the two populations of workers are different. In other words, the scores for the population of workers who have participated in continuing education seminars are higher than the scores for workers who have not. Thus, the two population means are different, indicating that seminars are leading to higher job skills scores.

Now that you have been introduced to the general logic of difference of means tests, we present the statistical steps involved in the process.

Difference of Means Procedure

The best way to illustrate the difference of means test is with an example. The Ware County librarian wants to increase circulation from the Ware County bookmobiles. The librarian thinks that poster ads in areas where the book-mobiles stop will attract more browsers and increase circulation. To test this idea, the librarian sets up an experiment. Ten bookmobile routes are selected at ran-dom; on those routes, poster ads are posted with bookmobile information. Ten other bookmobile routes are randomly selected; on those routes, no advertising is done. In effect, the librarian has set up the following experiment:

Group	Treatment	Comparison
Experimental group	Place ads	Measure circulation
Control group	No ads	Measure circulation

After a week-long experiment, the information listed in Table 13.1 is available to the librarian.

The null hypothesis is that the mean circulation of the experimental group is not higher than the mean circulation of the control group. Testing the difference between two means tells us the probability that both groups could be drawn from the same population. More formally, the analyst wants to know if μ_e (the experi-mental mean) is greater than μ_c (the control mean) or, alternatively, to calculate

$$d = \mu_e - \mu_c$$

to test if $d = 0$. The procedure is as follows:

Step 1: Calculate the mean and standard deviation for each group. These calculations have already been performed and are shown in Table 13.1. We use the sample means and standard deviations as estimates of the population parameters.

Table 13.1	Librarian's Data		
		Experimental Group	Control Group
	Mean	526 books	475 books
	Standard deviation	125	115

Step 2: Calculate the standard error of the mean estimate for each group.

$$\text{s.e.} = \frac{s}{\sqrt{n}}$$

Experimental group:

$$\text{s.e.} = \frac{125}{\sqrt{10}} = 39.5$$

Control group:

$$\text{s.e.} = \frac{115}{\sqrt{10}} = 36.4$$

Step 3: Calculate an overall or "pooled" standard error for both groups. The overall standard error is equal to the square root of the sum of the squared standard errors for each group. Symbolically, this can be expressed as

$$\text{s.e.}_d = \sqrt{\text{s.e.}_1^2 + \text{s.e.}_2^2}$$

For the present example, we have

$$\text{s.e.} = \sqrt{39.5^2 + 36.4^2} = \sqrt{1,560.25 + 1,324.96} = \sqrt{2,885.21} = 53.7$$

Step 4: Because we want to know the probability that the groups could have been drawn from the same population, and because we have a mean estimate and a standard error, we can calculate the following t score:

$$t = \frac{\overline{X}_1 - \overline{X}_2}{\text{s.e.}_d}$$

where $\overline{X}_1$ is the control group mean, $\overline{X}_2$ is the experimental group mean, and s.e. is the overall standard error. In the present example, we have

$$t = \frac{475 - 526}{53.7} = \frac{-51}{53.7} = -.95$$

Looking up a t score of $-.95$ in the t table presented as Table 3 in the Statistical Tables in the back of the book [degrees of freedom (df) is $n_1 + n_2 - 2$, or 18 in this case; the first column of Table 3 is labeled "df" for degrees of freedom], we find a probability of more than .1 (.18 if a computer is used). Statistically, we can say that there is more than 1 chance in 10 that the two samples could have been drawn from the same population (that is, there is no difference).

Step 5: If the research design shows no other possible causes, what can the librarian say managerially about the program?

Understanding the Three Major Difference of Means Tests

The preceding formula for a difference of means test is one of three such tests. It is the test that is used when the two samples are independent and the analyst is unwilling to assume that the two population variances are equal. There are two other tests: one for equal variances and one for dependent samples. To understand which test you should apply to a particular management question, you need to understand the difference between independent and dependent samples.

Independent samples are those in which cases across the two samples are not "paired" or matched in any way. The best procedure to obtain independent samples is through random sampling techniques. For example, if an analyst at the Internal Revenue Service (IRS) randomly selects two samples from a national database, each consisting of 250 tax returns, there is no reason to expect a one-to-one linkage or pairing between individual cases across the two samples. Case 1 from sample A might be a tax return filed by a male from Arkansas. Case 1 from sample B might be a tax return filed by a female from Nevada. The remaining 249 tax returns for each sample should be similarly diverse in terms of the background characteristics of filers. Because each sample is drawn randomly, we have no reason to expect paired relationships (such as each person in sample A being matched with a close relative in sample B) between individual cases across the two samples.

Dependent samples exist when each item in one sample is paired with an item in the second sample. A before-and-after test would generate dependent samples if the same cases were used both before and after. For example, an agency could select 50 employees with low performance scores and require them to attend mandatory performance workshops for a month. To see whether the workshops improve performance, the same 50 employees could be given performance exams after training has been completed. The scores for each employee are logically paired because each one has both a before and an after score.

The logic of dependent samples does not apply if the "before" and "after" cases are not paired. Let us assume that an agency with 1,000 employees has decided to select a random sample of 50 employees for drug testing. After obtaining the test results, agency officials undertake aggressive steps to reduce illegal drug usage among employees. Agency officials then draw a second random sample of 50 employees 3 months later to see whether the new policies are having an effect. The same 50 employees are not included in the before and after samples. Because cases for both samples were randomly selected, and there is no way to pair or connect the cases in the first sample with those in the second, the two samples are independent.

t Test Assuming Independent Samples with Unequal Variances

Of the three types of *t* tests, the independent samples, unequal variances *t* test is the most conservative; that is, it is less likely than the other two *t* tests to reject the null hypothesis. Sampling error is one reason why samples often have unequal variances. The problem this circumstance poses for inference is that sampling error makes it harder to determine whether two sample means are truly different or different mainly because of different variances that result from sampling error. The *t* test for independent samples with unequal variances is conservative in the sense that the calculations for the standard errors are designed to take large differences in sample variances into account. This procedure helps to clarify whether the sample means themselves are truly different. The calculations for degrees of freedom when using the *t* test for independent samples with unequal variances are also more conservative than those for the other *t* tests, as explained in Box 13.1.

The independent samples, unequal variances *t* test is particularly useful when the number of cases in each sample is different or when the number of cases in one or both of the samples is small (less than 30 or so). For example, if one sample consists of 150 cases and the other of 20, the amount of sampling error for the smaller sample might be much larger than that for the larger sample. If this were the case, the variances for the two samples would also be different.

Although a *t* test that makes it harder to reject the null hypothesis might seem like a disadvantage, a more rigorous standard makes the occurrence of Type I errors less likely. A public or nonprofit manager could spend his or her entire life using this *t* test and make adequate decisions (similar to using the binomial probability distribution when the hypergeometric should be used). We illustrate the use of this test with an example.

Sharon Pebble, the city manager of Stone Creek, South Dakota, wants to determine whether her new personnel procedures are decreasing the time it takes to hire an employee. She takes a sample of 10 city bureaus and calculates the average time to hire an employee, in days, before and after implementation of the new procedure. She gets the following results:

Bureau	Before	After
A	36.4	32.2
B	49.2	45.2
C	26.8	31.3
D	32.2	27.1
E	41.9	33.4
F	29.8	29.0
G	36.7	24.1
H	39.2	38.2
I	42.3	38.0
J	41.9	37.2

Box 13.1	Calculating Degrees of Freedom When Using the *t* Test for Independent Samples and Unequal Variances

One reason the *t* test for independent samples and unequal variances is more conservative than other *t* tests is the way degrees of freedom are calculated. The formula* for calculating degrees of freedom when using the independent samples unequal variances *t* test is as follows:

$$df = \frac{(s_1^2/N_1 + s_2^2/N_2)^2}{(s_1^2/N_1)^2/(N_1 - 1) + (s_2^2/N_2)^2/(N_2 - 1)}$$

where

s = sample variance

N = number of cases in sample

This formula generally produces lower df values than the formula that we have been using up to this point, df = $(n_1 + n_2 - 2)$. The lower the degrees of freedom, the larger the calculated *t* statistic must be when evaluating whether the null hypothesis can be rejected.

To simplify matters, we have used the less complex formula to calculate degrees of freedom for the problems at the end of the chapter. Although the degrees of freedom are sometimes the same using either formula (such as in the Stone Creek bureau example), you should not assume that this situation will always be the case when you are analyzing your own data. Thus, you should familiarize yourself with the steps involved in calculating degrees of freedom for the independent samples, unequal variances *t* test. Statistical software packages (such as SPSS) and spreadsheet programs (such as Microsoft Excel®) automatically calculate the correct degrees of freedom depending on the type of test (equal or unequal variances) that is selected.

*Formula for independent samples, unequal variances *t* test obtained from the National Institute of Standards and Technology Website: NIST/SEMATECH e-Handbook of Statistical Methods, http://www.itl.nist.gov/div898/handbook/.

The hypothesis, that personnel are being hired in less time than they were before the adoption of the new procedures, is the same for all three tests. The null hypothesis is also the same: There is no difference between the time it takes to hire new personnel before and after implementation of the new procedures.

First, we discuss the independent samples, unequal variances procedure.

Step 1: Estimate the mean and standard deviation for the period before the adoption of the new procedures and the period after:

Period	Mean	S
Before	37.64	6.71
After	33.57	6.23

Step 2: Calculate the standard error for each group:

$$\text{Before } \frac{6.71}{\sqrt{10}} = 2.12$$

$$\text{After } \frac{6.23}{\sqrt{10}} = 1.97$$

Step 3: Calculate the overall standard error:

$$\sqrt{2.12^2 + 1.97^2} = 2.89$$

Step 4: Calculate the t score for the difference of means:

$$\frac{37.64 - 33.57}{2.89} = \frac{4.07}{2.89} = 1.41$$

Step 5: Look up a t score of 1.41 with df (degrees of freedom) = 18 in Table 3 of the Statistical Tables. That value is statistically significant at less than .1. So there is less than 1 chance in 10 that the samples could have been drawn from the same population and, thus, that the means are equal. The resulting t score is not large enough to safely reject the null hypothesis (assuming an alpha value of .05; review "How Sure Should a Person Be" in Chapter 11). Thus, Ms. Pebble could conclude that the new procedures had no impact.

t Test Assuming Independent Samples with Equal Variances

The t test for independent samples and equal variances is less conservative than the t test for independent samples and unequal variances, because the former generates smaller standard errors and larger t scores. There is nothing wrong with using the t test for independent samples and equal variances if you are certain that the two sample variances are equal. If you assume that the sample variances are equal and they really are not, however, the overall standard error produced using this test will usually be smaller than it should be. This result increases the likelihood of making a Type I error when testing a hypothesis (i.e., rejecting the null hypothesis when it should be retained).

You can formally evaluate whether two sample variances are equal by performing the Levene test, which is an option available in most statistical software packages (see Box 13.2 for an explanation of how to interpret the Levene test). An even simpler approach is always to use the independent samples, unequal variances *t* test unless you are absolutely certain that the two sample variances are equal.

Box 13.2	How to Interpret the Levene Test for Equality of Variances

When interpreting the Levene test, the null hypothesis is that the two sample variances are equal. The alternative (research) hypothesis is that the two sample variances are not equal. The test statistic in this case is an *F* statistic. If you use a statistical software package to perform a difference of means test, the program will calculate the exact probability that the null hypothesis is correct. The following table is a sample SPSS output for a difference of means test that includes results for the Levene test.

Independent Samples Test

| | Levene's Test for Equality of Variances | | *t* Test for Equality of Means | | | | | | |
| | | | | | | | | 95% Confidence Interval of the Difference | |
	F	Sig.	t	df	Sig. (two-tailed)	Mean Difference	Std. Error Difference	Lower	Upper
Equal variances assumed	87.392	.000	−15.386	1,038	.000	−6.2228	.4044	−7.0164	−5.4292
Equal variances not assumed			−14.921	790.145	.000	−6.2228	.4171	−7.0415	−5.4041

In the present example, $F = 87.392$. With a level of significance of .000, this result indicates that the probability that the two sample variances are equal is extremely small. Thus, the null hypothesis should be rejected, and we should assume that the sample variances are not equal. Although a level of significance of .05 is commonly used to evaluate the test statistic, an analyst can also choose a more stringent threshold (such as .01) when testing the null hypothesis. For more information on how to calculate and interpret the Levene test, see Kurtz (1999, p. 185).

The *t* test for independent samples and equal variances operates as follows:

Step 1: Estimate the mean and standard deviation for the period before and the period after implementation of the new procedures, as shown in Step 1 in the prior example.

Step 2: Calculate an overall standard deviation by using the following formula:

$$s_d = \sqrt{\frac{[(n_1 - 1)s_1^2] + [(n_2 - 1)s_2^2]}{n_1 + n_2 - 2}}$$

The overall standard error is essentially a weighted average of the two standard deviations:

$$\sqrt{\frac{(9 \times 6.71^2) + (9 \times 6.23^2)}{10 + 10 - 2}} = 6.47$$

Step 3: Convert this overall standard deviation to a standard error with the following formula:

$$\text{s.e.} = s_d\sqrt{\frac{1}{n_1} + \frac{1}{n_2}}$$

$$6.47 \times \sqrt{\frac{1}{10} + \frac{1}{10}} = 2.89$$

In this case, the overall or pooled standard error is identical to the one in the preceding independent samples, unequal variances example because the sample sizes are equal. If the after sample had had 20 observations rather than 10, the final standard error would have been 1.99 for this method and 2.53 for the unequal variances method. The standard error for this method is always less than or equal to that of the other method; thus, the t score is always greater than or equal to the one for unequal variances. In the case of samples of 10 and 20, the t score for unequal variances would be 1.61 and for equal variances would be 2.05.

Step 4: Calculate the t score for the difference of means:

$$\frac{37.64 - 33.57}{2.89} = \frac{4.07}{2.89} = 1.41$$

Step 5: Look up a t score of 1.41 with df = 18. That value is statistically significant at less than .1. So there is less than 1 chance in 10 that the samples could have been drawn from the same population and, thus, that the means are equal.

t Test Assuming Dependent Samples

Finally, the t-test procedure for dependent samples is much different. In the present case, all of the items are paired because before and after data exist for each of the 10 bureaus. Because the items are paired, simply subtract one from the other to get d, the difference between the two items.

Step 1: Perform the pairwise subtractions to obtain the differences.

Bureau	Before	After	Difference
A	36.4	32.2	4.2
B	49.2	45.2	4.0
C	26.8	31.3	−4.5
D	32.2	27.1	5.1
E	41.9	33.4	8.5
F	29.8	29.0	.8
G	36.7	24.1	12.6
H	39.2	38.2	1.0
I	42.3	38.0	4.3
J	41.9	37.2	4.7

The remaining steps are performed on the differences, rather than on the original data. The results are treated as a case of statistical inference on the differences.

Step 2: Calculate the mean and standard deviation of the differences. In this case, the mean is 4.07, and the standard deviation is 4.56.

Step 3: Calculate the standard error using the normal formula of dividing the standard deviation by the square root of the sample size. In this case, the standard error is

$$\text{s.e.} = \frac{4.56}{\sqrt{10}} = 1.44$$

Step 4: Calculate a t score with $n = 10$, or 9 df to see whether the mean is different from zero:

$$t = \frac{4.07 - 0}{1.44} = 2.83$$

Step 5: This t score is statistically significant at less than .01. The dependent samples t test produces the most significant results, but it can be used only when the samples are dependent. In this case, Ms. Pebble would likely conclude that there was a decrease in the time to hire new employees after the new procedures were implemented.

For the remainder of this chapter and the problems, we will assume independent samples and unequal variances unless otherwise specified.

Proportions

The t test is a technique that can be used both for the difference between two sample means and for the difference between two sample proportions. For example, the Morgan City parole board has been running an experimental program on one-third of its parolees. The parolees in the experimental program are placed in halfway houses run by nonprofit organizations that try to ease the parolees' readjustment to society. All other parolees are simply released and asked to check in with their parole officer once a month. The parole board wanted to evaluate the experimental program and decided that if the experimental program significantly reduced the recidivism rate of parolees, then the program would be declared a success. A random sample of 100 parolees who were placed in halfway houses is selected. Their names are traced through the Nationwide Criminal Data System (NCDS); 68 have been arrested again and convicted. Two hundred randomly selected parolees who were not assigned to halfway houses were also traced through the NCDS, and 148 of these people were in jail. Is the recidivism rate for parolees sent to halfway houses lower than the rate for the other parolees?

The process of analysis of variance for proportions is identical to that for sample means:

Step 1: Calculate the sample proportions (means) and standard deviations. For the experimental group, we have

$$p = \frac{68}{100} = .68$$

$$s = \sqrt{p(1 - p)} = \sqrt{.68 \times .32} = .47$$

For the control group, we have

$$p = \frac{148}{200} = .74 \text{ and } s = \sqrt{.74 \times .26} = .44$$

Step 2: Calculate the standard error of the proportion estimate for each group.

$$\text{s.e.} = \frac{s}{\sqrt{n}}$$

Experimental group:

$$\text{s.e.} = \frac{.47}{\sqrt{100}} = .047$$

Control group:

$$\text{s.e.} = \frac{.44}{\sqrt{200}} = .031$$

Step 3: Calculate an overall standard error for both groups.

$$\text{s.e.}_d = \sqrt{\text{s.e.}_1^2 + \text{s.e.}_2^2} = \sqrt{.047^2 + .031^2} = \sqrt{.00317} = .056$$

Step 4: Convert the difference between the experimental and control groups into a t score with df = 298.

$$t = \frac{p_1 - p_2}{\text{s.e.}_d} = \frac{.74 - .68}{.056} = \frac{.06}{.056} = 1.07$$

Because the total number of cases far exceeds 30, we evaluate this t statistic by comparing it to the t values in the last row of Statistical Table 3 marked "∞" (indicating infinite degrees of freedom). The probability that the two samples could be drawn from the same population is greater than .10. We reach this conclusion because the value for the t statistic generated in step 4 ($t = 1.07$) does not exceed 1.282, the t score associated with the .10 level of significance in Table 3.

Step 5: Because we are dealing with crime, a manager should be more certain before acting. In this case a probability greater than .10 is not good enough to reject the null hypothesis; the result suggests that there is more than a .10 probability that the null hypothesis is correct. We thus conclude that the experimental program did not yield lower recidivism rates.

Let us look at one more example. Suppose the Morgan City parole board had a second experimental parole program in which parolees did community service work with local charities before they were granted parole. A sample of 100 of these parolees reveals 60 recidivists. Is the second experiment successfully reducing the recidivism rate in comparison to the control group? The calculations follow.

Experimental Group	Control Group
$n = 100$	$n = 200$
$p = .60$	$p = .74$
$s = .49$	$s = .44$
s.e. = .049	s.e. = .031

$$\text{s.e.}_d = \sqrt{.049^2 + .031^2} = .058$$
$$t = \frac{.74 - .60}{.058} = 2.41$$

This t score is statistically significant at less than .01, indicating that the probability of these samples being drawn from the same population is extremely small. What can you say from a research design perspective? What can you say from a management perspective? What decisions would you make?

Chapter Summary

Often a manager has samples from two groups (experimental and control, before and after, and so on) and wants to determine whether the two samples could be drawn from the same population and, hence, not differ significantly. This chapter illustrated the process of testing two sample means or two sample proportions to determine whether they could have been drawn from the same population. The procedure basically involves five steps. First, calculate the mean or proportion and standard deviation for each group. Second, calculate the standard error of the mean or proportion estimate for each group. Third, calculate an overall standard error for the groups. Fourth, calculate a t score and find its associated probability in the t table presented as Statistical Table 3 at the back of the book. Finally, make an informed decision based on the analysis.

There are three major difference-of-means tests. The t test assuming independent samples with unequal variances is the most conservative because it consistently produces larger overall standard errors than the other two t tests. The t test assuming independent samples with equal variances can be used if an analyst is sure that the sample variances in question are equal. The Levene test is a formal test of the equality of sample variances and should be used to evaluate this assumption if an analyst intends to use this difference of means test. The t test assuming dependent samples is most appropriate when values for the same cases can be paired; for example, they occur at two different points in time (as in a before-and-after comparison) or in two different sets of scores for the same sample (as in scores on standardized tests of reading and mathematics). A thorough grasp of the difference between dependent and independent samples is needed to understand which of these tests should be used to examine a particular research or management question.

Problems

13.1 John Johnson, the local sheriff, suspects that many of his city's residents are operating motor vehicles without current inspection stickers. To determine whether this is true, John has his boys, John, H. R., and Charles, randomly stop 100 cars. Of these 100 cars, 43 do not have current inspection stickers. John decides to put some fear into drivers and launches a public relations campaign threatening to crack down. A month later, John wants to know whether the program worked. A random sample of 100 cars showed that 21 did not have valid inspection stickers. What can you tell John about the program? (Ask the statistical, research design, and management questions.)

13.2 A state is considering using Global Positioning System (GPS) technology to track paroled sex offenders, but would like to conduct an experiment before adopting such a program on a larger scale. Seventy-five randomly selected parolees are ordered to wear bracelets with GPS tracking capabilities. Sixty-five randomly selected parolees are monitored by traditional methods (which consist of daily phone calls from parole officers). After 9 months, officials tabulate the following data on the proportion of re-offenders by group. What can state officials conclude from these data?

	GPS Group	Phone Group
Re-offenders	16	23
Non-offenders	59	42

13.3 The police chief wants to know whether the city's African Americans feel that the police are doing a good job. In comparison to whites' evaluations, this information will tell the police whether they have a community relations problem in the African American community. A survey reveals the information in the accompanying table. What can you tell the police chief?

Opinion	African American	White
Feel police do good job	74	223
Do not feel police do good job	76	73

13.4 General Kleinherbst is concerned with the VD (venereal disease) epidemic among soldiers in Europe. At a nonroutine inspection of 100 troops, 31 were found to have VD. Kleinherbst requires all troops to view the award-winning film *VD: Just between Friends*. At another inspection 180 days later, Kleinherbst finds that 43 of the 200 troops inspected have VD. What can you say about the program statistically, managerially, and from a research design point of view?

13.5 Morgan City Fire Chief Sidney Pyro is concerned about the low efficiency scores that his firefighters receive at the state testing institute. Chief Pyro believes that these scores result because some firefighters are not in good physical condition. Pyro orders 75 randomly selected firefighters to participate in an hour of exercise per day. Another 200 firefighters have no required exercise. After 60 days, all firefighters are tested again by the state; the results are shown in the accompanying table. What can you tell the chief based on this information?

	Exercise Group	No-Exercise Group
Mean	74.5	70.6
Standard deviation	31.4	26.3

13.6 Two hundred people on the public assistance rolls in Sunbelt County are randomly selected. One hundred are required to do public service work for the county; the other 100 continue as before. After 6 months, 63 of the public service workers are still on public assistance, as are 76 of the control group. What can you say about the effectiveness of this program? What facts may explain these results?

13.7 Ashville City Maintenance Chief Leon Tightwad wants to reduce the costs of maintaining the city automobile fleet. Knowing that city cars are kept for only 1 year, Leon feels that the city's periodic maintenance schedule may cost more than it is worth. Leon randomly selects 75 cars out of 300 and performs no maintenance on these cars unless they break down. At the end of the year, he finds the results shown in the accompanying table. What can you tell Leon about this experiment?

	Maintained Cars	No Maintenance
Mean	$625	$575
Standard deviation	150	200

13.8 Refer to Problem 13.7. Charlie Hustle is in charge of selling Ashville's cars after they have been used 1 year. He believes that Leon's policy costs the city money, and he presents the figures on the cars' sales prices shown in the accompanying table. Does Charlie have an argument? On an overall basis, who will save the city the most money, Leon Tightwad or Charlie Hustle?

	Maintained Cars	No Maintenance
Mean	$17,456	$16,821
Standard deviation	2,300	2,200

13.9 Both the Brethren Charity and the Lost Souls Mission are operating marriage counseling programs. The Brethren program has a man–woman team to counsel people, whereas Lost Souls uses single counselors. Last year, 12 of 84 randomly selected couples receiving counseling at Brethren ended up divorced. Ten of the 51 randomly selected couples at Lost Souls were divorced. As a policy analyst, what can you say about the programs?

13.10 The William G. Harding School of Public Affairs would like to evaluate its affirmative action program for students. After extended discussion, the faculty decides that all students will take the state civil service exam, and the scores on this exam will be used as the criterion of success. Write a memo discussing the results shown in the accompanying table.

	Regular Students	Affirmative Action Students
Mean	86.4	84.1
Standard deviation	17.3	28.2
n	44	19

13.11 A professor thinks that the MPA students at the University of Arizona (UA) are brighter than those at the University of Georgia (UGA). To examine this hypothesis, he gives the same midterm to UA students that he gave to UGA students the previous year. He finds the following results:

	UA	UGA
Mean	83.1	88.7
Standard deviation	11.4	7.8
n	36	24

Present a testable hypothesis and a null hypothesis, and evaluate them. Present a conclusion in plain English.

13.12 The state personnel bureau wants to know whether people resign if they are not promoted during the year. Bureau researchers take a sample of 30 people who were promoted and find that 6 of them resigned; a sample of 45 people who were not promoted includes 15 who resigned. State a hypothesis and a null hypothesis, and test them. State your conclusion in plain English.

13.13 Iowa has decided to run a quasi-experiment in regard to its workfare program and the program's impact on incentives. Officials think that workfare increases the incentives to individuals to earn more money in addition to welfare. Two hundred recipients are selected; 120 are randomly assigned to a workfare program, and 80 are assigned to a control group. By follow-up interviews, the state finds out how much outside income per week is earned by each individual, with the following results:

	Workfare	Control
Mean	$342.50	$297.30
s	137	95

Present a hypothesis and a null hypothesis, and evaluate them. State a conclusion in plain English.

13.14 Wisconsin contracts with private organizations to operate its job placement program. The state needs to evaluate the quality of the program offered by one of its vendors, the Beaver Dam Job Placement Center. One hundred unemployed individuals are selected at random. Sixty of these are run through the Beaver Dam program; the others serve as a control group. Sixty percent of the Beaver Dam program group get jobs; the average salary of those jobs is $29,847 (with a standard deviation of $1,800). Of the control group, 30% get jobs; the average salary of those jobs is $27,567 (standard deviation $3,600). This program can be evaluated by two different criteria. Perform the calculations for both criteria, and present your conclusions.

13.15 Enormous State University has an MPA program. The MPA director is concerned with the small number of MPA students who are being awarded Presidential Management Internships (PMIs). She thinks that this might be because MPA students lack interviewing skills. To experiment with this notion, 10 of the 20 PMI nominees are sent to a special interviewing workshop; the other 10 do not attend the workshop. Seven of the ten attending the workshop receive PMIs, and three of those not attending the workshop receive PMIs. Present a hypothesis and a null hypothesis, and evaluate them. State your conclusion in plain English.

13.16 The Department of Human Services (DHS) has contracted with the Institute for Research on Poverty to run an experimental job training program. A group of 200 individuals are randomly selected from among the hard-core unemployed. A control group of 50 is selected at the same time. The 200 individuals in the experimental group are assigned to a program that attempts to place them in jobs. DHS has defined placement of the individual in a job for 6 months as a success. Of this group, 38 are still employed after 6 months. Of the control group, 11 are employed after 6 months. Present a hypothesis and a null hypothesis, and test them. Present a conclusion in plain English.

13.17 As a National Institutes of Health administrator, you wish to evaluate an experiment at the University of Illinois concerning the impact of exercise on individuals with high-cholesterol diets. The Illinois researchers take 25 pigs that have high-cholesterol diets; 10 of these are randomly selected and made to jog on a treadmill for 2 miles a day. The other 15 pigs do not jog (although they might play golf or get exercise in other ways). After 6 months, each pig is tested for cholesterol in the bloodstream (measured in parts per million) with the following results:

	Exercise Group	Others
Mean	160	210
Standard deviation	40	60

Present a hypothesis and a null hypothesis, and evaluate them. Present a statistical conclusion in plain English.

13.18 The Austin Independent School District wants to know whether the LBJ Magnet School for the Sciences is improving student performance. One hundred students were admitted as sophomores last year to the LBJ school. These students scored a mean of 14.7 on the junior year math achievement test (14 years, 7 months, or about a college sophomore level) with a standard deviation of 1.1. Twenty-three of these students play football. Education researcher Lana "Ein" Stein selects a control group of students who, in their sophomore year, performed comparably to the LBJ students in their sophomore year. These 144 students did not attend a magnet school. Their junior math achievement test produced a mean of 13.6 and a standard deviation of 2.9. Their mean IQ score was 117. Present a hypothesis, test this hypothesis, and present a conclusion in plain English regarding the Magnet school students.

13.19 The Wisconsin legislature is considering a mandatory motorcycle helmet law. What legislators don't know is whether the law would encourage more people to use helmets. Senator I. C. Probability tells you that Minnesota has a law similar to the one that Wisconsin is considering. He would like you to compare the use of motorcycle helmets in Minnesota and Wisconsin. A survey is taken in both states, resulting in the statistics presented below. Present a hypothesis and a null hypothesis, and test them. Present your conclusion in plain English.

	Minnesota	Wisconsin
n	75	110
Number using helmets	37	28

13.20 Madonna Lewis's job in the Department of Sanitary Engineering is to determine whether new refuse collection procedures have improved the public's perception of the department. Public opinion surveys were taken both before and after the new procedures were implemented. The results are as follows:

	Before	After
The department is doing a good job	23	47
The department is doing a poor job	79	73

Present a hypothesis and a null hypothesis, and evaluate the hypotheses.

13.21 Edinburg attorney J. L. "Bubba" Pollinard is collecting data for a discrimination suit. He asks 500 Latino people whether they believe that the city is biased against them; 354 say it is. Bubba asks 300 Anglo residents the same question, and 104 residents state that the city is biased against them. Present a hypothesis and a null hypothesis, test the hypotheses, and present a conclusion in plain English.

13.22 Internal auditors for the city of Austin, Texas, periodically analyze patterns in parking meter collections. Specifically, the auditors focus on whether daily collection totals for the city's two collection teams are dramatically different. The auditors feel that the average daily receipt figures for each team should not be dramatically different; large differences between teams could indicate employee thefts or misreporting of receipts. The auditors ask you, as the chief statistician, to run a difference of means test on 200 randomly selected days of receipts (100 days for each team). Present a hypothesis and a null hypothesis, and conduct a difference of means test. Based on your analysis, what can you tell the auditors? (*Note: The data set for this problem is available on the book's companion website.*)

13.23 The director of the Wisconsin Department of Business Licensing is looking for ways to improve employee productivity. Specifically, she would like to see an improvement in the percentage of applications that employees process correctly. The director randomly selects 50 employees and gathers data on the percentage of applications each one correctly processed last month. On the recommendation of a consultant, the director has these 50 employees complete a 3-day workshop in Proactive Synergy Restructuring Techniques (PSRTs). At the end of the month following the PSRT training, the director collects the application processing data for the same 50 employees. Help the director analyze these data. From a statistical standpoint, what can you tell the director? (*Note: The data set for this problem is available on the book's companion website.*)

13.24 Dan Stout, a researcher at the Wisconsin Department of Public Health, has begun work on a study examining body mass index (BMI) values for Wisconsin residents. Mr. Stout is particularly interested in BMI variations across the state's two largest cities: Milwaukee and Madison. Mr. Stout believes that citizens in Madison are more physically fit and should thus have lower average BMI scores than citizens in Milwaukee. As a trial run before conducting the larger study, Mr. Stout has obtained two random samples of BMI data for 120 residents in each city (Milwaukee = BMIMIL, Madison = BMIMAD). What can Mr. Stout conclude from these data? (*Note: The data set for this problem is available on the book's companion website.*)

13.25 Dr. Sheila Roberts, head of the Department of Public Administration at Eastern Seaboard State University, is concerned about whether student performance in online courses is worse than student performance in traditional courses. Specifically, she believes that the lack of face-to-face student–instructor interaction in online courses may be an impediment to learning. To test this hypothesis, Dr. Roberts randomly selects the final grades from 240 students enrolled in Principles of Public Administration over the past year (120 students from online sections and 120 from traditional sections). What can Dr. Roberts conclude about her hypothesis? (*Note: The data set for this problem is available on the book's companion website.*)

13.26 The Department of Service Financing in the city of Belmont, New York, has been experimenting with having city units provide services in house versus having private contractors provide the same services. In the city Grounds Department, half of the landscaping work is performed by city crews, whereas the other half is performed by a private landscaping firm. The city manager has collected random samples of weekly expense report data for both providers. He asks you to conduct a difference of means test. What can the city manager conclude about the difference between in-house and private service provision? (*Note: The data set for this problem is available on the book's companion website.*)

13.27 John P. Smith, Director of the Texas Nonprofits Working Group, is interested in the emerging trend of small nonprofits (defined as those with budgets less than $2 million per year) collaborating with each other for the purpose of sharing administrative services (e.g., accounting, human resources, and information technology services). Mr. Smith hypothesizes that nonprofits engaged in collaborative relationships should be able to spend less on administrative services than nonprofits not engaged in collaborative cost-sharing agreements. To test this hypothesis, Mr. Smith collects data for a random sample of 150 small nonprofits in the state. Specifically, the variable of interest is the percent of each organization's annual budget spent on administrative services. In the sample, 75 of these organizations are engaged in collaborative cost-sharing agreements (SHARE); the other 75 are not (NOSHARE). Upon running a difference of means test, what can Mr. Smith conclude about his hypothesis? (*Note: The data set for this problem is available on the book's companion website.*)

13.28 A local foundation in Milwaukee has provided the Technical College of Milwaukee (TCM) with funding for a pilot program aimed at improving the academic performance of students who are single mothers. A number of these students have told school officials that laptop computers would help them immensely, due to unpredictable work and childcare scheduling issues that make it difficult for them to use the computer labs on campus. The foundation would like to see evidence on the program's effectiveness before making a larger financial commitment. Accordingly, administrators at TCM randomly assign the available laptops to 100 students from the group of students who requested laptops (COMSTUD). Another 100 of the students who requested (but did not receive) laptops were selected as a control group (NSTUD). At the end of the semester, the administrators conduct a difference of means test on the semester grade point averages (GPAs) for the two groups (the average GPAs were roughly the same for both groups at the start of the semester). What can they tell the foundation based on these results? (*Note: The data set for this problem is available on the book's companion website.*)

13.29 The federal government has asked officials in Milwaukee County to collect data on the Supplemental Nutrition Program for Women, Infants, and Children (WIC) in Milwaukee. Federal officials are concerned about whether children born to non-English-speaking parents are as healthy as those born to native speakers. County officials decide to conduct a pilot study to examine whether there are any differences between these groups. Specifically, officials will examine birth weight data for the two groups (measured in pounds and ounces). Two randomly selected samples of WIC participants are included in the study (each sample includes 100 individuals). The first sample of birth weight data is for babies born to non-English-speaking (NENGLISH) parents. The second sample is birth weight data for babies born to native speakers (ENGLISH). State the null and alternative hypotheses. Test the hypotheses using a difference of means test. (*Note: The data set for this problem is available on the book's companion website.*)

Analysis of Nominal and Ordinal Data

PART

5

Analysis of
Nominal and
Ordinal Data

Construction and Analysis of Contingency Tables

Chapter 2 introduced the three levels of measurement—nominal, ordinal, and interval—and discussed the measures of central tendency that can be used to describe and summarize variables of each type. Although this information provides a useful guide to the treatment of single variables, ordinarily such univariate statistics constitute only the first step in data analysis—and in the job of the public or nonprofit manager.

Imagine for a moment that you work in the department of public affairs for a large government or nonprofit agency. The department has just finished conducting its annual survey of public opinion about the agency. Some of the initial results show that most of the people interviewed now feel that the agency is doing a "very poor job," and the median opinion is not very cheery either, a "poor job." This assessment represents a dramatic downturn in public opinion compared with previous years. To be sure, this is important information, but obviously it is not the kind of news that you would want to give to your boss or to the mayor and the budget-minded city council or board of directors without some idea of how the public image of the agency might be improved. But how might this goal be attained?

One way to approach this question is to consider *why* public support has fallen. Perhaps the agency has cut a popular program that it used to administer in Avery County, California, one of several counties over which it has jurisdiction. If the loss of this program is responsible for the drop in agency prestige, then you would expect to find a lower level of public favor in Avery County than in other counties where it has not been necessary to cut programs. Or perhaps the fall in public esteem is a result of the recent appointment of a new director of the agency, "mean" Gene Medford, whose past political exploits received rough treatment in the local press. If so, then you would hypothesize that those citizens who disapproved of the appointment would be more critical of the job performance of the agency than would those who approved of the appointment. Fortunately, the survey of public opinion conducted by the agency elicited information pertaining to citizen residence and attitude toward the new director, so both of these ideas can be checked.

These proposed explanations for the decline in public opinion carry different implications for public policy. If data analysis yielded support for the first explanation, then the chief executive could be informed (gently!) that although public opinion of the agency is low evidence indicates that it could be improved through restoration of the program that had been cut in Avery County. By contrast, if the data showed support for the second explanation, the chief executive might advise Medford to clear the air about his past through public speeches and press conferences—or the chief executive might decide that less pleasant steps are necessary.

Regardless of which (if either) explanation turns out to be correct, the important point is that data analysis has moved from a concern with a single variable—public opinion toward the performance of the agency—to a focus on *relationships between variables*. This sequence is typical in the analysis of data. Generally, we would like to know not only the distribution of scores or responses on a variable of interest but also an explanation for this distribution. Are the county of residence of a citizen and attitude toward the agency related? Does a relationship exist between citizens' attitudes toward the new director and their attitudes toward the agency? In other words, do the responses on one variable help explain or account for responses on a second variable?

This chapter begins with the development of statistical methods to answer such questions. It is concerned with relationships between variables measured at the nominal and ordinal levels. (Relationships between interval-level variables are the subject of Part VI of this book.) The method that is generally employed to examine these relationships is called *contingency table analysis* or the analysis of *cross-tabulations*. In this chapter we show how to set up a contingency table— cross-tabulating the responses to a pair of nominal or ordinal variables—and how to interpret it. The next two chapters elaborate on this topic: Chapter 15 presents aids to the interpretation of contingency tables, such as "measures of association" between variables. Chapter 16 discusses a procedure called *control table analysis,* or *statistical controls*, through which the relationships among three or more variables can be examined.

Percentage Distributions

Before we can treat the construction and interpretation of contingency tables, we need to review *percentage distributions*. A contingency table is a bivariate (two-variable) percentage (or frequency) distribution. If you do not need the review, congratulations—please skip to the next section.

As shown in Chapter 4, a percentage distribution displays the percentage associated with each data value or group of data values. Consider the distribution of responses of a sample of individuals to a standard survey question that asks respondents to consider whether there are too many bureaucrats in the federal government. Table 14.1 presents the frequency distribution.

This distribution is difficult to interpret. Although it is evident that the mode is "agree" (the data value that occurs with greatest frequency; see Chapter 5 on

Table 14.1	Distribution of Responses	
	To what extent would you agree or disagree with the following statement? There are currently too many bureaucrats working for the federal government.	
	Response	Number of People
	Strongly agree	686
	Agree	979
	Neutral	208
	Disagree	436
	Strongly disagree	232

© Cengage Learning

measures of central tendency), the distribution does not give a clear presentation of this opinion's popularity. Is it held by half of the people interviewed? A third? Nor does the table communicate the relative frequency of occurrence of the other opinions (strongly disagree, disagree, and so on). What proportion of the sample voiced these responses?

Without this information, it is difficult not only to comprehend this distribution of responses but also to compare it with other distributions of attitudes. For example, it would be interesting to know how this particular distribution of opinion toward federal bureaucrats compares with distributions obtained when the question was put to different samples of people, in different regions of the country, or at different times. Has there been a trend among different groups, or in different regions, or over time toward the view that there are too many federal bureaucrats? Does the public feel the same way about local bureaucrats or state bureaucrats?

The raw response figures displayed in Table 14.1 cannot answer these questions. In order to address them, data analysts conventionally convert the raw figures to percentages, thus creating a percentage distribution.

Steps in Percentaging

The procedure for converting raw figures to percentages involves three steps:

Step 1: Add the number of people (frequencies) giving each of the responses to yield the total number of cases or **N**. In Table 14.1, this sum is equal to $686 + 979 + 208 + 436 + 232 = 2,541$.

Step 2: Divide each of the individual frequencies by this total and multiply the result by 100. For example, for the response "strongly agree" in Table 14.1, we divide 686 by 2,541 and obtain .26997. Then we multiply this result by 100, yielding 26.997. This figure is the *percentage* of the people interviewed who gave the response "strongly agree." Repeat the procedure for each of the other response categories.

Table 14.2	Percentage Distribution: Calculations

To what extent would you agree or disagree with the following statement?
There are currently too many bureaucrats working for the federal government.

Response	Frequency	Percentage	
Strongly agree	686	$(686 \div 2{,}541) \times 100 =$	27.0
Agree	979	$(979 \div 2{,}541) \times 100 =$	38.5
Neutral	208	$(208 \div 2{,}541) \times 100 =$	8.2
Disagree	436	$(436 \div 2{,}541) \times 100 =$	17.2
Strongly disagree	232	$(232 \div 2{,}541) \times 100 =$	9.1
Total	2,541		100.0

© Cengage Learning

Step 3: Round each of the percentages to one decimal place. If the second place to the right of the decimal point is greater than or equal to 5, add 1 to the first place to the right of the decimal. In this procedure, .16 becomes .2, .43 becomes .4, and 26.997 becomes 27.0. Table 14.2 shows the percentage distribution. (You may prefer to express the percentages as whole numbers, with no decimal places. Follow these rules for rounding.)

Displaying and Interpreting Percentage Distributions

The percentage distribution displays the percentage of respondents giving each of the responses to the survey item. The only frequency or raw number that should be presented in the table is the total number of cases, usually abbreviated **N**. The total frequency helps the reader evaluate the distribution of responses. In general, the larger the number of cases on which the percentages are based, the greater the confidence in the results. For example, you would normally have more confidence in a percentage distribution based on 2,541 respondents than in one based on 541 or 41. Table 14.3 shows the final "percentaged" table.

The percentage distribution facilitates interpretation and comparison. It is clear from the percentage distribution in Table 14.3 that approximately 40% of those interviewed (the mode) "agree" that there are currently too many federal bureaucrats and that 65.5% (27.0% + 38.5% = 65.5%), or nearly two-thirds, express agreement with this notion (either "strongly agree" or "agree"). The extent of agreement far outweighs the extent of disagreement—65.5% versus 26.3% (the percentage indicating either "disagree" or "strongly disagree"; 17.2% + 9.1% = 26.3%). Only a small proportion (8.2%) remains "neutral."

These percentages can be compared with those obtained in other surveys of public opinion (e.g., surveys conducted at other points in time or administered to different samples or populations) to assess how attitudes toward bureaucrats are

Table 14.3	Percentage Distribution: Final Table

To what extent would you agree or disagree with the following statement? There are currently too many bureaucrats working for the federal government.

Response	Percentage
Strongly agree	27.0
Agree	38.5
Neutral	8.2
Disagree	17.2
Strongly disagree	9.1
Total	100.0
	(**N** = 2,541)

changing. For instance, if 5 years ago a similar survey of public opinion indicated that only 40% of the public expressed agreement that there are too many federal bureaucrats, it would be evident that public opinion is becoming more negative.

Collapsing Percentage Distributions

Often, public and nonprofit managers combine, or *collapse*, several of the original response categories in order to form a smaller number of new categories and to calculate percentages based on the new categories. For example, in the preceding discussion, the response categories "strongly agree" and "agree" and the categories "strongly disagree" and "disagree" were collapsed into broader categories of "agreement" and "disagreement," respectively.

To calculate percentages in a collapsed distribution, you employ the procedure described earlier: (1) Compute the total frequency, (2) divide the frequency of each of the new categories by this total and multiply by 100, and (3) round to the first decimal place (or nearest whole percent). Alternatively, if the percentage distribution for the variable has already been calculated based on the original response categories, the percentages for the new collapsed categories can be found by adding the percentages for the categories that have been collapsed. (The percentages for categories that have not been collapsed will not change.) The latter method was employed in the preceding discussion. For example, because 27.0% of the sample stated that they "strongly agree" that there are too many federal bureaucrats and 38.5% "agree," a total of 65.5% fall into the new collapsed category of "agree." The first of these methods for percentaging a collapsed distribution is illustrated in Table 14.4.

There are two primary reasons for presenting the percentage distribution in collapsed form. First, it is easier to interpret a distribution based on a few response categories than one based on a lot. In many instances, such as the preparation of memoranda, the collapsed distribution presents all the information

| Table 14.4 | Collapsed Percentage Distribution |

To what extent would you agree or disagree with the following statement? There are currently too many bureaucrats working for the federal government.

Original Response Categories	(Original) Frequency	Collapsed Response Categories	(Collapsed) Frequency	Percentage
Strongly agree	686 ⎱	Agree	1,665	(1,665 ÷ 2,541) × 100 = 65.5
Agree	979 ⎰			
Neutral	208	Neutral	208	(208 ÷ 2,541) × 100 = 8.2
Disagree	436 ⎱			
Strongly disagree	232 ⎰	Disagree	668	(668 ÷ 2,541) × 100 = 26.3
Total	2,541	Total	2,541	100.0

© Cengage Learning

managers need to know, without burdening them with unnecessary complexity. Second, often in public and nonprofit administration, the data analyst or manager is not confident that the distinction between some response categories is very clear or meaningful; that is, you can generally be much more confident that, *in all*, 65.5% of those interviewed agree with a proposition than that *exactly* 27.0% "strongly agree" and *exactly* 38.5% "agree." To avoid communicating a false sense of precision, categories may be collapsed. Another good reason to get used to collapsed percentage distributions is that most contingency tables are based on this format (see below and Chapters 15 and 16).

When you collapse response categories of a variable, the collapsing must not pervert the meaning of the original categories. Response categories should be collapsed only if they are close in substantive meaning. Whereas the kind of collapsing we have done here—"strongly agree" and "agree," "strongly disagree" and "disagree"—is justified, collapsing the categories of "disagree" and "agree" would not be.

The major exception to this rule occurs in distributions of *nominal* variables that have many response categories. Frequently, only a few of the categories will have a large percentage of cases, whereas most of the categories will have only trivial numbers. In this situation, the analyst may choose to present each of the categories containing a substantial percentage and a category labeled "other," formed by collapsing all the remaining categories. For example, consider the variable "religion." In a given sample, the distribution of religion may be 62% Protestant, 22% Catholic, 13% Jewish, 1% Shinto, .5% Buddhist, .6% Hedonist, .5% Jainist, and .4% Central Schwenkenfelter. To summarize this distribution, the analyst may present the percentages as shown in Table 14.5; note the use of a collapsed "other" category.

An exercise is helpful to illustrate these points. The Shawnee Heights Independent Transit Authority has commissioned a poll of 120 persons to determine where Shawnee citizens do most of their shopping. This information is important to determine future transit routes in Shawnee Heights. The transit planners receive the data shown in Table 14.6.

Table 14.5	Collapsed Percentage Distribution for Religion

Religion	Percentage
Protestant	62
Catholic	22
Jewish	13
Other	3
Total	100
	(**N** = 1,872)

Table 14.6	Data for Shawnee Heights Poll

Main Store Named	Number of Persons
Cleo's (neighborhood store)	5
Morgan's (downtown)	18
Wiese's (eastern shopping center)	12
Cheatham's (neighborhood store)	2
Shop City (eastern shopping center)	19
Food-o-Rama (western shopping center)	15
Stermer's (downtown)	7
Binzer's (neighborhood store)	2
England's (western shopping center)	1
Bargainville's (eastern shopping center)	26
Whiskey River (downtown)	13
	120

In the space provided, construct a collapsed percentage distribution of the data in Table 14.6. (*Hint:* Consider collapsing categories based on common locations.)

Contingency Table Analysis

Analysis of contingency tables or cross-tabulations is the primary method public and nonprofit administrators use to examine relationships between variables measured at the ordinal and nominal levels and to make sense of them. The remainder of the chapter discusses the construction and interpretation of contingency tables. As you will see, percentaging is instrumental to contingency table analysis.

Constructing Contingency Tables

A **contingency table** or **cross-tabulation** is a bivariate frequency distribution. We have dealt with **univariate**, or single-variable, frequency distributions in examples earlier in this chapter and in previous chapters. A univariate frequency distribution presents the number of cases (or frequency) of each value of a variable. By analogy, a **bivariate**, or two-variable, frequency distribution presents the number of cases that fall into each possible pairing of the values or categories of two variables simultaneously. This definition is more readily visualized in an example.

Consider the cross-tabulation of the variables "race" (white, nonwhite) and "sex" (male, female) for volunteers to the Klondike Expressionist Art Museum. As these variables are defined here, there are four possible pairings: white and male, white and female, nonwhite and male, and nonwhite and female volunteers. Pairings across variables are easier to conceptualize if we first consider what the data look like prior to being summarized in a contingency table. For the Klondike volunteers, gender and race are coded as follows:

Sex	Race
1 = female	1 = white
2 = male	2 = nonwhite

Both variables are measured at the nominal level. Table 14.7 presents the raw data for 12 volunteers at the Art Museum.

The first row of data indicates that the first volunteer at the Art Museum has a score of "1" for both variables: This volunteer is a white female. The second

Table 14.7	Data for 12 Volunteers at the Klondike Expressionist Art Museum

Sex	Race
1	1
2	2
1	2
2	2
2	1
1	1
1	2
1	1
2	2
1	2
2	2
2	1

© Cengage Learning

row of data has values of "2" for both variables, so the second volunteer is a nonwhite male. To make sure you understand the pairings for sex and race, interpret the entries in this manner for volunteers 3 through 12.

The cross-tabulation of these two variables for all 451 volunteers at the Klondike Expressionist Art Museum displays the number of cases (volunteers) that fall into each of the race–sex pairings or combinations. In this sample of museum volunteers composed of 142 white males, 67 white females, 109 nonwhite males, and 133 nonwhite females, we obtain the contingency table displayed in Table 14.8. This type of table is called a *cross-tabulation* because it crosses (and tabulates) each of the categories of one variable with each of the categories of a second variable.

The numbers (frequency) in each cell of the table represent the aggregate results compiled from all 451 rows of data on volunteers, where each row corresponds to a volunteer. Although the cells within contingency tables such as Table 14.8 sometimes contain large numbers that may "look" like interval-level data, you should remember that these numbers represent total case counts for nominal- or ordinal-level variables. The data used to generate Table 14.8 look just like the data for the 12 volunteers displayed in Table 14.7, except that the data for all 451 rows (volunteers) are counted and summarized in Table 14.8.

At this point, some terminology is useful. The cross-classifications of the two variables—white–male, white–female, nonwhite–male, nonwhite–female—are called the **cells** of the table. The cell frequencies indicate the number of cases fitting the description specified by the categories of the row and column variables. The total number of respondents who are white or nonwhite is presented at the foot of the "White" and "Nonwhite" columns, respectively. Similarly, the total number of respondents who are male or female is presented at the far right of the respective rows. In reference to their position around the perimeter of the table, these total frequencies are called **marginals** (or marginal frequencies). These totals are calculated by adding the frequencies in the appropriate column or row. Finally, the **grand total**—the total number of cases represented in the table (**N**)—is displayed conventionally in the lower right corner of the table. It can be found by adding the cell frequencies, the row marginals, or the column marginals. You should satisfy yourself that all three of these additions give the same result. You should also make certain that you understand what each number in Table 14.8 represents.

Table 14.8	Contingency Table: Race and Sex of Volunteers to Klondike Expressionist Art Museum		
		Race	
Sex	White	Nonwhite	Total
Male	142	109	51
Female	67	133	200
Total	209	242	451

Table 14.9 Relationship between Type of Employment and Attitude toward Balancing the Federal Budget

Attitude toward Budget Balancing	Type of Employment			
	Public	Private	Nonprofit	Total
Disapprove				
Approve				
Total				

© Cengage Learning

Table 14.10 Relationship between Educational Level and Performance on Civil Service Examination

Performance on Civil Service Examination	Education		Total
	High School or Less	More Than High School	
Low	100	200	300
High	150	800	950
Total	250	1,000	1,250

© Cengage Learning

To ensure that you can assemble a cross-tabulation, fill in the cell, marginal, and grand total frequencies in Table 14.9. The variables of interest are "type of employment" (public sector, private sector, or nonprofit sector) and "attitude toward balancing the federal budget" (disapprove or approve). The cell frequencies are as follows: public–disapprove 126; public–approve 54; private–disapprove 51; private–approve 97; nonprofit–disapprove 25; nonprofit–approve 38.

Relationships between Variables

Public and nonprofit managers assemble and examine cross-tabulations because they are interested in the relationship between two ordinal- or nominal-level variables. A **statistical relationship** may be defined as a recognizable pattern of change in one variable as the other variable changes. In particular, the type of question that is usually asked is: As one variable increases in value, does the other also increase? Or, as one variable increases, does the other decrease?

The cell frequencies of a cross-tabulation provide some information regarding whether changes in one variable are associated statistically with (related to) changes in the other variable. The cross-tabulation presented in Table 14.10 of "education" (high school or less; more than high school) with "performance on the civil service examination" (low; high) illustrates this idea.

At first glance, the table seems to indicate that as education *increases* from high school or less ("low") to more than high school ("high"), performance on the civil service examination *decreases*, for twice as many individuals with high education (200) as individuals with low education (100) received low scores on the test. Because we would anticipate that education would *improve* scores on the examination, this initial finding seems counterintuitive. In fact, it is not only counterintuitive but also incorrect.

The reason for the faulty interpretation is that we have failed to take into account the *total number* of individuals who have low as compared with high education (that is, the marginal totals). Note that although this sample contained only 250 people with a high school education or less, 1,000 individuals—four times as many—had more than a high school education. Thus, when these figures are put in perspective, there are *four* times as many people with high education than with low education in the sample—yet only *twice* as many of the former as of the latter got low scores on the civil service examination. These data suggest that, in contrast to our initial interpretation, more highly educated people do earn higher scores on the civil service examination than do the less educated. This finding accords with intuition and is the primary conclusion supported by the table—when one analyzes it correctly.

How does one do so? The analysis process has three major steps. The problem with the initial interpretation of the contingency table was that it overlooked the relative number of cases in the categories of education (that is, the marginal totals). This problem can be remedied by percentaging the table appropriately—which is the key to analyzing and understanding cross-tabulations. The steps in the analysis process are as follows:

Step 1: Determine which variable is *independent* and which is *dependent*. As explained in Chapter 3, the independent variable is the anticipated causal variable, the one that is supposed to lead to changes or effects in the dependent or response or criterion variable. In the current example of the relationship between education and performance on the civil service examination, it is expected that higher education leads to improved performance on the test. Stated as a hypothesis: The higher the education, the higher the expected score on the civil service examination. Hence, education is the independent variable, and performance on the civil service examination is the dependent variable.

Step 2: Calculate percentages within the categories of the *independent* variable—in this case, education. We would like to know the percentage of people with high school education or less (low education) who received high scores on the civil service examination and the percentage of people with more than a high school education (high education) who received high scores. Then it would be possible to compare these percentages to determine whether those with high education receive higher scores on the examination in the aggregate than do those with low education. This comparison allows us to evaluate whether the expectation or hypothesis stated previously is correct, that education leads to improved scores on the civil service examination.

The procedure used to calculate percentages within the categories of education is the same as the univariate procedure elaborated earlier in the chapter. We are interested first in the percentage of people with high school education or less who received high scores on the civil service examination. Table 14.10 indicates that a total of 250 people fall into this category of education, and of these, 150 received high scores on the test. Thus, we find that $(150 \div 250) \times 100 = 60\%$ of those with low education earned high scores on the civil service examination. The other 100 of the 250 people with low education received low scores on the test; converting to a percentage, we find that $(100 \div 250) \times 100 = 40\%$ of those with low education earned low test scores.

Moving to those with more than a high school education, Table 14.10 shows that 800 of the 1,000 people with this level of education—or 80% $[(800 \div 1,000) \times 100]$—received high scores on the civil service examination, and the other 200—or 20% $[(200 \div 1,000) \times 100]$—earned low scores. Table 14.11 presents the cross-tabulation percentaged within the categories of education, including all calculations.

Step 3: Compare the percentages calculated within the categories of the *independent variable* (education) for *one* of the categories of the *dependent variable* (performance on the civil service examination). For example, whereas 80% of those with high education earned high scores on the civil service examination, only 60% of those with low education did so. Thus, our hypothesis is supported by these data: In general, those with high education received higher scores on the examination than did those with low education. As hypothesized, the higher the education, the higher is the score on the civil service examination.

To summarize the relationship between two variables in a cross-tabulation, public and nonprofit managers often calculate a **percentage difference** across one of the categories of the dependent variable. In this case, the percentage difference is equal to $80\% - 60\% = 20$ percentage points (the percentage of those with high education who earned high scores on the test minus the percentage of those with low education who did so). The conclusion is that education appears to make a

Table 14.11	**Percentage Distribution for Data of Table 14.10**	
Performance on Civil Service Examination	**Education**	
	High School or Less	More Than High School
Low	$(100 \div 250) \times 100 = 40\%$	$(200 \div 1,000) \times 100 = 20\%$
High	$(150 \div 250) \times 100 = 60\%$	$(800 \div 1,000) \times 100 = 80\%$
Total	$(n = 250)$ 100%	$(n = 1,000)$ 100%

© Cengage Learning

difference of 20 percentage points in performance on the civil service examination. As you will learn in Chapter 15, the percentage difference is a measure of the strength of the relationship between two variables.

Example: Automobile Maintenance in Berrysville

The city council of Berrysville, California, has been under considerable pressure to economize. Last year, the council passed an ordinance authorizing an experimental program for the maintenance of city-owned vehicles. The bill stipulates that for 1 year, a random sample of 150 of the city's 400 automobiles will receive no preventive maintenance and will simply be driven until they break down. The other 250 automobiles will receive regularly scheduled preventive maintenance. The council is interested in whether the expensive program of preventive maintenance reduces the number of breakdowns. After a year under the experimental maintenance program, the city council was presented with the data in Table 14.12, which summarizes the number of automobile breakdowns under the no maintenance and preventive maintenance plans. Analyze the data for the city council, and help the council by making a recommendation regarding whether the program should be continued (or expanded) or terminated.

Step 1: Determine which variable is independent and which is dependent. Because automobile maintenance is expected to affect the number of breakdowns, maintenance is the independent variable, and breakdowns is the dependent variable. Stated as a hypothesis, the greater the level of maintenance the less the rate of breakdowns.

Step 2: Calculate percentages within the categories of the independent variable, automobile maintenance. The calculations are shown in Table 14.13.

Step 3: Compare percentages for one of the categories of the dependent variable. More than half (52%) of the automobiles that received no maintenance broke down during the 1-year experimental program, compared to just 22.4% of the automobiles that received regularly scheduled maintenance, a difference of 29.6% (52% − 22.4%). Thus, automobile maintenance appears to make nearly a 30 percentage point difference in the rate of breakdowns. The data support the hypothesis:

Table 14.12	Automobile Maintenance Data		
	Automobile Maintenance		
Automobile Breakdowns	None	Regularly Scheduled	Total
No breakdown	72	194	266
Breakdown	78	56	134
Total	150	250	400

Table 14.13	Percentage Distribution for Data of Table 14.12	
	Automobile Maintenance	
Automobile Breakdowns	None	Regularly Scheduled
No breakdown	$(72 \div 150) \times 100 = 48\%$	$(194 \div 250) \times 100 = 77.6\%$
Breakdown	$(78 \div 150) \times 100 = 52\%$	$(56 \div 250) \times 100 = \underline{22.4\%}$
Total	$(n = 150)$ \quad 100%	$(n = 250)$ \quad 100.0%

© Cengage Learning

As maintenance increases, the rate of breakdowns decreases by almost 30%. From these data, should you recommend to the city council that it continues or terminates the experimental maintenance program?

Larger Contingency Tables

With one exception, the examples of contingency tables presented in this chapter have consisted of "two-by-two" tables—cross-tabulations in which both the independent and the dependent variables comprise just two values or response categories. Cross-tabulations can and often do consist of variables with a greater number of response categories. Table 14.14 presents the cross-tabulation of income (low, medium, and high) and job satisfaction (low, medium, and high) for the employees of Maslow City Post Office.

Although the analysis becomes somewhat more complicated, contingency tables based on variables with many response categories are analyzed in the same way as are the smaller two-by-two tables. First, determine which variable is independent and which is dependent. In this example, you would expect income to lead to job satisfaction: The greater the income, the higher the predicted job satisfaction. Income is the independent variable, and job satisfaction is the dependent variable. Thus in the second step, the percentage given in the table is within the categories of income. Table 14.15 presents the cross-tabulation, percentaged according to the steps elaborated earlier.

Table 14.14	Relationship between Income and Job Satisfaction			
	Income			
Job Satisfaction	Low	Medium	High	Total
Low	100	30	10	140
Medium	60	80	15	155
High	40	40	50	130
Total	200	150	75	425

© Cengage Learning

The final step in the analysis of contingency tables is to compare percentages for one of the categories of the dependent variable. Although the choice of a category in two-by-two tables is not a critical decision—both categories of the dependent variable will yield the *same* percentage difference—in larger tables, the selection of a category of the dependent variable for purposes of percentage comparison requires more care. In general, you should *not* choose an *intermediate* category, such as "medium" job satisfaction, for this purpose. Choosing either of the *endpoint* categories—"low" or "high" job satisfaction—will result in clearer understanding and interpretation of the contingency table.

Once the (endpoint) category of the dependent variable has been selected, compare the percentages calculated for the *endpoint* categories of the independent variable. Again, avoid intermediate categories of the independent (and dependent) variable for this purpose. In Table 14.15, this rule suggests that we compare the percentage of those with low income who have high job satisfaction (20%) with the percentage of those with high income who have high job satisfaction (66.7%). Alternatively, we could compare the percentage of those with low income who express low job satisfaction (50%) with the percentage of those with high income who express low job satisfaction (13.3%).

Which percentage comparison(s) should the public or nonprofit manager use to summarize the relationship found in the cross-tabulation? The percentage difference calculation typically yields different results depending on the endpoint category of the dependent variable chosen. In the current case, the percentage difference based on high job satisfaction is $66.7\% - 20.0\% = 46.7\%$, whereas the percentage difference for low job satisfaction is $50.0\% - 13.3\% = 36.7\%$. These percentage differences suggest varying levels of support for the relationship.

The best course of action for the public or nonprofit manager is to consider and report *both* percentage differences. They show that those with high income indicated high job satisfaction more often than did those with low income (by 47%) and, conversely, that those with low income indicated low job satisfaction more often than did their counterparts with high income (by 37%). Thus, income appears to make a difference of 37 to 47 percentage points in job satisfaction. These figures provide support for the hypothesis that the higher the income, the greater is the expected job satisfaction. Chapter 15 presents other techniques especially appropriate for the analysis of larger contingency tables.

Table 14.15	Percentage Distribution for Data of Table 14.14		
	Income		
Job Satisfaction	Low	Medium	High
Low	$(100 \div 200) \times 100 = 50\%$	$(30 \div 150) \times 100 = 20.0\%$	$(10 \div 75) \times 100 = 13.3\%$
Medium	$(60 \div 200) \times 100 = 30\%$	$(80 \div 150) \times 100 = 53.3\%$	$(15 \div 75) \times 100 = 20.0\%$
High	$(40 \div 200) \times 100 = 20\%$	$(40 \div 150) \times 100 = 26.7\%$	$(50 \div 75) \times 100 = 66.7\%$
Total	($n = 200$) 100%	($n = 150$) 100.0%	($n = 75$) 100.0%

Displaying Contingency Tables

A set of conventions has been developed for presenting contingency tables. First, contingency tables are rarely presented as bivariate frequency distributions (i.e., not percentaged). Instead, you should display the table in percentaged form; the percentages should be calculated and displayed according to the procedures described in the preceding section (do *not* show the percentage calculations). Second, the independent variable is placed along the *columns* of the table, and the dependent variable is positioned down the *rows*. Third, the substantive meaning of the categories of the independent variable should show a progression from least to most moving from left to right across the columns, and the categories of the dependent variable should show the same type of progression moving down the rows. In other words, the categories should be listed in the order "low," "medium," and "high"; or "disapprove," "neutral," and "approve"; or "disagree," "neutral," and "agree"; and so on. This procedure greatly facilitates the interpretation of measures of association (discussed in Chapter 15). See Table 14.15 for an illustration. Fourth, the percentages calculated within categories of the independent variable are summed down the column, and the total for each category is placed at the foot of the respective column. The sum should equal 100%, but because of rounding error, it may vary between 99% and 101%. Do not add the percentages across the rows of a table that has been percentaged in this manner (a meaningless operation). Finally, the total number of cases within each category of the independent variable is presented at the foot of the respective column. Usually, these totals are enclosed in parentheses and use the notation $n =$ ____. Table 14.16 presents schematically a contingency table displayed according to the conventional rules.

Two problems arise regarding the conventional display of contingency tables. First, these rules are widely accepted—but not always. Thus, in reading and studying contingency tables presented in books, journals, reports, memoranda, magazines, newspapers, and so on, you should not assume that the independent variable is always along the columns or that the dependent variable is always down the rows. Nor can you assume that the categories of the variables are ordered in the table according to the conventions. Instead, you should examine the table carefully, decide which variable is independent and which one is dependent, check to see whether the percentages have been calculated within the categories of the independent variable, and verify whether the author has compared percentages appropriately. You should recognize these procedures as the steps specified for analyzing and interpreting cross-tabulations presented in this chapter. Cultivating this habit will not only increase your understanding of contingency table results but will also sharpen your analytical skills.

The second problem arises as a consequence of computer utilization. On the job (or in class), you may be dealing with contingency tables constructed and percentaged by a computer. Not only is the computer oblivious to the distinction between independent and dependent variables, the ordering of response

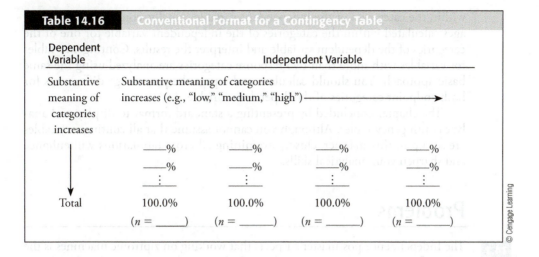

Table 14.16 Conventional Format for a Contingency Table

Dependent Variable	Independent Variable			
Substantive meaning of categories increases	Substantive meaning of categories increases (e.g., "low," "medium," "high") ⟶			
	——%	——%	——%	——%
	——%	——%	——%	——%
	⋮	⋮	⋮	⋮
Total	100.0%	100.0%	100.0%	100.0%
	(n = ____)	(n = ____)	(n = ____)	(n = ____)

© Cengage Learning

categories of variables, and so on, but also computers may be programmed to print out *three different sets of percentages*: percentages calculated (1) within the categories of the row variable; (2) within the categories of the column variable; and (3) according to the total number of cases represented in the contingency table, sometimes called *corner* or *total* percentaging. It is up to you as the manager to determine which set of percentages is most meaningful and, if necessary, to reconstruct the contingency table by hand from the computer printout according to the conventional form described previously. If you follow the steps for the analysis of contingency tables developed in this chapter, this task should not be difficult.

This chapter has elaborated a general method for determining whether two variables measured at the nominal or ordinal level are related statistically: contingency table or cross-tabulation analysis. It has not, however, addressed the question of *how strongly the* two variables are related. This question serves as the focus for the next chapter.

Chapter Summary

Contingency tables or cross-tabulations are used to display and analyze the relationship between two variables measured at the nominal or ordinal level. The simplest and often most useful technique for analyzing contingency tables is to calculate percentages appropriately and to compare them.

This chapter illustrated the analysis of contingency tables. A contingency table is a bivariate—or two-variable—frequency distribution. It presents the number of cases that fall into each possible pairing of the values of two variables. There are three major steps in the analysis process. First, determine which variable is independent and which is dependent. Second, calculate percentages within the categories of the independent variable. Finally, compare the percentages calculated within the categories of the independent variable for one of the categories of the dependent variable and interpret the results. Contingency tables for variables with more than two response categories are analyzed using the same basic approach. You should calculate and report the percentage differences for both endpoint categories of the dependent variable.

The chapter concluded by presenting a standard format to display and analyze contingency tables. Although you cannot assume that all contingency tables are set up in this manner, closely examining all cross-tabulations will enhance and sharpen your analytical skills.

Problems

14.1 The Independence postmaster suspects that working on ziptronic machines is the cause of high absenteeism. More than 10 absences from work without business-related reasons is considered excessive absenteeism. A check of employee records shows that 26 of the 44 ziptronic operators had 10 or more absences and 35 of 120 nonziptronic workers had 10 or more absences. Construct a contingency table for the postmaster. Does the table support the postmaster's suspicion that working on ziptronic machines is related to high absenteeism?

14.2 During last year's budget crunch, several deserving employees of the Bureau of Procedures (BP) were denied promotions. This year, an unusual number of BP employees retired. The bureau chief suspects that the denial of promotions resulted in increased retirements. Of the 115 employees denied promotion, 32 retired. Of the 58 employees promoted, 9 retired. Present a contingency table, and analyze this information.

14.3 The Syrian Air Force brass believe that overweight pilots have slow reaction times. They attribute the poor performance of their air force in recent war games to the pilots being overweight. The accompanying data were collected for all pilots. Analyze these data for the Syrian Air Force brass.

| | **Pilot Weight** | | |
Reaction Time	Normal	Up to 10 Pounds Overweight	More than 10 Pounds Overweight
Poor	14	36	45
Adequate	35	40	33
Excellent	46	25	15

14.4 Auditors for the Military Airlift Command (MAC) are checking the arrival times of the three charter airlines they used in the Pacific last year. Branflake Airways flew 135 flights and was late 78 times. Flying Armadillo Airlines flew 94 flights and was late 35 times. Air Idaho flew 115 flights, with 51 late arrivals. Set up a contingency table, and analyze it for MAC.

14.5 The state personnel office oversees the state's tuition assistance program, which pays the tuition of civil servants taking courses for an MPA. Only two schools offer an MPA degree in the state capital: Capital College of Law and East Winslow State University. Some concern is expressed by legislators that many tuition-assisted students do not graduate. Analyze the data in the accompanying table for the personnel office.

	Students Assisted for MPA Tution	
Status	Capital	East Winslow
Did not graduate	69	83
Adequate	23	37

14.6 Hyram Drant, a research analyst for the city fire department, suspects that old water pumps are more likely to fail. From the data in the accompanying table, construct a contingency table and check Drant's suspicion. How else could this problem be analyzed?

Age of Pump in Years		
Pump Failed	Pump Did Not Fail	
23	15	7
47	6	9
11	9	4
53	33	19
26	26	36
15	17	47
42	9	31
37	12	23
	31	6
	46	9
	15	3

14.7 As head scheduler of special events for the Incomparable Myriad (the city arena), your task is to schedule events that make a profit so that the city need not subsidize the arena. Analyze the data in the accompanying table, which is based on last year's data, and write a report to the city council.

	Type of Event				
Status	Hockey Games	Religious Rallies	Basketball Games	Rock Concerts	Public Administration Conventions
Not profitable	24	4	21	2	3
Profitable	18	32	6	8	0

14.8 As the newly appointed head of evaluation for the state agriculture experiment station, you are asked to evaluate the relative effectiveness of corn hybrids AX147 and AQ49. Of 32 test plots, AX147 had high yields on 21. AQ49 had high yields on 17 of 28 test plots. Construct a contingency table and make a recommendation.

14.9 The Cancer Institute is evaluating an experimental drug for controlling lip cancer. Eighty lip cancer victims are randomly selected and given the drug for 1 year. Sixty other lip cancer victims are randomly selected and given a placebo for a year. From the data in the accompanying table, what would you conclude?

| | **Treatment Group** | |
Cancer Status	Drug Group	Placebo Group
Active	58	42
Remission	22	18

14.10 A supervisor in the Department of Rehabilitative Services is critical of the performance of one of her counselors. The counselor is expected to arrange job training for those in need of vocational rehabilitation so that they may find employment. Yet the counselor has managed to place just 35% of his clients. The counselor argues that he is actually doing a good job and that the reason for his overall low rate of placement is that most of his clients are severely disabled, which makes them very difficult to place. The counselor's case load is presented in the accompanying table. Percentage the table appropriately, and evaluate who is correct—the supervisor or the counselor.

| | **Clients** | |
Job Placement	Not Severely Disabled	Severely Disabled
Not placed	17	118
Placed	47	26

14.11 A professor of public administration has kept records on the class participation of his students over the past several years. He has a strong feeling (hypothesis) that class participation is related to grade in the course. For this analysis he classifies course grades into two categories, fail and pass. He operationalizes class participation as "low" if the student participated in class discussion in fewer than 25% of class periods, and "high" if the student participated in 25% or more of the periods. Based on these definitions, he has assembled the cross-tabulation below. Does a relationship exist between class participation and course grades?

| | **Class Participation** | |
Grade in Course	Low	High
Fail	56	15
Pass	178	107

14.12 Susan Wolch and John Komer are interested in determining which of two books is more effective in teaching statistics to public administration students. They randomly assign a pool of 50 students to two groups of 25 students each. One group uses Meier, Brudney, and Bohte, *Applied Statistics for Public and Nonprofit Administration*. The other group uses Brand *X*. Their criterion for measuring success is student grades in the course. They get the results shown in the accompanying table. Evaluate these data and make a recommendation.

| | Book Used in Class | |
Grade	Brand X	Meier, Brudney, and Bohte
Students receiving C's, D's, or F's	18	9
Students receiving A's, or B's	7	16

14.13 Madonna Lewis is the head of public relations for the Department of Sanitary Engineering. Ms. Lewis is trying to determine whether new refuse collection procedures have improved the public's perception of the Department of Sanitary Engineering. She commissioned public opinion surveys before and after new customer service procedures were implemented in the Department. The results appear in the accompanying table. Analyze the table for Ms. Lewis, and evaluate whether public perception of the department has improved over time.

| | Survey | |
Opinion	Before	After
Department is doing a poor job	182	148
Department is doing a good job	55	94

14.14 The National Association of Schools of Higher Learning is concerned that the use of laptop computers, electronic notebooks, and similar devices by students in class is distracting them from paying attention. The association fears that the electronic technology may decrease students' learning and impede progress toward obtaining the undergraduate degree. To evaluate this relationship, the association obtains information from member schools regarding undergraduate performance. Two variables are available to the association: whether or not a student uses electronic devices in class (no, yes), and whether the student earns the undergraduate degree within 6 years (no, yes). These data appear below. Analyze the data for the National Association of Schools of Higher Learning. Based on your analysis, should the association be concerned about the use of electronic devices by students in class?

| | Use Electronic Devices in Class | |
Graduate in 6 Years	No	Yes
No	517	422
Yes	960	1140

15

Aids for the Interpretation of Contingency Tables

Chapter 14 developed a general method for constructing and analyzing contingency tables or cross-tabulations. It focused on procedures for percentaging these tables and determining whether two variables measured at the nominal or ordinal level are associated statistically.

This chapter begins where the previous one concluded. It elaborates methods for assessing the strength of a relationship between a pair of nominal or ordinal variables in a contingency table. These techniques are not substitutes for but *supplements* to those presented in Chapter 14. *All* of these procedures are useful for understanding the relationship between two variables measured at the nominal or ordinal level.

The chapter is divided into three major sections. The first part is devoted to the chi-square test. The chi-square is a test of statistical significance for relationships between variables measured at the nominal or ordinal level. Part 4, especially Chapters 10 and 11, discussed statistical inference. The chi-square test assesses whether the relationship observed in a cross-tabulation in a sample of data is sufficiently strong to infer that a relationship is likely to exist in the full population. The second part of the chapter develops methods for evaluating the strength of the relationship between two variables. The most straightforward of these techniques is the percentage difference, which was introduced in Chapter 14; it is discussed first. The final portion of the chapter explains measures of association: a group of statistics that summarize the strength of a relationship demonstrated in a cross-tabulation. The chapter presents a detailed development of frequently used measures of association: lambda and Cramér's V for nominal-level variables; and gamma, Kendall's tau-b and tau-c, and Somers's d_{yx} and d_{xy} for ordinal-level variables.

The Chi-Square Test: Statistical Significance for Contingency Tables

Chapter 10 introduced the issue of the correspondence between the results obtained in a sample of data and the actual situation in the population that the sample is intended to represent. *Statistical significance* is a procedure for establishing the degree of confidence that one can have in making an inference from a sample to its parent population.

The **chi-square test** is a procedure for evaluating the level of statistical significance attained by a bivariate relationship in a cross-tabulation. It assumes that there is no relationship between the two variables in the population (null hypothesis) and determines whether any relationship found in the sample cross-tabulation is so small as to be attributable to chance or large enough to suggest that a relationship does exist in the population (alternative hypothesis). This procedure involves three steps.

First, *expected frequencies* are calculated for each cell in the contingency table predicated on the assumption that the two variables are unrelated in the population. Second, based on the difference between the expected frequency and the actual frequency observed in each table cell, a test statistic called the *chi-square* is computed. Because the expected frequencies are premised on the assumption of no relationship, the greater the deviation between them and the actual frequencies, the greater is the departure of the observed relationship from the null hypothesis— hence the greater is our confidence in inferring the existence of a relationship between the two variables in the population. Third, the chi-square value computed for the actual data is compared with a table of theoretical chi-square values calculated and tabulated by statisticians. This comparison allows the analyst to determine the degree of confidence that he or she can have in inferring from the sample cross-tabulation that a relationship exists in the parent population.

Example: Incompetence in the Federal Government?

A disgruntled official working in the personnel department of a large federal bureaucracy is disturbed by the level of incompetence she perceives in the leadership of the organization. She is convinced that incompetence rises to the top, and she shares this belief with a coworker over lunch. The latter challenges her to substantiate her claim.

In order to do so, she selects from her personnel files a random sample of 400 people employed by the organization. From the formal education and civil service examination scores of these people, she classifies them into three levels of competence (low, medium, or high), and from their General Schedule (GS) ratings and formal job descriptions, she classifies them into three categories of hierarchical position in the organization (low, medium, or high). The cross-tabulation of these two variables for the sample of employees appears in Table 15.1. The official would like to know whether she can legitimately infer from this sample cross-tabulation that a relationship exists between competence and hierarchical position in the population of all workers in the organization. Accordingly, she decides to perform the chi-square test; the steps in this procedure follow.

Step 1: Calculate **expected frequencies** for each cell of the cross-tabulation based on the null hypothesis that competence and hierarchical position are not related in the population. (*Note:* If the table has been percentaged, then the data must be converted to raw frequencies before calculating the expected frequencies. Expected frequencies must be calculated on the basis of the raw figures.)

Table 15.1	Cross-Tabulation of Competence and Hierarchy			
	Competence			
Hierarchy	Low	Medium	High	Total
Low	113	60	27	200
Medium	31	91	38	160
High	8	8	24	40
Total	152	159	89	400

© Cengage Learning

If these two variables were unrelated, then we would expect to find the same distribution of hierarchical position in each category of competence as in the sample as a whole. For each level of competence, the percentages of hierarchical position would be identical. In that case, competence would have no impact on hierarchy; there would be percentage differences of 0% for each category of the dependent variable, indicating that the two variables are totally unrelated.

Although calculation of the expected frequencies is a bit cumbersome, it is not difficult. Consider the distribution of hierarchical position. Of the 400 people in the sample, 200 (50%) rank low in position; 160 (40%) hold medium-level positions; and the remaining 40 (10%) are at the top. The hypothetical no-relationship cross-tabulation is displayed in Table 15.2. Assuming that the null hypothesis of no relationship between competence and hierarchy is true, we would expect to find this same distribution of hierarchical position in each of the categories of competence. For example, of the 152 employees ranking low in competence, you would expect to find 50%, or 76.0, in low hierarchical positions (.50 × 152 = 76.0); 40%, or 60.8, in medium-level positions (.40 × 152 = 60.8); and 10%, or 15.2, in high-level positions in the hierarchy (.10 × 152 = 15.2). These are the expected frequencies for the low-competence category.

The expected frequencies for the medium- and high-competence categories are found analogously. Table 15.3 presents the detailed calculations.

Step 2: Compute the value of chi-square for the cross-tabulation. The **chi-square statistic** compares the frequencies actually observed with the expected frequencies (presuming no relationship between the variables) throughout the contingency table. The value of chi-square is found by (1) taking the difference between the observed and expected frequencies for each table cell, (2) squaring this difference, (3) dividing this result by the expected frequency, and (4) summing these quotients across all cells of the table. For example, in the low-competence–low-hierarchy cell of Table 15.1, the observed frequency is 113, as compared with

| Table 15.2 | Hypothetical No-Relationship Cross-Tabulation for Chi-Square |

		Competence		
Hierarchy	Low	Medium	High	Total
Low	50%	50%	50%	50%
Medium	40%	40%	40%	40%
High	10%	10%	10%	10%

© Cengage Learning

| Table 15.3 | Calculations for Expected Frequencies and Chi-Square |

Table Cell		Observed	Expected	(Observed − Expected)^2
Competence	Hierarchy	Frequency	Frequency	Expected
Low	Low	113	.50 × 152 = 76.0	18.01
Low	Medium	31	.40 × 152 = 60.8	14.61
Low	High	8	.10 × 152 = 15.2	3.41
Medium	Low	60	.50 × 159 = 79.5	4.78
Medium	Medium	91	.40 × 159 = 63.6	11.80
Medium	High	8	.10 × 159 = 15.9	3.93
High	Low	27	.50 × 89 = 44.5	6.88
High	Medium	38	.40 × 89 = 35.6	.16
High	High	24	.10 × 89 = 8.9	25.62
	Total	400	400.0	89.20 = chi-square

© Cengage Learning

an expected frequency of 76.0. Thus, as shown in the last column of Table 15.3: $(113 - 76.0)^2 \div 76.0 = 18.01$. Although in themselves these calculations are not likely to make a great deal of sense to you, their virtue is that they yield a sum—the value of chi-square—whose theoretical distribution is well known and can be used to evaluate the statistical significance of the relationship found in the contingency table. Table 15.3 indicates that the value of chi-square for the competence–hierarchy cross-tabulation is 89.20.

Step 3: Compare the value of chi-square calculated for the actual cross-tabulation with the appropriate value of chi-square tabulated in the table of theoretical values. The table of chi-square values is presented in Table 4 in the Statistical Tables at the back of this book.

To find the appropriate theoretical value of chi-square in Table 4 for a contingency table, two pieces of information must be specified: (1) the *degrees of freedom* associated with the table, and (2) the *level of statistical significance desired.*

The **degrees of freedom** is a number that gives some idea of the size of the empirical contingency table under study. It is found by multiplying one less than the number of rows in the table by one less than the number of columns (ignoring both marginal rows and columns). In the current example, the number of rows and the number of columns are both equal to 3, so there are $(3 - 1) \times (3 - 1) = 2 \times 2 = 4$ degrees of freedom. In the Statistical Tables, Table 4, the degrees of freedom (df) are printed in the far left column of the table.

The **level of statistical significance** is determined by the public or nonprofit manager according to his or her assessment of the decision-making situation (see Chapter 11). It is the probability of error that he or she is willing to tolerate in making an inference from the sample cross-tabulation to the parent population in the long run (i.e., if one were to use the same procedure over and over again to make decisions). For example, if the manager selects the frequently used level of .05, in the long run, he or she will make an incorrect inference that a relationship exists in the population when in fact it does not 5% of the time.

In other words, if the manager were to make 20 decisions based on the 5% rule, one is likely to be in error, and the other 19 are likely to be correct. Although the manager cannot be certain about any particular decision, she or he can be 95% confident in the long run. In the Statistical Tables, Table 4, the level of statistical significance (abbreviated *P,* for probability) is printed at the top of the table; these values cut off the specified area of the curve. Turning to this table, you should find that the theoretical value of chi-square for 4 degrees of freedom, allowing a probability of error of 5% (i.e., a level of statistical significance of .05), is equal to 9.49.

Now that the appropriate theoretical value of chi-square has been determined, it is possible to make the critical decision whether, based on the sample cross-tabulation, the existence of a relationship between competence and hierarchical position can be inferred to exist in the population of all agency employees. The table of theoretical values (Statistical Tables, Table 4) consists of *minimum* values of chi-square that must be obtained in empirical contingency tables to infer, with a given level of confidence (statistical significance), that a relationship exists in the population. The decision rules for chi-square are as follows:

- If the value of chi-square exceeds the appropriate minimum value in the chi-square distribution table, taking into account the degrees of freedom, you can reject the null hypothesis.

- If the value of chi-square does not exceed the appropriate minimum value in the chi-square distribution table, taking into account the degrees of freedom, you cannot reject the null hypothesis.

In this case, because the value of chi-square calculated for the cross-tabulation (89.20) is far greater than the appropriate minimum value stipulated by Table 4 with 4 degrees of freedom (9.49), allowing a 5% chance of error, we can infer that a relationship *does exist* between competence and hierarchical position in the population of agency employees. Had the calculated value of chi-square failed to surpass this minimum, the null hypothesis of no relationship in the population could *not* have been rejected, which would mean that there was probably no relationship between competence and hierarchy in the population.

Limitations of the Chi-Square Test

Although the chi-square test is very useful, the preceding example well illustrates one of its primary limitations. The test procedure led to the conclusion that a relationship does exist between competence and hierarchical position in the population of agency employees. Recall, however, that the disgruntled official in this example hypothesized that this relationship is *inverse* or *negative*: that is, the less the competence of the employee, the higher the level of the position attained in the hierarchy of the organization. In fact, when the cross-tabulation of these two variables in the sample of employees (Table 15.1) has been percentaged appropriately (see Chapter 14), the relationship between competence and hierarchical position is found to be *positive*. The percentaged cross-tabulation, presented in Table 15.4, shows that as competence increases, position in the hierarchy also increases. Thus, whereas the existence of a relationship can be inferred to exist in the population, it is in the *opposite* direction of the one hypothesized by the official. Therefore, the hypothesis is not supported.

The important point illustrated by this example is *not* that the chi-square test yields fallacious information but that it yields information of only a limited kind. The test is based solely on the deviation of an observed cross-tabulation from the condition of no relationship. The chi-square test is insensitive to the nature and direction of the relationship actually found in the contingency table. Public and nonprofit managers must be careful not to jump to the conclusion that a significant value of chi-square calculated in a contingency table indicates that the two variables are related in the hypothesized manner in the population. It may—and it may not. Supplementary

Table 15.4	Percentaged Cross-Tabulation for Competence–Hierarchy Relationship		
		Competence	
Hierarchy	Low	Medium	High
Low	74%	38%	30%
Medium	21%	57%	43%
High	5%	5%	27%
Total	100%	100%	100%
	($n = 152$)	($n = 159$)	($n = 89$)

analytical procedures such as percentaging the contingency table and computing a measure of association (as developed later in this chapter) are necessary for answering this question. As stated at the beginning of the chapter, the techniques presented here are supplements, not substitutes.

The other limitations of the chi-square test are typical of tests of statistical significance in general (see Part 4, "Inferential Statistics"). First, the chi-square test requires a method of sampling from the population—simple random sampling—that sometimes cannot be satisfied. Second, the value of chi-square calculated in a cross-tabulation is markedly inflated by sample size. As a result, in large samples, relationships are sometimes found to be statistically significant even when they are weak in magnitude. Hence, the test is not very discriminating.

Finally, although the chi-square test is frequently misinterpreted as a measure of strength of relationship, it does *not* assess the magnitude or substantive importance of empirical relationships. Instead, it provides information pertaining only to the probability of the *existence* of a relationship in the population. To be sure, this information is valuable, but it ignores the issue of size of relationship. (Later in this chapter, we present a measure of association derived from chi-square: Cramér's *V*.) For this reason, you should use the chi-square test in conjunction with other statistical procedures, especially those designed to evaluate strength of relationship. We turn to those techniques now.

Assessing the Strength of a Relationship

The Percentage Difference

Two transportation planners are locked in debate regarding the steps that should be implemented to increase ridership on public transportation, particularly line buses. The first insists that the major reason why people do not ride the bus to work is that they have not heard about it. Thus, she argues that the way to increase ridership is to advertise the availability of public transportation. The second planner contends that the situation is neither that simple nor that inexpensive. He believes that the primary obstacle to the success of public transportation is that it is not readily accessible to masses of potential riders. People will not leave their cars for a system they are unable to reach conveniently. From this point of view, the way to increase ridership is to expand existing bus routes and design and implement new ones so that public transportation is more readily accessible.

The measures proposed by the two transportation planners carry dramatically different implications—as well as price tags—for public policy; therefore, the federal government decided to fund a study to evaluate the relative validity of their claims. Data were collected from a random sample of 500 individuals. Among other questions, these individuals were asked whether they (1) rode the bus regularly to work, (2) had learned of the existence of public transportation through advertising, and (3) lived in close proximity to a bus stop (defined as within three blocks).

Table 15.5	Data for Bus Survey

Raw Data

	Heard Advertising				**Bus Accessible**		
Ride Bus	No	Yes	Total	**Ride Bus**	No	Yes	Total
No	225	134	359	No	269	90	359
Yes	75	66	141	Yes	81	60	141
Total	300	200	500	Total	350	150	500

Percentaged Cross-Tabulations

	Heard Advertising			**Bus Accessible**	
Ride Bus	No	Yes	**Ride Bus**	No	Yes
No	75%	67%	No	77%	60%
Yes	25%	33%	Yes	23%	40%
Total	100%	100%	Total	100%	100%
	($n = 300$)	($n = 200$)		($n = 350$)	($n = 150$)

© Cengage Learning

Table 15.5 presents the cross-tabulations between riding the bus to work and each of the other two variables. Both the raw, or nonpercentaged, tables and the percentaged tables are displayed. You should practice deriving the percentages from the raw figures. If any aspect of this process remains doubtful, you should review the steps for percentaging contingency tables explained in Chapter 14 before proceeding further.

Table 15.5 provides support for the hypotheses of both transportation planners. As hypothesized by the first planner, advertising is related positively to ridership. Whereas 33% of those who had heard advertising about public transportation rode the bus regularly to work, only 25% of those who had not heard such advertising did so. Thus, advertising was associated with an 8% increase in ridership. Similarly, as predicted by the second planner, accessibility is related positively to ridership; 40% of those living in close proximity to a bus stop rode the bus regularly, compared to only 23% of those for whom the bus was less convenient. Thus, accessibility was associated with a 17% increase in ridership.

These results raise the question "Which proposal is likely to have the greater impact on increasing ridership of public transportation?" Because accessibility seems to have made a difference of 17% in ridership, and advertising appears to have made a difference of 8%, the former has the larger impact; that is, changes in accessibility apparently lead to a larger change in ridership than do changes in advertising. Stated another way, accessibility is related *more strongly* to ridership than to advertising. In general, the greater the percentage difference, the stronger is the relationship between two variables. Accordingly, if the federal government intends to adopt one or the other of the two proposals (but not both) as a measure to increase the ridership of public transportation, these data suggest that improving accessibility is to be preferred.*

Perfect and Null Relationships

In a cross-tabulation, as the independent variable changes categories, the percentage difference for a given category of the dependent variable may range from 0% to 100%. Percentage differences of 100 for each of the categories of the dependent variable indicate that the two variables are associated *perfectly*. If you are given the score of a case on the independent variable, you can predict the score on the dependent variable with certainty.

As shown in Table 15.6, the relationship between two ordinal variables is perfect if all cases are located in the diagonal cells of the contingency table. Two types of perfect relationship exist. First, if the categories of both variables are arranged in ascending order (such as low, medium, and high), the relationship is perfect in the *positive* direction if all cases fall into the diagonal cells sloping downward from the top-left cell to the bottom-right one. (Refer to Table 14.16 for the conventional or standard format to set up and percentage contingency tables or cross-tabulations.) This pattern indicates that as scores on the independent variable increase, scores on the dependent variable also increase. Second, as Table 15.6 shows, if all cases fall into the diagonal cells sloping downward from the top-right cell to the bottom-left one, the relationship is perfect in the *negative* direction. This pattern indicates that as scores on the independent variable increase, scores on the dependent variable decrease. The closer the observed cross-tabulation comes to either of these configurations, the stronger is the association between the two variables. Because changes in the independent variable are hypothesized to be accompanied by changes in the dependent variable, this pattern is called the *covariation model of relationship*.

At the other extreme in a cross-tabulation, percentage differences of 0% within each of the categories of the dependent variable indicate that the independent and dependent variables are *not* associated. The more similar the distribution of the dependent variable across each of the categories of the independent variable, the less strongly the two variables are related. As was explained earlier in the discussion of the chi-square test, the strength of relationship between two variables reaches its lowest point when those distributions are identical. In that situation, the variables are totally unrelated.

Table 15.2, which was developed in conjunction with the chi-square test earlier in the chapter, provides an example. Note that knowing the value of the independent variable (competence) in Table 15.2 does not help in predicting

---

*To have greater confidence in this conclusion, one must examine the effects of advertising and accessibility on ridership simultaneously. Chapter 16 discusses the techniques necessary to do so, called statistical control table analysis.

| Table 15.6 | Perfect Relationships | | | |

Perfect Positive Relationship

	Independent Variable			
Dependent Variable	Category 1	Category 2	...	Category k
Category 1	100%	0%	...	0%
Category 2	0%	100%	...	0%
⋮	⋮	⋮	...	⋮
Category k	0%	0%	...	100%
Total	100%	100%	...	100%

...

Perfect Negative Relationship

	Independent Variable			
Dependent Variable	Category 1	Category 2	...	Category k
Category 1	0%	0%	...	100%
Category 2	⋮	⋮		⋮
⋮	0%	100%	...	0%
Category k	100%	0%	...	0%
Total	100%	100%	...	100%

values of the dependent variable (hierarchy) because the percentages are the same for each category of the independent variable. Even if you knew a person's level of competence, it would not help in predicting her or his position in the hierarchy. Table 15.7 illustrates that in contrast to the single model of perfect association, there are many empirical models of no association. As long as the percentages calculated on the dependent variable are identical for each category of the independent variable, no relationship exists.

In evaluating the strength of relationship between two variables, the critical question is, "Where on the continuum between the poles of no association and perfect association do the actual data fall?" Do they more closely resemble the model in Table 15.7 or the model in Table 15.6? The more that they correspond to the model of perfect association, the more strongly they are said to be related.

This discussion of extreme values of association raises a problem with respect to the percentage difference as a measure of strength of relationship. Because the models of perfect and null association are based on all cells of the cross-tabulation, it seems reasonable that a desirable quality of a measure intended to assess strength of relationship is that it take into account the configuration of data in the entire contingency table. Because it is based only on the endpoint categories of the

Table 15.7	No Relationship

No Association: General Model

$(a\% + b\% + c\% = 100\%)$

Dependent Variable	Independent Variable		
	Category 1	Category 2	Category 3
Category 1	$a\%$	$a\%$	$a\%$
Category 2	$b\%$	$b\%$	$b\%$
Category 3	$c\%$	$c\%$	$c\%$
Total	100%	100%	100%

No Association: Empirical Examples

Dependent Variable	Independent Variable			Dependent Variable	Independent Variable		
	Category 1	Category 2	Category 3		Category 1	Category 2	Category 3
Category 1	50%	50%	50%	Category 1	7%	7%	7%
Category 2	25%	25%	25%	Category 2	90%	90%	90%
Category 3	25%	25%	25%	Category 3	3%	3%	3%
Total	100%	100%	100%	Total	100%	100%	100%

© Cengage Learning

dependent variable, the percentage difference does not satisfy this desideratum; it takes into account only a portion of the data in the table (see Chapter 14). As a result, in larger cross-tabulations, the choice of the dependent variable category not only is somewhat arbitrary but also can lead to *different* results representing the strength of relationship between two variables in the *same* table. Depending on one's point of view, the category selected may understate or overstate the actual degree of relationship in the cross-tabulation. Accordingly, we strongly recommended (in Chapter 14) that you calculate and report both percentage differences.

It is important to place these points in perspective. In spite of its flaws, the percentage difference is perhaps the most widely used and certainly the most easily understood measure of strength of relationship. Used in combination with the other measures elaborated in this chapter, it can be extremely helpful for evaluating the nature and strength of relationship between two variables measured at the nominal or ordinal level. It is a hard fact of quantitative life that all statistics have flaws. An inevitable consequence of describing or summarizing or distilling a distribution into a single representative number or statistic is that some features of the data are captured very well, whereas others are slighted or overlooked completely. For this reason, we encourage you to think of the measures presented for understanding bivariate relationships as complementary rather than exclusive. In data analysis, use those *measures* that best elucidate the relationship under study.

Measures of Association

Measures of association are statistics whose magnitude and sign (positive or negative) provide an indication of the extent and direction of relationship between two variables in a cross-tabulation. In contrast to the percentage difference, measures of association are calculated on the basis of—and take into account—all data in the contingency table. These statistics are designed to indicate where an actual relationship falls on the scale from perfect to null.

To facilitate interpretation, statisticians define measures of association so that they follow these four conventions:

1. If the relationship between the two variables is perfect, the measure equals +1.0 (positive relationship) or −1.0 (negative relationship).

2. If there is no relationship between the two variables, the measure equals 0.0.

3. The sign of the measure indicates the direction of the relationship. A value greater than zero (a positive number) corresponds to a positive relationship; a value less than zero (a negative number) corresponds to a negative relationship. Again, refer to Table 14.6, which shows how to set up and percentage a cross-tabulation or contingency table so that the sign (direction) of a relationship can be interpreted correctly.

4. The stronger the relationship between the two variables, the greater is the magnitude of the measure. The absolute value of the statistic (ignoring sign) is what matters in assessing magnitude. A relationship measuring −.75 (or .75) is larger than one measuring −.25 (or .25).

Because the concept of direction (or sign) of relationship assumes that the categories of the variables are ordered (that is, they increase or decrease in substantive meaning, for example, from low, to medium, to high), this concept can be applied only to relationships between variables measured at the *ordinal* or *interval* levels. Direction of relationship has no meaning for nominal variables because the categories (for example, religion) have no numerical ordering. Based on the properties of measurement for each type of variable (see Chapter 2), different measures of association have been developed. Thus, there are interval measures of association, ordinal measures, and nominal measures. Some interval measures are considered in Part 6 on regression analysis. The remainder of this chapter describes several ordinal and nominal measures of association and provides examples illustrating their use.

An Ordinal Measure of Association: Gamma

We illustrate the computation of one of the more easily calculated ordinal measures of association, gamma. As will be shown, several other of the most frequently used measures of ordinal association have a similar development: the tau statistic of Kendall and the *d* statistics of Somers. We use gamma to assess the strength of relationship between education and seniority in a small sample of

Table 15.8	Cross-Tabulation of Education and Seniority for Southeast Animal Rights Association		
	Education		
Seniority	Low	High	Total
Low	20	10	30
High	5	15	20
Total	25	25	50

© Cengage Learning

50 employees in a nonprofit organization. These variables are cross-tabulated in Table 15.8.

To calculate the gamma statistic, we must first introduce the idea of **paired observations**. Consider two data cases in Table 15.8, one of an individual in the low education–low seniority cell, and the other of an individual in the high education–high seniority cell. (The data come from the Southeast Animal Rights Association.) With respect to one another, this pair of cases is ranked consistently on education and seniority—that is, for this pair of cases, as education increases, seniority increases. Thus, this pair provides support for the existence of a *positive* relationship between the two variables. If all cases were in these two cells of the table, we would have a perfect positive relationship (see Table 15.6). This situation is called a **concordant pair** of cases.

Now consider two different data cases in Table 15.8, one of an individual in the low education–high seniority cell, and the other of an individual in the high education–low seniority cell. In contrast to the first pair of cases, with respect to one another, this pair of cases is ranked inconsistently on education and seniority—that is, as education increases, seniority decreases, and vice versa. This pair provides support for the existence of a negative relationship between the two variables. It is called a **discordant pair**. If all cases fell into these two table cells, we would have a perfect negative relationship.

Gamma, (as well as many other ordinal measures of association), is based on the difference between the number of concordant or consistently ordered pairs and the number of discordant or inconsistently ordered pairs in the cross-tabulation. This difference indicates the relative support in the contingency table for a positive, as opposed to a negative, relationship between the two variables. If the number of concordant pairs exceeds the number of discordant pairs, there is greater support for a positive relationship in the table. In that case, the difference between the two will be positive, and the gamma statistic will have this (positive) sign. On the other hand, if the number of concordant pairs is less than the number of discordant pairs, there is greater support for a negative relationship. The difference between the two will be negative, and this result will be reflected in the (negative) sign of gamma. Regardless of the direction of the relationship, the larger the difference between the number of concordant pairs and the number of discordant pairs, the greater is the association between the two variables, and, hence, the greater is the magnitude (absolute value) of gamma.

With this understanding of concordant and discordant pairs, we are ready to calculate gamma. There are three steps:

Step 1: Calculate the number of concordant pairs and the number of discordant pairs of cases in the cross-tabulation.

In a small cross-tabulation, such as the one in Table 15.8, this calculation is not difficult. Consider first the concordant pairs. There are 20 cases in the low education–low seniority cell of the table. With respect to this group, the set of cases that is ordered consistently on both variables is the set of 15 observations in the high education–high seniority cell. Because each pairing of cases from these two table cells yields a concordant pair, in all there are 20 × 15 = 300 concordant pairs in Table 15.8.

The number of discordant pairs is found analogously. There are 10 cases in the high education–low seniority cell of Table 15.8. With respect to this set, the group of cases that is ordered inconsistently on the variables is the group of five observations in the low education–high seniority cell of the table. Because each pairing of cases from these two table cells gives a discordant pair, there are 10 × 5 = 50 discordant pairs in Table 15.8.

Step 2: Calculate the difference between the number of concordant pairs and the number of discordant pairs.

It is evident that the relationship between education and seniority in Table 15.8 is positive because there are more concordant pairs than discordant pairs. The difference between them is 300 − 50 = 250. This simple difference, however, is not very meaningful for interpreting the relative strength of relationship. For example, it would be misleading to compare the difference obtained in this small contingency table with that obtained in a larger table or in tables with many more cases because the latter will generate so many more pairs of cases.

For this reason, statisticians have standardized gamma, as well as most other measures of association, so that it will vary between −1.0 for a perfect negative relationship and +1.0 for a perfect positive relationship. Thus, the third and final step in calculating gamma is to standardize the measure.

Step 3: Divide the difference between the number of concordant pairs and the number of discordant pairs obtained in Steps 1 and 2 by their sum.

Division by the sum of the number of concordant pairs and the number of discordant pairs in the cross-tabulation ensures that gamma will vary between -1.0 and $+1.0$ (it will also follow the other conventions for measures of association discussed earlier). The three steps for calculating gamma can be summarized in a formula:

$$\text{gamma} = \frac{\text{number of concordant pairs} - \text{number of discordant pairs}}{\text{number of concordant pairs} + \text{number of discordant pairs}}$$

Accordingly, the value of gamma for Table 15.8 is equal to

$$\frac{300 - 50}{300 + 50} = \frac{250}{350} = .71$$

This value of gamma indicates a relatively strong positive relationship between education and seniority in the sample of employees of the Southeast Animal Rights Association. When the original cross-tabulation has been percentaged, as shown in Table 15.9, further support is found for this conclusion. The percentaged table shows that as education increases, employees are more likely to have high seniority by a difference of $60\% - 20\% = 40\%$.

Other Ordinal Measures of Association: Kendall's tau-*b* and tau-*c* and Somers's d_{yx} and d_{xy}

Several other commonly used measures of association for ordinal-level variables are similar to gamma: Kendall's tau-*b* and tau-*c*, and Somers's d_{yx} and d_{xy}. Because these measures are more cumbersome to calculate by hand, we will not do so here but will explain their use and interpretation. A computer will calculate them routinely.

Like gamma, all of these measures are based on comparing the number of concordant pairs with the number of discordant pairs in the contingency table. These differ from gamma by taking into account pairs of observations in the table that are *tied* on one or both of the variables. For example, a case in the low

Table 15.9	Percentaged Cross-Tabulation of Education and Seniority		
		Education	
Seniority		Low	High
Low		80%	40%
High		20%	60%
		($n = 25$)	($n = 25$)

© Cengage Learning

education–low seniority cell of the table is tied with a case in the low education–high seniority cell with respect to education because both cases have the same rank on education. Similarly, a case in the low education–high seniority cell is tied with a case in the high education–high seniority cell with respect to seniority because they both have the same rank on seniority.

Gamma takes into account only concordant and discordant pairs; it ignores tied pairs. The other measures of association do not. Instead, they are based on a more stringent conception of the types of data patterns in a contingency table that constitute a perfect relationship. In particular, they will yield lower values for a contingency table to the extent that the table contains pairs of cases tied on the variables. For this reason, unless a contingency table has no tied pairs (a very rare occurrence), gamma will always be greater than tau-*b*, tau-*c*, d_{yx}, and d_{xy}.

Kendall's tau-*b* is an appropriate measure of strict linear relationship for "square tables"—tables with the same number of rows as columns. The calculation of tau-*b* takes into account pairs of cases tied on each of the variables in the contingency table. For the education–seniority cross-tabulation in Table 15.8, the calculated value of tau-*b* is .41. **Kendall's tau-*c*** is an appropriate measure of linear relationship for "rectangular tables"—tables with different numbers of rows and columns. Note that in such a cross-tabulation, no clear diagonal exists for either a perfect positive or a perfect negative relationship (see Table 15.6)—so a different measure of association is needed for this situation. In the current example, tau-*c* is .40 (tau-*b* is preferred because the table is square).

Somers's d_{yx} presumes that seniority is the dependent variable and yields lower values to the degree that cases are tied on this variable only. The logic is that a tie on seniority indicates that a change in the independent variable (education) does not lead to a change in seniority as a perfect relationship would predict. Here, Somers's d_{yx} is .40. Conversely, **Somers's d_{yx}** presumes that education is the dependent variable and yields lower values to the degree that cases are tied on education only. The reasoning is that a tie on the dependent variable (now education) indicates that a change in the independent variable (now seniority) does not lead to a change in education, as a perfect relationship would predict. In this example, Somers's d_{xy} is .42, but it would not be the statistic of choice because the hypothesis was that education (independent variable) leads to seniority (dependent variable), not the reverse.

Recall that the gamma calculated for Table 15.8 is .71, which is much greater than the calculated value of any of the other measures of association. The reason is the tied pairs of cases. This situation is not at all unusual in the analysis of contingency tables. Among the measures of association, gamma will typically yield the largest value, whereas the others will be more modest. Which measure(s) should you use and interpret? In general, the tau measures are used more commonly than are the Somers's *d* measures. Many managers prefer to use both gamma and either tau-*b* or tau-*c*, depending on whether the contingency table is square or rectangular, respectively. In this manner, the measures give a good idea of the magnitude of the relationship found in the table evaluated according to less stringent as well as more stringent standards of association.

A Nominal Measure of Association: Lambda

Ordinal measures of association are based on a covariation model of relationship. To the extent that two variables change together, or *covary*, they are considered associated or related. Measures of covariation such as gamma assess the extent to which increases in one variable are accompanied by increases (positive relationship) or decreases (negative relationship) in a second variable.

Because nominal variables do not consist of ordered categories (the categories lack any sense of magnitude or intensity), application of the covariation model of association to relationships between nominal variables is precluded. Therefore, a different model of association is required. A frequently used model of association for nominal variables is called the *predictability* model, or the model of *predictive association*. It is based on the ability to predict the category of the dependent variable based on knowledge of the category of the independent variable.

One of the most helpful and frequently used nominal measures of association premised on the predictability model is lambda. **Lambda** is defined as the proportional reduction in error gained in predicting the category of the dependent variable when the value of the independent variable is taken into account. Lambda evaluates the extent to which prediction of the dependent variable is improved when the value of the independent variable is known. Because the worst case is one in which the independent variable provides no (zero) improvement in predicting the dependent variable, lambda cannot be negative but ranges from 0.0 to +1.0. The 0.0 to +1.0 scale is consistent with the idea that relationships between nominal variables do not have direction, only predictability. Measures of association that incorporate the "proportional reduction in error" interpretation are sometimes abbreviated *PRE statistics*.

An example will illustrate the calculation and interpretation of lambda. Consider the relationship between race (white, nonwhite) and whether an individual made a contribution to the Bureau of Obfuscation's United Way annual fund drive (no, yes). These variables are cross-tabulated for a random sample of 500 employees in Table 15.10.

Step 1: Calculate the number of errors in predicting the value of the dependent variable if the value of the independent variable were not known.

Table 15.10	Cross-Tabulation of Race and Contribution		
	Race		
Contribution	Nonwhite	White	Total
No	100	125	225
Yes	200	75	275
Total	300	200	500

© Cengage Learning

To calculate the value of lambda for the relationship shown in Table 15.10, we first disregard the race of the employee (independent variable). If race is disregarded, how many errors will we make in predicting whether the employee made a contribution to the United Way (dependent variable)? Because more employees made a contribution than did not, our best prediction is "contributed." This prediction is correct for 275 of the 500 employees in the sample who contributed, but it is in error for the remaining 225 who did not contribute. Thus, when the value of the independent variable is not taken into account (disregarded), the proportion of errors made in predicting the dependent variable is $225 \div 500 = .45$.

Step 2: Calculate the number of errors in predicting the value of the dependent variable, this time taking into account the value of the independent variable.

If the race of the employee is now introduced, how much better can we predict contributions to the United Way? If we knew that an employee was nonwhite, our best prediction would be that he or she made a contribution. We would be correct for 200 of the 300 nonwhites in the sample who made a contribution, but we would make errors in predicting for the other 100 who did not. If an employee is white, we would predict that he or she did not make a contribution. We would be correct for 125 of the 200 whites who did not contribute, leaving 75 errors in prediction for those who did. Thus, knowing the race of the employee, we would make a total of $100 + 75 = 175$ errors in predicting contributions to the United Way in a sample of 500 employees. This procedure yields a proportion of error equal to $175 \div 500 = .35$.

Step 3: Calculate the rate of improvement in predicting the value of the dependent variable when the value of the independent variable is known (Step 2) over the original prediction in which the value of the independent variable was ignored (Step 1). In other words, by how much has the rate of error in predicting the dependent variable been reduced by introducing knowledge of the independent variable?

We began with a proportion of error in predicting the dependent variable of .45, not taking into account the independent variable. By introducing the independent variable, we were able to reduce the proportion of error to .35. How much of an improvement do we have? Compared with the original proportion, the rate of improvement in predicting the dependent variable—or the proportional reduction in error—is

$$\frac{.45 - .35}{.45} = .22$$

which is the value of lambda for Table 15.10. This value suggests a moderate predictive relationship between race and contributions to the United Way.

An alternative way to understand and calculate lambda is to consider that without knowing the value of the independent variable, we made 225 errors in predicting the dependent variable; and that knowing the independent variable, we made 175 errors, a reduction of 50 errors. Thus, errors in prediction were reduced by the proportion $50 \div 225 = .22$, which again is the value of lambda for Table 15.10. Based on this logic, the formula for lambda can be written as

$$\text{lambda} = \frac{\begin{bmatrix} \text{number of errors in prediction} \\ \text{not knowing value of} \\ \text{independent variable} \end{bmatrix} - \begin{bmatrix} \text{number of errors in prediction} \\ \text{knowing value of independent} \\ \text{variable} \end{bmatrix}}{\begin{bmatrix} \text{number of errors in prediction} \\ \text{not knowing value} \\ \text{of independent variable} \end{bmatrix}}$$

A Nominal Measure of Association Based on Chi-Square: Cramér's *V*

The chi-square test of statistical significance elaborated at the beginning of this chapter is a measure of the existence of a relationship, not its strength. A variety of measures of association for nominal-level variables have been developed based on the chi-square. The measures include Pearson's contingency coefficient *C*, phi-square, Tschuprow's *T*, and Cramér's *V*. These measures are all related, and many computer statistical package programs display them routinely.

Probably the most useful, and most often used, of the measures is **Cramér's V**. It is given by the formula

$$V = \sqrt{\frac{\text{chi-square}}{m\mathbf{N}}}$$

where chi-square = value of chi-square calculated for the contingency table; m = (number of rows in the table − 1) or (number of columns in the table − 1) whichever is smaller; and $\mathbf{N}$ = size of the sample. Although the formula may seem complicated, it is easy to calculate Cramér's *V*, and we do so now for the cross-tabulation in Table 15.1.

Step 1: Calculate the value of chi-square for the cross-tabulation. For the data in Table 15.1, the value of chi-square is 89.20 (Table 15.3 shows the calculations).

Step 2: Calculate m. Determine which is smaller, the number of rows or the number of columns in the cross-tabulation, and subtract 1 from this number. Because Table 15.1 has the same number of rows as columns (3), this choice does not matter in this example. Subtracting 1 from 3 yields a difference of 2, which is the value of m.

Step 3: The remainder of the formula indicates that we must multiply m times $\mathbf{N}$; divide chi-square (from Step 1) by this product; and take the square root of the result.

In this example, $m = 2$ and $N = 400$, so $m \times N = 2 \times 400 = 800$. Dividing chi-square (89.20) by this product $= 89.20 \div 800 = 0.1115$; taking the square root of $0.1115 = 0.33$, which is the value of Cramér's V for Table 15.1.

Like all measures of association for nominal-level variables, Cramér's V is always a positive number (remember that the direction of relationship has no meaning for nominal data). The measure ranges from 0.0, indicating no relationship between the variables, to 1.0, indicating a perfect relationship.

Use of Nominal Measures of Association with Ordinal Data

For the analysis of relationships between variables measured at the ordinal level, public and nonprofit managers generally use ordinal measures of association. However, if the manager anticipates that the relationship is one not of covariation but of predictability, a nominal measure of association such as lambda can be employed. (This principle follows the Hierarchy of Measurement explained in Chapter 5.) For example, one might hypothesize that, because jobs at the bottom of the organizational hierarchy tend to be low paying and those at the top tend to be quite stressful, middle-level officials may have the highest level of job satisfaction. An empirical example is presented in Table 15.11; the data are for staff members of the Inward Institute, a small liberal arts college in central Iowa.

Because the cross-tabulation in Table 15.11 does not demonstrate a consistent pattern of increase in job satisfaction (dependent variable) with an increase in hierarchy (independent variable), the calculated value of an ordinal measure of association predicated on the covariation logic will be small. In contrast, because job satisfaction is highly predictable and based on the categories of hierarchy, the calculated value of lambda will be large. That is, if one knows an employee's level in the hierarchy, then a very good prediction can be made regarding job satisfaction. For example, for those low in the hierarchy, you would predict low satisfaction—you would be correct 75% of the time. What would you predict for the middle level in the hierarchy? How often would you be correct? (High satisfaction—80%.) For high-level positions? How often would you be correct for high-level positions? (Medium satisfaction—70%.) Although the relationship is not perfectly linear (see Table 15.6), it is quite predictable.

Table 15.11	Percentaged Cross-Tabulation of Hierarchy and Job Satisfaction		
		Hierarchy	
Job Satisfaction	Low	Middle	High
Low	75%	10%	20%
Medium	15%	10%	70%
High	10%	80%	10%
Total	100%	100%	100%
	($n = 200$)	($n = 200$)	($n = 200$)

In fact, in this example the calculated value of gamma, a measure based on covariation, is .25. By contrast, the calculated value of lambda, a measure based on predictability, is much greater, .62. This value of lambda suggests a much stronger relationship between hierarchy and job satisfaction than does the gamma value. Because the percentaged cross-tabulation (Table 15.11) does not reveal a consistent pattern of increase or decrease in employee job satisfaction across levels of the organizational hierarchy, measures of association based on covariation—such as gamma—will be small (Kendall's tau and the Somers's d measures are even smaller). By contrast, this relationship has high predictability, the model of association tapped by lambda. Given knowledge of employees' position in the organizational hierarchy, job satisfaction can be predicted very well. (See the discussion of predictability in relation to Table 15.11, which concluded the previous section.) As this example shows, a good strategy with table analysis is to use and interpret not only the percentaged cross-tabulation but also several measures of association.

If you would like to learn how to calculate measures of association such as gamma and lambda for larger tables, please see the website for this book.

Chapter Summary

This chapter elaborated important aids for the analysis and interpretation of contingency tables. The chi-square test of statistical significance assesses whether the relationship observed in a cross-tabulation based on a sample of data is sufficiently large to reject the null hypothesis that the variables are not related in the population. The chi-square test involves three steps. First, calculate expected frequencies for each cell of the cross-tabulation based on the null hypothesis that the variables are not related. Second, calculate the value of chi-square for the cross-tabulation, which assesses the departure from no relationship in the table. Finally, compare the value of the calculated chi-square with an appropriate value in the chi-square table of theoretical values to see whether it surpasses the threshold value necessary to reject the null hypothesis (Table 4 in the Statistical Tables in the back of the book).

One way to assess the strength of a relationship between two variables in a contingency table is by using percentage differences. The strength will range from a perfect relationship (percentage differences of 100) to a null relationship (percentage differences of 0).

Measures of association are statistics used to evaluate the extent and direction of a relationship between two variables in a contingency table. Gamma, which is based on pairs of observations, is a measure of association for ordinal data. It indicates the relative support in the contingency table for a positive, as opposed to a negative, relationship between the two variables. Related measures of association for ordinal-level variables are Kendall's tau-b and tau-c and Somers's d_{yx} and d_{xy}. All of these measures employ a covariation model of relationship: As the independent variable increases, the dependent variable increases (positive relationship) or decreases (negative relationship).

A different model of relationship is used for nominal-level data. This model of predictive association or predictability underlies lambda. Lambda evaluates the extent to which prediction of the dependent variable is improved when the value of the independent variable is taken into account. Cramér's *V*, which is based on the chi-square, is another measure of association for nominal-level variables.

Analysts can also use nominal measures of association to assess the degree of relationship between ordinal variables in a cross-tabulation. Examining both covariation statistics such as gamma and predictability statistics such as lambda for a contingency table can help public and nonprofit managers understand and interpret the relationship between the two variables.

Problems

15.1 The mayor wants to know whether the city's nonwhites feel that the police are doing a good job. In comparison to whites' evaluations, this information will tell the police whether they have a community relations problem in the nonwhite community. A survey reveals the data in the accompanying table. What can you tell the mayor? Base your statements on what you have learned in this chapter.

	Race		
Attitude toward Police	Nonwhite	White	Total
Police do not do good job	76	73	149
Police do good job	74	223	297
Total	150	296	446

15.2 The data for the competence–hierarchy example discussed earlier in the chapter are replicated in the accompanying table. Percentage the table and calculate gamma. Refer to the book's website page for the calculation of gamma in larger tables. Discuss the relationship between competence and level of organizational hierarchy as reflected in this table.

	Competence			
Hierarchy	Low	Medium	High	Total
Low	113	60	27	200
Medium	31	91	38	160
High	8	8	24	40
Total	152	159	89	400

15.3 Compute the value of chi-square for the data in the accompanying table, and percentage the cross-tabulation. From these data, would you say that the relationship between proximity of residence to the hospital and frequency of visits to the hospital for care is weak or strong? Explain your answer.

	Proximity to Hospital		
Frequency of Visits	Close	Medium	Far
Low	1,000	1,030	1,050
Medium	525	520	515
High	475	450	435

15.4 Two scholars are locked in debate regarding the interpretation of the accompanying data. One insists that the relationship between the age of a child and the child's perception of the parents is very strong; the other argues that no relationship exists. Why do the two scholars reach different conclusions? Analyze the table and resolve the dilemma. Is there a relationship between the age of a child and the child's perception of the parents?

Child's Perception of Parents	Age of Child (Years)		
	5–15	16–27	28 and Older
Negative	11%	53%	23%
Neutral	18%	27%	59%
Positive	71%	20%	18%
Total	100%	100%	100%

15.5 Devise a hypothesis of interest to you. Using percentages, construct cross—tabulations that show (a) perfect support for the hypothesis and (b) no support for the hypothesis. Construct three additional tables that show (c) strong, (d) medium, and (e) weak support for the hypothesis. After you have constructed the percentaged tables, make up marginal frequencies for each category of the independent variable and convert the percentages in the table cells to frequencies.

15.6 The city parks commission has decided to redevelop a community park. Some members of the commission feel that refurbishment of existing park facilities is sufficient to meet the needs of the community; therefore, they advocate minimal redevelopment. Other members feel that such a small-scale project is pointless. They contend that improvement of the park will create greater public satisfaction with the park and thus will draw many more people than currently use it. An increase in patrons could exhaust existing facilities, thus necessitating further redevelopment. To resolve this disagreement, the commission hires the consulting firm Dunewright and Associates to conduct a random sample survey of 1,000 adults living in the community. Among the questions asked are these: Do you regularly use the park? Do you consider park facilities satisfactory or unsatisfactory? Dunewright and Associates present the accompanying table to the city parks commission. Based on the table calculate gamma. What percent of the citizens use the park? What percent of the citizens are satisfied with the park? Based on the cross-tabulation of these questions presented in the accompanying table, should the city spend a lot of money to refurbish the park?

Use Park	Park Facilities	
	Unsatisfactory	Satisfactory
No	464	268
Yes	168	110
Total	632	378

15.7 The director of the state department of environmental affairs is concerned about the high level of employee dissatisfaction in the department. To alleviate this problem, he hires a statistical analyst to investigate the attitudes of employees. The analyst believes that the primary source of dissatisfaction is the type of job held by the employee—hourly wage or salary. To test this hypothesis, she obtains data pertaining to whether the employee is paid hourly or is salaried and whether he or she is satisfied or dissatisfied with the job. These data are cross-tabulated in the accompanying table. Percentage the table and calculate gamma. Refer to the book's website for the calculation of gamma in larger tables. Is there a relationship between type of job and job satisfaction?

	Type of Job		
Attitude toward Job	Hourly	Salary	Total
Dissatisfied	194	54	248
Satisfied	278	85	363
Total	472	139	611

15.8 The data analyst from Problem 15.7 also obtained information regarding whether the employee was on a standard 8-hour shift or on flextime. The cross-tabulation between these two variables appears below. Percentage the table and calculate gamma. Is there a relationship between the employment status of employees (shift versus flextime) and job satisfaction?

	Employment Status		
Attitude toward Job	Shift	Flextime	Total
Dissatisfied	194	55	249
Satisfied	186	176	362
Total	380	231	611

15.9 The personnel department of a small city has compiled the accompanying data regarding city employees. The data consist of the age of employees and the probability of their receiving a job promotion. On the basis of these data, how should the department advise job applicants who seek employment with the city?

	Age		
Probability of Promotion	30 or Less	31–50	51 or Greater
Low	17%	9%	65%
Medium	56%	15%	22%
High	27%	76%	13%
Total	100%	100%	100%

15.10 A Ph.D. student in public administration has studied the relationship between the quality of municipal bureaucracy and the economic development of cities. She hypothesizes that the higher the quality of the city bureaucracy (as measured by such factors as innovativeness, efficiency, and responsiveness), the greater the economic development. By this hypothesis, she assumes that bureaucratic quality leads to economic development. To test this hypothesis, she sent out questionnaires to a random sample of 120 cities with a population between 50,000 and 100,000. Based on these data, she assembles the accompanying cross-tabulation.

	Economic Development		
Bureaucratic Quality	Low	Medium	High
High	6	8	16
Medium	12	16	22
Low	16	14	10

Percentage the table appropriately and calculate gamma. Is there a relationship between bureaucratic quality and economic development? (*Hint:* First reorganize the table according to the standard format for constructing and analyzing contingency tables presented in Chapter 14.)

15.11 In her dissertation, the Ph.D. student from Problem 15.10 writes that the relationship between the quality of a municipal bureaucracy and the economic development of a city is causal—that is, that higher-quality bureaucracy leads to higher economic development. Evaluate her claim of causality. What conditions would have to be met in order to establish that this relationship is causal? Does the cross-tabulation between the two variables (presented in standard format) bear on the question of causality? How? Explain your answer. (*Hint:* See Chapter 3, on research design and causal inference.)

15.12 Professor Y. Doncha Findwork is in charge of placement of graduate students from the Barzini Institute of Business and Public Affairs (Sicily). Her goal is to find great job offers for students that they cannot refuse. Professor Findwork follows up with students one year post-placement to see if they are satisfied with their positions. She wants to know how effective the placements have been, as measured by student satisfaction. Help Professor Findwork by analyzing the data she has collected below. Are students more satisfied with placements in certain types of organizations more than others? In what types of organizations would you advise Professor Findwork to place her students? Calculate lambda and interpret its meaning.

	Placement Organization		
Job Satisfaction	Nonprofit	Public	For-profit
Not Satisfied	15	40	57
Satisfied	51	102	25

15.13 Organizational analyst Ann T. Gravity is examining the Peter Principle, which contends that people will rise in an organization until they reach their level of incompetence. She feels that this means that proportionately more competent people will be found at the lower level of the organization. To test this question, she decides to ask students to rate assistant professors, associate professors, and full professors. Based on these ratings, she classified the competence of professors as high, medium, or low. Interpret the accompanying table; calculate any necessary statistics. Refer to the book's website for the calculation of gamma in larger tables.

| | **Academic Rank** | | | |
Competence	**Assistant**	**Associate**	**Full**	**Total**
Low	27	38	24	89
Medium	60	91	8	159
High	106	38	8	152
Total	193	167	40	400

15.14 Dan Storch, a researcher at the Illinois Association of School Boards, wants to learn more about why some school bond referenda pass whereas others fail. Specifically, Mr. Storch believes that referendum measures that authorize funding for renovating existing buildings should be more successful than those that authorize funding for new buildings. Mr. Storch has gathered data on the last 100 public school bond referenda in Illinois. Referenda are divided into two categories, those authorizing renovations (coded 1) and those authorizing new school buildings (coded 2). The vote on each measure is coded as either "passed" (1), or "failed" (2). Based on these data, what can Mr. Storch conclude about his hypothesis? *(Note: The data set for this problem is available on the book's companion website.)*

15.15 The New Horizons Alcohol and Drug Abuse Center has begun to collect data on client satisfaction. In addition to offering individual counseling, the center has optional group-activities programs for its clients. The director of the center would like to know if clients who have participated in the group-activities programs are more satisfied with their treatment than those who have not participated in them. The director gathers data on 100 clients. Each client is classified as having participated in group programs (coded 1) or not (coded 0). Data on client satisfaction are taken from an exit survey that asked clients to rate their treatment as satisfactory (coded 1), neutral (coded 2), or unsatisfactory (coded 3). What can the director conclude about the link between participation in group programs and client satisfaction from these data? *(Note: The data set for this problem is available on the book's companion website.)*

15.16 Linda Dawkins, city manager of Pig Mountain, Connecticut, has instituted a public shaming campaign in hopes of getting delinquent taxpayers to pay their outstanding property tax bills. Ninety days after property tax bills are due, the city takes out a full-page newspaper announcement with the names of 50 randomly selected delinquent taxpayers in the Sunday edition of the *Pig Mountain Herald*. The names of 50 other randomly selected delinquent taxpayers are left out of the ad so that Ms. Dawkins can have a nonshamed control group for her experiment.

Ms. Dawkins gathers the delinquency data a month after the publication of the newspaper announcement. She divides delinquent taxpayers into two categories: publicly shamed (coded 1) and not publicly shamed (coded 0). The tax payment variable for each taxpayer is broken down into two categories: made some or all of tax payment (coded 1), and made no tax payment (coded 0). What can Ms. Dawkins conclude about the effectiveness of this program from these data? *(Note: The data set for this problem is available on the book's companion website.)*

15.17 James Anderson, director of the Tarrant County, Texas, public library system, hypothesizes that younger patrons prefer electronic media (DVDs, compact discs, MP3 downloads and/or Podcasts, etc.) over traditional printed materials (books, magazines, etc.), whereas older patrons prefer the traditional printed materials. Director Anderson wants to see if his hunch is true before deciding how to use next year's library acquisitions budget. He hires a consultant to conduct a survey of 100 randomly selected library patrons. The patrons are asked whether they favor having more of the library's acquisitions budget go toward electronic media at the expense of acquiring fewer printed items ("yes" responses coded 1, "no" responses coded 2). The survey asked respondents to place themselves in one of the following groups: young adult patron (coded 1); adult patron (coded 2); and senior citizen patron (coded 3). After conducting a cross-tabulation on these data, what can the director conclude? *(Note: The data set for this problem is available on the book's companion website.)*

15.18 Jeff Meier, director of research at the Wisconsin Council of Governments (WCG), is conducting a study on citizen perceptions of private sector and public sector service providers. Results from a survey commissioned by the WCG contain information on whether citizens have their trash collected by private refuse collection contractors or by traditional municipal trash collection crews: variable for "private collection" (coded 1) and for "municipal collection" (coded 2). The survey also asked citizens to state their service satisfaction level: variable for "satisfied with trash collection" (coded 1), for "dissatisfied" (coded 2). Based on these data, can Dr. Meier conclude that public perceptions of private and municipal trash collectors are significantly different? *(Note: The data set for this problem is available on the book's companion website.)*

15.19 A local Milwaukee research organization is conducting a study on the charitable activities of residents in the southeastern part of the state. For this purpose the research organization administered a survey. If respondents indicated that they had made financial contributions to any nonprofit organization in the past year, they were asked whether they intend to maintain (i.e., not change), increase, or decrease their charitable giving in the coming year. Survey respondents were asked to answer a variety of other questions as well (including gender and location or county).

The data for the dependent variable "charitable activities" are coded as follows:

1 = donate less
2 = no change
3 = donate more

Upon obtaining the results of the survey, the researchers look first at the relationship between gender and charitable giving behavior for the coming year: for "females" (coded 1) and for "males" (coded 2). Is there a statistically significant relationship between gender and charitable giving behavior? *(Note: The data set for this problem is available on the book's companion website.)*

15.20 Refer to Problem 15.19. The researchers in charge of the Southeastern Wisconsin charitable giving study have also collected data on the county of residents. They hypothesize that differences in the demographic makeup of the three major counties included in the study could influence residents' charitable giving behavior (the counties are simply labeled as "A," "B," and "C," for the purposes of the study). Upon generating a contingency table for county of resident and charitable giving behavior, what can the researchers conclude? *(Note: The data set for this problem is available on the book's companion website.)*

15.21 Tara Young, professor of management at Big State University, is interested in whether organizational size has an effect on leadership in nonprofit organizations. She has collected data on a random sample of 225 nonprofit organizations, using annual budgets to measure organizational size. The data are coded as follows:

1 = under $250,000
2 = $250,000 − $500,000
3 = $500,001 − $1,000,000
4 = over $1,000,000

Professor Young has collected data on a variety of characteristics for each of the organizations included in her sample, including the age of executive directors. Professor Young believes that larger nonprofits are more conservative when it comes to management issues and thus are more likely to have more seasoned executive directors. Conversely, she hypothesizes that smaller nonprofits are more entrepreneurial and are more likely to be run by younger individuals. She breaks down age of executive directors into three categories:

1 = 25–39
2 = 40–49
3 = 50 or older

Upon generating a contingency table, what can Professor Young conclude? *(Note: The data set for this problem is available on the book's companion website.)*

15.22 Refer to Problem 15.21. Professor Young is interested in testing the hypothesis of whether females are underrepresented as executive directors of large (again defined using annual budgets) nonprofit organizations. Accordingly, data on the gender of executive directors are included in her sample as well as their ages: "male" (coded 0), "female" (coded 1). Upon generating a contingency table for gender of executive directors and organizational size, what can Professor Young conclude about this hypothesis? *(Note: The data set for this problem is available on the book's companion website.)*

15.23 The board of directors of the Westville Community Center is interested in obtaining feedback from its donor base about various programmatic initiatives the center is contemplating. The board has hired a consultant to develop a survey instrument that will be sent to a random sample of 300 individuals in the donor base.

The consultant points to emerging research that finds that individuals who receive surveys via expedited delivery methods (such as next day delivery service) tend to complete surveys at a higher rate than individuals who receive surveys via traditional bulk-rate mail service (the standard way the Center has always administered surveys). The board is intrigued by this idea, but the board members want more evidence on how the expedited delivery methods would actually affect their donor base. Accordingly, the consultant devises an experiment. The survey is sent via expedited delivery to half of the individuals in the sample selected at random; the remaining 150 surveys are sent via bulk mail. A month after the survey has been sent, the consultant assembles a cross-tabulation on method of delivery and response rates. The data are coded as follows:

Delivery method

1 = survey sent using expedited service

0 = survey sent using standard delivery method

Response

1 = returned completed survey

0 = did not return survey

Based on the cross-tabulation, what can the consultant tell the board about the results of the experiment? *(Note: The data set for this problem is available on the book's companion website.)*

15.24 Rebecca Peters, head of a state procurement division, has heard rumors that minority contractors are being treated unfairly when competing for contracts. The specific claim is that minority contractors do not get their fair share of large contract awards (those over $250,000). The director asks her statistician to collect data on two variables. The first is a variable (AWARDS) for the size of 275 contract awards made since the start of the year. Large awards are defined as those greater than $250,000 and are coded as "1." Small contract awards are those equal to or less than $250,000 and are coded as "0." The second variable (FIRMS) measures contractor status, where "1" is used to represent minority-owned firms and "0" is used to represent all other firms. Upon generating a cross-tabulation, what can the statistician report to Ms. Peters? *(Note: The data set for this problem is available on the book's companion website.)*

Statistical Control Table Analysis

The previous two chapters discussed methods for examining the relationship between two variables measured at either the ordinal or the nominal level. In that discussion, when a pair of variables was found to be associated statistically, we inevitably assumed that they were, in fact, related, in the sense that changes in one could be expected to lead to changes in the other. Conversely, when the variables were not associated statistically, we assumed that the opposite was true.

These assumptions, however, are not always correct. A simple example should persuade you how they can lead you astray.

Suppose that you are a staff analyst working for the police department of a fairly large community. The mayor is concerned with a recent upsurge in juvenile crime and asks that you prepare a report advising her how the increase in crime can be combated. In researching the issue, you discover an interesting phenomenon. In those 25 precincts of the city in which ice cream consumption is high, the rate of juvenile crime is usually low, and in the 20 precincts in which consumption is low, juvenile crime typically reaches high levels. Thus, across the precincts of the city, the higher the ice cream consumption, the lower is the rate of juvenile crime. As Table 16.1 shows, according to any measure of association, this relationship is strong.

Using these data, should you advise the mayor that you have found the answer to the crime problem—to subsidize the sale of ice cream so that it may be offered at bargain prices to the rampaging juvenile hordes? Is satisfying their hunger for ice cream likely to appease their appetite for more costly antisocial behavior? After all, the data indicate that ice cream consumption and juvenile crime are strongly associated inversely.

Even though Table 16.1 would seem to support this policy response, somehow the proposed solution does not sit well. You would probably feel more than a little silly—not to mention fearful for your job—were you to inform the mayor that a scoop of chocolate (or perhaps rocky road or vanilla) is the answer to the problem of juvenile crime. But if ice cream is not the answer, then what is? And why are ice cream consumption and juvenile crime rates associated statistically, when, in fact, one almost certainly has nothing whatsoever to do with the other?

Table 16.1	Relationship between Juvenile Crime and Ice Cream Consumption	
	Ice Cream Consumption	
Rate of Juvenile Crime	Low	High
Low	25%	80%
High	75%	20%
Total	100%	100%
	($n = 20$ precincts)	($n = 25$ precincts)

© Cengage Learning

The answers to these two questions are interrelated. First, one variable that may bear on the rate of juvenile crime is the socioeconomic status (SES) of the precincts across the city. SES is a social science concept intended to assess the social status of a precinct based on the income, education, and occupational prestige of its residents (SES can also be measured at the level of individual respondents). For a number of reasons (such as stable home life, access to better education and job opportunities), juveniles living in high-SES precincts—those in which income, education, and occupational status are high—commit fewer crimes than do their peers living in less fortunate circumstances in low-SES precincts. As for the second question, in high-SES precincts parents and children have more money to purchase ice cream than do their counterparts living in low-SES precincts; therefore, ice cream consumption is higher in the former areas than in the latter. Note the circumstance created by these two relationships. In high-SES precincts, youths both eat more ice cream *and* commit fewer crimes than do youths living in low-SES precincts. Thus, because of the relationship of each variable to the SES of the precinct, ice cream consumption and the rate of juvenile crime *appear* to be related when, in fact, they are quite independent of one another. These relationships can be depicted graphically:

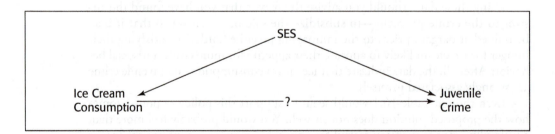

The type of reasoning illustrated in this example is typical of the data analysis process. The analyst finds that two variables are associated statistically (ice cream consumption and juvenile crime). She then tries to understand *why* the variables are associated. (Recall from Chapter 3 how important theory— a meaningful substantive explanation—is to understanding and interpreting a statistical relationship.) Are the two variables related in the sense that changes in one are likely to produce changes in the other, or is their apparent relationship attributable to the action of a *third* variable (SES of the precinct)? The analyst seeks to determine whether there is a relationship between the two variables or whether their association is accidental—due to a connection with some third variable. To address this issue, the researcher must introduce the third variable explicitly into the analysis. She then reexamines the relationship between the original two variables, taking into account the effect of the third variable. The technique used to incorporate a third variable into the analysis is called *controlling for* or *holding constant* the third variable (controlling for SES or holding constant SES) or, more simply, **statistical controls**, and the third variable is often called the **control variable**.

This chapter discusses statistical control techniques for the analysis of relationships among three or more variables measured at the ordinal or nominal level. The chapter both explains the use of these techniques and illustrates several likely results of introducing a third variable into the examination of a two-variable relationship. Different possible results are illustrated in a series of examples.

Controlling for a Third Variable

The procedure by which the analyst controls for the effect of a third variable on a bivariate (two variable) relationship is deceptively simple. He or she examines the relationship between the original two variables within each of the categories of the control variable and compares the results across the categories of the control. The examples that follow illustrate the procedure.

Example 1: Alcoholism in the Postal Service—The Effect of Hierarchical Position

The U.S. Postal Service has become alarmed by recent unsubstantiated reports from employees that the pressures of the workplace, such as large volumes of mail and very short time deadlines, contribute to alcoholism. The Postal Service has commissioned a blue-ribbon panel to investigate the problem. The panel collected data from post office employees working in offices in Ripple, Montana; Thunderbird, New Mexico; and Gallo, Mississippi.

As a first step, the panel hypothesized a positive relationship between position of the employee in the post office hierarchy and the rate of alcoholism. Panel members reasoned that those holding supervisory positions were under greater pressure than those holding nonsupervisory jobs and, therefore, would be more likely to turn to alcohol to relieve work tensions. The measure of alcoholism used by the study team is called the Harris Test. The test identifies with 95% accuracy whether the respondent is an alcoholic or a nonalcoholic. The relationship between hierarchical position (nonsupervisor or supervisor) and alcoholism (alcoholic or nonalcoholic) found by the study team is displayed in Table 16.2 in both raw (nonpercentaged) and percentaged form.

Table 16.2	Relationship between Hierarchy and Alcoholism		

Raw Data

Hierarchy

Alcoholism	Nonsupervisor	Supervisor	Total
Nonalcoholic	115	60	175
Alcoholic	5	20	25
Total	120	80	200

Percentaged Data

Hierarchy

Alcoholism	Nonsupervisor	Supervisor
Nonalcoholic	96%	75%
Alcoholic	4%	25%
Total	100%	100%
	($n = 120$)	($n = 80$)

© Cengage Learning

Because the table shows that supervisors are more likely than nonsupervisors to be alcoholics by a difference of 21% (25% − 4%), most members of the panel feel that these data offer support for the hypothesis that hierarchical position is related to alcoholism. One investigator, however, is not convinced. He maintains that it is not hierarchical position that leads post office employees to drink; rather, it is whether they have been selected and made to operate the ziptronic machine—a demanding device that puts high stress on the operator to identify zip codes printed on letters at an extremely rapid rate. Part of the process of selecting new supervisors is to identify employees who can succeed in this high-pressure job. Because supervisors operate the ziptronic more frequently than do nonsupervisors, the investigator argues that it only appears that hierarchical position leads to alcoholism. In fact, if one were to control for the effects of operating the ziptronic, one would find no relationship between hierarchy and alcoholism. The investigator's argument can be depicted graphically:

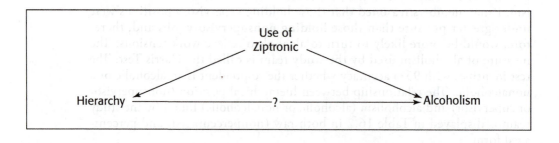

The statistical control procedure involves three major steps:

Step 1: Partition the sample according to the categories of the control variable. In the current example, 90 postal employees have operated the ziptronic, and the remaining 110 have not.

Step 2: Prepare the cross-tabulation between the original two variables for each of the subsamples defined by the control variable in Step 1. Percentage each of these tables separately (refer to Chapter 14 if you do not recall how to percentage a contingency table or cross-tabulation). In this example, the researcher would construct two distinct cross-tabulations between hierarchical position and alcoholism: one for those employees who have operated the ziptronic and the second for those who have not operated the ziptronic. Table 16.3 presents the results obtained according to this procedure for the post office data. Both the nonpercentaged and the percentaged cross-tabulations are displayed in the table.

It is important to recognize that the data presented in Table 16.3 are simply an *elaboration* of the cross-tabulation displayed in Table 16.2. Table 16.3 shows how the sample of 200 postal employees is distributed with respect to operation of the ziptronic (have operated the ziptronic, have not operated the ziptronic), that is, the control variable. For example, Table 16.2 shows that, in all, there are 175 nonalcoholics in the sample; Table 16.3 indicates that 74 of these employees have

Table 16.3	Cross-Tabulation of Subsamples Based on Operation of Ziptronic

Employees Who Have Operated Ziptronic (n = 90)

Employees Who Have Not Operated Ziptronic (n = 110)

Raw Data

	Hierarchy				Hierarchy		
Alcoholism	Non-supervisor	Supervisor	Total	**Alcoholism**	Non-supervisor	Supervisor	Total
Nonalcoholic	29	45	74	Nonalcoholic	86	15	101
Alcoholic	1	15	16	Alcoholic	4	5	9
Total	30	60	90	Total	90	20	110

Percentaged Data

	Hierarchy			Hierarchy	
Alcoholism	Nonsupervisor	Supervisor	**Alcoholism**	Nonsupervisor	Supervisor
Nonalcoholic	97%	75%	Nonalcoholic	96%	75%
Alcoholic	3%	25%	Alcoholic	4%	25%
Total	100%	100%	Total	100%	100%
	(n = 30)	(n = 60)		(n = 90)	(n = 20)

operated the ziptronic and the remaining 101 have not. Similarly, of the total of 25 alcoholics in the sample (Table 16.2), 16 have operated the ziptronic; 9 have not (Table 16.3). With respect to hierarchical position, of the total of 120 nonsupervisors in the sample (Table 16.2), 30 have operated the ziptronic, whereas the other 90 have not (Table 16.3). Finally, of the 80 supervisors in the sample (Table 16.2), 60 have operated the ziptronic, and the remaining 20 have not (Table 16.3).

Because Table 16.3 elaborates the original cross-tabulation presented in Table 16.2, this research method is sometimes called the *elaboration model*. Make sure that you can follow the correspondences relating the two tables outlined in the previous paragraph. You should be able to see that the figures displayed in the cross-tabulations of Table 16.3 are perfectly consistent with those of Table 16.2.

Step 3: Analyze and interpret the cross-tabulations obtained for each of the categories of the control variable. This step is the most demanding in the statistical control procedure, but a modicum of reasoning will simplify matters considerably.

Consider the argument made by the investigator on the study team who introduced the issue of the ziptronic machines. If he is correct in his hypothesis that operating the ziptronic (rather than hierarchical position) is the cause of alcoholism among postal employees, then once the effect of the ziptronic has been taken into account, hierarchical position should make no difference in the rate of alcoholism. Another way of stating this conclusion is that within the categories of the control variable (have operated the ziptronic, have not operated the ziptronic), one should find the same rate of alcoholism for supervisors and nonsupervisors: Supervisory and nonsupervisory personnel who have operated the ziptronic should *not* differ in the rate of alcoholism. Similarly, supervisors and nonsupervisors who have not operated the ziptronic also should not differ in the rate of alcoholism. These data would indicate that after taking into account (controlling for) the effect of operating the ziptronic, hierarchical position bears no relationship to the rate of alcoholism.

This logic encapsulates one side of the picture. The expectation is that operating the ziptronic machine, rather than hierarchical position, is the cause of alcoholism among postal employees. What would one expect to find if the *opposite* is true—that hierarchical position, rather than operation of the ziptronic, causes alcoholism? Because (now) the operation of the ziptronic is not related to alcoholism, then one would expect to find the same relationship between hierarchical position and alcoholism as displayed in the original cross-tabulation (Table 16.2)—regardless of whether the employees have operated the ziptronic machine or not. Thus, in each of the control tables (the separate tables cross-tabulating hierarchical position and alcoholism within each category of the control variable, operation of the ziptronic—Table 16.3), one should find that the relationship between hierarchical position and alcoholism is identical to that found in Table 16.2. These data would indicate that even when the effect of operating the ziptronic has been taken into account, hierarchical position and alcoholism remain related.

These two data expectations present opposite explanations for the causes of alcoholism among post office personnel. According to the first, if operation of the ziptronic machine (rather than hierarchical position) is the cause of alcoholism, then when the effect of operating the ziptronic is taken into account, the original relationship between hierarchy and alcoholism should disappear. That is, when use of the ziptronic is considered, hierarchical position is found to make no difference in the rate of alcoholism. According to the second, if hierarchical position (rather than operation of the ziptronic machine) is the cause of alcoholism, then when the effect of operating the ziptronic is taken into account, the original relationship between hierarchy and alcoholism should persist. Therefore, even when use of the ziptronic is considered, hierarchy continues to make a difference in the rate of alcoholism.

With these expectations in mind, we can interpret the data displayed in Table 16.3. Which of the opposite situations do the percentaged cross-tabulations more closely resemble? These data show overwhelming support for the second explanation. When the effects of operation of the ziptronic have been controlled, hierarchical position is related to alcoholism in exactly the same manner as in the original, uncontrolled cross-tabulation in Table 16.2. Regardless of whether or not they have used the ziptronic machines, 25% of the supervisors are alcoholics, as compared with only 3% of the nonsupervisors, a difference of 22%. Because the relationship between position in the hierarchy and rate of alcoholism is unaffected by the introduction of the ziptronic variable into the analysis, these data lend support to the conclusion that hierarchical position, rather than operation of the ziptronic, is a cause of alcoholism among postal employees. This finding offers some evidence of a nonspurious relationship between these two variables (see Chapter 3, on causal inference, for a full discussion of nonspuriousness).

Example 2A: Performance on the Civil Service Examination—A Case of Favoritism in Blakely?

The *Daily Mirror*, the newspaper for Blakely, Vermont, recently published a series of troubling articles accusing the Blakely city government of favoritism in testing and hiring job applicants. The articles charge Blakely officials with giving hiring preference to those whom they know rather than to the most qualified applicants. One article quotes an unsuccessful job candidate: "Unless you know someone in Blakely City Hall, you're not going to get a pass on the civil service examination. And without the pass, you don't make it onto the hire list. Check the list—most of the people on it have friends in city government. The key is to know somebody." Mayor Kent B. Fooled is disturbed by these charges and appoints his staff assistant, Evan Michael, to look into them.

To do so, Michael draws a random sample of 335 job applicants for analysis from the Blakely central personnel department. Fortunately, the application forms contain a number of questions useful for his purposes. One question asks whether the applicant knows anyone who works for Blakely, and another gathers the usual background information on education. Department records also show whether the applicant has passed or failed the Blakely civil service examination.

Michael begins by cross-tabulating the question of whether the applicant knew someone in Blakely city government (previous contact) with the information on whether she or he passed the civil service exam (test performance). Table 16.4 displays the cross-tabulation.

Like the mayor, Michael is disturbed by the results of the cross-tabulation. He had expected the charges aired in the newspaper articles to be unfounded, but in this sample, job applicants who did not know someone in city government failed the civil service examination at a rate 20% higher than did those with previous contact with a Blakely employee (54% − 34%). Michael, however, suspects that a third variable may be responsible for this surprising relationship: *education*. He reasons that level of education will certainly affect performance on the civil service exam. He feels that the only reason why those with previous contact appear to fare better on the test is that they are more likely to have completed higher levels of education.

| **Table 16.4** | **Relationship between Test Performance and Prior Contact** |

Raw Data

Test Performance	Prior Contact		
	No	Yes	Total
Fail	70	70	140
Pass	60	135	195
Total	130	205	335

Percentaged Data

Test Performance	Prior Contact	
	No	Yes
Fail	54%	34%
Pass	46%	66%
Total	100%	100%
	(*n* = 130)	(*n* = 205)

Michael knows that Blakely draws a lot of its job applicants from the local community college (Blakely Tech, home of the Fighting Financiers, a perennial athletic power). He and other Blakely employees have attended several job fairs at the college and spoken before classes and other groups there; Blakely also works with the college on an internship program. Thus, college education puts many potential job applicants in contact with Blakely city government, and higher education likewise helps them pass the civil service examination. To test these ideas empirically, Michael intends to introduce education (college graduate, not college graduate) into the analysis. The anticipated relationships among the three variables are shown in the figure below:

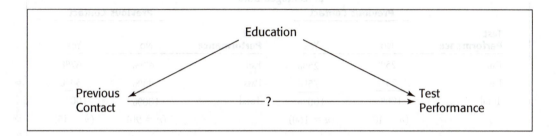

Michael then performs the following steps:

Step 1: Partition the sample according to the categories of the control variable. In this example, education is the control variable and consists of two categories: those who are college graduates and those who are not. Of the 335 individuals in the sample, 200 are college graduates and the remaining 135 are not.

Step 2: Assemble the cross-tabulation between the original two variables for each of the subsamples defined by the control variable in Step 1. Percentage each of these tables separately according to the procedure outlined in Chapter 14. In this instance, two cross-tabulations between previous contact and test performance would be obtained: the first based on those individuals who are college graduates and the second based on those individuals who are not. Table 16.5 displays the results obtained according to this procedure in the sample of applicants for positions in Blakely city government.

You should satisfy yourself that the elaboration of Table 16.4 presented in the cross-tabulations of Table 16.5 is consistent with the original data.

Step 3: Interpret the cross-tabulations obtained for each of the categories of the control variable. The logic of this process is the same as that elaborated in the previous example (hierarchy–ziptronic–alcoholism).

Table 16.5	Cross Tabulation of Subsamples Based on Education

Raw Data

College Graduates ($n = 200$)

Previous Contact

Test Performance	No	Yes	Total
Fail	10	40	50
Pass	30	120	150
Total	40	160	200

Not College Graduates ($n = 135$)

Previous Contact

Test Performance	No	Yes	Total
Fail	60	30	90
Pass	30	15	45
Total	90	45	135

Percentaged Data

Previous Contact

Test Performance	No	Yes
Fail	25%	25%
Pass	75%	75%
Total	100%	100%
	($n = 40$)	($n = 160$)

Previous Contact

Test Performance	No	Yes
Fail	67%	67%
Pass	33%	33%
Total	100%	100%
	($n = 90$)	($n = 45$)

© Cengage Learning

If education (rather than previous contact) is the cause of performance on the civil service examination, then when the effect of education is taken into account, the original relationship between contact and test performance should disappear; that is, when the effect of education has been controlled, previous contact should make no difference in test performance. Conversely, if contact (rather than education) is the cause of performance in the examination, then when education is taken into account, the original relationship found between previous contact and test performance in Table 16.4 should persist; that is, even when the effect of education has been considered, contact should continue to make a difference in performance in the civil service examination.

The percentaged cross-tabulations presented in Table 16.5 show that once education has been controlled, those with and without previous contact fail the civil service examination with equal frequency. Among the college graduates, 25% of both groups fail the exam, and among the noncollege graduates, 67% of both groups fail. Thus, because within the categories of education, previous contact makes no difference in test performance, these data warrant the conclusion that contact and performance on the civil service examination are not related. (If they were related, one would expect that previous contact would make a difference in test performance even when education was taken into account.)

Although prior contact with a Blakely city official *appeared* to affect test performance in the original bivariate cross-tabulation (Table 16.4), the introduction of the control variable (education) made the relationship disappear. Thus, in this example, contact is not a cause of test performance. Instead, previous contact is a *spurious* variable—one that initially appears to be related to the dependent variable but whose effect vanishes in the presence of the control variable.

Table 16.5 also demonstrates that, regardless of prior contact with a Blakely city official, the percentage of college graduates failing the examination (25%) is much smaller than the percentage of nongraduates who fail (67%). This finding indicates that it is education that leads to test performance. For both those who have and those who have not had prior contact, the higher the education, the better is the performance on the examination. The strength of this relationship can be seen in Table 16.6, which cross-tabulates education and performance on the civil service examination. This cross-tabulation is constructed from the control tables in Table 16.5. The relationship between education and test performance persists even when the effect of previous contact has been controlled.

Evan Michael reports these findings to the mayor. The mayor instructs him to write a letter to the *Daily Mirror* explaining that a careful look at all the data undermines the charges of favoritism in Blakely city

Table 16.6	Relationship between Education and Test Performance

Raw Data

	Education		
Test Performance	Not College Graduate	College Graduate	Total
Fail	90	50	140
Pass	45	150	195
Total	135	200	335

Percentaged Data

	Education	
Test Performance	Not College Graduate	College Graduate
Fail	67%	25%
Pass	33%	75%
Total	100%	100%
	($n = 135$)	($n = 200$)

© Cengage Learning

government. Indeed, the results show that Blakely has a strong commitment to merit because those with college education pass the civil service examination at a much higher rate. The editors agree to publish a follow-up article, placing the earlier series of articles in the proper context. Impressed by the analytic power of multivariate methods, Michael eagerly returns to Blakely Tech to take more courses in applied statistics for public and nonprofit administration (these courses use a certain beloved textbook).

Example 2B: Race, Education, and Complaints—A Developmental Sequence

Suppose that as an employee of Lillian County government, you were interested in why whites seem to complain more often about road conditions than do nonwhites. Imagine further that the county administrator had assembled data in a cross-tabulation, based on a survey of county residents, to support this claim. The relationship in the cross-tabulation might closely resemble the pattern found in Table 16.4, but in this case imagine that race (nonwhite versus white) is the independent variable and complaints about road conditions (no complaints versus complaints) is the dependent variable. If so, whites would appear to complain at a much higher rate than nonwhites (66% − 46% = 20%). Why?

As discussed in the previous example, a good next step would be to control for *education*. You might reason that whites have greater opportunity to attain higher levels of education, and education leads to higher expectations concerning the level of services government should provide and more confidence to voice these demands for better services to county officials (a polite phrase for "complain"). Following this logic, if you were to introduce education (college graduate, not college graduate) as a control variable into the analysis (as in the previous example), you would probably find a data pattern very similar to the one displayed in Table 16.5: Race would no longer make a difference in the frequency of complaints from residents, but level of education would make a huge difference.

In contrast to the previous example, however, race is *not* a spurious variable in this case. Instead, race leads to differences in access to education, and these differences, in turn, lead to differences in the rate of complaining to county officials. Thus, this example illustrates a *developmental sequence*, in which education acts as an *intervening* variable.

The difference between the two examples lies in the underlying causal structure of the variables. In this example, we are sure that race leads to education, which leads to complaints. In the previous example, education led to *both* prior contact with Blakely city officials and passing the civil service examination. Hence, prior contact was not the reason why applicants passed the exam—this factor actually obscured the effect of the true causal variable, education. Once education was introduced as the control variable, it quickly became apparent that prior contact was spurious.

What lesson do these two examples hold for public and nonprofit managers? When the effect of an independent variable disappears with the introduction of a control variable, the reason may be either a spurious relationship or a developmental sequence. Both situations produce the same pattern of relationships in the control tables. To decide which situation is more likely, you must carefully review and logically analyze the causal structure underlying the independent, control, and dependent variables. As we demonstrated in Chapter 3, having a substantive understanding of the likely causal structure is critical to understanding and interpreting statistical results correctly.

Example 3: Guaranteed Annual Income—A Case of Interaction

The previous two examples have illustrated polar opposite data analysis situations. In the first, introduction of a control variable (operation of the ziptronic) into the analysis had no effect on the original bivariate relationship (position in the hierarchy and alcoholism). In the second, the control variable (education) was totally responsible for the apparent—but not actual—relationship originally found between the two variables (previous contact with city officials and test performance).

A third situation that frequently occurs in the analysis of data is called *interaction* or *specification*. In this situation, the relationship between two variables changes markedly depending on the category of the control variable; that is, the categories of the control variable specify the nature of the relationship between the independent and dependent variables.

Several types of interactive relationships are possible. For example, in one category of a control variable, there may be no relationship between the independent and dependent variables, whereas in the second category of the control variable, there may be a strong positive or negative relationship. As an illustration, consider the likely effect on a student's college major of attending career planning sessions, controlling for the year of the student in college. Among new students, one is likely to find a strong relationship between attending the meetings and choice of major; however, among graduating seniors, one is likely to find no relationship.

In a second type of interaction, the relationship between the independent and dependent variables can change direction (positive to negative or vice versa) contingent on the category of the control variable. The following example illustrates a three-variable relationship of this kind.

The federal government has been experimenting with a guaranteed annual income program (GAI). Volatile policy debate revolves around the effects of this federal largesse. When people are guaranteed an income, are they more likely to spend all the money or to save at least a portion of it? To examine the effects of GAI, a staff analyst is appointed. He assembles data from 200 individuals who have participated in GAI and a matching sample of 200 who have not.

His first concern is whether those who participated in the GAI were more likely to save money than those who did not. Therefore, he cross-tabulates participation in GAI (no, yes) with money saved during the program (no, yes). The results are presented in Table 16.7.

This table reveals no relationship between participation in the GAI program and saving behavior. Those who participated in the program were just as likely to save (or not to save) money as those who did not. The analyst, however, is curious

Table 16.7	Relationship between GAI and Saving Money		

Raw Data

	Guaranteed Annual Income (GAI)		
Saved Money	No	Yes	Total
No	100	100	200
Yes	100	100	200
Total	200	200	400

Percentaged Data

	Guaranteed Annual Income (GAI)	
Saved Money	No	Yes
No	50%	50%
Yes	50%	50%
Total	100%	100%
	($n = 200$)	($n = 200$)

© Cengage Learning

about the effect on this relationship of the individual's past history of saving money. He believes that the ability to save money is learned over time; therefore, he reasons that those who have a past history of saving money will do so again under the GAI. Those who lack this history (or "learning") will fail in this pursuit once again. This hypothesis calls for the introduction of the saving history of the respondent (have saved in the past, have not saved in the past) into the analysis as a control variable. We omit detailed elaboration of the first two steps of the control procedure and simply present in Table 16.8 the two cross-tabulations obtained when this control variable is introduced. (If these steps remain unclear to you, review the detailed examples developed in the chapter.)

The control tables presented in Table 16.8 resemble neither of the polar situations we saw in the first two examples. Instead, Table 16.8 shows that the past history of saving *specifies* the relationship between participation in the GAI program and saving money. Among the individuals who had a past history of saving money, participation in the program is related positively to saving. Note that program participants saved money more frequently over the period of the study than did nonparticipants. In the subsample of respondents with a past history of saving, 64% of participants in the GAI saved money, compared with 55% of the nonparticipants. These data suggest that for this subsample, the GAI encouraged and led to saving behavior.

By contrast, for those individuals who had no past history of saving money, participation in the GAI had the opposite effect. In this subsample of

Table 16.8	Cross-Tabulation of Subsamples Based on Past Saving Behavior

Raw Data

Have Saved in Past (*n* = 220)

	GAI		
Saved Money	No	Yes	Total
No	50	40	90
Yes	60	70	130
Total	110	110	220

Have Not Saved in Past (*n* = 180)

	GAI		
Saved Money	No	Yes	Total
No	50	60	110
Yes	40	30	70
Total	90	90	180

Percentaged Data

	GAI	
Saved Money	No	Yes
No	45%	36%
Yes	55%	64%
Total	100%	100%
	(*n* = 110)	(*n* = 110)

	GAI	
Saved Money	No	Yes
No	56%	67%
Yes	44%	33%
Total	100%	100%
	(*n* = 90)	(*n* = 90)

© Cengage Learning

respondents, participants in the program saved money less frequently than did nonparticipants, 33% versus 44%, a difference in saving behavior of 11%. Thus, among those who had not saved money in the past, participation in the GAI is related negatively to saving during the period of the study. In this subsample, the GAI seemed to discourage saving behavior. In an interactive relationship such as this one, the control variable must be taken into account in order to understand the relationship between the independent and dependent variables.

This example is important not only because it demonstrates an interactive relationship but also because it shows that a relationship between two variables may not be evident *unless* a control variable is incorporated into the analysis. In the original, noncontrolled cross-tabulation displayed in Table 16.7, participation in the GAI program does *not* appear to be related to saving behavior. Participants in the program were just as likely to save (or not to save) money as were nonparticipants. The controlled cross-tabulations presented in Table 16.8, however, indicate that when the effect of past history of saving is considered, participation in the GAI is related to saving behavior. Among individuals who had saved in the past, the GAI led to further saving; among those who had no past history of saving, just the opposite occurred.

This example illustrates an important lesson in data analysis: Even when a bivariate cross-tabulation suggests that no relationship exists between two variables, the variables can still be related, but in a more complicated way. The introduction of a third, control variable can reveal a more subtle relationship. In the current example, failure to take into account a control variable suppressed the relationship between the independent and dependent variables. For this reason, this type of situation is sometimes called a *suppressor* relationship.

The converse is also true: A cross-tabulation that demonstrates a statistical association between two variables cannot ensure that the two variables are related. It was on this point that the chapter began. Whereas ice cream consumption appeared to be related to juvenile crime, controlling for the SES of the precinct will cause this relationship to disappear. In fact, SES—not ice cream consumption—is a cause of juvenile crime. Ice cream consumption only appeared to be related to crime, because individuals living in high-SES precincts are likely both to eat more ice cream and to commit fewer crimes than are those living in low-SES precincts. (Another example of such a spurious relationship was described earlier, based on the relationships among previous contact, education, and performance on the civil service examination.) It is these kinds of complexities that make data analysis frustrating and exciting at the same time.

Example 4: Support for Performance-Based Pay—Evidence of Joint Causation

The mayor of the city of Athenia has proposed to the city council that Athenia change compensation systems. As do many cities in the southeastern United States, Athenia determines employee pay primarily on the basis of years (seniority) in government service, in a grade-and-step system. The mayor believes that motivation and productivity of city workers would improve if Athenia were to shift to a performance-based pay system. Under the mayor's plan, supervisors would meet annually with individual employees to set performance goals for the year, employees would be evaluated 1 year later on accomplishment of the objectives, and pay increases would be tied to the performance evaluation. The city council is impressed with the pay plan, but before taking action, it authorizes the mayor to conduct a study of employee reaction to the plan and to report the results.

The mayor appoints two top MPAs in her office, Megan Samantha and Philip Joseph, to carry out the study. Because performance-based pay is thought to increase employee morale—because employees have greater involvement in establishing work goals and can move up the pay ladder more quickly than in a traditional grade-and-step system—the mayor expects to find strong support for her plan. Samantha and Joseph decide to survey a representative sample of 212 Athenia employees to ascertain their attitudes and opinions toward the mayor's proposal. They are surprised to find that only a bare majority of city workers, 52% ($n = 111$), favor the mayor's plan, whereas 48% ($n = 101$) oppose it. Good analysts that they are, Samantha and Joseph decide to undertake further study.

They believe that prior experience in the private sector may help to explain the results. Performance-based pay systems are much more common in private business than in government. Thus, Samantha and Joseph cross-tabulate support for performance-based pay (no, yes) in the Athenia sample by whether the employee has had work experience in the private sector (no, yes). They anticipate that city workers with a background in the private sector will be more favorable toward the new pay plan. Table 16.9 displays the cross-tabulation.

Table 16.9	Relationship between Employee Experience in the Private Sector and Support for Performance-Based Pay

Raw Data

Support for Performance-Based Pay	Private Sector Experience		
	No	Yes	Total
No	55	46	101
Yes	50	61	111
Total	105	107	212

Percentaged Data

Support for Performance-Based Pay	Private Sector Experience	
	No	Yes
No	52%	43%
Yes	48%	57%
Total	100%	100%
	($n = 105$)	($n = 107$)

Just as Samantha and Joseph had expected, support for performance-based pay is higher by 9% for employees who have work experience in the private sector (57%) than for those who do not (48%). Still, the researchers would like to identify other factors that may account for the attitudes of Athenia workers and that would help the researachers devise a strategy for building employee acceptance.

One variable that occurs to the researchers is job classification as either supervisory or nonsupervisory personnel. The mayor's pay plan would add to the burden on supervisors by giving them a larger role in setting annual goals with the employees and, especially, in evaluating their performance. According to city records, although Athenia supervisory personnel already have evaluation responsibilities, more than 95% of the time supervisors give employees performance ratings in the highest two categories. Samantha and Joseph would like to think that Athenia city government has a superior workforce—but they doubt that it's *that* good. Instead, they suspect that because pay is not strongly tied to performance appraisal in the present system, it has become largely a pro forma, routine exercise for supervisors and employees. By linking pay raises to performance, however, the mayor's plan could radically alter the nature of evaluation: Not only would it increase the workload on supervisors, but also—with pay at stake—it could make the process more confrontational and open the door to much-dreaded litigation. Of course, it might just as well produce greater teamwork and collaboration between supervisors and employees; yet Samantha and Joseph realize that when organizations introduce change without laying the appropriate groundwork, members often fear the worst. Their next step is to compare support for performance-based pay for supervisory versus nonsupervisory personnel, again taking into account prior work experience in the private sector, which has been shown to have an effect on these attitudes (Table 16.9). Table 16.10 presents the cross-tabulation of support for performance-based pay and work experience in the private sector, controlling for employee status as supervisory or nonsupervisory.

The percentaged data in the control tables lend insight into the attitudes of the Athenia employees. First, the tables show that even when job classification as supervisory versus nonsupervisory is taken into account (controlled statistically), prior work experience in the private sector continues to have the same effect on support for performance-based pay. Whether the employee is a supervisor or not, private sector job experience increases support for the proposed pay system by 10% and 9%, respectively. These findings reinforce the original relationship investigated in Table 16.9, which also yielded a 9% difference. Thus, the control tables provide evidence that the relationship between private sector work experience and support for performance-based pay is *nonspurious*; that is, when a third variable, employee job classification (supervisory versus nonsupervisory), is introduced into the analysis, the relationship persists. (The control tables cannot *prove*

Table 16.10	Cross-Tabulation of Subsamples Based on Employee Classification

Raw Data

Supervisory Personnel (*n* = 40)

Support for Performance-Based Pay	Private Sector Experience		
	No	Yes	Total
No	13	11	24
Yes	7	9	16
Total	20	20	40

Nonsupervisory Personnel (*n* = 172)

Support for Performance-Based Pay	Private Sector Experience		
	No	Yes	Total
No	42	35	77
Yes	43	52	95
Total	85	87	172

Percentaged Data

Support for Performance-Based Pay	Private Sector Experience	
	No	Yes
No	65%	55%
Yes	35%	35%
Total	100%	100%
	(*n* = 20)	(*n* = 10)

Support for Performance-Based Pay	Private Sector Experience	
	No	Yes
No	49%	40%
Yes	51%	60%
Total	100%	100%
	(*n* = 85)	(*n* = 87)

nonspuriousness, however, because other variables may turn out to be responsible for the relationship observed in Table 16.9.)

What about the effect of the job classification variable on support for performance-based pay? Samantha and Joseph had anticipated that supervisors would be less receptive to the new pay plan than would nonsupervisory personnel. Comparing supervisors with nonsupervisors across the two control tables, Samantha and Joseph find that the latter group is considerably more favorable. Among those without background in the private sector, nonsupervisors are more supportive of performance-based pay 51% to 35%, a difference of 16%. Similarly, among city employees who have worked in the private sector, nonsupervisors are again more favorable than supervisors by a margin of 15% (60% − 45%). For job classification, too, the table gives evidence of a *nonspurious* relationship: Classification produces substantial differences in support for performance-based pay, both for employees who have and for employees who do not have prior work experience in the private sector. (As before, the control tables cannot prove that this relationship is nonspurious because other variables may account for the association found.) Stated in another (equivalent) way, controlling for private sector work experience, supervisory status appears to decrease support for performance-based pay—just as Samantha and Joseph had expected.

Samantha and Joseph could proceed with further analysis of the employee survey data, identifying other variables that may affect employee attitudes on this dimension. In this instance the strength of the original relationship between prior work experience in the private sector and support for performance-based pay (Table 16.9) is maintained when supervisory status is introduced (Table 16.10): City employees with work experience in the private sector remained more favorable toward the mayor's pay plan by between 9% and 10%. Had prior work experience (independent variable) been related to supervisory status (control variable), however, the control tables would very likely have shown an attenuation in the original relationship. In that case, the issue that the analyst would have to consider is whether the percentage differences produced by the independent variable on the dependent variable, though reduced, are still large enough to conclude that the independent variable has an effect on the dependent variable. If, when the control variable is introduced, these percentage differences fall close to zero, the control tables give evidence of a spurious relationship (see, for example, Table 16.5), rather than of joint causation.

The difference between joint causation and interaction can sometimes be difficult to detect and interpret. Perhaps the easiest way to differentiate between the two situations is to note that if the relationship is one of joint causation, then the relationship between the independent variable and the dependent variable will be consistent in the control tables, and the relationship between the control variable and the dependent variable will also be consistent. In Table 16.10, for example, private sector experience had the same (positive) relationship to support for performance-based pay for both supervisory and nonsupervisory personnel. Similarly, nonsupervisory personnel, both those who have private sector experience and those who do not, were more supportive of performance-based pay.

By contrast, if the relationship is one of interaction, these relationships will not be consistent. You can see in Table 16.8, for example, that for those who had saved in the past, the GAI tended to increase saving behavior, but for those who had not saved in the past, the GAI tended to reduce saving behavior. If the independent and the control variables interact in affecting the dependent variable, the relationships will be very different within and across the control tables.

Results and Implications of Control Table Analysis

It is now possible to summarize four sets of possible empirical results (or perhaps five since one of them has two interpretations)—and their implications for further data analysis—of introducing a third (control) variable into a bivariate relationship. These sets are explained in Table 16.11. Examples of all of these types of three-variable relationships have been elaborated in this chapter.

Limitations of the Control Table Technique

Multivariate Relationships

Control table analysis is a relatively tractable procedure for the analysis of three-variable relationships. Beyond three variables, however, its utility as an analytical tool diminishes. For example, if a researcher is interested in the determinants of performance on the civil service examination, she might hypothesize that not only prior contact with city government and education might have effects (as in the example we considered earlier) but also sex and motivation. To assess the effect of each of these variables on test performance, she would have to examine the relationship between performance and one of the independent variables—say, prior contact—controlling simultaneously for the other two independent variables—sex and motivation. At a minimum, this procedure will generate four control tables: the cross-tabulation between prior contact and test performance for (1) males with high motivation, (2) males with low motivation, (3) females with high motivation, and (4) females with low motivation. If the motivation variable consists of three categories (such as low, medium, and high) rather than two, six control tables will result. The number of control tables is equal to the product of the number of categories of each of the control variables. Just as in the three-variable case, which has been the focus of this chapter, each of these control tables must be analyzed, compared, and interpreted for evidence not only of the simple effects of the independent variables but also of possible interactions among them. The number of control tables quickly becomes unwieldy. In addition, each control table requires sufficient cases for reliable analysis. As a result, the total number of cases necessary in the sample grows larger and, hence, more expensive to collect.

Table 16.11	Effects and Interpretation of Introducing a Third (Control) Variable into a Bivariate Relationship between an Independent Variable and a Dependent Variable		
Example	Empirical Effect of Introduction of Control Variable	Substantive Interpretation	Implications for Further Analysis
1.	Relationship between independent and dependent variables remains virtually unchanged (evidence of nonspuriousness).	Evidence that independent variable is related to dependent variable and that control variable is not related to dependent variable.	Eliminate control variable from further analysis. Continue analysis of relationship between independent and dependent variables.
2A.	Relationship between independent and dependent variables virtually disappears.	Evidence that independent variable is not related to dependent variable and that control variable is related to dependent variable; relationship between independent and dependent variables may be spurious.	Eliminate independent variable from analysis. Control variable becomes new independent variable in further analysis.
2B.	Same as in Example 2A.	Evidence that underlying causal structure may be developmental sequence linking independent, control, and dependent variables.	Independent variable affects control variable, which, in turn, affects dependent variable. Control variable becomes new independent variable in further analysis, but independent variable remains important in causal sequence.
3.	Relationship between independent and dependent variables changes markedly, depending on the category of the control variable (evidence of interaction or specification).	Evidence that relationship between the three variables is interactive. Control variable specifies relationship between independent and dependent variables.	Both independent and control variables must be considered in further analysis.
4.	Relationship between independent and dependent variables persists or is only somewhat attenuated in each control table; control variable is related to dependent variable (evidence of joint causation).	Evidence that both independent and control variables are related to dependent variable.	Both independent and control variables must be considered in further analysis.

For these reasons, control table analysis is performed only rarely for more than three variables simultaneously and almost never for more than four variables. Instead, in the face of multivariate complexity, researchers typically turn to more powerful, parsimonious methods, especially regression analysis (see Part 6). Although regression analysis is predicated on the interval measurement of variables, many researchers feel that the advantages of this technique more than compensate for any problems occasioned by treating ordinal data as interval (recall the discussion of the ordinal-interval debate in Chapter 5).

The Source of Control Variables

All of the examples presented in this chapter have begun with plausible relationships between two variables and then introduced sensible control variables into the analysis and interpretation of the resulting multivariate findings. An issue that has been ignored in this process is, Where do control variables originate?

Without question, the best source of meaningful control variables is good theory. Substantive theory that is intended to explain a given phenomenon will identify the crucial variables that must be considered in data analysis. In Chapter 3, on research design, theory was discussed as an essential component in drawing correct causal inferences. Other valuable sources of control variables are creative intuition, experience, previous research and published literature in an area, and expert opinion—including your boss's or your instructor's, even if you do not consider them experts.

This issue should be put in proper perspective. The source of appropriate control variables is a limitation of not only control table analysis but also all other forms of data analysis. The most powerful statistical techniques cannot compensate for a lack of solid substantive ideas and insights. Statistics is an excellent tool for testing hypothesized substantive relationships, but it is a poor one for suggesting these hypotheses.

Chapter Summary

Control table analysis is a technique for examining multivariate (three or more variable) relationships among nominal and ordinal variables. Control table analysis is used to determine how a third, "control" variable may affect the relationship between an independent variable and a dependent variable. Control table techniques illustrated in this chapter use percentage differences. The analyst examines the relationship between the independent and dependent variables within each of the categories of the control variable, and compares the results across the categories of the control. The process involves three steps. First, partition the sample according to the categories of the control variable. Second, assemble the cross-tabulation between the original independent and dependent variables for each of the subsamples defined by the control variable; percentage each of these tables separately. Third, compare and interpret the cross-tabulations obtained for each of the categories of the control variable.

The control table technique can help detect the major types of statistical effects emanating from the introduction of a control variable into a bivariate relationship: evidence of (1) nonspuriousness, (2A) spuriousness or (2B) a developmental sequence, (3) interaction or specification, and (4) joint causation. The general approach can be used with other analysis aids discussed in Chapter 15, such as the chi-square test and measures of association.

Problems

16.1 General Halftrack suspects that Colonel Sy Verleaf is discriminating in his promotions by promoting more whites than nonwhites. The following table illustrates this hypothesis:

	Race		
Status	Nonwhite	White	Total
Passed over	23	14	37
Promoted	27	86	113
Total	50	100	150

When called in to explain, Colonel Verleaf presents the following table:

	Non–West Pointers' Race				West Pointers' Race	
Status	Nonwhite	White		**Status**	Nonwhite	White
Passed over	20	12		Passed over	3	2
Promoted	19	12		Promoted	8	74

Analyze the preceding tables, and present a brief statement to General Halftrack about Colonel Verleaf's activities.

16.2 The Department of Defense is concerned about the number of Harrier crashes. The Air Force argues that the crashes result because many of these planes are piloted by marines. The data for this claim are shown in the following table:

	Pilot		
Result	Marine	Air Force	Total
Crash	46	32	78
Did not crash	187	155	342
Total	233	187	420

When the number of flight hours of the pilot is controlled, the following pattern appears:

	Pilot with Less Than 200 Hours			Pilot with More Than 200 Hours		
Result	Marine	Air Force	Total	Marine	Air Force	Total
Crash	36	26	62	10	6	16
Did not crash	62	51	113	125	104	229
Total	98	77	115	135	110	245

Analyze these tables and present your findings.

16.3 A health advocacy organization is trying to isolate the sources of health problems in the city. Some debate centers on whether health problems are related to family income or to frequency of city garbage collection. The accompanying tables display data for all neighborhoods in the city regarding average income of residents (low or high), frequency of city garbage collection (once per week or twice per week), and frequency of health problems reported in the neighborhood (low or high). Analyze these data and discuss the sources of health problems in the city.

	Average Income	
Frequency of Health Problems	Low	High
Low	103	180
High	147	120

Garbage Collection Once per Week				Garbage Collection Twice per Week		
	Average Income				Average Income	
Frequency of Health	Low	High		Frequency of Health	Low	High
Low	25	10		Low	78	170
High	56	12		High	91	108

16.4 A researcher is conducting an experiment to determine support for the feminist movement. The experimental procedure consists of playing a tape recording of a meeting of a feminist organization for a group of subjects and then comparing their attitudes with those of a matched control group of subjects who are not exposed to the tape. At the conclusion of the experiment, the researcher is amazed to find that the tape recording apparently made no difference in attitude toward the feminist movement. Check this result in the following table:

	Listened to Tape Recording	
Attitude toward Feminist Movement	No	Yes
Not favorable	40	39
Favorable	40	41

The researcher then decides to take into account the sex of the subjects and obtains the following tables:

Men				**Women**		
	Listened to Tape Recording				**Listened to Tape Recording**	
Attitude toward Feminist Movement	No	Yes		**Attitude toward Feminist Movement**	No	Yes
Not favorable	21	24		Not favorable	19	15
Favorable	19	16		Favorable	21	25

Did the tape recording have an effect on attitude toward the feminist movement? Explain your answer.

16.5 A state commission has been appointed to try to reduce crime. Commission analysts Philip Joseph and Rachel Maria have assembled data for 400 randomly selected cities. These data include whether police walk or do not walk a beat in the city, whether the city has fewer than the average number or more than the average number of streetlights for cities of the same size, and whether its crime rate is below the average or above the average for cities of the same size. Based on the accompanying data, what should Joseph and Maria recommend to the state commission in order to combat crime? Explain your answer.

	Streetlights	
Crime Rate	Below Average	Above Average
Below average	98	114
Above average	102	86

Police Do Not Walk Beat				**Police Walk Beat**		
	Streetlights				**Streetlights**	
Crime Rate	Below Average	Above Average		**Crime Rate**	Below Average	Above Average
Below Average	83	16		Below Average	15	98
Above Average	91	18		Above Average	11	68

16.6 A consumer advocate is trying to get legislation passed that will protect the environment of a large city. To increase the probability of success, the advocate researches the history of all legislation introduced in the city council in the last 5 years. She records whether the bill was favorable or not favorable to industry, whether the bill was introduced by a member of the city council or by the mayor, and whether it passed or was defeated. These variables are cross-tabulated in the accompanying tables. From these cross-tabulations, whom should the advocate try to persuade to introduce her legislation in the city council? Explain your answer.

Bill	Favorable to Industry	
	No	Yes
Defeated	132	43
Passed	138	87

Bill Introduced by Mayor

Bill	Favorable to Industry	
	No	Yes
Defeated	64	22
Passed	67	44

Bill Introduced by Member of City Council

Bill	Favorable to Industry	
	No	Yes
Defeated	68	21
Passed	71	43

16.7 A museum intends to construct a new wing. The board of directors is concerned that the new wing be a success in the sense of drawing many patrons. The museum staff has compiled data from 549 cities regarding how frequently museum collections are changed (infrequently or frequently), the size of the museum and surrounding grounds (small or large), and yearly attendance (low or high). From these data (see the accompanying cross-tabulations), what recommendations should be made to the board about constructing and maintaining the new wing?

Attendance	Size	
	Small	Large
Low	135	87
High	165	162

Infrequent Collection Changes

Attendance	Size	
	Small	Large
Low	78	47
High	82	51

Frequent Collection Changes

Attendance	Size	
	Small	Large
Low	57	40
High	83	111

16.8 A state welfare department has commissioned a survey to investigate the attitudes of its clients toward the department. For 1 week, upon completing a visit to the department, clients were asked whether they thought that they had to complete too many forms, whether they had to wait too long in line for service, and whether they felt the agency was run efficiently or inefficiently. From the accompanying cross-tabulations of their responses, what can the welfare department do to improve its image with clients?

	Too Many Forms	
Opinion	No	Yes
Inefficient	192	182
Efficient	128	78

Not Too Long in Line			**Too Long in Line**		
	Too Many Forms			**Too Many Forms**	
Opinion	No	Yes	**Opinion**	No	Yes
Inefficient	96	62	Inefficient	96	120
Efficient	96	49	Efficient	32	29

16.9 A school district is experimenting with two different methods of instruction to improve the performance of elementary school students. The first, "traditional" method emphasizes learning through memorization, and the second, "modern" method emphasizes learning through individual discovery. As the first cross-tabulation indicates, the two methods seem to be equally effective in their impact on student performance. Some educators, however, dispute this result; they argue that the best method depends on the intelligence of the student. To test this hypothesis, they examine the relationship between instructional method and performance in each of three groups—students with low, medium, and high intelligence. Do the accompanying cross-tabulations support this hypothesis? Which method should the school district employ for which type of student? Explain your answer. (*Hint*: Although this example has three control tables, the procedures used in analysis are analogous to those used in the case of two control tables, which were discussed at length in this chapter. The analyst must examine the relationship between the original two variables within each category of the third, or control, variable and note how the control tables differ from one another and from the original table. You can interpret the result according to the guidelines presented in Table 16.11.)

	Method	
Performance	Traditional	Modern
Low	268	269
High	272	271

Low Intelligence			**Medium Intelligence**		
	Method			**Method**	
Performance	Traditional	Modern	**Performance**	Traditional	Modern
Low	68	120	Low	78	79
High	102	70	High	102	101

High Intelligence

Performance	Method	
	Traditional	Modern
Low	122	70
High	68	100

16.10 The MPA director at a large university is interested in the factors that lead to successful placement of MPA students in employment. She defines successful placement of an MPA student as being offered the position that was his or her first choice for employment after completing the program. From student transcripts, she has classified students' grade point averages in the MPA program into two categories: 3.0 or below, and above 3.0 (on a 4.0 scale). From the transcripts, she also has determined whether the student took the courses in the quantitative concentration in the MPA program (these courses require the same beloved statistics book that you are using). These data appear in the accompanying tables. Based on the data, how should the MPA director advise students about how to receive successful placements?

Placement	Grade Point Average	
	3.0 or Below	Above 3.0
Not successful	78	97
Successful	104	184

Did Not Take Quantitative Concentration				Did Take Quantitative Concentration		
Placement	**Grade Point Average**			**Placement**	**Grade Point Average**	
	3.0 or Below	Above 3.0			3.0 or Below	Above 3.0
Not successful	44	58		Not successful	34	39
Successful	44	79		Successful	60	105

16.11 A researcher, Iwanna Know, is interested in how agency and bureau directors can achieve stronger control over their organizations. Using data from 500 of these organizations, Know finds a relationship between type of budget and control. By a large percentage difference, directors claim to have stronger control with a line-item budget than with any other type. This relationship persists even when the researcher introduces the third (control) variables of size of agency or bureau and number of hierarchical levels in the organization. Accordingly, Know concludes that the relationship between type of budget and director control must be causal. Explain why you agree or disagree with her conclusion.

16.12 The Valley View Volunteer Center (VVVC) is interested in mobilizing volunteers for community service. For this purpose the VVVC has conducted a random sample survey of Valley View to determine the sources of volunteering. Based on the literature the VVVC expects that people with higher education, and people who have children living in the household, are more likely to volunteer. The data from the Valley View survey are cross-tabulated below. The variables ask whether a person volunteered in the last year (no, yes), has a college degree (no, yes), and has children living in the household (no, yes). Based on the cross-tabulations, how should the VVVC target its recruitment efforts to attract more volunteers?

	College Degree	
Volunteered Last Year	No	Yes
No	187	147
Yes	63	73

	No Children				**Children**	
Volunteered Last Year	College No	Degree Yes		**Volunteered Last Year**	College No	Degree Yes
No	144	89		No	43	58
Yes	36	28		Yes	27	45

16.13 The Farango Civic Center holds an annual volunteer appreciation banquet. The head of the agency, Sarah Mony, MPA, would like to encourage more employees to attend the banquet. Ms. Mony has obtained data on whether the employee works with volunteers at the civic center (no, yes), volunteers on his or her own (no, yes), and attends the annual volunteer appreciation banquet (no, yes). These data are cross-tabulated below. Based on these data, Sarah Mony would like to know which has the greater influence on employees attending the annual volunteer appreciation banquet—working with volunteers at the civic center or volunteering on their own? To increase attendance at the annual volunteer appreciation banquet, what should Ms. Mony advise employees to do?

	Work with Volunteers	
Attend Volunteer Banquet	No	Yes
No	59	59
Yes	67	72

	Employee Does Not Volunteer			**Employee Volunteers**	
	Work with Volunteers			**Work with Volunteers**	
Attend Volunteer Banquet	No	Yes		No	Yes
No	34	33		25	26
Yes	28	30		39	42

Regression Analysis

PART

6

Regression
Analysis

Introduction to Regression Analysis

Often a public or nonprofit manager wants to know whether two interval-level variables are related. Interval-level data are variables that have a well-defined (equal) interval or unit of measurement, such as money (e.g., dollars), time (e.g., years), distance (e.g., miles), or countable quantities or occasions (e.g., number of volunteers or number of computer mouse clicks needed to make a donation on a nonprofit website). In general, an analyst should not use ordinal or nominal-level techniques, such as those discussed in Chapters 14 through 16, on interval-level data. Treating interval information as ordinal loses much of the information that the data contain. Collapsing interval data to present simple tables can be useful for simple reports and memoranda. An analyst should not take interval data (such as number of cars, revenue, highway speeds, hours volunteered, money donated, grant applications submitted, or crime rates), however, and collapse them into categories for analysis purposes.

A variety of public and nonprofit management problems can be interpreted as relationships between two interval variables. For example, the director of the highway patrol might want to know whether the average speed of motorists on a stretch of highway is related to the number of patrol cars on that stretch of highway. Knowing this information would allow the director to decide rationally whether or not to increase the number of patrol cars. In other situations, the public manager might want to know the relationship between two variables for prediction purposes. For example, a northeastern state is considering a sales tax on beer and would like to know how much revenue the tax would raise in the state. An analyst's strategy might be to see whether a relationship exists between a state's population and its tax revenues from beer sales. If a relationship is found, the analyst could then use the state's population to predict its potential revenue from a beer sales tax. Similarly, Habitat for Humanity might be interested in knowing if weather conditions (measured by inches of rainfall and so on) affect the number of construction volunteers.

This chapter presents an introduction to simple linear regression, a statistical technique to determine the relationship between two interval-level variables. Subsequent chapters build on this foundation.

Relationships between Variables

Relationships between two variables can be classified in two ways: as causal or predictive *and* as functional or statistical. In our first example, the relationship between police cars on the road and motorists' average speed, we have a causal relationship. The implicit hypothesis is that increasing the number of patrol cars on the road will reduce average speeds. In the beer sales tax example, a state's population will predict, or determine, tax revenues from beer sales. The variable that is predicted, or is caused, is referred to as the *dependent* variable (this variable is usually called Y). The variable that is used to predict, or is the cause of, change in another variable is referred to as the *independent* variable (this variable is usually called X).

In the following examples, determine which variable is the dependent variable and which is the independent variable:

A police chief believes that increasing expenditures for police will reduce crime.

independent variable _____

dependent variable _____

A librarian believes that circulation is related to advertising.

independent variable _____

dependent variable _____

MPA candidates who complete the nonprofit concentration perform better as summer interns in nonprofit agencies.

independent variable _____

dependent variable _____

The number of volunteers is affected by the weather.

independent variable _____

dependent variable _____

If you said the dependent variables were crime, circulation, good performance, and number of volunteers, congratulations.

Relationships may also be functional or statistical. A **functional relationship** is a relationship in which one variable (Y) is a direct function of another (X). For example, Russell Thomas, the longtime head of the city motor pool, believes that there is some type of relationship between the number of cars he sends over to Marquette's Tune Up Shop for tune-ups and the amount of the bill that he receives from Marquette's. Russell finds the information in Table 17.1 for the last five transactions with Marquette's.

Russell knows the first step in determining whether two variables are related is to graph the two variables. When graphing two variables, the independent variable (X) is always graphed along the bottom horizontally, and the dependent variable (Y) is always graphed along the side vertically. See Figure 17.1.

On the axes presented in Figure 17.2, graph the points representing the two variables.

Table 17.1	Data from Marquette's
Number of Cars	Amount of Bill
2	$ 192
1	96
5	480
4	384
2	192

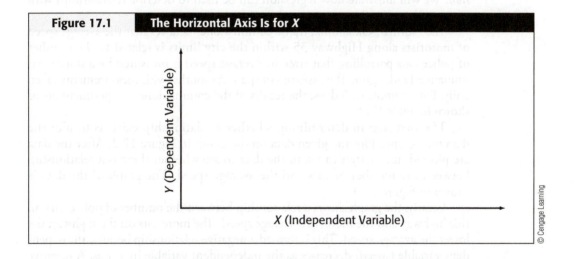

Figure 17.1   The Horizontal Axis Is for _X_

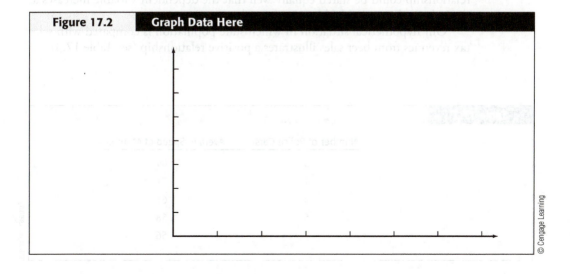

Figure 17.2   Graph Data Here

If you look carefully at the points you graphed in Figure 17.2, you will see that they fall without any deviation along a single line. This is a characteristic of a functional relationship. If someone knows the value of the independent variable, the value of the dependent variable can be predicted exactly. In the preceding example, Marquette's charges the city $96 to tune a car, so the bill is simply $96 times the number of cars.

Unfortunately, very few of the important relationships that public or non-profit managers must consider are functional. Most relationships are statistical. In a **statistical relationship**, knowing the value of the independent variable lets us estimate a value for the dependent variable, but the estimate is not exact. One process of determining the exact nature of a statistical relationship is called *regression*. We will illustrate how regression can be used to describe relationships with an example.

The Normal, Oklahoma, traffic commissioner believes that the average speed of motorists along Highway 35 within the city limits is related to the number of police cars patrolling that stretch. Average speed is measured by a stationary, unmanned radar gun. The experiment spans 2 months, with measurements taken daily. For a sample of 5 days, the results of the commissioner's experiment are as shown in Table 17.2.

The first step in determining whether a relationship exists is to plot the data on a graph. Plot the given data on the graph in Figure 17.2. After the data are plotted, the analyst can scan the data to see whether there is a relationship between the number of cars and the average speed. The graph of the data is shown in Figure 17.3.

Clearly, the graph shows a relationship between the number of police cars on this highway and the motorists' average speed: The more cars on the highway, the lower the average speed. This is termed a negative relationship because the dependent variable (speed) decreases as the independent variable increases. A negative relationship could be stated equally well that the dependent variable increases as the independent variable decreases (see Chapter 3).

Our hypothetical situation in which state population is compared with sales tax revenues from beer sales illustrates a positive relationship (see Table 17.3).

Table 17.2	Commissioner's Data	
	Number of Police Cars	Average Speed of Motorists
	3	64
	1	71
	4	61
	5	58
	7	56

© Cengage Learning

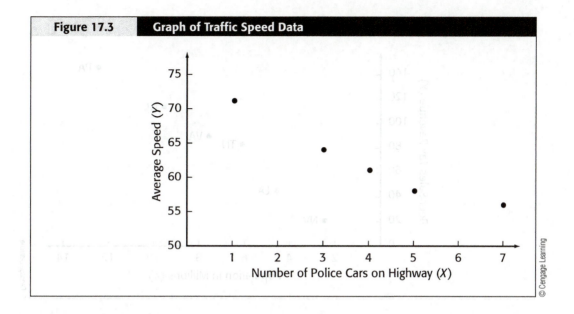

Figure 17.3 **Graph of Traffic Speed Data**

Average Speed (Y) vs. Number of Police Cars on Highway (X)

Table 17.3	Relationship between Tax Revenues and Population	
State	**Population (Millions)**	**Beer Revenue (Millions)**
Pennsylvania	12.4	146
Tennessee	6.1	85
Nevada	2.4	21
Louisiana	4.3	47
North Carolina	9.5	115
Virginia	7.6	90

The graph of these data is shown in Figure 17.4. From the graph, we see that as a state's population increases, so does the state's sales tax revenues from beer sales. Because both variables increase (or decrease) at the same time, the relationship is positive (see Chapter 3).

In many cases (far too many, for most managers), no relationship exists between the two variables. In Table 17.4, the number of police cars patrolling the streets of Normal, Oklahoma, is contrasted with the number of arrests for indecent exposure in Kansas City, Missouri.

A note of explanation is in order. On Wednesday, a regional public administration conference opened in Kansas City. Suspects are held for 24 hours, which also explains the Friday figures. Most of the Saturday incidents occurred at the airport.

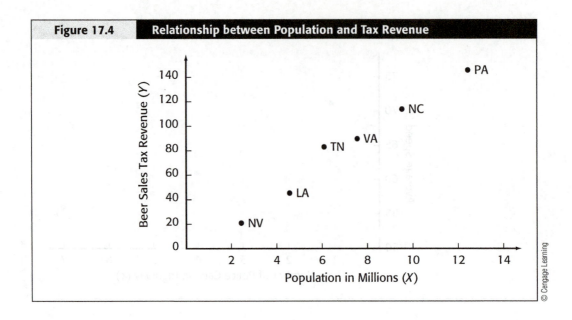

Figure 17.4 **Relationship between Population and Tax Revenue**

Beer Sales Tax Revenue (*Y*) vs Population in Millions (*X*)

Table 17.4	Patrol Cars and Number of Arrests	
Day	Cars on Patrol in Normal	Arrests for Indecent Exposure in Kansas City
Monday	2	27
Tuesday	3	12
Wednesday	3	57
Thursday	7	28
Friday	1	66
Saturday	6	60

The data are graphed in Figure 17.5. Clearly, no relationship exists between the number of police cars patrolling the streets of Normal and arrests for indecent exposure in Kansas City.

Ode to Eyeballing

When an analyst has only a few data points, the relationship between two variables can be determined visually. When the data sets become fairly large, however, eyeballing a relationship is extremely inaccurate. Statistics are needed that summarize the relationship between two variables. One variable, of course, can be summarized by a set of single figures—say, the mean and the standard deviation. The relationship between two variables can be summarized by a line.

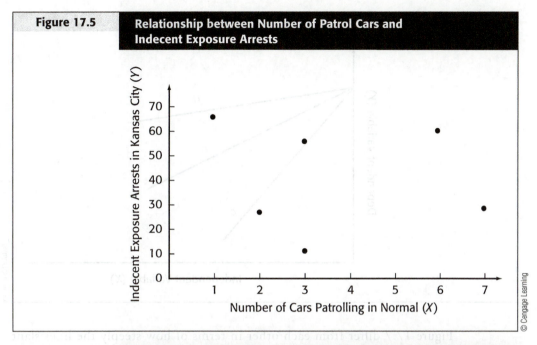

Figure 17.5 | **Relationship between Number of Patrol Cars and Indecent Exposure Arrests**

© Cengage Learning

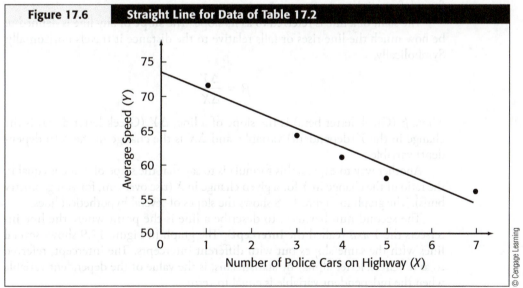

Figure 17.6 | **Straight Line for Data of Table 17.2**

© Cengage Learning

For our example of cars patrolling a stretch of Highway 35 and the average speed of traffic on that portion of highway, a straight line can be drawn that represents the relationship between the data (see Figure 17.6). The line generally follows the pattern of the data, sloping downward and to the right.

Any line can be described by two numbers, and the line describing the relationship between two variables is no exception. Lines *a*, *b*, and *c* in

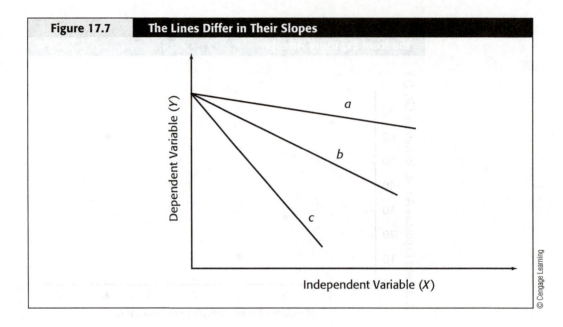

Figure 17.7 **The Lines Differ in Their Slopes**

Figure 17.7 differ from each other in terms of how steeply the lines slant from left to right.

The slant of a line is referred to as its slope. The **slope** of any line is defined to be how much the line rises or falls relative to the distance it travels horizontally. Symbolically,

$$\beta = \frac{\Delta Y}{\Delta X}$$

where β (Greek letter beta) is the slope of a line, ΔY (Greek letter delta) is the change in the Y (dependent) variable, and ΔX is the change in the X (independent) variable.

Another way to express this formula is to say that the slope of a line is equal to the ratio of the change in Y for a given change in X (rise over run, for you geometry buffs). The graph in Figure 17.8 shows the slopes of several hypothetical lines.

The second number used to describe a line is the point where the line intersects the *Y-axis* (called the **intercept**). The graph in Figure 17.9 shows several lines with the same slopes but with different intercepts. The intercept, referred to as α (Greek letter alpha) by statisticians, is the value of the dependent variable when the independent variable is equal to zero.

Any line can be fully described by its slope and its intercept:

$$Y = \alpha + \beta X$$

A line describing the relationship between two variables is represented by

$$\hat{Y} = \alpha + \beta X$$

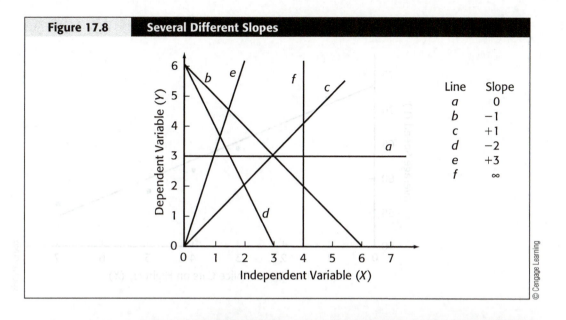

Figure 17.8 **Several Different Slopes**

Line	Slope
a	0
b	−1
c	+1
d	−2
e	+3
f	∞

© Cengage Learning

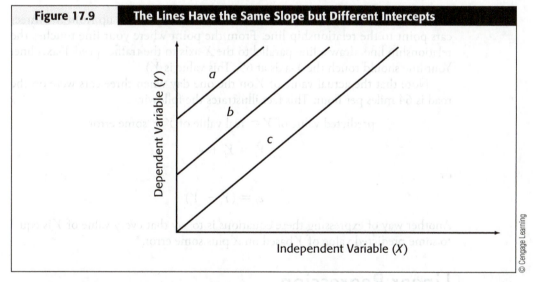

Figure 17.9 **The Lines Have the Same Slope but Different Intercepts**

© Cengage Learning

$\hat{Y}$ is a statistician's symbol for the predicted value of Y (called "Y hat"). $\hat{Y}$ for any value of X is a function of the intercept (α) and the slope (β), and it may or may not be equal to the actual value of Y.

To illustrate, let us return to our example of traffic speeds and patrol cars. The line drawn through the data in Figure 17.10 represents the relationship between the two variables. If we had only the line, what could we say about the expected average speed if three cars were on the road? $\hat{Y}$, the expected speed, is

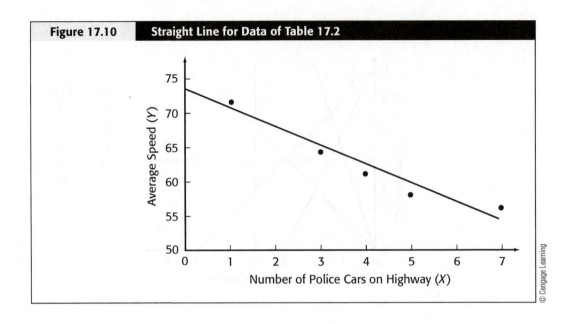

| **Figure 17.10** | **Straight Line for Data of Table 17.2** |

65 miles per hour. (To find this number, draw a line straight up from the three-cars point to the relationship line. From the point where your line touches the relationship line, draw a line parallel to the X-axis to the traffic speed Y-axis line. Your line should touch the Y-axis at 65. This value is $\hat{Y}$.)

Note that the actual value of Y on the one day when three cars were on the road is 64 miles per hour. This fact illustrates the following:

$$\text{predicted value of } Y = \text{real value of } Y + \text{ some error}$$

$$\hat{Y}_i = Y_i + e_i$$

or

$$e_i = (\hat{Y}_i - Y_i)$$

Another way of expressing these equations is to say that every value of Y is equal to some predicted value of Y based on X plus some error.*

Linear Regression

The pitfall of just drawing in a line to summarize a relationship is that numerous lines will look as if they summarize the relationship between two variables equally well. Statisticians have agreed that the best line to use to describe a relationship is

---

*We assume that error can be either negative or positive, so it does not matter whether error is added to $\hat{Y}_i$ (or Y_i) or subtracted from $\hat{Y}_i$ (or Y_i).

the line that minimizes the squared errors about it—that is, the line that makes the sum $(\hat{Y}_i - Y_i)^2$ of all the smallest possible numbers. This form of **regression** (or fitting a line to data) is called **ordinary least squares**, or you may call it just **linear regression**.

Linear regression using the principle of minimizing squared errors allows us to find one value of α and one value of β so that a unique regression line of the form $\hat{Y} = \alpha + \beta X$ can be determined. The calculations necessary to find α and β will be illustrated with an example.

Before considering the example, we should note that regression is a technique that is often used to make inferences from a sample to a population. Similar to other situations of inference, slightly different symbols are used. For a population regression, a line is denoted as

$$Y = \alpha + \beta X + \epsilon$$

Sometimes, rather than simply using Y, statisticians use the symbol $\mu_{y|x}$, which stands for the mean of y given x, or the mean value of y given the use of x to try to predict y. The population intercept is denoted α and the slope β. The symbol ϵ represents an error term meant to capture any errors in prediction. In statistics we rarely work with populations but rather with samples. In that case, the symbols are

$$Y = a + bX + e$$

The sample intercept is represented by the symbol a, the slope by b, and the error term by e. Similar to the case with means, the best estimate of the population slope and intercept are the sample slope and intercept.

Through some heavy mathematics based on calculus, statisticians have found that the formula for the slope b is as follows:

$$b = \frac{\sum(X_i - \bar{X})(Y_i - \bar{Y})}{\sum(X_i - \bar{X})^2}$$

Taken a piece at a time, this formula is not as intimidating as it looks. We will use the data on police cars and average speed to calculate b (see Table 17.5).

Table 17.5	Relationship between Police Cars and Average Speed	
	Number of Police Cars (X)	Average Speed (Y)
	3	64
	1	71
	4	61
	5	58
	7	56

© Cengage Learning

Step 1: Calculate the mean for both the dependent variable (Y) and the independent variable (X). If you have forgotten how to calculate a mean, please refer to Chapter 5. The mean for Y is 62, and the mean for X is 4.

Step 2: Subtract the mean of the dependent variable from each value of the dependent variable, yielding $(Y_i - \bar{Y})$. Do the same for the independent variable, yielding $(X_i - \bar{X})$.

$X_i - \bar{X}$	$Y_i - \bar{Y}$
$3 - 4 = -1$	$64 - 62 = 2$
$1 - 4 = -3$	$71 - 62 = 9$
$4 - 4 = 0$	$61 - 62 = -1$
$5 - 4 = 1$	$58 - 62 = -4$
$7 - 4 = 3$	$56 - 62 = -6$

Step 3: Multiply $(Y_i - \bar{Y})$ times $(X_i - \bar{X})$. That is, multiply the value that you get when you subtract the mean Y from Y_i by the value you get when you subtract the mean X from X_i.

$(X_i - \bar{X}) \times (Y_i - \bar{Y})$			
-1	$\times$	$2 =$	-2
-3	$\times$	$9 =$	-27
0	$\times$	$-1 =$	0
1	$\times$	$-4 =$	-4
3	$\times$	$-6 =$	-18

Step 4: Sum all the values of $(Y_i - \bar{Y})(X_i - \bar{X})$. You should get a sum of -51. This is the numerator of the formula for b.

Step 5: Use the $(X_i - \bar{X})$ column in Step 3, and square each of the values found in the column.

$(X_i - \bar{X})$	$(X_i - \bar{X})^2$
-1	1
-3	9
0	0
1	1
3	9

Step 6: Sum the squared values of $(X_i - X)$. The answer is 20.

Step 7: Divide $\Sigma(Y_i - \bar{Y})(X_i - \bar{X})$ or -51, by $\Sigma(X_i - \bar{X})^2$, or 20. This number -2.55 is the slope.

The intercept is much easier to calculate. Statisticians have discovered that

$$\alpha = \mu_y - \beta\mu_x$$

or

$$a = \bar{Y} - b\bar{X}$$

Substituting in the values of 62, -2.55, and 4 for $\bar{Y}$, b, and $\bar{X}$, respectively, we find

$$a = 62 - (-2.55) \times 4 = 62 - (-10.2) = 62 + 10.2 = 72.2$$

The regression equation that describes the relationship between the number of patrol cars on a stretch of Highway 35 and the average speed of motorists on that stretch of highway is

$$\hat{Y} = 72.2 - 2.55X$$

All sample regressions are of the general form

$$\hat{Y} = a + bX$$

In English, the predicted value of $Y(\hat{Y})$ is equal to X times the slope (b) plus the intercept (a). The slope and the intercept can be positive or negative. In the present example the intercept is positive (72.2) and indicates that if there are no patrol cars on a stretch of Highway 35, the average expected speed of motorists is 72.2. The slope is negative (-2.55) and indicates that for every patrol car on the road, the average speed of motorists is expected to decrease by 2.55.

Some Applications

The regression equation provides a wealth of information. Suppose the traffic commissioner wants to know the estimated average speed of traffic if six patrol cars are placed on duty. Another way of stating this question is, What is the value of $\hat{Y}$ (the estimated average speed) if the value of X (the number of cars) is 6? Using the formula

$$\hat{Y} = 72.2 - 2.55X$$

substitute 6 for X to obtain

$$\hat{Y} = 72.2 - 2.55 \times 6 = 72.2 - 15.3 = 56.9$$

The best estimate of the average speed for all cars on a stretch of Highway 35 is 56.9 if six patrol cars are placed on that stretch.

How much would the mean speed for all cars decrease if one additional patrol car were added? The answer is 2.55 miles per hour. The **regression coefficient** is the ratio of change in $\hat{Y}$ to the change in X. Where the change in X is 1 (car), the change in $\hat{Y}$ is -2.55 (miles per hour). In a management situation, this is how the slope should be interpreted. It is how much $\hat{Y}$ will change if X is changed (increased) 1 unit. Remember, though, that the regression line gives estimates, and there is error (e) in predicting actual Y scores.

What would the average speed be if no patrol cars were on the road? Substituting 0 into the regression equation for X, we find

$$\hat{Y} = 72.2 - 2.55X = 72.2 - 2.55(0) = 72.2$$

When X is 0, the value of $\hat{Y}$ is 72.2, or the intercept. The intercept is defined as the value of $\hat{Y}$ when X is equal to zero.

An Example

Most analysts rely on computer programs to calculate regression equations. We expect that you will do so, too. Just for practice, however, we ask you to calculate the regression equation for the population and beer sales tax example. Recall that for six states, the data are as given in Table 17.6. In the space provided, calculate the slope and the intercept of the regression line.

Table 17.6	Relationship between Tax Revenues and Population	
	Population, X (millions)	Beer Revenue, Y (millions)
	12.4	146
	6.1	85
	2.4	21
	4.3	47
	9.5	115
	7.6	90

© Cengage Learning

$$\overline{X} = \underline{\hspace{3cm}} \qquad \overline{Y} = \underline{\hspace{3cm}}$$

$X_i - \overline{X}$ $\qquad\qquad (X_i - \overline{X})^2 \quad Y_i - \overline{Y}$

$12.4 - \underline{\hspace{1.5cm}} = \underline{\hspace{1.5cm}} \quad \underline{\hspace{1.5cm}} \quad 146 - \underline{\hspace{1.5cm}} = \underline{\hspace{1cm}}$

$6.1 - \underline{\hspace{1.5cm}} = \underline{\hspace{1.5cm}} \quad \underline{\hspace{1.5cm}} \quad 85 - \underline{\hspace{1.5cm}} = \underline{\hspace{1cm}}$

$2.4 - \underline{\hspace{1.5cm}} = \underline{\hspace{1.5cm}} \quad \underline{\hspace{1.5cm}} \quad 21 - \underline{\hspace{1.5cm}} = \underline{\hspace{1cm}}$

$4.3 - \underline{\hspace{1.5cm}} = \underline{\hspace{1.5cm}} \quad \underline{\hspace{1.5cm}} \quad 47 - \underline{\hspace{1.5cm}} = \underline{\hspace{1cm}}$

$9.5 - \underline{\hspace{1.5cm}} = \underline{\hspace{1.5cm}} \quad \underline{\hspace{1.5cm}} \quad 115 - \underline{\hspace{1.5cm}} = \underline{\hspace{1cm}}$

$7.6 - \underline{\hspace{1.5cm}} = \underline{\hspace{1.5cm}} \quad \underline{\hspace{1.5cm}} \quad 90 - \underline{\hspace{1.5cm}} = \underline{\hspace{1cm}}$

$$(X_i - \overline{X}) \times (Y_i - \overline{Y})$$

$\underline{\hspace{1.5cm}} \times \underline{\hspace{1.5cm}} = \underline{\hspace{1.5cm}}$

$\underline{\hspace{1.5cm}} \times \underline{\hspace{1.5cm}} = \underline{\hspace{1.5cm}}$

$\underline{\hspace{1.5cm}} \times \underline{\hspace{1.5cm}} = \underline{\hspace{1.5cm}}$

$\underline{\hspace{1.5cm}} \times \underline{\hspace{1.5cm}} = \underline{\hspace{1.5cm}}$

$\underline{\hspace{1.5cm}} \times \underline{\hspace{1.5cm}} = \underline{\hspace{1.5cm}}$

$\underline{\hspace{1.5cm}} \times \underline{\hspace{1.5cm}} = \underline{\hspace{1.5cm}}$

$$\Sigma(X_i - \bar{X})(Y_i - \bar{Y}) = \underline{\hspace{3cm}}$$
$$\Sigma(X_i - \bar{X})^2 = \underline{\hspace{3cm}}$$
$$\beta = \frac{\Sigma(X_i - \bar{X})(Y_i - \bar{Y})}{\Sigma(X_i - \bar{X})^2} = \underline{\hspace{3cm}}$$
$$\alpha = \bar{Y} - \beta\bar{X} = \underline{\hspace{3cm}}$$

The answer to this exercise is presented at the end of the chapter, following the problems.

What would be the best estimate of Colorado's beer sales tax revenue if it had such a tax and had 5.5 million people?

Measures of Goodness of Fit

Any relationship between two variables can be summarized by linear regression. A regression line per se, however, does not tell us how well the regression line summarizes the data. To illustrate, the two sets of data in Figure 17.11 can both be summarized with the same regression line. In the graph of part (b), however, the data points cluster closely about the line; in the graph of part (a), the data points are much farther from the line. We can say that the regression line of (b) fits the data better than does the regression line of (a), even though the "best-fitting" regression line for the data in both Figures 17.11(a) and 17.11(b) is the same.

The distance a point is from the regression line is referred to as **error**. Recall that the regression line gives the value of $\hat{Y}_i$, whereas the data point represents Y_i.

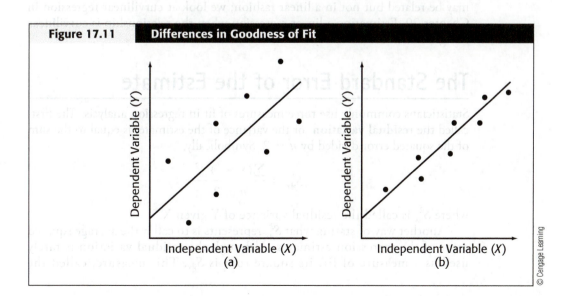

Figure 17.11	Differences in Goodness of Fit

In the following sections, we will discuss various ways that statisticians have devised to measure the goodness of fit of the regression line to the data. All these methods are based on the error.

Error in the context of regression analysis means unexplained variance (i.e., spread or dispersion in the values of Y that cannot be accounted for or "explained" by changes in X). A regression equation will almost always have some error, so trying to eliminate error entirely is not realistic. What are some of the causes of error in a regression equation?

First, a single independent variable rarely accounts for all of the variation in a dependent variable. For example, the unemployment rate might explain a substantial portion of the variation in demand for services at a local food bank, but other variables, including higher retail food prices and climate (such as cold weather), might also account for some of the variation in demand. Data values will not fall perfectly along a regression line if the independent variable explains only some of the variation in the dependent variable. This is why analysts often perform regression with several independent variables ("multiple regression"), a subject covered in Chapter 20.

Second, individual cases within our data do not always conform to the overall relationships we find when using regression analysis. For example, if most drivers slow down when the number of police cars on patrol goes up, a small number of drivers may throw caution to the wind and continue traveling at a high rate of speed. Even when a regression equation reveals a relationship between an independent and a dependent variable, deviations from the general pattern for individual cases are almost always inevitable.

Third, our measurements of important variables in public and nonprofit administration almost always contain error. Measuring such concepts as organization effectiveness and mission salience is very difficult. The presence of error in measurement contributes to errors in the regression equation. Fourth, variables may be related but not in a linear fashion; we look at curvilinear regression in Chapter 20. Estimating a linear regression when the relationship is curvilinear will generate substantial error.

The Standard Error of the Estimate

Statisticians commonly use three measures of fit in regression analysis. The first, called the **residual variation**, or the variance of the estimate, is equal to the sum of the squared error divided by $n - 2$. Symbolically,

$$S_{y|x}^2 = \frac{\Sigma(Y_i - \hat{Y}_i)^2}{n - 2}$$

where $S_{y|x}^2$ is called the residual variance of Y given X.

Another way of stating what $S_{y|x}^2$ represents is to call it the average squared error of the regression estimates. Although the residual variation is rarely used as a measure of fit, its square root is $S_{y|x}$. This measure, called the

standard error of the estimate (or sometimes root mean square error), is an estimate of the variation in $\hat{Y}$, the predicted value of Y. The standard error of the estimate can be used to place confidence intervals around an estimate that is based on a regression equation.

To illustrate the utility of this measure of fit of the regression line, we need to calculate the residual variance for a set of data. We will use the police cars and speed data of Table 17.5. In the worked-out example presented earlier, we found that the number of patrol cars on the highway was related to the average speed of all cars and that

$$\bar{X} = 4 \quad \bar{Y} = 62 \quad \hat{Y} = 72.2 - 2.55X$$

To calculate the residual variation, follow these steps:

Step 1: Using the values of X and the regression equation, calculate a $\hat{Y}$ value for every X value

$X \times b$	$Xb + a = \hat{Y}$
3×-2.55	$-7.65 + 72.2 = 64.6$
1×-2.55	$-2.55 + 72.2 = 69.7$
4×-2.55	$-10.2 + 72.2 = 62.0$
5×-2.55	$-12.75 + 72.2 = 59.5$
7×-2.55	$-17.85 + 72.2 = 54.4$

Step 2: Using the $\hat{Y}$ values and the Y values, calculate the total error for each value of Y.

$Y - \hat{Y}$
$64 - 64.6 = -0.6$
$71 - 69.7 = 1.3$
$61 - 62.0 = -1.0$
$58 - 59.5 = -1.5$
$56 - 54.4 = -1.6$

Step 3: Square the errors found in Step 2, and then sum these squares.

$(Y - \hat{Y})^2$
.36
1.69
1.00
2.25
2.56

$$\Sigma(Y - \hat{Y})^2 = 7.86$$

Step 4: Divide the sum of the squared errors by $n - 2$ to find the residual variation (or average squared error).

$$S_{y|x}^2 = \frac{7.86}{3} = 2.62$$

Step 5: Take the square root of this number to find the standard error of the estimate.

$$S_{y|x} = \sqrt{2.62} = 1.62$$

The standard error of the estimate may be interpreted as the amount of error that one makes when predicting a value of Y for a given value of X. The standard error of the estimate, however, applies only to predicting error at the exact middle of the distribution [that is, where X is equal to the mean of X; for a good explanation of why this is true, see Gujarati and Porter (2008), Chapter 5]. To predict a confidence limit around any single point, the following transformation of the standard error of the estimate is used:

$$S_{y|x} = \sqrt{1 + \frac{1}{n} + \frac{(X_0 - \overline{X})^2}{(n-1)S_x^2}}$$

where X_0 is the value of X being predicted, $\overline{X}$ is the mean of X, S_x is the standard deviation of X, and n is the sample size. Confidence limits can be placed around any predicted value of Y by using the following formula:

$$\overline{Y} \pm t \times S_{y|x}\sqrt{1 + \frac{1}{n} + \frac{(X_0 - \overline{X})^2}{(n-1)S_x^2}}$$

where t is the t score associated with whatever confidence limits are desired.

Suppose the highway commissioner wanted to predict the average speed of all cars when three patrol cars were on the road. Using the regression equation, he would find

$$Y = 72.2 - 2.55(3) = 72.2 - 7.65 = 64.55$$

This estimate of the average speed is not exact; it can be in error by a certain amount. To put 90% confidence limits around this estimate (64.55), we need to know the t score associated with 90% confidence limits. Simple (bivariate) regressions have $n - 2$ degrees of freedom, so we check Table 3 in the Statistical Tables for the .05 level (.05 + .05 = .10) with 3 degrees of freedom and find the value 2.35. Because we already know the value of x (it is 3), all we need is the standard deviation of x to do the calculations. That value is 2.23 (you need not believe us—you can calculate this yourself from the raw data). Thus, the formula reduces to

$64.55 \pm (2.35 \times 1.62) \times \sqrt{1.00 + (1/5) + [(3-4)^2/(5-1)(2.23)^2]}$

$64.55 \pm \qquad \times 3.81 \times \sqrt{1.00 + .2 + .05}$

$64.55 \pm \qquad \times 3.81 \times \sqrt{1.25}$

$64.55 \pm \qquad \times 3.81 \times 1.12$

60.28 to 68.82

We can be 90% sure that the mean speed of all cars (when three patrol cars are on the road) is between 60.28 and 68.82 miles per hour.

The Coefficient of Determination

The second goodness-of-fit measure adjusts for the total variation in Y. This measure, the coefficient of determination, is the ratio of the explained variation to the total variation in Y. Explained variation is nothing more than the total variation in the dependent variable minus the error variation. Statisticians have defined the ratio of explained to unexplained variation as equal to

$$r^2 = \frac{\Sigma(\hat{Y}_i - \overline{Y})^2}{\Sigma(Y_i - \overline{Y})^2}$$

This measure is called the **coefficient of determination**, or r^2. In bivariate (one independent variable) regression, we use r^2. In multiple (more than one independent variable) regression, the symbol R^2 is used (see Chapter 20). The coefficient of determination ranges from zero (the data do not fit the line at all) to one (the data fit the line perfectly).

The best way to interpret the coefficient of determination is as follows. If someone wanted you to guess the next value of Y but gave you no information, your best guess as to what Y is would be $\overline{Y}$ (the mean). The amount of error in this guess would be the total squared error for several guesses of Y which would be $\Sigma(Y_i - \overline{Y})^2$. If someone asked you to guess the next value of Y and gave you both the corresponding value of X and a regression equation, your best guess as to the value of Y_j would be $\hat{Y}_j$. How much of an improvement would $\hat{Y}$ be over just guessing the mean? Obviously, it is $(\hat{Y}_j - Y)$, or the difference between the estimated value of Y_j (or $\hat{Y}_j$) and the mean. The total improvement in squared error for several guesses would be $\Sigma(Y_i - \overline{Y})^2$. As you can tell, the coefficient of determination is the ratio of the reduction of the error by using the regression line to the total error by guessing the mean. Figure 17.12 shows the improvement in prediction achieved by using $\hat{Y}_i$ rather than $\overline{Y}$ to predict Y_j. The improvement in prediction is essential to calculating the coefficient of determination.

To calculate the coefficient of determination, follow these steps:

Step 1: Using the regression equation and each value of X, estimate a predicted value of $Y(\hat{Y})$. Such estimates were just made in the previous example; they are

X	$\hat{Y}$
3	64.6
1	69.7
4	62.0
5	59.5
7	54.4

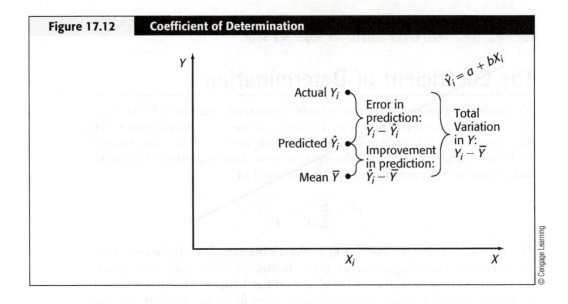

Figure 17.12 | **Coefficient of Determination**

Step 2: From each value of $\hat{Y}$ subtract the mean value of Y (in this case, 62), and square these differences.

$\hat{Y} - \bar{Y} = (\hat{Y} - \bar{Y})$	$(\hat{Y} - \bar{Y})^2$
$64.6 - 62 = 2.6$	6.8
$69.7 - 62 = 7.7$	59.3
$62.0 - 62 = .0$	.0
$59.5 - 62 = -2.5$	6.3
$54.4 - 62 = -7.6$	57.8

Step 3: Sum these squared differences to find the numerator of the coefficient of determination. In this case, the answer is 130.2.

Step 4: Subtract the mean value of Y from the individual values of Y, and square these differences.

$Y - \bar{Y} = (Y - \bar{Y})$	$(\hat{Y} - \bar{Y})^2$
$64 - 62 = 2$	4
$71 - 62 = 9$	81
$61 - 62 = -1$	1
$58 - 62 = -4$	16
$56 - 62 = -6$	36

Step 5: Sum these squared differences to get the denominator of the coefficient of determination. The answer is 138.

© Cengage Learning

Step 6: To find the coefficient of determination, divide the value found in Step 3 by the value found in Step 5.

$$r^2 = \frac{130.2}{138} = .94$$

To interpret the coefficient of determination, we can say that the number of patrol cars on a stretch of Highway 35 can explain 94% of the variance in the average speed of cars on that stretch of highway.

The square root of the coefficient of determination is called the **correlation coefficient**, or r. The value of r ranges from -1.0 for perfect negative correlation to $+1.0$ for perfect positive correlation. Despite its frequent use in many academic disciplines, the correlation coefficient has no inherent value because it is difficult to interpret. The coefficient of determination is far more useful.

The Standard Error of the Slope

The third measure of goodness of fit is the standard error of the slope. If we took several samples with an independent and a dependent variable and calculated a regression slope (b) for each sample, the sample slopes would vary somewhat. The standard deviation of these slope estimates is called the **standard error of the slope** estimate. The formula for the standard error of the slope estimate is

$$s_b = \frac{S_{y|x}}{\sqrt{\Sigma(X_i - \bar{X})^2}}$$

The standard error of the slope can be used in the same manner as other standard errors—to place a confidence interval around the slope estimate. The standard error of the slope estimate is calculated as follows:

Step 1: Calculate $S_{y|x}$, the standard error of the estimate. You will find that $S_{y|x}$ for the data we have been considering (see Table 17.1) is equal to 1.62.

Step 2: From each value of X, subtract the value of $\bar{X}$, and square these differences.

$X - \bar{X} = (X - \bar{X})$		$(X - \bar{X})^2$
$3 - 4 =$	-1	1
$1 - 4 =$	-3	9
$1 - 4 =$	0	0
$4 - 4 =$	1	1
$7 - 4 =$	3	9

Step 3: Sum all the squared differences: $\Sigma(X_i - \bar{X})^2 = 20$.

Step 4: Take the square root of the number found in Step 3: $= \sqrt{20} = 4.47$.

Step 5: Divide the standard error of the estimate (1.62) by the number found in Step 4 to get the standard error of the slope estimate.

$$s_b = \frac{1.62}{4.47} = .36$$

The standard error of the slope estimate can be used just like any other standard error. We can place 90% confidence limits around the slope estimate. The procedure for using the sample slope to place a 90% confidence limit around the slope estimate is

$$b \pm t \times s_b (df = 3)$$
$$-2.55 \pm 2.65 \times .36$$
$$-2.55 \pm .85$$
$$-3.40 \text{ to } -1.70$$

We can be 90% sure that the population slope falls between -1.70 and -3.40.

The standard error of the slope can also be used to answer the following question: What is the probability that one could draw a sample with a slope equal to the value of b obtained in a regression equation if the slope in the population equals zero? This is called *testing the statistical significance of the slope*. If $\beta = 0$, then there is no relationship between the variables in the population. If it is probable that the sample was drawn from such a population, we could not reject the null hypothesis that no relationship exists between the independent variable and the dependent variable.

To determine the probability in our example that a sample with a slope of -2.55 could have been drawn from a population where $\beta = 0$, we convert b into a t score by using 0 as the mean and by using the standard error of the slope

$$t = \frac{X - \mu}{s}$$

$$t = \frac{b - \beta}{s_b} = \frac{-2.55 - 0}{.36} = -7.1$$

A t value of 7.1 with 3 degrees of freedom is greater than the value for .005 ($t = 5.481$). The probability that a sample with a slope of -2.55 could have been drawn from a population with a slope of zero is less than .005. If there are no major research design problems (and there appear to be none here), the public or nonprofit manager would be justified in concluding that a relationship exists. (Research design is the subject of Chapter 3.)

Sometimes the entire population is used to calculate a regression line (e.g., an analysis based on all 50 U.S. states). In such cases, the preceding exercise of testing for statistical significance does not make theoretical sense because these procedures assume that only a sample of the data are available. Many analysts test for statistical significance anyway to illustrate that the relationship is not trivial or that it is very unlikely to occur by chance (i.e., the independent variable and the dependent variable are actually related).

Although you may not immediately see a link between the standard error of the slope and the coefficient of determination, the two are closely related. Think about why this is the case. The coefficient of determination reveals the amount of variation in the dependent variable that is explained by the independent variable. When we test the statistical significance of the slope and are unable to reject the null hypothesis ($\beta = 0$) the amount of variation in the dependent variable explained by the independent variable is typically small. In contrast, when we are able to reject the null hypothesis ($\beta = 0$) the coefficient of determination will be larger because the independent variable does indeed explain variation in the dependent variable.

To illustrate this point, we will perform a regression using the data in Table 17.4. Recall that when we graphed these data, we found no evidence of a relationship between the number of police cars on patrol in Normal, Oklahoma, and arrests for indecent exposure in Kansas City, Missouri.

$$\hat{Y} = 4.24 - .0138X$$

$$s_b = .0541 \qquad r^2 = .017$$

$$t = \frac{-.0138 - 0}{.0541} = .26$$

The regression equation confirms our initial finding of no relationship between the two variables. The slope coefficient is clearly not statistically significant. A t value of .26 with 4 degrees of freedom fails to exceed the t value associated with α at .05 ($t = 2.132$). The r^2 for the model is .017, indicating that the number of police cars on patrol in Normal explains less than 2% of the variation in indecent exposure arrest rates in Kansas City.

Generally speaking, if the independent variable does a poor job of explaining variation in the dependent variable, the r^2 value will also be quite low. A statistically insignificant slope and low r^2 are signs that the independent variable does a poor job explaining variation in the dependent variable.

Chapter Summary

Regression is a technique that can be used to describe the statistical relationship between two interval variables. This chapter illustrated the use of simple (bivariate) linear regression.

The relationship between two variables can be summarized by a line, and any line can be fully described by its slope and its intercept. The slope of a line is equal to the ratio of the change in Y to a given change in X. The intercept of the line is the point at which the line intersects the Y-axis. The technique of linear regression uses these concepts to find the best line to describe a relationship, which statisticians have agreed is the line that minimizes the squared errors about it. All regression equations are of the general form $\hat{Y} = \alpha + \beta X$, where α is the intercept and β is the slope. The chapter presented calculations for the slope and the intercept.

Once the regression line has been found, we usually want to see how well that line summarizes the data. To do so, we use what statisticians call measures of the goodness of fit. Three common measures are used. The standard error of the estimate, $S_{y|x}$, is an estimate of the variation in $\hat{Y}$, the predicted value of Y. The coefficient of determination, r^2 adjusts for the total variation in Y and ranges between 0 (no relationship/fit) to 1 (perfect relationship/fit). The standard error of the slope, s_b, gives the standard deviation of the sample slope estimates. The standard error of the slope can also be used to test (with a t test) the statistical significance of the slope. Using this test, we can evaluate whether a sample b deviates from the null hypothesis that the sample was drawn from a population in which the two variables are not related (i.e., $\beta = 0$).

Problems

17.1 The chief of automobile maintenance for the city of Normal feels that maintenance costs on high-mileage cars are much higher than those costs for low-mileage cars. The maintenance chief regresses yearly maintenance costs for a sample of 200 cars on each car's total mileage for the year. She finds the following:

$$\hat{Y} = \$50 + .030X \quad S_{y|x} = 150 \quad s_b = .005 \quad r^2 = .90$$
$$\overline{X} = 50,000 \quad s_x = 10,000$$

where Y is maintenance cost (in dollars) for the year and X is the mileage on a car.

(a) Is there a relationship between maintenance costs and mileage?

(b) What are the predicted maintenance costs of a car with 50,000 miles? Place a 95% confidence limit around this estimate.

(c) The maintenance chief considers $1,000 in maintenance a year excessive. For this criterion, how many miles will generate maintenance costs of $1,000?

17.2 James Jesse, the head of the Bureau of Animal Husbandry, perceives that several agencies received large increases in appropriations last year because they encouraged interest groups to testify for them before the House Appropriations Committee. The accompanying sample data for five agencies similar to Jesse's were gathered. Using regression analysis, calculate a regression equation. Does a relationship exist? The Bureau of Animal Husbandry could pressure 15 groups to testify for it. What percentage increase in appropriation would this number of groups predict? Place a 90% confidence interval around that estimate. How large an increase is each additional interest group worth?

Interest Groups Testifying	Percentage Increase in Appropriation
25	22
14	17
7	8
18	19
10	12

17.3 Martina Justice, the head of the state Bureau of Criminal Justice, feels that she could significantly reduce the crime rate in the state if the state doubled expenditures for police. To support her argument, Martina runs a regression of state crime rates (Y) (in crimes per 100,000 population) on per capita police expenditures (in dollars). She finds the following:

$$\hat{Y} = 2{,}475 + 5.1X \quad S_{y|x} = 425 \quad s_b = 1.3 \quad r^2 = .63 \quad n = 50$$

What has Martina found? Interpret the slope, intercept, and r^2.

17.4 The South Dakota Department of Game and Fish (SDDGF) wants to lengthen the pheasant-hunting season to bring in more tourist revenue. SDDGF's thinking is that most pheasants are killed during the first 2 weeks of the season; therefore, a longer season will not deplete the bird population. Using sample data from all past hunting seasons, Rodney Ringneck, the SDDGF's data analyst, regresses the number of birds surviving the season on the length in days in the season. He finds

$$\hat{Y} = 547{,}000 - 214X \quad s_b = 415 \quad r^2 = .15 \quad S_{y|x} = 15{,}000 \quad n = 35$$

What is Rodney's hypothesis? What did he find?

17.5 Lieutenant Edgar Beaver believes that officers who take master's-level courses receive higher officer efficiency ratings (OERs). Using a sample of 100 officers, Beaver regresses OERs (Y—it ranges from 0 to 100) on the number of courses each officer took beyond the BA. He finds

$$\hat{Y} = 95 + .1X \quad S_{y|x} = 1.4 \quad s_b = .07 \quad r^2 = .4 \quad \bar{X} = 5 \quad s_x = 8$$

What can Beaver say based on these results? Beaver has *a* 10-cour*se* master's degree. What is the best estimate of his OER? Place a 90% confidence limit around this estimate.

17.6 Caretakers, a local nonprofit organization, operates the concession stands for the Newland Baseball Park, home of the Newland Nuggets (a minor league baseball team). Doing so permits Caretakers to raise funds to operate its soup kitchen. Caretakers is concerned with waste in the concessions area. Too many precooked hot dogs are left over after a game. Heinz Canine, Caretakers's research analyst, feels that hot dog consumption (and other concession sales) can be predicted by the number of advance sale tickets purchased for a game (attendance is usually twice advance sales). Heinz gathers the accompanying data for a sample of 10 days. Run the regression for Heinz and tell him whether his hypothesis is correct. Predict how many hot dogs will be sold if 1,000 advance tickets are sold.

Advance Sales	Hot Dog Sales
247	503
317	691
1,247	2,638
784	1,347
247	602
1,106	2,493
1,749	3,502
875	2,100
963	1,947
415	927

17.7 The Nome City Personnel Office suspects that employees are staying home on cold days during the winter. The personnel office regresses the number of absences on the low temperature of the preceding night. Using a sample of 60 days, it finds

$$\hat{Y} = 485 - 5.1X \quad s_b = 1.1 \quad S_{yx} = 12.0 \quad r^2 = .86$$
$$X = 20 \quad s_x = 35$$

Interpret the intercept, the slope, and r^2.

Is the relationship significant? How many people will miss work if the overnight low is $-20°$? Place 90% confidence limits around this estimate.

17.8 Ridership on the North Salem Independent Transit System is increasing. The city's program evaluation office feels that the increase in the number of riders every day is due to the price of gasoline. Using data for the past 3 years, the evaluation office regresses daily ridership (Y) on the price of gasoline (in cents) for that day (X). It finds

$$\hat{Y} = 212 + 187X \quad s_b = 17.4 \quad S_{y|x} = 206 \quad r^2 = .91$$

Write a memo on the policy implications of a 50¢ increase in gasoline prices.

17.9 The Environmental Protection Agency (EPA) believes that the air quality in a city is directly related to the number of serious respiratory diseases. The agency regresses the number of reported cases of respiratory diseases per 1,000 population on the city's air quality index (ranges from 0 to 100; high scores indicate pollution) for 150 cities. It finds

$$\hat{Y} = 15.7 + .7X \quad s_b = .04 \quad S_{y|x} = 5.1 \quad r^2 = .71$$

Write a memo interpreting these results. What other factors affect this relationship?

17.10 The Office of Gerontology Policy (OGP) is considering a lawsuit against the Bureau of Investigations for age discrimination. OGP wants to base its suit on the following regression of civil service exam score (Y) on age of applicant (X) for the Bureau of Investigations. Write a memo evaluating OGP's case.

$$\hat{Y} = 92.4 - .3X \quad s_b = .007 \quad S_{y|x} = 5.2 \quad r^2 = .45 \quad n = 500$$

17.11 The Wisconsin Association of School Districts is interested in the relationship between school district population and funding for schools. From a sample of 300 school districts, the association uses simple regression to predict total school district expenditures in dollars (Y) using the school district's population (X = number of persons residing in the district). It finds

$$\hat{Y} = \$4,566 - \$824X$$
$$s_b = 135 \quad S_{y|x} = 34,788 \quad r^2 = .78$$
$$t = 6.10 \quad p < .0001$$

Express in plain English the substantive interpretations of the following:

(a) the intercept

(b) the slope

(c) the coefficient of determination

(d) the t score and how it is calculated

17.12 The State Department of Mental Health is doing a study of the use of drugs to control violent behavior among its patients. The case histories of 75 patients are selected for analysis. For each patient two variables are collected: the number of violent incidents the patient was involved in during the previous 3 months and the daily dosage of Valium given to each patient in milligrams. A regression analysis results in the following:

$$\hat{Y} = 126.6 - .0138X$$
$$s_b = .0053 \quad S_{y|x} = 2.4 \quad r^2 = .46$$
$$X = 500 \quad s_x = 200$$

What is the department's hypothesis? Interpret this regression. Is the hypothesis supported? Estimate the number of violent incidents that would be expected if a patient were given 1,000 milligrams of Valium per day. Put a 90% confidence limit around this estimate.

17.13 The Bureau of Personnel needs to predict how many employees will retire next month. Based on a sample of 35 past months, the bureau has run a regression using the number of employees older than age 60 as the independent variable and the number of retirements as the dependent variable. The bureau calculates the following regression:

$$\hat{Y} = .21 + .04X$$

$$r^2 = .35 \quad S_{y|x} = 4.5 \quad s_b = .006 \quad X = 540 \quad s_x = 90$$

Interpret the slope, intercept, and coefficient of determination, and test the slope for significance. What is your best estimate of the number of retirements next month if there are 620 employees older than 60? Could this number be as high as 30?

17.14 Dick Engstrom and Mike MacDonald are interested in the relationship between African-American representation on city councils and the structure of the electoral system. Their independent variable is the percentage of African Americans in the population; their dependent variable is the percentage of seats on the city council that are held by African Americans. Engstrom and MacDonald want to compare representation under single-member district election systems and under at-large election systems. They get the following results:

At-Large Systems

$$\hat{Y} = .348 + .495X$$

$$r^2 = .34 \quad n = 128 \quad s_b = .061 \quad S_{y|x} = 2.4 \quad X = 15 \quad s_x = 5.1$$

Single-Member District Systems

$$\hat{Y} = -.832 + .994X$$

$$r^2 = .816 \quad n = 36 \quad s_b = .075 \quad S_{y|x} = 2.1 \quad X = 20 \quad s_x = 8$$

For each equation, interpret the slope, intercept, and coefficient of determination. Test the slope to see whether it could be zero. Get the predicted city council representation of a city with 25% African-American population under both systems. Place a 95% confidence limit around your estimates. Present a hypothesis about the relative impact of electoral systems. What can you say about the relative representation of African Americans under each type of system?

17.15 Robert Stein of Brooklyn Associates argues that the per capita allocation of federal aid dollars to local governments is related to local needs. He measures *aid* as the number of dollars a city receives per person and *need* as the percentage of city residents who live in poverty. For 2013, he gets the following results:

$$\hat{Y} = 27.81 + 339.10X$$

$$r^2 = .43 \quad n = 243 \quad s_b = 93.4 \quad S_{y|x} = 124.066$$

Interpret this equation. Present a hypothesis and a null hypothesis, and evaluate the hypotheses based on this equation.

17.16 Over the past year, the Wisconsin Regional Sewage District (WRSD) has received considerable negative attention over incidents in which untreated sewage has been released into Lake Michigan. The director of WRSD argues that heavy rain, rather than actions taken by the district, is to blame for sewage release incidents. To prove her point, the director regresses the number of gallons of untreated sewage released into the lake per month (YUCK) on the total rainfall per month (RAIN) in inches (the data cover the last 72 months). Do the regression results support the director's claims? *(Note: The data set for this problem is available on the book's companion website.)*

17.17 Several years ago, officials at the Texas Department of Fish and Game implemented an aggressive advertising campaign with the goal of getting more hunters interested in hunting feral hogs. Officials would now like to evaluate whether the number of feral-hog-hunting permits issued per month has had any impact on the number of feral hogs killed each month. George Boyne, the department's chief feral hog expert, regresses the number of feral hogs killed per month (KHOG) on the number of hunting permits issued per month (LICENSE). What should Dr. Boyne conclude from these results? *(Note: The data set for this problem is available on the book's companion website.)*

17.18 In an effort to combat gun-related crimes, the city of Vancouver, Georgia, has initiated a guns-for-cash program in which citizens can turn in guns and receive cash in return (no questions asked). The city manager has collected data on the number of gun-related crimes per month (GCRIME) and the number of guns turned in per month (PGUN). Assist the manager by generating a regression equation with these data. What can you tell the manager about the effectiveness of the program? *(Note: The data set for this problem is available on the book's companion website.)*

17.19 Sue Borch, director of the Fowlerville, Maine, Center for Adult Recreational Activities, has long wondered whether there is a relationship between the number of complaints the center receives from patrons and volunteer staffing levels. To examine her hunch, Ms. Borch regresses the number of complaints received per week (COMP) on the number of volunteers on duty per week (NVOL). What can Ms. Borch conclude from these results? *(Note: The data set for this problem is available on the book's companion website.)*

17.20 Ms. Patricia Waldo, city manager of Big Cat, Texas, believes that she has discovered an effective strategy to combat the problem of loitering. Ms. Waldo believes that loitering will decrease dramatically when classical music is piped through the city's outdoor speaker system, which has been installed on a few main streets downtown. The program is phased in gradually. Music is played on the system on some days but is purposely not played on other days. This procedure enables the manager to compare differences in the number of individuals cited for loitering on music days and nonmusic days. Ms. Waldo runs a regression in which the number of individuals receiving either warnings or citations for loitering (LOIT) is the dependent variable. The independent variable is a dummy variable coded 1 for days when classical music is played on the outdoor speaker system and 0 for days when music is not played (MUSIC). What can Ms. Waldo conclude about the effectiveness of this program from the regression results? *(Note: The data set for this problem is available on the book's companion website.)*

17.21 Organizational theorist Ken Brier has obtained data on the composition of nonprofit boards of directors in the metro Chicago area. Professor Brier hypothesizes that the higher the percentage of major donors present on a board, the lower an organization's fund-raising expenses should be. Data are available for a sample of 77 nonprofits. The independent variable (DBOARD) is the percentage of board members per nonprofit identified as major donors to their respective organization; the dependent variable (FRAISE) is measured as the percentage of annual spending (out of total spending) devoted to fund-raising activities. Based on running a regression equation, what can Dr. Brier conclude? *(Note: The data set for this problem is available on the book's companion website.)*

17.22 Deborah Long, director of the Southeastern Wisconsin Nonprofits Coalition, is interested in why some nonprofits in the region collaborate more than others. Ms. Long believes that collaboration is negatively related to organizational size (i.e., the larger the nonprofit, the less likely the need to collaborate with other nonprofit organizations). To test her hypothesis, Ms. Long has collected data from a sample of 75 nonprofit organizations. Size is measured using each organization's annual budget in dollars (BUDGET). The dependent variable is the number of collaborative relationships each nonprofit is engaged in (CRELATE). Assist Ms. Long by generating a regression equation. What can you tell her about her hypothesis? *(Hint: Multiply the slope coefficient by 1,000,000 to assist with interpretation.)* *(Note: The data set for this problem is available on the book's companion website.)*

17.23 Dr. Sue Marsh, a physician at the Healthy Living Community Center, would like to obtain a better understanding of the factors that contribute to obesity in the community. Emerging research has suggested that proximity to convenience stores may be a contributing factor to obesity. To test this hypothesis, she asks one of her assistants to collect data for a sample of 50 randomly selected male clients. The first variable collected is the distance of each client's home to the nearest convenience store (in miles, DISTANCE). The dependent variable for the analysis is client weight (WEIGHT). Based on the regression output, what can be said about Dr. Marsh's hypothesis? *(Note: The data set for this problem is available on the book's companion website.)*

17.24 A public health researcher is interested in examining the economic effects of smoking. Specifically, she has data on two variables measured at the state level: the percentage of residents who smoke (PSMOKE) and annual average wages per capita (ANWAGES). Her hypothesis is that as the percentage of residents who smoke increases, average annual wages decrease. After running a regression (where PSMOKE is the independent variable), is there support for her hypothesis? *(Note: The data set for this problem is available on the book's companion website.)*

17.25 Refer to exercise **17.24**. The same researcher is also interested in examining why the percentage of residents who smoke (PSMOKE) varies by state. She hypothesizes that levels of education are negatively related to cigarette smoking. The percentage of 25- to 34-year-olds with any kind of college degree is the independent variable used to measure state education levels (COLED). Upon generating a regression, where COLED is the X variable and PSMOKE is the Y variable, what can the researcher conclude? *(Note: The data set for this problem is available on the book's companion website.)*

17.26 Data for the 25 largest school districts in the area in the metro Milwaukee area are available for analysis. The dependent variable is the percentage of students per district rated as proficient in reading (PREAD). The independent variable is the average attendance rate for each district (ATTEND). The results for this regression show that the magnitude of a one unit change in the independent variable on the dependent variable is quite large. Explain why this is the case. (Hint: Calculate and interpret the mean and standard deviation for the ATTEND variable before generating the regression.) *(Note: The data set for this problem is available on the book's companion website.)*

Answer to Regression Problem

$$\bar{X} = 7.1 \qquad \bar{Y} = 84$$

$X_i - \bar{X}$	$(X_i - \bar{X})^2$	$Y_i - \bar{Y}$	$(X_i - \bar{X}) \times (Y_i - \bar{Y})$
$12.4 - 7.1 = 5.3$	28.1	$146 - 84 = 62$	$5.3 \times 62 = 328.6$
$6.1 - 7.1 = -1.0$	1.0	$85 - 84 = 1$	$-1.0 \times 1 = -1.0$
$2.4 - 7.1 = -4.7$	22.1	$21 - 84 = -63$	$-4.7 \times -63 = 296.1$
$4.3 - 7.1 = -2.8$	7.8	$47 - 84 = -37$	$-2.8 \times 37 = -103.6$
$9.5 - 7.1 = 2.4$	5.8	$115 - 84 = 31$	$2.4 \times 31 = 74.4$
$7.6 - 7.1 = 0.5$	0.3	$90 - 84 = 6$	$.5 \times 6 = 3.0$

$$\Sigma(X_i - \bar{X})(Y_i - \bar{Y}) = 804.7$$
$$\Sigma(X_i - \bar{X})^2 = 65.1$$
$$b = \frac{804.7}{65.1} = 12.4$$
$$a = \bar{Y} - b\bar{X} = 84 - 12.4 \times 7.1 = 84 - 88.0 = -4.0$$
$$\hat{Y} = -4.0 + 12.4X$$

18

The Assumptions of Linear Regression

hapter 17 introduced an important statistical technique, linear regression analysis. Like any statistical procedure, regression analysis has assumptions and limitations. In the real world of work, actions, and decisions, analysts sometimes ignore or overlook these assumptions. They do so, however, at some managerial risk. All the uses of regression presented in the previous chapter and later ones become less reliable when any of the assumptions is not met.

In Chapter 17, recall that our highway patrol example yielded the following regression equation and coefficient of determination (r^2):

$$\hat{Y} = 72.2 - 2.55X \quad r^2 = .94$$

where $\hat{Y}$ is the predicted speed of all cars and X is the number of police patrol cars on the road. In our discussion in Chapter 17, we found that the predicted values $\hat{Y}_i$ did not exactly equal the real or actual values of $\hat{Y}_i$. According to the coefficient of determination, we accounted for 94% rather than all 100% of the variation in Y with $\hat{Y}$. What sorts of other factors account for average car speed in addition to the number of patrol cars on the road?

We can think of several factors. The weather conditions on any given day can slow traffic. The emergence and filling of potholes affect traffic speed. The number of other cars on the road restricts any one car's speed. The curves and hills and visibility on a stretch of highway affect traffic speed. These factors and others omitted from the regression equation probably account for the difference between Y_i and $\hat{Y}_i$. We can express this situation symbolically as

$$\hat{Y} = \alpha + \beta X + \beta_1(X_1, X_2, X_3, X_4)$$

where X_1, X_2, X_3, X_4 are the other factors, and β_1 is some weight (slope) representing their combined effect on Y. (*Note:* In any particular regression problem we can have more or fewer than four omitted factors.)

To simplify matters, we generally refer to all the other factors as e, or error.

$$Y = \alpha + \beta X + e$$

That is, the value of Y is equal to some constant (α) plus a slope (β) times X plus some error (e).

We introduce this terminology because most assumptions about linear regression are concerned with the error component. In this chapter, we will discuss the assumptions and limitations of linear regression.

Assumption 1

For any value of X, the errors in predicting Y are normally distributed with a mean of zero.

To illustrate, let us assume that we continue the Normal, Oklahoma, patrol car experiment for an entire year. Every day, between one and seven cars is sent out to patrol the local highway, and the average speed of all cars is measured. At the end of the year, let us assume that the overall regression equation remains the same:

$$\hat{Y} = 72.2 - 2.55X$$

By the end of the year, we probably have 50 days when four patrol cars were on the road. The average speed for each of these 50 days is listed in Table 18.1 in a frequency distribution.

Using the midpoint of the frequencies to represent each interval, we can calculate the error for each prediction because we know that the predicted speed for four patrol cars is 62 miles per hour ($72.2 - 2.55 \times 4 = 62$). The error calculations are given in Table 18.2. The mean error for all 50 cars is 0 (add the last column and divide by 50) and is distributed fairly close to normally.

Table 18.1	Frequency Distribution for Patrol Cars and Average Speeds (in mph)
Average Speed	Number of Days
58.5–59.0	1
59.0–59.5	2
59.5–60.0	2
60.0–60.5	4
60.5–61.0	4
61.0–61.5	6
61.5–62.0	6
62.0–62.5	6
62.5–63.0	6
63.0–63.5	4
63.5–64.0	4
64.0–64.5	2
64.5–65.0	2
65.0–65.5	1
65.5–66.0	0

Table 18.2		Error Calculations							
Average Speed	−	Predicted Speed	=	Error	×	Frequency	=	Total Error	
58.75	−	62	=	−3.25	×	1	=	−3.25	
59.25	−	62	=	−2.75	×	2	=	−5.50	
59.75	−	62	=	−2.25	×	2	=	−4.50	
60.25	−	62	=	−1.75	×	4	=	−7.00	
60.75	−	62	=	−1.25	×	4	=	−5.00	
61.25	−	62	=	−.75	×	6	=	−4.50	
61.75	−	62	=	−.25	×	6	=	−1.50	
62.25	−	62	=	.25	×	6	=	1.50	
62.75	−	62	=	.75	×	6	=	4.50	
63.25	−	62	=	1.25	×	4	=	5.00	
63.75	−	62	=	1.75	×	4	=	7.00	
64.25	−	62	=	2.25	×	2	=	4.50	
64.75	−	62	=	2.75	×	2	=	5.50	
65.25	−	62	=	3.25	×	1	=	3.25	

Whenever e has a mean of zero and is normally distributed, statisticians have found that sample slopes (b) have a mean equal to the population slope (β) and are distributed as a t distribution with a standard deviation s_b. When the sample size is fairly large ($N > 30$), the t distribution resembles the normal distribution, and z scores can be used as estimates of t scores. Because the t distribution is flatter than the normal distribution (the t has greater probability in the tails), it is important to use large samples whenever possible.

Assumption 2

This assumption is called "homoscedasticity," and its violation (nonconstant error) is called "heteroskedasticity": In other words, errors should not get larger as X gets larger. In Figure 18.1(a), errors have the same variance for all values of X_i; in Figure 18.1(b), the errors get larger as the value of X increases. Although Figure 18.1 shows a pattern for which the size of the error is positively related to the value of X (as X increases, e increases), the opposite situation is just as severe. If e decreases as X increases, the data are still heteroskedastic and violate this regression assumption. The same problem can affect the dependent variable; that is, the variance of the error term can increase as the values of Y increase. If this assumption of linear regression is violated, then both the standard error and t statistic associated with the slope coefficient (b) will be inaccurate. This violation can be serious because the standard error and the t statistic are used for testing the statistical significance of the slope; that

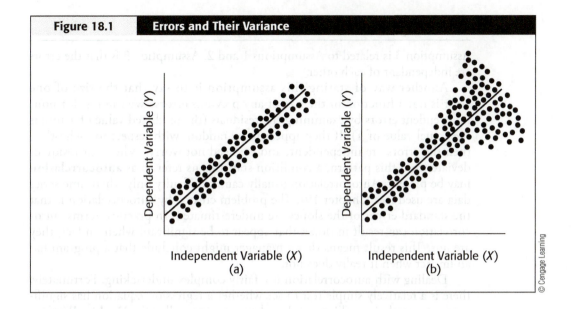

Figure 18.1   Errors and Their Variance

Independent Variable (X)
(a)

Independent Variable (X)
(b)

Dependent Variable (Y)

Dependent Variable (Y)

© Cengage Learning

is, whether there is a relationship between the independent variable X and the dependent variable Y (see Chapter 17). The fact that heteroskedasticity can occur for several reasons makes the topic complex. Apart from error terms that vary depending on the size of observations for a variable, the condition can result from "outliers," or extreme data values (see Chapter 5) and measurement error in either/both the dependent variable and/or the independent variable. In the case of multiple regression (see Chapter 20), heteroskedasticity can result from the exclusion of one or more relevant X variables from the regression equation (as discussed earlier in this chapter) or nonconstant error variance across one or more of the X variables.

Statisticians have developed some half dozen different tests for diagnosing heteroskedasticity. One must have an idea of what might be causing heteroskedastic error disturbances to know which of these diagnostic tests should be used to confirm if heteroskedasticity is indeed a problem. Techniques such as weighted least squares (WLS), robust standard errors, and variable transformations (such as logarithmic transformations of the X or Y variables; see Chapter 19) can be used to correct for heteroskedasticity. Much like the various statistical tests for diagnosing the problem, the user should have a good idea of what is responsible for the heteroskedastic error terms before deciding which of these fixes to use. Given the complexity of these issues, the reader should consult an advanced textbook on regression analysis (see Fox, 2008) for more thorough coverage of how to diagnose and correct for heteroskedasticity.

Assumption 3

Assumption 3 is related to Assumptions 1 and 2. Assumption 3 is that the errors are independent of each other.

Another way of stating this assumption is to say that the size of one error is not a function of the size of any previous errors. We can test for non-independent errors by examining the residuals (the predicted value of Y minus the actual value of Y). If they appear to be random with respect to each other, then the errors are independent, and we need not worry. When our residuals deviate from this pattern, a condition statisticians refer to as **autocorrelation** may be present. Autocorrelation usually causes difficulty only when time series data are used (see Chapter 19). The problem created by autocorrelation is that the standard errors of the slopes are underestimated. In practical terms, autocorrelation can result in slopes that appear to be significant when, in fact, they are not. This result means that a manager might conclude that a program has an impact when it really does not.

Dealing with autocorrelation is a fairly complex undertaking. Fortunately, there is a relatively simple test to see whether a regression equation has significant autocorrelation. This test is based on a statistic called the **Durbin–Watson**. Most regression programs will calculate a Durbin–Watson statistic. Durbin–Watson statistics are close to 2.0 if there is no autocorrelation, equal to 0 if there is perfect positive autocorrelation, and equal to 4.0 if there is perfect negative autocorrelation.

Table 5 in the Statistical Tables in the back of the book provides the Durbin–Watson table to test for autocorrelation at the .05 level of confidence. To use a Durbin–Watson table, you need to know the number of independent variables and the number of cases. Assume we have a regression equation with 3 independent variables and 16 cases. Using the table for $k = 3$ independent variables and $n = 16$ cases, we find two numbers, .857 and 1.728. The higher number, 1.728, is known as the upper limit (denoted d_U), the lower number is the lower limit (d_L). If the Durbin–Watson is greater than 1.728, you can reject the existence of autocorrelation with .05 confidence. If the number is less than .857, you can reject the hypothesis that there is no autocorrelation with .05 confidence. For numbers between .857 and 1.728, you cannot be certain whether autocorrelation exists.

What should you do if your Durbin–Watson value indicates autocorrelation is a problem? Fortunately, many statistical software packages have automatic routines for dealing with autocorrelation. Several of the methods for addressing autocorrelation work best only when there are a large number of cases in a data set. When the length of the time series is relatively short (e.g., 30 or fewer observations), the preferred technique for dealing with autocorrelation is called the **Prais–Winsten transformation**. The Prais–Winsten method applies ordinary least squares (OLS) regression to transformed variables that have been purged of autocorrelation. The coefficients in the resulting equation are interpreted just like coefficients in a traditional OLS regression equation (i.e., just as we have presented in the earlier chapters on regression). If your software package does not offer the Prais–Winsten method as an option, or if you want more information on other methods for addressing autocorrelation, you should consult an advanced statistics text (see Gujarati and Porter, 2008). Better yet, find a trained statistician to help you correct for this problem.

Assumption 4

Both the independent and the dependent variables must be interval variables (see Chapter 2).

The purist position is that regression cannot be performed with nominal or ordinal data. In a practical situation, however, regression with nominal or ordinal dependent and independent variables is possible. First, we will illustrate regression with a nominal independent variable.

The Homegrove City Parks superintendent wants to determine whether brand A or brand B riding mowers are more efficient. He tries three of each riding mower, testing them over normal city parks; he finds the data given in Table 18.3.

If the independent variable (the type of mower) is coded 1 when brand A is used and coded 0 when brand B is used, we have a nominal variable. Nominal variables with values of 1 or 0 are called **dummy variables** (see Chapter 21 for more discussion of dummy variables).

Table 18.3	Mower Brand and Acres of Grass Mowed
Mower	**Acres of Grass Mowed**
Brand $A1$	52
Brand $A2$	63
Brand $A3$	71
Brand $B1$	54
Brand $B2$	46
Brand $B3$	38

$X_i - \bar{X} =$	$(X_i - \bar{X})$	$(X_i - \bar{X})^2$	$Y_i - \bar{Y} = (Y_i - \bar{Y})$	
$1 - .5 =$	.5	.25	$52 - 54 =$	-2
$1 - .5 =$	.5	.25	$63 - 54 =$	9
$1 - .5 =$	.5	.25	$71 - 54 =$	17
$0 - .5 =$	$-.5$	.25	$54 - 54 =$	0
$0 - .5 =$	$-.5$	.25	$46 - 54 =$	-8
$0 - .5 =$	$-.5$	.25	$38 - 54 =$	-16

(continued)

Table 18.3	Mower Brand and Acres of Grass Mowed (*continued*)

$$\Sigma(X_i - \bar{X})^2 = 1.50$$

$(X_i - X)$	$\times$	$(Y_i - Y)$	$=$	$(X_i - \bar{X})(Y_i - \bar{Y})$
.5	$\times$	-2	$=$	-1
.5	$\times$	9	$=$	4.5
.5	$\times$	17	$=$	8.5
$-.5$	$\times$	0	$=$	0
$-.5$	$\times$	-8	$=$	4.0
$-.5$	$\times$	-16	$=$	-8.0

$$\Sigma(X_i - \bar{X})(Y_i - \bar{Y}) = 24$$

$$b = \frac{24}{1.5} = 16$$

$$a = \bar{Y} - b\bar{X} = 54 - (16 \times .5) = 46$$

$$\hat{Y} = 46 + 16X$$

© Cengage Learning

Brand of mower coded as a dummy variable appears with the data for the dependent variable below.

X	Y		
1	52	$\bar{X} = .5$	$\bar{Y} = 54$
1	63		
1	71		
0	54		
0	46		
0	38		

Recall from Chapter 17 that the formula for the slope of the regression line is

$$\frac{\Sigma(X_i - \bar{X})(Y_i - \bar{Y})}{\Sigma(X_i - \bar{X})^2}$$

The calculations follow.

Because X can be only two values, 0 and 1, $\hat{Y}$ can be only two values, 46 and 62. If we test for the statistical significance of the regression slope, we will find out whether the brand A mowers cut significantly more grass than brand B mowers. Recall that the formula for the standard error of the slope is

$$s_b = \frac{S_{y|x}}{\sqrt{\Sigma(X - \bar{X})^2}} = \frac{S_{y|x}}{\sqrt{1.5}} = \frac{S_{y|x}}{1.22}$$

Recall that S_{yx} can be calculated by the following formula:

$$S_{yx}^2 = \frac{\Sigma(Y_i - \hat{Y}_i)^2}{n - 2}$$

The calculations follow.

$Y_i -$	$\hat{Y}_i =$	$(Y_i - \hat{Y}_i)$	$(Y_i - \hat{Y}_i)^2$
52 −	62 =	−10	100
63 −	62 =	1	1
71 −	62 =	9	81
54 −	46 =	8	64
46 −	46 =	0	0
38 −	46 =	−8	64

$$S_{yx}^2 = \frac{\Sigma(Y_i - \hat{Y}_i)^2}{n - 2} = \frac{310}{4} = 77.5$$

$$S_{yx} = 8.8$$

Substituting this value into the preceding formula yields

$$s_b = \frac{8.8}{1.22} = 7.2$$

Converting $b = 16.0$ to a t score, we have

$$t = \frac{16.0 - 0}{7.2} = 2.22$$

With a t score of 2.22, the probability of brand A being no better than brand B is approximately .05 (t test, df = 4).

When the mower problem was first presented, you may have thought that this problem could have been solved with a test of means (see Chapter 13). Indeed, it can.

Brand A	Brand B
$\bar{X} = 62$	$\bar{Y} = 46$
$S = 9.5$	$s = 8.0$

$$\text{s.e.} = 5.48 \quad \text{s.e.} = 4.61$$

$$\text{s.e.}_d = \sqrt{5.48^2 + 4.61^2} = 7.2$$

$$t = \frac{62 - 46}{7.2} = \frac{16}{7.2} = 2.22$$

Notice that we get the same answer that we obtained using regression. This result occurs because a difference of means test is similar to regression with dummy variables (a dummy variable is a nominal variable with codes 1 and 0). You should also note that the regression intercept (46) is the same value as one of the means; the slope (16) is equal to the difference between the means; and the standard error of the slope (7.2) is equal to the overall standard error in the difference of means test.

Regression can also be performed with a nominal dependent variable. Suppose a personnel office tests the data entry skills of 10 job applicants, who are then hired. After 1 year, five of these processors have been fired. A personnel manager hypothesizes that the processors were fired because they lacked good keyboard skills. The job situation and data processing scores are listed in Table 18.4.

After subjecting these data to a regression computer program, the analyst found the following relationship:

$$\hat{Y} = -1.19 + .0248X \quad s_b = .009$$

$$S_{y|x} = .4 \quad r^2 = .49$$

Clearly a relationship exists ($t = 2.8$, df = 8). To understand the results of this regression, we must interpret as the probability that a processor is not fired. For example, substituting the first person's data processing score into the regression equation, we find

$$\hat{Y} = -1.19 + .0248(85) = -1.19 + 2.11 = .92$$

The probability that the first person will not be fired is .92. Similar calculations could be made for all data processors, and confidence limits could be placed around the probability by using the standard error of the estimate.

Regression with dummy dependent variables does have some pitfalls. If we substitute the word processing score of the fifth person (94) into the regression equation, we find

$$\hat{Y} = 1.19 + .0248(94) = -1.19 + 2.33 = 1.44$$

Table 18.4	Job Situation and Data Processing Score	
	Job Situation, Y (0 = Fired; 1 = Not Fired)	Data Processing Score, X (Words per Minute)
	1	85
	0	48
	1	63
	0	57
	1	94
	0	56
	1	65
	0	58
	0	72
	1	82

© Cengage Learning

The probability that this person will not be fired is 1.14, a meaningless probability. Using regression with dummy dependent variables often results in probabilities greater than 1 or less than 0. Managerially, we might want to interpret probabilities of more than 1.0 as equal to .99. Similarly, probabilities of less than 0 can be reset to .01. For most management situations, these adjustments will eliminate uninterpretable predictions. Special types of analysis called *probit and logit analysis* can be used to restrict probabilities to values between 0 and 1. These techniques are fairly sophisticated and, therefore, should not be used without expert assistance. (If you want to learn more about them, please see Long, 1997.)

Assumption 5

The final assumption of regression is that the relationships are linear.

Linear relationships are those that can be summarized by a straight line (without any curve). If linear regression is used to summarize a nonlinear relationship, the regression equation will be inaccurate. To determine whether a relationship is linear, we must plot the data on a set of coordinate axes, just as we have been doing in this chapter and in Chapter 17. The data plotted in Figure 18.2 represent linear relationships.

Nevertheless, many relationships that a manager must consider are not linear. For example, the city manager may want to project city revenues for next year. The growth of city revenues may well look like the graph in Figure 18.3. Revenues increase in this example faster than a linear relationship would predict. The graph represents a **logarithmic relationship**. Such relationships and how they can be treated in regression are the subject of the next chapter.

Another relationship sometimes found in the public and nonprofit sectors is the *quadratic* relationship. In situations in which adding another worker will improve the productivity of all workers (because workers can then specialize and

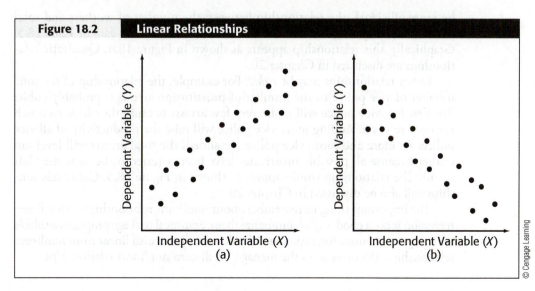

| Figure 18.2 | Linear Relationships |

© Cengage Learning

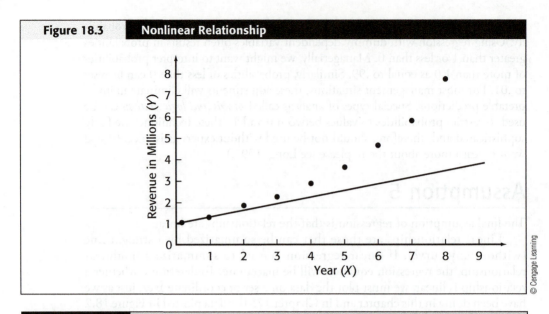

Figure 18.3 **Nonlinear Relationship**

Number of Welfare Workers (X)	Number of Cases Processed per Day (Y)
1	1
2	4
3	9
4	16
5	25

Table 18.5 Data Representing a Quadratic Relationship

be more efficient), the relationship between the number of workers and total productivity may be quadratic. This idea is illustrated by the data in Table 18.5. Graphically, this relationship appears as shown in Figure 18.4. Quadratic relationships are discussed in Chapter 20.

Other relationships may be *cubic*. For example, the relationship of the total number of vice police to the number of prostitution arrests is probably cubic. The first few vice police will make very few arrests because they have so much territory to cover. Adding more vice police will raise the productivity of all vice police. As more and more vice police are added, the total arrests will level out (either because all possible prostitutes have been arrested or because they left town). The relationship would appear as shown in Figure 18.5. Cubic relationships will also be discussed in Chapter 20.

The important thing to remember about nonlinear relationships is that linear regression is not a good way to summarize them. Statistical package programs available on computers cannot (or, rather, usually do not) distinguish linear from nonlinear relationships; the onus is on the manager to discern nonlinear relationships.

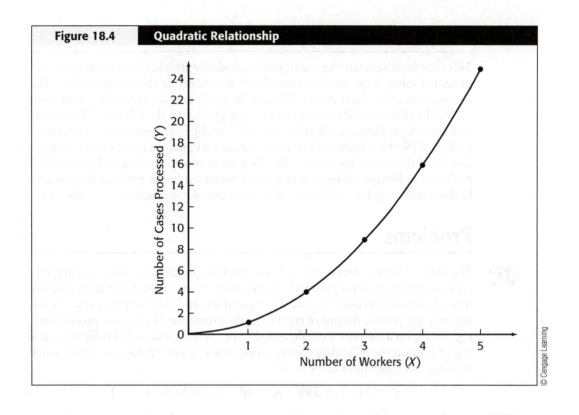

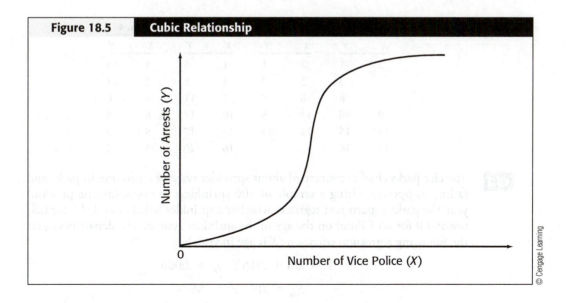

Chapter Summary

This chapter discussed five assumptions made by simple linear regression and presented some of the problems associated with violating these assumptions. The assumptions are as follows: (1) All errors in prediction are normally distributed, (2) the distribution of the errors is constant regardless of the value of X, (3) the errors are independent of each other, (4) both variables are measured at the interval level, and (5) the relationship is linear. Sometimes analysts ignore these assumptions in their day-to-day routine, but they do so at some managerial risk. All the analytical techniques of regression analysis presented in the previous chapter and in those following become less reliable when any of the assumptions is not met.

Problems

18.1 The Normal police chief wants to know whether police car cruising has any impact on crime rates. Of the city's 10 precincts, 5 are cruised regularly, and the other 5 are never cruised (police do respond to calls in these precincts). At the end of a test period, the police chief takes the crime rate (Y) in each precinct and regresses it on a dummy variable coded 1 for cruising and coded 0 for no cruising (X). From the following regression equation, what can you say about police cruising and crime rates in Normal?

$$\hat{Y} = 247.5 + 24X \quad s_b = 48 \quad S_{y|x} = 35.0 \quad r^2 = .12$$

18.2 Graph each set of data shown in the accompanying table. Determine whether the relationships are linear or nonlinear. If nonlinear, state what type of relationship it is.

No. 1		No. 2		No. 3		No. 4	
X	Y	X	Y	X	Y	X	Y
2	1	2	1	1	5	1	15
5	3	5	3	4	8	2	11
7	6	8	5	7	11	4	6
9	10	11	9	10	14	6	4
14	15	14	14	13	17	9	3
17	16			16	20	15	2

18.3 The city parks chief is concerned about sprinkler systems corroding in parks and failing to operate. Using a sample of 100 sprinklers in operation the previous year, the parks department regresses whether a sprinkler failed (Y coded 1 for failure and 0 for no failure) on the age of the sprinkler system. The department gets the following regression equation (X is age in years):

$$\hat{Y} = .06 + .016X \quad s_b = .0006$$

$$S_{y|x} = .04 \quad r^2 = .56$$

(a) Is there a relationship between corrosion and sprinkler failure?

(b) The sprinkler system in Frolic Park is 52 years old. What is the probability that this sprinkler system will fail?

(c) A sprinkler system that is only 2 years old fails in Barren Park. What is the probability that this will happen?

(d) What is the probability that the 65-year-old sprinkler system in Choirpractice Park will fail?

18.4 Too many U.S. Army mechanics are failing their yearly skills tests. Colonel Maxwell Brown believes that this failure rate results because mechanics do not learn anything from experience. His hypothesis is that time spent in an occupational specialty is unrelated to performance on the yearly skills exam. He regresses whether a mechanic failed the test (0 = failure, and 1 = no failure) on the mechanic's time as a mechanic (X) in years. For a sample of 400 troops, he finds

$$\hat{Y} = .63 + .03X \quad S_{y|x} = .41 \quad s_b = .61 \quad r^2 = .09$$

Evaluate Brown's argument by interpreting the regression.

18.5 Refer to Problem 18.4. Sergeant Desk believes the failures are related to reading ability. She regresses whether these same 400 troops failed (Y) on their reading test scores (X, scored in terms of school grade levels). She finds

$$\hat{Y} = .15 + .071X \quad S_{y|x} = .06 \quad s_b = .011 \quad r^2 = .80$$

Interpret Desk's regression. Compare her argument with Brown's. Can you reconcile them?

18.6 Refer to Problem 18.5. What is the probability that a troop reading at the fifth-grade level will pass the mechanics' exam? To be 80% sure that 75% of the mechanics pass the exam, what would the reading level need to be raised to? Comment on the validity of the mechanics' exam.

18.7 The Department of Health and Human Services (HHS) wants to compare average per capita health care costs for four cities that have health maintenance organizations (HMOs) with four similar cities that do not have HMOs. Using the accompanying data, run a regression, and prepare a brief memo to HHS about the findings.

HMO Cities	Non-HMO Cities
$14,120	$15,160
$13,860	$12,500
$13,700	$14,090
$14,040	$14,600

18.8 The Intercity Bus Company is concerned with the high cost of fuel. The company believes that fuel is being wasted because drivers are exceeding the speed limit. A series of tests ($N = 85$) shows the following relationship between bus speed (X) and miles per gallon of fuel (Y) for speeds between 35 and 85 miles per hour (mph):

$$\hat{Y} = 12.4 - .11X \quad s_b = .007 \quad S_{y|x} = .41 \quad r^2 = .98$$
$$\overline{X} = 50 \quad s_x = 15$$

Intercity is considering placing a governor on all buses, limiting their speed to 55 mph. At an average speed of 55 mph, how many miles per gallon would a bus get? Place a 95% confidence limit around this estimate.

18.9 Refer to Problem 18.8. Intercity buses travel 8,200 miles a week. The current miles per gallon for buses are 5.1. Provide an estimate of the amount of money that could be saved in a week (with a 55-mph governor) if fuel costs $4 per gallon. Place 95% confidence limits around this estimate.

18.10 The White Hawk Indian Tribe wants to know whether its Head Start program is having any impact. To examine this question, an analyst regresses the reading scores in class grade equivalents of all fourth-grade students (Y) on whether the student was enrolled in a Head Start program (1 = enrolled; 0 = not enrolled). Interpret the following regression for the tribe.

$$\hat{Y} = 3.2 - .06X \quad s_b = .1 \quad S_{y|x} = 1.1 \quad r^2 = .16$$

18.11 The South Carolina Insurance Commission wants to know whether states that have no-fault insurance for automobiles have lower insurance rates. The commission takes a survey of 20 states and asks whether they have a no-fault insurance law (coded 1 if they do) and determines the cost (in dollars) of an automobile insurance policy for a 30-year-old male driver who drives 15,000 miles per year and owns a 2014 Ford Focus. It gets the following results:

$$\hat{Y} = \$265.00 - 74.33X$$
$$s_b = 29.4 \quad S_{y|x} = 14.9 \quad r^2 = .34$$

Present a hypothesis and a null hypothesis, and evaluate them. Present a conclusion in plain English. Do not forget to interpret the regression.

18.12 A study by the Occupational Safety and Health Administration seeks to know whether the probability that an industrial plant is inspected is affected by the number of accidents at the plant. An analyst regresses whether a plant is inspected (1 = inspected) on the number of accidents resulting in a lost day of work (X). He finds

$$\hat{Y} = .04 + .012X$$
$$s_b = .0021 \quad S_{y|x} = .19 \quad r^2 = .48 \quad n = 320$$
$$\overline{X} = 47 \quad s_x = 22$$

Interpret this regression. If Ace Manufacturing has 14 accidents resulting in lost work days, what can you say about whether it will be inspected?

18.13 A statistician at a school district has data on student enrollments for the past 28 years. She feels that past enrollments are the best predictor of future enrollments. To test her hunch, she regresses enrollments against time (where the data cover the years 1987 through 2014 and the values for the X variable are coded 1 through 28). She finds the following:

$$\hat{Y} = 25399 + 463X$$

$$s_b = 14.392 \quad S_{yx} = 615 \quad r^2 = .976 \quad n = 28$$

$$\text{Durbin} - \text{Watson} = .094$$

Assist the statistician by interpreting this regression for her. Does autocorrelation appear to be a problem? Explain.

19

Time Series Analysis

Any public manager who can accurately predict the future will become a member of the Senior Executive Service before he or she is 35 years old. Any nonprofit manager who can do so is likely to become the executive director of an agency before he or she reaches that age. In many situations, a manager must make decisions today that will not be implemented until next year, and the success of those decisions will depend on factors unknown at the time of the decision. A personnel manager needs to know the agency's total employment for next year to negotiate health care plans with private insurers. A city budget officer needs to know next year's revenue to make current budget decisions. A public works planner needs to know the demand for sewage disposal over the next 20 years so that disposal systems can be designed and constructed. The director of volunteers at the local Red Cross needs to know when demand for volunteers is likely to be highest (or lowest) to plan a recruitment campaign for the coming year.

Projecting the future state of some managerially relevant variable is called **forecasting**. The major building block that permits data-based forecasting is called **time series analysis**. This chapter illustrates a variety of time series techniques. First, the general principles of time series analysis are presented. Second, simple time series linear regression models are illustrated, followed by a more common logarithmic regression model. Third, the forecasting ability of these models is illustrated. Finally, the bivariate time series model is discussed.

Introduction to Time Series

A **time series** is nothing more than a sequence of observations on some variable (Y) when the observations occur at equally spaced time intervals. To illustrate the general principles of time series, we use the following example. Kerry Jones, the head of the Flagler City Public Works Department, needs to know the number of absences by sanitation engineers. Kerry uses this information to hire substitutes, who are then assigned to refuse-policing units (garbage crews) when a member of the crew does not show up for work. Substitutes are assigned because the efficiency of a crew drops dramatically when the crew is shorthanded. At the same time, Kerry announces an incentive program to reduce absenteeism.

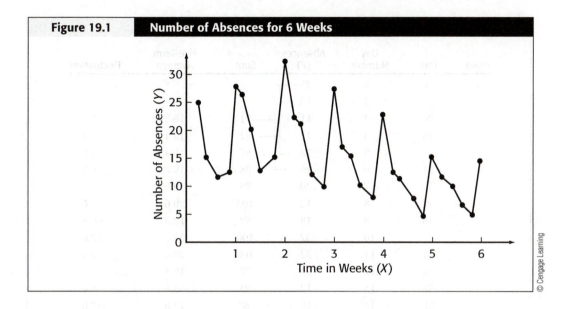

| **Figure 19.1** | **Number of Absences for 6 Weeks** |

Any employee who does not use his or her sick leave by the end of the year will receive a cash payment. The graph in Figure 19.1 shows the number of absent sanitary engineers for the 6 weeks following the announcement of the incentive program.

The first noticeable aspect of the absenteeism graph is that a **cyclical pattern** based on the day of the week is present. Monday consistently has the second highest number of absentees. Absenteeism then drops on Tuesday and falls still further on Wednesday. After a slight increase on Thursday, absenteeism skyrockets to its weekly high on Friday. The cyclical pattern is the first important aspect that the analyst reports. It tells the analyst that absenteeism follows the same pattern for the public works department that it follows for most businesses, government agencies, and nonprofits (that is, much absenteeism appears to result from long weekends).

A second, perhaps more important, question for Kerry Jones is: Did the absenteeism rate decline after the incentive system was introduced? This question is difficult to answer from the graph because the day-to-day fluctuations (*short-term variation*) obscure any long-term trend. If the short-term fluctuations could be removed from the data, however, the long-term trend would be visible.

The accepted way to filter out a short-term fluctuation is by using a **moving average**. The first step is to determine how long the short-term cycle is. In this situation, the length of the short-term trend is obvious—5 days. Absenteeism follows a 5-day pattern, peaking on Mondays and Fridays. In this situation, then, a five-term moving average is needed.

To get a five-term moving average, simply take each day's number of absences and add the absences for the 2 previous days and the 2 following days. Divide this sum by 5. The resulting number is the five-term moving average.

Table 19.1		Calculations for a Five-Term Moving Average				
Week	Day	Day Number	Absences (Y)	Sum	Five-Term Average	Fluctuation
1	M	1	25			
	Tu	2	15			
	W	3	11	91	18.2	−7.2
	Th	4	12	92	18.4	−6.4
	F	5	28	97	19.4	8.6
2	M	6	26	98	19.6	6.4
	Tu	7	20	99	19.8	.2
	W	8	12	103	20.6	−8.6
	Th	9	13	99	19.8	−6.8
	F	10	32	100	20.0	12.0
3	M	11	22	100	20.0	2.0
	Tu	12	21	97	19.4	1.6
	W	13	12	93	18.6	−6.6
	Th	14	10	88	17.6	−7.6
	F	15	28	82	16.4	11.6
4	M	16	17	80	16.0	1.0
	Tu	17	15	78	15.6	−.6
	W	18	10	73	14.6	−4.6
	Th	19	8	68	13.6	−5.6
	F	20	23	64	12.8	10.2
5	M	21	12	61	12.2	−.2
	Tu	22	11	58	11.6	−.6
	W	23	7	50	10.0	−3.0
	Th	24	5	49	9.8	−4.8
	F	25	15	48	9.6	5.4
6	M	26	11	47	9.4	1.6
	Tu	27	10	47	9.4	.6
	W	28	6	46	9.2	−3.2
	Th	29	5			
	F	30	14			

These calculations are performed in Table 19.1. (Note that the first 2 days and the last 2 days in the table do not have five-term moving averages.) The five-term moving average can then be graphed to determine whether the absenteeism rate is declining. See Figure 19.2.

From the graph in Figure 19.2, we can clearly see a trend in absences. If Kerry were interested in a further specification of the relationship, he could

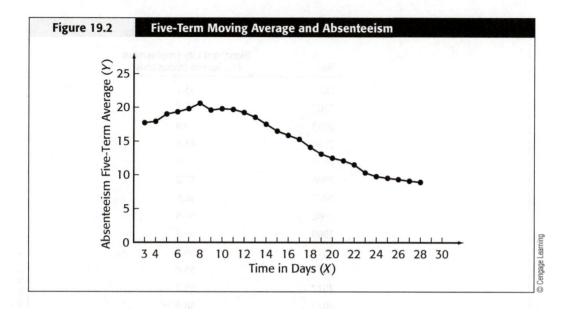

Figure 19.2   **Five-Term Moving Average and Absenteeism**

apply regression analysis to the data. This result would tell him how strong the relationship between time and absenteeism is (or, within the context of this problem, how great a decline in absenteeism followed the incentive program).

Whenever the length of a short-term fluctuation is an odd number, computing a moving average is easy. In our example, the value for the third observation was the average of observations 1, 2, 3, 4, and 5. For a three-term moving average, the value of the third observation is the average of observations 2, 3, and 4. For a short-term fluctuation of an even number of terms, we run into a problem. Using the previous data for a four-term moving average model, we find that the first moving average is 15.8—but this is the value for the 2½ observation. A 2½ observation does not make sense. In this situation, we first calculate the four-term moving average for the 3½ observation (16.5). Then we take the average of the 2½ observation and the 3½ observation and assign this value to the third observation $[(15.8 + 16.5) \div 2 = 16.2]$. We continue this procedure for all items, as illustrated here.

Observation:	1	2	3	4	5	6	7
Four-term average:		15.8	16.5	19.3	21.5	21.5	
Adjusted average:			16.2	17.9	20.4	21.5	

Forecasting without Fluctuation

The chief personnel officer of Blanchard needs to know approximately how many employees Blanchard will have each year for the next 5 years. The only information that Ms. Jean Cruncher, the head personnel analyst, has is the city's employment figures since 2001. These data appear in Table 19.2.

Table 19.2	Blanchard Employment Data	

Year	Blanchard City Employment Employees (thousands)
2001	35.7
2002	38.8
2003	40.9
2004	43.4
2005	44.9
2006	47.2
2007	48.8
2008	50.8
2009	50.8
2010	50.7
2011	55.0
2012	55.3
2013	58.6
2014	59.9

© Cengage Learning 2015

Ms. Cruncher assumes that the same factors that have caused employment to increase in the past 15 years (mandated federal programs, population growth, citizen demands for services, and so on) will continue to influence employment over the next 5 years. By assuming that the future will resemble the past, Ms. Cruncher can use some fairly simple techniques to forecast the city's employment in 2015, 2016, 2017, 2018, and 2019.

Step 1: The first step in time series analysis (just like the first step in any bivariate analysis) is to plot the data. Employment should be considered the dependent variable, and the year should be considered the independent variable. See Figure 19.3.

Step 2: Examine the plot of the data and determine whether any short-term fluctuations exist. The data show no appreciable short-term fluctuation, so go on to Step 4.

Step 3: If the data show a cyclical trend, as the absenteeism data did, you will need to determine the length of the short-term trend. Using this length (L) construct an L-term moving average model. Short-term fluctuations create some problems in the next few steps; the problems will be discussed later in this chapter.

Step 4: Determine whether a relationship exists. From the data shown in Figure 19.3, you can discern a positive linear relationship between time and employment in Blanchard.

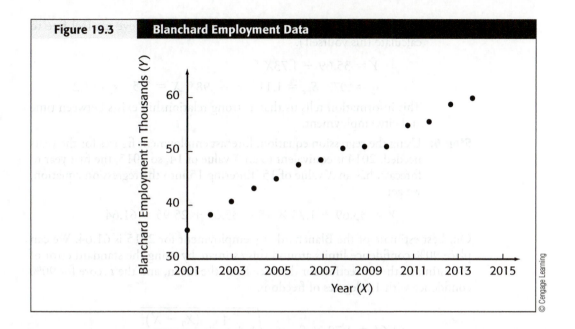

Step 5: Use linear regression to estimate the relationship between time and the variable that is being analyzed. To do this, label the first year (2001) as 1, the second year as 2, and so on. After this renumbering, we have the following data set:

X	Y
1	35.7
2	38.8
3	40.9
4	43.4
5	44.9
6	47.2
7	48.8
8	50.8
9	50.8
10	50.7
11	55.0
12	55.3
13	58.6
14	59.9

Now perform linear regression, with Y (employment) as the dependent variable. Because we will need the mean and standard deviation for X for confidence limits, calculate those also. A regression program produces the following results (if you do not believe us, feel free to calculate this yourself).

$$\hat{Y} = 35.69 + 1.73X$$

$$s_b = .07 \quad S_{y|x} = 1.11 \quad r^2 = .98 \quad X = 7.5 \quad s_x = 4.2$$

This information tells us that a strong relationship exists between time and city employment.

Step 6: Using the regression equation, forecast employment figures for the years needed. 2014 is equivalent to an X value of 14, so 2015, the first year to forecast, has an X value of 15. Entering 15 into the regression equation, we get

$$\hat{Y} = 35.69 + 1.73 \times 15 = 35.69 + 25.95 = 61.64$$

Our best estimate of the Blanchard city employment for 2015 is 61.64. We can place 90% confidence limits around this estimate by using the standard error of the estimate, the correction for distance from the mean, and the t score for 90% confidence with 12 degrees of freedom:

$$61.64 \pm 1.78 \times S_{y|x} \times \sqrt{1 + \frac{1}{n} + \frac{(X_0 - \overline{X})^2}{(n - 1)s_x^2}}$$

$$61.64 \pm 1.78 \times 1.11 \times \sqrt{1 + \frac{1}{14} + \frac{(15 - 7.5)^2}{(14 - 1)(4.2)^2}}$$

$$61.64 \pm 1.78 \times 1.11 \times 1.15$$

$$61.64 \pm 2.27$$

$$59.37 \text{ to } 63.91$$

The 90% confidence limits on the Blanchard city employment are 59.37 to 63.91.

A word of caution is in order. Forecasting forces us to go beyond the available data. Under normal circumstances, this process is to be avoided with regression models. Only if we can logically assume that the future will closely resemble the past can we forecast with confidence. In fact, the 90% confidence limits hold only if the future is an extrapolation of the past. If any major changes occur, the confidence limits are meaningless. Even so, the confidence limits are very wide.

The Blanchard city employment forecasts for 2016, 2017, 2018, and 2019 are as follows.

Year	$X \times b$	$bX + a$	$= \hat{Y}$
2016	16×1.73	$27.68 + 35.69 =$	63.37
2017	17×1.73	$29.41 + 35.69 =$	65.10
2018	18×1.73	$31.14 + 35.69 =$	66.83
2019	19×1.73	$32.87 + 35.69 =$	68.56

The 90% confidence limits of these forecasts are as follows:

2016: 61.04 to 65.70

2017: 62.71 to 67.49

2018: 64.37 to 69.29

2019: 66.02 to 71.10

Ms. Cruncher can now use these forecasts to plan a variety of personnel decisions, including size of health care benefits, amount of money that needs to be set aside for pensions, and affirmative action goals.

Forecasting an Exponential Trend

B. Tom Line, chief budgeting officer for Palmdale, Florida, needs to forecast city revenue for next year so that the city budget can be based on city revenue. The mayor also wants 5 years of revenue projections because he wants to know whether sufficient revenue will be generated to purchase a $100,000 park without a bond issue. The current year's budget is $2.1 million, and current revenues are $2.138 million. The mayor tells Mr. Line to assume that past revenue trends will continue and that expenditures will increase 7% per year for the next 5 years. The question to be answered is: Can Palmdale accumulate $100,000 in excess revenue? (Revenue saved last year cannot be used as part of the $100,000.) The revenue data are shown in Table 19.3.

Before forecasting revenue, Mr. Line needs a forecast of expenditures. The mayor said to assume a 7% annual increase. This growth rate results in the projections shown in Table 19.4.

Given the data in Table 19.4, Mr. Line follows the forecasting procedure outlined previously.

Step 1: First, Mr. Line plots the data. The plot is shown in Figure 19.4.

Step 2: Does a short-term fluctuation exist? None is apparent in the graph, so Mr. Line assumes that no short-term fluctuations exist. He skips to Step 4.

Step 4: Does a time series relationship exist? Clearly one does. Unfortunately, the data do not appear to be linear; rather, they appear to increase by a greater amount each year. For the moment, Mr. Line decides to ignore this fact and proceed to Step 5.

Step 5: Using linear regression, Mr. Line estimates the equation for the line. To do this, he converts 2001 to year 1 and numbers all following years accordingly (2014 is year 14). He estimates the following regression line:

$$\hat{Y} = 412 + 108.1X$$

$$s_b = 7.29 \quad S_{y|x} = 110 \quad r^2 = .95$$

Table 19.3	Palmdale Revenue Data	
	Year	Revenue (thousands)
	2001	678
	2002	679
	2003	743
	2004	837
	2005	949
	2006	982
	2007	1,081
	2008	1,205
	2009	1,317
	2010	1,416
	2011	1,479
	2012	1,637
	2013	1,968
	2014	2,138

© Cengage Learning 2015

Table 19.4	Projected Expenditures	
	Year	Expenditures (millions)
	2014	2.1 (actual)
	2015	2.247
	2016	2.404
	2017	2.573
	2018	2.753
	2019	2.945

© Cengage Learning 2015

Step 6: Using the regression equation, Mr. Line forecasts revenues for 2015 through 2019:

Year	$X \times b$	$bX + a$	$= \hat{Y}$
2015	15×108.1	$1,621.5 + 412$	$= 2,033.5$
2016	16×108.1	$1,729.6 + 412$	$= 2,141.6$
2017	17×108.1	$1,837.7 + 412$	$= 2,249.7$
2018	18×108.1	$1,945.8 + 412$	$= 2,357.8$
2019	19×108.1	$2,053.9 + 412$	$= 2,465.9$

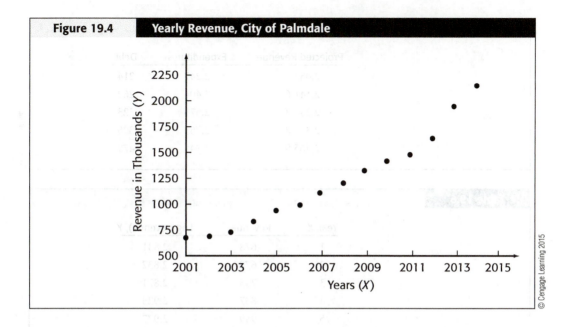

Figure 19.4 **Yearly Revenue, City of Palmdale**

© Cengage Learning 2015

Clearly something is wrong with the forecasts. Revenue for 2015 is forecast to be $105,000 less than 2014 revenue. When a time series that is not linear, such as this one, is estimated with linear regression, the forecasts will generally be underestimations. The underestimation occurs because the linear regression cannot account for the upswing in revenues for the most recent few years (this violates the linearity assumption; see "Assumption 5," Chapter 18). If Mr. Line's forecasts are compared with expenditures, the mayor will receive quite a shock (see Table 19.5).

The correct procedure to follow when the time series increases at a constant rate is to convert the time series variable into logarithms. The problem in this case is that the error variance of individual observations tends to increase as the magnitude of individual observations increases (see "Assumption 2," Chapter 18). A logarithmic transformation addresses this problem by stabilizing the error variance across all of the observations in the series (compared to the original data) while preserving the underlying pattern inherent in the original data.

Logarithms address this problem by condensing the variance or dispersion of numbers. A logarithm is a power; a base-10 logarithm is the power to which 10 must be raised to yield a given number of interest. For example, the base-10 logarithm of 100 is 2 (10 raised to the second power, i.e., squared, is 100); the base-10 logarithm of 1,000 is 3 (10 raised to the third power, i.e., cubed, is 1,000). Note that the raw numbers range from 100 to 1,000, but the logarithms range from just 2 to 3. Table 19.6 presents the logarithmic transformation of revenue. As shown in the table, the raw revenue numbers vary from 678 to 2,138, but the logarithms vary from just 2.831 to 3.330. [For more information on using and interpreting logarithms, see Allison (1999, 154–55) or Fox (2008, Chapter 4)].

Table 19.5	Revenue and Expenditures		
	Projected Revenue	Expenditures	Debt
	2,033.5	2,247	214
	2,141.6	2,404	262
	2,249.7	2,573	323
	2,357.8	2,753	395
	2,465.9	2,945	479

© Cengage Learning

Table 19.6	Converting to Logarithms		
	Year, X	Revenue	Log (revenue), Y
	1	678	2.831
	2	679	2.832
	3	743	2.871
	4	837	2.923
	5	949	2.977
	6	982	2.992
	7	1,081	3.033
	8	1,205	3.081
	9	1,317	3.120
	10	1,416	3.151
	11	1,479	3.170
	12	1,637	3.214
	13	1,968	3.294
	14	2,138	3.330

© Cengage Learning

Performing regression on the values of X and Y in Table 19.6, Mr. Line finds

$$\hat{Y} = 2.767 + .0389X$$

$$s_b = .0011 \quad S_{y|x} = .016 \quad r^2 = .99$$

Notice that r^2 increased when a log transformation of Y was regressed on time. This result occurs because a log transformation bends the line upward to fit the values of the data.

How can the preceding regression line be interpreted? If we convert the regression slope into an antilog (in this case, the antilog of .0389 is 1.094) and subtract 1 from the antilog, the resulting number tells us the percentage that Y increases every year.

$$1.094 - 1.0 = .094 \text{ or } 9.4\%$$

Palmdale city revenues are increasing at a rate of 9.4% per year.

To forecast city revenues with a logarithmic regression, follow the usual procedure to get predicted logarithms of expenditures.

Year	$X \times b$	$bX + a$	$= \hat{Y}$
2015	15×0.0389	$0.584 + 2.267$	$= 3.351$
2016	16×0.0389	$0.622 + 2.267$	$= 3.389$
2017	17×0.0389	$0.661 + 2.267$	$= 3.428$
2018	18×0.0389	$0.700 + 2.267$	$= 3.467$
2019	19×0.0389	$0.739 + 2.267$	$= 3.506$

The predicted values of $\hat{Y}$ must now be converted from logarithms to regular numbers. This conversion can be accomplished with a calculator that has a power key. One merely takes 10 to the $\hat{Y}$ power to obtain the regular number (see Table 19.7).

Contrasting the revenue projections in Table 19.7 with expenditure predictions, we find the results shown in Table 19.8. The surplus figures show that Palmdale, Florida, will accumulate the needed $100,000 for the park sometime near the middle of 2017. The figures also show that the city will run a budget surplus of $262,000 if no new programs are added and taxes are not cut. Why might this information be valuable to the mayor?

Table 19.7	Converting $\hat{Y}$ to Revenue	
Year	**$\hat{Y}$**	**Projected Revenue**
2015	3.351	2,241
2016	3.389	2,451
2017	3.428	2,681
2018	3.467	2,932
2019	3.506	3,207

© Cengage Learning 2015

Table 19.8	Revenues and Expenditures		
Year	**Revenues**	**Expenditures**	**Surplus**
2015	2,241	2,247	−6
2016	2,451	2,404	47
2017	2,681	2,573	108
2018	2,932	2,753	179
2019	3,207	2,945	262

© Cengage Learning 2015

Forecasting with a Short-Term Fluctuation

To this point, we have illustrated two fairly simple forecasts of trends. Neither set of data had any noticeable short-term fluctuation. To illustrate how forecasting is done when a time series contains some short-term fluctuation, let us return to our example of Flagler Public Works Department absences introduced at the beginning of this chapter. Refer to Figure 19.5, which shows the number of absences from work for a 6-week period.

Step 1: The first step is to plot the data, as shown in Figure 19.5.

Step 2: By examining the graph, determine whether any short-term fluctuation exists. In this instance, absences peak on Friday, remain high on Monday, drop on Tuesday and Wednesday, and show a slight increase on Thursday. Clearly a short-term trend exists.

Step 3: Determine the length of the short-term fluctuation. In this example, the length of the short-term fluctuation is 5 days. To remove this short-term fluctuation, calculate a five-term moving average. These calculations, explained earlier in this chapter, are shown in Table 19.9.

Step 4: Graph the five-term moving average; this figure represents the number of absences that occur each day when the short-term fluctuation is removed. Examining the graph in Figure 19.6, we see that a negative relationship exists between time and absenteeism. The absenteeism rate is clearly downward.

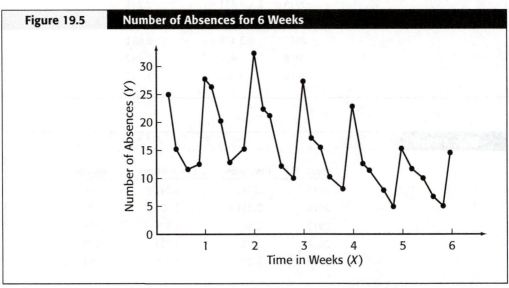

Figure 19.5   Number of Absences for 6 Weeks

Table 19.9		Calculations for a Five-Term Moving Average				
Week	Day	Day Number	Absences (Y)	Sum	Five-Term Average	Fluctuation
1	M	1	25			
	Tu	2	15			
	W	3	11	91	18.2	−7.2
	Th	4	12	92	18.4	−6.4
	F	5	28	97	19.4	8.6
2	M	6	26	98	19.6	6.4
	Tu	7	20	99	19.8	.2
	W	8	12	103	20.6	−8.6
	Th	9	13	99	19.8	−6.8
	F	10	32	100	20.0	12.0
3	M	11	22	100	20.0	2.0
	Tu	12	21	97	19.4	1.6
	W	13	12	93	18.6	−6.6
	Th	14	10	88	17.6	−7.6
	F	15	28	82	16.4	11.6
4	M	16	17	80	16.0	1.0
	Tu	17	15	78	15.6	−.6
	W	18	10	73	14.6	−4.6
	Th	19	8	68	13.6	−5.6
	F	20	23	64	12.8	10.2
5	M	21	12	61	12.2	−.2
	Tu	22	11	58	11.6	−.6
	W	23	7	50	10.0	−3.0
	Th	24	5	49	9.8	−4.8
	F	25	15	48	9.6	5.4
6	M	26	11	47	9.4	1.6
	Tu	27	10	47	9.4	.6
	W	28	6	46	9.2	−3.2
	Th	29	5			
	F	30	14			

© Cengage Learning

Step 5: Using linear regression, estimate the relationship between time and the five-term moving average. In this case, use all values of X from $X = 3$ to $X = 28$. The regression estimate of the relationship is

$$\hat{Y} = 23.3 - .508X$$

$$s_b = .0392 \quad S_{y|x} = 1.497 \quad r^2 = .87$$

where X is the day and Y is the number of absences.

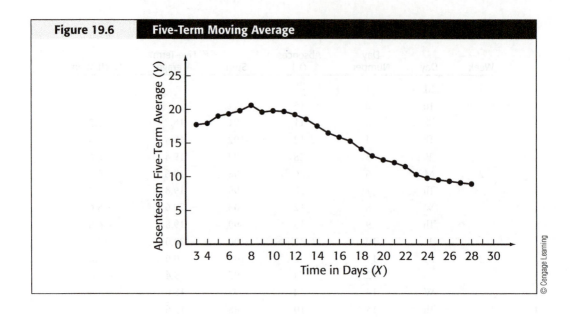

Figure 19.6 — **Five-Term Moving Average**

You now have a forecast for the moving average of the number of absences. At this point, if you want to forecast specific days, the short-term fluctuation must be put back into the model. This procedure is fairly advanced and needs to be done with the assistance of a statistician [see Kutner, Nachtsheim, and Neter (2004)].

Bivariate Forecasting

In the previous three examples of forecasting, the independent variable was always time. This need not be the case. The independent variable can, in fact, be a variable that causes the dependent variable to vary. This section illustrates forecasting when the independent variable is not time. Such forecasting is called **bivariate forecasting**.

Stermerville is a bedroom suburb located 15 miles north of Jackson. J. R. "Dusty" Rhodes, the Stermerville director of sewage treatment, wants to forecast the volume of sewage per day his plant will need to treat for the next 5 years. The Stermerville Treatment Plant has a capacity of 500 tons of sewage per day. At this time, the plant is treating 375 tons per day. To expand the plant, it will take about 4 years (counting funding, Environmental Protection Agency [EPA] clearance, construction, and testing). For this reason Mr. Rhodes needs to forecast future demands on his sewage treatment plant. If demand will exceed 500 tons per day in the next 5 years, Mr. Rhodes must begin the process to expand the plant now.

Because Stermerville is a bedroom community with no industry and little commercial development, the volume of sewage is highly correlated with the number of households in Stermerville. Dusty's data analyst, Morticia "Severe"

Year	Tons of Sewage per Day	Houses	Building Permits	Next Year's Projected Houses
2001		1,100	300	1,370
2002	158	1,370	150	1,505
2003	188	1,500	570	2,013
2004	192	2,000	600	2,540
2005	230	2,510	511	2,970
2006	234	3,000	754	3,679
2007	252	3,700	310	3,979
2008	285	4,050	680	4,662
2009	293	4,620	318	4,906
2010	315	4,885	815	5,619
2011	335	5,500	510	5,959
2012	353	6,040	603	6,582
2013	358	6,580	590	7,111
2014	375	7,150	475	7,578

Table 19.10 Stermerville Data

Storms, has discovered that she can accurately predict next year's demand for sewage treatment by combining the present number of houses in Stermerville with 90% of the number of building permits issued for new houses (90% is used because 10% of new houses for which permits are issued are not built). Storms gathers the data given in Table 19.10.

Storms explains what she wants to do. She wants to forecast next year's demand for sewage treatment in tons per day. Because the actual number of houses is highly correlated with sewer use, Storms needs an estimate of next year's number of houses to forecast next year's demand. This value appears in the "Projected Houses" column. Projected houses for 2002 (1,370) is equal to the number of houses in 2001 (1,100) plus 90% of the building permits ($300 \times .9 + 1,100 = 270 + 1,100 = 1,370$). Note that "Projected Houses" fairly accurately predicts the next year's total housing. Storms then aligns the variables in two columns so that tons of sewage per day for a given year is lined up with next year's projected houses for the previous year (i.e., the value for 2001 projected houses is actually the projected number of houses for 2002; see Table 19.11). The number of projected houses for 2015 is withdrawn from the data set for the moment.

Storms then runs a regression of sewage in tons (Y) on the projected number of houses, with the following results:

$$\hat{Y} = 125.2 + .0367X$$

$$s_b = .0016 \quad S_{y|x} = 10.5 \quad r^2 = .98 \quad \bar{X} = 4.069, \quad s_x = 1,923$$

Table 19.11	Sewage and Projected Houses	
	Tons of Sewage per Day (Y)	Projected Houses (X)
	158	1,370
	188	1,505
	192	2,013
	230	2,540
	234	2,970
	252	3,679
	285	3,979
	293	4,662
	315	4,906
	335	5,619
	353	5,959
	358	6,582
	375	7,111

© Cengage Learning

Storms has no trouble using this information to project sewage treatment demand for 2015 because she has a projected housing value for 2015 (it is 7,578). Substituting this value for X, Storms gets the following projection for 2015:

$$\hat{Y} = 125.2 + .0367X = 125.2 + .0367(7,578) = 403.3$$

Using the standard error of the estimate and the correction factor for distance from the mean of X, Storms can place 90% confidence limits around this estimate (df = 11).

$$403.3 \pm t \times S_{y|x} \times \sqrt{1 + \frac{1}{n} + \frac{(X_0 - \bar{X})^2}{(n-1)S_x^2}}$$

$$403.3 \pm 1.796 \times 10.5 \times \sqrt{1 + (1/13) + \frac{(7,578 - 4,069)^2}{(13-1)(1,923^2)}}$$

$$403.3 \pm 1.796 \times 10.5 \times 1.16$$

$$403.3 \pm 21.9$$

$$381.4 \text{ to } 425.2$$

How can Storms forecast sewage treatment demand for 2016 to 2019? Storms needs the estimated number of houses in Stermerville. The estimated number of houses is the current number plus 90% of the building permits issued. If Storms could estimate the number of building permits for the next 5 years, then she could extrapolate the number of houses. Storms consults several local builders, who tell her that they expect to reduce new starts to about 450 per year for the next 4 years. Storms makes the following estimates of housing:

Projected Houses	=	Last Year's Projection	+	.9 × Estimated Yearly Permits	Total Estimated Housing Permits
Projected 2016 houses	=	7,578	+	(.9 × 450) =	7,983
Projected 2017 houses	=	7,983	+	(.9 × 450) =	8,388
Projected 2018 houses	=	8,388	+	(.9 × 450) =	8,793
Projected 2019 houses	=	8,793	+	(.9 × 450) =	9,198

Storms then uses these estimates to project future demand for sewage treatment.

Year	$X \times b$	$Xb + a$	$= \hat{Y}$
2016	7,983 × .0367	293.0 + 125.2 =	418.2
2017	8,388 × .0367	307.8 + 125.2 =	433.0
2018	8,793 × .0367	322.7 + 125.2 =	447.9
2019	9,198 × .0367	337.6 + 125.2 =	462.8

The projections show that Stermerville will not exceed its capacity of 500 tons per day in the next 5 years. Storms shows these data to Mr. Rhodes. Mr. Rhodes asks Storms how sure she is that demand in 2019 will not exceed 500 tons per day. Storms uses the standard error of the estimate and the adjustment for the value of X to determine the probability that the 2019 estimate exceeds 500. This is

$$10.5 \times \sqrt{1 + (1/13) + \frac{(9,198 - 4,069)^2}{(13 - 1)(1,923^2)}}$$

$$10.5 \times \sqrt{1 + .08 + .59}$$

$$10.5 \times 1.29$$

$$13.6$$

This figure can be used as a standard error to calculate a t score in the following formula:

$$t = \frac{Y - \hat{Y}}{s} = \frac{500 - 462.8}{13.6} = 2.74$$

Looking up this value in the t table, Storms concludes that the probability is less than .01. She reports this information to Mr. Rhodes.

Rhodes then wants to know what year to expect the demand to exceed 500 so that he can plan. Storms substitutes a value of 500 for Y into the regression equation:

$$500 = 125.2 + .0367X$$
$$374.8 = .0367X$$
$$10{,}212 = X$$

Storms finds that when projected housing exceeds 10,212, sewage will exceed 500 tons per day. When will this be? Storms consults her builder friends, who tell her that 450 new starts a year will hold for the next 10 years. Using this figure, Storms projects the following housing figures:

2020: 9,603

2021: 10,008

2022: 10,413

These figures indicate that the capacity of the sewage treatment plant will be adequate until 2022. Forecasts involve greater risks the farther that they extend into the future; therefore, 2020 or 2021 may well be a more appropriate year for plant expansion to be completed. Note that any changes in building permits should be monitored; any change in permits will require new forecasts.

Chapter Summary

Forecasting is an attempt to predict the future, usually through some reliance on statistical techniques. This chapter introduced some simple forecasting techniques based on linear regression.

The foundation on which data-based forecasting rests is time series analysis. A time series is a sequence of observations on a variable of interest when the observations occur at equally spaced time intervals. Most time series will have some short-term fluctuations, which can be filtered out by using a moving average.

There are six basic steps in a time series analysis. First, plot the data. Second, examine the plot and determine whether any short-term fluctuations exist. Third, if the data show a cyclical trend, determine the length of the short-term trend and filter the trend. Fourth, determine whether a relationship exists. Fifth, estimate the relationship between time and the variable being analyzed. Sixth, make a forecast by using the regression equation.

When the forecast involves an exponential trend—that is, the time series increases at a constant rate—the time series variable must be converted to logarithms. If the forecast involves short-term fluctuations, a moving average should be calculated.

When the independent variable in a set of observations is not time but another variable, the forecasting method is called bivariate forecasting. The analysis process for this situation is somewhat similar to that for time series analysis; again, linear regression techniques are used.

Problems

19.1 John Johnson, warden of Ramsey Prison, believes that a relationship exists between the size of the state's population between the ages of 18 and 35 and the number of inmates assigned to Ramsey. John has his trusty analyst, Marc Wallace, go down to the Census Bureau's local office to get census estimates for the past 50 years. Marc then regresses Ramsey's prison population on the size of the state's 18- to 35-year-old population. He finds the following:

$$\hat{Y} = -14 + .0005X$$

$$s_b = .0000003 \quad S_{y|x} = 12.6 \quad r^2 = .93$$

(a) The Census Bureau estimates that next year's population between the ages of 18 and 35 will be 934,000. What is the projected prison population?

(b) Ramsey's capacity is 500 persons. The old wing of the prison contains room for 100 persons. John would like to close this wing to save on maintenance. How small would the state's 18- to 35-year-old population need to be for this to be done?

19.2 The Indiana State Department of Agriculture is concerned about the number of acres of farmland being withdrawn from farming. The department would like to propose new legislation to prevent this but would like to show the legislature what would happen if it does not act. Dewey Compost, the department's statistician, regresses the number of acres used for farming in the state on time (1982 = year 1). Dewey finds the following:

$$\hat{Y} = 2.743 - .027X$$

$$s_b = .0007 \quad S_{y|x} = .013 \quad r^2 = .89 \quad s_x = 16 \quad \bar{X} = 29 \quad n = 33$$

(a) How strong is the relationship?

(b) If Y is in millions of acres, how many acres of farmland will be lost in the next 10 years if the legislature does not act and if past practices continue?

(c) How many acres will be used for farming in 2015? Place a 90% confidence interval around this estimate.

19.3 I. L. Iterate High School is the only high school in Milward, Iowa. The superintendent hires you to forecast future school enrollments so that the school can plan ahead. Using the accompanying data, what can you tell the superintendent? *(Note: The data set for this problem is available on the book's companion website.)*

Year	Students
2000	810
2001	1,094
2002	1,402
2003	1,893
2004	2,205
2005	2,687
2006	3,115
2007	3,324
2008	3,496
2009	3,531
2010	3,412
2011	3,174
2012	2,963
2013	2,810
2014	2,794

19.4 The Chelsea City Police budget appears to be increasing at a rate of 10% per year. Could the city use linear regression to forecast this budget? By what percentage will the budget increase in 10 years?

19.5 The Aurora city economist, I. C. Recession, uses the previous year's growth in the money supply (in percent) to forecast the inflation rate (in percent) for Aurora. Using data for 35 years, Recession has built the following regression model (Y is inflation in percentage; X is money supply growth in percentage).

$$\hat{Y} = -5.4 + 2.1X$$

$$s_b = .007 \quad S_{y|x} = 2.0 \quad r^2 = .99 \quad \bar{X} = 3.2 \quad s_x = 3.0$$

Interpret this regression equation; then forecast next year's inflation rate if the money supply grows by 8.2%. Place 90% confidence limits around this estimate. What is the probability that the rate of inflation will be over 15%?

19.6 The Fifth Division of the U.S. Army wants to forecast personnel costs for the next 5 years. A search of the records reveals the accompanying data. Using these data, forecast the personnel costs for 2015, 2016, 2017, 2018, and 2019. Place 90% confidence limits around these estimates. *(Note: The data set for this problem is available on the book's companion website.)*

Year	Costs (thousands)
2014	51,576
2013	49,015
2012	40,845
2011	34,497
2010	28,625
2009	25,376
2008	21,163
2007	18,468
2006	14,992
2005	13,633
2004	12,069
2003	11,452
2002	10,321
2001	9,329
2000	7,982
1999	7,877
1998	7,648
1997	7,071
1996	6,411
1995	5,409
1994	4,657
1993	4,017

19.7 The number of patients at the Bluefield State Mental Hospital (Y) appears to be related to the state's population (X):

$$\hat{Y} = .07 + .0031X$$

$$s_b = .00013 \quad S_{y|x} = 46 \quad r^2 = .99 \quad N = 35$$

Interpret the regression and forecast the number of patients if the state's population is predicted to be 876,451. How many additional patients would a population increase of 20,000 bring?

19.8 From the accompanying data on the Yanktoni Sioux Indian Tribe, project the tribal population for 2016 and 2021. Place a 90% confidence limit around both projections. (*Note: The data set for this problem is available on the book's companion website.*)

Year	Population
2005	812
2006	831
2007	863
2008	901
2009	925
2010	963
2011	989
2012	1,016
2013	1,037
2014	1,062

19.9 Metro City Police believe that the number of domestic disputes on any summer night is highly correlated with the temperature that night (the hotter the night, the more family fights there are). If the number of disputes can be forecast, the police department can use the results to allocate personnel. Research analyst Silvia Jones regresses the number of domestic disputes *(Y)* on the Fahrenheit-temperature at 4:00 in the afternoon *(X)*. Interpret this regression for the Metro City Police.

$$\hat{Y} = 216 + 3.1X$$

$$s_b = 1.5 \quad S_{y|x} = 18 \quad r^2 = .81 \quad N = 150$$

Forecast the number of disputes if the temperature is 95° at 4:00 P.M.

19.10 Using the number of traffic fatalities for the 30-year period beginning in 1985 (1985 = year 1), a western state wants to forecast traffic fatalities for 2015, 2016, and 2017. Using the following regression, make these forecasts and place an 80% confidence limit around the forecasts.

$$\hat{Y} = 1,246 + 36.4X$$

$$s_b = 1.9 \quad S_{y|x} = 154 \quad r^2 = .97 \quad \bar{X} = 15.5 \quad s_x = 8.8$$

19.11 The city building permit agency is concerned about its future workloads. Initially, the agency thinks that it can predict the number of building permits that will be issued next year by simply using the year as the independent variable (1987 is year 1). This regression results in the following:

$$\hat{Y} = 2,256 + 234.6X$$

$$s_b = 23.1 \quad S_{y|x} = 154 \quad r^2 = .65$$

The agency then uses the unemployment rate (percentage of unemployed), rather than the year, as the independent variable to predict building permits. This produces the following:

$$\hat{Y} = 13{,}413 - 678X$$

$$s_b = 21.4 \quad S_{y|x} = 108 \quad r^2 = .78$$

Interpret each of these regressions. Predict the number of building permits that will be issued in 2015 if unemployment is 7.2%. Which of these equations is the better one from a managerial perspective?

19.12 The Mansfield School District wants to predict student enrollments for next year. It hires Daniel Mazmanian Educational Consultants to do this work. Using data from 1992 through 2014 (1992 = year 1), the consultants assume that all past trends will continue and use a time series regression to predict the total number of students enrolled (Y). They get the following:

$$Y = 781 + 28.8X$$

$$s_b = .68 \quad S_{y|x} = 6.2 \quad N = 23 \quad r^2 = .9955 \quad \overline{X} = 10 \quad s_x = 6$$

Interpret the slope, intercept, and r^2. Is there a relationship between time and enrollments?

20

Multiple Regression

In the three preceding chapters, all regression problems were solved with simple regression (regression with only one independent variable). By contrast, in many management situations, a dependent variable will have more than one cause. Under such circumstances, simple regression is an inadequate technique. **Multiple regression** is a statistical procedure designed to incorporate more than one independent variable. In this chapter we discuss the techniques of multiple regression.

Recall from our discussion of causality in Chapter 3 that one of the key issues in demonstrating a causal relationship between two variables is taking other explanatory variables into account as possible causes of variation in the variable being explained. The chief limitation of bivariate regression is that only one independent variable is used to explain variation in the dependent variable. Assuming that one variable is the cause of another without thinking about other possible explanatory variables is usually not a wise research strategy. Multiple regression is a valuable research tool because it allows for the inclusion of several independent variables to explain a dependent variable.

Bivariate regression is a good starting point for constructing causal relationships. If statistically significant results are obtained in a bivariate regression, it may seem like the task of constructing a causal model is complete. The results obtained from bivariate models, however, are often just the starting point for constructing more inclusive causal models.

When statistically significant results are obtained using bivariate regression, the next logical step is to select other relevant independent variables and perform multiple regression. But what if we really do not care about other independent variables and are interested only in finding out whether the initial independent variable we selected is related to the dependent variable? Should we still consider multiple regression in cases like this?

The answer is yes. Causal explanations are stronger when we include control variables in our analyses. We can have more faith in the idea that a particular independent variable explains variation in a dependent variable if, after generating a multiple regression that includes other relevant explanatory variables, the original independent variable remains statistically significant. If we end our modeling efforts after performing a bivariate regression and finding statistically significant results, we run the risk of attributing too much explanatory power to one variable. Sometimes statistically significant relationships from bivariate models "wash out" in the presence of other explanatory variables (see "The Logic of Controls" in this chapter). Bivariate regression is a very useful tool, but one should take care before making definitive statements about the existence of causal relationships using this technique alone.

An Example

The best way to illustrate the use of multiple regression is with an example. Charles Pyro, fire chief of Stermerville, has divided Stermerville into nine fire districts of approximately equal size. Pyro's problem is that Stermerville is planning to offer fire service to Boonsville, a neighboring town about the size of one of Stermerville's fire districts. Pyro would like to know how many fires a month he can expect to fight in Boonsville so that he can allocate his firefighters accordingly.

As an old hand at firefighting, Chief Pyro knows that older houses are more likely to burn than are newer houses. He decides to see whether he can predict the number of monthly fires in a fire district by using the average age of district housing. Pyro has the data shown in Table 20.1.

After graphing these data, Pyro performs a regression analysis on them and gets the following results:

$$\hat{Y} = 28.6 + 1.12X$$

$$s_b = .41 \quad S_{y|x} = 18.4 \quad r^2 = .51 \quad \overline{X} = 27.0 \quad s_x = 15.7$$

Using this information to predict the number of fires in Boonsville, which has an average housing age of 42 years, Pyro finds

$$\hat{Y} = 28.6 + 1.12(42) = 28.6 + 47.02 = 75.6$$

Table 20.1	Stermerville Fire Data	
District	Number of Fires (Y)	Average Housing Age (X)
1	44	23
2	94	35
3	38	4
4	65	49
5	95	48
6	57	12
7	20	14
8	52	33
9	64	25

© Cengage Learning

Placing a 90% confidence limit around this prediction (df = 7), Pyro receives a shock:

$$75.6 \pm t \times S_{y|x} \times \sqrt{1 + \frac{1}{n} + \frac{(X - \bar{X})^2}{(n - 1)s_x^2}}$$

75.6 ± 1.895 × 18.4 × 1.11

75.6 ± 38.7

36.9 to 114.3

The confidence interval on this estimate is so wide that it is of little value to Chief Pyro.

One way to interpret a regression with a low r^2 is to conclude that some factors in addition to, or perhaps instead of, the independent variable explain the variation in Y. To identify these factors, one uses experience, intuition, theory, or even trial and error. In the present instance, Chief Pyro knows that fewer fires occur in homes that are owner occupied than in homes that are rented. Pyro believes that he could accurately predict fires if he knew both the average age of housing in a fire district and the percentage of houses that are owner occupied. In short, Pyro would like a prediction equation of the following form:

$$\hat{Y} = \alpha + \beta_1 X_1 + \beta_2 X_2$$

where $\hat{Y}$ is the number of fires, X_1 is the average age of housing, X_2 is the percentage of owner-occupied housing, α is the intercept, and β_1 and β_2 are weights or slopes.

Obviously, Pyro could set up the prediction equation just stated; the key is the selection of the weights. Pyro would like to select weights so that his predictions of Y are as accurate as possible. In short, Pyro would like to minimize the squared error, or $(\hat{Y}_i - Y_i)^2$. This is the familiar principle of least squares that we use in simple regression (see Chapter 17). In fact, multiple regression is nothing more than the assignment of weights so that $(\hat{Y}_i - Y_i)^2$ is minimized.

We consider specifically how these regression coefficients are calculated shortly. But first we discuss the interpretation of a multiple regression. Pyro's data analyst runs a multiple regression on the data in Table 20.2.

The regression program provides the following information:

$$\hat{Y} = 38.1 + 1.57X_1 - .49X_2$$

$$s_{b_1} = .087 \quad s_{b_2} = .036 \quad S_{y|x} = 3.55 \quad R^2 = .98$$

The interpretation of this regression equation focuses on the estimated values of β_1 and β_2. These are the values of slopes, just as b was in simple regression, only now the slopes are in three dimensions (and thus difficult to graph) rather than in two. The regression coefficient for age of housing (b_1) is equal to the increase in the number of fires in a district if the average age of all housing in the district increases by 1 year *and* the percentage of owner-occupied housing remains the same. In other words, b_1 is the increase in the number of fires resulting

Table 20.2	Fire Data Including Owner-Occupied Homes		

			Housing	
Fire District	Fires per Month (Y)	Age (X_1)	Percentage Owned (X_2)
1	44	23	70
2	94	35	3
3	38	4	10
4	65	49	96
5	95	48	40
6	57	12	4
7	20	14	80
8	52	33	78
9	64	25	15

from increases in housing age, controlling for the percentage of owner-occupied housing. In this case, a district will have 1.57 more fires for every year older its houses are if the percentage of houses that are owner occupied remains the same. Statisticians often refer to this slope as a **partial slope**.

The regression coefficient for percentage of housing that is owner occupied (b_2) has a similar interpretation. For every percentage point increase in owner-occupied housing in a district, the district will have .49 fewer fires if the average age of houses remains the same. (Note that the sign of b_2 is negative, $-.49$.)

Although the intercept remains the value of $\hat{Y}$ if both average age and per-centage of owner-occupied houses are zero, $\hat{Y}$ can also have a value of 38.1 for numerous other values of X_1 and X_2. For example, if X_1 is equal to 10 and X_2 is equal to 32, Y is also equal to 38.1.

A variety of other factors must also be considered when interpreting a multiple regression. If all the assumptions of regression hold (see Chapter 18), sample estimates of the regression slopes are t-distributed. This means that each slope will have its own standard error. Note that two standard errors of the slope estimates have been presented. These standard errors can be used to determine the probability that the data came from a population with partial slopes equal to 0. When a partial slope equals 0, it means that the X variable in question is unrelated to Y when the other X variables are controlled.

For b_1 the probability that the data came from a population with slope = 0 can be found as follows:

$$t = \frac{b_1 - 0}{s_{b_1}} = \frac{1.57 - 0}{.087} = 18.0$$

To look up this t value in Table 3 of the Statistical Tables, you need to know the number of degrees of freedom. For a multiple regression, the degrees of freedom are equal to the number of cases (in this case, 9) minus the number of parameters estimated (in this case, 3—one intercept and two slopes). Using 6 degrees of freedom, this t value has a probability of less than .0005. We can be fairly sure the slope in question is not zero. In the space provided, calculate the probability that b_2 came from a population with slope $= 0$.

If you found a probability of less than .0005 ($t = 13.6$), congratulations.

In the results just reported, you might have noticed this equality: $R^2 = .98$. R^2 is the symbol for the *multiple coefficient of determination*. R^2 is the percentage of variance in Y that is explained by X_1 and X_2. Another interpretation of R^2 is that it is equal to the r^2 between Y and $\hat{Y}$. Notice that R^2 is larger than r^2 in the simple regression of fires on age. This will always happen. When more variables are used to explain or predict the dependent variable, the coefficient of determination will increase.

Because of the way it is calculated, R^2 goes up even if we add independent variables that have little or no explanatory power. In other words, even if the partial slope for the independent variable equals zero, the value of R^2 will still go up. If R^2 is low, we could essentially add variables at random, with each one pushing R^2 higher, even if each new partial slope was statistically insignificant. This result obviously can give a false sense of the real explanatory power of a model.

To remedy this problem, statistical programs generate a statistic called an **Adjusted R^2**. The Adjusted R^2 provides a more accurate picture of the explanatory power of a model because it adjusts for the presence of partial slopes with insignificant t values. If a model includes both statistically significant and insignificant partial slopes, the Adjusted R^2 will be lower than the R^2. If a model includes only partial slope coefficients with significant t values, the Adjusted R^2 and R^2 values will typically be quite similar. There are valid reasons for including partial slopes with insignificant t values in your regression model, so you should not automatically remove independent variables from the model simply because they lower the Adjusted R^2. We explain the reasons for this advice later in the chapter.

Finally, notice that the value of the standard error of the estimate has dropped. If Boonsville has housing that is 42 years old on the average and is 80% owner occupied, the number of fires per month can be predicted:

$$\hat{Y} = 38.1 + 1.57X_1 - .49X_2$$

For Boonsville, $X_1 = 42$ and $X_2 = 80$:

$$\hat{Y} = 38.1 + 1.57(42) - .49(80) = 38.1 + 65.9 - 39.2 = 64.8$$

Note that this estimate is different from the simple regression estimate of 75.6.

Unfortunately, putting a confidence limit around an estimate for a multiple regression is fairly difficult. Many advanced statistics books do not even cover its calculation because the formula is highly complex and, for more than two variables, requires the use of matrix algebra. The standard error of the estimate is a reasonably good estimate for the amount of the error when the sample size is large and the X values are close to their respective means. So, for practical purposes, managers can often use plus or minus twice the standard error of the estimate to approximate 95% confidence limits. The actual limits are likely to be somewhat larger than this, especially if the X values are far from their means. Some computer programs are designed to automatically calculate confidence limits on predictions. When these limits are available, they should be used. Using the two-times rule of thumb, Chief Pyro gets confidence limits of

$$64.8 \pm 2 \times 3.55$$

$$57.7 \text{ to } 71.9$$

This narrower range of confidence (in comparison to simple bivariate regression with a standard error of 18.4) is one that Chief Pyro can use with greater confidence.

Calculating Partial Slopes

If we wish to calculate the slope values in a multiple regression, it is helpful to change the standard designation of a regression line to the following:

$$\hat{X}_1 = a + b_{12.3}X_2 + b_{13.2}X_3$$

where $b_{12.3}$ means the regression slope of X_1 on X_2 controlling for X_3 and $b_{13.2}$ means the regression slope of X_1 on X_3 controlling for X_2. Statisticians, using the principles of least squares, have found that

$$b_{12.3} = \frac{b_{12} - (b_{13})(b_{32})}{1 - (b_{23})(b_{32})}$$

If we performed all the simple regressions indicated on the right-hand side of the equation using the Stermerville fire data, we would find that

$$b_{12} = 1.12 \quad b_{13} = -.24 \quad b_{23} = .16 \quad b_{32} = .92$$

If you do not believe that these are the correct slopes, feel free to calculate them yourself. Substituting these values into the equation for $b_{12.3}$, we find

$$b_{12.3} = \frac{1.12 - (-.24)(.92)}{1 - (.16)(.92)} = \frac{1.12 + .22}{1 - .15} = \frac{1.34}{.85} = 1.57$$

For $b_{13.2}$, the calculations are

$$b_{13.2} = \frac{b_{13} - (b_{12})(b_{23})}{1 - (b_{32})(b_{23})} = \frac{-.24 - (1.12)(.16)}{1 - (.92)(.16)} = \frac{-.41}{.85} = -.49$$

To calculate the value of the intercept, we use the following formula:

$$a = \bar{Y} - b_1\bar{X}_1 - b_2\bar{X}_2 = 58.8 - 1.57(27.0) - (-.49)44$$
$$= 58.8 - 42.4 + 21.6 = 38$$
$$\hat{Y} = 38 + 1.57X_1 - .49X_2$$

In the real world, very few analysts calculate the slopes and intercepts in multiple regression by hand. Computer programs can perform the calculations far more quickly and accurately than can any normal human being. The role of a manager, after all, is to make decisions based on the information available rather than to calculate regression coefficients.

The Logic of Controls

In Chapter 16, we introduced the logic of controls for nominal and ordinal data. The logic of control relationships applies equally well to interval-level data and multiple regression.

A Spurious Relationship

The head statistician for North Zulch City Police, Mr. A. Nalist, has made a startling discovery. When Mr. Nalist regresses the number of juvenile crimes in a precinct on the number of household pets in that precinct, he finds the following:

$$\hat{Y} = 15.4 - .075X \quad s_b = .009 \quad r^2 = .70$$

Pet ownership in a precinct appears to be a fairly good predictor of juvenile crimes. While Mr. Nalist was drafting a memo advocating the free distribution of pets to prevent crime, I. C. Fallacy (a research assistant) suggested that a multiple regression with both pet ownership (X_1) and median income in the precinct (X_2) be used to predict juvenile crime (Y). A multiple regression reveals the following:

$$\hat{Y} = 16.5 - .003X_1 - .32X_2$$
$$s_{b_1} = .047 \quad s_{b_2} = .006 \quad R^2 = .85$$

Note that the regression slope for pet ownership in a precinct has fallen to zero (t score $= .06$), whereas median income is strongly related to juvenile crime ($t = 53.3$). Whenever a relationship is spurious between an independent variable and a dependent variable, the regression slope between the two variables will fall to zero if one includes in the regression model a variable that causes both the other variables (in this case, high income causes pet ownership and low crime rates).

A Specification

A relationship is specified if two variables appear unrelated but become related in the presence of a third variable (see Chapter 16). For example, when absenteeism rates (Y) are regressed on the age of letter carriers (X) for the Ripple, North Dakota, post office, no relationship exists:

$$\hat{Y} = 8.6 + .03X$$
$$s_b = .58 \quad r^2 = .01$$

But when an analyst controls for the length of routes (X_2) by entering it into the regression equation, the following pattern emerges:

$$\hat{Y} = 4.7 - .18X_1 + 2.1X_2$$
$$s_{b_1} = .021 \quad s_{b_2} = 1.1 \quad R^2 = .50$$

When length of routes (in miles) is controlled, a relationship appears between absenteeism and age. Obviously, older letter carriers with longer routes have higher absenteeism rates. In the best of all possible worlds, the Ripple postmaster would reassign routes so that older letter carriers would have shorter routes. In theory, the result would be lower absenteeism and, thus, higher productivity.

Dummy Variable Regression

In Chapter 18, simple regression with a dichotomous independent variable was demonstrated. The results were identical to a difference of means test. Can regression be used with nominal independent variables when the independent variable has more than two categories? Yes, but only when the analyst constructs the regression carefully.

Suppose a police chief wants to see whether precinct crime rates are related to different areas of the city. The chief is particularly concerned about the crime rates in the inner city, downtown, and middle-class residential areas. One way to determine whether the area of the city affects precinct crime rates is to regress crime rates in each precinct on area of the city. To do this, create a dummy variable X_1 that is coded 1 if the precinct in question is in the inner city and is coded 0 if it is not. Another dummy variable, X_2, is created that is coded 1 if the precinct is downtown and coded 0 if it is not.

Do not create a third dummy variable for middle-class areas. Two dummy variables account for all three types of precincts, as illustrated here:

If $X_1 = 1$ and $X_2 = 0$, then the precinct is *inner city*.

If $X_1 = 0$ and $X_2 = 1$, then the precinct is *downtown*.

If $X_1 = 0$ and $X_2 = 0$, then the precinct is *middle class*.

A regression of precinct crime rates on X_1 and X_2 might reveal the following:

$$\hat{Y} = 5,463 + 2,471X_1 - 1,362X_2$$
$$S_{b_1} = 236 \quad S_{b_2} = 147$$

This regression equation can be interpreted as follows. The intercept, 5,463, is the mean number of crimes for all middle-class precincts ($X_1 = 0$ and $X_2 = 0$).

The mean number of crimes for all inner-city precincts is $\alpha + \beta_1$, or 7,934. The mean number of crimes for downtown precincts is $\alpha + \beta_2$, or 4,101. The standard errors of the regression slopes indicate that crime rates in the inner city and downtown are significantly different from those in the middle-class precincts. These results would match those for analysis of variance (see Chapter 13) and are much easier to interpret.

Regression with Three Independent Variables

Multiple regression can be used with an unlimited number of independent variables so long as there are sufficient cases or observations for analysis. Regression with three or more independent variables is nothing more than a straightforward extension of the two-independent-variables case.

An Example

Jack Sixgun, the police chief of Metropolis, is concerned about the number of assaults made on police officers in Metropolis. Chief Sixgun asks his data analysts to study the assaults on Metropolis police over the past 10 years. As the dependent variable, the analysts use a dummy variable coded 1 if a police officer was assaulted in a year and coded 0 if he or she was not.

Chief Sixgun suggests that the analysts use three independent variables. The first is the height of the police officer: Chief Sixgun feels that taller officers command more authority and, therefore, are less likely to be assaulted. The analysts operationalize this variable as the number of inches in height a police officer is over the 5-foot, 4-inch minimum. Second, Chief Sixgun believes that officers are less likely to be assaulted if they are operating in teams. This is a dummy variable coded 1 if the officer was teamed with another officer and coded 0 if the officer was not. Third, Chief Sixgun believes that rookies are more likely to make mistakes that will result in assaults. This variable was operationalized as the number of years the officer has served on the force.

Using a multiple regression computer program, Sixgun's analysts find the following:

$$\hat{Y} = .11 + .05X_1 + .21X_2 - .03X_3$$

$$s_{b_1} = .016 \quad s_{b_2} = .062 \quad s_{b_3} = .008 \quad S_{y|x} = .08 \quad R^2 = .73 \quad \mathbf{N} = 200$$

where X_1 is the police officer's height, X_2 is the team variable, and X_3 is the number of years on the force.

The regression equation is interpreted in the same way as was the equation for the two-independent-variable case. The regression coefficient for height (.05) shows the amount that the probability of assault increases (Y is a dummy variable; thus, $\hat{Y}$ becomes a probability) with each inch in height over 5 feet, 4 inches if teams and time on the force are held constant. This finding shocks

Chief Sixgun because a 6-foot, 6-inch police officer has a .7 greater probability of being assaulted than does a 5-foot, 4-inch police officer.

The second regression coefficient is the increase in the probability of assault by being assigned to a team (.21) if height and time on the force remain constant. Again Chief Sixgun is surprised because officers in teams are more likely to be assaulted than officers alone.

Finally, the third regression coefficient indicates that the probability of being assaulted drops .03 for every year the officer serves on the force (all other things being equal).

The intercept (.11) is the probability of being assaulted when X_1, X_2, and X_3 are all zero. In other words, our best estimate is that a 5-foot, 4-inch police officer who is not teamed with another officer and is a rookie (0 years) has a .11 probability of being assaulted in the line of duty in a year's time.

Note that all three regression coefficients have standard errors. By determining the probability that each could be drawn from a population where $\beta = 0$, the strength of the relationships can be assessed. Perform the necessary calculations in the space provided.

The preceding regression equation can be used in the same way that any other regression equation can be used. For example, we can predict the probability that a 6-foot-tall officer with 3 years on the force and assigned to a team would be assaulted. We substitute the values of 8 (number of inches over 5 feet, 4 inches), 1, and 3 for X_1, X_2, and X_3, respectively.

$$\hat{Y} = .11 + .05(8) + .21(1) - .03(3)$$
$$= .11 + .40 + .21 - .09 = .51 + .12 = .63$$

This particular officer has a .63 probability of being assaulted this year. Using the same standard error of the estimate (.08), we could place a rough 95% confidence limit around this estimate (a t value of 2.0 will provide a good approximation).

$$.63 \pm t \times S_{y|x}$$
$$.63 \pm 2.0 \times .08$$
$$.63 \pm .16$$
$$.47 \text{ to } .79$$

Chief Sixgun can also use the regression equation to make management decisions. Because teams increase the probability of assaults by .21, he may decide to eliminate team patrols. Because taller officers are more likely to be assaulted, he may decide to relax the height requirement for police officers.

Calculating Regression Coefficients

When you, as an analyst, must perform a regression with three or more independent variables, we strongly recommend that you use one of numerous computer programs to calculate the regression. Most programs will provide the values for all slopes, the intercept, all slope standard errors, the standard error of the estimate, and the coefficient of determination. For those who prefer to calculate regression slopes by hand, use the following formula:

$$b_{12.34} = \frac{b_{12.3} - (b_{14.3})(b_{42.3})}{1 - (b_{24.3})(b_{42.3})}$$

Note that this is only one slope needed for a regression with three independent variables. Other formulas for the intercept and the standard errors can be found in statistics texts (see the Annotated Bibliography at the end of the book).

Testing a Hypothesis

Several minority groups have charged that the Capers City civil service exam discriminates against minorities. In fact, whites are twice as likely to pass the exam as are minorities. Harlan Fitzgerald, Capers civil service commissioner, counters these claims with the argument that minorities taking the exam have less education, less job-related experience, and lower school grades and thus are more likely to fail for these reasons. Minority groups contend that even when these factors are considered, the exam still discriminates against minorities.

The dispute could be resolved if we could test Mr. Fitzgerald's hypothesis:

H_0: When education, job experience, and grades are controlled, race is unrelated to performance on the Capers City civil service exam.

Regression can be used to test this hypothesis. For each civil service applicant, the following information must be gathered:

Y = score on the civil service exam
X_1 = number of years of formal education
X_2 = years of relevant job experience
X_3 = grade point average in college
X_4 = minority status (1 = minority, 0 = nonminority)

A regression line estimated for this information would be

$$\hat{Y} = a + \beta_1 X_1 + \beta_2 X_2 + \beta_3 X_3 + \beta_4 X_4$$

Mr. Fitzgerald's hypothesis can be restated as follows:

H_0: β_4 is equal to zero.

β_4 is the relationship of race to civil service exam scores when education, experience, and grades are controlled. If β_4 equals zero, then race is unrelated to exam scores when the other factors are controlled. As Mr. Fitzgerald would say, the relationship between race and civil service exam scores is spurious. One can test whether β_4 is equal to zero by calculating a t score and finding the probability of this t score in Table 3 of the Statistical Tables.

For the minority groups to prove their contention, not only would β_4 have to not be equal to zero, but it would also have to have a negative value. A negative slope demonstrates that minorities do worse on the exam than whites do when education, experience, and grades are controlled. If β_4 is positive, Mr. Fitzgerald still wins his argument (at least in regard to minority groups).

Two Additional Regression Assumptions

Recall our discussion of the assumptions of regression analysis in Chapter 18. Each of the assumptions for bivariate regression also applies in the case of multiple regression. Multiple regression differs from bivariate regression in that two additional assumptions must be considered when developing equations with more than one independent variable.

Assumption 1: Model Is Specified Correctly

An important assumption in multiple regression is correct model specification. In simple terms, a well-specified regression equation contains all or most of the independent variables known to be relevant predictors of the dependent variable.

As a starting point in specifying a model, it is quite common to look at existing research on a topic to see what others examining the same (or a similar) question have used as explanatory variables. The more substantive knowledge you possess about the topic in question, the better your ability to select relevant independent variables.

Although existing research can help inform the selection of explanatory variables, there is hardly ever a case where one objectively "correct" set of explanatory variables for a particular regression model exists. Model specification involves good judgment. Above all, you should have sound reasons for choosing the explanatory variables used in a multiple regression analysis and should be prepared to defend your choices. As a beginning data analyst, you should think about a few fairly obvious questions when selecting explanatory variables for a multiple regression equation.

Have Key Variables Been Omitted from the Equation?

Given our knowledge of the factors that affect the dependent variable, does it appear that key explanatory variables have been omitted from the model? If so, why? The reason might be something as simple as an inability to locate data for the variable. Input from a colleague or supervisor who might see things from a different point of view can be helpful when an analyst wonders whether she or he has considered all relevant explanatory variables.

How do we know whether our model is "underspecified"—that is, does not contain enough important independent variables? One way to spot an underspecified model is by looking at the R^2 and Adjusted R^2. The closer either of these values is to zero, the lower the explanatory power of the model. The omission of key independent variables results in the error term absorbing much of the variance that would otherwise be explained by missing independent variables. The size of the error term tends to decrease as relevant explanatory variables are added to the equation. The following example illustrates the problem of an underspecified model.

The director of the Westville, Tennessee, homeless shelter wants to obtain a better understanding of program costs. He has data on operating costs for the last 15 weeks. The director knows that when unemployment is high, demand for services tends to increase. Accordingly, he obtains weekly data on new unemployment claims from the state unemployment office and uses the number of new claims as the first independent variable. At times, the shelter experiences a drop-off in volunteers, which results in paid employees working more hours. The director decides to include the number of volunteer hours worked per week as the second independent variable. He generates the following regression equation:

$$\hat{Y} = 9,780 + 2.44X_1 - 55.14X_2$$

$$s_{b_1} = 1.5 \quad s_{b_2} = 31.8 \quad R^2 = .34 \quad \text{Adj. } R^2 = .23$$

where X_1 is the number of new unemployment claims and X_2 is the number of hours worked by volunteers.

The director is somewhat disappointed that his model explains only about a third of the variation in operating costs. He meets with his staff and asks for feedback on the results. One member of the staff notices that the director seems to have missed the most obvious determinant of operating costs—the number of clients served. The director reruns the regression equation using the number of clients served per week as the third independent variable:

$$\hat{Y} = 8,540 + 1.98X_1 - 9.914X_2 + 44.51X_3$$

$$s_{b_1} = 1.2 \quad s_{b_2} = 5.8 \quad s_{b_3} = 6.5 \quad R^2 = .87 \quad \text{Adj. } R^2 = .84$$

where X_1 is the number of new unemployment claims, X_2 is the number of hours worked by volunteers, and X_3 is the number of clients served.

When the number of clients served per week was included, the R^2 and Adjusted R^2 values for the model rose dramatically. In addition to increasing the explanatory power of a model, the inclusion of important omitted variables results in more accurate estimates of the effects on the dependent variable of all the independent variables included in the regression equation.

Can I Explain Why I Selected Each Independent Variable?

Theory should always guide the choice of possible explanatory variables. "Fishing" for results by haphazardly adding independent variables to, or subtracting them from, the regression equation in hopes of obtaining statistically significant findings is not sound practice. The chances of finding spurious relationships increase when little forethought is put into model specification. In Chapter 3 we discussed theory as a key component used to determine causality. A good data analyst should always be prepared to explain the substantive rationale for the statistical relationship between an independent variable and a dependent variable. Maximizing the number of statistically significant slopes or maximizing R^2 for the sake of obtaining impressive-looking results is not the goal of multiple regression.

You should keep in mind, however, that fishing for results and searching for novel explanations are very different things. You should not be afraid to test different model specifications if you have sound reasons for adding explanatory variables to, or removing them from, an equation. Sometimes the theories guiding our research are poorly developed, which opens the door to innovative attempts at model specification. The key is to have a rationale underlying the choice of each independent variable used in a regression equation.

When Should a Variable Be Dropped from an Equation?

A common belief among data analysts is that after one performs a multiple regression and finds a variable with an insignificant slope coefficient, the variable should be removed and the regression rerun. Statistically, this may help improve the "fit" of the model because a variable with low explanatory power has been removed from the equation. The Adjusted R^2 value typically goes up when statistically insignificant slope coefficients are removed from a model.

Removing independent variables with insignificant slope coefficients has value, especially when selecting a final set of explanatory variables to be included in a model. If the partial slope for a particular variable is not statistically significant, removing the variable and rerunning the regression may provide a more accurate depiction of the relationships among the remaining independent variables and the dependent variable.

A crucial point to keep in mind, however, is that statistically insignificant slope coefficients can be very significant substantively from a managerial standpoint. In policy analysis, knowing what is *not* statistically significant is often as important as knowing what is statistically significant.

For example, a program analyst in a state department of public instruction is interested in determining the factors that shape student performance. She performs a multiple regression (with district-level data from across the state) where student test scores are the dependent variable. The analyst selects average class size, teacher experience (in years), and average state aid per pupil as independent variables. She generates the following regression equation:

$$\hat{Y} = 78 + .41X_1 + .28X_2 + .14X_3$$

$$s_{b_1} = .11 \quad s_{b_2} = .09 \quad s_{b_3} = .98 \quad R^2 = .81 \quad \text{Adj. } R^2 = .70$$

where X_1 is average class size, X_2 is teacher experience, and X_3 is state aid per pupil.

The t values for the first two partial slopes are significant at the .05 probability level. With a t value of .143, the partial slope coefficient for the state aid per pupil variable is not statistically significant. Does this mean that the analyst should automatically drop the variable from the equation and rerun the model in hopes of increasing the Adjusted R^2? If the analyst takes this route, she may be throwing away very important information about how a policy is working. Knowing that state aid per pupil is unrelated to student performance (at least in terms of statistical significance) may be useful information for revising policy in the future.

An unfavorable connotation sometimes is associated with the term *statistically insignificant*. Statistical significance or insignificance should not trigger automatic response sets when interpreting partial slopes in a regression equation. It is perfectly acceptable to remove independent variables from a model if they lack explanatory power. Yet care and judgment should be used to assess the substantive importance of findings, regardless of whether the results are statistically significant. If gaining knowledge about the effects of a particular independent variable is important, it is a good idea to leave the variable in the equation even if the partial slope coefficient is not statistically significant. If gaining knowledge about the effects of a particular independent variable is not central to the research question at hand, then removing a statistically insignificant variable may be appropriate. A manager should always interpret the substantive meaning of partial slope coefficients before dropping independent variables from a regression equation.

Assumption 2: Low Multicollinearity

A second important assumption in multiple regression is low **multicollinearity**. This term refers to a case in which two or more independent variables are highly correlated (have a linear relationship). Examples of variables that can be expected to be highly correlated are agency budget size and number of agency employees, and population size and number of traffic accidents.

Multicollinearity makes it difficult for the regression equation to estimate unique partial slopes for each independent variable. Partial slope estimates and the associated t values can be misleading if one independent variable is highly correlated with another. Not only is it difficult to distinguish the effect of one independent variable from another, but high multicollinearity also typically results in partial slope coefficients with inflated standard errors, thus making it hard to obtain statistically significant results.

Multicollinearity can be diagnosed in a regression equation by looking for two things: The equation may produce a high Adjusted R^2 but slope coefficients that are not statistically significant, or the value of the coefficients may change (sometimes dramatically) when independent variables are added to or subtracted from the equation. The unstable variables are likely to be collinear.

One of the simplest ways to avoid or address multicollinearity is to assess logically whether each independent variable included in a model is really measuring something different from the others. If you think one independent variable might be measuring the same thing as another, you can test this hunch by calculating a correlation coefficient (with a computer program, if possible) for the variables in question (see Chapter 17). Values for correlation coefficients range from -1.0 (perfect negative correlation) to $+1.0$ (perfect positive correlation).

The closer values are to either end of the range, the more closely the two variables move together, or covary. Alternatively, if you suspect that multicollinearity between two independent variables is a problem, you can run a bivariate regression in which one of the explanatory variables is used to explain the other. The closer the R^2 value for the equation is to 1.0, the more likely multicollinearity is a problem. (Because both of these techniques are based on the correlation coefficient, they are highly related.)

The effects of multicollinearity are best illustrated with an example. Frank Watson, the director of the Arizona State Audit Bureau, is interested in finding out why some auditors perform better on annual auditor skills tests than others. Dr. Watson selects three independent variables to explain exam scores for a random sample of 19 auditors. "Years of job experience" at the bureau is selected as the first independent variable because the director feels that more experienced employees should possess a deeper knowledge of auditing procedures than their less experienced counterparts. Dr. Watson selects "employee age" as the second independent variable because he believes that there is no substitute for life experience when dealing with complex program evaluation issues. Finally, Dr. Watson feels that salaried workers should have more knowledge about auditing procedures than hourly workers, so a dummy variable coded 1 if an employee is salaried and 0 if not is included in the analysis. The following regression equation is generated:

$$\hat{Y} = 75.2 + .56X_1 + .25X_2 + 1.36X_3$$
$$s_{b_1} = .66 \quad s_{b_2} = .35 \quad s_{b_3} = .90 \quad R^2 = .81 \quad \text{Adj. } R^2 = .79$$

where X_1 is employee experience, X_2 is employee age, and X_3 is a salaried/hourly dummy variable.

The director is puzzled by the results. The R^2 and Adjusted R^2 values indicate that the model explains approximately 80% of the variation in employee exam scores, yet none of the partial slope coefficients is statistically significant. The director's assistant points out that multicollinearity may be affecting the results because employee age and years of job experience are probably correlated with each other to some extent. To confirm her hunch, the assistant calculates a correlation coefficient and finds a .95 correlation between employee experience and employee age. Upon regressing years of job experience on employee age, an R^2 value of .91 is obtained. Based on these results, the assistant recommends that Dr. Watson remove one of the independent variables from the equation. Dr. Watson decides to remove employee age from the model because he feels that years of experience at the bureau provides a more precise measure of actual job skills. The new regression equation is as follows:

$$\hat{Y} = 80.9 + 1.03X_1 + 1.32X_2$$
$$s_{b_1} = .13 \quad s_{b_2} = .79 \quad R^2 = .80 \quad \text{Adj. } R^2 = .77$$

where X_1 is employee experience and X_2 is the salaried/hourly dummy variable.

The results of the second regression model indicate that employee experience in years has a positive and statistically significant effect on employee exam scores.

Recall that in the first model, the partial slope coefficients for both the employee experience and age variables were not statistically significant because of high multicollinearity.

Although logical reasoning can be helpful for identifying which of the independent variables are affected by multicollinearity, sometimes an analyst will not have prior knowledge about relationships between or among particular independent variables. Because we often do not know ahead of time whether multicollinearity might be a problem, it is always a good idea to generate the correlations between each pair of independent variables included in a regression equation (called a *correlation matrix*). An even more advanced approach for detecting multicollinearity is analysis of variance inflation factors (VIFs), which most statistical software programs provide.

It may seem that the obvious solution to high multicollinearity is the removal of one or more independent variables from the regression equation, but a manager should not let his or her statistician make such changes automatically. Changing how a model is specified requires sound judgment because removing important independent variables may make it more difficult to study the management question at hand. Sometimes a loss of precision in estimating partial slope coefficients is preferable to removing highly correlated independent variables from a model. Other options commonly pursued by analysts include combining the collinear variables into a scale or index using the values of both variables or transforming a suspect variable using a mathematical calculation (such as taking the logarithm of each value). All options must be carefully considered to ensure that the concept each variable represents (for instance, age, budget size, number of employees, or test scores) is not lost in the transformation. Diagnosing and reducing multicollinearity is a fairly advanced topic, so if you suspect it is a problem, you should consult a statistician or statistical textbook (see Fox, 2008).

Polynomial Curve Fitting

Linear regression is appropriate only where the relationship between variables is linear. In Chapter 19, nonlinear regression with logarithms was demonstrated. Two other forms of nonlinear regression, also called **polynomial curve fitting**, are important to know: quadratic relationships and cubic relationships.

Quadratic Relationships

Boomtown, Wyoming, a fast-growing new town in the western coal fields, has experienced a phenomenal increase in its crime rate as the city's population has skyrocketed. The data in Table 20.3 show this increase.

The county sheriff, Seymour "Tex" Critter, would like to forecast the number of crimes in Boomtown so that he can decide how many deputies to assign to Boomtown. Tex begins his analysis by graphing the data. Do this on the graph in Figure 20.1.

Table 20.3	Crime Rate in Boomtown

Year	Number of Crimes
2007	1
2008	3
2009	10
2010	31
2011	69
2012	124
2013	183
2014	234

© Cengage Learning 2015

Figure 20.1	Graph Data Here

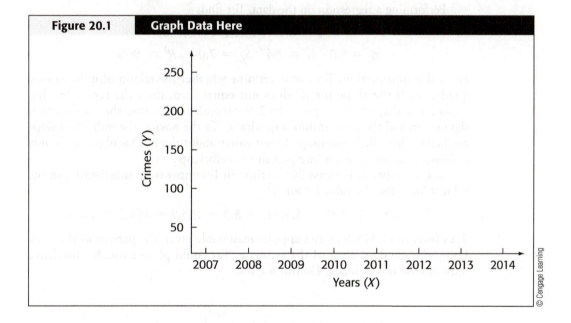

© Cengage Learning

When Tex examines the graph of the data, he sees that the relationship is not linear; crime is increasing at an accelerating rate. This is the general form of a quadratic relationship. To fit a curved line to these data, Tex must convert years to regular numbers for new X values (i.e., 1 for 2007, 2 for 2008, 3 for 2009, and so on). Then these X values must be squared. See Table 20.4.

To calculate a regression equation that will accurately describe the data, Tex must estimate the following regression:

$$\hat{Y} = \alpha + \beta_1 X + \beta_2 X^2$$

Notice that both X and X^2 are included in the equation.

Table 20.4	Calculations for Boomtown Data			
	Year	X	X^2	Y
	2007	1	1	1
	2008	2	4	3
	2009	3	9	10
	2010	4	16	31
	2011	5	25	69
	2012	6	36	124
	2013	7	49	183
	2014	8	64	234

© Cengage Learning 2015

Performing a regression on the data, Tex finds

$$\hat{Y} = 8.9 - 15.1X + 5.5X^2$$

$$s_{b_1} = 5.0 \quad s_{b_2} = .54 \quad S_{y|x} = 7.04 \quad R^2 = .996$$

From this information, Tex can determine whether the relationship is, in fact, quadratic. If the slope for X^2 does not equal zero, then the regression has a quadratic shape ($5.5 \div .54 = 10.2 = t$ score). In this case the coefficient is significant, and the relationship is quadratic. To the novice, the individual slope coefficients have little meaning; do not worry about them. Our objective is only to forecast, so we need not interpret these coefficients.

Tex attempts to forecast 2015 crime in Boomtown by substituting in the value 9 for X and the value 81 for X^2.

$$\hat{Y} = 8.9 - 15.1(9) + 5.5(81) = 8.9 - 135.9 + 445.5 = 318.5$$

Tex's forecast of 318.5 crimes appears reasonable given the pattern of the data. Using the standard error of the estimate, Tex could place a rough confidence limit around this estimate. Do this for Tex.

To illustrate the utility of the quadratic forecast, Tex determined a straight linear forecast for crime in Boomtown.

$$\hat{Y} = -74.1 + 34.7X$$

$$s_b = 4.6 \quad S_{y|x} = 30.0 \quad r^2 = .90$$

Notice that for the linear regression, r^2 is lower and the standard error of the estimate is higher. Forecasts with this model would be less accurate than those arrived at with the quadratic model. The forecast for 2015 would be as follows:

$$\hat{Y} = -74.1 + 34.7(9) = -74.1 + 312.3 = 238.2$$

Table 20.5	Xenith City Data on Prostitution Arrests	
	Arrests	Number of Vice Squad Officers
	25	1
	34	2
	43	3
	98	4
	123	5
	194	6
	253	7
	271	8
	294	9
	292	10
	298	11

The linear forecast for 2015 is only five crimes more than the 2014 figure. Clearly this forecast would not be accurate if past trends continued. Hence, the manager should use the quadratic model for forecasting.

Cubic Regression

The city of Xenith has been experimenting over the past year with the number of officers assigned to the vice squad. For the past 11 months, the city has gathered the information on prostitution arrests shown in Table 20.5.

Currently the city council wants the police department to double its vice squad to drive prostitution off the streets. The police chief would rather use these additional officers on homicide because she does not believe that an increase in vice squad officers would have any impact on prostitution arrests.

The police chief begins her analysis by graphing the data. Do this for the police chief on the graph in Figure 20.2.

The police chief recognizes the pattern of a cubic relationship, as illustrated in Chapter 18. She then decides to run three regressions, one linear (bivariate) with X, one a quadratic, and one a cubic, as follows:

$$\text{linear} \quad \hat{Y} = a + \beta X$$
$$\text{quadratic:} \ \hat{Y} = a + \beta_1 X + \beta_2 X^2$$
$$\text{cubic:} \quad \hat{Y} = a + \beta_1 X + \beta_2 X^2 + \beta_3 X^3$$

To do this, the police chief squares and cubes the X values, as shown in Table 20.6. The following regressions result.

Linear:

$$\hat{Y} = -22.8 + 33.0X$$
$$s_b = 2.8 \quad S_{y|x} = 29.0 \quad r^2 = .94$$

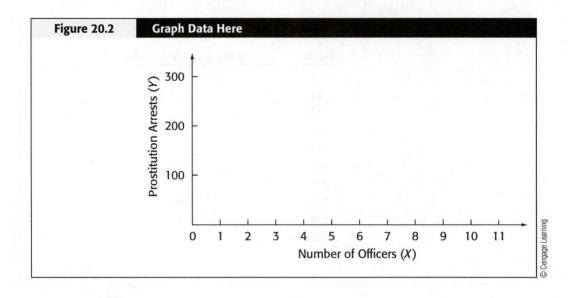

Figure 20.2 **Graph Data Here**

Prostitution Arrests (Y) vs *Number of Officers (X)*

© Cengage Learning

Table 20.6 Calculations for Xenith City Data

Y	X	X^2	X^3
25	1	1	1
34	2	4	8
43	3	9	27
98	4	16	64
123	5	25	125
194	6	36	216
253	7	49	343
271	8	64	512
294	9	81	729
292	10	100	1,000
298	11	121	1,331

© Cengage Learning

Quadratic:

$$\hat{Y} = -55.3 + 48.0X - 1.3X^2$$

$$s_{b_1} = 11.7 \quad s_{b_2} = .95 \quad S_{y|x} = 27.9 \quad R^2 = .95$$

Cubic:

$$\hat{Y} = 43.9 - 34.0X - 15.1X^2 - .91X^3$$

$$s_{b_1} = 15.4 \quad s_{b_2} = 2.9 \quad s_{b_3} = .16 \quad S_{y|x} = 12.6 \quad R^2 = .991$$

Notice the increase in the coefficient of determination for the cubic equation and the decrease in the standard error of the estimate. These results plus the standard errors of the slopes indicate that the relationship is cubic.

The real advantage of the cubic form lies in forecasting. If the police chief forecasts the number of arrests with 11 officers by using the linear and cubic models, she finds

$$\text{Linear: } \hat{Y} = -23.4 + 33(11) = 340.2$$
$$\text{Cubic: } \hat{Y} = -43.9 - 34.0(11) + 15.1(121) - .91(1,331)$$
$$= 42.8 - 374 + 1,827 - 1,211 = 285$$

Notice that not only is the cubic forecast more accurate, but also the linear forecast is far too high. This result is important in decision making because a linear forecast of 22 police officers would show a large increase in arrests, whereas the cubic forecast would not. (Note that forecasting arrests by 22 police officers is extremely risky when the data contain information for only 1 to 11 officers.)

Chapter Summary

Multiple regression is a technique used for interval-level data when the analyst has more than one independent variable and wants to explain or predict scores on the dependent variable. This chapter discussed the interpretation of multiple regression and the application of regression to two or more independent variables.

Two concepts involved in multiple regression are partial slopes and the multiple coefficient of determination. Each is analogous to its counterpart, the (bivariate) slope and coefficient of determination (r^2), in simple linear regression based on a single independent variable. Adjusted R^2 values reveal the reduction in explanatory power of a model after taking statistically insignificant partial slope coefficients into account. This chapter illustrated the interpretation of these terms when a dependent variable is regressed on two or more independent variables. The logic of control relationships, introduced in Chapter 16, applies equally well here to multiple regression.

Multiple regression is a very flexible statistical technique. Multiple regression can be used to test hypotheses involving more than one independent variable. Dummy variable regression can be used with nominal independent variables having two or more categories. Multiple regression can also be used to estimate relationships that are not linear, a technique known as polynomial curve fitting. In addition to all the assumptions for bivariate regression (see Chapter 18), in multiple regression analysis, sound and valid results depend on two further assumptions: that the regression equation includes all of the independent variables that theory or experience suggest will influence the dependent variable (specification), and that the predictor variables are not so closely related that their independent effects on the dependent variable cannot be distinguished (multicollinearity).

Problems

20.1 Forrest Tucker, the head statistician for the National Parks Service, believes that park usage as measured by number of visitors (Y) is a function of the number of people who live within 200 miles of the park (X_1), the number of camping hookups available (X_2), and the mean annual temperature at the park (X_3). For a sample of 200 parks under Forrest's supervision, the following regression is calculated:

$$\hat{Y} = 147 + .0212X_1 + 15.4X_2 + 186X_3$$

$$s_{b_1} = .0157 \quad s_{b_2} = 12.4 \quad s_{b_3} = 10.4 \quad R^2 = .50 \quad \text{Adj. } R^2 = .43$$

For this regression, what can you tell Forrest? Write a one-page memo with your assessment.

20.2 If Janice Position-Classification, personnel officer for the Bureau of Forms, can forecast agency separations 6 months from now, she can plan recruitment efforts to replace these people. Janice believes that separations 6 months from now are determined by the number of agency people passed over for promotion (X_1), the number of agency people 64 years old or older (X_2), and the ratio of government salaries to private sector salaries (X_3). Using regression, Janice finds the following:

$$\hat{Y} = 27.4 + .35X_1 + .54X_2 - 271X_3$$

$$s_{b_1} = .0031 \quad s_{b_2} = 0.136 \quad s_{b_3} = 263 \quad S_{y|x} = 54$$

$$R^2 = .89 \quad \text{Adj. } R^2 = .85 \quad N = 214$$

Write a one-page memo explaining the results, and then forecast the number of separations if 418 people are passed over for promotion, 327 people are 64 years old or older, and government salaries equal those in the private sector.

20.3 The Forest Service believes that it can predict the number of forest fires per month in a forest, knowing the amount of rainfall that fell the previous month (X_1) and the average daily temperature for that month (X_2), taken from historical records. A regression yields the following:

$$\hat{Y} = 2.0 - 1.1X_1 + .14X_2$$

$$s_{b_1} = .021 \quad s_{b_2} = .003 \quad S_{y|x} = 1.4$$

$$R^2 = .96 \quad \text{Adj. } R^2 = .96 \quad N = 136$$

(a) Write a brief memo interpreting the slopes, the intercept, and R^2.

(b) Barren National Forest has had 4 inches of rain in the last month and has a historical mean temperature of 84 degrees for this month. What is the best estimate of the number of fires in Barren this month?

20.4 The McKeesport Fire Department wants to know how likely it is that a truck pump will fail. The fire chief, George Pyro (no relation), thinks pump failure is a function of age (X_1) and water hardness (X_2 measured on a scale of 1 to 10).

The department statistician runs a regression on a dummy variable (coded 1 for failure and 0 for no failure) for 217 pumps. She finds the following:

$$\hat{Y} = .14 + .01X_1 + 05X_2$$

$$s_{b_1} = .0002 \quad s_{b_2} = .025 \quad s_{y|x} = .04 \quad R^2 = .93 \quad \text{Adj. } R^2 = .92$$

Write a memo explaining what the regression means. If the average water hardness is 3 and the chief would like to replace any pump with a probability of failing of .80 or more, at what age should pumps be replaced?

20.5 Lieutenant Colonel Syl Verleaf is placed in charge of base security at all 240 military bases in Europe. Verleaf believes that the crime rate is positively correlated to the size of the base, the percentage of troops without high school degrees, and the number of women on base. Verleaf's statistician finds the following:

$$\hat{Y} = 47.3 + .031X_1 + 2.4X_2 - .065X_3$$

$$s_{b_1} = .0021 \quad s_{b_2} = 3.0 \quad s_{b_3} = .0027 \quad S_{y|x} = 17.1$$
$$R^2 = .80 \quad \text{Adj. } R^2 = .78$$

where X_1 is the number of troops on the base, X_2 is the percentage of troops without high school degrees, X_3 is the number of women on the base, and Y is the number of serious crimes in a month. Interpret all the regression coefficients, R^2 and the intercept. What is the most important independent variable? Ramstein Air Base has 15,000 troops, 42% of its troops have no high school degree, and there are 3,000 women on base. What is your best estimate of the number of crimes per month for this base?

20.6 Refer to Problem 20.5. The information for Rathesberg Base and Krasmic Kaserne appears in the accompanying table.

Statistic	Rathesberg	Krasmic
X_1 (troops)	12,000	14,000
X_2 (% without high school degree)	34	28
X_3 (women)	2,000	3,000
Y (number of crimes)	517	290

Calculate Y for each base. Why might it be interesting to study both bases in depth?

20.7 The Missouri Department of Education has hired a program evaluation team to investigate why the average reading scores for all seniors vary from 9.4 to 13.1 for different high schools ($N = 326$). The program evaluation team believes that reading scores are affected by pupil–teacher ratios (X_1) and per-student spending on education in a school district (X_2). Using regression analysis, the team finds

$$\hat{Y} = 10.6 - .091X_1 + .0031X_2$$

$$s_{b_1} = .017 \quad s_{b_2} = .00061 \quad s_{y|x} = .17 \quad R^2 = .75 \quad \text{Adj. } R^2 = .74$$

Interpret this equation for the department of education. The education department's budget has enough money to lower the pupil–teacher ratio by 5 or to increase the per-student spending by $50. Which should it do?

20.8 Several states have argued that the 65-mph speed limit has no justification and have refused to enforce it. The federal Department of Transportation (DOT) believes that the 65-mph limit saves lives. To illustrate its contention, the department regressed the number of traffic fatalities last year in a state (Y) on the state's population (X_1), the number of days of snow cover (X_2), and the average speed of all cars (X_3). It found

$$\hat{Y} = 1.4 + .00029X_1 + 2.4X_2 + 10.3X_3$$

$$s_{b_1} = .00003 \quad s_{b_2} = .62 \quad s_{b_3} = 1.1 \quad S_{y|x} = 36.1$$

$$R^2 = .78 \quad \text{Adj. } R^2 = .78 \quad N = 50$$

Does reducing the average speed of cars have an impact? All other things being equal, how many lives would be saved in a state if the average speed were reduced from 75 to 65 mph?

20.9 Redlands Blue Cross wants to hold down hospital costs in the area hospitals. It regresses the average cost of a hospital stay (Y) on the number of days the person stayed in the hospital (X_1), the number of lab tests made (X_2), and the number of prescription drugs ordered (X_3). Interpret the following regression and decide whether any policy changes can be recommended.

$$\hat{Y} = 325.36 + 5196.40X_1 + 1224.90X_2 + 111.41X_3$$

$$s_{b_1} = 640 \quad s_{b_2} = 320 \quad s_{b_3} = 20 \quad S_{y|x} = 112.50$$

$$R^2 = .96 \quad \text{Adj. } R^2 = .93 \quad N = 75$$

20.10 The Buford State University chapter of the American Association of University Professors (AAUP) regressed the salaries of all BSU faculty (Y) on the number of articles each faculty member has published (X_1) and the number of years the person has served on the faculty (X_2). Interpret the following regression:

$$\hat{Y} = 65,200 + 1,250X_1 + 1,750X_2$$

$$S_{b_1} = 902 \quad S_{b_2} = 152$$

$$R^2 = .91 \quad \text{Adj. } R^2 = .87 \quad N = 517$$

20.11 Ohio has had an urban enterprise zone program in operation for the past 5 years. Local governments are free to set up three types of zones to attract new industry: zone A (businesses are exempt from taxes for 10 years), zone B (industries are exempt from taxes for 10 years, and they may use tax-free industrial development bonds), and zone C (the local government contributes to the capital investment of the industry). Local governments can set up one and only one type of urban enterprise zone. The state wants to know the impact of the zones on local unemployment rates (Y). To do this, it set up a dummy variable X_1 (coded 1 if the zone is a B-type zone and coded 0 otherwise) and another dummy variable X_2 (coded 1 if the zone is a C-type zone and 0 otherwise). It wants to control for the following variables: X_3, the percentage of unemployment in the counties surrounding the urban area with the zone; X_4, the median education level of the urban area in years; and X_5, the percentage of the urban area's employed population that is employed in services. Y is measured in percentage unemployed. A regression for 136 cities reveals the following results:

$$\hat{Y} = 5.4 + 1.32X_1 - .64X_2 - .82X_3 - .07X_4 - .13X_5$$

$$s_{b_1} = .31 \quad s_{b_2} = .32 \quad s_{b_3} = .03 \quad s_{b_4} = .13 \quad s_{b_5} = .031$$

$$S_{y|x} = .62 \quad R^2 = .53 \quad \text{Adj. } R^2 = .51$$

Interpret all slopes, the intercept, and R^2. Analyze the slopes, including tests of significance, and express in clear English what this regression reveals. Youngstown has a zone C enterprise zone, with unemployment in the surrounding counties of 8.9%, median education of 10.8 years, and 31% of the city's employed working in services. What is your best guess of the percentage of unemployment in Youngstown?

21.12 The Strategic Air Command (SAC) is concerned about the possibility that missiles will not launch successfully. Utilizing test data, it regresses X_1 (the temperature at launch in degrees Fahrenheit), X_2 (the number of months since the last overhaul of the launch mechanism), and X_3 (the number of ICBMs sited within 800 meters). SAC gets the following results with Y (a dummy variable that is coded 1 if the launch fails):

$$\hat{Y} = .06 - 0.12X_1 + .006X_2 - .094X_3$$

$$s_{b_1} = .0021 \quad s_{b_2} = .0015 \quad s_{b_3} = .087 \quad S_{y|x} = .034$$

$$R^2 = .69 \quad \text{Adj. } R^2 = .65 \quad N = 214$$

Interpret the slopes, intercept, and R^2, and test the slopes for significance. SAC wants the probability of failure to be no more than 20%. If launches will proceed at -10 degrees with no other missiles within 800 meters, how often should launch mechanisms be serviced?

21.13 At Eastern State University, a study of sex discrimination in salaries is undertaken. The analyst regresses the salary of each teaching professional on the number of years of experience (X_1), the number of publications (X_2), and the sex of the person (X_3, a dummy variable with male coded as 1). She gets the following results:

$$\hat{Y} = \$28,563 + \$2,235X_1 + \$65X_2 + \$1,150X_3$$

$$s_{b_1} = 386 \quad s_{b_2} = 39 \quad s_{b_3} = 316 \quad S_{y|x} = 2,690$$

$$R^2 = .68 \quad \text{Adj. } R^2 = .67$$

Interpret the slopes, intercept, and R^2. Estimate the salary of a male professor with 7 years of experience and three publications.

20.14 The state tax division is evaluating the money raised by state sales taxes. Using data from all states, division members regress the amount of money raised by the sales tax per capita on the average per-capita income (X_1) and a dummy variable coded 1 if the state taxed the sale of groceries (X_2). They get the following results:

$$\hat{Y} = .03 + .0218X_1 + 147.18X_2$$

$$s_{b_1} = .0043 \quad s_{b_2} = 36.3 \quad S_{y|x} = 31.40 \quad R^2 = .86 \quad \text{Adj. } R^2 = .85$$

Interpret this regression. Present a hypothesis about placing a tax on the sale of groceries and evaluate this hypothesis. How much could a state with a per-capita income of $33,947 and a tax on groceries raise per capita with a sales tax?

20.15 You have been hired by the U.S. Supreme Court to find out if any racial bias affects whether persons who are convicted of capital murder receive the death penalty. Your data are 194 persons who were convicted of murder in six southern states. The dependent variable is a dummy variable coded 1 if the person received the death penalty and coded 0 otherwise. The independent variables are X_1, the number of persons killed by the convictee (ranges from 1 to 8); X_2, a dummy variable coded 1 if the person was able to pay for his or her own attorney (rather than having a court-assigned public defender); X_3, the number of years of formal education the person has; and X_4, a race variable coded 1 if the convictee was white and coded 0 otherwise. A regression analysis finds the following:

$$\hat{Y} = .54 + .05X_1 - .23X_2 - .02X_3 - .31X_4$$

$$s_{b_1} = .042 \quad s_{b_2} = .083 \quad s_{b_3} = .006 \quad s_{b_4} = .012 \quad S_{y|x} = .14$$

$$R^2 = .52 \quad \text{Adj. } R^2 = .49$$

(a) Interpret this regression, including slopes, intercept, and R^2. Are the slopes significant? What does this regression say about the research question?

(b) How likely is it that a white man with a college degree, who paid for his own attorney and who killed two people, will get the death penalty?

(c) How likely is it that a nonwhite man with an eighth-grade education, who had a public defender and who killed one person, will receive the death penalty?

(d) How would you change this study to find out whether the victim's race mattered?

20.16 Tax expert Bob Erikson is interested in the reliance of state governments on "sin taxes"—taxes on the purchase of alcohol and tobacco and on gambling. The dependent variable is the percentage of state revenue that is raised from sin taxes. Three research hypotheses guide Bob's analysis. First, Bob believes that Catholics are generally "good-time" people who drink, smoke, and play bingo a lot; X_1 is the percentage of the state population who are Catholic. Second, Bob notes that Republicans seem less concerned than Democrats do that sin taxes might be regressive; X_2 is the percentage of the state legislature who are Republicans. Third, Bob suspects that sin taxes could be used to hold down the level of property taxes; X_3 is the per-capita property tax in thousands of dollars. A regression program produces the following results:

$$\hat{Y} = .54 + .23X_1 + .11X_2 - 1.41X_3$$
$$s_{b_1} = .04 \quad s_{b_2} = .087 \quad s_{b_3} = .15 \quad S_{y|x} = .74$$
$$R^2 = .74 \quad \text{Adj. } R^2 = .71$$

(a) Interpret the slopes, intercept, and R^2.

(b) What are the research hypotheses? Evaluate these hypotheses.

(c) Michigan has 20% Catholic constituents, 47% Republicans in the state legislature, and a property tax of $2.5 per thousand. What is your best guess as to the sin tax rate in Michigan?

(d) The actual sin tax rate in Michigan is 16.1%. What would you conclude about that?

20.17 Marv Johnson, city manager of Filkburg, Virginia, wants to develop a better understanding of the factors that influence vehicle maintenance and costs. Mr. Johnson has data on 100 vehicles in the city's vehicle fleet. The dependent variable is the annual maintenance cost per vehicle (MCOST). The independent variables include total vehicle mileage (TMILE), a dummy variable coded 1 for emergency service vehicles and coded 0 for all other types of vehicles (VTYPE), and the total number of days the vehicle was in use over the year (TDAYS). Assist Mr. Johnson by generating a regression equation using these data. What substantive conclusions can be reached about factors that affect vehicle maintenance costs? *(Note: The data set for this problem is available on the book's companion website.)*

20.18 Rita Sharp, operations director of the Farnsworth Museum of Industrial Arts, has gathered weekly visitor data for the past year. Ms. Sharp is interested in explaining why the number of visitors varies from week to week (NUMV). Ms. Sharp has data on two independent variables. The first is a dummy variable coded 1 for weeks when new items went on display and coded 0 for all other weeks (NITEM). The second is a variable for the price of an admissions ticket because part of the museum's marketing strategy is to have weekly reduced-price admission promotions (TPRICE). The director asks you to generate a regression equation using these data. In summarizing the findings, what should you tell the director? *(Note: The data set for this problem is available on the book's companion website.)*

20.19 Stephanie Albini, chief risk manager of Action Park, Illinois, has collected data on the number of accidents occurring on city property over the last 72 months. The mayor of Action Park thinks accidents occur at random, but Ms. Albini believes that statistical analysis of the data is in order before such conclusions can be made. Ms. Albini runs a regression using the number of accidents per month as the dependent variable (NAC). For the first independent variable, Ms. Albini collects data on total monthly snowfall in inches (SNOW) because she believes that snow and ice are important contributors to accidents. To get a sense of whether variations in spending on facilities maintenance might be a contributing factor, Ms. Albini includes total monthly facilities and maintenance spending as the second independent variable in the analysis (MSPEND). After analyzing these data, what should Ms. Albini tell the mayor? *(Note: The data set for this problem is available on the book's companion website.)*

20.20 Officials in the Michigan Department of Education want to determine why student performance varies across school districts in the state. Department officials ask their chief statistician to run a regression analysis where the average district pass rate on the state-mandated standardized skills test is the dependent variable (TEST). The independent variables are the average teacher salary per school district (TSAL), the average class size (CLSIZE), and the average district daily attendance rate (ATTEND). What can the chief statistician report to her supervisors after running the analysis? *(Note: The data set for this problem is available on the book's companion website.)*

20.21 Ms. Patricia Waldo, city manager of Big Cat, Texas (you met Ms. Waldo in Problem 17.20), is working on policy interventions designed to discourage loitering in her town. In her regression analysis, the number of individuals receiving either warnings or citations for loitering (LOIT) is the dependent variable. The first independent variable (examined in Problem 17.20) is a dummy variable coded 1 for days when classical music was played on the town's outdoor speaker system and coded 0 for days when music was not played (MUSIC). Big Cat has installed a speaker system on a few main streets downtown.

Ms. Waldo wants to find other factors that can explain loitering activity. Because she believes that rain decreases loitering activity, she creates a new dummy variable coded 1 for days when it rained and coded 0 for all other days (RAIN). Ms. Waldo also includes an independent variable for the daily high temperature (TEMP) because she believes that loitering activity decreases on extremely hot days (because people are more likely to stay indoors when it is uncomfortably hot). After running the revised regression, what conclusions can Ms. Waldo draw? *(Note: The data set for this problem is available on the book's companion website.)*

20.22 Two colleagues in the economics department at Big State University are having a debate over the factors that influence per-capita charitable donation totals across the states (SDONATE, defined as per-capita donations reported on federal tax returns, by state). One of the scholars believes that economic variables, such as state per-capita income (INCOME) and state unemployment rates (UNEMP, defined as the average unemployment rate for the first 11 months of the year, by state), are the main forces that explain the variation in per-capita charitable donation totals by state. The other scholar believes this variation is best explained by the percentage of residents in each state who define themselves as religious (measured as the percentage of residents who consider themselves Christian church adherents (CHURCH)). Generate a regression model using these data. Based on the results, which argument has the most empirical support? *(Note: The data set for this problem is available on the book's companion website.)*

20.23 The Shorewood Community Center runs a substance abuse counseling program. Over the course of the 8-week program, clients are expected to attend three counseling sessions per week. Because attendance ultimately affects whether clients succeed, the director of the program would like to obtain a better understanding of why some clients attend more than others. The director asks her research intern to run a regression on the available data for the most recent group of clients ($n = 75$) who started (but did not necessarily complete) the program. Days attended is the dependent variable (ATTEND). The independent variables include the following:

REFERRAL = A dummy variable for whether the client was referred by the criminal justice system (coded 1 if yes, 0 if not).

AGE = Age of client (in years)

After generating a regression equation, what can the intern tell the director about the explanatory power of these independent variables? *(Note: The data set for this problem is available on the book's companion website.)*

20.24 The leaders of a community health clinic want to evaluate the impact of a weight loss program for clients initiated a year ago. The program consisted of weekly low-impact group exercise sessions offered three times a week. Clients varied greatly in their attendance at these sessions.

Program administrators decide to analyze data from the program using multiple regression. The dependent variable in the analysis is total pounds lost per client over the course of the program (WLOSS).

Program administrators have a variety of independent variables. The primary independent variable is the number of exercise sessions attended (EXERCISE). Weight (in pounds) at the start of the program (WEIGHT) is included as an independent variable because clients differ greatly on this measure. Age (in years) is also entered into the model (AGE). Administrators have mixed views on the effects of this variable. Some feel that younger individuals might be more motivated to lose weight, whereas others feel motivation might rise with age.

Finally, the administrators in charge of the study ask an intern to use an Internet mapping tool to determine the distance (in miles) from each client's residence to the facility (MILES). The administrators control for this variable because they believe clients who live further away from the center's facilities may be less motivated to consistently participate in the program.

After generating a regression equation, prepare a brief memo summarizing the analysis of the weight loss program. *(Note: The data set for this problem is available on the book's companion website.)*

20.25 Darcie Warner, an analyst at the U.S. Census Bureau, is researching why the percentage of households without access to the Internet varies by state. This measure (NOINT) will be the dependent variable in her empirical analysis. She has collected data on what she believes are two relevant explanatory variables: the percentage of foreign-born residents by state (PFORB) and the poverty rate (POVERTY) by state. These are her independent variables. Ms. Warner hypothesizes that states with higher percentages of foreign-born residents are more urban and cosmopolitan; therefore, she expects this variable to be negatively related to the dependent variable. In the case of poverty, Ms. Warner expects to see a positive relationship between poverty rates and lack of household Internet access. Upon generating a regression equation with these data, what can Ms. Warner say about her hypotheses? *(Note: The data set for this problem is available on the book's companion website.)*

20.26 Refer to Exercise 17.24. In that example, a public health researcher attempted to explain why the percentage of residents who smoke (PSMOKE) varies by state. Her original hypothesis was that education levels are negatively related to cigarette smoking. The percentage of 25- to 34-year-olds with any kind of college degree was the independent variable used to measure state education levels (COLED). Unsatisfied with simply running a bivariate regression, the researcher collects data for two additional independent variables. The first new independent variable comes from survey data on the percentage of smokers per state who attempted to quit smoking in the previous year (QUITS). The second new variable is the state excise tax per pack of cigarettes, measured in cents/dollars (ETAX). The hypothesis for this variable is that higher excise taxes should discourage smoking. After running the revised model (where COLED, QUITS, and ETAX are the X variables and PSMOKE is the Y variable), what has the researcher found? *(Note: The data set for this problem is available on the book's companion website.)*

Regression Output and Data Management

In Chapters 17 through 20, we presented the results of various regression analyses in equation form to illustrate how a relationship between an independent and a dependent variable can be expressed in terms of a slope, intercept, and error term. You should be aware that most statistical software packages do not present regression results this way. To show you how regression output is displayed using statistical software, we have generated computer output for some of the examples presented in Chapter 17 using SPSS.

Bivariate Regression Output

Example 1

Computer-generated regression reports typically contain a lot of information, including some terms and statistics not discussed in the body of this chapter. You generally do not need to discuss all of the information displayed in the output when presenting and describing regression results. We feel it is important, however, for beginner analysts to know what all of these data mean. Our first sample SPSS output page in Table 21.1 is for the police cars and average speed data from Table 17.2. We will explain each section of the output, moving from the bottom of the table to the top.

Coefficients

The coefficients section of the output displays the values for the intercept and slope. Many statistical package programs use the term *constant* instead of *intercept* (including one of the most popular programs, SPSS), but they mean the same thing.

The first thing you should notice is that the values for the constant and slope (the CARS variable) are the same as those found in the equation in the "Some Applications" section in Chapter 17. They are not presented, however, in actual equation form on the computer output. If we wanted to present these or any regression results in equation form, the output contains all the information necessary to do so. We simply take the unstandardized regression coefficients from the rows labeled "(Constant)" and "CARS" and produce the equation

$$\hat{Y} = 72.2 - 2.55X$$

Table 21.1	SPSS Output for Police Cars and Average Speed Regression

Model Summary

Model	R	R^2	Adjusted R^2	Std. Error of the Estimate
1	.971[a]	.942	.923	1.62788

[a]Predictors: (Constant), CARS.

ANOVA[b]

Model		Sum of Squares	df	Mean Square	F	Significance
1	Regression	130.050	1	130.050	49.075	.006[a]
	Residual	7.950	3	2.650		
	Total	138.000	4			

[a]Predictors: (Constant), CARS.
[b]Dependent variable: SPEED.

Coefficients[a]

Model		Unstandardized Coefficients		Standardized Coefficients		
		B	Std. Error	Beta	t	Significance
1	(Constant)	72.200	1.628		44.352	.000
	CARS	−2.550	.364	−.971	−7.005	.006

[a]Dependent variable: SPEED.

© Cengage Learning

Remember that a negative sign in front of the slope coefficient indicates a negative relationship. Accordingly, in this case the equation is stated as an intercept minus a slope: $\hat{Y} = 72.2 - 2.55X$. Statistical package programs do not print out positive signs in front of positive slope coefficients. When the relationship (slope) is positive, the equation will be stated as an intercept plus a slope.

Notice that the standard error of the slope is displayed to the right of the slope coefficient. If you divide the slope coefficient by the standard error of the slope, the result is the t statistic seen in the column labeled "t." The level of statistical significance for rejecting the null hypothesis is provided on the output itself, which means we do not have to consult a t table to interpret the probability associated with the t value for the slope, as we did in earlier chapters (in those chapters we consulted the t table provided at the end of the book). The "Sig." column reveals that the level of statistical significance for the cars variable is .006. This means that there is less than a 1% chance that the null hypothesis of no relationship is actually true. Therefore, you should reject the null hypothesis of no relationship.

Although information for the standard error and t score is also provided for the intercept, most analysts do not report these data (other than the intercept itself). Because the goal of regression analysis is usually to determine whether an independent variable is statistically related to a dependent variable, it is far more important to interpret tests of statistical significance for the slope coefficient. The final column heading is for standardized coefficients. Standardized coefficients are more relevant in the case of multiple regression; we will discuss the meaning of standardized coefficients when we consider multiple regression output later in the chapter.

ANOVA

The "ANOVA" (analysis of variance) section of the output provides information on the percentage of explained versus unexplained variance for the regression model. The "Sum of Squares" column provides information for both the independent variable and the error term. In the row labeled "Regression," you will see a value of 130.05. If we divide this number by the total sum of squares, we can determine the proportion of variance explained by the model. Notice that when we divide 130.05 by 138, the result is .942. In the "Model Summary" section of the output, you will find that the R^2 value is also .942. This is not a coincidence. When you divide the sum of squares for the regression by the total sum of squares, the result will always be equal to R^2.

We did not show you a real error term in Chapter 17, so those of you who eagerly awaited one will now be rewarded. The row labeled "Residual" provides important information about the error term. Recall that the error term refers to the amount of variance in the dependent variable that cannot be explained by the independent variable. The value for the sum of squares for the residual is 7.95. If we divide this number by 138, the result is .058. How is this number related to R^2? If we subtract the R^2 of .942 from 1.0 (the proportion of explained variance plus the proportion of unexplained variance in the dependent variable must sum to 1.0), we obtain a result of .058. This tells us that approximately 6% of the variation in the dependent variable remains unexplained.

Although analysts traditionally report R^2 instead of ANOVA output, information from the "Sum of Squares" column is useful for evaluating the fit of a model. If the sum of squares for the residual is low in relation to the sum of squares for the regression, the implication is that the independent variable explains at least some of the variation in the dependent variable. An easy way to spot weak results is if the sum of squares for the residual approaches the total sum of squares itself.

The column labeled "Mean Square" is simply the data from the sum of "Sum of Squares" column divided by the degrees of freedom (df). In general, analysts rarely interpret the output in this column. You should be aware, however, that it is undesirable for the value for the "Regression" df to be anywhere near the value for the "Total" df. Each time we add an explanatory variable to a model, the df value for the regression increases by one. If the degrees of freedom for the regression approach the degrees of freedom for the entire model, we have included almost as many independent variables as there are total observations for the dependent variable. Thus, "explained variance" becomes meaningless.

The column labeled "F" displays the F statistic. Because the F statistic is more relevant to multiple regression, we will defer explaining the meaning of this term until later in the chapter.

Model Summary

This section provides information about the overall "fit" of the model.

The column labeled "R" displays the correlation coefficient. As we noted in Chapter 17, we rarely interpret the correlation coefficient when analyzing regression output. It is much more common to report the R^2, which appears in the column to the right of the "R" column. Remember that you can calculate the value for R^2 by using the data from the "Sum of Squares" column found in the ANOVA section. Even though an adjusted R^2 value appears on the output, it has far more meaning in the context of multiple regression models. Finally, the standard error of the estimate (see Chapter 17) appears in the last column.

Example 2

The regression output for the police cars and average speed example was ideal for demonstrating the results of a statistically significant relationship. Table 21.2 displays regression results for the data in Table 17.4, where the independent variable is the number of police cars on patrol in Normal, Oklahoma, and the dependent variable is the number of indecent exposure arrests in Kansas City, Missouri. Common sense tells us that it is silly to hypothesize a relationship between these two variables. We generate a regression with these data to give you a sense of what output looks like when there is no relationship between the independent and dependent variables.

This example should also serve as a reminder of a point we made in Chapter 3 regarding the use of statistical tools for testing causal relationships. Computers and statistical software packages will generate output, even if the hypothesized relationship examined is completely ridiculous. The fact that computers can quickly generate results does not mean you should use them in place of common sense. As an analyst you should always have a sound rationale for studying particular research questions.

Coefficients

The results from the coefficients section clearly indicate that a relationship does not exist between the number of police cars in Normal and indecent exposure arrest rates in Kansas City. The t score for the slope is $-.263$, with a probability of .805. The probability figure indicates that there is about an 81% chance that the null hypothesis of $B = 0$ (that is, no relationship) is true.

ANOVA

An easy way to determine whether an independent variable does a good job of explaining variation in a dependent variable is to look at the sum of squares

Table 21.2 SPSS Output for Police Cars and Arrests Data

Model Summary

Model	R	R^2	Adjusted R^2	Std. Error of the Estimate
1	.130[a]	.017	0	24.51462

[a]Predictors: (Constant), CARS.

ANOVA[b]

Model		Sum of Squares	df	Mean Square	F	Significance
	Regression	41.467	1	41.467	.069	.806[a]
1	Residual	2,403.866	4	600.966		
	Total	2,445.333	5			

[a]Predictors: (Constant), CARS.
[b]Dependent variable: ARRESTS.

Coefficients[a]

Model		Unstandardized Coefficients		Standardized Coefficients		
		B	Std. Error	Beta	t	Significance
1	(Constant)	46.183	19.894		2.321	.081
	CARS	−1.232	4.689	−.130	−.263	.806

[a]Dependent variable: ARRESTS.

© Cengage Learning

values. In this case, the sum of squares for the residual or error is 2,403.86. The total sum of squares is 2,445.33. When we divide the first number by the second, we get a result of .983; this means that over 98% of the variation in the dependent variable remains unexplained. The sum of squares for the regression is 41.46. When we divide this number by the total sum of squares, the result is .017. This figure indicates that the "police cars" variable explains less than 2% of the variation in the dependent variable "indecent exposure arrests."

Model Summary

The R^2 and adjusted R^2 values mirror the results found in the ANOVA section. The R^2 of .017 shows that the number of police cars on patrol in Normal explains less than 2% of the variance in arrest rates in Kansas City.

If the two variables are unrelated, you may be wondering why the R^2 is greater than zero. Even though the slope coefficient is not statistically significant, the independent variable still absorbs 1 df. In cases like this, R^2 values above zero are possible simply because of the way R^2 is calculated. The adjusted R^2 of zero indicates that the small amount of explanatory power indicated by the R^2 is purely the result of the insignificant independent variable absorbing a degree of freedom, rather than having any meaningful explanatory power.

Multiple Regression Output

For the next example, we will explain multiple regression output. The legislative audit bureau for the state of Arkansas has gathered data for 15 community mental health centers across the state. State officials want to obtain a better understanding of differences in employee satisfaction rates across branch locations. Employee satisfaction is measured as the percentage of total employees at each branch who are satisfied with their jobs (SATISF).

Three independent variables are included in the regression equation. The number of clients served per year is used to see how differences in workload affect satisfaction rates (CLIENTS). The second variable is the average years of experience of supervisory and managerial employees (JOBEXPR). State officials hypothesize that more experienced managers are better able to motivate their employees. Finally, the age of the facility is used to assess whether the setting itself affects employee satisfaction rates (AGEFACT). The results for this regression are shown in Table 21.3. Because we have already explained what the terms displayed on the output mean, we will move directly to interpretation.

Coefficients

The value for the intercept is 110. Sometimes the intercept term takes on unrealistic values. In the present case, the literal interpretation is that if the number of clients, managerial experience, and age of facility were all equal to zero, 110% of employees would be satisfied with their jobs. This is clearly impossible, given that the maximum percentage of satisfied employees cannot exceed 100%. Unrealistic values for the intercept are not uncommon, so you should not be concerned when you come across cases like this.

The coefficients for the independent variables indicate that the number of clients served and the years of managerial experience are statistically significant. The coefficient for age of facility is not statistically significant, as indicated by the t score of $-.48$. The "Significance" column shows the probabilities associated with each partial slope. With the level of significance at .64, the partial slope for facility age is clearly not even close to the traditional .05 cutoff for statistical significance. Remember that in each case, the t statistics for each partial slope is calculated by dividing the partial slope coefficient by its standard error.

As we noted in Chapter 20, model specification issues should be considered before automatically removing statistically insignificant independent variables from a regression equation. In this case, the knowledge that the age of the facility does not seem to affect employee satisfaction rates could be valuable by pointing state officials toward other variables that are more likely to improve the explanatory performance of the regression model.

Table 21.3	SPSS Multiple Regression Output

Model Summary

Model	R	R^2	Adjusted R^2	Std. Error of the Estimate
1	.965[a]	.930	.911	4.117

[a]Predictors: (Constant), AGEFACT, JOBEXPR, CLIENTS.

ANOVA[b]

Model		Sum of Squares	df	Mean Square	F	Significance
	Regression	2,490.459	3	830.153	48.970	.000[a]
1	Residual	186.475	11	16.952		
	Total	2,676.933	14			

[a]Predictors: (Constant), AGEFACT, JOBEXPR, CLIENTS.
[b]Dependent variable: SATISF.

Coefficients[a]

Model		Unstandardized Coefficients		Standardized Coefficients	t	Significance
		B	Std. Error	Beta		
	(Constant)	110.093	27.846		3.954	.002
1	CLIENTS	−.127	.055	−.461	−2.317	.041
	JOBEXPR	3.260	1.114	.543	2.900	.014
	AGEFACT	−.037	.076	−.045	−.480	.641

[a]Dependent variable: SATISF.

Of course, the other option is simply to remove the age of facility variable and reestimate the regression equation. If you drop insignificant variables from a model, you should be aware that the audience who sees the final results might ask why certain variables were left out or excluded. For example, legislators who read a summary report might assume that age of facility was not considered at all when conducting the analysis. To ensure the intended audience knows which independent variables were used in the final equation, you may want to report and discuss the results for the original model briefly or in a footnote.

Standardized Coefficients

The "Standardized Coefficients" column presents partial slope and intercept values in standard deviation units. Standardized coefficients are more commonly referred to as *beta weights*. Beta weights are more useful in the case of multiple regression than they are for bivariate regression.

Beta weights are used to assess the relative effect of each partial slope coefficient. From our discussion of standard normal scores in Chapter 7, you may remember that when variables are measured on different scales, they are often difficult to compare. In the present case, the number of clients served ranges from 320 to 502, whereas managerial experience ranges from 3 to 9 years. Determining the relative impact of each variable can be difficult because the scales are very different. Beta weights address this problem by transforming the values for each partial slope into a common metric: standard deviation units.

A beta weight reveals the amount of change in the dependent variable (expressed in standard deviations) for every one standard deviation change in the independent variable. For example, the beta weight for the number of clients is $-.46$. This means that a one standard deviation change in the number of clients will result in a $-.46$ standard deviation decrease in employee satisfaction. The beta weight for managerial experience is .54, indicating that a one standard deviation change in this variable leads to a .54 standard deviation increase in employee satisfaction.

Regarding the unstandardized coefficients for these two variables, the coefficient for managerial experience is much larger than the coefficient for the number of employees. When the variables are expressed as beta weights, the magnitude of change for managerial experience is still larger than it is for the number of employees, but not by nearly as much. A one standard deviation change in either variable results in approximately half a standard deviation change in the dependent variable.

Although beta weights can be useful for assessing the relative impact of independent variables in a regression equation, analysts often report unstandardized coefficients because they are easier to interpret. Even when the beta weight for a particular variable is larger than the beta weights for all of the other variables in an equation, you have not necessarily discovered *the* independent variable that will always be most influential in explaining variation in the dependent variable. The independent variable with the largest beta weight is most influential only relative to the other independent variables *currently* included in the regression equation. The magnitude of beta weights can change when new variables are added or existing variables are removed from an equation. Values for beta weights can also change when the number of observations in a data set changes. For example, the number of cases in a data set might change if an analyst is updating a data set after new data have become available.

The *F* Statistic

In multiple regression, the *F* statistic shows whether the partial slope coefficients for all of the independent variables taken together as a group are equal to zero. If all of the partial slope coefficients in a multiple regression lack explanatory power, the *F* statistic will be very low. The "Significance" column next to the *F* statistic reveals the probability of all partial slope coefficients in the equation being equal to zero. The larger the *F* statistic, the more likely it is that at least one of the independent variables is statistically significant (i.e., not equal to 0).

In the current example, the F statistic of 48.97 indicates that there is virtually no chance that all of the partial slopes are equal to zero.

The F statistic is useful for assessing whether multicollinearity (i.e., high intercorrelation or interrelationship among the independent variables) is a problem (see Chapter 20). If the value for the F statistic indicates a low probability that all partial slopes are equal to zero but none of the partial slope coefficients is statistically significant, this combination often indicates the presence of high multicollinearity (intercorrelation) between two or more of the independent variables.

ANOVA

The ANOVA section for multiple regression is interpreted in the same way as it is for bivariate regression. The overall explanatory power of the model can be assessed by comparing the sum of squares for the regression and for the residual to the total sum of squares. When we divide the sum of squares for the regression, 2,490, by the total sum of squares value, 2,676, the result is .9305. This figure indicates that all three independent variables together explain about 93% of the variation in employee satisfaction rates. The sum of squares for the residual is 186. When we divide this number by the total sum of squares, the result is .0695. This figure indicates that about 7% of the variation in employee satisfaction rates remains unexplained.

Model Summary

Although R^2 and adjusted R^2 values are provided for both bivariate and multivariate regression equations, the adjusted R^2 is more useful for interpreting the latter. The R^2 of .93 indicates that the number of clients, managerial experience, and age of facility explain about 93% of the variation in employee satisfaction rates. Earlier we found that the partial slope coefficient for the age of facility variable was not statistically significant. The slightly lower adjusted R^2 of .91 reflects this finding.

The drop-off in explanatory power for this model is not very dramatic. When the adjusted R^2 is substantially lower than the R^2, it is usually a good idea to identify the partial slope coefficients with insignificant t scores to determine whether these variables should remain in the model.

Dummy Variable Regression Output

For the final example in this chapter, we will interpret the results of multiple regression output where a dummy variable is included as an independent variable (Table 21.4). In this example, a research intern at a state agency is asked to analyze the impact holding a master's degree has on employee salaries. The dependent variable is simply employee salaries in dollars (SALARY). The first independent variable is a dummy variable, coded "1" if the employee has a master's degree and "0" if not (MASTERS). The intern also includes a second independent variable in the analysis: employee experience, measured in years (YEARS).

Table 21.4	SPSS Multiple Regression Output Containing a Dummy Variable

Model Summary

Model	R	R^2	Adjusted R^2	Std. Error of the Estimate
1	.818[a]	.670	.640	7,973.406

[a]Predictors: (Constant), MASTERS, YEARS.

ANOVA[a]

Model		Sum of Squares	df	Mean Square	F	Sig.
	Regression	2,834,946,129.30	2	1,417,473,064.65	22.296	.000[b]
1	Residual	1,398,654,632.06	22	63,575,210.548		
	Total	4,233,600,761.36	24			

[a]Dependent variable: SALARY.
[b]Predictors: (Constant), MASTERS, YEARS.

Coefficients[a]

Model		Unstandardized Coefficients		Standardized Coefficients	t	Sig.
		B	Std. Error	Beta		
	(Constant)	32,214.835	3,084.589		10.444	.000
1	YEARS	2,487.731	389.076	.784	6.394	.000
	MASTERS	7,645.084	3,422.594	.274	2.234	.036

[a]Dependent variable: SALARY.

Coefficients

While the coefficients for both of the independent variables are statistically significant ($p < .05$), we are particularly interested in the interpretation of the dummy variable. As discussed in Chapter 18, a *dummy variable* is a two-category variable that is usually coded 1 if a condition is met (for example, an organization is nonprofit) versus 0 if the condition is not met (the organization is not nonprofit). The value for the "master's" dummy coefficient is 7,645. To properly interpret this or any other dummy variable, an analyst always needs to record how the variable was originally coded (i.e., what the 0 and 1 codes mean substantively).

When working with a dummy variable in a statistical software package, remember that the slope coefficient will always express the effect of the variable in terms of the category that is coded as a "1." In the present case, the coefficient indicates that employees with a master's degree have salaries $7,645 higher than those without a master's degree (controlling for employee experience). Because the t statistic is significant ($p < .05$), this result indicates that there is a difference in salaries for the two groups of employees.

Table 21.5	Different Ways to Code a Dummy Variable	
	Original Dummy	New Dummy
	1 = Master's Degree	1 = no Master's Degree
	0 = no Master's Degree	0 = Master's Degree
	0	1
	1	0
	0	1
	1	0
	0	1
	0	1
	1	0
	0	1
	0	1
	0	1
	0	1
	1	0
	0	1
	0	1
	1	0
	0	1
	1	0
	0	1
	0	1
	1	0
	1	0
	0	1
	0	1
	1	0

How would the results be affected if an analyst decided to code the possession of a master's degree as 0 and the lack of a master's degree as 1? Each version of the dummy variable is presented in Table 21.5. Each row represents one case or observation. The SPSS output with the new version of the "master's degree" dummy variable appears in Table 21.6 on page 432.

The only thing that changes in the regression output when the new version of the dummy variable is used is the direction or sign (positive or negative) of the

| Table 21.6 | SPSS Regression Output with Recoded Dummy Variable |

Model Summary

Model	R	R^2	Adjusted R^2	Std. Error of the Estimate
1	.818[a]	.670	.640	7,973.406

[a]Predictors: (Constant), MASTERSB, YEARS.

ANOVA[a]

Model		Sum of Squares	df	Mean Square	F	Sig.
	Regression	2,834,946,129.30	2	1,417,473,064.65	22.296	.000[b]
1	Residual	1,398,654,632.06	22	63,575,210.548		
	Total	4,233,600,761.36	24			

[a]Dependent variable: SALARY.
[b]Predictors: (Constant), MASTERSB, YEARS.

Coefficients[a]

Model		Unstandardized Coefficients		Standardized Coefficients	t	Sig.
		B	Std. Error	Beta		
	(Constant)	39,859.919	3,598.876		11.076	.000
1	YEARS	2,487.731	389.076	.784	6.394	.000
	MASTERSB	−7,645.084	3,422.594	−.274	−2.234	.036

[a]Dependent variable: SALARY.

coefficient. The magnitude (−7,645) is still exactly the same as it was in the first equation. Because "no master's degree" is coded as "1" in this case, the substantive interpretation of the coefficient is that employees who do *not* hold a master's degree have salaries $7,645 lower than those who do have a master's degree (controlling for years of experience).

For purposes of consistency and interpretation, we recommend that the values for the "1" category in a dummy variable be reserved for cases that possess a particular attribute, or where a condition does exist. The values for the "0" category should be reserved for cases that do not possess a particular attribute, or where a condition does not exist. If an analyst uses several dummy variables and does not stick to a consistent definition for whether the 1's or 0's indicate the presence or absence of an attribute, interpretation of the results will be very confusing—both to the audience and the analyst.

You should not interpret or report standardized regression coefficients for regression equations containing dummy variables. Unstandardized coefficients should always be reported when a regression model contains dummy variables.

What to Report when Discussing Regression Output

The short answer to what you should report when discussing regression output is to report anything your supervisor asks you to report. In the problems presented in Chapters 17 through 20, we focused on interpreting values for the intercept, slopes, and partial slopes. When summarizing regression results, you should be able to discuss the meaning of these coefficients in ordinary language without using a lot of jargon or technical terms. You should also note whether the slope or partial slope coefficients are statistically significant. Finally, you should discuss the R^2 or adjusted R^2 values to provide a sense of the overall explanatory power of the model.

Data Management Issues

At this point, you are probably eager to perform statistical analyses using a computer software package such as SPSS, SAS, or Stata. A statistical package program can produce regression output for a data set containing thousands of observations in seconds. Although you may be tempted to move immediately to advanced statistical analyses, you should first take some important data management issues into account.

Managing Data Sets

It is always good practice to have both a working data set and a master data set. Considerable time, effort, and money can be wasted if you make irreversible changes to a data set only to find later that you need a copy of the data set in its original form. To make a working data set, you can simply save your working data set by using a name that is different from the name of the master data set.

Creating a working file is important because you may find it necessary to recode or transform variables in the master (original) data set. For example, you may decide to recode an interval-level variable into an ordinal variable to create a contingency table. Or you may decide to collapse an ordinal-level variable with 10 categories into an ordinal variable with only three categories.

If you overwrite a variable when recoding data, a problem can arise if you save the data set and later find that you need the variable in its original form. Aside from recoding variables only in a working data set, it is good practice not to overwrite existing variables in a database. Instead, you should leave variables in their original form and create new recoded variables with new names. For example, a recoded version of VAR1 could be created, named, and saved as VAR1RECODED.

Creating subsets of larger data sets is another reason for having both working and master data sets. Analysts sometimes find it necessary to truncate data sets to include only a subset of cases. For example, if an analyst has a large data set with thousands of observations for dozens of branch offices, he or she may want to conduct an analysis using only cases for one or two specific branch locations. It would be very risky and ill-advised for an analyst to delete large numbers of cases in the master data set while trying to remember not to click on the "save file" button as he or she is working with the data set. A large number of cases could be lost if an error were made in saving.

Missing Values

Missing values for a variable are those for which no legitimate responses or scores are available. SPSS refers to nonmissing cases as "valid cases." Missing values occur for a variety of reasons: a respondent refuses to answer a question in a survey, data are lost or miscoded, the data may not be available for all cases, and so forth. Note that the amount of missing data and the particular cases with missing data usually vary across the variables in a data set. For example, gender may be available for all cases, education level may be available for most cases, but a more sensitive variable on age may have a large amount of missing data.

Missing data values should always be addressed before conducting statistical analyses. For example, only 65% of clients who complete a survey administered by a social services agency might answer the question, "What is your annual income?" Or when working with a time series data set that contains 20 variables covering 72 months, all 72 data points may not be available for all 20 variables.

Identifying missing data values prior to analysis is important for several reasons. First, if a key variable has a substantial number of missing values, making valid conclusions about statistical relationships becomes more difficult. For example, if the values for a key variable consist mostly of missing values, it may be difficult to make inferences or study causal relationships with so few cases. If an analyst performs multiple regression analysis using SPSS, the default setting is to include only those cases with nonmissing values for each variable. SPSS will produce an equation based only on those cases for which data are available for all variables. As a result, in a data set where many variables have missing data, the number of cases that are actually analyzed could be substantially reduced. For example, in a data set with 100 cases, where the variable for gender has 100 cases, the variable for education has 85 cases, and the variable for age has 60 cases, you are likely to end up with fewer than 60 valid cases (the cases with missing data on some variables may be different from the cases with missing data on other variables).

Second, identifying missing values is especially useful for spotting potential problems with survey questions. If a small percentage of survey respondents provide answers to certain questions, the large number of missing responses might be due to poorly worded questions. The individuals filling out the survey questionnaires may simply leave confusing, ambiguous, or loaded questions blank. When the data set contains a great amount of missing data, the analyst may need to send out new survey forms with different questions in order to increase response rates and completion rates on individual items.

Because statistical software packages treat missing observations differently, you should not assume that the software package you are using will automatically recognize missing observations and make the necessary adjustments, such as removing cases with missing data from analytical procedures. Many software packages require that missing values be defined as a number, such as 9 or 99 (depending on the number of digits in data values for a variable) before the observations are defined as missing. You should not define missing values as 0's because in many cases zero values are legitimate responses. Prior to performing any statistical analyses, you should familiarize yourself with the procedures employed to recognize and label missing data values in the particular statistical package you use. For more information on dealing with missing data when conducting statistical analyses, consult a textbook on the subject (e.g., McKnight et al., 2007).

The Importance of Examining Descriptive Statistics Prior to Using More Advanced Statistical Techniques

One of the biggest mistakes beginning analysts make is jumping straight to techniques such as contingency tables or regression analysis without first running descriptive statistics for the variables used in the analysis. Running descriptive statistics is important because doing so can help identify outliers or data entry errors.

The Range and Other Descriptive Statistics

The range is one of the most useful diagnostic tools for spotting outliers or data entry errors (see Chapter 6). Spotting data entry errors would be easy if data sets contained only 10 to 15 rows of data and only a few variables. What happens, however, when a data set contains several thousand rows of data and dozens of variables? "Eyeballing" the data is not practical in such instances.

The range is useful because it provides information about the lowest and highest values for a variable. This statistic is extremely helpful for discovering miscoded data or outliers. The utility of identifying the highest and lowest values for the variables in a data set is that we usually know ahead of time the legitimate range of values a variable can take. For example, two of the authors of this text were once working with data on average teacher salaries for a set of public schools. When we calculated the range for this variable, the minimum value was $29,000 and the maximum value was $360,000. Before you decide to quit your MPA program to become a public school teacher, you should realize that what actually happened in this case was that an extra zero was accidentally added to the numbers for some school districts. After correcting the data entry errors, we found that the actual range was $29,000 to $36,000.

As an analyst in a government or nonprofit setting, you may have to work with data that have passed through several hands. For example, clients or citizens fill out forms, which are then processed by administrative clerks, which are then matched with other data to create a data set. In other cases, you may be working with a data set that was originally put together by another party, such as a state or federal agency. As data pass through many hands, data entry errors can be made along the way. The point is that you should confirm, rather than assume, that your data set is free of errors before undertaking any statistical analyses.

When outliers have been identified, it is important not to delete or change outlying observations automatically. You should first determine the reason why the values are so extreme in relation to the other data points. Sometimes outliers are not the result of data-coding errors but are instead substantively important observations that should not be deleted or recoded. For example, in international relations studies, the United States may stand out on measures of average wealth; in studies of the states, the larger states may take extreme values on measures of urban population.

In addition to using the range to detect outliers, you should calculate descriptive statistics for all variables prior to performing more advanced data analysis techniques. If the values for a particular measure of central tendency or measure of dispersion seem abnormally high or low, a closer look at the data may be warranted. Analysts sometimes accompany the results obtained from more advanced statistical techniques such as regression analysis with a table that lists the means and standard deviations for all of the variables used in the analysis. This procedure is useful for the audience—and the analyst.

The Importance of Plotting Data before Analysis

An analyst can get a better idea of the shape of a data distribution or relationship by plotting the data on a set of coordinate axes prior to analysis. Data plots provide analysts with two useful pieces of information. First, data plots can be used to locate outliers. Even when the number of observations is large, extreme values tend to stand out on graphs.

Second, plotting variables on a set of coordinate axes helps an analyst get a sense of the functional form of a relationship. Although regression analysis should be used to assess formally whether a relationship exists between an independent variable and a dependent variable, plotting the variables beforehand can provide clues about whether the relationship (if any) is linear. Recall from Chapter 18 that one of the assumptions of regression analysis is that the relationship between an independent variable and a dependent variable should be linear. If the relationship is quadratic, cubic, or logarithmic, traditional regression analysis without the necessary adjustments will provide misleading results (see Chapter 20). A graphical plot is a simple tool that can tell the analyst whether nonlinear estimation methods or transformation of the data may be necessary. Those interested in learning more about how to detect patterns in the data visually should see Few (2009).

Chapter Summary

When regression analysis is performed using statistical software packages such as SPSS, SAS, or Stata, the output generated will provide a large amount of information about each regression equation. At a minimum, analysts usually report and describe the substantive meaning of regression coefficients and R^2 values.

The ANOVA section of regression output allows an analyst to assess the amount of error present in a model and the proportion of variance in the dependent variable that is explained by the independent variable(s). Although ANOVA output provides useful information about the overall fit of a regression model, analysts more commonly report and discuss R^2 and adjusted R^2 values.

Standardized regression coefficients are useful for multiple regression. Standardized coefficients or beta weights make it possible to compare the relative magnitude of partial slope coefficients within a model by expressing the slopes in terms of standard deviation units. Analysts generally prefer reporting unstandardized rather than standardized coefficients because the former are easier to interpret.

A good analyst will always run descriptive statistics and look for data entry errors or missing values prior to performing regression analysis or any other advanced data analysis techniques. Missing data, outliers, or miscoded data can affect the quality of the results obtained from more advanced statistical analysis techniques—which, in turn, can affect the quality of the inferences and conclusions made using the statistical output. Statistical software packages can calculate all of these key diagnostic tools very quickly. An analyst should never jump straight to more advanced techniques before taking these basic preliminary steps.

Problems

21.1 The Director of Economic Development in Potto Gulch, Wisconsin, is interested in studying the relationship between business activity and spending on social welfare programs. Specifically, she hypothesizes that as business activity increases the boost to the local economy (mainly through job creation) should result in lower spending on programs for the poor. To test this hypothesis, the director gathers annual data for the last 11 years on three variables. The dependent variable is annual spending on social welfare programs (in millions of dollars). The director feels that the number of business permits issued each year is a good indicator of economic activity and selects this as the first independent variable (BPRMT). The second independent variable is the number of residents in Potto Gulch (POP). The regression output is displayed below.

Model Summary

Model	R	R^2	Adj. R^2	Std. Error of the Estimate
1	.791[a]	.626	.532	800,770.013

[a]Predictors: (Constant), BPRMT, POP.

ANOVA[b]

Model		Sum of Squares	df	Mean Square	F	Significance
	Regression	8,568,393,095,762.110	2	4,284,196,547,881.058	6.681	.020[a]
1	Residual	5,129,860,913,328.790	8	641,232,614,166.099		
	Total	13,698,254,009,090.910	10			

[a]Predictors: (Constant), BPRMT, POP.
[b]Dependent variable: EXPENDIT.

Coefficients[a]

Model		Unstandardized Coefficients		Standardized Coefficients	t	Significance
		B	Std. Error	Beta		
	(Constant)	3,655,278.783	8,482,054.890		.431	.678
1	POP	109.855	100.721	.293	1.091	.307
	BPRMT	−5,049.119	2,339.638	−.581	−2.158	.063

[a]Dependent variable: EXPENDIT.

(a) Interpret the slopes and intercept for this model. What substantive conclusion can the director make about the relationship between business activity and spending on social welfare programs?

(b) The director is concerned about the drop in the explanatory power of the model indicated by the adjusted R^2 value. What is probably the reason why the adjusted R^2 is lower than R^2?

(c) The director has located data on the actual number of Potto Gulch citizens receiving social welfare assistance each year. If the director includes this new variable in the model, which of the current independent variables should be removed from the model? Explain.

21.2 The director of the Northern Tennessee Association of Local Governments is conducting a study on differences in average property taxes (in thousands of dollars) that residents in 15 local communities pay on their homes. The director believes that variations in property taxes are a function of two variables: the number of government employees on staff in each city (EMPLOYEES) and city size, measured in square miles (SIZE). The director uses SPSS to generate the following regression, where the average property tax per residence is the dependent variable.

Model Summary

Model	R	R^2	Adj. R^2	Std. Error of the Estimate
1	.983[a]	.967	.961	112.85532

[a]Predictors: (Constant), SIZE, EXPLOYEES.

ANOVA[b]

Model		Sum of Squares	df	Mean Square	F	Significance
	Regression	4,421,115.713	2	2,210,557.857	173.563	.000[a]
1	Residual	152,835.887	12	12,736.324		
	Total	4,573,951.600	14			

[a]Predictors: (Constant), SIZE EMPLOYEES.
[b]Dependent variable: PTAX.

Coefficients[a]

Model		Unstandardized Coefficients		Standardized Coefficients		
		B	Std. Error	Beta	t	Significance
	(Constant)	938.736	336.866		2.787	.016
1	Employees	8.225	2.631	.564	3.126	.009
	Size	47.532	19.794	−.430	2.380	.035

[a]Dependent variable: PTAX.

(a) Interpret the intercept, slopes, and R^2 values.

(b) Interpret the standardized coefficients. Explain how the standardized coefficients differ in magnitude from the unstandardized coefficients.

21.3 The director of exhibits at the Grosse Out Pointe Institute of Modern and Trashy Art wants to know what drives monthly attendance figures. She believes that the number of new exhibits each month (EXHIBITS) is an important variable because the public has a large appetite for new and innovative trashy art. For the second independent variable, the director decides to study the impact of the season on attendance, reasoning that in cold-weather months, residents are more likely to attend the museum because there are fewer outdoor and recreational options available. The director creates a dummy variable (SEASON), coded 1 if the month is a cold-weather month (November through March) and 0 if not. The director uses SPSS to generate the following regression, where monthly attendance is the dependent variable.

Model Summary

Model	R	R^2	Adj. R^2	Std. Error of the Estimate
1	.925[a]	.857	.783	311.53355

[a]Predictors: (Constant), SEASON EXHIBIT.

ANOVA[b]

Model		Sum of Squares	df	Mean Square	F	Significance
	Regression	6,953,045.135	2	3,476,522.568	35.821	.000[a]
1	Residual	1,164,637.798	12	97,053.150		
	Total	8,117,682.933	14			

[a]Predictors: (Constant), SEASON, EXHIBIT.
[b]Dependent variable: ATTEND.

Coefficients[a]

Model		Unstandardized Coefficients		Standardized Coefficients		
		B	Std. Error	Beta	t	Significance
	(Constant)	2,659.058	304.018		8.746	.000
1	Exhibit	360.714	42.8560	.942	8.417	.000
	Season	153.784	168.032	.102	.915	.378

[a]Dependent variable: ATTEND.

(a) Interpret the intercept, slopes, and R^2.

(b) Interpret the adjusted R^2 value. What is probably the reason why the adjusted R^2 is somewhat lower than R^2?

21.4 Refer to the EDUCATION data set available at the book's companion website. Use the following set of independent variables—ALTEACH, REVPUP, CLASS, and PECD—to explain teacher turnover rates, or TETURN.

(a) Interpret the slopes, intercept, and R^2.

(b) Based on your interpretation of the standardized regression coefficients, which independent variable has the greatest impact on teacher turnover rates?

(Note: The data set for this problem is available on the book's companion website.)

21.5 Refer to the EDUCATION data set available at the book's companion website. Use the following set of independent variables—PAFR, PHISP, CLASS, and TETURN—to explain overall student pass rates, or PASSALL.

(a) Interpret the slopes, intercept, and R^2 for the model. Based on your interpretation of R^2, does it seem that relevant explanatory variables might be missing from the model? Explain.

(b) Add ATTEND to the existing set of independent variables and generate a second regression. Interpret the slopes, intercept, and R^2 for the model. Has the addition of a new independent variable improved the explanatory power of the model? Explain. *(Note: The data set for this problem is available on the book's companion website.)*

Annotated Bibliography

Allison, Paul D. *Multiple Regression: A Primer* (Thousand Oaks, CA: Pine Forge Press, 1999). A very good overview of regression analysis and regression assumptions. Clearly written, with an emphasis on explaining regression in a way that assumes little background in mathematics.

Ammons, David N. *Tools for Decision Making: A Practical Guide for Local Government,* 2nd ed. (Washington, DC: Congressional Quarterly Press, 2009). A clear and concise overview of a wide variety of analytical tools with useful public management applications.

Babbie, Earl R. *The Practice of Social Research,* 13th ed. (Belmont, CA: Wadsworth, 2012). An excellent introductory guide to the design, conduct, and evaluation of research.

Babbie, Earl R. *Survey Research Methods,* 2nd ed. (Belmont, CA: Wadsworth, 1990). Focuses on the design of surveys and the analysis of results. Contains a chapter on survey ethics.

Blom, Barry, and Salomon A. Guajardo. *Revenue Analysis and Forecasting* (Chicago, IL: Government Finance Officers Association, 2001). An excellent overview of applied forecasting techniques. A practical guide for the beginner that does not contain a lot of advanced math or complex formulas.

Campbell, Donald T., and Julian C. Stanley. *Experimental and Quasi-Experimental Designs for Research* (Boston, MA: Houghton Mifflin, 1975). Classic presentation of the strengths and weaknesses of important research designs.

Cook, Thomas, and Donald T. Campbell. *Quasi-Experimentation* (Boston, MA: Houghton Mifflin, 1979). A thorough discussion of the analysis of public programs in field settings.

Few, Stephen. *Now You See It: Simple Visualization Techniques for Quantitative Analysis* (Oakland, CA: Analytics Press, 2009). An excellent reference on how to use spreadsheets to detect and understand patterns in graphically displayed data.

Fowler, Floyd. *Survey Research Methods,* 4th ed. (Newbury Park, CA: Sage, 2008). A good overview of how to prepare and administer surveys.

Fox, John. *Regression Diagnostics: An Introduction* (Newbury Park, CA: Sage. Sage University Paper Series on Quantitative Applications in the Social Sciences, 07-079, 1991). An excellent overview of how to diagnose and address violations of regression assumptions. Provides practical advice on how to deal with multicollinearity, errors in model specification, heteroskedasticity, and other issues related to the assumptions of regression analysis.

Fox, John. *Applied Regression Analysis and Generalized Linear Models,* 2nd ed. (Thousand Oaks, CA: Sage Publications, 2008). A text with thorough coverage of regression diagnostics; best for those with strong background in math.

Frankfort-Nachmias, Chava, and David Nachmias. *Research Methods in the Social Sciences,* 6th ed. (New York: Freeman, 2000). A good introductory book on research methods and statistics. Emphasizes social science problems.

Graybill, Franklin A., and Hariharan K. Iyer. *Regression Analysis: Concepts and Applications* (Belmont, CA: Duxbury Press, 1994). An advanced text with emphasis on regression applications. A good reference book.

Gujarati, Dadomar N., and Dawn Porter. *Basic Econometrics,* 5th ed. (New York: McGraw-Hill, 2008). An intermediate econometrics text with in-depth coverage of regression analysis.

Hamilton, James D. *Time Series Analysis* (Princeton, NJ: Princeton University Press, 1994). A good overview of a wide variety of techniques for analyzing time series data.

Hamilton, Lawrence. *Regression with Graphics* (Pacific Grove, CA: Brooks/Cole, 1995). The hands-down best advanced book for using exploratory data analysis, graphics approaches, and regression diagnostics. One of the authors uses it, along with Pindyck and Rubinfeld, for his advanced class.

Hays, William L. *Statistics,* 5th ed. (Fort Worth, TX: Harcourt Brace, 1994). A very complete, basic treatment of statistics.

Johnson, Gail. *Research Methods for Public Administrators,* 2nd ed. (Armonk, NY: M. E. Sharpe, 2009). A solid, introductory book for beginning MPA students and practitioners that focuses on the interpretation and use of research findings and recognizes both the promise and the limitations of research within a political environment.

Kennedy, Peter. *A Guide to Econometrics,* 4th ed. (Malden, MA: Wiley-Blackwell, 2008). For those who want a good, intuitive description of some of the most advanced statistical procedures in economics.

Kerlinger, Fred N. *Foundations of Behavioral Research,* 4th ed. (Belmont, CA: Wadsworth, 1999). A classic text in research methods for the social sciences.

King, Gary. *Unifying Political Methodology: The Likelihood Theory of Statistical Inference* (New York: Cambridge

University Press, 1989). A sustained argument that the logic of least squares may be inappropriate, and that statistics based on maximum likelihood estimators are more appropriate in most instances. An advanced book that should be required reading for doctoral students in public administration and other fields.

Kleinbaum, David G., Lawrence L. Kupper, Keith E. Muller, and Azhar Nazim. *Applied Regression Analysis and Other Multivariate Methods,* 4th ed. (Florence, KY: Cengage Learning, 2008). For advanced students who want a detailed discussion of regression and analysis of variance.

Kurtz, Norman. *Statistical Analysis for the Social Sciences* (Needham Heights, MA: Allyn & Bacon, 1999). Provides straightforward, in-depth coverage of hypothesis testing and difference of means tests. A good source for those seeking in-depth knowledge of the principles of statistical inference.

Kutner, Michael, Christopher Nachtsheim, and John Neter. *Applied Linear Statistical Models,* 5th ed. (New York: McGraw-Hill, 2004). A solid applied statistics text. Excellent on probability, inference, and introduction to time series.

Langbein, Laura. *Public Program Evaluation: A Statistical Guide,* 2nd ed. (Armonk, NY: M. E. Sharpe, 2012). A comprehensive and somewhat advanced text designed to equip students and practitioners with the statistical skills needed to conduct program evaluation.

Lawrence, John A., and Pasternack, Barry A. *Applied Management Science: Modeling, Spreadsheet Analysis, and Communication for Decision Making* (Hoboken, NJ: John Wiley & Sons, Inc., 2002). The text focuses on modeling management science problems, analyzing the models, and communicating the results.

Long, J. Scott. *Regression Models for Categorical and Limited Dependent Variables* (Thousand Oaks, CA: Sage Publications, 1997). A very thorough guide to logit, probit, and other approaches for modeling limited dependent variables.

Maddala, G. S., and Kajal Lahiri. *Introduction to Econometrics,* 4th ed. (New York: Wiley, 2009). The most readable, but not all that readable for the novice, econometric book on the market.

Manheim, Jarol B., Richard C. Rich, and Lars Willnat. *Empirical Political Analysis: Research Methods in Political Science,* 7th ed. (New York: Longman, 2007). A readable discussion of how to plan, conduct, and write up a data-based study.

McDavid, James C., Irene Huse, and Laura R. L. Hawthorne. *Program Evaluation and Performance Measurement: An Introduction to Practice,* 2nd ed. (Los Angeles, CA: Sage Publications, 2013). A readable text and one of the few that covers program evaluation, performance evaluation, qualitative analysis, and economic approaches in the same volume.

McKnight, Patrick E., Katherine M. McKnight, Souraya Sidani, and Aurelio Jose Figueredo. *Missing Data: A Gentle Introduction* (New York: Guilford Press, 2007). A clearly written text that discusses both the consequences of missing data and methods for dealing with missing data in statistical analyses.

McLaughlin, Thomas A. *Streetsmart Financial Basics for Nonprofit Managers,* 3rd ed. (New York: Wiley, 2009). Hands down, the clearest treatment of quantitative management techniques useful for nonprofit financial management. Topics include financial ratio analysis, break-even analysis, and basic accounting. One of the best books for students who want to gain practical knowledge of how to analyze and interpret financial data for nonprofit organizations.

McNabb, David E. *Research Methods for Political Science: Quantitative and Qualitative Approaches*, 2nd ed. (Armonk, NY: M. E. Sharpe, 2009). A good introductory text focusing on political science that integrates both quantitative and qualitative approaches to research and covers a variety of topics in research methods, such as research design and specification of research problems.

Meier, Kenneth J., and Jeff Gill. *What Works? A New Approach to Program and Policy Analysis* (Boulder, CO: Westview Press, 2000). An innovative approach to the analysis that argues that most traditional regression approaches do not meet the needs of managers.

The book merges optimization techniques with regression.

Mendenhall, William, James E. Reinmuth, and Robert J. Beaver. *Statistics for Management and Economics,* 7th ed. (Belmont, CA: Duxbury Press, 1993). Focuses on parametric statistics. Good reference book for probability and applied regression.

Michel, R. Gregory. *Decision Tools for Budgetary Analysis* (Chicago: Government Finance Officers Association, 2001). An excellent overview of quantitative techniques useful for evaluating financial aspects of policy decisions. Topic coverage includes cost-effectiveness analysis, net present value analysis, and break-even analysis, among others. A nice complement to more theory-based discussions of decision-making techniques.

Miller, Delbert C., and Neil J. Salkind. *Handbook of Research Design and Social Measurement,* 6th ed. (Newbury Park, CA: Sage, 2002). An excellent, comprehensive reference on the research process, especially study design, measurement, data collection, and reporting results.

Mohr, Lawrence B. *Impact Analysis for Program Evaluation,* 2nd ed. (Thousand Oaks, CA: Sage Publications, 1995). A good resource for how to use various research designs when conducting program evaluations.

Mooney, Christopher Z., and Robert D. Duval. *Bootstrapping: A Nonparametric Approach to Statistical Inference* (Newbury Park, CA: Sage,

1993). A primer on a computationally intensive alternative to classical statistics.

Ott, Lyman, and Michael Longnecker. *An Introduction to Statistical Methods and Data Analysis,* 6th ed. (Belmont, CA: Brooks/Cole, 2010). Text contains a wide variety of problems from agriculture, politics, medicine, and so on. Intended for the beginning student.

Paulos, John A. *Innumeracy: Mathematical Illiteracy and Its Consequences* (New York: Farrar, Straus & Giroux, 2001). Provides an intuitive overview of various principles in probability using clever and amusing examples.

Paulos, John A. *A Mathematician Reads the Newspaper* (New York: Doubleday, 1997). An entertaining and informative look at the misuse of statistical data by the media. A good intuitive guide on how to evaluate probabilities and other statistical evidence.

Pindyck, Robert S., and Daniel L. Rubinfeld. *Econometric Models and Economic Forecasts,* 4th ed. (New York: McGraw-Hill/Irwin, 2000). A good advanced book, especially effective on time series.

Poister, Theodore H. *Measuring Performance in Public and Nonprofit Organizations* (San Francisco, CA: Jossey-Bass, 2003). A thorough overview of key issues in performance measurement, including the development of program logic models, guidelines for creating performance indicators, techniques for analyzing performance data, and the application of performance measurement to strategic management. General theories are illustrated with data and examples from a variety of governmental and nonprofit organizations.

Rea, Louis M., and Richard A. Parker. *Designing and Conducting Survey Research: A Comprehensive Guide,* 3rd ed. (San Francisco, CA: Jossey-Bass, 2005). A good, nontechnical guide to survey construction and implementation.

Secrest, Lee, Donald Campbell, and Richard D. Schwartz. *Unobtrusive Measures,* vol. 2 (Newbury Park, CA: Sage, 1999). A discussion of measurement under circumstances where good measures are difficult to find.

Tufte, Edward R. *The Visual Display of Quantitative Information,* 2nd ed. (Englewood Cliffs, NJ: Graphics Press, 2001). A classic text on how to effectively describe and summarize data using graphical techniques.

Webb, Eugene J., Donald T. Campbell, Richard D. Schwartz, and Lee Sechrest. *Unobtrusive Measures,* revised edition (Los Angeles: Sage Publications, 1999). The classic statement of the meaning and use of unobtrusive, nonreactive measures in the social sciences.

Welch, Susan, and John C. Comer. *Quantitative Methods for Public Administration: Techniques and Applications,* 3rd ed. (Long Grove, IL: Waveland Press, 2001). An introductory statistics book that primarily uses public policy examples.

Statistical Tables

| Table 1 | The Normal Distribution |

Each entry in the table indicates the proportion of the total area under the normal curve contained in the segment bounded by a perpendicular raised at the mean and a perpendicular raised at a distance of *z* standard deviation units.

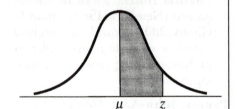

To illustrate: 40.99% of the area under a normal curve lies between the maximum ordinate and a point 1.34 standard deviation units away.

z	0.00	0.01	0.02	0.03	0.04	0.05	0.06	0.07	0.08	0.09
0.0	0.0000	0.0040	0.0080	0.0120	0.0160	0.0199	0.0239	0.0279	0.0319	0.0359
0.1	0.0398	0.0438	0.0478	0.0517	0.0557	0.0596	0.0636	0.0675	0.0714	0.0753
0.2	0.0793	0.0832	0.0871	0.0910	0.0948	0.0987	0.1026	0.1064	0.1103	0.1141
0.3	0.1179	0.1217	0.1255	0.1293	0.1331	0.1368	0.1406	0.1443	0.1480	0.1517
0.4	0.1554	0.1591	0.1628	0.1664	0.1700	0.1736	0.1772	0.1808	0.1844	0.1879
0.5	0.1915	0.1950	0.1985	0.2019	0.2054	0.2088	0.2123	0.2157	0.2190	0.2224
0.6	0.2257	0.2291	0.2324	0.2357	0.2389	0.2422	0.2454	0.2486	0.2518	0.2549
0.7	0.2580	0.2612	0.2642	0.2673	0.2704	0.2734	0.2764	0.2794	0.2823	0.2852
0.8	0.2881	0.2910	0.2939	0.2967	0.2995	0.3023	0.3051	0.3078	0.3106	0.3133
0.9	0.3159	0.3186	0.3212	0.3238	0.3264	0.3289	0.3315	0.3340	0.3365	0.3389
1.0	0.3413	0.3438	0.3461	0.3485	0.3508	0.3531	0.3554	0.3577	0.3599	0.3621
1.1	0.3643	0.3665	0.3686	0.3708	0.3729	0.3749	0.3770	0.3790	0.3810	0.3830
1.2	0.3849	0.3869	0.3888	0.3907	0.3925	0.3944	0.3962	0.3980	0.3997	0.4015

(continued)

Table 1		The Normal Distribution (continued)							
z	0.00	0.01	0.02	0.03	0.04	0.05	0.06	0.07	0.08	0.09
1.3	0.4032	0.4049	0.4066	0.4082	0.4099	0.4115	0.4131	0.4147	0.4162	0.4177
1.4	0.4192	0.4207	0.4222	0.4236	0.4251	0.4265	0.4279	0.4292	0.4306	0.4319
1.5	0.4332	0.4345	0.4357	0.4370	0.4382	0.4394	0.4406	0.4418	0.4429	0.4441
1.6	0.4452	0.4463	0.4474	0.4484	0.4495	0.4505	0.4515	0.4525	0.4535	0.4545
1.7	0.4554	0.4564	0.4573	0.4582	0.4591	0.4599	0.4608	0.4616	0.4625	0.4633
1.8	0.4641	0.4649	0.4656	0.4664	0.4671	0.4678	0.4686	0.4693	0.4699	0.4706
1.9	0.4713	0.4719	0.4726	0.4732	0.4738	0.4744	0.4750	0.4756	0.4761	0.4767
2.0	0.4772	0.4778	0.4783	0.4788	0.4793	0.4798	0.4803	0.4808	0.4812	0.4817
2.1	0.4821	0.4826	0.4830	0.4834	0.4838	0.4842	0.4846	0.4850	0.4854	0.4857
2.2	0.4861	0.4864	0.4868	0.4871	0.4875	0.4878	0.4881	0.4884	0.4887	0.4890
2.3	0.4893	0.4896	0.4898	0.4901	0.4904	0.4906	0.4909	0.4911	0.4913	0.4916
2.4	0.4918	0.4920	0.4922	0.4925	0.4927	0.4929	0.4931	0.4932	0.4934	0.4936
2.5	0.4938	0.4940	0.4941	0.4943	0.4945	0.4946	0.4948	0.4949	0.4951	0.4952
2.6	0.4953	0.4955	0.4956	0.4957	0.4959	0.4960	0.4961	0.4962	0.4963	0.4964
2.7	0.4965	0.4966	0.4967	0.4968	0.4969	0.4970	0.4971	0.4972	0.4973	0.4974
2.8	0.4974	0.4975	0.4976	0.4977	0.4977	0.4978	0.4979	0.4979	0.4980	0.4981
2.9	0.4981	0.4982	0.4982	0.4983	0.4984	0.4984	0.4985	0.4985	0.4986	0.4986
3.0	0.4986	0.4987	0.4987	0.4988	0.4988	0.4989	0.4989	0.4989	0.4990	0.4990
3.1	0.4990	0.4991	0.4991	0.4991	0.4992	0.4992	0.4992	0.4992	0.4993	0.4993
3.2	0.4993	0.4993	0.4994	0.4994	0.4994	0.4994	0.4994	0.4995	0.4995	0.4995
3.3	0.4995	0.4995	0.4995	0.4996	0.4996	0.4996	0.4996	0.4996	0.4996	0.4997
3.4	0.4997	0.4997	0.4997	0.4997	0.4997	0.4997	0.4997	0.4997	0.4998	0.4998
3.5	0.4998	0.4998	0.4998	0.4998	0.4998	0.4998	0.4998	0.4998	0.4998	0.4998
3.6	0.4998	0.4998	0.4999	0.4999	0.4999	0.4999	0.4999	0.4999	0.4999	0.4999
3.7	0.4999	0.4999	0.4999	0.4999	0.4999	0.4999	0.4999	0.4999	0.4999	0.4999
3.8	0.4999	0.4999	0.4999	0.4999	0.4999	0.4999	0.4999	0.5000	0.5000	0.5000
3.9	0.5000	0.5000	0.5000	0.5000	0.5000	0.5000	0.5000	0.5000	0.5000	0.5000

Table 2 Poisson Probability Distributions

Entry is probability mass $F(x)$ corresponding to $X = x$, where $F(x) = \lambda^x \exp(-\lambda)/x!$

					λ				
x	.1	.2	.3	.4	.5	.6	.7	.8	.9
0	0.9048	0.8187	0.7408	0.6703	0.6065	0.5488	0.4966	0.4493	0.4066
1	0.0905	0.1637	0.2222	0.2681	0.3033	0.3293	0.3476	0.3595	0.3659
2	0.0045	0.0164	0.0333	0.0536	0.0758	0.0988	0.1217	0.1438	0.1647
3	0.0002	0.0011	0.0033	0.0072	0.0126	0.0198	0.0284	0.0383	0.0494
4	0.0000	0.0001	0.0003	0.0007	0.0016	0.0030	0.0050	0.0077	0.0111
5	0.0000	0.0000	0.0000	0.0001	0.0002	0.0004	0.0007	0.0012	0.0020
6	0.0000	0.0000	0.0000	0.0000	0.0000	0.0000	0.0001	0.0002	0.0003

					λ				
x	1.0	1.5	2.0	2.5	3.0	3.5	4.0	4.5	5.0
0	0.3679	0.2231	0.1353	0.0821	0.0498	0.0302	0.0183	0.0111	0.0067
1	0.3679	0.3347	0.2707	0.2052	0.1494	0.1057	0.0733	0.0500	0.0337
2	0.1839	0.2510	0.2707	0.2565	0.2240	0.1850	0.1465	0.1125	0.0842
3	0.0613	0.1255	0.1804	0.2138	0.2240	0.2158	0.1954	0.1687	0.1404
4	0.0153	0.0471	0.0902	0.1336	0.1680	0.1888	0.1954	0.1898	0.1755
5	0.0031	0.0141	0.0361	0.0668	0.1008	0.1322	0.1563	0.1708	0.1755
6	0.0005	0.0035	0.0120	0.0278	0.0504	0.0771	0.1042	0.1281	0.1462
7	0.0001	0.0008	0.0034	0.0099	0.0216	0.0385	0.0595	0.0824	0.1044
8	0.0000	0.0001	0.0009	0.0031	0.0081	0.0169	0.0298	0.0463	0.0653
9	0.0000	0.0000	0.0002	0.0009	0.0027	0.0066	0.0132	0.0232	0.0363
10	0.0000	0.0000	0.0000	0.0002	0.0008	0.0023	0.0053	0.0104	0.0181
11	0.0000	0.0000	0.0000	0.0000	0.0002	0.0007	0.0019	0.0043	0.0082
12	0.0000	0.0000	0.0000	0.0000	0.0001	0.0002	0.0006	0.0016	0.0034
13	0.0000	0.0000	0.0000	0.0000	0.0000	0.0001	0.0002	0.0006	0.0013
14	0.0000	0.0000	0.0000	0.0000	0.0000	0.0000	0.0001	0.0002	0.0005
15	0.0000	0.0000	0.0000	0.0000	0.0000	0.0000	0.0000	0.0001	0.0002

(continued)

Table 2	Poisson Probability Distributions (continued)							

					λ				
x	5.5	6.0	6.5	7.0	7.5	8.0	9.0	10.0	11.0
0	0.0041	0.0025	0.0015	0.0009	0.0006	0.0003	0.0001	0.0000	0.0000
1	0.0225	0.0149	0.0098	0.0064	0.0041	0.0027	0.0011	0.0005	0.0002
2	0.0618	0.0446	0.0318	0.0223	0.0156	0.0107	0.0050	0.0023	0.0010
3	0.1133	0.0892	0.0688	0.0521	0.0389	0.0286	0.0150	0.0076	0.0037
4	0.1558	0.1339	0.1118	0.0912	0.0729	0.0573	0.0337	0.0189	0.0102
5	0.1714	0.1606	0.1454	0.1277	0.1094	0.0916	0.0607	0.0378	0.0224
6	0.1571	0.1606	0.1575	0.1490	0.1367	0.1221	0.0911	0.0631	0.0411
7	0.1234	0.1377	0.1462	0.1490	0.1465	0.1396	0.1171	0.0901	0.0646
8	0.0849	0.1033	0.1188	0.1304	0.1373	0.1396	0.1318	0.1126	0.0888
9	0.0519	0.0688	0.0858	0.1014	0.1144	0.1241	0.1318	0.1251	0.1085
10	0.0285	0.0413	0.0558	0.0710	0.0858	0.0993	0.1186	0.1251	0.1194
11	0.0143	0.0225	0.0330	0.0452	0.0585	0.0722	0.0970	0.1137	0.1194
12	0.0065	0.0113	0.0179	0.0263	0.0366	0.0481	0.0728	0.0948	0.1094
13	0.0028	0.0052	0.0089	0.0142	0.0211	0.0296	0.0504	0.0729	0.0926
14	0.0011	0.0022	0.0041	0.0071	0.0113	0.0169	0.0324	0.0521	0.0728
15	0.0004	0.0009	0.0018	0.0033	0.0057	0.0090	0.0194	0.0347	0.0534
16	0.0001	0.0003	0.0007	0.0014	0.0026	0.0045	0.0109	0.0217	0.0367
17	0.0000	0.0001	0.0003	0.0006	0.0012	0.0021	0.0058	0.0128	0.0237
18	0.0000	0.0000	0.0001	0.0002	0.0005	0.0009	0.0029	0.0071	0.0145
19	0.0000	0.0000	0.0000	0.0001	0.0002	0.0004	0.0014	0.0037	0.0084
20	0.0000	0.0000	0.0000	0.0000	0.0001	0.0002	0.0006	0.0019	0.0046
21	0.0000	0.0000	0.0000	0.0000	0.0000	0.0001	0.0003	0.0009	0.0024
22	0.0000	0.0000	0.0000	0.0000	0.0000	0.0000	0.0001	0.0004	0.0012
23	0.0000	0.0000	0.0000	0.0000	0.0000	0.0000	0.0000	0.0002	0.0006
24	0.0000	0.0000	0.0000	0.0000	0.0000	0.0000	0.0000	0.0001	0.0003
25	0.0000	0.0000	0.0000	0.0000	0.0000	0.0000	0.0000	0.0000	0.0001

(continued)

Table 2		Poisson Probability Distributions (continued)							

					λ				
x	12	13	14	15	16	17	18	19	20
0	0.0000	0.0000	0.0000	0.0000	0.0000	0.0000	0.0000	0.0000	0.0000
1	0.0001	0.0000	0.0000	0.0000	0.0000	0.0000	0.0000	0.0000	0.0000
2	0.0004	0.0002	0.0001	0.0000	0.0000	0.0000	0.0000	0.0000	0.0000
3	0.0018	0.0008	0.0004	0.0002	0.0001	0.0000	0.0000	0.0000	0.0000
4	0.0053	0.0027	0.0013	0.0006	0.0003	0.0001	0.0001	0.0000	0.0000
5	0.0127	0.0070	0.0037	0.0019	0.0010	0.0005	0.0002	0.0001	0.0001
6	0.0255	0.0152	0.0087	0.0048	0.0026	0.0014	0.0007	0.0004	0.0002
7	0.0437	0.0281	0.0174	0.0104	0.0060	0.0034	0.0019	0.0010	0.0005
8	0.0655	0.0457	0.0304	0.0194	0.0120	0.0072	0.0042	0.0024	0.0013
9	0.0874	0.0661	0.0473	0.0324	0.0213	0.0135	0.0083	0.0050	0.0029
10	0.1048	0.0859	0.0663	0.0486	0.0341	0.0230	0.0150	0.0095	0.0058
11	0.1144	0.1015	0.0844	0.0663	0.0496	0.0355	0.0245	0.0164	0.0106
12	0.1144	0.1099	0.0984	0.0829	0.0661	0.0504	0.0368	0.0259	0.0176
13	0.1056	0.1099	0.1060	0.0956	0.0814	0.0658	0.0509	0.0378	0.0271
14	0.0905	0.1021	0.1060	0.1024	0.0930	0.0800	0.0655	0.0514	0.0387
15	0.0724	0.0885	0.0989	0.1024	0.0992	0.0906	0.0786	0.0650	0.0516
16	0.0543	0.0719	0.0866	0.0960	0.0992	0.0963	0.0884	0.0772	0.0646
17	0.0383	0.0550	0.0713	0.0847	0.0934	0.0963	0.0936	0.0863	0.0760
18	0.0255	0.0397	0.0554	0.0706	0.0830	0.0909	0.0936	0.0911	0.0844
19	0.0161	0.0272	0.0409	0.0557	0.0699	0.0814	0.0887	0.0911	0.0888
20	0.0097	0.0177	0.0286	0.0418	0.0559	0.0692	0.0798	0.0866	0.0888
21	0.0055	0.0109	0.0191	0.0299	0.0426	0.0560	0.0684	0.0783	0.0846
22	0.0030	0.0065	0.0121	0.0204	0.0310	0.0433	0.0560	0.0876	0.0769
23	0.0016	0.0037	0.0074	0.0133	0.0216	0.0320	0.0438	0.0559	0.0669
24	0.0008	0.0020	0.0043	0.0083	0.0144	0.0226	0.0328	0.0442	0.0557
25	0.0004	0.0010	0.0024	0.0050	0.0092	0.0154	0.0237	0.0336	0.0446

(continued)

Table 2		Poisson Probability Distributions (continued)						

					λ				
x	12	13	14	15	16	17	18	19	20
26	0.0002	0.0005	0.0013	0.0029	0.0057	0.0101	0.0164	0.0240	0.0343
27	0.0001	0.0002	0.0007	0.0016	0.0034	0.0063	0.0109	0.0173	0.0254
28	0.0000	0.0001	0.0003	0.0009	0.0019	0.0038	0.0070	0.0117	0.0181
29	0.0000	0.0001	0.0002	0.0004	0.0011	0.0023	0.0044	0.0077	0.0125
30	0.0000	0.0000	0.0001	0.0002	0.0006	0.0013	0.0026	0.0049	0.0083
31	0.0000	0.0000	0.0000	0.0001	0.0003	0.0007	0.0015	0.0030	0.0054
32	0.0000	0.0000	0.0000	0.0001	0.0001	0.0004	0.0009	0.0018	0.0034
33	0.0000	0.0000	0.0000	0.0000	0.0001	0.0002	0.0005	0.0010	0.0020
34	0.0000	0.0000	0.0000	0.0000	0.0000	0.0001	0.0002	0.0006	0.0012
35	0.0000	0.0000	0.0000	0.0000	0.0000	0.0000	0.0001	0.0003	0.0007
36	0.0000	0.0000	0.0000	0.0000	0.0000	0.0000	0.0001	0.0002	0.0004
37	0.0000	0.0000	0.0000	0.0000	0.0000	0.0000	0.0000	0.0001	0.0002
38	0.0000	0.0000	0.0000	0.0000	0.0000	0.0000	0.0000	0.0000	0.0001
39	0.0000	0.0000	0.0000	0.0000	0.0000	0.0000	0.0000	0.0000	0.0001

Source: From J. Neter, W. Wasserman, and G. A. Whitmore, *Applied Statistics, 4th.* Copyright ©1993. Printed and Electronically reproduced by permission of Pearson Education, Inc., Upper Saddle River, New Jersey.

Table 3   The *t* Distribution

	Level of Significance for One-Tailed Test						
df	.10	.05	.025	.01	0.005	.001	.0005
1	3.078	6.314	12.71	31.821	63.657	—	636.619
2	1.886	2.920	4.31	6.965	9.925	—	31.598
3	1.638	2.353	3.19	4.541	5.841	—	12.941
4	1.533	2.132	2.78	3.747	4.604	7.18	8.610
5	1.476	2.015	2.57	3.365	4.032	5.90	6.859
6	1.440	1.943	2.45	3.143	3.707	5.21	5.959
7	1.415	1.895	2.37	2.998	3.499	4.79	5.405
8	1.397	1.860	2.31	2.896	3.355	4.51	5.041
9	1.383	1.833	2.27	2.821	3.250	4.30	4.781
10	1.372	1.812	2.23	2.764	3.169	4.15	4.587
11	1.363	1.796	2.20	2.718	3.106	4.03	4.437
12	1.356	1.782	2.18	2.681	3.055	3.93	4.318
13	1.350	1.771	2.16	2.650	3.012	3.86	4.221
14	1.345	1.761	2.15	2.624	2.977	3.79	4.140
15	1.341	1.753	2.13	2.602	2.947	3.74	4.073
16	1.337	1.746	2.12	2.583	2.921	3.69	4.015
17	1.333	1.740	2.11	2.567	2.898	3.65	3.965
18	1.330	1.734	2.10	2.552	2.878	3.62	3.922
19	1.328	1.729	2.09	2.539	2.861	3.58	3.883
20	1.325	1.725	2.09	2.528	2.845	3.56	3.850
21	1.323	1.721	2.08	2.518	2.831	3.53	3.819
22	1.321	1.717	2.07	2.508	2.819	3.51	3.792
23	1.319	1.714	2.07	2.500	2.807	3.49	3.767
24	1.318	1.711	2.06	2.492	2.797	3.47	3.745
25	1.316	1.708	2.06	2.485	2.787	3.45	3.725
26	1.315	1.706	2.06	2.479	2.779	3.44	3.707
27	1.314	1.703	2.05	2.473	2.771	3.43	3.690
28	1.313	1.701	2.05	2.467	2.763	3.41	3.674
29	1.311	1.699	2.05	2.462	2.756	3.40	3.659
30	1.310	1.697	2.04	2.457	2.750	3.39	3.646
∞	1.282	1.645	1.96	2.326	2.576	3.08	3.291

Source: Adapted from David G. Kleinbaum and Lawrence L. Kupper, *Applied Regression Analysis and Other Multivariable Methods*. Copyright © 1978. Published by Wadsworth/Duxbury Press.

Table 4	The Chi-Square Distribution				
p	0.10	0.05	0.025	0.01	0.005	df
	2.71	3.84	5.02	6.63	7.88	1
	4.61	5.99	7.38	9.21	10.60	2
	6.25	7.81	9.35	11.34	12.84	3
	7.78	9.49	11.14	13.28	14.86	4
	9.24	11.07	12.83	15.09	16.75	5
	10.64	12.59	14.45	16.81	18.55	6
	12.02	14.07	16.01	18.48	20.3	7
	13.36	15.51	17.53	20.1	22.0	8
	14.68	16.92	19.02	21.7	23.6	9
	15.99	18.31	20.5	23.2	25.2	10
	17.28	19.68	21.9	24.7	26.8	11
	18.55	21.0	23.3	26.2	28.3	12
	19.81	22.4	24.7	27.7	29.8	13
	21.1	23.7	26.1	29.1	31.3	14
	22.3	25.0	27.5	30.6	32.8	15
	23.5	26.3	28.8	32.0	34.3	16
	24.8	27.6	30.2	33.4	35.7	17
	26.0	28.9	31.5	34.8	37.2	18
	27.2	30.1	32.9	36.2	38.6	19
	28.4	31.4	34.2	37.6	40.0	20
	29.6	32.7	35.5	38.9	41.4	21
	30.8	33.9	36.8	40.3	42.8	22
	32.0	35.2	38.1	41.6	44.2	23
	33.2	36.4	39.4	43.0	45.6	24
	34.4	37.7	40.6	44.3	46.9	25
	35.6	38.9	41.9	45.6	48.3	26
	36.7	40.1	43.2	47.0	49.6	27
	37.9	41.3	44.5	48.3	51.0	28
	39.1	42.6	45.7	49.6	52.3	29
	40.3	43.8	47.0	50.9	53.7	30
	51.8	55.8	59.3	63.7	66.8	40
	63.2	67.5	71.4	76.2	79.5	50

(continued)

Table 4		The Chi-Square Distribution (continued)			
p	0.10	0.05	0.025	0.01	0.005	df
	74.4	79.1	83.3	88.4	92.0	60
	85.5	90.5	95.0	100.4	104.2	70
	96.6	101.9	106.6	112.3	116.3	80
	107.6	113.1	118.1	124.1	128.3	90
	118.5	124.3	129.6	135.8	140.2	100

Source: Adapted from David G. Kleinbaum and Lawrence L. Kupper, *Applied Regression Analysis and Other Multivariable Methods*. Copyright © 1978. Published by Wadsworth/Duxbury Press.

Table 5		Durbin-Watson Statistic Test Bounds									

Probability = .05

	k = 1		k = 2		k = 3		k = 4		k = 5		k = 6	
n	d_L	d_U	d_L	d_U	d_L	d_U	d_L	d_U	d_L	d_U	d_L	d_U
6	0.610	1.400	—	—	—	—	—	—	—	—	—	—
7	0.700	1.356	0.467	1.896	—	—	—	—	—	—	—	—
8	0.763	1.332	0.559	1.777	0.368	2.287	—	—	—	—	—	—
9	0.824	1.320	0.629	1.699	0.455	2.128	0.296	2.588	—	—	—	—
10	0.879	1.320	0.697	1.641	0.525	2.016	0.376	2.414	0.243	2.822	—	—
11	0.927	1.324	0.758	1.604	0.595	1.928	0.444	2.283	0.316	2.645	0.203	3.005
12	0.971	1.331	0.812	1.579	0.658	1.864	0.512	2.177	0.379	2.506	0.268	2.832
13	1.010	1.340	0.861	1.562	0.715	1.816	0.574	2.094	0.445	2.390	0.328	2.692
14	1.045	1.350	0.905	1.551	0.767	1.779	0.632	2.030	0.505	2.296	0.389	2.572
15	1.077	1.361	0.946	1.543	0.814	1.750	0.685	1.977	0.562	2.220	0.447	2.472
16	1.106	1.371	0.982	1.539	0.857	1.728	0.734	1.935	0.615	2.157	0.502	2.388
17	1.133	1.381	1.015	1.536	0.897	1.710	0.779	1.900	0.664	2.104	0.554	2.318
18	1.158	1.391	1.046	1.535	0.933	1.696	0.820	1.872	0.710	2.060	0.603	2.257
19	1.180	1.401	1.074	1.536	0.967	1.685	0.859	1.848	0.752	2.023	0.649	2.206
20	1.201	1.411	1.100	1.537	0.998	1.676	0.894	1.828	0.792	1.991	0.692	2.162
21	1.221	1.420	1.125	1.538	1.026	1.669	0.927	1.812	0.829	1.964	0.732	2.124
22	1.239	1.429	1.147	1.541	1.053	1.664	0.958	1.797	0.863	1.940	0.769	2.090
23	1.257	1.437	1.168	1.543	1.078	1.660	0.986	1.785	0.895	1.920	0.804	2.061
24	1.273	1.446	1.188	1.546	1.101	1.656	1.013	1.775	0.925	1.902	0.837	2.035
25	1.288	1.454	1.206	1.550	1.123	1.654	1.038	1.767	0.953	1.886	0.868	2.012
26	1.302	1.461	1.224	1.553	1.143	1.652	1.062	1.759	0.979	1.873	0.897	1.992
27	1.316	1.469	1.240	1.556	1.162	1.651	1.084	1.753	1.004	1.861	0.925	1.974
28	1.328	1.476	1.255	1.560	1.181	1.650	1.104	1.747	1.028	1.850	0.951	1.958
29	1.341	1.483	1.270	1.563	1.198	1.650	1.124	1.743	1.050	1.841	0.975	1.944
30	1.352	1.489	1.284	1.567	1.214	1.650	1.143	1.739	1.071	1.833	0.998	1.931

(continued)

| Table 5 | Durbin-Watson Statistic Test Bounds (continued) |

Probability = .05

	k = 1		k = 2		k = 3		k = 4		k = 5		k = 6	
n	d_L	d_U	d_L	d_U	d_L	d_U	d_L	d_U	d_L	d_U	d_L	d_U
31	1.363	1.496	1.297	1.570	1.229	1.650	1.160	1.735	1.090	1.825	1.020	1.920
32	1.373	1.502	1.309	1.574	1.244	1.650	1.177	1.732	1.109	1.819	1.041	1.909
33	1.383	1.508	1.321	1.577	1.258	1.651	1.193	1.730	1.127	1.813	1.061	1.900
34	1.393	1.514	1.333	1.580	1.271	1.652	1.208	1.728	1.144	1.808	1.080	1.891
35	1.402	1.519	1.343	1.584	1.283	1.653	1.222	1.726	1.160	1.803	1.097	1.884
36	1.411	1.525	1.354	1.587	1.295	1.654	1.236	1.724	1.175	1.799	1.114	1.877
37	1.419	1.530	1.364	1.590	1.307	1.655	1.249	1.723	1.190	1.795	1.131	1.870
38	1.427	1.535	1.373	1.594	1.318	1.656	1.261	1.722	1.204	1.792	1.146	1.864
39	1.435	1.540	1.382	1.597	1.328	1.658	1.273	1.722	1.218	1.789	1.161	1.859
40	1.442	1.544	1.391	1.600	1.338	1.659	1.285	1.721	1.230	1.786	1.175	1.854
45	1.475	1.566	1.430	1.615	1.383	1.666	1.336	1.720	1.287	1.776	1.238	1.835
50	1.503	1.585	1.462	1.628	1.421	1.674	1.378	1.721	1.335	1.771	1.291	1.822
55	1.528	1.601	1.490	1.641	1.452	1.681	1.414	1.724	1.374	1.768	1.334	1.814
60	1.549	1.616	1.514	1.652	1.480	1.689	1.444	1.727	1.408	1.767	1.372	1.808
65	1.567	1.629	1.536	1.662	1.503	1.696	1.471	1.731	1.438	1.767	1.404	1.805
70	1.583	1.641	1.554	1.672	1.525	1.703	1.494	1.735	1.464	1.768	1.433	1.802
75	1.598	1.652	1.571	1.680	1.543	1.709	1.515	1.739	1.487	1.77	1.458	1.801
80	1.611	1.662	1.586	1.688	1.560	1.715	1.534	1.743	1.507	1.772	1.480	1.801
85	1.624	1.671	1.600	1.696	1.575	1.721	1.550	1.747	1.525	1.774	1.500	1.801
90	1.635	1.679	1.612	1.703	1.589	1.726	1.566	1.751	1.542	1.776	1.518	1.801
95	1.645	1.687	1.623	1.709	1.602	1.732	1.579	1.755	1.557	1.778	1.535	1.802
100	1.654	1.694	1.634	1.715	1.613	1.736	1.592	1.758	1.571	1.780	1.550	1.803
150	1.720	1.746	1.706	1.760	1.693	1.774	1.679	1.788	1.665	1.802	1.651	1.817
200	1.758	1.778	1.748	1.789	1.738	1.799	1.728	1.810	1.718	1.820	1.707	1.831

Source: "Testing in Serial Correlation in Least Squares Regression. II" by J. Durbin et al., *Biometrika*, Vol. 38, June 1951, pp. 159–178. Reprinted by permission of Oxford University Press through Rightslink.

Glossary

adjusted R^2 (coefficient of determination) a measure of goodness of fit in regression that adjusts for the inclusion of variables with little or no explanatory power in a model.

alpha the probability level selected as the cutoff point for rejecting the null hypothesis.

assumptions untested propositions (usually within a theory).

asymmetric distribution a frequency or percentage distribution that is not perfectly balanced about its midpoint.

autocorrelation a condition where the error terms in a regression model with longitudinal data are correlated with each other.

average deviation the average (absolute) difference between the mean and all other values in a set of data, ignoring the sign of the difference.

bar chart a bar graph for a variable that can take on only a very limited set of values.

benchmarking a technique used to compare an organization's performance on a particular criterion to performance of similar organizations on the same criterion.

Bernoulli process a process in which the outcome of any trial can be classified into one of two mutually exclusive and jointly exhaustive outcomes, and each trial is independent of all other trials.

bimodal distribution a data distribution with two distinct peaks where observations tend to cluster.

binomial probability distribution a discrete probability distribution for phenomena that can be described by a Bernoulli process.

bivariate using two variables; contingency tables are bivariate presentations; simple regression is a bivariate technique.

bivariate forecasting a time series in which the independent variable is an actual variable rather than time.

case study an in-depth examination of an event or locale, often conducted after (because) something dramatic has happened.

cells the cross-classifications of two variables in a contingency table.

central limit theorem a foundational concept in statistical inference which states that if a sampling distribution is made up of samples containing more than 30 cases (each), the sample means will be normally distributed.

chi-square statistic the calculated value of chi-square that is compared with the chi-square distribution table (Statistical Table 4 in the back of the book) to determine statistical significance.

chi-square test a measure of statistical significance for contingency tables.

class one of the group categories used to cluster data in a frequency distribution.

class boundary the lowest or highest value of a variable that falls within a class or grouping of a variable.

class frequency the number of items in any given class in a frequency distribution.

class interval the distance between the upper class boundary and the lower class boundary in a frequency distribution.

class midpoint the point halfway between the lower and upper boundaries of a class.

coefficient of determination a measure of goodness of fit for a regression line based on the ratio of explained variation to total variation.

combination the number of ways a group of items can be clustered into subsets of similar size (such as a combination of five things taken three at a time).

concept the basic building block of research or theory that abstracts or summarizes a critical characteristic or aspect of a class of events.

concordant pair used in some measures of association for a contingency table, a pair of observations that provides support for the existence of a positive relationship between two variables.

confidence limits the upper and lower boundaries that one is X percent sure (confident) that the estimate falls within (as in 95% confidence limits).

consensual validity an indicator has consensual validity when numerous researchers accept the indicator as valid.

context in research design, the setting in which a study is conducted, important for external validity.

contingency table a table that shows how two or more variables are related by cross-tabulating the variables.

continuous variable a variable that can take on values that are not whole numbers (fractional values).

control variable a third variable introduced to evaluate the relationship between two other variables (e.g., spuriousness).

convergent validity if indicators of a concept produce similar results, the indicators have convergent validity.

correlation coefficient a measure of association equal to the square root of the coefficient of determination with a plus or minus sign to indicate the direction of the relationship (positive versus negative).

correlational validity validity established when an indicator correlates strongly with other accepted valid indicators.

covariation a statistical relationship between variables, necessary (but not sufficient) to infer causality.

Cramér's *V* a measure of association based on chi-square for cross-tabulations that include variables measured at the nominal or higher levels of measurement.

cross-sectional (correlational) study a quasi-experimental research design in which data are obtained for one point in time, often from a large sample of subjects.

cubic relationship a relationship between two variables that resembles an S-shaped curve.

cumulative frequency distribution a frequency distribution that progressively adds the numbers of observations that fall above or below a certain standard.

cumulative percentage distribution a percentage distribution that progressively adds the percentages of observations that fall above or below a certain standard.

cyclical pattern in time series analysis, a trend or cycle in the data points that repeats regularly over time.

degrees of freedom a measure needed to use many probability distributions, such as the chi-square or the *t* distributions.

dependent samples samples where individual cases from one sample are paired or matched with cases from the second sample.

dependent variable the variable that is caused or predicted by the independent variable (in regression, the *Y* variable).

descriptive statistics statistics used to summarize a body of data; contrasted with inferential statistics used to generalize from a sample to the population.

discordant pair used in some measures of association for a contingency table, a pair of observations that provides support for the existence of a negative relationship between two variables.

discrete variable a variable that has a minimum-sized unit that cannot be further subdivided.

discriminant validity if an indicator distinguishes one concept from another similar but different concept, it has discriminant validity.

dispersion (measures of) statistics that measure how closely data cluster about the mean or other measure of central tendency (see *standard deviation*).

dummy variable a nominal-level variable coded with values of 1 and 0, often used in regression.

Durbin-Watson a statistical test used to determine the presence of autocorrelation in regression models.

efficiency measures information about costs on a per-client or per-event basis.

error in regression analysis, the distance a data point is from the regression line.

expected frequencies in calculating the chi-square statistic, the hypothetical frequencies that would be predicted for each cell of the contingency table if the two variables were not related.

expected value the sum of the products of all the values that can be attained and the respective probabilities of their attainment.

experimental design a research design that features random assignment of cases to the experimental and control groups.

exponential probability distribution a probability distribution used to estimate the length of time between events.

external validity the degree to which research findings or results can be generalized to hold true in other populations, settings, or times.

face validity an indicator has face validity when the researcher accepts the indicator as valid.

forecasting the use of statistical techniques—usually time series regression—to predict future events or results.

frequency distribution a table that pairs data values with their respective number of cases or observations.

frequency polygon a graphical method of presenting a frequency distribution.

functional relationship a relationship in which one variable is an exact weighted combination of one or more variables or constants (a relationship without statistical error).

gamma an ordinal measure of association sensitive to curvilinear relationships.

grand total the total number of cases contained in a contingency table.

histogram a bar graph representing a frequency distribution.

homoscedasticity an assumption of linear regression that the size of the errors is not affected by the size of the values of the independent variable.

hypergeometric probability distribution a probability distribution used when trials are independent and the universe is finite.

hypothesis an educated guess or conjecture about the world that can be shown to be either true or false based on data analysis.

independent samples samples where individual cases across two samples are not paired or matched.

independent variable the variable that causes or predicts the dependent variable (in regression, the X variable).

indicator a measurable aspect of a concept.

inferential statistics sample statistics used to infer characteristics about the population.

inputs resources that an organization uses to achieve its goals.

inter-rater reliability a technique used to assess the degree of consistency among individuals who are applying a measurement scheme to collect and code data.

intercept the point at which the regression line crosses the axis of the dependent (Y) variable.

internal validity the degree to which research findings or results satisfy all conditions for establishing causality.

interquartile deviation in a frequency or percentage distribution, the two data values that cut off the middle 50% of all values.

interval estimate in statistical inference, a range or interval determined so that the probability that a parameter falls within it is acceptably high (e.g., 95%).

interval level a highly precise level of measurement based on a unit or interval accepted as a common standard.

Kendall's tau-*b* and tau-*c* measures of association based on covariation for cross-tabulations that include variables measured at the ordinal level; tau-*b* is appropriate for square tables, and tau-*c* is appropriate for rectangular tables.

lack of precision a threat to the reliability of measurement arising from the use of small samples or measurement scales lacking sufficient gradations.

lambda a nominal measure of association based on the principle of proportional reduction in error (PRE).

law of large numbers a concept in probability theory that states that large samples are more likely than small samples to approach normality.

level of statistical significance the probability of error (i.e., type I error) the researcher is willing to tolerate in making an inference from the sample to the population.

levels of measurement the precision inherent in the measurement of different types of variables.

linear regression regression in which the relationship between the variables is assumed to be linear.

logarithmic relationship a relationship between two variables in which one variable increases at a constant rate.

marginals the row or column frequency totals in a contingency table.

mean the arithmetic average for a group of data.

measurement the systematic assignment of numbers or categories to some phenomenon of interest for purposes of analysis.

measurement reliability an indicator is reliable to the degree that it consistently assigns the same numbers to similar phenomena.

measurement validity a measure is valid to the degree that it taps the concept it is intended to measure.

measures of association statistics designed to measure the magnitude and direction of the relationship between two variables in a cross-tabulation.

measures of central tendency statistics designed to represent the average or middle in a distribution of data.

measures of dispersion statistics designed to reveal how closely the data do or do not cluster around the mean.

median the middle item in a group of data when the data are ranked in order of magnitude.

mode the most common value in a distribution.

model a simplified version of a theory that captures its key components and is amenable to empirical testing.

model specification the idea in multiple regression that relevant explanatory variables are included, while irrelevant ones are excluded, when predicting variation in a dependent variable.

moving average in time series analysis, a procedure based on averaging contiguous observations to filter out short-term fluctuations, especially cycles.

multicollinearity the situation in multiple regression analysis in which two independent variables significantly overlap, affecting the accuracy of slope estimates.

multiple causation the social science position that an event or phenomenon can have several causes.

multiple indicators a strategy of measurement in which several indicators are used to measure a single concept.

multiple regression an interval-level statistical technique that uses several independent variables to predict or explain the dependent variable based on minimizing squared error.

negatively skewed data a frequency distribution that has a few extremely low numbers or data values that distort the mean.

nominal definition defines a concept in terms of other concepts.

nominal level a measurement level that allows only a determination that phenomena are the same or different, lacking any sense of relative size or magnitude.

nonspuriousness a criterion for a causal relationship requiring that a covariation or association between two variables or phenomena cannot be explained by a third factor.

normal curve a classic bell-shaped curve or distribution indicating that observations at or close to the mean occur with highest probability, and that the probability of occurrence progressively decreases as observations deviate from the mean.

null hypothesis the hypothesis that there is no impact or change (nothing happened); the working hypothesis phrased negatively.

objective indicator an indicator based on reports or documents that do not require judgment on the researcher's part.

ogive a graphical presentation of a cumulative frequency distribution.

one-tailed test a significance test in which the hypothesis specifies a direction (and, therefore, uses only one tail of the normal curve or other probability distribution).

operational definition a definition that specifies how a concept will be measured for purposes of the study in question.

ordinal level a level of measurement at which it is possible to say that one object (or event or phenomenon) has more or less of a given characteristic than another, but not how much more or less.

ordinary least squares in regression analysis, the principle of minimizing the sum of squared errors to fit the regression line to the data.

outcomes more precise indicators of performance than outputs that focus more on quality than on quantity and more on results outside the organization than inside.

outlier an extreme value in a frequency distribution; can have a disproportionate influence on the mean.

outputs tangible indicators that show how an organization uses its resources.

paired observations a procedure used in the calculation of some measures of association for contingency tables that relates observations in different cells of the table.

panel study a type of study in which a series of cross-sectional studies is conducted on the same sample of individuals over time; that is, a group of individuals is surveyed at repeated intervals over time.

parallel forms reliability the correlation between responses obtained on two sets of items as a measure of reliability.

parameter a measure used to summarize characteristics of a population based on all items in the population (such as a population mean).

partial slope another name for regression coefficients in a multiple regression.

percentage difference in contingency table analysis, an elemental measure of association based on calculating and comparing percentages in appropriate cells of the table.

percentage distribution a frequency distribution that contains a column listing the percentage of items for each data value or class.

Poisson distribution a probability distribution used when events occur at varying intervals of time, space, or distance.

polynomial curve fitting the use of regression to estimate nonlinear relationships.

population the total set of items that one wants to analyze (all bus users, all citizens of a city, etc.).

positively skewed data a frequency distribution that has a few extremely high numbers or data values that distort the mean.

Prais–Winsten transformation a statistical technique used to correct for the presence of autocorrelation in regression models.

predicted value in regression analysis, the expected (predicted) value of the dependent variable for a given value of the independent variable based on the calculated regression line.

predictive validity a type of measurement validity based on the degree to which an indicator correctly predicts a specified outcome in the future.

quasi-experimental designs research designs that lack the requirements of experimental designs but are structured in a similar fashion.

random assignment in research design, a procedure that gives each subject an equal chance of placement in the experimental group or the control group so that no systematic difference exists between the groups prior to administration of the treatment.

range a measure of dispersion calculated by subtracting the smallest value in a distribution from the largest value.

regression a statistical technique used to describe the relationship between two variables based on the principle of minimizing errors in prediction.

regression coefficient the weight assigned to independent variables in a regression (the beta or slope).

reliable indicator an indicator that consistently assigns the same scores to some phenomenon that has not, in fact, changed, regardless of who is doing the measuring, where the measuring is conducted, or other extraneous factors.

research design a systematic program for empirically testing proposed causal relationships that guides the collection, analysis, and interpretation of the relevant data.

research hypothesis the opposite of the null hypothesis, typically phrased positively ("impact or change" rather than "no impact or no change").

residual variation the average squared error in prediction with a regression equation.

sample a subset of the population that is sometimes selected randomly. Measures that summarize a sample are called sample statistics.

scale a composite measure that combines several variables into a single unified measure of a concept.

slope the degree that a regression line rises or falls moving from left to right (often called beta or the regression coefficient).

Somers's d_{yx} and d_{xy} measures of association based on covariation for cross-tabulations that include variables measured at the ordinal level.

split-half reliability measure of reliability in which the set of items intended to measure a given concept is divided into two parts.

spurious relationship a relationship between two variables that is caused by a third variable.

standard deviation a measure of dispersion; the square root of the average squared deviation from the mean (i.e., the variance).

standard error of the estimate an estimate of the error (equivalent to one standard deviation) in an estimate of Y derived from a regression equation; a measure of goodness of fit.

standard error of the mean an estimate of the amount of error in a sample estimate of a population mean.

standard error of the slope a measure of goodness of fit in a regression; a measure of error in a slope estimated from sample data.

statistic a measure that is used to summarize a sample of data.

statistical controls a procedure used to check and evaluate the relationship between an independent variable and a dependent variable by introducing a third, control variable into the analysis.

statistical relationship a recognizable pattern of change in one variable as the other variable changes.

Student's *t* distribution a sampling distribution used for testing hypotheses on small samples.

subjective indicator an indicator based on the judgment of one or more persons.

subjective measure a measure that relies on the judgment of the analyst or of a respondent in a survey.

symmetric distribution a frequency or percentage distribution that is perfectly balanced about its midpoint.

test–retest reliability method for assessing measurement reliability by measuring the same phenomenon or set of variables twice over a reasonably short time period.

theory an integrated set of propositions intended to explain or account for a given phenomenon.

time order a criterion for a causal relationship requiring that the independent variable or phenomenon must precede the dependent variable or phenomenon in time.

time series a variable measured at regular time intervals.

time series analysis a variety of statistical techniques for analyzing and forecasting the observations of a variable measured at equally spaced intervals over time.

total frequency the total number of observations or cases in an analysis, usually denoted by the symbol **N**.

trend studies studies that monitor and attempt to account for shifts over time in various indicators, usually indicators that are highly aggregated (e.g., gross national product).

***t* test** a statistical test that is based on the t distribution and is used for slopes and for means when n is less than 30 and the population is not normally distributed.

two-tailed test a significance test in which the hypothesis does not specify direction (and, therefore, uses both tails of a probability distribution).

Type I error rejecting the null hypothesis when it is true.

Type II error accepting the null hypothesis when it is false.

uniform distribution a frequency (percentage) distribution in which each data value or set of values occurs with equal frequency (percentage).

univariate referring to the presentation or analysis of one variable at a time; for example, frequency distributions and measures of central tendency.

unobtrusive indicator a variable or measure collected without the knowledge or reactivity of the subject, such as fingerprint smudges on museum display cases to evaluate the popularity of different exhibits.

unobtrusive measures nonreactive measuring instruments in which the act of measuring a phenomenon does not alter the behavior or attribute being assessed.

valid indicator an indicator that accurately measures the concept it is intended to measure.

variable a measured quantity or characteristic that can take on a variety of values (i.e., it varies).

variance the average squared deviation from the mean; the square of the standard deviation.

z score the number of standard deviations an item is from the mean; z scores can be calculated for raw data, means, slopes, regression estimates, and so on.

Answers to Odd-Numbered Computational Problems

The following are the answers to selected problems in which computations play an important role. Where the answers to questions are based on interpretation (e.g., Chapters 1–4) or management judgment, the answers are not included.

For Chapters 10–13, exact probabilities for most of the answers have been calculated using a statistical software package. Because the t-distribution table provides only seven levels of statistical significance ranging from .10 to .0005, exact probabilities cannot be calculated by hand. When working out the problems for these chapters, it is sufficient to evaluate whether the t statistic obtained falls above or below a particular level of significance (such as > or < .05).

Chapter 2

2.9 A different number should be selected to represent each category. Because there are four categories, numbering the categories 1 through 4 is logical, but other numbers are acceptable.

1 = Friend
2 = Silver
3 = Gold
4 = Platinum

Interval Version	Ordinal Version 1
$25	1
$150	2
$75	1
$450	3
$100	2
$750	4
$90	1
$175	2
$250	3
$50	1

2.11 Translating the numbers into words yields the following results for each employee.

Employee   1: female, full time, and professional

2: male, full time, general labor

3: female, part time, administrative

4: male, full time, administrative

5: female, part time, professional

6: female, part time, professional

7: male, part time, general labor

8: female, full time, general labor

2.13 Answers for outputs and outcomes will vary for each indicator. The key is that indicators should not confuse these two concepts.

Chapter 5

5.1 Mean = 59; median = 59

5.3

Number of Days of Sick Leave Taken	Number of Employees	Percentage
0–2	4	10.5
3–5	7	18.4
6–8	7	18.4
9–11	14	36.8
12–14	6	15.8

Categories 6–8 and 9–11. It appears that the department is abusing its sick days.

5.5

Income	Number of Families	Percentage
0–300	25	1.14
300–600	163	7.49
600–900	354	16.27
900–1,200	278	12.78
1,200–1,500	421	19.35
1,500–1,800	603	27.71
1,800–2,100	211	9.70
2,100–2,400	84	3.86
2,400–2,700	32	1.47
2,700–3,000	5	.229

Category of median is 1,200–1,500. Category of mode is 1,500–1,800.

5.7 Mean for first 9 months = 34.67. To meet target of monthly average of 34 employees for entire year, the bureau can employ up to 32 employees over the next 3 months.

5.9 Mean = 46; median = 47. The police chief appears to be correct.

5.11 Mean GRE verbal = 643.75; median GRE verbal = 640; mean GRE quantitative = 570; median GRE quantitative = 575. Complaint is warranted.

5.13 Percentage distribution:

0	37.3%
1	31.4%
2	16.5%
3	8.6%
4	6.2%

Level of measurement = interval; mean = 1.15; median = 1 (1.40 with interpolation); mode = 0; standard deviation = 1.19. Depending on which statistic(s) is (are) cited, a recommendation can be made for allocating—or not allocating—money to refurbish the civic center.

5.15 Percentage distribution:

White	34%
Black	25%
Hispanic	20%
Asian	13%
Other	8%

Level of measurement: nominal; the only measure of central tendency is the mode: whites with 34%. The city workforce is reasonably diverse.

Chapter 6

6.1 Brand B has greater variation despite its higher mean; it may not be as useful as Brand A.

6.3 Some crews are hauling a lot less garbage than others and skewing the distribution in a negative direction.

6.5 Select System A. System A is better than System C because it has smaller mean and standard deviation. System A is also better than System B because System B is erratic.

6.7 On average (mean), it takes 193 days to close a case, but the mean is inflated by some especially long closures.

6.9 Mean = 20.94; median = 19.5; mode = 15; standard deviation = 8.55. Evidence shows that a few employees do much more work than all of the others.

6.11 Mean = 35.29; median = 31; standard deviation = 12.12. Report median because of positive skewness in data (one case is nearly twice as large as next largest case).

6.13 The city manager should be provided with the standard deviation for each sample. For the police, the standard deviation equals 41.66; for the firefighters, it has a value of 104.12. Wide variation around the mean for firefighters suggests there might be a problem.

Chapter 7

7.1 $z = (50 - 67) \div 7 = -17 \div 7 = -2.43$. $p(z = 2.43) = .4925$; $.5 - .4925 = .0075$. So 0.75% process fewer forms, and 99.25% process more forms. Complaint seems justified.

7.3 $z = (42 - 36) \div 5 = 6 \div 5 = 1.20$ $p(z = 1.20) = .3849$. So the probability of reimbursement within 42 days $= .5 + .3849 = .8849$. The probability of reimbursement after 42 days $= 1 - .8849 = .1151$. Because score is only slightly more than one standard deviation above mean, probably should not be apprehensive.

7.5 For 25 mpg, $z = (25 - 27.3) \div 3.1 = -2.3 \div 3.1 = -0.74$. $p(z = 0.74) = .2704$. The probability of cars that will get at least 25 mpg $= .2704 + .5 = .7704$, or 77.04%. For 24 mpg, $z = (24 - 27.3) \div 3.1 = -3.3 \div 3.1 = -1.06$. $p(z = 1.06) = .3554$. The probability of cars that will get at least 25 mpg $= .3554 + .5 = .8554$, or 85.54%.

7.7 .90 criterion corresponds to ($p = .45$). $z(p = .45) = 1.65$. Convert z to actual scores: lower limit $= 76 - (1.65 \times 5.7) = 76 - 9.4 = 66.6$; upper limit $= 76 + (1.65 \times 5.7) = 76 + 9.4 = 85.4$.

7.9 $z = (24{,}832 - 25{,}301) \div 986 = 469 \div 986 = -0.48$. $p(z = 0.48) = .1844$. Ima's salary is within one-half of one standard deviation of average salary. She is not seriously underpaid.

7.11 $z = (15 - 17) \div 3.1 = -2 \div 3.1 = 2.645$. $p(z = .64) = .2422$. $z = (21 - 17) \div 3.1 = 4 \div 3.1 = 1.29$. $p(z = 1.29) = .4015$; $.5 - .4015 = .0985$. Less than 10% of clients need 21 or more days of counseling, so this does not seem to be a major concern at the present.

Chapter 8

8.1 $n = 12$, $p = .4$, $r = 3$ or less; $p(3) = .141894$, $p(2) = .063852$, $p(1) = .017414$, $p(0) = .002177$; answer $= .225337$ or .23.

8.3 94.32

8.5 $n = 182$, $p = .51$, $r = 177$ +, normal curve method; mean $= 92.82$, standard deviation $= 6.74$, $z = 12.49$, $p < .0001$

8.7 $n = 20$, $p = .25$, $r = 16$ +; answer $= .0000003865$

8.9 $n = 5$, $p = .34$ (or 212/620), $r = 5$, $p = .00467$

8.11 $n = 9, p = .6, r = 8,9; p(8) = .060, p(9) = .010, p(8,9) = .07$

8.13 $n = 8, p = .91, r = 2$ or less, $p = .000013$

8.15 $n = 100, p = .25, n = 29 +$, normal curve method; mean $= 25$, standard deviation $= 4.23, z = .92, p = .1588$

8.17 $n = 6, p = .33, r = 1,0; p(1) = .27, p(0) = .09, p(0,1) = .36$

Chapter 9

9.1 $n = 50, p = .6, r = 40 +, Np = 100$, mean $= 30$, standard deviation $= 2.46$, $z = 4.07, p < .0001$

9.3 $n = 35, p = .3, r = 17 +, Np = 200$, mean $= 10.5$, standard deviation $= 2.47$, $z = 2.63, p = .0043$

9.5 $n = 120, p = .23, r = 24 +, Np = 150$; mean $= 27.6$, standard deviation $= 2.07$, $z = 1.74, p = .0409$

9.7 Asperin; $n = 200, p = .5, r = 60$ or less, $Np = 1,000$; mean $= 100$, standard deviation $= 6.33, z = 6.32, p < .0001$

9.9 $n = 211, p = .34, r = 91 +, Np = 620$; mean $= 71.74$, standard deviation $= 5.59, z = 3.44, p = .0003$

9.11 $\lambda = 6.0$ (a) .1526 (b) .0025 (c) .0149 (d) .0446 (e) .1512

9.13 $\lambda = .1; .0954$

9.15 $n = 100, p = .25, r = 29 +, Np = 1,000$; mean $= 25$, standard deviation $= 3.97, z = 1.01, p = .1562$

Chapter 10

10.1 s.e. $= 9.83$; mean $= 30$; standard deviation $= \$31.10$; 95% confidence, $\$7.78$ to $\$52.22$ using $t = 2.26$ for 9 df

10.3 s.e. $= 3.0, t = 2.0, p = .0228$

10.5 Best estimate $= 6.96, s = 2.1$, s.e. $= .94, t = 3.22$ with 4 df, p $< .025$

10.7 Best estimate $= \$1,810.80, s = \$378$, s.e. $= 119.56$, 80% confidence limits (using $t = 1.38$ with $df = 9$) $= \$1,645.80$ to $\$1,975.80$

10.9 Mean $= 20.0, s = 25.3$, s.e. $= 5.66$

10.11 (a) s.e. $= 407$, confidence limits $17,400 \pm 1.65 \times 407$, or $16,729$ to $18,071$

(b) $z = 2.70, p < .0004$

(c) $z = .983, p = .1635$

10.13 s.e. $= 1.5, t = 2.67, p = .0038$

10.15 s.e. $= 3.6, t = 2.06, p = .0197$

10.17 s.e. $= .156, t = 3.84, p < .0005$

Chapter 11

11.1 Hypothesis: Jack costs less than $364 per car.

Null hypothesis: Jack does not cost less than $364 per car.

s.e. = 20, t = 1.7, p = .0445; possible discussion points: inflation, quality of repairs, costs of terminating public employees.

11.3 Survey of 96

11.5 Best estimate = 40.34, s = 7.68, s.e. = 2.43, t = 2.41 (9 df), p < .025

11.7 Hypothesis: Students are averaging less than 7.3 hours of volunteer work. Null hypothesis: Students are not averaging less than 7.3 hours of volunteer work. Mean = 6.8, s = 1.5, s.e. = .173, t = 2.89 (74 df), p < .005; conclusion: reject the null hypothesis.

11.9 Hypothesis: Absenteeism is less than 12.8 workdays.

Null hypothesis: Absenteeism is not less than 12.8 workdays.

s.e. = 1.03, t = 3.98, (19 df), p < .005; conclusion: reject the null hypothesis. This would happen by chance only rarely, so the number of absences is probably less than 12.8.

11.11 Hypothesis: This year's corn crop yields are less than 32.4 bushels/acre.

Null hypothesis: This year's corn crop yields are not less than 32.4 bushels/acre.

s.e. = 1.57, t = 6.37, p < .0001; 80% confidence limits = 22.4 ± 1.28 × 1.57, or 20.4 to 24.4.

11.13 s.e. = 13,750; 99% confidence limits = 74,500 ± 2.95 × 13,750, or 115,063 to 33,938.

Hypothesis: Punitive damages average less than $100,000 per case.

Null hypothesis: Punitive damages do not average less than $100,000 per case. t = 1.85

p < .05; conclusion: punitive damages are not likely to average more than $100,000 per case.

Chapter 12

12.1 1,702

12.3 s = .32, s.e. = .023, t = 2.17, p = .015

12.5 Hypothesis: After the public service ads, less than 74% of drivers violate the speed limit.

Null hypothesis: After the public service ads, 74% (or more) of drivers violate the speed limit.

s = .44, s.e. = .0098, t = 2.04, p = .0207; note that this finding is statistically significant yet substantively trivial.

12.7 140

12.9 Best estimate = .25

12.11 Best estimate of error rate = 7.2, s = .258, s.e. = .016; 90% confidence = .072 ± 1.65 × .016, or .0984 to .0456.

Hypothesis: The error rate is greater than 5%, or .05.

Null hypothesis: The error rate is not greater than 5%, or .05.

Need to calculate new deviation and s.e.: They are .218 and .014, t = 1.57, p = .0582.

12.13 Best estimate of paid is 82%, or .82.

What is the probability that this percentage could result if the population proportion were .9 or larger? Standard deviation = .3 (use square root of .9 × .1), s.e. = .03, t = 2.67, p = .0038

12.15 Hypothesis: pregnancy rate is lower than 21% TPPC

S = .407 (use population percentage), s.e. = .05, t = 1.74

Chapter 13

13.1 Hypothesis: After the PR campaign, fewer people do not have inspection stickers.

Null hypothesis: After the PR campaign, there is no change in the number of people lacking inspection stickers.

	Proportion	s	s.e	s.e.$_d$	t	p
Before	.43	.50	.050			
After	.21	.41	.041	.065	3.38	.0004

13.3 Hypothesis: African Americans are less likely to feel that the police are doing a good job.

Null hypothesis: There is no difference in the proportion of African Americans and whites who feel the police are doing a good job.

	Proportion	s	s.e	s.e.$_d$	t	p
African Americans	.49	.50	.041			
After	.75	.43	.025	.048	5.42	<.0001

13.5 Hypothesis: The exercise group will perform better than the nonexercise group.

Null hypothesis: There is no difference in performance between the exercise and nonexercise groups.

Exercise group s.e. = 3.63, nonexercise group s.e. = 1.86, s.e.$_d$ = 4.08, t = .96, p = .1685

13.7 Hypothesis: Maintenance costs will be less on cars that do not get routine maintenance.

Null hypothesis: There is no difference in maintenance costs for cars that receive service and those that do not.

Maintained s.e. = 10, not maintained s.e. = 23.1, s.e.$_d$ = 25.2, t = 1.99, p = .0239

13.9 Hypothesis: Brethren will have a lower divorce rate.

Null hypothesis: There is no difference in divorce rates for Brethren and Lost Souls.

	Proportion	s	s.e	s.e.$_d$	t	p
Brethren	.14	.35	.038			
Lost Souls	.196	.39	.055	.067	.84	.2005

13.11 Hypothesis: UA students score higher than UGA students.

Null hypothesis: There is no difference in the scores of UA and UGA students.

(*Note:* This hypothesis is rejected by the results because UGA students have a higher mean.)

UA s.e. = 1.9, UGA s.e. = 1.6, s.e.$_d$ = 2.48, t = 2.26, p = .0122

13.13 Hypothesis: People on workfare earn more money.

Null hypothesis: There is no difference in earnings for those on workfare and those not on workfare.

Workfare s.e. = 10.6, control s.e. = 8.94, s.e.$_d$ = 16.41, t = 2.75, p = .0020

13.15 Hypothesis: Workshop students are more likely to receive PMIs.

Null hypothesis: Workshop attendance has no effect on the likelihood of receiving PMIs.

	Proportion	s	s.e	s.e.$_d$	t	p
Workshop Group	.7	.46	.145			
Control Group	.3	.46	.145	.205	.1.95	<.0.5
					(df = 18)	

13.17 Hypothesis: Jogging pigs have lower cholesterol levels.

Null hypothesis: The cholesterol levels of jogging and nonjogging pigs are not different.

Joggers s.e. = 12.65, control s.e. = 15.49, s.e.$_d$ = 20.0, t = 2.5 with 23 df, p = .01

13.19 Hypothesis: Seat belt use is higher in Minnesota.

Null hypothesis: There is no difference in the proportion of residents using seat belts in Minnesota and Wisconsin.

	Proportion	s	s.e	s.e.$_d$	t	p
Minnesota	.49	.50	.058			
Wisconsin	.25	.44	.042	.072	3.33	.0004

13.21 Hypothesis: Latinos are more likely to feel the city is biased.

Null hypothesis: There is no difference in the proportion of Latino and Anglo residents who feel the city is biased.

	Proportion	s	s.e	s.e.$_d$	t	p
Latinos	.71	.45	.020			
Anglos	.35	.48	.028	.034	10.59	<.0001

Chapter 14

14.1 Cross-tabulation (frequencies):

	Work on Ziptronic?	
Number of Absences	No	Yes
Fewer than 10	85	18
10 or more	35	26
Total	120	44

Cross-tabulation (percentaged):

	Work on Ziptronic?	
Number of Absences	No	Yes
Fewer than 10	71%	41%
10 or more	29%	59%

Conclusion: Hypothesis is supported. Employees who operate ziptronic are more likely to have 10 or more absences than those who do not by 30%.

14.3 Cross-tabulation (percentaged):

		Pilot Weight	
Reaction Time	Normal	Up to 10 Pounds Overweight	More Than 10 Pounds Overweight
Poor	15%	36%	48%
Adequate	37%	40%	36%
Excellent	48%	25%	16%

Conclusion: Egyptian Air Force brass is correct. Overweight pilots are more likely to have poor reaction time than normal-weight pilots by 33% (48% − 15% = 33%) Overweight pilots are also less likely to have excellent reaction time than normal-weight pilots by 32% (48% − 16% = 32%).

14.5 Cross-tabulation (percentaged):

	Students Assisted for MPA Tuition	
Status	Capital	East Winslow
Did no graduate	75%	69%
Graduated	25%	31%

Conclusion: Legislators have reason for concern. Most tuition-assisted students do not graduate. East Winslow does slightly better than Capital in graduation rate (by 6%), but 72% of these students do not graduate.

14.7 Cross-tabulation (percentaged):

	Type of Event				
Status	Hockey Rallies	Religious Rallies	Basketball Games	Rock Concerts	Public Administration Conventions
Not Profitable	57%	11%	78%	20%	100%
Profitable	43%	89%	22%	80%	0%

Conclusion: Religious rallies rank highest with respect to the rate of profitable events (89%), followed closely by rock concerts (80%). Hockey games (43%) and basketball games (22%) lag far behind, and public administration conventions (0%), alas, rank dead last.

14.9 Cross-tabulation (percentaged):

	Treatment Group	
Cancer Status	Drug Group	Placebo Group
Active	72%	70%
Remission	28%	30%

Conclusion: Virtually no difference between drug group and placebo group in achieving remission. The drug does not appear to be effective.

14.11 Cross-tabulation (percentaged):

	Class Participation	
Grade in Course	Low	High
Fail	24%	12%
Pass	76%	88%

Conclusion: The professor's hypothesis is supported. Students who had a high rate of class participation were more likely to pass the course than students with a low rate of participation by 12%.

14.13 Percentage cross-tabulation:

Opinion	Before	After
Department is doing a poor job	77%	61%
Department is doing a good job	23%	39%

Hypothesis: New refuse collection procedures have improved the public's perception of the Department of Sanitary Engineering.

Null hypothesis: New refuse collection procedures have not improved the public's perception of the Department of Sanitary Engineering.

Conclusion: New refuse collection procedures appear to have improved the public's perception of Department of Sanitary Engineering. The second (after) survey shows that 39% feel that the department is doing a good job, compared with 23% in the first (before) survey, a difference of 16%.

Chapter 15

15.1 Percentaged cross-tabulation:

	Race	
Attitude toward Police	Nonwhite	White
Police Do Not Do Good Job	51%	25%
Police Do Good Job	49%	75%

Conclusion: The police have a community relations problem in the nonwhite community.

15.3 Percentaged cross-tabulation:

	Proximity to Hospital		
Frequency of Visits	Close	Medium	Far
Low	50%	52%	53%
Medium	26%	26%	26%
High	24%	23%	22%

Chi-square = 3.13; not statistically significant.

Conclusion: Percentaged table and chi-square show that no relationship exists between these variables.

15.7 Percentaged cross-tabulation:

	Type of Job	
Attitude toward Job	Hourly	Salary
Dissatisfied	41%	39%
Satisfied	59%	61%

For gamma, C = 16,490; D = 15,012:

$$\frac{16{,}490 - 15{,}012}{16{,}490 + 15{,}012} = .05$$

No relationship exists between type of job and job satisfaction. C refers to concordant pairs of cases, and D refers to discordant pairs.

15.9 Probability of promotion is much greater for younger employees (age 30 or less), and especially for middle-aged employees (age 31−50), than for the oldest group of employees (age 51 or greater).

15.11 The four conditions of causality are covariation, time order, nonspuriousness, and theory (see Chapter 3). Cross-tabulation satisfies covariation condition, and theoretical justification probably exists for this relationship. However, Ph.D. student gives no evidence that she has satisfied time order condition (does bureaucratic quality lead to economic development or the reverse?), and nonspuriousness condition (might third variables be responsible for the observed covariation?).

15.13 Percentaged cross-tabulation:

	Rank		
Commence	Assistant	Associate	Full
Low	14%	23%	60%
Medium	31%	54%	20%
High	55%	23%	20%

Conclusion: McClain's hypothesis gains support. Assistant professors (55%) have the highest percentage of high competence, with associate professors (23%) and full professors (20%) far behind. Associate professors (54%) have the highest percentage of medium competence, with professors (20%) again far behind. Professors (60%) lead in only one category—low competence!

Chapter 16

16.1 Percentaged cross-tabulation (no control variable):

	Race	
Status	Nonwhite	White
Passed Over	46%	14%
Promoted	54%	86%

Percentaged control tables:

	Non-West Pointers			West Pointers	
Status	Nonwhite	White	**status**	Nonwhite	White
Passed Over	51%	50%	Passed Over	27%	3%
Promoted	49%	50%	Promoted	73%	97%

Conclusion: Original table suggests discrimination because whites promoted at a much higher rate than nonwhites, 86% versus 54%. Control tables show that non–West Pointers—whether nonwhite or white—have 50–50 chance of promotion (no discrimination). However, among West Pointers, whites have much higher rate of promotion than nonwhites, 97% versus 73%. This finding again suggests racial discrimination, although a larger sample of nonwhite West Pointers would have been desirable.

16.3 Percentaged cross-tabulation (no control variable):

	Average Income	
Frequency of Health Problems	Low	High
Low	41%	60%
High	59%	40%

Percentaged control tables:

Frequency of Health Problems	Garbage Collection Once per Week			Frequency of Health Problems	Garbage Collection Twice per Week	
	Average Income				Average Income	
	Low	High			Low	High
Low	31%	45%		Low	46%	61%
High	69%	55%		High	54%	39%

Conclusion: Original cross-tabulation shows that higher-income individuals have lower rate of health problems by 19%. Control tables show that both income and frequency of garbage collection affect rate of health problems: High-income individuals have lower rate of health problems than low-income individuals by 14% to 15%, and those with garbage collected twice per week have lower rate of health problems than those with once-per-week collection by 15% to 16%.

16.5 Percentaged cross-tabulation (no control variable):

Crime Rate	Streetlights	
	Below Average	Above Average
Below Average	49%	57%
Above Average	51%	43%

Percentaged control tables:

Crime Rate	Police Do Not Walk Beat			Crime Rate	Police Walk Beat	
	Streetlights				Streetlights	
	Below Average	Above Average			Below Average	Above Average
Below Average	48%	47%		Below Average	58%	59%
Above Average	52%	53%		Above Average	42%	41%

Conclusion: Original table suggests that cities with above-average streetlights are more likely to have below-average crime rates by 8%. However, control tables show that when police walking (or not walking) a beat is controlled, streetlights have no effect on crime rate. Instead, cities that have police walking a beat more often have below-average crime rates than cities without police on the beat by 10% to 12%. According to these data, cities are better advised to increase beat-walking than streetlights to reduce crime.

16.7 Percentaged cross-tabulation (no control variable):

Attendance	Size	
	Small	Large
Low	45%	35%
High	55%	65%

Percentaged control tables:

Infrequent Collection Changes			Frequent Collection Changes		
	Size			**Size**	
Attendance	Small	Large	**Attendance**	Small	Large
Low	49%	48%	Low	41%	26%
High	51%	52%	High	59%	74%

Conclusion: Original cross-tabulation suggests that large-size museums are more likely to have high attendance by 10%. However, control tables show that if the museum collection changes infrequently, size makes no difference with respect to attendance. By contrast, if the collection changes frequently, attendance tends to be high, especially for large-size museums. Recommend that the city change the collection frequently, regardless of size of new museum, and, if possible, build large museum.

16.9 Percentaged cross-tabulation (no control variable):

	Method	
Performance	Traditional	Modern
Low	50%	50%
High	50%	50%

Percentaged control tables:

	Low Intelligence	
Performance	Traditional	Modern
Low	40%	63%
High	60%	37%

	Medium Intelligence	
Performance	Traditional	Modern
Low	43%	44%
High	57%	56%

	High Intelligence	
Performance	Traditional	Modern
Low	64%	41%
High	36%	59%

Conclusion: Original cross-tabulation suggests no relationship between method of instruction and student performance. However, control tables show that if student has low intelligence, traditional method of instruction more often leads to high performance than does modern method by 23%. If student has medium intelligence, traditional and modern methods are equally effective in achieving high performance. If student has high intelligence, modern method is more effective in achieving high performance by 23%. These data support the hypothesis that the best method of instruction depends on the intelligence of the student.

16.13 The percentaged cross-tabulations follow.

	Work with Volunteers	
Attend Volunteer Banquet	No	Yes
No	47%	45%
Yes	53%	55%
	100%	100%
	(126)	(131)

Employee Does Not Volunteer		**Employee Volunteers**	
	Work with Volunteers		Work with Volunteers	
Attend Volunteer Banquet	No	Yes	No	Yes
No	55%	52%	39%	38%
Yes	45%	48%	61%	62%
	100%	100%	100%	100%
	(62)	(63)	(64)	(68)

Controlling for working with volunteers at the civic center, employees who volunteer on their own are more likely to attend the annual volunteer appreciation banquet than those who do not volunteer by 11–12%. Controlling for whether or not the employee volunteers on his or her own, employees who work with volunteers at the civic center are more likely to attend the annual volunteer appreciation banquet than those who do not work with volunteers at the center by 2–3%. Therefore, if Sarah Mony wants to encourage employees to attend the annual volunteer appreciation banquet, she should encourage them to volunteer on their own.

Chapter 17

17.1 (a) Yes, a relationship exists, $t = 60$; for each additional mile driven, maintenance costs increase by 3 cents.

(b) $1,550 \pm 295$ or $1,845 to $1,295

(c) If $Y = 1,000$, then what is X?

Substitute into the equation and solve. $X = 31,667$

17.3 Slope: For each increase of $1.00 in per capita police expenditures, the state crime rate *increases* by 5.1. Intercept: If per capita police expenditures are equal to 0 (not a likely situation), then the best guess as to the crime rate is 2,475. Coefficient of determination: If you know the per capita expenditures for crime, you can explain 63% of the variation in crime rates. There is a positive correlation between crime rates and expenditures; this probably exists because states increase budgets to combat crime whenever crime increases.

17.5 Beaver can say the following:

(a) For every additional course taken, the OER increases by .1.

(b) If a person takes 0 courses, the best estimate of the OER is 95.

(c) Knowing the number of courses taken can explain 40% of the variation in OERs.

(d) $t = 1.43$, $p = .0778$; a relationship exists, but it is weak.

Estimate of Beaver's OER $= 96 \pm (1.65 \times 1.4 \times 1.05)$, or 98.43 to 93.57.

17.7 Intercept: If the temperature is 0 degree, our best guess as to the number of absent workers is 485. Slope: For each increase of 1 degree in temperature, absences drop by 5.1. Coefficient of determination: If you know the low temperature for the preceding night, you can explain 86% of the variation in absences. The relationship is significant; $t = 4.63$; workers absent $= 587 \pm (1.65 \times 12 \times 1.02)$, or 607 to 567.

17.9 Slope: An increase of 1 in the air quality index is associated with a .7 increase in respiratory diseases per 1,000 population. Intercept: If the air quality index is 0, the best guess as to the number of respiratory diseases per 1,000 population is 15.7. If you know the air quality index for the city, you can explain 71% of the variation in respiratory disease rates. The relationship is significant; $t = 17.5$.

17.11 Intercept: The best guess of the expenditures in a school district even if the district had no people is $4,566 (an unlikely situation). Slope: For each person in the school district, expenditures increase by $824. Coefficient of determination: If you know the number of people in the school district, you can explain 78% of the variation in school expenditures. t score: Calculated by dividing the slope by the standard error of the slope; it indicates a statistically significant relationship.

17.13 Intercept: If no employees are age 60 or older, the best guess as to the number of retirements next month is 2.1 persons. Slope: For each additional person age 60 or older in the agency, retirements will increase by .04 next month. $t = 6.67$; significant. You can explain 35% of the variation in retirements by knowing how many persons are age 60 or older. Retirements $= 26.9$ or 27; could the number be as large as 30? $t = (27 - 30)/(4.6) = .69$; $p = .2578$; very likely.

17.15 Hypothesis: Federal aid dollars increase as poverty levels increase. Interpretation: intercept: If 0% of the city's residents live in poverty, the city will still receive $27.81 per person in federal aid. Slope: For every one percentage point increase in residents living in poverty, federal aid increases by $339.10 per person. If you know the percentage of residents living in poverty, you can explain 43% of the variation in per capita federal aid. $t = 3.63$; the relationship is significant.

Chapter 18

18.1   There is a positive but nonsignificant relationship between cruising and crime rates ($t = .5$ *with* 8 df). The analyst should conclude that cruising is unrelated to crime rates.

18.3   Yes, there is a relationship; $t = 26.67$.

Frolic Park, $p = .892$; Barren Park, $p = .092$; Choirpractice Park, $p = 1.10$. (This should be interpreted as a probability of .99; in other words, the sprinkler in this park should be replaced immediately.)

18.5   Desk is correct. This is a strong relationship between reading ability and test scores ($t = 6.45$). In fact, reading scores can explain 80% of the variation in test scores. The slope shows that the probability of passing the exam increases by .071 for each increase of one grade in reading ability. Both persons can be correct because their hypotheses are compatible. Brown does not find a relationship between experience and exam scores because exam scores are strongly affected by the reading ability of the troop.

18.7 $Y = \$14,087.5 - \$157.5X$, $r^2 = .012$. $S_{y|x} = 820$, $s_b = 580$. There is no relationship between HMOs and health care costs.

18.9   At 6.35 miles per gallon, buses consume 1,291 gallons per week rather than 1,608 per week. But using the 95% confidence limits of 5.55 to 7.15, the consumption of fuel range is 1,477 to 1,147; this means a savings of between 131 gallons, or \$524, and 461 gallons, or \$1844.

18.11 Hypothesis: States with no-fault laws have lower insurance costs. Intercept: The average cost for a policy of this nature in states without no-fault insurance is \$265. Intercept: No-fault insurance states have policy costs of \$74.33 less. $t = 2.53$ with 18 df, $p < .05$.

18.13 The value of .094 for the Durbin–Watson statistic indicates that positive autocorrelation is a problem in this equation.

Chapter 19

19.1   (a) $453 \pm (2.58 \times 12.6)$, or 485.5 to 420.5

(b) If $Y = 400$, what is X? $X = 828,000$

19.3   The relationship is not linear. Forecasting enrollments from these data would result in predictions that are not particularly useful.

19.5   Intercept: If the money supply grows at a rate of 0%, then your best guess as to the inflation rate would be -5.4 (or deflation of 5.4%). Slope: A 1 percentage point increase in the money supply is associated with a 2.1 percentage point increase in inflation. The relationship is significant; $t = 300$. If you know the change in the money supply, you can explain 99% of the variation in the inflation rate. Inflation rate of $11.82 \pm (1.65 \times 2 \times 1.05)$, or 15.29 to 8.35.

Could the rate be 15%? $t = (11.82 - 15)/2.1 = 1.51$, $p = .0655$.

19.7 Slope: for every additional person in the state population, the patients at Bluefield State will increase by .0031 (or by 31 for every 10,000 persons); this relationship is significant; $t = 23.85$ **(a)** 2,718 **(b)** 62.

19.9 Intercept: Your best guess as to the number of domestic disputes on a night when the temperature at 4:00 P.M. is 0 degrees is 216. Slope: For each degree increase in temperature, the number of domestic disputes increases by 3.1; $t = 2.07$, which is significant. If you know the temperature at 4 P.M., you can explain 81% of the variation in the number of domestic disputes in Metro $= 510.5 \pm (t \times 18)$.

19.11 Regression 1: Intercept: If the year is 1986, your best guess as to the number of building permits issued is 2,256. Slope: For each year that passes, building permits issued will increase by 234.6; $t = 10.16$. If you know the year, you can explain 65% of the variation in the number of building permits issued.

Regression 2: If the unemployment rate is 0, your best guess as to the number of building permits issued is 13,413. Slope: For each 1 percentage point increase in unemployment, building permits drop by 678; $t = 31.68$, which is significant. If you know the percent unemployment, you can explain 78% of the variation in the number of building permits.

Prediction; Equation 1: 9,059; Equation 2: 8,531.4. The second equation is more useful. It has a lower overall standard error of the estimate.

Chapter 20

20.1 All regression interpretations are fairly similar, so 20.1 will be done in depth. Intercept: If the number of people who live within 200 miles of the camp is 0, the number of camping hookups is 0, and the mean annual temperature at the park is 0 (not a likely situation), then your best estimate of park usage will be 147 (people). Slope 1: For each additional person living within 200 miles of the park, an additional .0212 persons will visit the park, controlling for hookups and temperature. $t = 1.35$; this relationship is barely significant. Slope 2: For each additional camping hookup available, an additional 15.4 people will visit the camp, controlling for residents within 200 miles and temperature. $t = 1.24$; this relationship is barely significant. Slope 3: For each additional degree higher the mean annual temperature is, a park can expect an additional 186 visitors if you control for residents within 200 miles and temperature. $t = 17.55$; this relationship is significant. Coefficient of determination: knowing the number of residents within 200 miles, the number of camping hookups, and the mean annual temperature at the park allows one to explain 50% of the variation in park usage. The assessment should note that weather conditions seem to be the major influence on park usage.

20.3 The t scores are 52.4 for rainfall and 46.7 for temperature. Best estimate for Barren is 9.36.

20.5 t scores are 14.76 for troops, .8 for education, and 24.1 for women. Note that education is not significant. Best estimate of number of crimes $= 418.1$.

20.7 t-scores are 5.35 for pupil–teacher ratios and 5.08 for spending. Decreasing the pupil–teacher ratio by 5 improves reading scores by .455, whereas increasing spending by \$50 improves them by .155.

20.9 t-scores are 8.11 for days stayed, 3.83 for lab tests, and 5.57 for prescription drugs. The results suggest that the number of days stayed and the number of lab tests are the biggest determinants of costs, so management might want to pay particular attention to these variables.

20.11 t-scores are 4.26 for B-type zone, 2.0 for C-type zone, 27.3 for neighboring unemployment, .54 for median education (not significant), and 4.19 for service employment. Best estimate for Youngstown $= 7.272\%$.

20.13 t-scores are 5.79 for years of experience, 1.67 for articles, and 3.64 for sex. The important finding is that males are paid on the average \$1,150 more than females. Best guess is \$45,553.

20.15 Test of slopes: number of persons killed, $t = 1.19$; ability to pay for attorney, $t = 2.77$; number of years of formal education, $t = 3.33$; and race, $t = 25.83$. The regression clearly shows that the race of the convicted is associated with receiving the death penalty. Whites are less likely to receive the death penalty, all other things being equal. If $X_1 = 2$, $X_2 = 1$, $X_3 = 16$, and $X_4 = 1$, then $Y = -.22$. Because a probability cannot be less than 0, one should conclude that there is little chance that such a person would receive the death penalty. Second person: If $X_1 = 1$, $X_2 = 0$, $X_3 = 8$, and $X_4 = 0$, then $Y = .43$. To find out if the race of the victim mattered, gather data on a fifth variable, the race of the victim, and add this variable to the equation.

Chapter 21

21.1 (a) Intercept: If population and the number of business permits were both equal to zero, Potto Gulch would spend about \$3.65 million on social welfare programs each year.

Slopes: The slope coefficient for population is not statistically significant. For every additional business permit issued, social welfare expenditures go down by \$5,049. There is a relationship between new business permits and social welfare expenditures ($t = 2.16$), but the overall impact is rather small.

(b) The adjusted R^2 is lower than the R^2 due to the presence of the insignificant population variable.

(c) Because the population variable is not statistically significant, replacing this variable with the actual number of residents receiving social welfare assistance is an appropriate strategy.

21.3 (a) Intercept: If the number of new exhibits were equal to zero and it were a warm-weather month, the average number of visitors would be 2,659. Slopes: For every one additional new exhibit, the number of visitors goes up by about 361 per month. The season coefficient is not statistically significant.

(b) The R^2 of .857 indicates that these two variables explain about 86% of the variation in the number of visitors. The reason why the adjusted R^2 is lower than R^2 is probably that the coefficient for the season dummy variable is not statistically significant.

21.5 (a) Intercept: If class size, teacher turnover, percentage of African American students, and percentage of Hispanic students were all equal to zero, the expected pass rate would be 94.5%.

Slopes: For every 1% increase in the percentage of African American students, overall student pass rates decline by $-.194$ of a percentage point (about 2/10 of a percentage point). For every 1% increase in the percentage of Hispanic students, overall student pass rates decline by $-.116$ of a percentage point (about 1/10 of a percentage point). For every 1% increase in the teacher turnover rate, overall student pass rates decline by $-.184$ of a percentage point. All three slope coefficients are significant at the .05 level. The coefficient for class size is not statistically significant at the .05 level.

The R^2 value indicates that the model explains about 30% of the variation in pass rates on state-mandated tests. With only 30% of the variance explained, other variables that affect pass rates are probably not currently included in the model.

(b) When attendance is included as an explanatory variable ($t = 10.5$), the R^2 rises to .37. This is a clear improvement in explanatory power over the original model.

Index